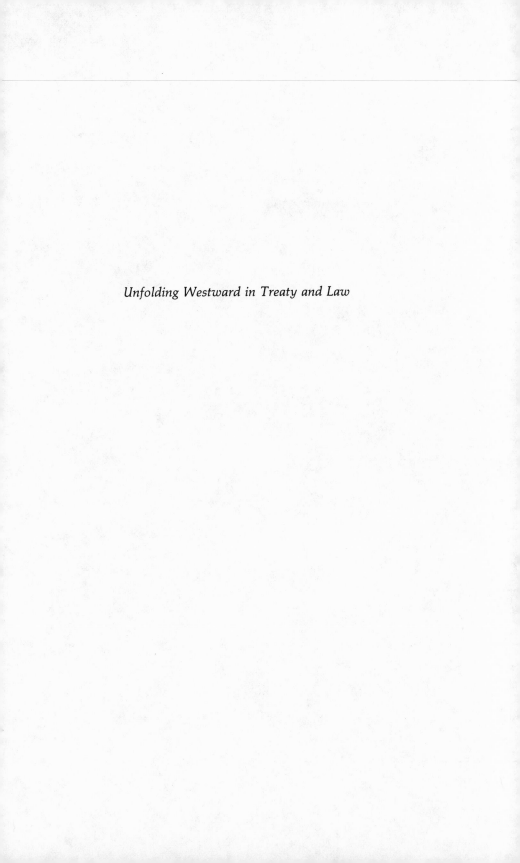

Unfolding Westward in Treaty and Law

Unfolding Westward in Treaty and Law

Land Documents in United States History from the Appalachians to the Pacific, 1783–1934

by

Frederick E. Hosen

McFarland & Company, Inc., Publishers
Jefferson, North Carolina, and London

Library of Congress Cataloguing-in-Publication Data

Hosen, Frederick E., 1938–
    Unfolding westward in treaty and law : land documents in United States history from the Appalachians to the Pacific, 1783–1934
/ by Frederick E. Hosen.
     p. cm.
    Bibliography: p.
    Includes index.
    ISBN 0-89950-308-X
    1. Law – United States – Territories and possessions. 2. United States – Constitutional law, State. 3. United States – Territorial expansion. 4. United States – Territories and possessions.
I. Title.
KF4635.H67   1988
342.73'0412 – dc19
[347.302412]   87-29879
                                                    CIP

Printed in the United States of America (acid-free natural paper)

McFarland   Box 611   Jefferson NC 28640

Contents

Preface

The objective of this book is to make available to the reader basic documents that provide a continuum of information, in treaty and law, sufficient to track the geographical growth of the contiguous United States.

The work provides a flow of history and points of departure for more engaging study. Piece by piece, major boundary agreements and settlements formed, by the early twentieth century, the United States as it essentially is today.

For the most part, the boundaries were established by treaty at various times with France, Great Britain, Mexico, Spain, and the Republic of Texas. Further division was made by territorial acts and state acts of the Congress of the United States, and, on occasion, by proclamation of the president. With the physical formation of the country determined essentially by treaty and territorial act, the state boundaries provided both geographic and political divisions within the already existing boundaries.

With one exception, which is mentioned later, the period of documentation in this work is from September 3, 1783, the date of the Treaty Between the United States of America and His Britannic Majesty (Treaty of Paris), to February 16, 1911, the date of the Joint Resolution reaffirming the boundary line between Texas and the territory of New Mexico. Since this period of documentation, changes have occurred in both state and national boundaries, but, by February 14, 1912, when the state of Arizona was admitted into the Union, the basic geographical features of the United States had solidified.

One pre- and one post–1912 act that are sociopolitical rather than geographical are included because of their particular influence on the westward movement. First, there is the act of May 20, 1862, which provided for the establishment of homesteads on the lands of public domain, and second, the act of June 28, 1934, which provided for up to eighty million acres of land to be set aside for grazing. While the former of these two acts might be credited with opening the West, the latter could well be credited with its closure.

Except for the "homestead" and "grazing" acts, all documents presented identify various geographic boundaries. Also, except for two excerpts (provided as excerpts because they were referenced by principal boundary acts), all documents are given in their entirety. As a body, these documents provide complete coverage, beyond the thirteen original states, of the contiguous United States at the times of its earliest stages of formation.

Again with two exceptions, the sources of all treaties and acts were publications of the Congress and the Department of State of the United States.

Those exceptions are: (1) An Act Passed at a General Assembly of the Commonwealth of Virginia, December 18, 1789 (Excerpt), and (2) An agreement Between the Republic of Texas and the Mexican Army (Treaty of Velasco), May 14, 1836.

Additionally, several states and the District of Columbia, located east of the Appalachian mountains, are included in this documentation since they were created or organized after the formation of the thirteen original states.

Every effort has been made to remain true to the source documents. It should be recognized that what may appear to be an error may well be the practice of the time and place that the document was produced. For example, in the Treaty Between the United States and Great Britain, September 3, 1783, the word Mississipp: is consistently spelled Missisippi (i.e. one of the last two of the letters "s" is left out). Therefore, spelling and capitalization have not been changed except where it is obvious that a typographical error occurred.

Introduction

There are numerous books about the movement of Americans beyond the Appalachian Mountains to the Pacific Ocean. Most of these books, when referring to the various treaties and laws of the westward movement, give only excerpts, whereas, in this work those documents are presented in their entirety. Thus, this compilation of treaties and laws should enhance the reader's understanding of specific areas, as well as the whole, of American history.

The various documents may provide new perspectives for the reader with such passages as:

> His Britannic Majesty acknowledges the said United States, viz. New-Hampshire, Massachusetts-Bay, Rhode-Island and Providence Plantations, Connecticut, New-York, New-Jersey, Pennsylvania, Delaware, Maryland, Virginia, North-Carolina, South-Carolina, and Georgia, to be free, sovereign and independent States; that he treats with them as such; and for himself, his heirs and successors, relinquishes all claims to the government, propriety and territorial rights of the same, and every part thereof [Treaty Between the United States of America and His Britannic Majesty — Article I, September 3, 1783].

> *And be it further enacted,* That every free white male inhabitant above the age of twenty-one years, who shall be an actual resident of said Territory, and shall possess the qualifications hereinafter prescribed, shall be entitled to vote at the first election, and shall be eligible to any office within the said Territory, . . . [An Act to Organize the Territories of Nebraska and Kansas — Section 23, May 30, 1854].

> . . . The utmost good faith shall always be observed towards the Indians; their lands and property shall never be taken from them without their consent; and in their property, rights, and liberty they never shall be invaded or disturbed, unless in just and lawful wars authorized by Congress; but laws founded in justice and humanity shall, from time to time, be made, for preventing wrongs being done them, and for preserving peace and friendship with them [An Ordinance for the Government of the Territory of the United States, Northwest of the River Ohio — Section 14, Article III, July 13, 1787].

> . . . That perfect toleration of religious sentiment shall be secured,

1

and that no inhabitant of said State shall ever be molested in person or property on account of his or her mode of religious worship: *Provided,* That polygamous or plural marriages are forever prohibited [An Act to Enable the People of Utah to Form a Constitution and State Government, and to Be Admitted into the Union on an Equal Footing with the Original States — Section 3, July 16, 1894].

During the period of formation of geographic and political division of the West other events influenced the country's growth, and the time at which those events occurred should provide an added dimension to this flow of history. Some of the most significant events, in chronological order, are:

1796	George Washington's farewell address in which he pointed out the importance of national unity.
1804–1806	Lewis and Clark explored the northwest United States.
1825	The Erie Canal, which opened the Great Lakes to commerce, was placed in service.
1841–1842	The first wagon train travelled from Independence, Missouri, to California.
1848	Gold was discovered in California.
1860	The pony express, between Sacramento, California, and St. Joseph, Missouri was started.
1861	The first transcontinental telegraph was placed in operation.
1869	The transcontinental railroad was completed.

There are eight physiographic regions within the contiguous United States. Starting at the Atlantic coast and moving toward the Pacific coast they are successively: the Coastal Plain; the Appalachian Highlands; the Interior Highlands of Arkansas, Missouri, and eastern Oklahoma; the Superior Upland in the area of Lake Superior; the Interior Plains; the Rocky Mountain System; the Intermontane Plateaus; and finally, the Pacific Mountain System.

These physiographic regions represent quite a variety of landscape, including forests, grasslands, deserts, mountains, and swamps, with the climate ranging from subarctic to subtropic. Many states are in more than one region. The Coastal Plain incorporates all or part of eighteen states; the Appalachian Highlands, all or part of seventeen states; the Interior Highlands, all or part of three states; the Superior Upland, the region that is the smallest in area, all or part of two states; the Interior Plains, by far the largest region in area, all or part of twenty-three states; the Rocky Mountain System, all or part of seven states; the Intermontane Plateaus, all or part of ten states; and the Pacific Mountain System, all or part of three states.

National, territorial, and state boundaries generally coincide with the meandering of rivers and streams, the location of lakes, ocean shores, mountain ranges, latitudinal and longitudinal lines and coordinates. When established, boundaries should be clearly marked with monuments that are as permanent as they can reasonably be. Unfortunately, blazed trees or relatively small stones have at times been used, a practice which led to uncertainty and inevitable resurvey.

A brief comment about another book is called for. A publication of the United States Geological Survey, entitled *Boundaries of the United States and the Several States, Bulletin 1212,* provides an official summary of the said boundaries and should certainly be referred to in any study of the subject at hand. In *Bulletin 1212,* relevant treaties and laws are referenced or quoted in part. The United States Geological Survey has produced a valuable work that identifies the various boundaries of, and within, the United States. However, although intentional, by not presenting the various documents in their entirety the *Bulletin* is of less use to the historian than it might otherwise be. In the work presented here, an attempt is made to avoid the technical approach of *Bulletin 1212* and rather provide a historical symphony which gives the reader a broader perspective of the nation's growth.

Treaties

Treaty Between the United States of America and His Britannic Majesty (Treaty of Paris), September 3, 1783

Treaty Between the United States of America and Spain (Treaty of San Lorenzo), October 27, 1795

Treaty Between the United States of America and the French Republic (Louisiana Purchase), April 30, 1803

A Proclamation by the President of the United States of America Regarding the Territory South of the Mississippi Territory and Eastward of the River Mississippi and Extending to the River Perdido, October 27, 1810

Treaty Between the United States of America and Great Britain (Treaty of Ghent), December 24, 1814

Treaty Between the United States of America and Great Britain, October 20, 1818

Treaty Between the United States of America and Spain (Adams-Onis Treaty), February 22, 1819

Treaty Between the United States of America and Mexico, January 12, 1828, and April 5, 1831

An Agreement Between the Republic of Texas and the Mexican Army (Treaty of Velasco), May 14, 1836

Convention Between the United States of America and the Republic of Texas, April 25, 1838

Treaty Between the United States of America and Great Britain (Webster-Ashburton Treaty), August 9, 1842

Treaty Between the United States of America and Great Britain, June 15, 1846

Treaty Between the United States of America and the Mexican Republic (Treaty of Guadalupe Hidalgo), February 2, 1848

Treaty Between the United States of America and Mexico (The Gadsden Purchase), December 30, 1853

Territorial Acts

An Ordinance for the Government of the Territory of the United States, Northwest of the River Ohio, July 13, 1787

An Act for the Government of the Territory of the United States, South of the River Ohio, May 26, 1790

An Act for an Amicable Settlement of Limits with the State of Georgia, and Authorizing the Establishment of a Government in the Mississippi Territory, April 7, 1798

An Act to Divide the Territory of the United States, Northwest of the Ohio, into Two Separate Governments, May 7, 1800

An Act Erecting Louisiana into Two Territories, and Providing for the Temporary Government Thereof, March 26, 1804

An Act to Divide the Indiana Territory into Two Separate Governments, January 11, 1805

An Act Further Providing for the Government of the District of Louisiana, March 3, 1805

An Act for Dividing the Indiana Territory into Two Separate Governments, February 3, 1809

An Act to Enlarge the Boundaries of the Mississippi Territory, May 14, 1812

An Act Providing for the Government of the Territory of Missouri, June 4, 1812

An Act to Establish a Separate Territorial Government for the Eastern Part of the Mississippi Territory, March 3, 1817

An Act Establishing a Separate Territorial Government in the Southern Part of the Territory of Missouri, March 2, 1819

An Act for the Establishment of a Territorial Government in Florida, March 30, 1822

An Act to Fix the Western Boundary Line of the Territory of Arkansas, and for Other Purposes, May 26, 1824

An Act to Authorize the President of the United States to Run and Mark a Line Dividing the Territory of Florida from the State of Georgia, May 4, 1826

An Act to Ascertain and Mark the Line Between the State of Alabama and the Territory of Florida, and the Northern Boundary of the State of Illinois, and for Other Purposes, March 2, 1831

An Act to Attach the Territory of the United States West of the Mississippi River, and North of the State of Missouri, to the Territory of Michigan, June 28, 1834

An Act Establishing the Territorial Government of Wisconsin, April 20, 1836

7

An Act to Divide the Territory of Wisconsin and to Establish the Territorial Government of Iowa, June 12, 1838

An Act to Define and Establish the Eastern Boundary Line of the Territory of Iowa, March 3, 1839

An Act to Establish the Territorial Government of Oregon, August 14, 1848

An Act to Establish the Territorial Government of Minnesota, March 3, 1849

An Act Proposing to the State of Texas the Establishment of Her Northern and Western Boundaries, the Relinquishment by the Said State of All Territory Claimed by Her Exterior to Said Boundaries, and of All Her Claims Upon the United States, and to Establish a Territorial Government for New Mexico, September 9, 1850

An Act to Establish a Territorial Government for Utah, September 9, 1850

An Act to Establish the Territorial Government of Washington, March 2, 1853

An Act to Organize the Territories of Nebraska and Kansas, May 30, 1854

An Act Declaring the Southern Boundary of New Mexico, August 4, 1854

An Act to Provide a Temporary Government for the Territory of Colorado, February 28, 1861

An Act to Organize the Territory of Nevada, March 2, 1861

An Act to Provide a Temporary Government for the Territory of Dakota, and to Create the Office of Surveyor General Therein, March 2, 1861

An Act to Extend the Territorial Limits of the Territory of Nevada, July 14, 1862

An Act to Provide a Temporary Government for the Territory of Arizona, and for Other Purposes, February 24, 1863

An Act to Provide a Temporary Government for the Territory of Idaho, March 3, 1863

An Act to Provide a Temporary Government for the Territory of Montana, May 26, 1864

An Act Providing a Temporary Government for the Territory of Wyoming, July 25, 1868

An Act to Re-define a Portion of the Boundary Line Between the State of Nebraska and the Territory of Dakota, April 28, 1870

An Act to Readjust the Western Boundary of Dakota Territory, February 17, 1873

An Act to Provide a Temporary Government for the Territory of Oklahoma, to Enlarge the Jurisdiction of the United States Court in the Indian Territory, and for Other Purposes, May 2, 1890

Joint Resolution Reaffirming the Boundary Line Between Texas and the Territory of New Mexico, February 16, 1911

State Acts

An Act Passed at a General Assembly of the Commonwealth of Virginia, December 18, 1789 (Excerpt)

An Act to Accept a Cession of the Claims of the State of North Carolina to a Certain District of Western Territory, April 2, 1790

An Act for Establishing the Temporary and Permanent Seat of the Government of the United States, July 16, 1790

An Act Declaring the Consent of Congress, That a New State Be Formed Within the Jurisdiction of the Commonwealth of Virginia, and Admitted into This Union, by the Name of the State of Kentucky, February 4, 1791

An Act for the Admission of the State of Vermont into This Union, February 18, 1791

An Act to Amend "An Act for Establishing the Temporary and Permanent Seat of Government of the United States," March 3, 1791

An Act for the Admission of the State of Tennessee into the Union, June 1, 1796

An Act to Enable the People of the Eastern Division of the Territory Northwest of the River Ohio to Form a Constitution and State Government, and for the Admission of Such State into the Union, on an Equal Footing with the Original States, and for Other Purposes, April 30, 1802

An Act to Enable the People of the Territory of Orleans to Form a Constitution and State Government, and for the Admission of Such State into the Union, on an Equal Footing with the Original States, and for Other Purposes, February 20, 1811

An Act to Enlarge the Limits of the State of Louisiana, April 14, 1812

An Act to Enable the People of the Indiana Territory to Form a Constitution and State Government, and for the Admission of Such State into the Union on an Equal Footing with the Original States, April 19, 1816

An Act to Enable the People of the Western Part of the Mississippi Territory to Form a Constitution and State Government, and for the Admission of Such State into the Union, on an Equal Footing with the Original States, March 1, 1817

An Act to Enable the People of the Illinois Territory to Form a Constitution and State Government, and for the Admission of Such State into the Union on an Equal Footing with the Original States, April 18, 1818

An Act to Enable the People of the Alabama Territory to Form a Constitution and State Government, and for the Admission of Such State into the Union on an Equal Footing with the Original States, March 2, 1819

An Act for the Admission of the State of Maine into the Union, March 3, 1820

An Act to Authorize the People of the Missouri Territory to Form a Constitution and State Government, and for the Admission of Such State into the Union on an Equal Footing with the Original States, and to Prohibit Slavery in Certain Territories, March 6, 1820

Treaty Between the United States of America and the Western Cherokee, May 6, 1828 (Excerpt)

An Act to Authorize the President of the United States to Run and Mark a Line, Dividing the Territory of Arkansas from the State of Louisiana, May 19, 1828

An Act to Extend the Western Boundary of the State of Missouri to the Missouri River, June 7, 1836

An Act to Establish the Northern Boundary Line of the State of Ohio, and to Provide for Admission of the State of Michigan into the Union upon the Conditions Therein Expressed, June 15, 1836

An Act for the Admission of the State of Arkansas into the Union, and to Provide for the Due Execution of the Laws of the United States, within the Same, and for Other Purposes, June 15, 1836

An Act to Settle and Establish the Northern Boundary Line of the State of Ohio, June 23, 1836

An Act for the Admission of the States of Iowa and Florida into the Union, March 3, 1845

An Act to Define the Boundaries of the State of Iowa, and to Repeal So Much of the Act of the Third of March, One Thousand Eight Hundred and Forty-Five as Relates to the Boundaries of Iowa, August 4, 1846

An Act to Enable the People of Wisconsin Territory to Form a Constitution and State Government, and for the Admission of Such State into the Union, August 6, 1846

An Act Giving the Consent of the Government of the United States to the State of Texas to Extend Her Eastern Boundary, So as to Include Within Her Limits One Half of Sabine Pass, Sabine Lake, and Sabine River, as Far North as the Thirty-Second Degree of North Latitude, July 5, 1848

An Act Proposing to the State of Texas the Establishment of Her Northern and Western Boundaries, the Relinquishment by Said State of all Territory Claimed by Her Exterior to Said Boundaries, and of All Her Claims Upon the United States, and to Establish a Territorial Government for New Mexico, September 9, 1850

An Act to Authorize the People of the Territory of Minnesota to Form a Constitution and State Government, Preparatory to Their Admission in the Union on an Equal Footing with the Original States, February 26, 1857

An Act to Authorize the President of the United States in Conjunction with the State of Texas, to Run and Mark the Boundary Lines Between the Territories of the United States and the State of Texas, June 5, 1858

An Act for the Admission of Oregon into the Union, February 14, 1859

An Act to Authorize the President of the United States in Conjunction with the State of California, to Run and Mark the Boundary Lines Between the

Territories of the United States and the State of California, May 26, 1860

An Act for the Admission of Kansas into the Union, January 29, 1861

An Act for the Admission of the State of "West Virginia" into the Union, and for Other Purposes, December 31, 1862

An Act to Enable the People of Nevada to Form a Constitution and State Government, and for the Admission of Such State into the Union on an Equal Footing with the Original States, March 21, 1864

An Act to Enable the People of Nebraska to Form a Constitution and State Government, and for the Admission of Such State into the Union on an Equal Footing with the Original States, April 19, 1864

An Act Concerning the Boundaries of the State of Nevada, May 5, 1866

An Act to Enable the People of Colorado to Form a Constitution and State Government, and for the Admission of the Said State into the Union on an Equal Footing with the Original States, March 3, 1875

An Act Giving the Consent of Congress to an Agreement or Compact Entered into Between the States of New York and Vermont Respecting the Boundary Between Said States, April 7, 1880

An Act to Extend the Northern Boundary of the State of Nebraska, March 28, 1882

An Act to Provide for the Division of Dakota into Two States and to Enable the People of North Dakota, South Dakota, Montana, and Washington to Form Constitutions and State Governments and to Be Admitted into the Union on an Equal Footing with the Original States, and to Make Donations of Public Lands to Such States, February 22, 1889

An Act to Provide for the Admission of the State of Idaho into the Union, July 3, 1890

An Act to Provide for the Admission of the State of Wyoming into the Union, and for Other Purposes, July 10, 1890

An Act to Enable the People of Utah to Form a Constitution and State Government, and to Be Admitted into the Union on an Equal Footing with the Original States, July 16, 1894

An Act to Give the Consent of Congress to a Compact Entered into Between the States of South Dakota and Nebraska Respecting the Boundary Between Said States, July 24, 1897

Joint Resolution Ratifying Agreement Between Tennessee and Virginia with Reference to the Boundary Line of Said States, March 3, 1901

An Act to Extend the Western Boundary Line of the State of Arkansas, February 10, 1905

An Act Establishing That Portion of the Boundary Line Between the State of South Dakota and the State of Nebraska South of Union County, South Dakota, March 1, 1905

An Act to Enable the People of Oklahoma and of the Indian Territory to Form a Constitution and State Government and Be Admitted into the Union on an Equal Footing with the Original States; and to Enable the People of New Mexico and of Arizona to Form a Constitution and State Government and Be Admitted into the Union on an Equal Footing with the Original States, June 16, 1906

Table of Territories and the Date of the Primary Organic Act in Chronological Order

Territory	*Date of Organic Act*
Northwest Territory	July 13, 1787
Territory Southwest of River Ohio	May 26, 1790
Mississippi	April 7, 1798
Indiana	May 7, 1800
Orleans	March 26, 1804
Michigan	January 11, 1805
Louisiana	March 3, 1805
Illinois	February 3, 1809
Missouri	June 4, 1812
Alabama	March 3, 1817
Arkansas	March 2, 1819
Florida	March 30, 1822
Wisconsin	April 20, 1836
Iowa	June 12, 1838
Oregon	August 14, 1848
Minnesota	March 3, 1849
New Mexico	September 9, 1850
Utah	September 9, 1850
Washington	March 2, 1853
Nebraska	May 30, 1854
Kansas	May 30, 1854
Colorado	February 28, 1861
Nevada	March 2, 1861
Dakota	March 2, 1861
Arizona	February 24, 1863
Idaho	March 3, 1863
Montana	May 26, 1864
Wyoming	July 25, 1868
Oklahoma	May 2, 1890

Note: Only those territories of the contiguous United States are listed.

Table of States in Order of Rank of Entry into the Union and the Date of Entry

Order	Date	State
1	December 7, 1787	Delaware
2	December 12, 1787	Pennsylvania
3	December 18, 1787	New Jersey
4	January 2, 1788	Georgia
5	January 9, 1788	Connecticut
6	February 6, 1788	Massachusetts
7	April 28, 1788	Maryland
8	May 23, 1788	South Carolina
9	June 21, 1788	New Hampshire
10	June 25, 1788	Virginia
11	July 26, 1788	New York
12	November 21, 1789	North Carolina
13	May 29, 1790	Rhode Island
14	March 4, 1791	Vermont
15	June 1, 1792	Kentucky
16	June 1, 1796	Tennessee
17	March 1, 1803	Ohio
18	April 30, 1812	Louisiana
19	December 11, 1816	Indiana
20	December 10, 1817	Mississippi
21	December 3, 1818	Illinois
22	December 14, 1819	Alabama
23	March 15, 1820	Maine
24	August 10, 1821	Missouri
25	June 15, 1836	Arkansas
26	January 26, 1837	Michigan
27	March 3, 1845	Florida
28	December 29, 1845	Texas
29	December 28, 1846	Iowa
30	May 29, 1848	Wisconsin
31	September 9, 1850	California
32	May 11, 1858	Minnesota
33	February 14, 1859	Oregon
34	January 29, 1861	Kansas

15

Order	Date	State
35	June 20, 1863	West Virginia
36	October 31, 1864	Nevada
37	March 1, 1867	Nebraska
38	August 1, 1876	Colorado
39	November 2, 1889	North Dakota
40	November 2, 1889	South Dakota
41	November 8, 1889	Montana
42	November 11, 1889	Washington
43	July 3, 1890	Idaho
44	July 10, 1890	Wyoming
45	January 4, 1896	Utah
46	November 16, 1907	Oklahoma
47	January 6, 1912	New Mexico
48	February 14, 1912	Arizona

Note: Only those states of the contiguous United States are listed.

List of the Principal State Organic Acts 1789–1911

(* Included in This Book)

Vermont — admitted into the Union, March 4, 1791

*February 18, 1791 — An Act for the Admission of the State of Vermont into This Union

*April 7, 1880 — An Act Giving the Consent of Congress to an Agreement or Compact Entered into Between the States of New York and Vermont Respecting the Boundary Between Said States

Kentucky — admitted into the Union, June 1, 1792

*December 18, 1789 — An Act Passed at a General Assembly of the Commonwealth of Virginia (Excerpt)

*February 4, 1791 — An Act Declaring the Consent of Congress, That a New State Be Formed Within the Jurisdiction of the Commonwealth of Virginia, and Admitted into This Union, by the Name of the State of Kentucky

Tennessee — admitted into the Union, June 1, 1796

*April 2, 1790 — An Act to Accept a Cession of the Claims of the State of North Carolina to a Certain District of Western Territory

*June 1, 1796 — An Act for the Admission of the State of Tennessee into the Union

*March 3, 1901 — Joint Resolution Ratifying Agreement Between Tennessee and Virginia with Reference to the Boundary Line of Said States

Ohio — admitted into the Union, March 1, 1803

*April 30, 1802 — An Act to Enable the People of the Eastern Division of the Territory Northwest of the River Ohio to Form a Constitution and State Government, and for the Admission of Such State into the Union,

on an Equal Footing with the Original States, and for Other Purposes

March 3, 1803 – An Act in Addition to, and in Modification of, the Propositions Contained in the Act Entitled "An Act to Enable the People of the Eastern Division of the Territory Northwest of the River Ohio, to Form a Constitution and State Government, and for the Admission of Such State into the Union, on an Equal Footing with the Original States, and for Other Purposes"

July 14, 1832 – An Act to Provide for the Taking of Certain Observations Preparatory to the Adjustment of the Northern Boundary Line of the State of Ohio

*June 15, 1836 – An Act to Establish the Northern Boundary Line of the State of Ohio, and to Provide for the Admission of the State of Michigan into the Union upon the Conditions Therein Expressed

*June 23, 1836 – An Act to Settle and Establish the Northern Boundary Line of the State of Ohio

June 23, 1836 – An Act Supplementary to the Act Entitled "An Act to Establish the Northern Boundary Line of the State of Ohio, and to Provide for the Admission of the State of Michigan into the Union upon the Conditions Therein Expressed"

Louisiana – admitted into the Union, April 30, 1812

*February 20, 1811 – An Act to Enable the People of the Territory of Orleans to Form a Constitution and State Government, and for the Admission of Such State into the Union, on an Equal Footing with the Original States, and for Other Purposes

April 8, 1812 – An Act for the Admission of the State of Louisiana into the Union, and to Extend the Laws of the United States to the Said State

*April 14, 1812 – An Act to Enlarge the Limits of the State of Louisiana

May 22, 1812 – An Act Supplementary to an Act Entitled "An Act for the Admission of the State of Louisiana into the Union, and to Extend the Laws of the United States to the Said State"

*May 19, 1828 – An Act to Authorize the President of the United States to Run and Mark a Line, Dividing the Territory of Arkansas from the State of Louisiana

Indiana – admitted into the Union, December 11, 1816

*April 19, 1816 – An Act to Enable the People of the Indiana Territory to Form a Constitution and State Government, and for the Admission of Such State into the Union on an Equal Footing with the Original States

December 11, 1816 – Joint Resolution of Congress for the Admission of the State of Indiana into the Union

Mississippi – admitted into the Union, December 10, 1817

*March 1, 1817 — An Act to Enable the People of the Western Part of the Mississippi Territory to Form a Constitution and State Government, and for the Admission of Such State into the Union, on an Equal Footing with the Original States

December 10, 1817 — Joint Resolution of Congress for the Admission of the State of Mississippi into the Union

Illinois — admitted into the Union, December 3, 1818

*April 18, 1818 — An Act to Enable the People of the Illinois Territory to Form a Constitution and State Government, and for the Admission of Such State into the Union on an Equal Footing with the Original States

December 3, 1818 — Joint Resolution of Congress Declaring the Admission of the State of Illinois into the Union

March 2, 1831 — An Act to Ascertain and Mark the Line Between the State of Alabama and the Territory of Florida, and the Northern Boundary of the State of Illinois, and for Other Purposes

Alabama — admitted into the Union, December 14, 1819

*March 2, 1819 — An Act to Enable the People of the Alabama Territory to Form a Constitution and State Government, and for the Admission of Such State into the Union on an Equal Footing with the Original States

December 14, 1819 — Joint Resolution of Congress Declaring the Admission of the State of Alabama into the Union

March 2, 1831 — An Act to Ascertain and Mark the Line Between the State of Alabama and the Territory of Florida, and the Northern Boundary of the State of Illinois, and for Other Purposes

Maine — admitted into the Union, March 15, 1820

*March 3, 1820 — An Act for the Admission of the State of Maine into the Union

Missouri — admitted into the Union, August 10, 1821

*March 6, 1820 — An Act to Authorize the People of the Missouri Territory to Form a Constitution and State Government, and for the Admission of Such State into the Union on an Equal Footing with the Original States, and to Prohibit Slavery in Certain Territories

March 2, 1821 — Joint Resolution of Congress Providing for the Admission of the State of Missouri into the Union on a Certain Condition

August 10, 1821 — A Proclamation by the President of the United States Admitting the State of Missouri into the Union

*June 7, 1836 — An Act to Extend the Western Boundary of the State of Missouri to the Missouri River

June 7, 1910 — Joint Resolution of Congress to Enable the States of Missouri and Kansas to Agree upon a Boundary Line and to Determine the

Jurisdiction of Crimes Committed on the Missouri River and Adjacent Territories

Arkansas — admitted into the Union, June 15, 1836

*May 6, 1828 — Treaty Between the United States of America and the Western Cherokee (Excerpt)

*May 19, 1828 — An Act to Authorize the President of the United States to Run and Mark a Line Dividing the Territory of Arkansas from the State of Louisiana

*June 15, 1836 — An Act for the Admission of the State of Arkansas into the Union, and to Provide for the Due Execution of the Laws of the United States, Within the Same, and for Other Purposes

June 23, 1836 — An Act Supplementary to the Act Entitled "An Act for the Admission of the State of Arkansas into the Union, and to Provide for the Due Execution of the Laws of the United States, Within the Same, and for Other Purposes"

*February 10, 1905 — An Act to Extend the Western Boundary Line of the State of Arkansas

Michigan — admitted into the Union, January 26, 1837

*June 15, 1836 — An Act to Establish the Northern Boundary Line of the State of Ohio, and to Provide for the Admission of the State of Michigan into the Union upon the Conditions Therein Expressed

June 23, 1836 — An Act Supplementary to the Act Entitled "An Act to Establish the Northern Boundary Line of the State of Ohio, and to Provide for the Admission of the State of Michigan into the Union on Certain Conditions"

June 26, 1837 — An Act to Admit the State of Michigan into the Union, upon an Equal Footing with the Original States

June 12, 1838 — An Act to Ascertain and Designate the Boundary Line Between the State of Michigan and the Territory of Wisconsin

Florida — admitted into the Union, March 3, 1845

*March 3, 1845 — An Act for the Admission of the States of Iowa and Florida into the Union (Chap. XLVIII)

March 3, 1845 — An Act Supplemental to the "Act for the Admission of the States of Iowa and Florida into the Union," and for Other Purposes (Chap. LXXV)

March 3, 1845 — An Act Supplemental to the "Act for the Admission of the States of Iowa and Florida into the Union" (Chap. LXXVI)

Texas — admitted into the Union, December 29, 1845

March 1, 1845 — Joint Resolution of Congress for Annexing Texas to the United States

December 29, 1845 – Joint Resolution of Congress for the Admission of the State of Texas into the Union

*July 5, 1848 – An Act Giving the Consent of the Government of the United States to the State of Texas to Extend Her Eastern Boundary, So as to Include Within Her Limits One Half of Sabine Pass, Sabine Lake, and Sabine River, as Far North as the Thirty-Second Degree of North Latitude

*September 9, 1850 – An Act Proposing to the State of Texas the Establishment of Her Northern and Western Boundaries, the Relinquishment by the Said State of all Territory Claimed by Her Exterior to Said Boundaries, and of All Her Claims upon the United States, and to Establish a Territorial Government for New Mexico

*June 5, 1858 – An Act to Authorize the President of the United States, in Conjunction with the State of Texas, to Run and Mark the Boundary Lines Between the Territories of the United States and the State of Texas

January 31, 1885 – An Act to Authorize the Appointment of a Commission by the President of the United States to Run and Mark the Boundary Lines Between a Portion of the Indian Territory and the State of Texas, in Connection with a Similar Commission to Be Appointed by the State of Texas

*February 16, 1911 – Joint Resolution Reaffirming the Boundary Line Between Texas and the Territory of New Mexico

Iowa – admitted into the Union, December 28, 1846

*March 3, 1845 – An Act for the Admission of the States of Iowa and Florida into the Union (Chap. XLVIII)

March 3, 1845 – An Act Supplemental to the "Act for the Admission of the States of Iowa and Florida into the Union," and for Other Purposes (Chap. LXXV)

March 3, 1845 – An Act Supplemental to the "Act for the Admission of the States of Iowa and Florida into the Union" (Chap. LXXVI)

*August 4, 1846 – An Act to Define the Boundaries of the State of Iowa, and to Repeal So Much of the Act of the Third of March, One Thousand Eight Hundred and Forty-Five as Relates to the Boundaries of Iowa

December 28, 1846 – An Act for the Admission of the State of Iowa into the Union

Wisconsin – admitted into the Union, May 29, 1848

*August 6, 1846 – An Act to Enable the People of Wisconsin Territory to Form a Constitution and State Government, and for the Admission of Such State into the Union

March 3, 1847 – An Act for the Admission of the State of Wisconsin into the Union

May 29, 1848 – An Act for the Admission of the State of Wisconsin into the Union

California — admitted into the Union, September 9, 1850

September 9, 1850 — An Act for the Admission of the State of California into the Union

*May 26, 1860 — An Act to Authorize the President of the United States in Conjunction with the State of California, to Run and Mark the Boundary Lines Between the Territories of the United States and the State of California

Minnesota — admitted into the Union, May 11, 1858

*February 26, 1857 — An Act to Authorize the People of the Territory of Minnesota to Form a Constitution and State Government Preparatory to Their Admission into the Union on an Equal Footing with the Original States

May 11, 1858 — An Act for the Admission of the State of Minnesota into the Union

Oregon — admitted into the Union, February 14, 1859

*February 14, 1859 — An Act for the Admission of Oregon into the Union

June 10, 1910 — Joint Resolution of Congress to Enable the States of Oregon and Washington to Agree upon a Boundary Line Between Said States Where the Columbia River Forms Said Boundary

Kansas — admitted into the Union, January 29, 1861

May 4, 1858 — An Act for the Admission of the State of Kansas into the Union

*January 29, 1861 — An Act for the Admission of the State of Kansas into the Union

June 7, 1910 — Joint Resolution of Congress to Enable the States of Missouri and Kansas to Agree upon a Boundary Line and to Determine the Jurisdiction of Crimes Committed on the Missouri River and Adjacent Territories

West Virginia — admitted into the Union, June 20, 1863

*December 31, 1862 — An Act for the Admission of the State of West Virginia into the Union and for Other Purposes

April 20, 1863 — A Proclamation by the President of the United States Admitting the State of West Virginia into the Union

Nevada — admitted into the Union, October 31, 1864

*March 21, 1864 — An Act to Enable the People of Nevada to Form a Constitution and State Government, and for the Admission of Such State into the Union on an Equal Footing with the Original States

May 21, 1864 — An Act to Amend an Act Entitled "An Act to Enable the People of Nevada to Form a Constitution and State Government, and for the Admission of Such State into the Union on an Equal Footing with the Original States"

October 31, 1864 — A Proclamation by the President of the United States Admitting the State of Nevada into the Union

*May 5, 1866 — An Act Concerning the Boundaries of the State of Nevada

Nebraska — admitted into the Union, March 1, 1867

*April 19, 1864 — An Act to Enable the People of Nebraska to Form a Constitution and State Government, and for the Admission of Such State into the Union on an Equal Footing with the Original States

February 9, 1867 — An Act for the Admission of the State of Nebraska into the Union

March 1, 1867 — A Proclamation by the President of the United States Admitting the State of Nebraska into the Union

April 28, 1870 — An Act to Re-define a Portion of the Boundary Line Between the State of Nebraska and the Territory of Dakota

*March 28, 1882 — An Act to Extend the Northern Boundary of the State of Nebraska

*July 24, 1897 — An Act to Give the Consent of Congress to a Compact Entered into Between the States of South Dakota and Nebraska Respecting the Boundary Between Said States

*March 1, 1905 — An Act Establishing That Portion of the Boundary Line Between the State of South Dakota and the State of Nebraska South of Union County, South Dakota

Colorado — admitted into the Union, August 1, 1876

March 21, 1864 — An Act to Enable the People of Colorado to Form a Constitution and State Government, and for the Admission of Such State into the Union on an Equal Footing with the Original States

June 18, 1864 — An Act to Amend an Act Entitled "An Act to Enable the People of Colorado to Form a Constitution and State Government, and for the Admission of Such State into the Union on an Equal Footing with the Original States"

*March 3, 1875 — An Act to Enable the People of Colorado to Form a Constitution and State Government, and for the Admission of the Said State into the Union on an Equal Footing with the Original States

March 3, 1876 — An Act to Amend the Act Entitled "An Act to Enable the People of Colorado to Form a Constitution and State Government, and for the Admission of Said State into the Union on an Equal Footing with the Original States." Approved March 3, 1875

August 1, 1876 — A Proclamation by the President of the United States Proclaiming Colorado a State of the Union

North Dakota — admitted into the Union, November 2, 1889

*February 22, 1889 — An Act to Provide for the Division of Dakota into Two States and to Enable the People of North Dakota, South Dakota,

Montana, and Washington to Form Constitutions and State Governments and to Be Admitted into the Union on an Equal Footing with the Original States, and to Make Donations of Public Lands to Such States

November 2, 1889 — A Proclamation by the President of the United States Admitting the State of North Dakota into the Union

September 25, 1890 — An Act to Authorize the Secretary of the Interior to Survey and Mark the Seventh Standard Parallel Between the States of North and South Dakota

South Dakota — admitted into the Union, November 2, 1889

*February 22, 1889 — An Act to Provide for the Division of Dakota into Two States and to Enable the People of North Dakota, South Dakota, Montana, and Washington to Form Constitutions and State Governments and to Be Admitted into the Union on an Equal Footing with the Original States, and to Make Donations of Public Lands to Such States

November 2, 1889 — A Proclamation by the President of the United States Admitting the State of South Dakota into the Union

September 25, 1890 — An Act to Authorize the Secretary of the Interior to Survey and Mark the Seventh Standard Parallel Between the States of North and South Dakota

*July 24, 1897 — An Act to Give the Consent of Congress to a Compact Entered into Between the States of South Dakota and Nebraska Respecting the Boundary Between Said States

*March 1, 1905 — An Act Establishing That Portion of the Boundary Line Between the State of South Dakota and the State of Nebraska South of Union County, South Dakota

Montana — admitted into the Union, November 8, 1889

*February 22, 1889 — An Act to Provide for the Division of Dakota into Two States and to Enable the People of North Dakota, South Dakota, Montana, and Washington to Form Constitutions and State Governments and to Be Admitted into the Union on an Equal Footing with the Original States, and to Make Donations of Public Lands to Such States

November 8, 1889 — A Proclamation by the President of the United States Admitting the State of Montana into the Union

Washington — admitted into the Union, November 11, 1889

*February 22, 1889 — An Act to Provide for the Division of Dakota into Two States and to Enable the People of North Dakota, South Dakota, Montana, and Washington to Form Constitutions and State Governments and to Be Admitted into the Union on an Equal Footing with the Original States, and to Make Donations of Public Lands to Such States

November 11, 1889 — A Proclamation by the President of the United States Admitting the State of Washington into the Union

June 10, 1910 — Joint Resolution of Congress to Enable the States of Oregon and Washington to Agree Upon a Boundary Line Between Said States Where the Columbia River Forms Said Boundary

Idaho — admitted into the Union, July 3, 1890

*July 3, 1890 — An Act to Provide for the Admission of the State of Idaho into the Union

Wyoming — admitted into the Union, July 10, 1890

*July 10, 1890 — An Act to Provide for the Admission of the State of Wyoming into the Union, and for Other Purposes

Utah — admitted into the Union, January 4, 1896

*July 16, 1894 — An Act to Enable the People of Utah to Form a Constitution and State Government, and to Be Admitted into the Union on an Equal Footing with the Original States

January 4, 1896 — A Proclamation by the President of the United States Admitting the State of Utah into the Union

Oklahoma — admitted into the Union, November 16, 1907

*June 16, 1906 — An Act to Enable the People of Oklahoma and of the Indian Territory to Form a Constitution and State Government and Be Admitted into the Union on an Equal Footing with the Original States; and to Enable the People of New Mexico and of Arizona to Form a Constitution and State Government and Be Admitted into the Union on an Equal Footing with the Original States

New Mexico — admitted into the Union, January 6, 1912

*June 16, 1906 — An Act to Enable the People of Oklahoma and of the Indian Territory to Form a Constitution and State Government and Be Admitted into the Union on an Equal Footing with the Original States; and to Enable the People of New Mexico and of Arizona to Form a Constitution and State Government and Be Admitted into the Union on an Equal Footing with the Original States

*June 20, 1910 — An Act to Enable the People of New Mexico to Form a Constitution and State Government and Be Admitted into the Union on an Equal Footing with the Original States; and to Enable the People of Arizona to Form a Constitution and State Government and Be Admitted into the Union on an Equal Footing with the Original States

August 21, 1911 — Joint Resolution of Congress to Admit the Territories of New Mexico and Arizona as States into the Union upon an Equal Footing with the Original States

Arizona — admitted into the Union, February 14, 1912

*June 16, 1906 — An Act to Enable the People of Oklahoma and of the Indian

Territory to Form a Constitution and State Government and Be Admitted into the Union on an Equal Footing with the Original States; and to Enable the People of New Mexico and of Arizona to Form a Constitution and State Government and Be Admitted into the Union on an Equal Footing with the Original States

*June 20, 1910 — An Act to Enable the People of New Mexico to Form a Constitution and State Government and Be Admitted into the Union on an Equal Footing with the Original States; and to Enable the People of Arizona to Form a Constitution and State Government and Be Admitted into the Union on an Equal Footing with the Original States

August 21, 1911 — Joint Resolution of Congress to Admit the Territories of New Mexico and Arizona as States into the Union upon an Equal Footing with the Original States

District of Columbia

*July 16, 1790 — Act for Establishing the Temporary and Permanent Seat of the Government of the United States

*March 3, 1791 — An Act to Amend "An Act for Establishing the Temporary and Permanent Seat of the Government of the United States"

Map Showing the Thirteen Original States and the Territory Claimed by Those States

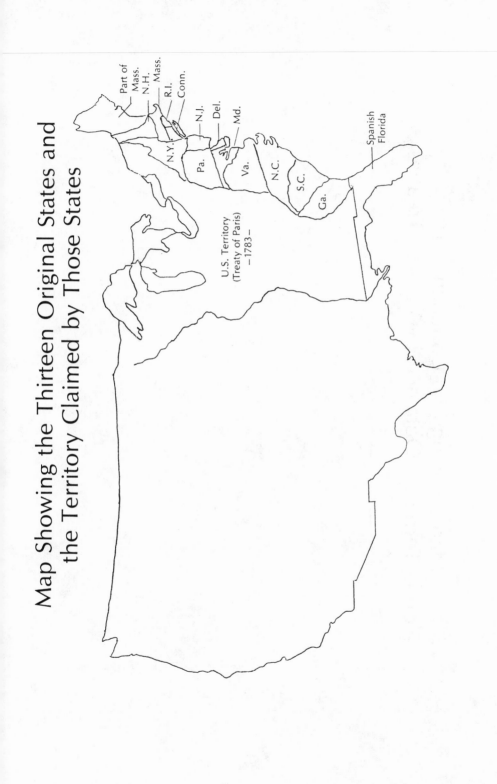

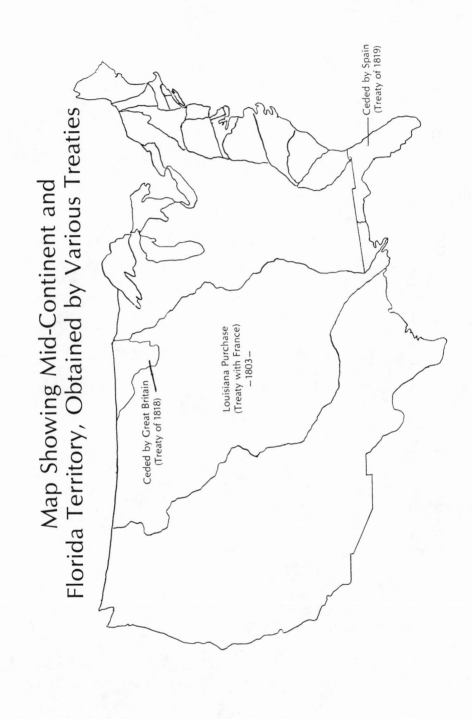

Map Showing Mid-Continent and
Florida Territory, Obtained by Various Treaties

Ceded by Great Britain
(Treaty of 1818)

Louisiana Purchase
(Treaty with France)
— 1803 —

Ceded by Spain
(Treaty of 1819)

Map Showing Territory, Essentially West of the Louisiana Purchase, Obtained by Various Treaties

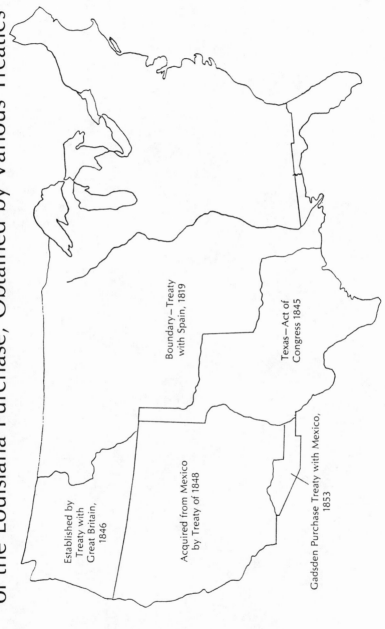

Established by Treaty with Great Britain, 1846

Boundary—Treaty with Spain, 1819

Texas—Act of Congress 1845

Acquired from Mexico by Treaty of 1848

Gadsden Purchase Treaty with Mexico, 1853

The Documents

TREATY BETWEEN THE UNITED STATES OF AMERICA AND HIS BRITANNIC MAJESTY — SEPTEMBER 3, 1783

In the name of the Most Holy and Undivided Trinity.

It having pleased the Divine Providence to dispose the hearts of the most serene and most potent Prince George the Third, by the Grace of God King of Great-Britain, France and Ireland, Defender of the Faith, Duke of Brunswick and Lunebourg, Arch-Treasurer and Prince Elector of the Holy Roman Empire, &c. and of the United States of America, to forget all past misunderstandings and differences that have unhappily interrupted the good correspondence and friendship which they mutually wish to restore; and to establish such a beneficial and satisfactory intercourse between the two countries, upon the ground of reciprocal advantages and mutual convenience, as may promote and secure to both perpetual peace and harmony: And having for this desirable end, already laid the foundation of peace and reconciliation, by the provisional articles, signed at Paris, on the thirtieth of November, one thousand seven hundred and eighty-two, by the commissioners empowered on each part, which articles were agreed to be inserted in, and to constitute the treaty of peace proposed to be concluded between the crown of Great-Britain and the said United States, but which treaty was not to be concluded until terms of peace should be agreed upon between Great-Britain and France, and his Britannic Majesty should be ready to conclude such treaty accordingly; and the treaty between Great-Britain and France, having since been concluded, his Britannic Majesty and the United States of America, in order to carry into full effect the provisional articles abovementioned, according to the tenor thereof, have constituted and appointed, that is to say, His Britannic Majesty on his part, David Hartley, Esquire, Member of the Parliament of Great-Britain; and the said United States on their part, John Adams, Esquire, late a Commissioner of the United States of America at the Court of Versailles, late Delegate in Congress from the state of Massachusetts, and Chief Justice of the said state, and Minister Plenipotentiary of the said United States to their High Mightinesses the States General of the United Netherlands; Benjamin Franklin, Esquire, late Delegate in Congress from the state of Pennsylvania, President of the Convention of the said state, and Minister Plenipotentiary from the United States of America at the Court of Versailles; John Jay, Esquire, late President of

Congress, and Chief Justice of the state of New-York, and Minister Plenipotentiary from the said United States at the Court of Madrid, to be the Plenipotentiaries for the concluding and signing the present definitive treaty; who after having reciprocally communicated their respective full powers, have agreed upon and confirmed the following articles.

ARTICLE I.

His Britannic Majesty acknowledges the said United States, viz. New-Hampshire, Massachusetts-Bay, Rhode-Island and Providence Plantations, Connecticut, New-York, New-Jersey, Pennsylvania, Delaware, Maryland, Virginia, North-Carolina, South-Carolina, and Georgia, to be free, sovereign and independent States; that he treats with them as such; and for himself, his heirs and successors, relinquishes all claims to the government, propriety and territorial rights of the same, and every part thereof.

ARTICLE II.

And that all disputes which might arise in future, on the subject of the boundaries of the said United States, may be prevented, it is hereby agreed and declared, that the following are, and shall be their boundaries, viz. From the north-west angle of Nova-Scotia, viz. that angle which is formed by a line, drawn due north from the source of St. Croix river to the Highlands; along the said Highlands which divide those rivers, that empty themselves into the river St. Lawrence, from those which fall into the Atlantic ocean, to the north-westernmost head of Connecticut river, thence down along the middle of that river, to the forty-fifth degree of north latitude; from thence, by a line due west on said latitude, until it strikes the river Iroquois or Cataraquy; thence along the middle of said river into lake Ontario, through the middle of said lake until it strikes the communciation by water between that lake and lake Erie; thence along the middle of said communication into lake Erie, through the middle of said lake until it arrives at the water-communication between that lake and lake Huron; thence along the middle of said water-communication into the lake Huron; thence through the middle of said lake to the water-communication between that lake and lake Superior; thence through lake Superior northward of the isles Royal and Phelipeaux, to the Long Lake; thence through the middle of said Long Lake, and the water-communication between it and the Lake of the Woods, to the said Lake of the Woods; thence through the said lake to the most north-western point thereof, and from thence on a due west course to the river Missisippi; thence by a line to be drawn along the middle of the said river Missisippi until it shall intersect the northernmost part of the thirty-first degree of north latitude. South by a line to be drawn due east from the determination of the line last mentioned, in the latitude of thirty-one degrees north of the Equator, to the middle of the river Apalachicola or Catahouche; thence along the middle thereof to its junction with the Flint river; thence strait to the head of St. Mary's river; and thence down along the middle of St. Mary's river to the Atlantic ocean. East by a line to be drawn along the middle of the river St. Croix, from its mouth in the Bay of Fundy to its source, and from its source directly north to the aforesaid Highlands which divide the rivers that fall into the Atlantic ocean, from those which fall into the river St. Lawrence; comprehending all islands within twenty leagues of any part of the shores of the United States, and lying between lines to be drawn due east from the points where the aforesaid boundaries between Nova-Scotia on the one part, and East-Florida on the other, shall respectively touch the Bay of Fundy and the Atlantic ocean; excepting such islands as now are, or heretofore have been within the limits of the said province of Nova-Scotia.

ARTICLE III.

It is agreed that the people of the United States shall continue to enjoy unmolested the right to take fish of every kind on the Grand Bank, and on all the other banks of Newfoundland; also in the gulph of St. Lawrence, and at all other places in the sea, where the inhabitants of both countries used at any time heretofore to fish; and also that the inhabitants of the United States shall have liberty to take fish of every kind on such part of the coast of Newfoundland as British fishermen shall use (but not to dry or cure the same on that island); and also on the coasts, bays and creeks of all other of his Britannic Majesty's dominions in America; and that American fishermen shall have liberty to dry and cure fish in any of the unsettled bays, harbours and creeks of Nova-Scotia, Magdalen islands, and Labrador, so long as the same shall remain unsettled; but so soon as the same or either of them shall be settled, it shall not be lawful for the said fishermen to dry or cure fish at such settlement, without a previous agreement for that purpose with the inhabitants, proprietors or possessors of the ground.

ARTICLE IV.

It is agreed that creditors or either side, shall meet with no lawful impediment to the recovery of the full value in sterling money, of all bona fide debts heretofore contracted.

ARTICLE V.

It is agreed that the Congress shall earnestly recommend it to the legislatures of the respective states, to provide for the restitution of all estates, rights and properties, which have been confiscated, belonging to real British subjects, and also of the estates, rights and properties of persons resident in districts in the possession of his Majesty's arms, and who have not borne arms against the said United States. And that persons of any other description shall have free liberty to go to any part or parts of any of the thirteen United States, and therein to remain twelve months, unmolested in their endeavours to obtain the restitution of such of their estates, rights and properties, as may have been confiscated; and that Congress shall also earnestly recommend to the several states a reconsideration and revision of all acts or laws regarding the premises, so as to render the said laws or acts perfectly consistent, not only with justice and equity, but with that spirit of conciliation, which on the return of the blessings of peace should universally prevail. And that Congress shall also earnestly recommend to the several states, that the estates, rights and properties of such last mentioned persons, shall be restored to them, they refunding to any persons who may be now in possession, the bona fide price (where any has been given) which such persons may have paid on purchasing any of the said lands, rights or properties, since the confiscation. And it is agreed, that all persons who have any interest in confiscated lands, either by debts, marriage settlements, or otherwise, shall meet with no lawful impediment in the prosecution of their just rights.

ARTICLE VI.

That there shall be no future confiscations made, nor any prosecutions commenced against any person or persons for, or by reason of the part which he or they may have taken in the present war; and that no person shall, on that account, suffer any future loss or damage, either in his person, liberty or property; and that those who may be in confinement on such charges, at the time of the ratification of the treaty in America, shall be immediately set at liberty, and the prosecutions so commenced be discontinued.

ARTICLE VII.

There shall be a firm and perpetual peace between his Britannic Majesty and the said States, and between the subjects of the one and the citizens of the other, wherefore all hostilities, both by sea and land, shall from henceforth cease: all prisoners on both sides shall be set at liberty, and his Britannic Majesty shall, with all convenient speed, and without causing any destruction, or carrying away any negroes or other property of the American inhabitants, withdraw all his armies, garrisons and fleets from the said United States, and from every post, place and harbour within the same; leaving in all fortifications the American artillery that may be therein; and shall also order and cause all archives, records, deeds and papers, belonging to any of the said states, or their citizens, which in the course of the war may have fallen into the hands of his officers, to be forthwith restored and delivered to the proper states and persons to whom they belong.

ARTICLE VIII.

The navigation of the river Missisippi, from its source to the ocean, shall for ever remain free and open to the subjects of Great-Britain, and the citizens of the United States.

ARTICLE IX.

In case it should so happen that any place or territory belonging to Great-Britain or to the United States, should have been conquered by the arms of either from the other, before the arrival of the said provisional articles in America, it is agreed, that the same shall be restored without difficulty, and without requiring any compensation.

ARTICLE X.

The solemn ratifications of the present treaty, expedited in good and due form, shall be exchanged between the contracting parties, in the space of six months, or sooner if possible, to be computed from the day of the signature of the present treaty. In witness whereof, we the undersigned, their Ministers Plenipotentiary, have in their name and in virtue of our full powers, signed with our hands the present definitive treaty, and caused the seals of our arms to be affixed thereto.

Done at Paris, this third day of September, in the year of our Lord one thousand seven hundred and eighty-three.

D. Hartley,	(L.S.)
John Adams,	(L.S.)
B. Franklin,	(L.S.)
John Jay,	(L.S.)

AN ORDINANCE FOR THE GOVERNMENT
OF THE TERRITORY OF THE UNITED STATES
NORTHWEST OF THE RIVER OHIO
(THE CONFEDERATE CONGRESS, JULY 13, 1787)

SECTION 1. *Be it ordained by the United States in Congress assembled,* That the said Territory, for the purpose of temporary government, be one district, subject, however, to be divided into two districts, as future circumstances may, in the opinion of congress, make it expedient.

SEC. 2. *Be it ordained by the authority aforesaid,* That the estates both of resident and non-resident proprietors in the said territory, dying intestate, shall descend to, and be distributed among, their children and the descendants of a deceased child in equal parts, the descendants of a deceased child or grandchild to take the share of their deceased parent in equal parts among them; and where there shall be no children or descendants, then in equal parts to the next of kin, in equal degree; and among collaterals, the children of a deceased brother or sister of the intestate shall have, in equal parts among them, their deceased parent's share; and there shall, in no case, be a distinction between kindred of the whole and half blood; saving in all cases to the widow of the intestate, her third part of the real estate for life, and one-third part of the personal estate; and this law relative to descents and dower, shall remain in full force until altered by the legislature of the district. And until the governor and judges shall adopt laws as hereinafter mentioned, estates in the said territory may be devised or bequeathed by wills in writing, signed and sealed by him or her in whom the estate may be, (being of full age,) and attested by three witnesses; and real estates may be conveyed by lease and release, or bargain and sale, signed, sealed, and delivered by the person, being of full age, in whom the estate may be, and attested by two witnesses, provided such wills be duly proved, and such conveyances be acknowledged, or the execution thereof duly proved, and be recorded within one year after proper magistrates, courts, and registers, shall be appointed for that purpose; and personal property may be transferred by delivery, saving, however, to the French and Canadian inhabitants, and other settlers of the Kaskaskies, Saint Vincents, and the neighboring villages, who have heretofore professed themselves citizens of Virginia, their laws and customs now in force among them, relative to the descent and conveyance of property.

SEC. 3. *Be it ordained by the authority aforesaid,* That there shall be appointed, from time to time, by Congress, a governor whose commission shall continue in force for the term of three years, unless sooner revoked by Congress; he shall reside in the district, and have a freehold estate therein, in one thousand acres of land, while in the exercise of his office.

SEC. 4. There shall be appointed from time to time, by Congress, a secretary, whose commission shall continue in force for four years, unless sooner revoked; he shall reside in the district, and have a freehold estate therein, in five hundred acres of land, while in the exercise of his office. It shall be his duty to keep and preserve the acts and laws passed by the legislature, and the public records of the district, and the proceedings of the governor in his executive department, and transmit authentic copies of such acts and proceedings every six months to the Secretary of Congress. There shall also be appointed a court, to consist of three judges, any two of whom to form a court, who shall have a common-law jurisdiction, and reside in the district, and have each therein a freehold estate, in five hundred acres of land, while in the exercise of their offices; and their commissions shall continue in force during good behavior.

SEC. 5. The governor and judges, or a majority of them, shall adopt and publish in the district such laws of the original States, criminal and civil, as may be necessary, and best suited to the circumstances of the district, and report them to Congress from time to time, which laws shall be in force in the district until the organization of the general assembly therein, unless disapproved of by Congress; but afterwards the legislature shall have authority to alter them as they shall think fit.

SEC. 6. The governor, for the time being, shall be commander-in-chief of the militia, appoint and commission all officers in the same below the rank of general officers; all general officers shall be appointed, and commissioned by Congress.

SEC. 7. Previous to the organization of the general assembly the governor shall appoint such magistrates, and other civil officers, in each county or township, as he shall find necessary for the preservation of the peace and good order in the same. After the general assembly shall be organized the powers and duties of magistrates and other civil officers shall be regulated and defined by the said assembly; but all magistrates and other civil officers, not herein otherwise directed, shall, during the continuance of this temporary government, be appointed by the governor.

SEC. 8. For the prevention of crimes and injuries, the laws to be adopted or made shall have force in all parts of the district, and for the execution of process, criminal and civil, the governor shall make proper divisions thereof, and he shall proceed, from time to time, as circumstances may require, to lay out the parts of the district in which the Indian titles shall have been extinguished, into counties and townships, subject, however, to such alterations as may thereafter be made by the legislature.

SEC. 9. So soon as there shall be five thousand free male inhabitants, of full age, in the district, upon giving proof thereof to the governor, they shall receive authority, with time and place, to elect representatives from their counties or townships, to represent them in the general assembly: *Provided,* That for every five hundred free male inhabitants there shall be one representative, and so on, progressively, with the number of free male inhabitants, shall the right of representation increase, until the number of representatives shall amount to twenty-five; after which the number and proportion of representatives shall be regulated by the legislature: *Provided,* That no person be eligible or qualified to act as a representative, unless he shall have been a citizen of one of the United States three years, and be a resident in the district, or unless he shall have resided in the district three years, and, in either case, shall likewise hold in his own right, in fee-simple, two hundred acres of land within the same: *Provided also,* That a freehold in fifty acres of land in the district, having been a citizen of one of the States, and being resident in the district, or the like freehold and two years' residence in the district, shall be necessary to qualify a man as an elector of a representative.

SEC. 10. The representatives thus elected shall serve for the term of two years; and in case of the death of a representative, or removal from office, the governor shall issue a writ to the county or township, for which he was a member, to elect another in his stead, to serve for the residue of the term.

SEC. 11. The general assembly, or legislature, shall consist of the governor, legislative council, and a house of representatives. The legislative council shall consist of five members, to continue in office five years, unless sooner removed by Congress; any three of whom to be a quorum; and the members of the council shall be nominated and appointed in the following manner, to wit: As soon as representatives shall be elected the governor shall appoint a time and place for them to meet together, and, when met they shall nominate ten persons, resident in the district, and each possessed of a freehold in five hundred acres of land, and return their names to Congress, five of whom Congress shall appoint and commission to serve as aforesaid; and whenever a vacancy shall happen in the council, by death or removal from office, the house of representatives shall nominate two persons, qualified as aforesaid, for each vacancy, and return their names to Congress, one of whom Congress shall appoint and commission for the residue of the term; and every five years, four months at least before the expiration of the time of service of the members of the council, the said house shall nominate ten persons, qualified as aforesaid, and return their names to Congress, five of whom Congress shall appoint and commission to serve as members of the council five years, unless sooner removed. And the governor, legislative council, and house of representatives shall have authority to make laws in all cases for the good government of the district, not repugnant to the principles and articles in this ordinance established and declared. And all bills, having passed by a majority in the house, and by a majority in the council, shall be referred to the governor for his assent; but no bill or legislative act whatever, shall be of any force without his assent. The governor shall have power to convene, prorogue, and dissolve the general assembly, when, in his opinion, it shall be expedient.

SEC. 12. The governor, judges, legislative council, secretary, and such other officers as Congress shall appoint in the district, shall take an oath or affirmation of fidelity, and of office; the governor before the President of Congress, and all other officers before the governor. As soon as a legislature shall be formed in the district, the council and house assembled, in one room, shall have authority, by joint ballot, to elect a delegate to Congress, who shall have a seat in Congress, with a right of debating, but not of voting, during this temporary government.

SEC. 13. And for extending the fundamental principles of civil and religious liberty, which form the basis whereon these republics, their laws and constitutions, are erected; to fix and establish those principles as the basis of all laws, constitutions, and governments, which forever hereafter shall be formed in the said territory; to provide, also, for the establishment of States, and permanent government therein, and for their admission to a share in the Federal councils on an equal footing with the original States, at as early periods as may be consistent with the general interest:

SEC. 14. It is hereby ordained and declared, by the authority aforesaid, That the following articles shall be considered as articles of compact, between the original States and the people and States in the said territory, and forever remain unalterable, unless by common consent, to wit:

ARTICLE I

No person, demeaning himself in a peaceable and orderly manner, shall ever be molested on account of his mode of worship, or religious sentiments, in said territories.

ARTICLE II

The inhabitants of the said territory shall always be entitled to the benefits of the writs of *habeas corpus,* and of the trial by jury; of a proportionate representation of the people in the legislature, and of judicial proceedings according to the course of the common law. All persons shall be bailable, unless for capital offences, where the proof shall be evident, or presumption great. All fines shall be moderate; and no cruel or unusual punishments shall be inflicted. No man shall be deprived of his liberty or property, but by the judgement of his peers, or the law of the land, and should the public exigencies make it necessary, for the common preservation, to take any person's property, or to demand his particular services, full compensation shall be made for the same. And, in the just preservation of rights and property, it is understood and declared, that no law ought ever to be made or have force in said territory, that shall, in any manner whatever, interfere with or affect private contracts, or engagements, *bona fide*, and without fraud previously formed.

ARTICLE III

Religion, morality, and knowledge being necessary to good government, and the happiness of mankind, schools and the means of education shall forever be encouraged. The utmost good faith shall always be observed towards the Indians; their lands and property shall never be taken from them without their consent; and in their property, rights, and liberty they never shall be invaded or disturbed, unless in just and lawful wars authorized by Congress; but laws founded in justice and humanity shall, from time to time, be made, for preventing wrongs being done to them, and for preserving peace and friendship with them.

ARTICLE IV

The said territory, and the States which may be formed therein, shall forever remain a part of this confederacy of the United States of America, subject to the Articles of Confederation, and to such alterations therein as shall be constitutionally made; and to all the acts and ordinances of the United States in Congress assembled, conformable thereto. The inhabitants and settlers in the said territory shall be subject to pay a part of the Federal debts, contracted, or to be contracted, and a proportional part of the expenses of government to be apportioned on them by Congress, according to the same common rule and measure by which apportionments thereof shall be made on the other States; and the taxes for paying their proportion shall be laid and levied by the authority and direction of the legislatures of the district, or districts, or new States, as in the original States, within the time agreed upon by the United States in Congress assembled. The legislatures of those districts, or new States, shall never interfere with the primary disposal of the soil by the United States in Congress assembled, nor with any regulations Congress may find necessary for securing the title in such soil to the *bona-fide* purchasers. No tax shall be imposed on lands the property of the United States; and in no case shall nonresident proprietors be taxed higher than residents. The navigable waters leading into the Mississippi and Saint Lawrence, and the carrying places between the same, shall be common highways, and forever free, as well to the inhabitants of the said territory as to the citizens of the United States, and those of any other States that may be admitted into the confederacy, without any tax, impost, or duty therefor.

ARTICLE V

There shall be formed in the said territory not less than three nor more than five States; and the boundaries of the States, as soon as Virginia shall alter her act of cession and consent to the same, shall become fixed and established as follows, to wit: The western State, in the said territory, shall be bounded by the Mississippi, the Ohio, and the Wabash Rivers; a direct line drawn from the Wabash and Post Vincents, due north, to the territorial line between the United States and Canada; and by the said territorial line to the Lake of the Woods and Mississippi. The middle State shall be bounded by the said direct line, the Wabash from Post Vincents to the Ohio, by the Ohio, by a direct line drawn due north from the mouth of the Great Miami to the said territorial line, and by the said territorial line. The eastern State shall be bounded by the last-mentioned direct line, the Ohio, Pennsylvania, and the said territorial line: *Provided, however,* And it is further understood and declared, that the boundaries of these three States shall be subject so far to be altered that, if Congress shall hereafter find it expedient, they shall have authority to form one or two States in that part of the said territory which lies north of an east and west line drawn through the southerly bend or extreme of Lake Michigan. And whenever any of the said States shall have sixty thousand free inhabitants therein, such State shall be admitted, by its delegates, into the Congress of the United States, on an equal footing with the original States, in all respects whatever; and shall be at liberty to form a permanent constitution and State government: *Provided,* The constitution and government, so to be formed, shall be republican, and in conformity to the principles contained in these articles, and, so far as it can be consistent with the general interests of the Confederacy, such admission shall be allowed at an earlier period, and when there may be a less number of free inhabitants in the State than sixty thousand.

ARTICLE VI

There shall be neither slavery nor involuntary servitude in the said territory, otherwise than in the punishment of crimes, whereof the party shall have been duly convicted: *Provided always,* That any person escaping into the same, from whom labor or service is lawfully claimed in any one of the original States, such fugitive may be lawfully reclaimed, and conveyed to the person claiming his or her labor service as aforesaid.

Be it ordained by the authority aforesaid, That the resolutions of the 23d of April, 1784, relative to the subject of this ordinance, be, and the same are hereby, repealed, and declared null and void.

Done by the United States, in Congress assembled, the 13th day of July, in the year of our Lord 1787, and of their sovereignty and independence the 12th.

CHARLES THOMSON,

Sec'y.

AN ACT PASSED AT A GENERAL ASSEMBLY OF THE COMMONWEALTH OF VIRGINIA DECEMBER 18, 1789 (EXCERPT) CHAP. XIV.

An ACT Concerning the Erection of the District of Kentucky into an Independent State. Passed the 18th of December, 1789.

Sect. IV. The said convention shall be held at Danville on the twenty sixth day of July next, and shall and may proceed, after choosing a president and other proper officers, and settling the proper rules of proceeding, to consider and determine whether it be expedient for, and the will of the good people of the said district that the same be enacted into an independent state, on the terms and conditions following:

Sect. V. First, that the boundary between the proposed state and Virginia, shall remain the same as at present separates the district from the residue of this Commonwealth.

. . . . . .

AN ACT TO ACCEPT A CESSION OF THE CLAIMS OF THE STATE OF NORTH CAROLINA TO A CERTAIN DISTRICT OF WESTERN TERRITORY APRIL 2, 1790

A deed of cession having been executed, and in the Senate offered for acceptance to the United States, of the claims of the state of North Carolina, to a district of territory therein described; which deed is in the words following, viz.

To all who shall see these Presents

We the underwritten Samuel Johnston and Benjamin Hawkins, Senators in the Congress of the United States of America, duly and constitutionally chosen by the legislature of the State of North Carolina, send greeting. Whereas the General Assembly of the State of North Carolina, on the _____ day of December, in the year of our Lord one thousand seven hundred and eighty-nine, passed an act, entituled "An Act for the purpose of ceding to the United States of America, certain western lands therein described," in the words following, to wit:

Whereas the United States in Congress assembled, have repeatedly and earnestly recommended to the respective states in the Union, claiming or owning vacant western territory, to make cession of part of the same, as a further means, as well hastening the extinguishment of the debts, as of establishing the harmony of the United States; and the inhabitants of the said western territory being also desirous that such cession should be made, in order to obtain a more ample protection than they have heretofore received: now this state, being ever desirous of doing ample justice to the public creditors, as well as the establishing the harmony of the United States, and complying with the reasonable desires of her citizens; *Be it enacted by the General Assembly of the State of North Carolina, and it is hereby enacted by the authority of the same,* That the Senators of this state, in the Congress of the United States, or one of the Senators and any two of the Representatives of this state in the Congress of the United States, are hereby authorized, empowered and required to execute a deed or deeds on the part and behalf of this state, conveying to the United States of America, all right, title and claim which this state has to the sovereignty and territory of the lands situated within the chartered limits of this state, west of a line beginning on the extreme height of the Stone Mountain, at the place where the Virginia line intersects it; running thence along the extreme height of the said mountain, to the place where Wataugo river breaks through it; thence a direct course to the top of the Yellow Mountain, where Bright's road crosses the same; thence along the ridge of said mountain, between the waters of Doe river and the waters of Rock Creek, to the place where the road crosses the Iron Mountain; from thence along the extreme height of said mountain, to where Nolichucky river runs through the same; thence to the top of the Bald Mountain; thence along the extreme height of the said mountain to the Painted Rock, on French Broad river; thence along the highest ridge of the said mountain, to the place where it is called the Great Iron or Smoaky Mountain: thence along the extreme height of the said mountain, to the place where it is called Unicoy or Unaka Mountain, between the Indian towns of Cowee and Old Chota; thence along the main ridge of the said mountain, to the southern boundary of this state, upon the following express conditions, and subject thereto — that is to say: *First,* That neither the lands nor inhabitants westward of the said mountain shall be estimated after the cession made by virtue of this act shall be accepted, in the ascertaining the proportion of this state with the United States, in the common expense occasioned by the late war. *Secondly,* That the lands laid off, or directed to be laid off by any act or acts of the General Assembly of this state, for the officers and soldiers thereof, their heirs and assigns respectively, shall be and enure to the use and benefit of the said officers, their heirs and assigns respectively; and if the bounds of the said lands already prescribed for the officers and soldiers of the continental line of this state, shall not contain a sufficient quantity of lands fit for cultivation, to make good the several provisions intended by law, that such officer or soldier, or his assignee, who shall fall short of his allotment or proportion, after all the lands fit for cultivation within the said bounds are appropriated, be permitted to take his quota, or such part thereof as may be deficient, in any other part of the said territory intended to be ceded by virtue of this act, not already appropriated. And where entries have been made agreeable to law, and titles under them not perfected by grant or otherwise, then, and in that case, the governor for the time being shall, and he is hereby required to perfect, from time to time, such titles, in such manner as if this act had never been passed. And that all entries made by, or grants made to all and every person or persons whatsoever, agreeable to law, and within the limits hereby intended to be ceded to the United States, shall have the same force and effect as if such cession had not been made; and that all and every right of occupancy and pre-emption, and every other right reserved by any act or acts to persons settled on, and occupying lands within the limits of the lands hereby intended to be ceded as aforesaid, shall continue to be in full force, in the same manner as if the cession had not been made, and as conditions upon which the said lands are ceded to the United States. And further, it shall be understood, that if any person or persons shall have, by virtue of the act, entitled "An act for opening the land-office for the redemption of specie and other certificates, and discharging the arrears due to the army," passed in the year one thousand seven hundred and eighty-three, made his or their entry in the office usually called John Armstrong's office, and located the same to any spot or piece of ground, on which any other person or persons shall have previously located any entry or entries, that then, and in that case, the person or persons having made such entry or entries, or their assignee or assignees, shall have leave, and be at full liberty to remove the location of such entry or entries, to any lands on which no entry has been specially located, or on any vacant lands included within the limits of the lands hereby intended to be ceded: *Provided,* That nothing herein contained shall extend or be construed to extend to the making good any entry or entries, or any grant or grants heretofore declared void, by any act or acts of the General Assembly of this state. *Thirdly,* That all the lands intended to be ceded by virtue of this act to the United States of America, and not appropriated as before mentioned, shall be considered as a common fund for the use and benefit of the United States of America, North Carolina inclusive, according to their respective and usual proportion in the general charge and expenditure, and shall be faithfully disposed of for that purpose, and for no other use or purpose whatever. *Fourthly,* That the territory so ceded, shall be laid out and formed into a state or states, containing a suitable extent of territory, the inhabitants of which shall enjoy all the privileges, benefits and advantages set forth in the ordinance of the late Congress, for the government of the western territory of the United States, that is to say; whenever the Congress of the United States shall cause to be officially transmitted to the executive authority of this state, an authenticated copy of the act to be passed by the Congress of the United States, accepting the cession of territory made by virtue of this act, under the express conditions hereby specified; the said Congress shall at the same time assume the government of the said ceded territory, which they shall execute in a manner similar to that which they support in the territory west of the Ohio; shall protect the inhabitants against enemies, and shall never bar or deprive them of any privileges which the people in the territory west of the Ohio enjoy: *Provided always,* That no regulations made or to be made by Congress, shall tend to emancipate slaves. *Fifthly,* That the inhabitants of the said ceded territory shall be liable to pay such sums of money, as may, from taking their census, be their just proportion of the debt of the United States, and the arrears of the requisitions of Congress on this state. *Sixthly,* That all persons indebted to this state, residing in the territory intended to be ceded by virtue of this act, shall be held and deemed liable to pay such debt or debts in the same manner, and under the same penalty or penalties as if this act had never been passed. *Seventhly,* That if the Congress of the United States do not accept the cession hereby intended to be made, in due form, and give official notice thereof to the executive of this state, within eighteen months from the passing of this act, then this act shall be of no force or effect whatsoever. *Eighthly,* That the laws in force and use in the State of North Carolina, at the time of passing this act, shall be, and continue in full force within the territory hereby ceded, until the same shall be repealed, or otherwise altered by the legislative authority of the said territory. *Ninthly,* That the lands of non-resident proprietors within the said ceded territory, shall not be taxed higher than the lands of residents. *Tenthly,* That this act shall not prevent the people now residing south of French Broad, between the rivers Tennessee and Big Pigeon, from entering their pre-emptions in that tract, should an office be opened for that purpose, under an act of the present General Assembly. *And be it further enacted by the authority aforesaid,* That the sovereignty and jurisdiction of this state, in and over the territory aforesaid, and all and every the inhabitants thereof, shall be and remain the same in all respects, until the Congress of the United States shall accept the cession to be made by virtue of this act, as if this act had never passed.

Read three times, and ratified in General Assembly, the _____ day of December, A.D. 1789.

> Chas. Johnson, *Sp. Sen.*
> S. Cabarrus, *Sp. H.C.*"

Now therefore know ye, That we, Samuel Johnston and Benjamin Hawkins, senators aforesaid, by virtue of the power and authority committed to us by the said act, and in the name, and for and on behalf of the said state, do, by these presents, convey, assign, transfer, and set over unto the United States of America, for the benefit of the said states, North Carolina inclusive, all right, title, and claim which the said state hath to the sovereignty and territory of the lands situated within the chartered limits of the said state, as bounded and described in the above recited act of the General Assembly, to and for the uses and purposes, and on the conditions mentioned in the said act.

In witness whereof, we have hereunto subscribed our names, and affixed our seals, in the senate-chamber, at New York, this twenty-fifth day of

February, in the year of our Lord, one thousand seven hundred and ninety, and in the fourteenth year of the independence of the United States of America.

Sam. Johnston.   (L.S.)

Benjamin Hawkins.   (L.S.)

Signed, sealed, and delivered
  in the presence of
Sam. A. Otis.

Be it enacted by the Senate and House of Representatives of the United States of America in Congress assembled, That the said deed be, and the same is hereby accepted.

Approved, April 2, 1790.

AN ACT FOR THE GOVERNMENT
OF THE TERRITORY OF THE UNITED STATES,
SOUTH OF THE RIVER OHIO
MAY 26, 1790

SECTION 1. *Be it enacted by the Senate and House of Representatives of the United States of America in Congress assembled,* That the territory of the United States south of the river Ohio, for the purposes of temporary government, shall be one district; the inhabitants of which shall enjoy all the privileges, benefits and advantages set forth in the ordinance of the late Congress, for the government of the territory of the United States northwest of the river Ohio. And the government of the said territory south of the Ohio, shall be similar to that which is now exercised in the territory northwest of the Ohio; except so far as is otherwise provided in the conditions expressed in an act of Congress of the present session entitled "An act to accept a cession of the claims of the State of North Carolina, to a certain district of western territory."

SECTION 2. *And be it further enacted,* That the salaries of the officers, which the President of the United States shall nominate, and with the advice and consent of the Senate appoint, by virtue of this act, shall be the same as those, by law established, of similar officers in the government northwest of the river Ohio. And the powers, duties and emoluments of a superintendent of Indian affairs for the southern department, shall be united with those of the governor.

Approved, May 26, 1790.

AN ACT FOR ESTABLISHING THE
TEMPORARY AND PERMANENT SEAT OF THE
GOVERNMENT OF THE UNITED STATES
JULY 16, 1790

SECTION 1. *Be it enacted by the Senate and House of Representatives of the United States of America in Congress assembled,* That a district of territory, not exceeding ten miles square, to be located as hereafter directed on the river Potomac, at some place between the mouths of the Eastern Branch and Connogochegue, be, and the same is hereby accepted for the permanent seat of the government of the United States. *Provided nevertheless,* That the operation of the laws of the state within such district shall not be affected by this acceptance, until the time fixed for the removal of the government thereto, and until Congress shall otherwise by law provide.

SEC. 2. *And be it further enacted,* That the President of the United States be authorized to appoint, and by supplying vacancies happening from refusals to act or other causes, to keep in appointment as long as may be necessary, three commissioners, who, or any two of whom, shall, under the direction of the President, survey, and by proper metes and bounds define and limit a district of territory, under the limitations above mentioned; and the district so defined, limited and located, shall be deemed the district accepted by this act, for the permanent seat of the government of the United States.

SEC. 3. *And be it [further] enacted,* That the said commissioners, or any two of them, shall have power to purchase or accept such quantity of land on the eastern side of the said river, within the said district, as the President shall deem proper for the use of the United States, and according to such plans as the President shall approve, the said commissioners, or any two of them, shall, prior to the first Monday in December, in the year one thousand eight hundred, provide suitable buildings for the accommodation of Congress, and of the President, and for the public offices of the government of the United States.

SEC. 4. *And be it [further] enacted,* That for defraying the expense of such purchase and buildings, the President of the United States be authorized and requested to accept grants of money.

SEC. 5. *And be it [further] enacted,* That prior to the first Monday in December next, all offices attached to the seat of the government of the United States, shall be removed to, and until the said first Monday in December, in the year one thousand eight hundred, shall remain at the city of Philadelphia, in the state of Pennsylvania, at which place the session of Congress next ensuing the present shall be held.

SEC. 6. *And be it [further] enacted,* That on the said first Monday in December, in the year one thousand eight hundred, the seat of the government of the United States shall, by virtue of this act, be transferred to the district and place aforesaid. And all offices attached to the said seat of government, shall accordingly be removed thereto by their respective holders, and shall, after the said day, cease to be exercised elsewhere; and that the necessary expense of such removal shall be defrayed out of the duties on imposts and tonnage, of which a sufficient sum is hereby appropriated.

Approved, July 16, 1790.

AN ACT DECLARING THE CONSENT OF CONGRESS, THAT A NEW STATE BE FORMED WITHIN THE JURISDICTION OF THE COMMONWEALTH OF VIRGINIA AND ADMITTED INTO THIS UNION, BY THE NAME OF THE STATE OF KENTUCKY

FEBRUARY 4, 1791

WHEREAS the legislature of the commonwealth of Virginia, by an act entitled "An act concerning the erection of the district of Kentucky into an independent state," passed the eighteenth day of December, one thousand seven hundred and eighty-nine, have consented, that the district of Kentucky, within the jurisdiction of the said commonwealth, and according to its actual boundaries at the time of passing the act aforesaid, should be formed into a new state: And whereas a convention of delegates, chosen by the people of the said district of Kentucky, have petitioned Congress to consent, that, on the first day of June, one thousand seven hundred and ninety-two, the said district should be formed into a new state, and received into the Union, by the name of "The State of Kentucky:"

SECTION 1. *Be it enacted by the Senate and House of Representatives of the United States of America in Congress assembled, and it is hereby enacted and declared,* That the Congress doth consent, that the said district of Kentucky, within the jurisdiction of the commonwealth of Virginia, and according to its actual boundaries, on the eighteenth day of December, one thousand seven hundred and eighty-nine, shall, upon the first day of June, one thousand seven hundred and ninety-two, be formed into a new State, separate from and independent of, the said commonwealth of Virginia.

SEC. 2. *And be it further enacted and declared,* That upon the aforesaid first day of June, one thousand seven hundred and ninety-two, the said new State, by the name and style of the State of Kentucky, shall be received and admitted into this Union, as a new and entire member of the United States of America.

Approved, February 4, 1791.

AN ACT FOR THE ADMISSION
OF THE STATE OF VERMONT INTO THIS UNION
FEBRUARY 18, 1791

The state of Vermont having petitioned the Congress to be admitted a member of the United States, *Be it enacted by the Senate and House of Representatives of the United States of America in Congress assembled, and it is hereby enacted and declared,* That on the fourth day of March, one thousand seven hundred and ninety-one, the said state, by the name and style of "The State of Vermont," shall be received and admitted into this Union, as a new and entire member of the United States of America.

Approved, February 18, 1791.

AN ACT TO AMEND "AN ACT FOR
ESTABLISHING THE TEMPORARY AND PERMANENT
SEAT OF THE GOVERNMENT OF THE UNITED STATES"
MARCH 3, 1791

Be it enacted by the Senate and House of Representatives of the United States of America in Congress assembled, That so much of the act, intitled "An act for establishing the temporary and permanent seat of the government of the United States," as requires that the whole of the district of territory, not exceeding ten miles square, to be located on the river Potomac, for the permanent seat of the government of the United States, shall be located above the mouth of the Eastern Branch, be and is hereby repealed, and that it shall be lawful for the President to make any part of the territory below the said limit, and above the mouth of Hunting Creek, a part of the said district, so as to include a convenient part of the Eastern Branch, and of the lands lying on the lower side thereof, and also the town of Alexandria, and the territory so to be included, shall form a part of the district not exceeding ten miles square, for the permanent seat of the government of the United States, in like manner and to all intents and purposes, as if the same had been within the purview of the above recited act: *Provided,* That nothing herein contained, shall authorize the erection of the public buildings otherwise than on the Maryland side of the river Potomac, as required by the aforesaid act.

Approved, March 3, 1791.

TREATY BETWEEN
THE UNITED STATES OF AMERICA AND SPAIN
OCTOBER 27, 1795

His Catholic Majesty and the United States of America desiring to consolidate on a permanent basis the Friendship and good correspondence which happily prevails between the two Parties, have determined to establish by a convention several points, the settlement whereof will be productive of general advantage and reciprocal utility to both Nations.

With this intention his Catholic Majesty has appointed the most Excellent Lord Don Manuel de Godoy and Alvarez de Faria, Rios, Sanchez Zarzosa, Prince de la Paz Duke de la Alcudia Lord of the Soto de Roma and of the State of Albalá: Grandee of Spain of the first class: perpetual Regidor of the Citty of Santiago: Knight of the illustrious Order of the Golden Fleece, and Great Cross of the Royal and distinguished Spanish order of Charles the III. Commander of Valencia del Ventoso, Rivera, and Aceuchal in that of Santiago: Knight and Great Cross of the religious order of S! John: Counsellor of State: First Secretary of State and Despacho: Secretary to the Queen: Superintendent General of the Posts and High Ways: Protector of the Royal Academy of the Noble Arts, and of the Royal Societies of natural history, Botany, Chemistry, and Astronomy: Gentleman of the King's Chamber in employement: Captain General of his Armies: Inspector and Major of the Royal Corps of Body Guards &ª &ª &ª and the President of the United States with the advice and consent of their Senate, has appointed Thomas Pinckney a Citizen of the United States, and their Envoy Extraordinary to his Catholic Majesty. And the said Plenipotentiaries have agreed upon and concluded the following Articles.

ART. I.

There shall be a firm and inviolable Peace and sincere Friendship between His Catholic Majesty his successors and subjects, and the United Estates and their Citizens without exception of persons or places.

ART. II.

To prevent all disputes on the subject of the boundaries which separate the territories of the two High contracting Parties, it is hereby declared and agreed as follows: to wit: The Southern boundary of the United States which divides their territory from the Spanish Colonies of East and West Florida, shall be designated by a line beginning on the River Mississippi at the Northermost part of the thirty first degree of latitude North of the Equator, which from thence shall be drawn due East to the middle of the River Apalachicola or Catahouche, thence along the middle thereof to its junction with the Flint, thence straight to the head of S<u>t</u> Mary's River, and thence down the middle there of to the Atlantic Occean. And it is agreed that if there should be any troops, Garrisons or settlements of either Party in the territory of the other according to the above mentioned boundaries, they shall be withdrawn from the said territory within the term of six months after the ratification of this treaty or sooner if it be possible and that they shall be permitted to take with them all the goods and effects which they possess.

ART. III.

In order to carry the preceding Article into effect one Commissioner and one Surveyor shall be appointed by each of the contracting Parties who shall meet at the Natchez on the left side of the River Mississippi before the expiration of six months from the ratification of this convention, and they shall proceed to run and mark this boundary according to the stipulations of the said Article. They shall make Plats and keep journals of their proceedings which shall be considered as part of this convention, and shall have the same force as if they were inserted therein. And if on any account it should be found necessary that the said Commissioners and Surveyors should be accompanied by Guards, they shall be furnished in equal proportions by the Commanding Officer of his Majesty's troops in the two Floridas, and the Commanding Officer of the troops of the United States in their Southwestern territory, who shall act by common consent and amicably, as well with respect to this point as to the furnishing of provissions and instruments and making every other arrangement which may be necessary or useful for the execution of this article.

ART. IV.

It is likewise agreed that the Western boundary of the United States which separates them from the Spanish Colony of Louisiana, is in the middle of the channel or bed of the River Mississippi from the Northern boundary of the said States to the completion of the thirty first degree of latitude North of the Equator; and his Catholic Majesty has likewise agreed that the navigation of the said River in its whole breadth from its source to the Occean shall be free only to his Subjects, and the Citizens of the United States, unless he should extend this privilege to the Subjects of other Powers by special convention.

ART. V.

The two High contracting Parties shall by all the means in their power maintain peace and harmony among the several Indian Nations who inhabit the country adjacent to the lines and Rivers which by the preceeding Articles form the boundaries of the two Floridas; and the beter to obtain this effect both Parties oblige themselves expressly to restrain by force all hostilities on the part of the Indian Nations living within their boundaries: so that Spain will not suffer her Indians to attack the Citizens of the United States, nor the Indians inhabiting their territory; nor will the United States permit these last mentioned Indians to commence hostilities against the Subjects of his Catholic Majesty, or his Indians in any manner whatever.

And whereas several treaties of Friendship exist between the two contracting Parties and the said Nations of Indians, it is hereby agreed that in future no treaty of alliance or other whatever (except treaties of Peace) shall be made by either Party with the Indians living within the boundary of the other; but both Parties will endeavour to make the advantages of the Indian trade common and mutually beneficial to their respective Subjects and Citizens observing in all things the most complete reciprocity: so that both Parties may obtain the advantages arising from a good understanding with the said Nations, without being subject to the expence which they have hitherto occasioned.

ART. VI.

Each Party shall endeavour by all means in their power to protect and defend all Vessels and other effects belonging to the Citizens or Subjects of the other, which shall be within the extent of their jurisdiction by sea or by land, and shall use all their efforts to recover and cause to be restored to the right owners their Vessels and effects which may have been taken from them within the extent of their said jurisdiction whether they are at war or not with the Power whose Subjects have taken possession of the said effects.

ART. VII.

And it is agreed that the Subjects or Citizens of each of the contracting Parties, their Vessels, or effects shall not be liable to any embargo or detention on the part of the other for any military expedition or other public or private purpose whatever; and in all cases of seizure, detention, or arrest for debts contracted or offences commited by any Citizen or Subject of the one Party within the jurisdiction of the other, the same shall be made and prosecuted by order and authority of law only, and according to the regular course of proceedings usual in such cases. The Citizens and Subjects of both Parties shall be allowed to employ such Advocates, Sollicitors, Notaries, Agents, and Factors, as they may judge proper in all their affairs and in all their trials at law in which they may be concerned before the tribunals of the other Party, and such Agents shall have free access to be present at the proceedings in such causes, and at the taking of all examinations and evidence which may be exhibited in the said trials.

ART. VIII.

In case the Subjects and inhabitants of either Party with their shipping whether public and of war or private and of merchants be forced through stress of weather, pursuit of Pirates, or Enemies, or any other urgent necessity for seeking of shelter and harbor to retreat and enter into any of the Rivers, Bays, Roads, or Ports belonging to the other Party, they shall be received and treated with all humanity, and enjoy all favor, protection and help, and they shall be permitted to refresh and provide themselves at reasonable rates with victuals and all things needful for the sustenance of their persons or reparation of their Ships, and prosecution of their voyage; and they shall no ways be hindered from returning out of the said Ports, or Roads, but may remove and depart when and whither they please without any let or hindrance.

ART. IX.

All Ships and merchandize of what nature soever which shall be rescued out of the hands of any Pirates or Robbers on the high seas shall be brought into some Port of either State and shall be delivered to the custody of the Officers of that Port in order to be taken care of and restored entire to the true proprietor as soon as due and sufficient proof shall be made concerning the property there of.

ART. X.

When any Vessel of either Party shall be wrecked, foundered, or otherwise damaged on the coasts or within the dominion of the other, their respective Subjects or Citizens shall receive as well for themselves as for their Vessels and effects the same assistence which would be due to the inhabitants of the Country where the damage happens, and shall pay the same charges and dues only as the said inhabitants would be subject to pay in a like case: and if the operations of repair should require that the whole or any part of the cargo be unladen they shall pay no duties, charges, or fees on the part which they shall relade and carry away.

ART. XI.

The Citizens and Subjects of each Party shall have power to dispose of their personal goods within the jurisdiction of the other by testament, dona-tion, or otherwise; and their representatives being Subjects or Citizens of the other Party shall succeed to their said personal goods, whether by testament or ab intestato and they may take possession thereof either by themselves or others acting for them, and dispose of the same at their will paying such dues only as the inhabitants of the Country wherein the said goods are shall be subject to pay in like cases, and in case of the absence of the representatives, such care shall be taken of the said goods as would be taken of the goods of a native in like case, until the lawful owner may take measures for receiving them. And if question shall arise among several claimants to which of them the said goods belong the same shall be decided finally by the laws and Judges of the Land wherein the said goods are. And where on the death of any person holding real estate within the territories of the one Party, such real estate would by the laws of the Land descend on a Citizen or Subject of the other were he not disqualified by being an alien, such subject shall be allowed a reasonable time to sell the same and to withdraw the proceeds without molestation, and exempt from all rights of detraction on the part of the Government of the respective states.

ART. XII.

The merchant Ships of either of the Parties which shall be making into a Port belonging to the enemy of the other Party and concerning whose voyage and the species of goods on board her there shall be just grounds of suspicion shall be obliged to exhibit as well upon the high seas as in the Ports and havens not only her passports but likewise certificates expressly shewing that her goods are not of the number of those which have been prohibited as contraband.

ART. XIII.

For the beter promoting of commerce on both sides, it is agreed that if a war shall break out between the said two Nations one year after the proclamation of war shall be allowed to the merchants in the Cities and Towns where they shall live for collecting and transporting their goods and merchandizes, and if any thing be taken from them, or any injury be done them within that term by either Party, or the People or Subjects of either, full satisfaction shall be made for the same by the Government.

ART. XIV.

No subject of his Catholic Majesty shall apply for or take any commission or letters of marque for arming any Ship or Ships to act as Privateers against the said United States or against the Citizens, People, or inhabitants of the said United States, or against the property of any of the inhabitants of any of them, from any Prince or State with which the said United States shall be at war.

Nor shall any Citizen, Subject, or Inhabitant of the said United States apply for or take any commission or letters of marque for arming any Ship or Ships to act as Privateers against the subjects of his Catholic Majesty or the property of any of them from any Prince or State with which the said King shall be at war. And if any person of either Nation shall take such commissions or letters of marque he shall be punished as a Pirate.

ART. XV.

It shall be lawful for all and singular the Subjects of his Catholic Majesty, and the Citizens People, and inhabitants of the said United States to sail with their Ships with all manner of liberty and security, no distinction being made who are the proprietors of the merchandizes laden thereon from any Port to the Places of those who now are or hereafter shall be at enmity with his Catholic Majesty or the United States. It shall be likewise lawful for the Subjects and inhabitants aforesaid to sail with the Ships and merchandizes aforementioned, and to trade with the same liberty and security from the Places, Ports, and Havens of those who are Enemies of both or either Party without any opposition or disturbance whatsoever, not only directly from the Places of the Enemy aforementioned to neutral Places but also from one Place belonging to an Enemy to another Place belonging to an Enemy, whether they be under the jurisdiction of the same Prince or under several, and it is hereby stipulated that Free Ships shall also give freedom to goods, and that every thing shall be deemed free and exempt which shall be found on board the Ships belonging to the Subjects of either of the contracting Parties although the whole lading or any part thereof should appartain to the Enemies of either; contraband goods being always excepted. It is also agreed that the same liberty be extended to persons who are on board a free Ship, so that, although they be Enemies to either Party they shall not be made Prisoners or taken out of that free Ship unless they are Soldiers and in actual service of the Enemies.

ART. XVI.

This liberty of navigation and commerce shall extend to all kinds of merchandizes excepting those only which are distinguished by the name contraband; and under this name of contraband or prohibited goods shall be comprehended arms, great guns, bombs, with the fusees, and other things belonging to them, cannon ball, gun powder, match, pikes, swords, lances, speards, halberds, mortars, petards, granades, salpetre, muskets, musket ball bucklers, helmets, breast plates, coats of mail, and the like kind of arms proper for arming soldiers, musket rests, belts, horses with their furniture and all other warlike instruments whatever. These merchandizes which follows shall not be reconed among contraband or prohibited goods; that is to say, all sorts of cloths and all other manufactures woven of any wool, flax, silk, cotton, or any other materials whatever, all kinds of wearing aparel together with all species whereof they are used to be made, gold and silver as well coined as uncoined, tin, iron, latton, copper, brass, coals, as also wheat, barley, oats, and any other kind of corn and pulse: tobacco and likewise all manner of spices, salted and smoked flesh, salted fish, cheese and butter, beer, oils, wines, sugars, and all sorts of salts, and in general all provisions which serve for the sustenance of life. Furthermore all kinds of cotton, hemp, flax, tar, pitch, ropes, cables, sails, sail cloths, anchors, and any parts of anchors, also ships masts, planks, wood of all kind, and all other things proper either for building or repairing ships, and all other goods whatever which have not been worked into the form of any instrument prepared for war by land or by sea, shall not be reputed contraband, much less such as have been already wrought and made up for any other use: all which shall be wholy reckoned among free goods, as likewise all other merchandizes and things which are not comprehended and particularly mentioned in the foregoing enumeration of contraband goods: so that they may be transported and carried in the freest manner by the subjects of both parties, even to Places belonging to an Enemy, such towns or Places being only excepted as are at that time besieged, blocked up, or invested. And except the cases in which any Ship of war or Squadron shall in consequence of storms or other accidents at sea be under the necessity of taking the cargo of any trading Vessel or Vessels, in which case they may stop the said Vessel or Vessels and furnish themselves with necessaries, giving a receipt in order that the Power to whom the said ship of war belongs may pay for the articles so taken according to the price thereof at the Port to which they may appear to have been destined by the Ship's papers: and the two contracting Parties engage that the Vessels shall not be detained longer than may be absolutely necessary for their said Ships to supply themselves with necessaries: that they will immediately pay the value of the receipts: and indemnify the proprietor for all losses which he may have sustained in consequence of such transaction.

ART. XVII.

To the end that all manner of dissentions and quarels may be avoided and prevented on one side and the other, it is agreed that in case either of the Parties hereto should be engaged in a war, the ships and Vessels belonging to the Subjects or People of the other Party must be furnished with sea letters or passports expressing the name, property, and bulk of the Ship, as also the name and place of habitation of the master or commander of the said Ship, that it may appear thereby that the Ship really and truly belongs to the Subjects of one of the Parties; which passport shall be made out and granted according to the form* annexed to this Treaty. They shall likewise be recalled every year, that is, if the ship happens to return home within the space of a year. It is likewise agreed that such ships being laden, are to be provided not only with passports as above mentioned but also with certificates containing the several particulars of the cargo, the place whence the ship sailed, that so it may be known whether any forbidden or contraband goods be on board the same; which certificates shall be made out by the Officers of the place whence the ship sailed in the accustomed form; and if any one shall think it fit or adviseable to express in the said certificates the person to whom the goods on board belong he may freely do so: without which requisites they may be sent to one of the Ports of the other

*No form of passport is annexed to the treaty.

contracting Party and adjudged by the competent tribunal according to what is above set forth, that all the circumstances of this omission having been well examined, they shall be adjudged to be legal prizes, unless they shall give legal satisfaction of their property by testimony entirely equivalent.

ART. XVIII.

If the Ships of the said subjects, People or inhabitants of either of the Parties shall be met with either sailing along the Coasts on the high Seas by any Ship of war of the other or by any Privateer, the said Ship of war or Privateer for the avoiding of any disorder shall remain out of cannon shot, and may send their boats aboard the merchant Ship which they shall so meet with, and may enter her to number of two or three men only to whom the master or Commander of such ship or vessel shall exhibit his passports concerning the property of the ship made out according to the form* inserted in this present Treaty: and the ship when she shall have shewed such passports shall be free and at liberty to pursue her voyage, so as it shall not be lawful to molest or give her chase in any manner or force her to quit her intended course.

ART. XIX.

Consuls shall be reciprocally established with the privileges and powers which those of the most favoured Nations enjoy in the Ports where their consuls reside, or are permitted to be.

ART. XX.

It is also agreed that the inhabitants of the territories of each Party shall respectively have free access to the Courts of Justice of the other, and they shall be permitted to prosecute suits for the recovery of their properties, the payment of their debts, and for obtaining satisfaction for the damages which they may have sustained, whether the persons whom they may sue be subjects or Citizens of the Country in which they may be found, or any other persons whatsoever who may have taken refuge therein; and the proceedings and sentences of the said Court shall be the same as if the contending parties had been subjects or Citizens of the said Country.

ART. XXI.

In order to terminate all differences on account of the losses sustained by the Citizens of the United States in consequence of their vessels and cargoes having been taken by the Subjects of his Catholic Majesty during the late war

*No form of passport is annexed to the treaty.

between Spain and France, it is agreed that all such cases shall be referred to the final decision of Commissioners to be appointed in the following manner. His Catholic Majesty shall name one Commissioner, and the President of the United States by and with the advice and consent of their Senate shall appoint another, and the said two Commissioners shall agree on the choice of a third, or if they cannot agree so they shall each propose one person, and of the two names so proposed one shall be drawn by lot in the presence of the two original Commissioners, and the person whose name shall be so drawn shall be the third Commissioner, and the three Commissioners so appointed shall be sworn inpartially to examine and decide the claims in question according to the merits of the several cases, and to justice, equity, and the laws of Nations. The said Commissioners shall meet and sit at Philadelphia and in the case of the death, sickness, or necessary absence of any such commissioner his place shall be supplied in the same manner as he was first appointed, and the new Commissioner shall take the same oaths, and do the same duties. They shall receive all complaints and applications, authorized by this article during eighteen months from the day on which they shall assemble. They shall have power to examine all such persons as come before them on oath or affirmation touching the complaints in question, and also to receive in evidence all written testimony authenticated in such manner as they shall think proper to require or admit. The award of the said Commissioners or any two of them shall be final and conclusive both as to the justice of the claim and the amount of the sum to be paid to the claimants; and his Catholic Majesty undertakes to cause the same to be paid in specie without deduction, at such times and Places and under such conditions as shall be awarded by the said Commissioners.

ART. XXII.

The two high contracting Parties hoping that the good correspondence and friendship which happily reigns between them will be further increased by this Treaty, and that it will contribute to augment their prosperity and opulence, will in future give to their mutual commerce all the extension and favor which the advantage of both Countries may require; and in consequence of the stipulations contained in the IV. article his Catholic Majesty will permit the Citizens of the United States for the space of three years from this time to deposit their merchandize and effects in the Port of New Orleans, and to export them from thence without paying any other duty than a fair price for the hire of the stores, and his Majesty promises either to continue this permission if he finds during that time that it is not prejudicial to the interest of Spain, or if he should not agree to continue it there, he will assign to them on another part of the banks of the Mississippi an equivalent establishment.

ART. XXIII.

The present Treaty shall not be in force until ratified by the Contracting Parties, and the ratifications shall be exchanged in six months from this time, or sooner if possible.

In Witness whereof We the underwritten Plenipotentiaries of His Catholic Majesty and of the United States of America have signed this present Treaty of Friendship, Limits and Navigation and have thereunto affixed our seals respectively.

Done at San Lorenzo el Real this seven and twenty day of October one thousand seven hundred and ninety five.

       Thomas Pinckney
       (Seal)
       El Principe de la Paz
       (Seal)

AN ACT FOR THE ADMISSION
OF THE STATE OF TENNESSEE INTO THE UNION
JUNE 1, 1796

WHEREAS by the acceptance of the deed of cession of the state of North Carolina, Congress are bound to lay out into one or more states, the territory thereby ceded to the United States:

Be it enacted by the Senate and House of Representatives of the United States of America in Congress assembled, That the whole of the territory ceded to the United States by the state of North Carolina, shall be one state, and the same is hereby declared to be one of the United States of America, on an equal footing with the original states, in all respects whatever, by the name and title of the State of Tennessee. That until the next general census, the said state of Tennessee shall be entitled to one Representative in the House of Representatives of the United States; and in all other respects, as far as they may be applicable, the laws of the United States shall extend to, and have force in the state of Tennessee, in the same manner, as if that state had originally been one of the United States.

Approved, June 1, 1796.

AN ACT FOR AN AMICABLE SETTLEMENT OF LIMITS WITH THE STATE OF GEORGIA, AND AUTHORIZING THE ESTABLISHMENT OF A GOVERNMENT IN THE MISSISSIPPI TERRITORY
APRIL 7, 1798

SECTION 1. *Be it enacted by the Senate and House of Representatives of the United States of America in Congress assembled,* That the President of the United States be, and he hereby is authorized to appoint three commissioners; any two of whom shall have power to adjust and determine with such commissioners as may be appointed under the legislative authority of the state of Georgia, all interfering claims of the United States and that state, to territory situate west of the river Chatahouchee, north of the thirty-first degree of north latitude, and south of the cession made to the United States by South Carolina: And also to receive any proposal for the relinquishment or cession of the whole or any part of the other territory claimed by the state of Georgia, and out of the ordinary jurisdiction thereof.

SEC. 2. *Be it further enacted,* That all the lands thus ascertained as the property of the United States, shall be disposed of in such manner as shall be hereafter directed by law; and the nett proceeds thereof shall be applied to the sinking and discharging the public debt of the United States, in the same manner as the proceeds of the other public lands in the territory northwest of the river Ohio.

SEC. 3. *Be it further enacted,* That all that tract of country bounded on the west by the Mississippi; on the north by a line to be drawn due east from the mouth of the Yasous to the Chatahouchee river; on the east by the river Chatahouchee; and on the south by the thirty-first degree of north latitude, shall be, and hereby is constituted one district, to be called the Mississippi Territory: and the President of the United States is hereby authorized to establish therein a government in all respects similar to that now exercised in the territory northwest of the river Ohio, excepting and excluding the last article of the ordinance made for the government thereof by the late Congress on the thirteenth day of July one thousand seven hundred and eighty-seven, and by and with the advice and consent of the Senate to appoint all the necessary officers therein, who shall respectively receive the same compensation for their services; to be paid in the same manner as by law established for similar officers in the territory northwest of the river Ohio; and the powers, duties and emoluments of a superintendent of Indian affairs for the southern department, shall be united with those of governor: *Provided always,* that if the President of the United States should find it most expedient to establish this government in the recess of Congress, he shall nevertheless have full power to appoint and commission all officers herein authorized; and their commissions shall continue in force until the end of the session of Congress next ensuing the establishment of the government.

SEC. 4. *Be it further enacted*, That the territory hereby constituted one district for the purposes of government, may at the discretion of Congress be hereafter divided into two districts, with separate territorial governments in each, similar to that established by this act.

SEC. 5. *Be it further enacted*, That the establishment of this government shall in no respect impair the right of the state of Georgia, or of any person or persons either to the jurisdiction or the soil of the said territory, but the rights and claims of the said state and of all persons interested, are hereby declared to be as firm and available, as if this act had never been made.

SEC. 6. *And be it further enacted*, That from and after the establishment of the said government, the people of the aforesaid territory, shall be entitled to and enjoy all and singular the rights, privileges and advantages granted to the people of the territory of the United States, northwest of the river Ohio, in and by the aforesaid ordinance of the thirteenth day of July, in the year one thousand seven hundred and eighty-seven, in as full and amply a manner as the same are possessed and enjoyed by the people of the said last mentioned territory.

SEC. 7. *And be it further enacted*, That from and after the establishment of the aforesaid government, it shall not be lawful for any person or persons to import or bring into the said Mississippi territory, from any port or place, without the limits of the United States, or to cause or procure to be so imported or brought, or knowingly to aid or assist in so importing or bringing any slave or slaves, and that every person so offending, and being thereof convicted before any court within the said territory, having competent jurisdiction, shall forfeit and pay, for each and every slave so imported or brought, the sum of three hundred dollars; one moiety for the use of the United States, and the other moiety for the use of any person or persons who shall sue for the same; and that every slave, so imported or brought, shall thereupon become entitled to, and receive his or her freedom.

SEC. 8. *And be it further enacted*, That the sum of ten thousand dollars be, and hereby is appropriated, for the purpose of enabling the President of the United States to carry into effect the provisions of this act; and that the said sum be paid out of any monies in the treasury not otherwise appropriated.

Approved, April 7, 1798.

AN ACT TO DIVIDE THE TERRITORY
OF THE UNITED STATES NORTHWEST OF THE OHIO,
INTO TWO SEPARATE GOVERNMENTS
MAY 7, 1800

SECTION 1. *Be it enacted by the Senate and House of Representatives of the United States of America in Congress assembled*, That from and after the fourth day of July next, all that part of the territory of the United States north-west of the Ohio river, which lies to the westward of a line beginning at the Ohio, opposite to the mouth of Kentucky river, and running thence to Fort Recovery, and thence north until it shall intersect the territorial line between the United States and Canada, shall, for the purposes of temporary government, constitute a separate territory, and be called the Indiana Territory.

SEC. 2. *And be it further enacted*, That there shall be established within the said territory a government in all respects similar to that provided by the ordinance of Congress, passed on the thirteenth day of July one thousand seven hundred and eighty-seven, for the government of the territory of the United States northwest of the river Ohio; and the inhabitants thereof shall be entitled to, and enjoy all and singular the rights, privileges and advantages granted and secured to the people by the said ordinance.

SEC. 3. *And be it further enacted*, That the officers for the said territory, who by virtue of this act shall be appointed by the President of the United States, by and with the advice and consent of the Senate, shall respectively exercise the same powers, perform the same duties, and receive for their services the same compensations as by the ordinance aforesaid and the laws of the United States, have been provided and established for similar officers in the territory of the United States northwest of the river Ohio. And the duties and emoluments of superintendent of Indian affairs shall be united with those of governor: *Provided*, that the President of the United States shall have full power, in the recess of Congress, to appoint and commission all officers herein authorized; and their commissions shall continue in force until the end of the next session of Congress.

SEC. 4. *And be it further enacted*, That so much of the ordinance for the government of the territory of the United States northwest of the Ohio river, as relates to the organization of a general assembly therein, and prescribes the powers thereof, shall be in force and operate in the Indiana territory, whenever satisfactory evidence shall be given to the governor thereof, that such is the wish of a majority of the freeholders, notwithstanding there may not be therein five thousand free male inhabitants of the age of twenty-one years and upwards: *Provided*, that until there shall be five thousand free male inhabitants of twenty-one years and upwards in said territory, the whole number of representatives to the general assembly shall not be less than seven, nor more than nine, to be apportioned by the governor to the several counties in the said territory, agreeably to the number of free males of the age of twenty-one years and upwards which they may respectively contain.

SEC. 5. *And be it further enacted*, That nothing in this act contained shall be construed so as in any manner to affect the government now in force in the territory of the United States northwest of the Ohio river; further than to prohibit the exercise thereof within the Indiana territory, from and after the aforesaid fourth day of July next: *Provided*, that whenever that part of the territory of the United States which lies to the eastward of a line beginning at the mouth of the Great Miami river, and running thence due north to the territorial line between the United States and Canada, shall be erected into an independent state, and admitted into the Union on an equal footing with the original states, thenceforth said line shall become and remain permanently the boundary line between such state and the Indiana territory; any thing in this act contained to the contrary notwithstanding.

SEC. 6. *And be it further enacted,* That until it shall be otherwise ordered by the legislatures of the said territories respectively, Chilicothe, on Scioto river, shall be the seat of the government of the territory of the United States northwest of the Ohio river; and that Saint Vincennes on the Wabash river, shall be the seat of the government for the Indiana territory.

Approved, May 7, 1800.

AN ACT TO ENABLE THE PEOPLE OF THE EASTERN DIVISION OF THE TERRITORY NORTHWEST OF THE RIVER OHIO TO FORM A CONSTITUTION AND STATE GOVERNMENT, AND FOR THE ADMISSION OF SUCH STATE INTO THE UNION, ON AN EQUAL FOOTING WITH THE ORIGINAL STATES, AND FOR OTHER PURPOSES
APRIL 30, 1802

Be it enacted by the Senate and House of Representatives of the United States of America in Congress assembled, That the inhabitants of the eastern division of the territory northwest of the river Ohio, be, and they are hereby authorized to form for themselves a constitution and state government, and to assume such name as they shall deem proper, and the said state, when formed, shall be admitted into the Union, upon the same footing with the original states, in all respects whatever.

SEC. 2. *And be it further enacted,* That the said state shall consist of all the territory included within the following boundaries, to wit: bounded on the east by the Pennsylvania line, on the south by the Ohio river, to the mouth of the Great Miami river, on the west by the line drawn due north from the mouth of the Great Miami, aforesaid, and on the north by an east and west line, drawn through the southerly extreme of Lake Michigan, running east after intersecting the due north line aforesaid, from the mouth of the Great Miami, until it shall intersect Lake Erie, or the territorial line, and thence with the same through Lake Erie to the Pennsylvania line, aforesaid: *Provided,* that Congress shall be at liberty at any time hereafter, either to attach all the territory lying east of the line to be drawn due north from the mouth of the Miami, aforesaid, to the territorial line, and north of an east and west line drawn through the southerly extreme of Lake Michigan, running east as aforesaid to Lake Erie, to the aforesaid state, or dispose of it otherwise, in conformity to the fifth article of compact between the original states, and the people and states to be formed in the territory northwest of the river Ohio.

SEC. 3. *And be it further enacted,* That all that part of the territory of the United States, northwest of the river Ohio, heretofore included in the eastern division of said territory, and not included within the boundary herein prescribed for the said state, is hereby attached to, and made a part of the Indiana territory, from and after the formation of the said state, subject nevertheless to be hereafter disposed of by Congress, according to the right reserved in the fifth article of the ordinance aforesaid, and the inhabitants therein shall be entitled to the same privileges and immunities, and subject to the same rules and regulations, in all respects whatever, with all other citizens residing within the Indiana territory.

SEC. 4. *And be it further enacted,* That all male citizens of the United States, who shall have arrived at full age, and resided within the said territory at least one year previous to the day of election, and shall have paid a territorial or county tax, and all persons having in other respects, the legal qualifications to vote for representatives in the general assembly of the territory, be, and they are hereby authorized to choose representatives to form a convention, who shall be apportioned amongst the several counties within the eastern division aforesaid, in a ratio of one representative to every twelve hundred inhabitants of each county, according to the enumeration taken under the authority of the United States, as near as may be, that is to say: from the county of Trumbull, two representatives; from the county of Jefferson, seven representatives, two of the seven to be elected within what is now known by the county of Belmont, taken from Jefferson and Washington counties; from the county of Washington, four representatives; from the county of Ross, seven representatives, two of the seven to be elected in what is now known by Fairfield county, taken from Ross and Washington counties; from the county of Adams, three representatives; from the county of Hamilton, twelve representatives, two of the twelve to be elected in what is now known by Clermont county, taken entirely from Hamilton county; and the elections for the representatives aforesaid, shall take place on the second Tuesday of October next, the time fixed by a law of the territory, intituled "An act to ascertain the number of free male inhabitants of the age of twenty-one, in the territory of the United States northwest of the river Ohio, and to regulate the elections of representatives for the same," for electing representatives to the general assembly, and shall be held and conducted in the same manner as is provided by the aforesaid act, except that the qualifications of electors shall be as herein specified.

SEC. 5. *And be it further enacted,* That the members of the convention, thus duly elected, be, and they are hereby authorized to meet at Chilicothe on the first Monday in November next; which convention, when met, shall first determine by a majority of the whole number elected, whether it be or be not expedient at that time to form a constitution and state government for the people, within the said territory, and if it be determined to be expedient, the convention shall be, and hereby are authorized to form a constitution and state government, or if it be deemed more expedient, the said convention shall provide by ordinance for electing representatives to form a constitution or frame of government; which said representatives shall be chosen in such manner, and in such proportion, and shall meet at such time and place, as shall be prescribed by the said ordinance; and shall form for the people of the said state, a constitution and state government; provided the same shall be republican, and not repugnant to the ordinance of the thirteenth of July, one thousand seven hundred and eighty-seven, between the original states and the people and states of the territory northwest of the river Ohio.

SEC. 6. *And be it further enacted,* That until the next general census shall be taken, the said state shall be entitled to one representative in the House of Representatives of the United States.

SEC. 7. *And be it further enacted,* That the following propositions be, and the same are hereby offered to the convention of the eastern state of the said territory, when formed, for their free acceptance or rejection, which, if accepted by the convention, shall be obligatory upon the United States.

First, That the section, number sixteen, in every township, and where such section has been sold, granted or disposed of, other lands equivalent thereto, and most contiguous to the same, shall be granted to the inhabitants of such township, for the use of schools.

Second, That the six miles reservation, including the salt springs, commonly called the Scioto salt springs, the salt springs near the Muskingum river, and in the military tract, with the sections of land which include the same, shall be granted to the said state for the use of the people thereof, the same to be used under such terms and conditions and regulations as the legislature of the said state shall direct: *Provided,* the said legislature shall never sell nor lease the same for a longer period than ten years.

Third, That one twentieth part of the nett proceeds of the lands lying within the said state sold by Congress, from and after the thirtieth day of June next, after deducting all expenses incident to the same, shall be applied to the laying out and making public roads, leading from the navigable waters emptying into the Atlantic, to the Ohio, to the said state, and through the same, such roads to be laid out under the authority of Congress, with the consent of the several states through which the road shall pass: *Provided always,* that the three foregoing propositions herein offered, are on the conditions that the convention of the said state shall provide, by an ordinance irrevocable, without the consent of the United States, that every and each tract of land sold by Congress, from and after the thirtieth day of June next, shall be and remain exempt from any tax laid by order or under authority of the state, whether for state, county, township or any other purpose whatever, for the term of five years from and after the day of sale.

Approved, April 30, 1802.

TREATY BETWEEN THE UNITED STATES
OF AMERICA AND THE FRENCH REPUBLIC
APRIL 30, 1803

The President of the United States of America and the First Consul of the French Republic in the name of the French People desiring to remove all Source of misunderstanding relative to objects of discussion mentioned in the second and fifth articles of the Convention of the 8th Vendémiaire an 9/30 September 1800 relative to the rights claimed by the United States in virtue of the Treaty concluded at Madrid the 27 of October 1795, between His Catholic Majesty, & the Said United States, & willing to Strengthen the union and friendship which at the time of the Said Convention was happily reestablished between the two nations have respectively named their Plenipotentiaries to wit The President of the United States, by and with the advice and consent of the Senate of the Said States; Robert R. Livingston Minister Plenipotentiary of the United States and James Monroe Minister Plenipotentiary and Envoy extraordinary of the Said States near the Government of the French Republic; And the First Consul in the name of the French people, Citizen Francis Barbé Marbois Minister of the public treasury who after having respectively exchanged their full powers have agreed to the following Articles.

ARTICLE I

Whereas by the Article the third of the Treaty concluded at St Idelfonso the 9th Vendémiaire an 9/1st October 1800 between the First Consul of the French Republic and his Catholic Majesty it was agreed as follows.

"His Catholic Majesty promises and engages on his part to cede to the "French Republic six months after the full and entire execution of the conditions "and Stipulations herein relative to his Royal Highness the Duke of Parma, the "Colony or Province of Louisiana with the Same extent that it now has in the "hands of Spain, & that it had when France possessed it; and Such as it Should "be after the Treaties subsequntly entered into between Spain and other States".

And whereas in pursuance of the Treaty and particularly of the third article the French Republic has an incontestible title to the domain and to the possession of the said Territory—The First Consul of the French Republic desiring to give to the United States a strong proof of his friendship doth hereby cede to the said United States in the name of the French Republic for ever and in full Sovereignty the said territory with all its rights and appurtenances as fully and in the Same manner as they have been acquired by the French Republic in virtue of the above mentioned Treaty concluded with his Catholic Majesty.

ART: II

In the cession made by the preceding article are included the adjacent Islands belonging to Louisiana all public lots and Squares, vacant lands and all public buildings, fortifications, barracks and other edifices which are not private property. — The Archives, papers & documents relative to the domain and Sovereignty of Louisiana and its dependances will be left in the possession of the Commissaries of the United States, and copies will be afterwards given in due form to the Magistrates and Municipal officers of Such of the said papers and documents as may be necessary to them.

ART: III

The inhabitants of the ceded territory shall be incorporated in the Union of the United States and admitted as soon as possible according to the principles of the federal Constitution to the enjoyment of all the rights, advantages and immunities of citizens of the United States, and in the mean time they shall be maintained and protected in the free enjoyment of their liberty, property and the Religion which they profess.

ART: IV

There Shall be Sent by the Government of France a Commissary to Louisiana to the end that he do every act necessary as well to receive from the Officers of his Catholic Majesty the Said country and its dependances in the name of the French Republic if it has not been already done as to transmit it in the name of the French Republic to the Commissary or agent of the United States.

ART: V

Immediately after the ratification of the present Treaty by the President of the United States and in case that of the first Consul's shall have been previously obtained, the Commissary of the French Republic shall remit all military posts of New Orleans and other parts of the ceded territory to the Commissary or Commissaries named by the President to take possession — the troops whether of France or Spain who may be there shall cease to occupy any military post from the time of taking possession and shall be embarked as soon as possible in the course of three months after the ratification of this treaty.

ART: VI

The United States promise to execute Such treaties and articles as may have been agreed between Spain and the tribes and nations of Indians until by mutual consent of the United States and the said tribes or nations other Suitable articles Shall have been agreed upon.

ART: VII

As it is reciprocally advantageous to the commerce of France and the United States to encourage the communication of both nations for a limited time in the country ceded by the present treaty until general arrangements relative to the commerce of both nations may be agreed on; it has been agreed between the contracting parties that the French Ships coming directly from France or any of her colonies loaded only with the produce and manufactures of France or her Said Colonies; and the Ships of Spain coming directly from Spain or any of her colonies loaded only with the produce or manufactures of Spain or her Colonies Shall be admitted during the Space of twelve years in the Port of New-Orleans and in all other legal ports-of-entry within the ceded territory in the Same manner as the Ships of the United States coming directly from France or Spain or any of their Colonies without being Subject to any other or greater duty on merchandize or other or greater tonnage than that paid by the citizens of the United States.

During the Space of time above mentioned no other nation Shall have a right to the Same privileges in the Ports of the ceded territory — the twelve years Shall commence three months after the exchange of ratifications if it Shall take place in France or three months after it Shall have been notified at Paris to the French Government if it Shall take place in the United States; It is however well understood that the object of the above article is to favour the manufactures, Commerce, freight and navigation of France and of Spain So far as relates to the importations that the French and Spanish Shall make into the Said Ports of the United States without in any Sort affecting the regulations that the United States may make concerning the exportation of the produce and merchandize of the United States, or any right they may have to make Such regulations.

ART: VIII

In future and for ever after the expiration of the twelve years, the Ships of France shall be treated upon the footing of the most favoured nations in the ports above mentioned.

ART: IX

The particular Convention Signed this day by the respective Ministers having for its object to provide for the payment of debts due to the Citizens of the United States by the French Republic prior to the 30th Septr 1800 (8th Vendémiaire an 9) is approved and to have its execution in the Same manner as if it had been inserted in this present treaty and it Shall be ratified in the Same form and in the Same time So that the one Shall not be ratified distinct from the other.

Another particular Convention Signed at the Same date as the present treaty relative to a definitive rule between the contracting parties is in the like manner approved and will be ratified in the Same form, and in the Same time and jointly.

ART: X

The present treaty Shall be ratified in good and due form and the ratifications Shall be exchanged in the Space of Six months after the date of the Signature of the Ministers Plenipotentiary or Sooner if possible.

In faith whereof the respective Plenipotentiaries have Signed these articles in the French and English languages; declaring nevertheless that the present Treaty was originally agreed to in the French language; and have thereunto affixed their Seals.

Done at Paris the tenth day of Floreal in the eleventh year of the French Republic; and the 30th of April 1803.

Robt R Livingston
(Seal)
Ja^s Monroe
(Seal)
        Barbé Marbois
        (Seal)

AN ACT ERECTING LOUISIANA INTO TWO TERRITORIES, AND PROVIDING FOR THE TEMPORARY GOVERNMENT THEREOF
MARCH 26, 1804

Be it enacted by the Senate and House of Representatives of the United States of America in Congress assembled, That all that portion of country ceded by France to the United States, under the name of Louisiana, which lies south of the Mississippi territory, and of an east and west line to commence on the Mississippi river, at the thirty-third degree of north latitude, and to extend west to the western boundary of the said cession, shall constitute a territory of the United States, under the name of the territory of Orleans; the government whereof shall be organized and administered as follows:

SEC. 2. The executive power shall be vested in a governor, who shall reside in the said territory, and hold his office during the term of three years, unless sooner removed by the President of the United States. He shall be commander in chief of the militia of the said territory; shall have power to grant pardons for offences against the said territory, and reprieves for those against the United States, until the decision of the President of the United States thereon, shall be made known; and to appoint and commission all officers civil and of the militia, whose appointments are not herein otherwise provided for, and which shall be established by law. He shall take care that the laws be faithfully executed.

SEC. 3. A secretary of the territory shall also be appointed, who shall hold his office during the term of four years, unless sooner removed by the President of the United States, whose duty it shall be, under the direction of the governor, to record and preserve all the papers and proceedings of the executive, and all the acts of the governor and legislative council, and transmit authentic copies of the proceedings of the governor in his executive department, every six months, to the President of the United States. In case of the vacancy of the office of governor, the government of the said territory shall devolve on the secretary.

SEC. 4. The legislative powers shall be vested in the governor, and in thirteen of the most fit and discreet persons of the territory, to be called the legislative council, who shall be appointed annually by the President of the United States from among those holding real estate therein, and who shall have resided one year at least, in the said territory, and hold no office of profit under the territory or the United States. The governor, by and with advice and consent of the said legislative council, or of a majority of them, shall have power to alter, modify, or repeal the laws which may be in force at the commencement of this act. Their legislative powers shall also extend to all the rightful subjects of legislation; but no law shall be valid which is inconsistent with the constitution and laws of the United States, or which shall lay any person under restraint, burthen, or disability, on account of his religious opinions, professions or worship; in all which he shall be free to maintain his own, and not burthened for those of another. The governor shall publish throughout the said territory, all the laws which shall be made, and shall from time to time, report the same to the President of the United States, to be laid before Congress; which, if disapproved of by Congress, shall thenceforth be of no force. The governor or legislative council shall have no power over the primary disposal of the soil, nor to tax the lands of the United States, nor to interfere with the claims to land within the said territory. The governor shall convene and prorogue the legislative council, whenever he may deem it expedient. It shall be his duty to obtain all the information in his power, in relation to the customs, habits, and dispositions of the inhabitants of the said territory, and communicate the same from time to time, to the President of the United States.

SEC. 5. The judicial power shall be vested in a superior court, and in such inferior courts, and justices of the peace, as the legislature of the territory may from time to time establish. The judges of the superior court and the justices of the peace, shall hold their offices for the term of four years. The superior court shall consist of three judges, any one of whom shall constitute a court; they shall have jurisdiction in all criminal cases, and exclusive jurisdiction in all those which are capital; and original and appellate jurisdiction in all civil cases of the value of one hundred dollars. Its sessions shall commence on the first Monday of every month, and continue till all the business depending before them shall be disposed of. They shall appoint their own clerk. In all criminal prosecutions which are capital, the trial shall be by a jury of twelve good and lawful men of the vicinage; and in all cases criminal and civil in the superior court, the trial shall be by a jury, if either of the parties require it. The inhabitants of the said territory shall be entitled to the benefits of the writ of habeas corpus; they shall be bailable, unless for capital offences where the proof shall be evident, or the presumption great; and no cruel and unusual punishments shall be inflicted.

SEC. 6. The governor, secretary, judges, district attorney, marshal, and all general officers of the militia, shall be appointed by the President of the United States, in the recess of the Senate; but shall be nominated at their next meeting for their advice and consent. The governor, secretary, judges, members of the legislative council, justices of the peace, and all other officers, civil and of the militia, before they enter upon the duties of their respective offices, shall take an oath or affirmation to support the constitution of the United States, and for the faithful discharge of the duties of their office; the governor, before the President of the United States, or before a judge of the supreme or district court of the United States, or before such other person as the President of the Unites States shall authorize to administer the same; the secretary, judges, and members of the legislative council, before the governor; and all other officers before such persons as the governor shall direct. The governor shall receive an annual salary of five thousand dollars; the secretary of two thousand dollars; and the judges of two thousand dollars each; to be paid quarter yearly out of the revenues of impost and tonnage, accruing within the said territory. The members of the legislative council shall receive four dollars each per day, during their attendance in council.

SEC. 7. *And be it further enacted,* That the following acts, that is to say:

An act for the punishment of certain crimes against the United States.

An act, in addition to an act, for the punishment of certain crimes against the United States.

An act to prevent citizens of the United States from privateering against nations in amity with, or against citizens of the United States.

An act for the punishment of certain crimes therein specified.

An act respecting fugitives from justice, and persons escaping from service of their masters.

An act to prohibit the carrying on the slave trade from the United States to any foreign place or country.

An act to prevent the importation of certain persons into certain states, where by the laws thereof, their admission is prohibited.

An act to establish the post-office of the United States.

An act further to alter and establish certain post roads, and for the more secure carriage of the mail of the United States.

An act for the more general promulgation of the laws of the United States.

An act, in addition to an act, intituled an act for the more general promulgation of the laws of the United States.

An act to promote the progress of useful arts, and to repeal the act heretofore made for that purpose.

An act to extend the privilege of obtaining patents for useful discoveries and inventions to certain persons therein mentioned, and to enlarge and define the penalties for violating the rights of patentees.

An act for the encouragement of learning, by securing the copies of maps, charts, and books, to the authors and proprietors of such copies, during the time therein mentioned.

An act, supplementary to an act, intituled An act for the encouragement of learning, by securing the copies of maps, charts, and books, to the authors and proprietors of such copies, during the time therein mentioned; and extending the benefits thereof to the arts of designing, engraving, and etching historical and other prints.

An act providing for salvage in cases of recapture.

An act respecting alien enemies.

An act to prescribe the mode in which the public acts, records, and judicial proceedings in each state shall be authenticated, so as to take effect in every other state.

An act for establishing trading houses with the Indian tribes.

An act for continuing in force a law, intituled An act for establishing trading houses with the Indian tribes, And

An act making provision relative to rations for Indians, and to their visits to the seat of government, shall extend to, and have full force and effect in the above mentioned territories.

SEC. 8. There shall be established in the said territory a district court, to consist of one judge, who shall reside therein, and be called the district judge, and who shall hold, in the city of Orleans, four sessions annually; the first to commence on the third Monday in October next, and the three other sessions, progressively, on the third Monday of every third calendar month thereafter. He shall, in all things, have and exercise the same jurisdiction and powers, which are by law given to, or may be exercised by the judge of Kentucky district; and shall be allowed an annual compensation of two thousand dollars, to be paid quarter yearly out of the revenues of impost and tonnage accruing within the said territory. He shall appoint a clerk for the said district, who shall reside, and keep the records of the court, in the city of Orleans, and shall receive for the services performed by him, the same fees to which the clerk of Kentucky district is entitled for similar services.

There shall be appointed in the said district, a person learned in the law, to act as attorney for the United States, who shall, in addition to his stated fees, be paid six hundred dollars, annually, as a full compensation for all extra services. There shall also be appointed a marshal for the said district, who shall perform the same duties, be subject to the same regulations and penalties, and be entitled to the same fees to which marshals in other districts are entitled for similar services; and shall moreover be paid two hundred dollars, annually, as a compensation for all extra services.

SEC. 9. All free male white persons, who are housekeepers, and who shall have resided one year, at least, in the said territory, shall be qualified to serve as grand or petit jurors, in the courts of the said territory; and they shall, until the legislature thereof shall otherwise direct, be selected in such manner as the judges of the said courts, respectively, shall prescribe, so as to be most conducive to an impartial trial, and to be least burthensome to the inhabitants of the said territory.

SEC. 10. It shall not be lawful for any person or persons to import or bring into the said territory, from any port or place without the limits of the United States, or cause or procure to be imported or brought, or knowingly to aid or assist in so importing or bringing any slave or slaves. And every person so offending, and being thereof convicted before any court within said territory, having competent jurisdiction, shall forfeit and pay for each and every slave so imported or brought, the sum of three hundred dollars; one moiety for the use of the United States, and the other moiety for the use of the person or persons who shall sue for the same; and every slave so imported or brought, shall thereupon become entitled to, and receive his or her freedom. It shall not be lawful for any person or persons to import or bring into the said territory, from any port or place within the limits of the United States, or to cause or procure to be so imported or brought, or knowningly to aid or assist in so importing or bringing any slave or slaves, which shall have been imported since the first day of May, one thousand seven hundred and ninety-eight, into any port or place within the limits of the United States, or which may hereafter be so imported, from any port or place without the limits of the United States; and every person so offending, and being thereof convicted before any court within said territory, having competent jurisdiction, shall forfeit and pay for each and every slave so imported or brought, the sum of three hundred dollars, one moiety for the use of the United States, and the other moiety for the use of the person or persons who shall sue for the same; and no slave or slaves shall directly or indirectly be introduced into said territory, except by a citizen of the United States, removing into said territory for actual settlement, and being at the time of such removal bona fide owner of such slave or slaves; and every slave imported or brought into the said territory, contrary to the provisions of this act, shall thereupon be entitled to, and receive his or her freedom.

SEC. 11. The laws in force in the said territory, at the commencement of this act, and not inconsistent with the provisions thereof, shall continue in force, until altered, modified, or repealed by the legislature.

SEC. 12. The residue of the province of Louisiana, ceded to the United States, shall be called the district of Louisiana, the government whereof shall be organized and administered as follows:

The executive power now vested in the governor of the Indiana territory, shall extend to, and be exercised in the said district of Louisiana. The governor and judges of the Indiana territory shall have power to establish, in the said district of Louisiana, inferior courts, and prescribe their jurisdiction and duties, and to make all laws which they may deem conducive to the good government of the inhabitants thereof: *Provided however*, that no law shall be valid which is inconsistent with the constitution and laws of the United States, or which shall lay any person under restraint or disability on account of his religious opinions, profession, or worship; in all of which he shall be free to maintain his own, and not burthened for those of another: *And provided also*, that in all criminal prosecutions, the trial shall be by a jury of twelve good and lawful men of the vicinage, and in all civil cases of the value of one hundred dollars, the trial shall be by jury, if either of the parties require it. The judges of the

Indiana territory, or any two of them, shall hold annually two courts within the said district, at such place as will be most convenient to the inhabitants thereof in general, shall possess the same jurisdiction they now possess in the Indiana territory, and shall continue in session until all the business depending before them shall be disposed of. It shall be the duty of the secretary of the Indiana territory to record and preserve all the papers and proceedings of the governor, of an executive nature, relative to the district of Louisiana, and transmit authentic copies thereof every six months to the President of the United States. The governor shall publish throughout the said district, all the laws which may be made as aforesaid, and shall from time to time report the same to the President of the United States, to be laid before Congress, which, if disapproved of by Congress, shall thence forth cease, and be of no effect.

The said district of Louisiana shall be divided into districts by the governor, under the direction of the President, as the convenience of the settlements shall require, subject to such alterations hereafter as experience may prove more convenient. The inhabitants of each district, between the ages of eighteen and forty-five, shall be formed into a militia, with proper officers, according to their numbers, to be appointed by the governor, except the commanding officer, who shall be appointed by the President, and who whether a captain, a major or a colonel, shall be the commanding officer of the district, and as such, shall, under the governor, have command of the regular officers and troops in his district, as well as of the militia, for which he shall have a brevet commission, giving him such command, and the pay and emoluments of an officer of the same grade in the regular army; he shall be specially charged with the employment of the military and militia of his district, in cases of sudden invasion or insurrection, and until the orders of the governor can be received, and at all times with the duty of ordering a military patrol, aided by militia if necessary, to arrest unauthorized settlers in any part of his district, and to commit such offenders to jail to be dealt with according to law.

SEC. 13. The laws in force in the said district of Louisiana, at the commencement of this act, and not inconsistent with any of the provisions thereof, shall continue in force until altered, modified or repealed by the governor and judges of the Indiana territory, as aforesaid.

SEC. 14. *And be it further enacted,* That all grants for lands within the territories ceded by the French Republic to the United States, by the treaty of the thirtieth of April, in the year one thousand eight hundred and three, the title whereof was, at the date of the treaty of St. Ildefonso, in the crown, government or nation of Spain, and every act and proceeding subsequent thereto, of whatsoever nature, towards the obtaining any grant, title, or claim to such lands, and under whatsoever authority transacted, or pretended, be, and the same are hereby declared to be, and to have been from the beginning, null, void, and of no effect in law or equity. *Provided nevertheless,* that any thing in this section contained shall not be construed to make null and void any bona fide grant, made agreeably to the laws, usages and customs of the Spanish government to an actual settler on the lands so granted, for himself, and for his wife and family; or to make null and void any bona fide act or proceeding done by an actual settler agreeably to the laws, usages and customs of the Spanish government, to obtain a grant for lands actually settled on by the person or persons claiming title thereto, if such settlement in either case was actually made prior to the twentieth day of December, one thousand eight hundred and three: *And provided further*, that such grant shall not secure to the grantee or his assigns more than one mile square of land, together with such other and further quantity as heretofore hath been allowed for the wife and family of such actual settler, agreeably to the laws, usages and customs of the Spanish government. And that if any citizen of the United States, or other person, shall make a settlement on any lands belonging to the United States, within the limits of Louisiana, or shall survey, or attempt to survey, such lands, or to designate boundaries by marking trees, or otherwise, such offender shall, on conviction thereof, in any court of record of the United States, or the territories of the United States, forfeit a sum not exceeding one thousand dollars, and suffer imprisonment not exceeding twelve months; and it shall, moreover, be lawful for the President of the United States to employ such military force as he may judge necessary to remove from lands belonging to the United States any such citizen or other person who shall attempt a settlement thereon.

SEC. 15. The President of the United States is hereby authorized to stipulate with any Indian tribes owning lands on the east side of the Mississippi, and residing thereon, for an exchange of lands, the property of the United States, on the west side of the Mississippi, in case the said tribes shall remove and settle thereon; but in such stipulation, the said tribes shall acknowledge themselves to be under the protection of the United States, and shall agree that they will not hold any treaty with any foreign power, individual state, or with the individuals of any state or power; and that they will not sell or dispose of the said lands, or any part thereof, to any sovereign power, except the United States, nor to the subjects or citizens of any other sovereign power, nor to the citizens of the United States. And in order to maintain peace and tranquillity with the Indian tribes who reside within the limits of Louisiana, as ceded by France to the United States, the act of Congress, passed on the thirtieth day of March, one thousand eight hundred and two, intituled "An act to regulate trade and intercourse with the Indian tribes, and to preserve peace on the frontiers," is hereby extended to the territories erected and established by this act; and the sum of fifteen thousand dollars of any money in the treasury not otherwise appropriated by law, is hereby appropriated to enable the President of the United States to effect the object expressed in this section.

SEC. 16. The act, passed on the thirty-first day of October, one thousand eight hundred and three, intituled "An act to enable the President of the United States to take possession of the territories ceded by France to the United States, by the treaty concluded at Paris, on the thirtieth day of April last, and for the temporary government thereof," shall continue in force until the first day of October next, any thing therein to the contrary notwithstanding; on which said first day of October, this act shall commence, and have full force, and shall continue in force for and during the term of one year, and to the end of the next session of Congress which may happen thereafter.

Approved, March 26, 1804.

AN ACT TO DIVIDE THE INDIANA TERRITORY
INTO TWO SEPARATE GOVERNMENTS
JANUARY 11, 1805

Be it enacted by the Senate and House of Representatives of the United States of America in Congress assembled, That from and after the thirtieth day of June next, all that part of the Indiana territory, which lies north of a line drawn east from the southerly bend or extreme of Lake Michigan, until it shall intersect Lake Erie, and east of a line drawn from the said southerly bend through the middle of said lake to its northern extremity, and thence due north to the northern boundary of the United States, shall, for the purpose of temporary government, constitute a separate territory, and be called Michigan.

SEC. 2. *And be it further enacted,* That there shall be established within the said territory, a government in all respects similar to that provided by the ordinance of Congress, passed on the thirteenth day of July, one thousand seven hundred and eighty-seven, for the government of the territory of the United States, northwest of the river Ohio; and by an act passed on the seventh day of August, one thousand seven hundred and eighty-nine, entitled "An act to provide for the government of the territory northwest of the river Ohio;" and the inhabitants thereof shall be entitled to, and enjoy all and singular the rights, privileges, and advantages granted and secured to the people of the territory of the United States, northwest of the river Ohio, by the said ordinance.

SEC. 3. *And be it further enacted,* That the officers for the said territory, who by virtue of this act shall be appointed by the President of the United States, by and with the advice and consent of the Senate, shall respectively exercise the same powers, perform the same duties, and receive for their services the same compensations, as by the ordinance aforesaid and the laws of the United States, have been provided and established for similar officers in the Indiana territory; and the duties and emoluments of superintendent of Indian affairs, shall be united with those of governor.

SEC. 4. *And be it further enacted,* That nothing in this act contained, shall be construed so as, in any manner, to affect the government now in force in the Indiana territory, further than to prohibit the exercise thereof within the said territory of Michigan, from and after the aforesaid thirtieth day of June next.

SEC. 5. *And be it further enacted,* That all suits, process, and proceedings, which, on the thirtieth day of June next, shall be pending in the court of any county, which shall be included within the said territory of Michigan; and also all suits, process, and proceedings, which on the said thirtieth day of June next, shall be pending in the general court of the Indiana territory, in consequence of any writ of removal, or order for trial at bar, and which had been removed from any of the counties included within the limits of the territory of Michigan aforesaid, shall, in all things concerning the same, be proceeded on, and judgements and decrees rendered thereon, in the same manner as if the said Indiana territory had remained undivided.

SEC. 6. *And be it further enacted*, That Detroit shall be the seat of government of the said territory, until Congress shall otherwise direct.
Approved, January 11, 1805.

AN ACT FURTHER PROVIDING FOR THE GOVERNMENT OF THE DISTRICT OF LOUISIANA

MARCH 3, 1805

Be it enacted by the Senate and House of Representatives of the United States of America in Congress assembled, That all that part of the country ceded by France to the United States, under the general name of Louisiana, which, by an act of the last session of Congress, was erected into a separate district, to be called the district of Louisiana, shall henceforth be known and designated by the name and title of the Territory of Louisiana, the government whereof shall be organized and administered as follows:

The executive power shall be vested in a governor, who shall reside in said territory, and hold his office during the term of three years, unless sooner removed by the President of the United States. He shall be commander in chief of the militia of the said territory, superintendent ex officio of Indian affairs, and shall appoint and commission all officers in the same, below the rank of general officers; shall have power to grant pardons for offences against the same, and reprieves for those against the United States, until the decision of the President thereon shall be known.

SEC. 2. There shall be a secretary, whose commission shall continue in force for four years, unless sooner revoked by the President of the United States, who shall reside in the said territory, and whose duty it shall be, under the direction of the governor, to record and preserve all the papers and proceedings of the executive, and all the acts of the governor and of the legislative body, and transmit authentic copies of the same every six months, to the President of the United States. In case of a vacancy of the office of governor, the government of the said territory shall be exercised by the secretary.

SEC. 3. The legislative power shall (be) vested in the governor and in three judges, or a majority of them, who shall have power to establish inferior courts in the said territory, and prescribe their jurisdiction and duties, and to make all laws which they may deem conducive to the good government of the inhabitants thereof: *Provided however*, that no law shall be valid which is inconsistent with the constitution and laws of the United States, or which shall lay any person under restraint or disability on account of his religious opinions, profession, or worship, in all of which he shall be free to maintain his own and not be burthened with those of another. *And provided also*, that in all criminal prosecutions, the trial shall be by a jury of twelve good and lawful men of the vicinage, and in all civil cases of the value of one hundred dollars, the trial shall be by jury, if either of the parties require it. And the governor shall publish throughout the said territory, all the laws which may be made as aforesaid, and shall from time to time report the same to the President of the United States, to be laid before Congress, which, if disapproved of by Congress, shall thenceforth cease and be of no effect.

SEC. 4. There shall be appointed three judges, who shall hold their offices for the term of four years, who, or any two of them, shall hold annually two courts within the said district, at such place as will be most convenient to the inhabitants thereof in general: shall possess the same jurisdiction which is possessed by the judges of the Indiana territory, and shall continue in session until all the business depending before them shall be disposed of.

SEC. 5. *And be it further enacted,* That for the more convenient distribution of justice, the prevention of crimes and injuries, and execution of process criminal and civil, the governor shall proceed from time to time as circumstances may require, to lay out those parts of the territory in which the Indian title shall have been extinguished, into districts, subject to such alteration as may be found necessary; and he shall appoint thereto such magistrates and other civil officers as he may deem necessary, whose several powers and authorities shall be regulated and defined by law.

SEC. 6. *And be it further enacted,* That the governor, secretary and judges, to be appointed by virtue of this act, shall respectively receive the same compensations for their services as are by law established for similar offices in the Indiana territory, to be paid quarter yearly out of the treasury of the United States.

SEC. 7. *And be it further enacted,* That the governor, secretary, judges, justices of the peace, and all other officers civil or military, before they enter upon the duties of their respective offices, shall take an oath, or affirmation, to support the constitution of the United States, and for the faithful discharge of the duties of their office; the governor before the President of the United States, or before a judge of the supreme or district court of the United States, or before such other person as the President of the United States shall authorize to administer the same; the secretary and judges before the governor; and all other officers'before such person as the governor shall direct.

SEC. 8. *And be it further enacted,* That the governor, secretary, and judges, to be appointed by virtue of this act, and all the additional officers authorized thereby, or by the act for erecting Louisiana into two territories, and providing for the temporary government thereof, shall be appointed by the President of the United States, in the recess of the Senate, but shall be nominated at their next meeting for their advice and consent.

SEC. 9. *And be it further enacted,* That the laws and regulations, in force in the said district, at the commencement of this act, and not inconsistent with the provisions thereof, shall continue in force, until altered, modified, or repealed by the legislature.

SEC. 10. *And be it further enacted,* That so much of an act, intituled "An act erecting Louisiana into two territories, and providing for the temporary government thereof," as is repugnant to this act, shall, from and after the fourth day of July next, be repealed, on which said fourth day of July, this act shall commence and have full force.

Approved, March 3, 1805.

AN ACT FOR DIVIDING THE INDIANA TERRITORY INTO TWO SEPARATE GOVERNMENTS

FEBRUARY 3, 1809

Be it enacted by the Senate and House of Representatives of the United States of America in Congress assembled, That from and after the first day of March next, all that part of the Indiana territory which lies west of the Wabash river, and a direct line drawn from the said Wabash river and Post Vincennes, due north to the territorial line between the United States and Canada, shall, for the purpose of temporary government, constitute a separate territory, and be called Illinois.

SEC. 2. *And be it further enacted,* That there shall be established within the said territory a government in all respects similar to that provided by the ordinance of Congress, passed on the thirteenth day of July, one thousand seven hundred and eighty-seven, for the government of the territory of the United States, northwest of the river Ohio; and by an act passed on the seventh day of August, one thousand seven hundred and eighty-nine, intituled "An act to provide for the government of the territory northwest of the river Ohio;" and the inhabitants thereof shall be entitled to, and enjoy all and singular the rights, privileges and advantages, granted and secured to the people of the territory of the United States northwest of the river Ohio, by the said ordinance.

SEC. 3. *And be it further enacted,* That the officers for the said territory, who, by virtue of this act, shall be appointed by the President of the United States, by and with the advice and consent of the Senate, shall respectively exercise the same powers, perform the same duties, and receive for their services the same compensations, as by the ordinance aforesaid, and the laws of the United States, have been provided and established for similar officers in the Indiana territory. And the duties and emoluments of superintendent of Indian affairs, shall be united with those of governor: *Provided,* that the President of the United States shall have full power, in the recess of Congress, to appoint and commission all officers herein authorized, and their commissions shall continue in force until the end of the next session of Congress.

SEC. 4. *And be it further enacted,* That so much of the ordinance for the government of the territory of the United States northwest of the Ohio river, as relates to the organization of a general assembly therein, and prescribes the powers thereof, shall be in force and operate in the Illinois territory, whenever satisfactory evidence shall be given to the governor thereof that such is the wish of a majority of the freeholders, notwithstanding there may not be therein five thousand free male inhabitants of the age of twenty-one years and upwards: *Provided,* that until there shall be five thousand free male inhabitants of twenty-one years and upwards in said territory, the whole number of representatives to the general assembly shall not be less than seven, nor more than nine, to be apportioned by the governor to the several counties in the said territory, agreeably to the number of free males of the age of twenty-one years and upwards, which they may respectively contain.

SEC. 5. *And be it further enacted,* That nothing in this act contained shall be construed so as in any manner to affect the government now in force in the Indiana territory, further than to prohibit the exercise thereof within the Illinois territory, from and after the aforesaid first day of March next.

SEC. 6. *And be it further enacted,* That all suits, process and proceedings, which, on the first day of March next, shall be pending in the court of any county which shall be included within the said territory of Illinois, and also all suits, process and proceedings, which, on the said first day of March next, shall be pending in the general court of the Indiana territory, in consequence of any writ of removal, or order for trial at bar, and which had been removed from any of the counties included within the limits of the territory of Illinois aforesaid, shall, in all things concerning the same, be proceeded on, and judgments and decrees rendered thereon, in the same manner as if the said Indiana territory had remained undivided.

SEC. 7. *And be it further enacted,* That nothing in this act contained shall be so construed as to prevent the collection of taxes, which may on the first day of March next, be due to the Indiana territory or lands lying in the said territory of Illinois.

SEC. 8. *And be it further enacted,* That until it shall be otherwise ordered by the legislature of the said Illinois territory, Kaskaskia on the Mississippi river, shall be the seat of government for the said Illinois territory.

Approved, February 3, 1809.

A PROCLAMATION BY THE PRESIDENT OF THE UNITED STATES OF AMERICA REGARDING THE TERRITORY SOUTH OF THE MISSISSIPPI TERRITORY AND EASTWARD OF THE RIVER MISSISSIPPI AND EXTENDING TO THE RIVER PERDIDO OCTOBER 27, 1810

Whereas the territory south of the Mississippi Territory and eastward of the river Mississippi, and extending to the river Perdido, of which possession was not delivered to the United States in pursuance of the treaty concluded at Paris on the 30th April, 1803, has at all times, as is well known, been considered and claimed by them as being within the colony of Louisiana conveyed by the said treaty in the same extent that it had in the hands of Spain and that it had when France originally possessed it; and

Whereas the acquiescence of the United States in the temporary continuance of the said territory under the Spanish authority was not the result of any distrust of their title, as has been particularly evinced by the general tenor of their laws and by the distinction made in the application of those laws between that territory and foreign countries, but was occasioned by their conciliatory views and by a confidence in the justice of their cause and in the success of candid discussion and amicable negotiation with a just and friendly power; and

Whereas a satisfactory adjustment, too long delayed, without the fault of the United States, has for some time been entirely suspended by events over which they had no control; and

Whereas a crises has at length arrived subversive of the order of things under the Spanish authorities, whereby a failure of the United States to take the said territory into its possession may lead to events ultimately contravening the views of both parties, whilst in the meantime the tranquillity and security of our adjoining territories are endangered and new facilities given to violations of our revenue and commercial laws and of those prohibiting the introduction of slaves;

Considering, moreover, that under these peculiar and imperative circumstances a forbearance on the part of the United States to occupy the territory in question, and thereby guard against the confusions and contingencies which threaten it, might be construed into a dereliction of their title or an insensibility to the importance of the stake; considering that in the hands of the United States it will not cease to be a subject of fair and friendly negotiation and adjustment; considering, finally that the acts of Congress, though contemplating a present possession by a foreign authority, have contemplated also an eventual possession of the said territory by the United States, and are accordingly so framed as in that case to extend in their operation to the same:

Now be it known that I, James Madison, President of the United States of America, in pursuance of these weighty and urgent considerations, have deemed it right and requisite that possession should be taken of the said territory in the name and behalf of the United States. William C.C. Claiborne, governor of the Orleans Territory, of which the said Territory is to be taken as part, will accordingly proceed to execute the same and to exercise over the said Territory the authorities and functions legally appertaining to his office; and the good people inhabiting the same are invited and enjoined to pay due respect to him in that character, to be obedient to the laws, to maintain order, to cherish harmony, and in every manner to conduct themselves as peaceable citizens, under full assurance that they will be protected in the enjoyment of their liberty, property, and religion.

In testimony whereof I have caused the seal of the United States to be hereunto affixed, and signed the same with my hand.

Done at the city of Washington, the 27th day of October A.D.

(Seal)   1810, and in the thirty-fifth year of the Independence of the said
              United States.

                                          JAMES MADISON
              By the President:
              R. Smith
                 Secretary of State.

AN ACT TO ENABLE THE PEOPLE OF THE TERRITORY OF ORLEANS TO FORM A CONSTITUTION AND STATE GOVERNMENT, AND FOR THE ADMISSION OF SUCH STATE INTO THE UNION, ON AN EQUAL FOOTING WITH THE ORIGINAL STATES, AND FOR OTHER PURPOSES
FEBRUARY 20, 1811

Be it enacted by the Senate and House of Representatives of the United States of America in Congress assembled, That the inhabitants of all that part of the territory or country ceded under the name of Louisiana, by the treaty made at Paris on the thirtieth day of April, one thousand eight hundred and three, between the United States and France, contained within the following limits, that is to say: beginning at the mouth of the river Sabine, thence by a line to be drawn along the middle of the said river, including all islands to the thirty-second degree of latitude; thence due north, to the northernmost part of the thirty-third degree of north latitude; thence along the said parallel of latitude to the river Mississippi; thence down the said river to the river Iberville; and from thence along the middle of the said river and lakes Maurepas and Ponchartrain, to the gulf of Mexico; thence bounded by the said gulf to the place of beginning: including all islands within three leagues of the coast, be, and they are hereby authorized to form for themselves a constitution and state government, and to assume such name as they may deem proper, under the provisions and upon the conditions herein after mentioned.

SEC. 2. *And be it further enacted,* That all free white male citizens of the United States, who shall have arrived at the age of twenty-one years, and resided within the said territory, at least one year previous to the day of election, and shall have paid a territorial, county, district or parish tax: and all persons having in other respects the legal qualifications to vote for representatives in the general assembly of the said territory, be, and they are hereby authorized to choose representatives to form a convention, who shall be apportioned amongst the several counties, districts and parishes, within the said territory of Orleans, in such manner as the legislature of the said territory shall by law direct. The number of representatives shall not exceed sixty; and the elections for the representatives aforesaid shall take place on the third Monday in September next, and shall be conducted in the same manner as is now provided by the laws of the said territory for electing members for the House of Representatives.

SEC. 3. *And be it further enacted,* That the members of the convention, when duly elected, be, and they are hereby authorized to meet at the city of New Orleans, on the first Monday of November next, which convention, when met, shall first determine, by a majority of the whole number elected, whether it be expedient or not, at that time, to form a constitution and state government, for the people within the said territory, and if it be determined to be expedient, then the convention shall in like manner declare, in behalf of the people of the said territory, that it adopts the constitution of the United States; whereupon the said convention shall be, and hereby is authorized to form a constitution and state government, for the people of the said territory: *Provided,* the constitution to be formed, in virtue of the authority herein given, shall be republican, and consistent with the constitution of the United States; that it shall contain the fundamental principles of civil and religious liberty; that it shall secure to the citizen the trial by jury in all criminal cases, and the privilege of the writ of *habeas corpus,* conformably to the provisions of the constitution of the United States; an that after the admission of the said territory of Orleans as a state into the Union, the laws which such state may pass shall be promulgated, and its records of every description shall be preserved, and its judicial and legislative written proceedings conducted, in the language in which the laws and the judicial and legislative written proceedings of the United States are now published and conducted: *And provided also,* that the said convention shall provide by an ordinance, irrevocable without the consent of the United States, that the people inhabiting the said territory do agree and declare, that they for ever disclaim all right or title to the waste or unappropriated lands, lying within the said territory; and that the same shall be and remain at the sole and entire disposition of the United States; and, moreover, that each and every tract of land, sold by Congress, shall be and remain exempt from any tax, laid by the order or under the authority of the state, whether for state, county, township, parish or any other purpose whatever, for the term of five years from and after the respective days of the sales thereof; and that the lands belonging to citizens of the United States, residing without the said state, shall never be taxed higher than the lands belonging to persons residing therein; and that no taxes shall be imposed on lands the property of the United States; and that the river Mississippi and the navigable rivers and waters leading into the same or into the gulf of Mexico, shall be common highways and for ever free, as well to the inhabitants of the said state as to other citizens of the United States, without any tax, duty, impost or toll therefor, imposed by the said state.

SEC. 4. *And be it further enacted,* That in case the convention shall declare its assent, in behalf of the people of the said territory, to the adoption of the constitution of the United States, and shall form a constitution and state government for the people of the said territory of Orleans, the said convention, as soon thereafter as may be, is hereby required to cause to be transmitted to Congress the instrument, by which its assent to the constitution of the United States is thus given and declared, and also a true and attested copy of such constitution or frame of state government, as shall be formed and provided by said convention, and if the same shall not be disapproved by Congress, at their next session after the receipt thereof, the said state shall be admitted into the Union, upon the same footing with the original states.

SEC. 5. *And be it further enacted,* That five per centum of the net proceeds of the sales of the lands of the United States, after the first day of January, shall be applied to laying out and constructing public roads and levees in the said state, as the legislature thereof may direct.

Approved, February 20, 1811.

AN ACT TO ENLARGE THE LIMITS
OF THE STATE OF LOUISIANA
APRIL 14, 1812

Be it enacted by the Senate and House of Representatives of the United States of America in Congress assembled, That in case the legislature of the state of Louisiana shall consent thereto, all that tract of country comprehended within the following bounds, to wit: Beginning at the junction of the Iberville, with the river Mississippi; thence along the middle of the Iberville, the river Amite, and of the lakes Maurepas and Pontchartrain to the eastern mouth of the Pearl river; thence up the eastern branch of Pearl river to the thirty-first degree of north latitude; thence along the said degree of latitude to the river Mississippi; thence down the said river to the place of beginning, shall become and form a part of the said state of Louisiana, and be subject to the constitution and laws thereof, in the same manner, and for all intents and purposes as if it had been included within the original boundaries of the said state.

SEC. 2. *And be it further enacted,* That it shall be incumbent upon the legislature of the state of Louisiana, in case they consent to the incorporation of the territory aforesaid, within their limits, at their first session, to make provision by law for the representation of the said territory in the legislature of the state, upon the principles of the constitution, and for the securing to the people of the said territory, equal rights, privileges, benefits and advantages with those enjoyed by the people of the other parts of the state; which law shall be liable to revision, modification and amendment by Congress, and also in the manner provided for the amendment of the state constitution, but shall not be liable to change or amendment by the legislature of the state.

Approved, April 14, 1812.

AN ACT TO ENLARGE THE BOUNDARIES
OF THE MISSISSIPPI TERRITORY
MAY 14, 1812

Be it enacted by the Senate and House of Representatives of the United States of America in Congress assembled, That all that portion of territory lying east of Pearl river, west of the Perdido, and south of the thirty-first degree of latitude, be, and the same is hereby annexed to the Mississippi territory; to be governed by the laws now in force therein, or which may hereafter be enacted, and the laws and ordinances of the United States, relative thereto, in like manner as if the same had originally formed a part of said territory; and until otherwise provided by law, the inhabitants of the said district hereby annexed to the Mississippi territory, shall be entitled to one representative in the general assembly thereof.

Approved, May 14, 1812.

AN ACT PROVIDING FOR THE GOVERNMENT
OF THE TERRITORY OF MISSOURI
JUNE 4, 1812

Be it enacted by the Senate and House of Representatives of the United States of America in Congress assembled, That the territory heretofore called Louisiana shall hereafter be called Missouri, and that the temporary government of the territory of Missouri shall be organized and administered in the manner herein after prescribed.

SEC. 2. *And be it further enacted,* That the executive power shall be vested in a governor, who shall reside in the said territory; he shall hold his office during the term of three years, unless sooner removed by the President of the United States; shall be commander in chief of the militia of the said territory; shall have power to appoint and commission all officers civil and of the militia, whose appointments are not herein otherwise provided for, which shall be established by law; shall take care that the laws be faithfully executed; shall have power to grant pardons for offences against the said territory, and reprieves for those against the United States, until the decision of the President of the United States thereon shall be made known; shall have power on extraordinary occasions to convene the general assembly, and he shall ex officio be superintendent of Indian affairs.

SEC. 3. *And be it further enacted,* That there shall be a secretary, whose commission shall continue in force for four years, unless sooner revoked by the President of the United States; he shall reside in the said territory; it shall be his duty, under the direction of the governor, to record and preserve all the proceedings and papers of the executive, and all the acts of the general assembly, and to transmit authentic copies of the same every six months to the President of the United States. In case of a vacancy of the office of governor, the government of the said territory shall be executed by the secretary.

SEC. 4. *And be it further enacted,* That the legislative power shall be vested in a general assembly, which shall consist of the governor, a legislative council and a house of representatives. The general assembly shall have power to make laws in all cases, both civil and criminal, for the good government of the people of the said territory, not repugnant to or inconsistent with the constitution and laws of the United States; and shall have power to establish inferior courts, and to prescribe their jurisdiction and duties; to define the powers and duties of justices of the peace and other civil officers in the said territory, and to regulate and fix the fees of office, and to ascertain and provide for payment of the same, and for all other services rendered to the said territory, under the authority thereof. All bills having passed by a majority in the house of representatives, and by a majority in the legislative council, shall be referred to the governor for his assent, but no bill or legislative act whatever shall be of any force without his approbation.

SEC. 5. *And be it further enacted,* That the legislative council shall consist of nine members to continue in office five years, unless sooner removed by the President of the United States, any five of them shall be a quorum. The members of the legislative council shall be nominated and appointed in the manner following: as soon as representatives shall be elected, they shall be convened by the governor as hereafter prescribed, and when met, shall nominate eighteen persons, residents in the said territory one year preceding their nomination, holding no office of profit under the territory or the United States, the office of justice of the peace excepted, and each possessing in his own right two hundred acres of land therein, and return the names to the President of the United States, nine of whom the President, by and with the advice and consent of the Senate, shall appoint and commission to serve as aforesaid; and when a vacancy shall happen in the legislative council, by death or removal from office, the house of representatives shall nominate two persons qualified as aforesaid for each vacancy, and return their names to the President of the United States, one of whom he, by and with the advice and consent of the Senate, shall appoint and commission for the residue of the term: and every five years, four months at least before the expiration of the time of service of the members of the legislative council, the house of representatives shall nominate eighteen persons, qualified as aforesaid, and return their names to the President of the United States, nine of whom shall be appointed and commissioned as aforesaid, to serve as members of the legislative council five years, if not sooner removed. No person shall be a member of the legislative council who hath not attained to the age of twenty-five years.

SEC. 6. *And be it further enacted,* That the house of representatives shall be composed of members elected every second year by the people of the said territory, to serve for two years. For every five hundred free white male inhabitants there shall be one representative, and so on progressively with the number of free white male inhabitants shall the right of representation increase until the number of the representatives shall amount to twenty-five, after which the number and proportion of representatives shall be regulated by the general assembly. No person shall be eligible or qualified to be a representative, who shall not have attained to the age of twenty-one years, and who shall not have resided in the territory one year next preceding the day of election, and who shall not be a freeholder within the county in which he may be elected; and no person holding an office under the United States or an office of profit under the territory shall be a representative. In case of vacancy by death, resignation, removal or otherwise of a representative, the governor shall issue a writ to the county, whenever a vacancy may be as aforesaid, to elect another person to serve the residue of the term. That all free white male citizens of the United States, above the age of twenty-one years, who have resided in said territory twelve months next preceding an election, and who shall have paid a territorial or county tax, assessed at least six months previous thereto, shall be entitled to vote for representatives to the general assembly of said territory.

SEC. 7. *And be it further enacted,* That in order to carry the same into operation, the governor of the said territory shall cause to be elected thirteen representatives, and for that purpose shall proceed, as circumstances may require, to lay off the parts of the said territory to which the Indian title hath been extinguished, into convenient counties, on or before the first Monday in October next, and give notice thereof throughout the same, and shall appoint the most convenient time and place within each of the said counties for holding the elections, and shall nominate a proper officer or officers to preside at and conduct the same, and to return to him the names of the persons who shall have been elected. All subsequent elections shall be regulated by the general assembly, and the number of representatives shall be determined and the apportionment made in the manner herein before prescribed.

SEC. 8. *And be it further enacted,* That the representatives elected as aforesaid, shall be convened by the governor in the town of St. Louis on the first Monday in December next; and the first general assembly shall be convened by the governor, as soon as may be convenient, at St. Louis, after the members of the legislative council shall be appointed and commissioned. The general assembly shall meet once in each year, at St. Louis, and such meeting shall be on the first Monday in December annually, unless they shall by law appoint a different day. The legislative council and house of representatives, when assembled, shall each choose a speaker and its other officers, and determine the rules of its proceedings. Each house shall sit on its own adjournments from day to day. Neither house shall during the session, without consent of the other, adjourn for more than two days, nor to any other place than that where the two houses shall be sitting. The members of the general assembly shall, in all cases except treason, felony or breach of the peace, be privileged from arrest during their attendance at their respective houses, and in going to and returning from the same; and for any speech or debate in either house, they shall not be questioned in any other place.

SEC. 9. *And be it further enacted,* That all and every free white male person who, on the twentieth day of December, in the year one thousand eight hundred and three, was an inhabitant of the territory of Louisiana, and all free white male citizens of the United States, who, since the said twentieth day of December, in the year one thousand eight hundred and three emigrated, or who hereafter may emigrate to the said territory, being otherwise qualified according to the provisions of this act, shall be capable to hold any office of honour, trust or profit, in the said territory, under the United States, or under the said territory, and to vote for members of the general assembly and a delegate to Congress during the temporary government provided for by this act.

SEC. 10. *And be it further enacted,* That the judicial power shall be vested in a superior court, and in inferior courts and justices of the peace. The judges of the superior court and justices of the peace shall hold their offices for the term of four years, unless sooner removed; the superior court shall consist of three judges, who shall reside in the said territory, and two of whom shall constitute a court; the superior courts shall have jurisdiction in all criminal cases, and exclusive jurisdiction in all those that are capital; and original and appellate jurisdiction in all civil cases of the value of one hundred dollars; the said judges shall hold their courts at such times and places as shall be prescribed by the general assembly. The sessions of the superior and inferior courts shall continue until all the business depending shall be disposed of, or for such time as shall be prescribed by the general assembly. The superior and inferior courts shall respectively appoint their clerks, who shall be commissioned by the governor, and shall hold their offices during the temporary government of the said territory, unless sooner removed by the court.

SEC. 11. *And be it further enacted,* That all free male white persons of the age of twenty-one years, who shall have resided one year in the said territory, and are not disqualified by any legal proceeding, shall be qualified to serve as grand or petit jurors in the courts of the said territory; and they shall, until the general assembly thereof shall otherwise direct, be selected in such manner as the said courts shall respectively prescribe, so as to be most conducive to an impartial trial, and least burthensome to the inhabitants of the said territory.

SEC. 12. *And be it further enacted,* That the governor, secretary and judges for the territory of Missouri, authorized by this act, and all general officers of the militia, during the temporary government thereof, shall be appointed and commissioned by the President of the United States, by and with the advice and consent of the Senate; and the governor, secretary and judges shall respectively receive for their services the compensations established by law, to be paid quarter yearly out of the treasury of the United States; the governor, secretary, judges, members of the legislative council, members of the house of representatives, justices of the peace, and all other officers civil and military, before they enter on the duties of their respective offices, shall take an oath or affirmation to support the constitution of the United States, and for the faithful discharge of the duties of their office; the governor before a judge of the supreme or a district court of the United States, or a judge of the said territory; the secretary and judges before the governor; the members of the legislative council and house of representatives before a judge of the said territory; and the justices of the peace and all other officers before such person as the governor shall appoint and direct.

SEC. 13. *And be it further enacted,* That the citizens of the said territory entitled to vote for representatives to the general assembly thereof, shall, at the time of electing their representatives to the said general assembly, also elect one delegate from the said territory to the Congress of the United States; and the delegate so elected, shall possess the same powers, shall have the same privileges and compensation for his attendance in Congress, and for going to and returning from the same, as heretofore have been granted to and provided for a delegate from any territory of the United States.

SEC. 14. *And be it further enacted*, That the people of the said territory shall always be entitled to a proportionate representation in the general assembly; to judicial proceedings according to the common law and the laws and usages in force in the said territory; to the benefit of the writ of habeas corpus. In all criminal cases the trial shall be by jury of good and lawful men of the vicinage. All persons shall be bailable unless for capital offences where the proof shall be evident or the presumption great. All fines shall be moderate, and no cruel or unusual punishment shall be inflicted. No man shall be deprived of his life, liberty or property, but by the judgement of his peers and the law of the land. If the public exigencies make it necessary for the common preservation to take the property of any person, or to demand his particular services, full compensation shall be made for the same. No ex post facto law or law impairing the obligation of contracts shall be made. No law shall be made which shall lay any person under restraint, burthen or disability, on account of his religious opinions, professions or mode of worship, in all which he shall be free to maintain his own, and not burthened for those of another. Religion, morality and knowledge being necessary to good government and the happiness of mankind, schools and the means of education shall be encouraged and provided for from the public lands of the United States in the said territory, in such manner as Congress may deem expedient.

SEC. 15. *And be it further enacted*, That the general assembly shall never interfere with the primary disposal of the soil by the United States in Congress assembled, nor with any regulation Congress may find necessary to make for securing the title in the bona fide purchasers: no tax shall ever be imposed on lands the property of the United States. The lands of non-resident proprietors shall never be taxed higher than those of residents. The Mississippi and Missouri rivers, and the navigable waters flowing into them, and the carrying places between the same, shall be common highways and forever free to the people of the said territory and to the citizens of the United States, without any tax, duty or impost therefor.

SEC. 16. *And be it further enacted*, That the laws and regulations in force in the territory of Louisiana, at the commencement of this act, and not inconsistent with the provisions thereof, shall continue in force until altered, modified or repealed by the general assembly. And it is hereby declared that this act shall not be construed to vacate the commission of any officer in the said territory, acting under the authority of the United States, but that every such commission shall be and continue in full force as if this act had not been made. And so much of an act, entitled "An act further providing for the government of the territory of Louisiana," approved on the third day of March, one thousand eight hundred and five, and so much of an act, entitled "An act for erecting Louisiana into two territories and providing for the temporary government thereof," approved the twenty-sixth of March, one thousand eight hundred and four, as is repugnant to this act, shall from and after the first Monday in December next be repealed. On which first Monday in December next this act shall commence and have full force: *Provided*, so much of it as requires the governor of said territory to perform certain duties previous to the said first Monday of December next shall be in force from the passage thereof.

Approved, June 4, 1812.

TREATY BETWEEN THE UNITED STATES OF AMERICA AND GREAT BRITAIN DECEMBER 24, 1814

His Britannic Majesty and the United States of America desirous of terminating the war which has unhappily subsisted between the two Countries, and of restoring upon principles of perfect reciprocity, Peace, Friendship, and good Understanding between them, have for that purpose appointed their respective Plenipotentiaries, that is to say, His Britannic Majesty on His part has appointed the Right Honourable James Lord Gambier, late Admiral of the White now Admiral of the Red Squadron of His Majesty's Fleet; Henry Goulburn Esquire, a Member of the Imperial Parliament and Under Secretary of State; and William Adams Esquire, Doctor of Civil Laws: And the President of the United States, by and with the advice and consent of the Senate thereof, has appointed John Quincy Adams, James A. Bayard, Henry Clay, Jonathan Russell, and Albert Gallatin, Citizens of the United States; who, after a reciprocal communication of their respective Full Powers, have agreed upon the following Articles.

ARTICLE THE FIRST.

There shall be a firm and universal Peace between His Britannic Majesty and the United States, and between their respective Countries, Territories, Cities, Towns, and People of every degree without exception of places or persons. All hostilities both by sea and land shall cease as soon as this Treaty shall have been ratified by both parties as hereinafter mentioned. All territory, places, and possessions whatsoever taken by either party from the other during the war, or which may be taken after the signing of this Treaty, excepting only the Islands hereinafter mentioned, shall be restored without delay and without causing any destruction or carrying away any of the Artillery or other public property originally captured in the said forts or places, and which shall remain therein upon the Exchange of the Ratifications of this Treaty, or any Slaves or other private property; And all Archives, Records, Deeds, and Papers, either of a public nature or belonging to private persons, which in the course of the war may have fallen into the hands of the Officers of either party, shall be, as far as may be practicable, forthwith restored and delivered to the proper authorities and persons to whom they respectively belong. Such of the Islands in the Bay of Passamaquoddy as are claimed by both parties shall remain in the possession of the party in whose occupation they may be at the time of the Exchange of the Ratifications of this Treaty until the decision respecting the title to the said Islands shall have been made in conformity with the fourth Article of this Treaty. No disposition made by this Treaty as to such possession of the Islands and territories claimed by both parties shall in any manner whatever be construed to affect the right of either.

ARTICLE THE SECOND.

Immediately after the ratifications of this Treaty by both parties as hereinafter mentioned, orders shall be sent to the Armies, Squadrons, Officers, Subjects, and Citizens of the two Powers to cease from all hostilities: and to prevent all causes of complaint which might arise on account of the prizes which may be taken at sea after the said Ratifications of this Treaty, it is reciprocally agreed that all vessels and effects which may be taken after the space of twelve days from the said Ratifications upon all parts of the Coast of North America from the Latitude of twenty three degrees North to the Latitude of fifty degrees North, and as far Eastward in the Atlantic Ocean as the thirty sixth degree of West Longitude from the Meridian of Greenwich, shall be restored on each side: — that the time shall be thirty days in all other parts of the Atlantic Ocean North of the Equinoctial Line or Equator: — and the same time for the British and Irish Channels, for the Gulf of Mexico, and all parts of the West Indies: — forty days for the North Seas for the Baltic, and for all parts of the Mediterranean: — sixty days for the Atlantic Ocean South of the Equator as far as the Latitude of the Cape of Good Hope: — ninety days for every other part of the world South of the Equator, and one hundred and twenty days for all other parts of the world without exception.

ARTICLE THE THIRD.

All Prisoners of war taken on either side as well by land as by sea shall be restored as soon as practicable after the Ratifications of this Treaty as hereinafter mentioned on their paying the debts which they may have contracted during their captivity. The two Contracting Parties respectively engage to discharge in specie the advances which may have been made by the other for the sustenance and maintenance of such prisoners.

ARTICLE THE FOURTH.

Whereas it was stipulated by the second Article in the Treaty of Peace of one thousand seven hundred and eighty three between His Britannic Majesty and the United States of America that the boundary of the United States should comprehend "all Islands within twenty leagues of any part of the shores of the United States and lying between lines to be drawn due East from the points where the aforesaid boundaries between Nova Scotia on the one part and East Florida on the other shall respectively touch the Bay of Fundy and the Atlantic Ocean, excepting such Islands as now are or heretofore have been within the limits of Nova Scotia," and whereas the several Islands in the Bay of Passama-quoddy, which is part of the Bay of Fundy, and the Island of Grand Menan in the said Bay of Fundy, are claimed by the United States as being compre-hended within their aforesaid boundaries, which said Islands are claimed as be-longing to His Britannic Majesty as having been at the time of and previous to the aforesaid Treaty of one thousand seven hundred and eighty three within the limits of the Province of Nova Scotia: In order therefore finally to decide upon these claims it is agreed that they shall be referred to two Commissioners to be appointed in the following manner: viz: One Commissioner shall be ap-pointed by His Britannic Majesty and one by the President of the United States, by and with the advice and consent of the Senate thereof, and the said two Commissioners so appointed shall be sworn impartially to examine and decide upon the said claims according to such evidence as shall be laid before them on the part of His Britannic Majesty and of the United States respectively. The said Commissioners shall meet at S! Andrews in the Province of New Brunswick, and shall have power to adjourn to such other place or places as they shall think fit. The said Commissioners shall by a declaration or report under their hands and seals decide to which of the two Contracting parties the several Islands aforesaid do respectively belong in conformity with the true in-tent of the said Treaty of Peace of one thousand seven hundred and eighty three. And if the said Commissioners shall agree in their decision both parties shall consider such decision as final and conclusive. It is further agreed that in the event of the two Commissioners differing upon all or any of the matters so referred to them, or in the event of both or either of the said Commissioners refusing or declining or wilfully omitting to act as such, they shall make jointly or separately a report or reports as well to the Government of His Britannic Majesty as to that of the United States, stating in detail the points on which they differ, and the grounds upon which their respective opinions have been formed, or the grounds upon which they or either of them have so refused de-clined or omitted to act. And His Britannic Majesty and the Government of the United States hereby agree to refer the report or reports of the said Commis-sioners to some friendly Sovereign or State to be then named for that prupose, and who shall be requested to decide on the differences which may be stated in the said report or reports, or upon the report of one Commissioner together with the grounds upon which the other Commissioner shall have refused, de-clined or omitted to act as the case may be. And if the Commissioner so re-fusing, declining, or omitting to act, shall also wilfully omit to state the grounds upon which he has so done in such manner that the said statement may be referred to such friendly Sovereign or State together with the report of such other Commissioner, then such Sovereign or State shall decide ex parte upon the said report alone. And His Britannic Majesty and the Government of the United States engage to consider the decision of such friendly Sovereign or State to be final and conclusive on all the matters so referred.

ARTICLE THE FIFTH.

Whereas neither that point of the Highlands lying due North from the source of the River S! Croix, and designated in the former Treaty of Peace between the two Powers as the North West Angle of Nova Scotia, nor the North Westernmost head of Connecticut River has yet been ascertained; and whereas that part of the boundary line between the Dominions of the two Powers which extends from the source of the River S! Croix directly North to the abovementioned North West Angle of Nova Scotia, thence along the said Highlands which divide those Rivers that empty themselves into the River S! Lawrence from those which fall into the Atlantic Ocean to the North Westernmost head of Connecticut River, thence down along the middle of that River to the forty fifth degree of North Latitude, thence by a line due West on said latitude until it strikes the River Iroquois or Cataraquy, has not yet been surveyed: it is agreed that for these several purposes two Commissioners shall be appointed, sworn, and authorized to act exactly in the manner directed with respect to those mentioned in the next preceding Article unless otherwise specified in the present Article. The said Commissioners shall meet at S! Andrews in the Province of New Brunswick, and shall have power to adjourn to such other place or places as they shall think fit. The said Commissioners shall have power to ascertain and determine the points above mentioned in conformity with the provisions of the said Treaty of Peace of one thousand seven hundred and eighty three, and shall cause the boundary aforesaid from the source of the River S! Croix to the River Iroquois or Cataraquy to be surveyed and marked according to the said provisions. The said Commissioners shall make a map of the said boundary, and annex to it a declaration under their hands and seals certifying it to be the true Map of the said boundary, and particularizing the latitude and longitude of the North West Angle of Nova Scotia, of the North Westernmost head of Connecticut River, and of such other points of the said boundary as they may deem proper. And both parties agree to consider such map and declaration as finally and conclusively fixing the said boundary. And in the event of the said two Commissioners differing, or both, or either of them refusing, declining, or wilfully omitting to act, such reports, declarations, or statements shall be made by them or either of them, and such reference to a friendly Sovereign or State shall be made in all respects as in the latter part of the fourth Article is contained, and in as full a manner as if the same was herein repeated.

ARTICLE THE SIXTH.

Whereas by the former Treaty of Peace that portion of the boundary of the United States from the point where the forty fifth degree of North Latitude strikes the River Iroquois or Cataraquy to the Lake Superior was declared to be "along the middle of said River into Lake Ontario, through the middle of said Lake until it strikes the communication by water between that Lake and Lake Erie, thence along the middle of said communication into Lake Erie, through the middle of said Lake until it arrives at the water communication into the Lake Huron; thence through the middle of said Lake to the water communication between that Lake and Lake Superior:" and whereas doubts have arisen what was the middle of the said River, Lakes, and water communications, and whether certain Islands lying in the same were within the Dominions of His Britannic Majesty or of the United States: In order therefore finally to decide these doubts, they shall be referred to two Commissioners to be appointed, sworn, and authorized to act exactly in the manner directed with respect to those mentioned in the next preceding Article unless otherwise specified in this present Article. The said Commissioners shall meet in the first instance at Albany in the State of New York, and shall have power to adjourn to such other place or places as they shall think fit. The said Commissioners shall by Report or Declaration under their hands and seals, designate the boundary through the said River, Lakes, and water communications, and decide to which of the two Contracting parties the several Islands lying within the said Rivers, Lakes, and water communications, do respectively belong in conformity with the true intent of the said Treaty of one thousand seven hundred and eighty three. And both parties agree to consider such designation and decision as final and conclusive. And in the event of the said two Commissioners differing or both or either of them refusing, declining, or wilfully omitting to act, such reports, declarations, or statements shall be made by them or either of them, and such reference to a friendly Sovereign or State shall be made in all respects as in the latter part of the fourth Article is contained, and in as full a manner as if the same was herein repeated.

ARTICLE THE SEVENTH.

It is further agreed that the said two last mentioned Commissioners after they shall have executed the duties assigned to them in the preceding Article, shall be, and they are hereby, authorized upon their oaths impartially to fix and determine according to the true intent of the said Treaty of Peace of one thousand seven hundred and eighty three, that part of the boundary between the dominions of the two Powers, which extends from the water communication between Lake Huron and Lake Superior to the most North Western point of the Lake of the Woods; — to decide which of the two Parties the several Islands lying in the Lakes, water communications, and Rivers forming the said boundary do respectively belong in conformity with the true intent of the said Treaty of Peace of one thousand seven hundred and eighty three, and to cause such parts of the said boundary as require it to be surveyed and marked. The said Commissioners shall by a Report or declaration under their hands and seals, designate the boundary aforesaid, state their decision on the points thus referred to them, and particularize the Latitude and Longitude of the most North Western point of the Lake of the Woods, and of such other parts of the said boundary as they may deem proper. And both parties agree to consider such designation and decision as final and conclusive. And in the event of the said two Commissioners differing, or both or either of them refusing, declining, or wilfully omitting to act, such reports, declarations or statements shall be made by them or either of them, and such reference to a friendly Sovereign or State shall be made in all respects as in the latter part of the fourth Article is contained, and in as full a manner as if the same was herein repeated.

ARTICLE THE EIGHTH.

The several Boards of two Commissioners mentioned in the four preceding Articles shall respectively have power to appoint a Secretary, and to employ such Surveyors or other persons as they shall judge necessary. Duplicates of all their respective reports, declarations, statements, and decisions, and of their accounts, and of the Journal of their proceedings shall be delivered by them to the Agents of His Britannic Majesty and to the Agents of the United States, who may be respectively appointed and authorized to manage the business on behalf of their respective Governments. The said Commissioners shall be respectively paid in such manner as shall be agreed between the two contracting parties, such agreement being to be settled at the time of the Exchange of the Ratifications of this Treaty. And all other expenses attending the said Commissions shall be defrayed equally by the two parties. And in the case of death, sickness, resignation, or necessary absence, the place of every such Commissioner respectively shall be supplied in the same manner as such Commissioner was first appointed; and the new Commissioner shall take the same oath or affirmation and do the same duties. It is further agreed between the two contracting parties that in case any of the Islands mentioned in any of the preceding Articles, which were in the possession of one of the parties prior to the commencement of the present war between the two Countries, should by the decision of any of the Boards of Commissioners aforesaid, or of the Sovereign or State so referred to, as in the four next preceding Articles contained, fall within the dominions of the other party, all grants of land made previous to the commencement of the war by the party having had such possession, shall be as valid as if such Island or Islands had by such decision or decisions been adjudged to be within the dominions of the party having had such possession.

ARTICLE THE NINTH.

The United States of America engage to put an end immediately after the Ratification of the present Treaty to hostilities with all the Tribes or Nations of Indians with whom they may be at war at the time of such Ratification, and forthwith to restore to such Tribes or Nations respectively all the possessions, rights, and privileges which they may have enjoyed or been entitled to in one thousand eight hundred and eleven previous to such hostilities. Provided always that such Tribes or Nations shall agree to desist from all hostilities against the United States of America, their Citizens, and Subjects upon the Ratification of the present Treaty being notified to such Tribes of Nations, and shall so desist accordingly. And His Britannic Majesty engages on his part to put an end immediately after the Ratification of the present Treaty to hostilities with all the Tribes or Nations of Indians with whom He may be at war at the time of such Ratification, and forthwith to restore to such Tribes or Nations respectively all the possessions, rights, and privileges, which they may have enjoyed or been entitled to in one thousand eight hundred and eleven previous to such hostilities. Provided always that such Tribes or Nations shall agree to desist from all hostilities against His Britannic Majesty and His Subjects upon the Ratification of the present Treaty being notified to such Tribes or Nations, and shall so desist accordingly.

ARTICLE THE TENTH.

Whereas the Traffic in Slaves is irreconcilable with the principles of humanity and Justice, and whereas both His Majesty and the United States are desirous of continuing their efforts to promote its entire abolition, it is hereby agreed that both the contracting parties shall use their best endeavours to accomplish so desirable an object.

ARTICLE THE ELEVENTH.

This Treaty when the same shall have been ratified on both sides without alteration by either of the contracting parties, and the Ratifications mutually exchanged, shall be binding on both parties, and the Ratifications shall be exchanged at Washington in the space of four months from this day or sooner if practicable.

In faith whereof, We the respective Plenipotentiaries have signed this Treaty, and have thereunto affixed our Seals.

Done in triplicate at Ghent the twenty fourth day of December one thousand eight hundred and fourteen.

Gambier.	(Seal)
Henry Goulburn	(Seal)
William Adams	(Seal)
John Quincy Adams	(Seal)
J.A. Bayard	(Seal)
H. Clay.	(Seal)
Jona Russell	(Seal)
Albert Gallatin	(Seal)

AN ACT TO ENABLE THE PEOPLE OF THE INDIANA TERRITORY TO FORM A CONSTITUTION AND STATE GOVERNMENT, AND FOR THE ADMISSION OF SUCH STATE INTO THE UNION ON AN EQUAL FOOTING WITH THE ORIGINAL STATES APRIL 19, 1816

Be it enacted by the Senate and House of Representatives of the United States of America, in Congress assembled, That the inhabitants of the territory of Indiana be, and they are hereby authorized to form for themselves a constitution and state government, and to assume such name as they shall deem proper; and the said state, when formed, shall be admitted into the union upon the same footing with the original states, in all respects whatever.

SEC. 2. *And be it further enacted,* That the said state shall consist of all the territory included within the following boundaries, to wit: bounded on the east, by the meridian line which forms the western boundary of the state of Ohio; on the South, by the river Ohio, from the mouth of the Great Miami river, to the mouth of the river Wabash; on the west, by a line drawn along the middle of the Wabash, from its mouth to a point, where a due north line drawn from the town of Vincennes, would last touch the north western shore of the said river; and from thence by a due north line, until the same shall intersect an east and west line, drawn through a point ten miles north of the southern extreme of lake Michigan; on the north, by the said east and west line, until the same shall intersect the first mentioned meridian line which forms the western boundary of the state of Ohio: *Provided,* That the convention hereinafter provided for, when formed, shall ratify the boundaries aforesaid; otherwise they shall be and remain as now prescribed by the ordinance for the government of the territory northwest of the river Ohio: *Provided, also,* That the said state shall have concurrent jurisdiction on the river Wabash, with the state to be formed west thereof, so far as the said river shall form a common boundary to both.

SEC. 3. *And be it further enacted,* That all male citizens of the United States, who shall have arrived at the age of twenty-one years, and resided within the said territory, at least one year previous to the day of election, and shall have paid a county or territorial tax; and all persons having in other respects the legal qualifications to vote for representatives in the general assembly of the said territory be, and they are hereby authorized to choose representatives to form a convention, who shall be apportioned amongst the several counties within the said territory, according to the apportionment made by the legislature thereof, at their last session, to wit: from the county of Wayne, four representatives; from the county of Franklin, five representatives; from the county of Dearborn, three representatives; from the county of Switzerland, one representative; from the county of Jefferson, three representatives; from the county of Clark, five representatives; from the county of Harrison, five representatives; from the county of Washington, five representatives; from the county of Knox, five representatives; from the county of Gibson, four representatives; from the county of Posey, one representative; from the county of Warrick, one representative; and from the county of Perry, one representative. And the election for the representatives aforesaid, shall be holden on the second Monday of May, one thousand eight hundred and sixteen, throughout the several counties in the said territory; and shall be conducted in the same manner, and under the same penalties, as prescribed by the laws of the said territory, regulating elections therein for members of the House of representatives.

SEC. 4. *And be it further enacted*, That the members of the convention, thus duly elected be, and they are hereby authorized to meet at the seat of the government of the said territory, on the second Monday of June next, which convention, when met, shall first determine, by a majority of the whole number elected, whether it be, or be not expedient, at that time, to form a constitution and state government, for the people within the said territory, and if it be determined to be expedient, the convention shall be, and hereby are authorized, to form a constitution and state government: or if it be deemed more expedient, the said convention shall provide by ordinance for electing representatives to form a constitution, or frame of government; which said representatives shall be chosen in such manner, and in such proportion, and shall meet at such time and place, as shall be prescribed by the said ordinance, and shall then form, for the people of said territory, a constitution and state government: *Provided*, That the same, whenever formed, shall be republican, and not repugnant to those articles of the ordinance of the thirteenth of July, one thousand seven hundred and eighty-seven, which are declared to be irrevocable between the original states, and the people and states of the territory northwest of the river Ohio; excepting so much of said articles as relate to the boundaries of the states therein to be formed.

SEC. 5. *And be it further enacted*, That, until the next general census shall be taken, the said state shall be entitled to one representative in the House of Representatives of the United States.

SEC. 6. *And be it further enacted*, That the following propositions be, and the same are hereby offered to the convention of the said territory of Indiana, when formed, for their free acceptance or rejection, which, if accepted by the convention, shall be obligatory upon the United States.

First. That the section numbered sixteen, in every township, and when such section has been sold, granted or disposed of, other lands, equivalent thereto, and most contiguous to the same, shall be granted to the inhabitants of such township for the use of schools.

Second. That all salt springs within the said territory, and the land reserved for the use of the same, together with such other lands as may, by the President of the United States, be deemed necessary and proper for working the said salt springs, not exceeding, in the whole, the quantity contained in thirty-six entire sections, shall be granted to the said state, for the use of the people of the said state, the same to be used under such terms, conditions, and regulations as the legislature of the said state shall direct: provided the said legislature shall never sell nor lease the same, for a longer period than ten years at any one time.

Third. That five per cent. of the net proceeds of the lands lying within the said territory, and which shall be sold by Congress from and after the first day of December next, after deducting all expenses incident to the same, shall be reserved for making public roads and canals, of which three-fifths shall be applied to those objects within the said state, under the direction of the legislature thereof, and two-fifths to the making of a road or roads leading to the said state under the direction of Congress.

Fourth. That one entire township, which shall be designated by the President of the United States, in addition to the one heretofore reserved for that purpose, shall be reserved for the use of a seminary of learning, and vested in the legislature of the said state, to be appropriated solely to the use of such seminary by the said legislature.

Fifth. That four sections of land be, and the same are hereby granted to the said state, for the purpose of fixing their seat of government thereon, which four sections shall, under the direction of the legislature of said state, be located at any time, in such township and range, as the legislature aforesaid may select, on such lands as may hereafter be acquired by the United States, from the Indian tribes within the said territory: *Provided,* That such locations shall be made prior to the public sale of the lands of the United States, surrounding such location: *And provided always,* That the five foregoing provisions, herein offered, are on the conditions that the convention of the said state shall provide by an ordinance irrevocable, without the consent of the United States, that every and each tract of land sold by the United States, from and after the first day of December next, shall be and remain exempt from any tax, laid by order or under any authority of the state, whether for state, county or township, or any other purpose whatever, for the term of five years, from and after the day of sale.

Approved, April 19, 1816.

AN ACT TO ENABLE THE PEOPLE OF THE WESTERN PART OF THE MISSISSIPPI TERRITORY TO FORM A CONSTITUTION AND STATE GOVERNMENT, AND FOR THE ADMISSION OF SUCH STATE INTO THE UNION, ON AN EQUAL FOOTING WITH THE ORIGINAL STATES MARCH 1, 1817

Be it enacted by the Senate and House of Representatives of the United States of America, in Congress assembled, That the inhabitants of the western part of the Mississippi territory be, and they hereby are, authorized to form for themselves a constitution and state government, and to assume such name as they shall deem proper; and the said state, when formed, shall be admitted into the union upon the same footing with the original states, in all respects whatever.

SEC. 2. *And be it further enacted,* That the said state shall consist of all the territory included within the following boundaries, to wit: Beginning on the river Mississippi at the point where the southern boundary line of the state of Tennessee strikes the same, thence east along the said boundary line to the Tennessee river, thence up the same to the mouth of Bear Creek, thence by a direct line to the north-west corner of the county of Washington, thence due south to the Gulf of Mexico, thence westwardly, including all the islands within six leagues of the shore, to the most eastern junction of Pearl river with Lake Borgne, thence up said river to the thirty-first degree of north latitude, thence west along the said degree of latitude to the Mississippi river, thence up the same to the beginning.

SEC. 3. *And be it further enacted,* That all free white male citizens of the United States, who shall have arrived at the age of twenty-one years, and resided within the said territory at least one year previous to the time of holding the election, and shall have paid a county or territorial tax, and all persons having in other respects the legal qualifications to vote for Representatives in the general assembly of the said territory, be, and they are hereby authorized to choose Representatives to form a convention, who shall be apportioned among the several counties within the said territory, as follows, to wit: from the county of Warren, two Representatives; from the county of Claiborne, four Representatives; from the county of Jefferson, four Representatives; from the county of Adams, eight Representatives; from the county of Franklin, two Representatives; from the county of Wilkinson, six Representatives; from the county of Amite, six Representatives; from the county of Pike, four Representatives; from the county of Lawrence, two Representatives; from the county of Marion, two Representatives; from the county of Hancock, two Representatives; from the county of Wayne, two Representatives; from the county of Greene, two Representatives; from the county of Jackson, two Representatives; and the election of the Representatives aforesaid shall be holden on the first Monday and Tuesday in June next, throughout the several counties above mentioned, and shall be conducted in the same manner as is prescribed by the laws of said territory, regulating elections therein for members of the House of Representatives.

SEC. 4. *And be it further enacted,* That the members of the convention, thus duly elected, be, and they hereby are authorized to meet at the town of Washington, on the first Monday in July next: which convention, when met, shall first determine, by a majority of the whole number elected; whether it be or be not expedient, at that time, to form a constitution and state government for the people within the said territory; and if it be determined to be expedient, the convention shall be, and hereby are, authorized to form a constitution and state government: *Provided,* That the same, when formed, shall be republican, and not repugnant to the principles of the ordinance of the thirteenth of July, one thousand seven hundred and eighty-seven, between the people and states of the territory north-west of the river Ohio, so far as the same has been extended to the said territory by the articles of agreement between the United States and the state of Georgia, or of the constitution of the United States: *And provided also*, That the said convention shall provide, by an ordinance irrevocable without the consent of the United States, that the people inhabiting the said territory do agree and declare that they for ever disclaim all right or title to the waste or unappropriated lands lying within the said territory, and that the same shall be and remain at the sole and entire disposition of the United States; and moreover, that each and every tract of land sold by Congress, shall be and remain exempt from any tax laid by the order, or under the authority, of the state, whether for state, county, township, parish or any other purpose whatever, for the term of five years, from and after the respective days of the sales thereof, and that the lands belonging to citizens of the United States, residing without the said state, shall never be taxed higher than the lands belonging to persons residing therein; and that no taxes shall be imposed on lands the property of the United States, and that the river Mississippi, and the navigable rivers and waters leading into the same, or into the Gulf of Mexico, shall be common highways, and for ever free, as well to the inhabitants of the said state, as to other citizens of the United States, without any tax, duty, impost, or toll, therefor, imposed by the said state.

SEC. 5. *And be it further enacted*, That five per cent. of the net proceeds of the lands lying within the said territory, and which shall be sold by Congress from and after the first day of December next, after deducting all expenses incident to the same, shall be reserved for making public roads and canals; of which three-fifths shall be applied to those objects within the said state, under the direction of the legislature thereof, and two-fifths to the making of a road or roads leading to the said state, under the direction of Congress: *Provided*, That the application of such proceeds shall not be made until after payment is completed of the one million two hundred and fifty thousand dollars due to the state of Georgia, in consideration of the cession to the United States, nor until the payment of all the stock which has been or shall be created by the act, entitled "An act providing for the indemnification of certain claimants of public lands in the Mississippi territory," shall be completed: *And provided also*, That the said five per cent. shall not be calculated on any part of such proceeds as shall be applied to the payment of the one million two hundred and fifty thousand dollars due to the state of Georgia, in consideration of the cession to the United States, or in payment of the stock which has or shall be created by the act, entitled "An act providing for the indemnification of certain claimants of public lands in the Mississippi territory."

SEC. 6. *And be it further enacted*, That until the next general census shall be taken, the said state shall be entitled to one Representative in the House of Representatives of the United States.

Approved, March 1, 1817.

AN ACT TO ESTABLISH A
SEPARATE TERRITORIAL GOVERNMENT FOR THE
EASTERN PART OF THE MISSISSIPPI TERRITORY
MARCH 3, 1817

Be it enacted by the Senate and House of Representatives of the United States of America, in Congress assembled, That all that part of the Mississippi territory which lies within the following boundaries, to wit: beginning at the point where the line of the thirty-first degree of north latitude intersects the Perdido river, thence east to the western boundary line of the state of Georgia, thence along said line to the southern boundary line to the state of Tennessee, thence west along said boundary line to the Tennessee river, thence up the same to the mouth of Bear creek, thence by a direct line to the north-west corner of Washington county, thence due south to the Gulf of Mexico, thence eastwardly, including all the islands within six leagues of the shore, to the Perdido river, and thence up the same to the beginning, shall, for the purpose of a temporary government, constitute a separate territory, and be called "Alabama."

SEC. 2. *And be it further enacted,* That all offices which may exist, and all laws which may be in force, in said territory, within the boundaries above described, at the time this act shall go into effect, shall continue to exist, and be in force, until otherwise provided by law. And the President of the United States shall have power to appoint a governor and secretary for the said Alabama territory, who shall respectively exercise the same power, perform the same duties, and receive for their services the same compensation, as are provided for the governor and secretary of the Mississippi territory: *Provided,* that the appointment of said governor, and secretary, shall be submitted to the Senate, for their advice and consent, at the next session of Congress.

SEC. 3. *And be it further enacted,* That there shall be appointed an additional judge for the Mississippi territory, who shall reside in the eastern part thereof, and receive the same compensation as the other judges; and that the judge appointed by virtue of an act, passed the twenty-seventh day of March, one thousand eight hundred and four, for the appointment of an additional judge for the Mississippi territory, together with the judge appointed for Madison county, and the judge to be appointed by virtue of this act, shall possess and exercise exclusive original jurisdiction in the superior courts of Washington, Baldwin, Clarke, Monroe, Montgomery, Wayne, Green, Jackson, Mobile, Madison, and of such new counties as may be formed out of them, and shall arrange the same among themselves, from time to time: *Provided,* that no judge shall sit more than twice in succession in the same court; and that the other judges of the Mississippi territory shall exercise, as heretofore authorized by an act of Congress, or of the territorial legislature, exclusive jurisdiction in the superior courts of the other counties. That a general court, to be composed of the judge appointed by the virtue of the act of twenty-seventh of March, one thousand eight hundred and four, the judge appointed for Madison county, and the judge to be appointed by virtue of this act, or any two of them, shall be holden at St. Stephens, commencing on the first Mondays of January and July, annually, who shall have the same power of issuing writs of error to the superior courts of the counties mentioned in this section, or which shall hereafter be formed in the eastern division of the territory, which was given by the act for the appointment of an additional judge, passed the year one thousand eight hundred and four, to the superior court of Adams district, and which shall possess, exclusively of the courts of the several counties, the federal jurisdiction given to the superior courts of the territories, by an act passed the third day of March, one thousand eight hundred and five, entitled "An act to extend jurisdiction in certain cases to the territorial courts."

SEC. 4. *And be it further enacted,* That the governor, to be appointed under the authority of this act, shall, immediately after entering into office, convene, at the town of St. Stephens, such of the members of the legislative council and house of representatives, of the Mississippi territory, as may then be the representatives from the several counties within the limits of the territory to be established by this act; and the said members shall constitute the legislative council, and house of representatives for the aforesaid Alabama territory, whose powers, in relation to the said territory, shall be, until the expiration of the term for which they shall have been chosen, or until Congress shall otherwise provide, the same in all respects as are now possessed by the legislative council, and house of representatives of the Mississippi territory; and the said legislative council, and house of representatives of the Alabama territory, so formed, shall have power to nominate six persons to the President of the United States, three of whom shall be selected by him for members of the legislative council, in addition to the number which the said territory may possess, agreeably to the foregoing provisions of this section. The said legislative council and house of representatives, shall also have power to elect a delegate to Congress, who shall, in all respects, possess the same rights and immunities as other delegates from territories of the United States.

SEC. 5. *And be it further enacted,* That this act shall commence and be in force, so soon as the convention, the appointment whereof has been authorized by Congress at their present session, shall have formed a constitution and state government, for that part of the Mississippi territory lying west of the territory herein described; of which act of convention the governor of the Mississippi, for the time being, shall give immediate notice to the President of the United States, who shall thereupon forthwith proceed to the execution of the powers vested in him by the second section of this act; but in case said convention shall fail to form a constitution and state government, as aforesaid, then this act shall become null and void, except so far as relates to the third section thereof, which shall take effect, and be in force, from and after the passage of this act.

SEC. 6. *And be it further enacted,* That all persons who shall be in office, within the territory hereby established, when the said convention shall have formed a constitution and state government, as aforesaid, shall continue to hold and exercise their offices, in all respects as if this act had never been made; and the governor and secretary of the Mississippi territory, for the time being, shall continue to exercise the duties of their respective offices, in relation to the territory hereby established, until a governor and secretary shall be appointed therefor, in pursuance to this act.

SEC. 7. *And be it further enacted,* That all judicial process in the said territory of Alabama, shall be issued, and bear test, as heretofore; nor shall any suit be discontinued, or the proceedings of any cause stayed, or in any wise affected by any thing contained in this act, or in the act, entitled, "An act to enable the people of the western part of the Mississippi territory to form a constitution and state government, and for the admission of such state into the union on an equal footing with the original states."

SEC. 8. *And be it further enacted,* That the town of St. Stephens shall be the seat of government for the said Alabama territory, until it shall be otherwise ordered by the legislature thereof.

SEC. 9. *And be it further enacted,* That whatever balance may remain in the treasury of the Mississippi territory, at the time when the convention authorized to form a constitution and state government, for the western part of said territory, may have formed a constitution and state government for the same, shall be divided between the new state and territory, according to the amount which may have been paid into said treasury, from the counties lying within the limits of such state and territory respectively.

Approved, March 3, 1817.

AN ACT TO ENABLE THE PEOPLE OF THE ILLINOIS TERRITORY TO FORM A CONSTITUTION AND STATE GOVERNMENT, AND FOR THE ADMISSION OF SUCH STATE INTO THE UNION ON AN EQUAL FOOTING WITH THE ORIGINAL STATES APRIL 18, 1818

Be it enacted by the Senate and House of Representatives of the United States of America, in Congress assembled, That the inhabitants of the territory of Illinois be, and they are hereby, authorized to form for themselves a constitution and state government, and to assume such name as they shall deem proper; and the said state, when formed, shall be admitted into the union upon the same footing with the original states, in all respects whatever.

SEC. 2. *And be it further enacted,* That the said state shall consist of all the territory included within the following boundaries, to wit: Beginning at the mouth of the Wabash river; thence, up the same, and with the line of Indiana, to the north-west corner of said state; thence, east with the line of the same state, to the middle of Lake Michigan; thence, north along the middle of said lake, to north latitude forty-two degrees thirty minutes; thence, west to the middle of the Mississippi river; and thence, down, along the middle of the river, to its confluence with the Ohio river; and thence, up the latter river, along its north-western shore, to the beginning: *Provided,* That the convention hereinafter provided for, when formed, shall ratify the boundaries aforesaid; otherwise they shall be and remain as now prescribed by the ordinance for the government of the territory north-west of the river Ohio: *Provided also,* That the said state shall have concurrent jurisdiction with the state of Indiana on the Wabash river, so far as said river shall form a common boundary to both, and also concurrent jurisdiction on the Mississippi river, with any state or states to be formed west thereof, so far as said river shall form a common boundary to both.

SEC. 3. *And be it further enacted,* That all white male citizens of the United States, who shall have arrived at the age of twenty-one years, and have resided in said territory six months previous to the day of election, and all persons having in other respects the legal qualifications to vote for representatives in the general assembly of the said territory, be, and they are hereby, authorized to choose representatives to form a convention, who shall be apportioned amongst the several counties as follows:

From the county of Bond, two representatives:
From the county of Madison, three representatives:
From the county of St. Clair, three representatives:
From the county of Monroe, two representatives:
From the county of Randolph, two representatives:
From the county of Jackson, two representatives:
From the county of Johnson, two representatives:
From the county of Pope, two representatives:
From the county of Gallatin, three representatives:
From the county of White, two representatives:
From the county of Edwards, two representatives:
From the county of Crawford, two representatives:
From the county of Union, two representatives:
From the county of Washington, two representatives:
And from the county of Franklin, two representatives:
And the election for the representatives aforesaid shall be holden on the first Monday of July next, and the two following days, throughout the several counties in the said territory, and shall be conducted in the same manner, and under the same regulations, as prescribed by the laws of the said territory regulating elections therein, for members of the House of Representatives.

SEC. 4. *And be it further enacted,* That the members of the convention, thus duly elected, be, and they are hereby, authorized to meet at the seat of government of the said territory, on the first Monday of the month of August next, which convention, when met, shall first determine, by a majority of the whole number elected, whether it be, or be not, expedient at that time to form a constitution and state government for the people within the said territory, and, if it be expedient, the convention shall be and hereby is authorized to form a constitution and state government; or, if it be deemed more expedient, the said convention shall provide by ordinance for electing representatives to form a constitution or frame of government; which said representatives shall be chosen in such manner, and in such proportion, and shall meet at such time and place, as shall be prescribed by the said ordinance, and shall then form for the people of said territory a constitution and state government: *Provided,* That the same, whenever formed, shall be republican, and not repugnant to the ordinance of the thirteenth of July, seventeen hundred and eighty-seven, between the original states and the people and states of the territory north-west of the river Ohio: excepting so much of said articles as relate to the boundaries of the states therein to be formed: *And provided also,* That it shall appear, from the enumeration directed to be made by the legislature of the said territory, that there are, within the proposed state, not less than forty thousand inhabitants.

SEC. 5. *And be it further enacted,* That until the next general census shall be taken, the said state shall be entitled to one representative in the House of Representatives of the United States.

SEC. 6. *And be it further enacted,* That the following propositions be and the same are hereby, offered to the convention of the said territory of Illinois, when formed, for their free acceptance or rejection, which if accepted by the convention, shall be obligatory upon the United States and the said state.

First. That section numbered sixteen, in every township, and, when such section has been sold or otherwise disposed of, other lands, equivalent thereto, and as contiguous as may be, shall be granted to the state, for the use of the inhabitants of such township, for the use of schools.

Second. That all salt springs within such state, and the land reserved for the use of the same, shall be granted to the said state, for the use of the said state, and the same to be used under such terms, and conditions, and regulations, as the legislature of the said state shall direct: *Provided,* The legislature shall never sell nor lease the same for a longer period than ten years, at any one time.

Third. That five per cent. of the net proceeds of the lands lying within such state, and which shall be sold by Congress, from and after the first day of January, one thousand eight hundred and nineteen, after deducting all expenses incident to the same, shall be reserved for the purposes following, viz: two-fifths to be disbursed, under the direction of Congress, in making roads leading to the state; the residue to be appropriated, by the legislature of the state, for the encouragement of learning, of which one-sixth part shall be exclusively bestowed on a college or university.

Fourth. That thirty-six sections, or one entire township, which shall be designated by the President of the United States, together with the one heretofore reserved for that purpose, shall be reserved for the use of a seminary of learning, and vested in the legislature of the said state, to be appropriated solely to the use of such seminary by the said legislature. *Provided always,* That the four foregoing propositions, herein offered, are on the conditions that the convention of the said state shall provide, by an ordinance irrevocable without the consent of the United States, that every and each tract of land sold by the United States, from and after the first day of January, one thousand eight hundred and nineteen, shall remain exempt from any tax laid by order, or under any authority of, the state, whether for state, county, or township, or any other purpose whatever, for the term of five years from and after the day of sale: *And further,* That the bounty lands granted, or hereafter to be granted, for military services during the late war, shall, while they continue to be held by the patentees, or their heirs, remain exempt, as aforesaid, from all taxes, for the term of three years, from and after the date of the patents respectively; and that all the lands belonging to the citizens of the United States, residing without the said state, shall never be taxed higher than lands belonging to persons residing therein.

SEC. 7. And be it further enacted, That all that part of the territory of the United States lying north of the state of Indiana, and which was included in the former Indiana territory, together with that part of the Illinois territory which is situated north of and not included within the boundaries prescribed by this act, to the state thereby authorized to be formed, shall be, and hereby is, attached to, and made a part of the Michigan territory, from and after the formation of the said state, subject, nevertheless, to be hereafter disposed of by Congress, according to the right reserved in the fifth article of the ordinance aforesaid, and the inhabitants therein shall be entitled to the same privileges and immunities, and subject to the same rules and regulations, in all respects, with the other citizens of the Michigan territory.

Approved, April 18, 1818.

TREATY BETWEEN THE UNITED STATES OF AMERICA AND GREAT BRITAIN OCTOBER 20, 1818

The United States of America, and His Majesty The King of the United Kingdom of Great Britain and Ireland, desirous to cement the good Understanding which happily subsists between them, have, for that purpose, named their respective Plenipotentiaries, that is to say: The President of the United States, on his part, has appointed, Albert Gallatin, Their Envoy Extraordinary and Minister Plenipotentiary to the Court of France; and Richard Rush, Their Envoy Extraordinary and Minister Plenipotentiary to the Court of His Britannic Majesty: And His Majesty has appointed The Right Honorable Frederick John Robinson, Treasurer of His Majesty's Navy, and President of the Committee of Privy Council for Trade and Plantations; and Henry Goulburn Esquire, One of His Majesty's Under Secretaries of State: Who, after having exchanged their respective Full Powers, found to be in due proper Form, have agreed to and concluded the following Articles.

ARTICLE I.

Whereas differences have arisen respecting the Liberty claimed by the United States for the Inhabitants thereof, to take, dry, and cure Fish on certain Coasts, Bays, Harbours, and Creeks of His Britannic Majesty's Dominions in America, it is agreed between The High Contracting Parties, that the Inhabitants of the said United States shall have for ever, in common with the Subjects of His Britannic Majesty, the Liberty to take Fish of every kind on that part of the Southern Coast of Newfoundland which extends from Cape Ray to the Rameau Islands, on the Western and Northern Coast of Newfoundland, from the said Cape Ray to the Quirpon Islands on the Shores of the Magdalen Islands, and also on the Coasts, Bays, Harbours, and Creeks from Mount Joly on the Southern Coast of Labrador, to and through the Streights of Belleisle and thence Northwardly indefinitely along the Coast, without prejudice however, to any of the exclusive Rights of the Hudson Bay Company: and that the American Fishermen shall also have liberty for ever, to dry and cure Fish in any of the unsettled Bays, Harbours, and Creeks of the Southern part of the Coast of Newfoundland hereabove described, and of the Coast of Labrador; but so soon as the same, or any Portion thereof, shall be settled, it shall not be lawful for the said Fisherman to dry or cure Fish at such Portion so settled, without previous Agreement for such purpose with the Inhabitants, Proprietors, or Possessors of the Ground. And the United States hereby renounce for ever, any Liberty heretofore enjoyed or claimed by the Inhabitants thereof, to take, dry, or cure Fish on, or within three marine Miles of any of the Coasts, Bays, Creeks, or Harbours of His Britannic Majesty's Dominions in America not included within the above mentioned Limits; provided however, that the American Fishermen shall be admitted to enter such Bays or Harbours for the purpose of Shelter and of repairing Damages therein, of purchasing Wood, and of obtaining Water, and for no other purpose whatever. But they shall be under such Restrictions as may be necessary to prevent their taking, drying or curing Fish therein, or in any other manner whatever abusing the Privileges hereby reserved to them.

ARTICLE II.

It is agreed that a Line drawn from the most North Western Point of the Lake of the Woods, along the Forty Ninth Parallel of North Latitude, or, if the said Point shall not be in the Forty Ninth Parallel of North Latitude, then that a Line drawn from the said Point due North or South as the Case may be, until the said Line shall intersect the said Parallel of North Latitude, and from the Point of such Intersection due West along and with the said Parallel shall be the Line of Demarcation between the Territories of the United States, and those of His Britannic Majesty, and that the said Line shall form the Northern Boundary of the said Territories of the United States, and the Southern Boundary of the Territories of His Britannic Majesty, from the Lake of the Woods to the Stony Mountains.

ARTICLE III.

It is agreed, that any Country that may be claimed by either Party on the North West Coast of America, Westward of the Stony Mountains, shall, together with it's Harbours, Bays, and Creeks, and the Navigations of all Rivers within the same, be free and open, for the term of ten Years from the date of the Signature of the present Convention, to the Vessels, Citizens, and Subjects of the Two Powers: it being well understood, that this Agreement is not to be construed to the Prejudice of any Claim, which either of the Two High Contracting Parties may have to any part of the said Country, nor shall it be taken to affect the Claims of any other Power or State to any part of the said Country; the only Object of The High Contracting Parties, in that respect, being to prevent disputes and differences amongst Themselves.

ARTICLE IV.

All the Provisions of the Convention "to regulate the Commerce between the Territories of the United States and of His Britannic Majesty" concluded at London on the third day of July in the Year of Our Lord One Thousand Eight Hundred and Fifteen, with the exception of the Clause which limited it's duration to Four Years, & excepting also so far as the same was affected by the Declaration of His Majesty respecting the Island of St Helena, are hereby extended and continued in force for the term of ten Years from the date of the Signature of the present Convention, in the same manner, as if all the Provisions of the said Convention were herein specially recited.

ARTICLE V.

Whereas it was agreed by the first Article of the Treaty of Ghent, that "All Territory, Places, and Possessions whatsoever taken by either Party from the other during the War, or which may be taken after the signing of this Treaty, excepting only the Islands hereinafter mentioned, shall be restored without delay; and without causing any destruction, or carrying away any of the Artillery or other public Property originally captured in the said Forts or Places which shall remain therein upon the Exchange of the Ratifications of this Treaty, or any Slaves or other private Property"; and whereas under the aforesaid Article, the United States claim for their Citizens, and as their private Property, the Restitution of, or full Compensation for all Slaves who, at the date of the Exchange of the Ratifications of the said Treaty, were in any Territory, Places, or Possessions whatsoever directed by the said Treaty to be restored to the United States, but then still occupied by the British Forces, whether such Slaves were, at the date aforesaid, on Shore, or on board any British Vessel lying in Waters within the Territory or Jurisdiction of the United States; and whereas differences have arisen, whether, by the true intent and meaning of the aforesaid Article of the Treaty of Ghent the United States are entitled to the Restitution of, or full Compensation for all or any Slaves as above described, the High Contracting Parties hereby agree to refer the said differences to some Friendly Sovereign or State to be named for that purpose; and The High Contracting Parties further engage to consider the decision of such Friendly Sovereign or State, to be final and conclusive on all the Matters referred.

ARTICLE VI.

This Convention, when the same shall have been duly ratified by The President of the United States, by and with the Advice and Consent of their Senate, and by His Britannic Majesty, and the respective Ratifications mutually exchanged, shall be binding and obligatory on the said United States and on His Majesty; and the Ratifications shall be exchanged in Six Months from this date, or sooner, if possible.

In witness whereof the respective Plenipotentiaries have signed the same, and have thereunto affixed the Seal of their Arms.

Done at London this Twentieth day of October, in the Year of Our Lord One Thousand Eight Hundred and Eighteen.

Albert Gallatin	(Seal)
Richard Rush.	(Seal)
Frederick John Robinson	(Seal)
Henry Goulburn	(Seal)

TREATY BETWEEN THE UNITED STATES OF AMERICA AND SPAIN

FEBRUARY 22, 1819

Treaty of Amity, Settlement and Limits Between the United States of America, and His Catholic Majesty.

The United-States of America and His Catholic Majesty desiring to consolidate on a permanent basis the friendship and good correspondence which happily prevails between the two Parties, have determined to settle and terminate all their differences and pretensions by a Treaty, which shall designate with precision the limits of their respective bordering territories in North-America.

With this intention the President of the United-States has furnished with their full Powers John Quincy Adams, Secretary of State of the said United-States; and His Catholic Majesty has appointed the Most Excellent Lord Don Luis de Onis, Gonzalez, Lopez y Vara, Lord of the Town of Rayaces, Perpetual

Regidor of the Corporation of the City of Salamanca, Knight Grand-Cross of the Royal American Order of Isabella, the Catholic, decorated with the Lys of La Vendée, Knight-Pensioner of the Royal and distinguished Spanish Order of Charles the Third, Member of the Supreme Assembly of the said Royal Order; of the Counsel of His Catholic Majesty; his Secretary with Exercise of Decrees, and his Envoy Extraordinary and Minister Plenipotentiary near the United-States of America.

And the said Plenipotentiaries, after having exchanged their Powers, have agreed upon and concluded the following Articles.

ARTICLE. 1.

There shall be a firm and inviolable peace and sincere friendship between the United-States and their Citizens, and His Catholic Majesty, his Successors and Subjects, without exception of persons or places.

ART. 2.

His Catholic Majesty cedes to the United-States, in full property and sovereignty, all the territories which belong to him, situated to the Eastward of the Mississippi, known by the name of East and West Florida. The adjacent Islands dependent on said Provinces, all public lots and Squares, vacant Lands, public Edifices, Fortifications, Barracks and other Buildings, which are not private property, Archives and Documents, which relate directly to the property and sovereignty of said Provinces, are included in this Article. The said Archives and Documents shall be left in possession of the Commissaries, or Officers of the United-States, duly authorized to receive them.

ART. 3.

The Boundary Line between the two Countries, West of the Mississippi, shall begin on the Gulph of Mexico, at the mouth of the River Sabine in the Sea, continuing North, along the Western Bank of that River, to the 32$^{\underline{d}}$ degree of Latitude; thence by a Line due North to the degree of Latitude, where it strikes the Rio Roxo of Nachitoches, or Red-River, then following the course of the Rio-Roxo Westward to the degree of Longitude, 100 West from London and 23 from Washington, then crossing the said Red-River, and running thence by a Line due North to the River Arkansas, thence, following the Course of the Southern bank of the Arkansas to its source in Latitude, 42. North, and thence by that parallel of Latitude to the South-Sea*. The whole being as laid down in Melish's Map of the United-States, published at Philadelphia, improved to the first of January 1818. But if the Source of the Arkansas River shall be found to fall North or South of Latitude 42, then the Line shall run from the said Source due South or North, as the case may be, till it meets the said

*Pacific Ocean

Parallel of Latitude 42, and thence along the said Parallel to the South Sea: all the Islands in the Sabine and the said Red and Arkansas Rivers, throughout the Course thus described, to belong to the United-States; but the use of the Waters and the navigation of the Sabine to the Sea, and of the said Rivers, Roxo and Arkansas, throughout the extent of the said Boundary, on their respective Banks, shall be common to the respective inhabitants of both Nations. The Two High Contracting Parties agree to cede and renounce all their rights, claims and pretensions to the Territories described by the said Line: that is to say. — The United States hereby cede to His Catholic Majesty, and renounce forever, all their rights, claims, and pretensions to the Territories lying West and South of the above described Line; and, in like manner, His Catholic Majesty cedes to the said United-States, all his rights, claims, and pretensions to any Territories, East and North of the said Line, and, for himself, his heirs and successors, renounces all claim to the said Territories forever.

ART. 4.

To fix this Line with more precision, and to place the Land marks which shall designate exactly the limits of both Nations, each of the Contracting Parties shall appoint a Commissioner, and a Surveyor, who shall meet before the termination of one year from the date of the Ratification of this Treaty, at Nachitoches, on the Red River, and proceed to run and mark the said Line from the mouth of the Sabine to the Red River, and from the Red River to the River Arkansas, and to ascertain the Latitude of the source of the said river Arkansas, in conformity to what is above agreed upon and stipulated, and the Line of Latitude 42. to the South Sea: they shall make out plans and keep Journals of their proceedings, and the result agreed upon by them shall be considered as part of this Treaty, and shall have the same force as if it were inserted therein. The two Governments will amicably agree respecting the necessary Articles to be furnished to those persons, and also as to their respective escorts, should such be deemed necessary.

ART. 5.

The Inhabitants of the ceded Territories shall be secured in the free exercise of their Religion, without any restriction, and all those who may desire to remove to the Spanish Dominions shall be permitted to sell, or export their Effects at any time whatever, without being subject, in either case, to duties.

ART. 6.

The Inhabitants of the Territories which His Catholic Majesty cedes to the United-States by this Treaty, shall be incorporated in the Union of the United-States, as soon as may be consistent with the principles of the Federal Constitution, and admitted to the enjoyment of all the privileges, rights and immunities of the Citizens of the United-States.

ART. 7.

The Officers and Troops of His Catholic Majesty in the Territories hereby ceded by him to the United-States shall be withdrawn, and possession of the places occupied by them shall be given within six months after the exchange of the Ratifications of this Treaty, or sooner if possible, by the Officers of His Catholic Majesty, to the Commissioners or Officers of the United-States, duly appointed to receive them; and the United-States shall furnish the transports and escort necessary to convey the Spanish Officers and Troops and their baggage to the Havana.

ART. 8.

All the grants of land made before the 24th of January 1818. by His Catholic Majesty or by his lawful authorities in the said Territories ceded by His Majesty to the United-States, shall be ratified and confirmed to the persons in possession of the lands, to the same extent that the same grants would be valid if the Territories had remained under the Dominion of His Catholic Majesty. But the owners in possession of such lands, who by reason of the recent circumstances of the Spanish Nation and the Revolutions in Europe, have been prevented from fulfilling all the conditions of their grants, shall complete them within the terms limited in the same respectively, from the date of this Treaty; in default of which the said grants shall be null and void. All grants made since the said 24th of January 1818. when the first proposal on the part of His Catholic Majesty, for the cession of the Floridas was made, are hereby declared and agreed to be null and void.

ART. 9.

The two High Contracting Parties animated with the most earnest desire of conciliation and with the object of putting an end to all the differences which have existed between them, and of confirming the good understanding which they wish to be forever maintained between them, reciprocally renounce all claims for damages or injuries which they, themselves, as well as their respective citizens and subjects may have suffered, until the time of signing this Treaty.

The renunciation of the United-States will extend to all the injuries mentioned in the Convention of the 11th of August 1802.

2. To all claims on account of Prizes made by French Privateers, and condemned by French Consuls, within the Territory and Jurisdiction of Spain.

3. To all claims of indemnities on account of the suspension of the right of Deposit at New-Orleans in 1802.

4. To all claims of Citizens of the United-States upon the Government of Spain, arising from the unlawful seizures at Sea, and in the ports and territories of Spain or the Spanish Colonies.

5. To all claims of Citizens of the United-States upon the Spanish

Government, statements of which, soliciting the interposition of the Government of the United-States have been presented to the Department of State, or to the Minister of the United-States in Spain, since the date of the Convention of 1802, and until the signature of this Treaty.

The renunciation of His Catholic Majesty extends,

1. To all the injuries mentioned in the Convention of the 11th of August 1802.

2. To the sums which His Catholic Majesty advanced for the return of Captain Pike from the Provincias Internas.

3. To all injuries caused by the expedition of Miranda that was fitted out and equipped at New-York.

4. To all claims of Spanish subjects upon the Government of the United-States arising from unlawful seizures at Sea or within the ports and territorial Jurisdiction of the United-States.

Finally, to all the claims of subjects of His Catholic Majesty upon the Government of the United-States, in which the interposition of His Catholic Majesty's Government has been solicited before the date of this Treaty, and since the date of the Convention of 1802, or which may have been made to the Department of Foreign Affairs of His Majesty, or to His Minister in the United-States.

And the High Contracting Parties respectively renounce all claim to indemnities for any of the recent events or transactions of their respective Commanders and Officers in the Floridas.

The United-States will cause satisfaction to be made for the injuries, if any, which by process of Law, shall be established to have been suffered by the Spanish Officers, and individual Spanish inhabitants, by the late operations of the American Army in Florida.

ART. 10.

The Convention entered into between the two Governments on the 11th of August 1802, the Ratification of which were exchanged the 21st December 1818, is annulled.

ART. 11.

The United-States, exonerating Spain from all demands in future, on account of the claims of their Citizens, to which the renunciations herein contained extend, and considering them entirely cancelled, undertake to make satisfaction for the same, to an amount not exceeding Five Millions of Dollars. To ascertain the full amount and validity of those claims, a Commission, to consist of three Commissioners, Citizens of the United-States, shall be appointed by the President, by and with the advice and consent of the Senate; which Commission shall meet at the City of Washington, and within the space of three years, from the time of their first meeting, shall receive, examine and decide upon the amount and validity of all the claims included within the descriptions above mentioned. The said Commissioners shall take an oath or affirmation, to be entered on the record of their proceedings, for the faithful and diligent discharge of their duties; and in case of the death, sickness, or necessary absence of any such Commissioner, his place may be supplied by the appointment, as aforesaid, or by the President of the United-States during the recess of the Senate, of another Commissioner in his stead. The said Commissioners shall be authorized to hear and examine on oath every question relative to the said claims, and to receive all suitable authentic testimony concerning the same. And the Spanish Government shall furnish all such documents and elucidations as may be in their possession, for the adjustment of the said claims, according to the principles of Justice, the Laws of Nations, and the stipulations of the Treaty between the two Parties of 27th October 1795; the said Documents to be specified, when demanded at the instance of the said Commissioners.

The payment of such claims as may be admitted and adjusted by the said Commissioners, or the major part of them, to an amount not exceeding Five Millions of Dollars, shall be made by the United-States, either immediately at their Treasury or by the creation of Stock bearing an interest of Six per Cent per annum, payable from the proceeds of sales of public lands within the Territories hereby ceded to the United-States, or in such other manner as the Congress of the United-States may prescribe by Law.

The records of the proceedings of the said Commissioners, together with the vouchers and documents produced before them, relative to the claims to be adjusted and decided upon by them, shall, after the close of their transactions, be deposited in the Department of State of the United-States; and copies of them or any part of them, shall be furnished to the Spanish Government, if required, at the demand of the Spanish Minister in the United-States.

ART. 12.

The Treaty of Limits and Navigation of 1795. remains confirmed in all and each one of its Articles, excepting the 2, 3, 4, 21 and the second clause of the 22^{d} Article, which, having been altered by this Treaty, or having received their entire execution, are no longer valid.

With respect to the 15th Article of the same Treaty of Friendship, Limits and Navigation of 1795, in which it is stipulated, that the Flag shall cover the property, the Two High Contracting Parties agree that this shall be so understood with respect to those Powers who recognize this principle; but if either of the two Contracting Parties shall be at War with a Third Party, and the other Neutral, the Flag of the Neutral shall cover the property of Enemies, whose Government acknowledge this principle, and not of others.

ART. 13.

Both Contracting Parties wishing to favour their mutual Commerce, by affording in their ports every necessary Assistance to their respective Merchant

Vessels, have agreed, that the Sailors who shall desert from their Vessels in the ports of the other, shall be arrested and delivered up, at the instance of the Consul-who shall prove nevertheless, that the Deserters belonged to the Vessels that claimed them, exhibiting the document that is customary in their Nation: that is to say, the American Consul in a Spanish Port, shall exhibit the Document known by the name of *Articles*, and the Spanish Consul in American Ports, the Roll of the Vessel; and if the name of the Deserter or Deserters, who are claimed, shall appear in the one or the other, they shall be arrested, held in custody and delivered to the Vessel to which they shall belong.

ART. 14.

The United-States hereby certify, that they have not received any compensations from France for the injuries they suffered from her Privateers, Consuls, and Tribunals, on the Coasts and in the Ports of Spain, for the satisfaction of which provision is made by this Treaty; and they will present an authentic statement of the prizes made, and of their true value, that Spain may avail herself of the same in such manner as she may deem just and proper.

ART. 15.

The United-States to give to His Catholic Majesty, a proof of their desire to cement the relations of Amity subsisting between the two Nations, and to favour the Commerce of the Subjects of His Catholic Majesty, agree that Spanish Vessels coming laden only with productions of Spanish growth, or manufactures directly from the Ports of Spain or of her Colonies, shall be admitted for the term of twelve years to the Ports of Pensacola and S͟t Augustine in the Floridas, without paying other or higher duties on their cargoes or of tonnage than will be paid by the vessels of the United-States. During the said term no other Nation shall enjoy the same privileges within the ceded Territories. The twelve years shall commence three months after the exchange of the Ratifications of this Treaty.

ART. 16.

The present Treaty shall be ratified in due form by the Contracting Parties, and the Ratifications shall be exchanged in Six Months from this time or sooner if possible.

In Witness whereof, We the Underwritten Plenipotentiaries of the United-States of America and of His Catholic Majesty, have signed, by virtue of Our Powers, the present Treaty of Amity, Settlement and Limits, and have thereunto affixed our Seals respectively.

Done at Washington, this Twenty-Second day of February, One Thousand Eight Hundred and Nineteen.

(Seal)   John Quincy Adams
(Seal)   Luis de Onis

AN ACT ESTABLISHING A
SEPARATE TERRITORIAL GOVERNMENT IN THE
SOUTHERN PART OF THE TERRITORY OF MISSOURI
MARCH 2, 1819

Be it enacted by the Senate and House of Representatives of the United States of America, in Congress assembled, That from and after the fourth day of July next, all that part of the territory of Missouri which lies south of a line, beginning on the Mississippi river, at thirty-six degrees, north latitude, running thence west to the river St. Francois; thence, up the same, to thirty-six degrees thirty minutes north latitude; and thence, west, to the western territorial boundary line; shall, for the purposes of a territorial government, constitute a separate territory, and be called the Arkansaw territory.

SEC. 2. *And be it further enacted,* That there shall be established in the said territory of Arkansaw, a temporary government, to consist of three departments, the executive, the legislative, and the judiciary.

SEC. 3. *And be it further enacted,* That the executive power shall be vested in a governor, who shall reside in the said territory, and shall hold his office during three years, unless sooner removed by the President of the United States: he shall be commander in chief of the militia of said territory, shall have power to appoint and commission all officers required by law to be appointed for said territory, whose appointments are not otherwise provided for by this act; shall take care that the laws be faithfully executed; shall have power to grant pardons for offences against the said territory, and reprieves for those against the United States, until the decision of the President thereon shall have been made known; shall, on extraordinary occasions, have power to convene the general assembly, hereinafter provided for, after one shall have been organized in conformity to law; shall ex-officio, be superintendent of Indian affairs, and shall have such other powers, and perform such further duties, as are by law given to, and imposed on, the governor of the Missouri territory, in all cases in which they shall become legally applicable to the territory of Arkansaw.

SEC. 4. *And be it further enacted,* That there shall be a secretary for the said territory, who shall reside therein, and continue in office for the term of four years, unless sooner removed by the President: he shall perform all the duties imposed on the secretary for the territory of Missouri, by an act of Congress of the fourth of June, eighteen hundred and twelve, entitled "An act providing for the government of Missouri."

SEC. 5. *And be it further enacted,* That the legislative power shall, until the organization of the general assembly, hereinafter provided for, be vested in the governor and the judges of the superior court of the territory, who shall have power to pass any law for the administration of justice in said territory, which shall not be repugnant to this act, or inconsistent with the constitution of the United States: *Provided,* that whenever the general assembly shall be organized, all the legislative power of the territory shall be vested in, and exercised by, the said general assembly.

SEC. 6. *And be it further enacted,* That so much of the act of Congress of the fourth of June, eighteen hundred and twelve, entitled "An act providing for the government of the territory of Missouri," as relates to the organization of a general assembly therein, prescribes the powers and privileges thereof, the mode of election, and period of service, of the members thereof, and defines the qualifications and privileges of the electors and elected, shall be in full force and operation in the Arkansaw territory, to the extent of its application, so soon as the governor thereof shall be satisfied that such is the desire of a majority of the freeholders thereof, and not until then: *Provided,* That until there shall be five thousand free white males, of the age of twenty-one years and upwards, resident in the said territory, the whole number of representatives shall not exceed nine.

SEC. 7. *And be it further enacted,* That the judicial power of the territory shall be vested in a superior court, and in such inferior courts as the legislative department of the territory shall, from time to time, institute and establish, and in justices of the peace. The superior court shall be composed of three judges, who shall reside in the territory and continue in office for the term of four years, unless sooner removed by the President. The superior court shall have jurisdiction in all criminal and penal cases, and exclusive cognisance of all capital cases, and shall have and exercise original jurisdiction, concurrently with the inferior courts, and exclusive appellate jurisdiction in all civil cases in which the amount in controversy shall be one hundred dollars or upwards. The superior court shall be holden at such times and place, or places, as the legislative department shall direct, and continue in session until the business therein shall be disposed of, or as long as shall be prescribed by law. *Provided,* That any two of the judges shall constitute a court of appellate, and any one a court of original jurisdiction.

SEC. 8. *And be it further enacted,* That the governor, secretary, judges and all other officers, of the territory, civil and military, shall, before they enter on the duties of their respective offices, take an oath or affirmation to support the constitution of the United States, and to discharge, with fidelity, the duties of their offices; the governor before a judge of the supreme or district court of the United States, or a judge of the superior court of the said territory; the secretary and judges, before the said governor, or a judge of the supreme or district court of the United States; and all other officers, before the governor, or any of the judges of the supreme or inferior courts, or justices of the peace, of said territory.

SEC. 9. *And be it further enacted,* That the governor, secretary, and judges of the superior court authorized for said territory, during the temporary government thereof, shall be appointed by the President of the United States, with the advice and consent of the Senate: *Provided,* That the President shall have full power, during the recess of the Senate, to commission all or any of the said officers, until the end of the session of Congress next succeeding the date of the commission. The governor, secretary, and judges of the superior court, shall receive the same compensation, payable quarter yearly, which the governor, secretary, and superior judges, of the Missouri territory are entitled to by law.

SEC. 10. *And be it further enacted,* That all the laws which shall be in force in the territory of Missouri, on the fourth day of July next, not inconsistent with the provisions of this act, and which shall be applicable to the territory of Arkansaw, shall be, and continue, in force in the latter territory, until modified or repealed by the legislative authority thereof.

SEC. 11. *And be it further enacted*, That the bounty lands granted, or hereafter to be granted, for military services during the late war, shall, while they continue to be held by the patentees or their heirs, remain exempt from all taxes, for the term of three years from and after the date of the patents respectively.

SEC. 12. *And be it further enacted*, That whenever, according to the provisions of this act, the people of the Arkansaw territory shall have a right to elect members of the house of representatives of their general assembly, they shall also have the right to elect a delegate from the said territory to the Congress of the United States, who shall possess the same powers, enjoy the same privileges, and receive the same compensation, granted and secured by law to the delegates from other territories.

SEC. 13. *And be it further enacted*, That until otherwise directed by the legislative department of the said territory of Arkansaw, the seat of the territorial government thereof shall be the post of Arkansaw, on the Arkansaw river.

SEC. 14. *And be it further enacted*, That the line now established by law, between the land offices at the seat of justice in the county of Lawrence, and at the town of Jackson, in the county of Cape Gireadeau, shall, from and after the passage of this act, be so altered as to run, be the same and correspond with the northern line of the said territory of Arkansaw, any thing in the act, entitled "An act making provisions for the establishment of additional land offices in the territory of Missouri," passed the seventeenth day of February, one thousand eight hundred and eighteen, to the contrary notwithstanding.

Approved, March 2, 1819.

AN ACT TO ENABLE THE PEOPLE OF THE ALABAMA TERRITORY TO FORM A CONSTITUTION AND STATE GOVERNMENT, AND FOR THE ADMISSION OF SUCH STATE INTO THE UNION ON AN EQUAL FOOTING WITH THE ORIGINAL STATES MARCH 2, 1819

Be it enacted by the Senate and House of Representatives of the United States of America, in Congress assembled, That the inhabitants of the territory of Alabama be, and they are hereby, authorized to form for themselves a constitution and state government, and to assume such name as they may deem proper; and that the said territory, when formed into a state, shall be admitted into the union, upon the same footing with the original states, in all respects whatever.

SEC. 2. *And be it further enacted,* That the said state shall consist of all the territory included within the following boundaries, to wit: Beginning at the point where the thirty-first degree of north latitude intersects the Perdido river; thence, east, to the western boundary line of the state of Georgia; thence along said line, to the southern boundary line of the state of Tennessee; thence, west, along said boundary line, to the Tennessee river; thence, up the same, to the mouth of Bear creek; thence, by a direct line, to the north-west corner of Washington county; thence, due south, to the Gulf of Mexico; thence, eastwardly, including all island within six leagues of the shore, to the Perdido river; and thence, up the same to the beginning.

SEC. 3. *And be it further enacted,* That it shall be the duty of the surveyor of the lands of the United States south of the state of Tennessee, and surveyor of the public lands in the Alabama territory, to run and cut out the line of demarcation, between the state of Mississippi and the state to be formed of the Alabama territory; and if it should appear to said surveyors, that so much of said line designated in the preceding section, running due south, from the north-west corner of Washington county to the Gulf of Mexico, will encroach on the counties of Wayne, Green, or Jackson, in said state of Mississippi, then the same shall be so altered as to run in a direct line from the north-west corner of Washington county to a point on the Gulf of Mexico, ten miles east of the mouth of the river Pascagola.

SEC. 4. *And be it further enacted,* That all white male citizens of the United States, who shall have arrived at the age of twenty-one years, and have resided in said territory three months previous to the day of election, and all persons having, in other respects, the legal qualifications to vote for representatives in the General Assembly of the said territory, be, and they are hereby, authorized to choose representatives to form a constitution, who shall be appointed among the several counties as follows:

From the county of Madison, eight representatives.
From the county of Monroe, four representatives.
From the county of Blount, three representatives.
From the county of Limestone, three representatives.
From the county of Shelby, two representatives.
From the county of Montgomery, two representatives.
From the county of Washington, two representatives.
From the county of Tuskaloosa, two representatives.
From the county of Lawrence, two representatives.
From the county of Franklin, two representatives.
From the county of Cotaco, two representatives.
From the county of Clark, two representatives.
From the county of Baldwin, one representative.
From the county of Cawhauba, one representative.
From the county of Conecah, one representative.

From the county of Dallas, one representative.
From the county of Marengo, one representative.
From the county of Marion, one representative.
From the county of Mobile, one representative.
From the county of Lauderdale, one representative.
From the county of St. Clair, one representative.
From the county of Autauga, one representative.

And the election for the representatives aforesaid, shall be holden on the first Monday and Tuesday in May next, throughout the several counties in the said territory, and shall be conducted in the same manner, and under the same regulations, as prescribed by the laws of the said territory, regulating elections therein for the members of the House of Representatives.

SEC. 5. *And be it further enacted*, That the members of the convention, thus duly elected, be, and they are hereby, authorized to meet at the town of Huntsville, on the first Monday in July next; which convention, when met, shall first determine, by a majority of the whole number elected, whether it be, or be not, expedient at that time, to form a constitution and state government for the people within the said territory; And if it be determined to be expedient, the convention shall be, and hereby are, authorized to form a constitution and state government: *Provided*, That the same when formed, shall be republican, and not repugnant to the principles of the ordinance of the thirteenth of July, one thousand seven hundred and eighty-seven, between the people and states of the territory north-west of the river Ohio, so far as the same has been extended to the said territory, by the articles of agreement between the United States and the state of Georgia, or of the constitution of the United States.

SEC. 6. *And be it further enacted*, That the following propositions be, and the same are hereby, offered to the convention of the said territory of Alabama, when formed, for their free acceptance or rejection, which, if accepted by the convention, shall be obligatory upon the United States.

First. That the section numbered sixteen in every township, and when such section has been sold, granted, or disposed of, other lands equivalent thereto, and most contiguous to the same, shall be granted to the inhabitants of such townships for the use of schools.

Second. That all salt springs within the said territory, and the lands reserved for the use of the same, together with such other lands as may, by the President of the United States, be deemed necessary and proper for working the said salt springs, not exceeding in the whole the quantity contained in thirty-six entire sections, shall be granted to the said state, for the use of the people of the said state, the same to be used, under such terms, conditions, and regulations, as the legislature of the said state shall direct: *Provided*, The said legislature shall never sell, nor lease the same for a longer term than ten years at any one time.

Third. That five per cent. of the net proceeds of the lands lying within the said territory, and which shall be sold by Congress, from and after the first day of September, in the year one thousand eight hundred and nineteen, after deducting all expenses incident to the same, shall be reserved for making public roads, canals, and improving the navigation of rivers, of which three-fifths shall be applied to those objects within the said state, under the direction of the legislature thereof, and two-fifths to the making of a road or roads leading to the said state, under the direction of Congress.

Fourth. That thirty-six sections, or one entire township, to be designated by the Secretary of the Treasury, under the direction of the President of the United States, together with the one heretofore reserved for that purpose, shall be reserved for the use of a seminary of learning, and vested in the legislature of the said state, to be appropriated solely to the use of such seminary by the said legislature. And the Secretary of the Treasury, under the direction as aforesaid, may reserve the seventy-two sections or two townships, hereby set apart for the support of a seminary of learning, in small tracts: *Provided*, That no tract shall consist of less than two sections: *And provided always*, That the said convention shall provide, by an ordinance irrevocable without the consent of the United States, that the people inhabiting the said territory, do agree and declare that they forever disclaim all right and title to the waste or unappropriated lands lying within the said territory; and that the same shall be and remain at the sole and entire disposition of the United States; and moreover, that each and every tract of land sold by the United States, after the first day of September, in the year one thousand eight hundred and nineteen, shall be and remain exempt from any tax laid by the order, or under the authority of the state, whether for state, county, township, parish, or any other purpose whatever, for the term of five years, from and after the respective days of the sales thereof; and that the lands belonging to citizens of the United States, residing without the said state, shall never be taxed higher than the lands belonging to persons residing therein; and that no tax shall be imposed on lands, the property of the United States; and that all navigable waters within the said state shall for ever remain public highways, free to the citizens of said state and of the United States, without any tax, duty, impost, or toll, therefor, imposed by the said state.

SEC. 7. *And be it further enacted*, That, in lieu of a section of land, provided to be reserved for the seat of government of the said territory, by an act, entitled "An act respecting the surveying and sale of the public lands in the Alabama territory," there be granted to the said state, for the seat of the government thereof, a tract of land containing sixteen hundred and twenty acres, and consisting of sundry fractions and a quarter section, in sections thirty-one and thirty-two, in township sixteen, and range ten, and in sections five and six, in township fifteen, and range ten, and in sections twenty-nine and thirty, in the same township and range, lying on both sides of the Alabama and Cahawba rivers, and including the mouth of the river Cahawba, and which heretofore has been reserved from public sale, by order of the President of the United States.

SEC. 8. *And be it further enacted*, That, until the next general census shall be taken, the said state shall be entitled to one representative in the House of Representatives of the United States.

SEC. 9. *And be it further enacted*, That, in case the said convention shall form a constitution and state government for the people of the territory of Alabama, and said convention, as soon thereafter as may be, shall cause a true and attested copy of such constitution or frame of government as shall be formed or provided, to be transmitted to Congress, for its approbation.

Approved, March 2, 1819.

AN ACT FOR THE ADMISSION OF THE STATE OF MAINE INTO THE UNION

MARCH 3, 1820

WHEREAS, by an act of the state of Massachusetts, passed on the nineteenth day of June, in the year one thousand eight hundred and nineteen, entitled "An act relating to the separation of the district of Maine from Massachusetts proper, and forming the same into a separate and independent state," the people of that part of Massachusetts heretofore known as the district of Maine, did, with the consent of the legislature of said state of Massachusetts, form themselves into an independent state, and did establish a constitution for the government of the same, agreeably to the provisions of said act — Therefore,

Be it enacted by the Senate and House of Representatives of the United States of America, in Congress assembled, That from and after the fifteenth day of March, in the year one thousand eight hundred and twenty, the state of Maine is hereby declared to be one of the United States of America, and admitted into the Union on an equal footing with the original states, in all respects whatever.

Approved, March 3, 1820.

AN ACT TO AUTHORIZE THE PEOPLE OF THE MISSOURI TERRITORY TO FORM A CONSTITUTION AND STATE GOVERNMENT, AND FOR THE ADMISSION OF SUCH STATE INTO THE UNION ON AN EQUAL FOOTING WITH THE ORIGINAL STATES, AND TO PROHIBIT SLAVERY IN CERTAIN TERRITORIES

MARCH 6, 1820

Be it enacted by the Senate and House of Representatives of the United States of America, in Congress assembled, That the inhabitants of that portion of the Missouri territory included within the boundaries hereinafter designated, be, and they are hereby, authorized to form for themselves a constitution and state government, and to assume such name as they shall deem proper; and the said state, when formed, shall be admitted into the Union, upon an equal footing with the original states, in all respects whatsoever.

SEC. 2. *And be it further enacted,* That the said state shall consist of all the territory included within the following boundaries, to wit: Beginning in the middle of the Mississippi river, on the parallel of thirty-six degrees of north latitude; thence west, along that parallel of latitude, to the St. Francois river; thence up, and following the course of that river, in the middle of the main channel thereof, to the parallel of latitude of thirty-six degrees and thirty minutes; thence west, along the same, to a point where the said parallel is intersected by a meridian line passing through the middle of the mouth of the Kansas river, where the same empties into the Missouri river, thence, from the point aforesaid north, along the said meridian line, to the intersection of the parallel of latitude which passes throught the rapids of the river Des Moines, making the said line to correspond with the Indian boundary line; thence east, from the point of intersection last aforesaid, along the said parallel of latitude, to the middle of the channel of the main fork of the said river Des Moines; thence down and along the middle of the main channel of the said river Des Moines, to the mouth of the same, where it empties into the Mississippi river; thence, due east, to the middle of the main channel of the Mississippi river; thence down, and following the course of the Mississippi river, in the middle of the main channel thereof, to the place of beginning: *Provided*, The said state shall ratify the boundaries aforesaid; *And provided also*, That the said state shall have concurrent jurisdiction on the river Mississippi, and every other river bordering on the said state, so far as the said rivers shall form a common boundary to the said state; and any other state or states, now or hereafter to be formed and bounded by the same, such rivers to be common to both; and that the river Mississippi, and the navigable rivers and waters leading into the same, shall be common highways, and for ever free, as well to the inhabitants of the said state as to other citizens of the United States, without any tax, duty, impost, or toll, therefor, imposed by the said state.

SEC. 3. *And be it further enacted*, That all free white male citizens of the United States, who shall have arrived at the age of twenty-one years, and have resided in said territory three months previous to the day of election, and all other persons qualified to vote for representatives to the general assembly of the said territory, shall be qualified to be elected, and they are hereby qualified and authorized to vote, and choose representatives to form a convention, who shall be appropriated amongst the several counties as follows:

From the county of Howard, five representatives. From the county of Cooper, three representatives. From the county of Montgomery, two representatives. From the county of Pike, one representative. From the county of Lincoln, one representative. From the county of St. Charles, three representatives. From the county of Franklin, one representative. From the county of St. Louis, eight representatives. From the county of Jefferson, one representative. From the county of Washington, three representatives. From the county of St. Genevieve, four representatives. From the county of Madison, one representative. From the county of Cape Girardeau, five representatives. From the county of New Madrid, two representatives. From the county of Wayne, and that portion of the county of Lawrence which falls within the boundaries herein designated, one representative.

And the election for the representatives aforesaid shall be holden on the first Monday, and two succeeding days of May next, throughout the several counties aforesaid in the said territory, and shall be, in every respect, held and conducted in the same manner, and under the same regulations as is prescribed by the laws of the said territory regulating elections therein for members of the general assembly, except that the returns of the election in that portion of Lawrence county included in the boundaries aforesaid, shall be made to the county of Wayne, as is provided in other cases under the laws of said territory.

SEC. 4. *And be it further enacted,* That the members of the convention thus duly elected, shall be, and they are hereby authorized to meet at the seat of government of said territory on the second Monday of the month of June next; and the said convention, when so assembled, shall have power and authority to adjourn to any other place in the said territory, which to them shall seem best for the convenient transaction of their business; and which convention, when so met, shall first determine by a majority of the whole number elected, whether it be, or be not, expedient at that time to form a constitution and state government for the people within the said territory, as included within the boundaries above designated; and if it be deemed expedient, the convention shall be, and hereby is, authorized to form a constitution and state government; or, if it be deemed more expedient, the said convention shall provide by ordinance for electing representatives to form a constitution or frame of government; which said representatives shall be chosen in such manner, and in such proportion as they shall designate; and shall meet at such time and place as shall be prescribed by the said ordinance; and shall then form for the people of said territory, within the boundaries aforesaid, a constitution and state government: *Provided,* That the same whenever formed, shall be republican, and not repugnant to the constitution of the United States; and that the legislature of said state shall never interfere with the primary disposal of the soil by the United States, nor with any regulations Congress may find necessary for securing the title in such soil to the *bona fide* purchasers; and that no tax shall be imposed on lands the property of the United States; and in no case shall non-resident proprietors be taxed higher than residents.

SEC. 5. *And be it further enacted,* That until the next general census shall be taken, the said state shall be entitled to one representative in the House of Representatives of the United States.

SEC. 6. *And be it further enacted,* That the following propositions be, and the same are hereby, offered to the convention of the said territory of Missouri, when formed, for their free acceptance or rejection, which, if accepted by the convention, shall be obligatory upon the United States:

First. That section numbered sixteen in every township, and when such section has been sold, or otherwise disposed of, other lands equivalent thereto, and as contiguous as may be, shall be granted to the state for the use of the inhabitants of such township, for the use of schools.

Second. That all salt springs, not exceeding twelve in number, with six sections of land adjoining to each, shall be granted to the said state for the use of said state, the same to be selected by the legislature of the said state, on or before the first day of January, in the year one thousand eight hundred and twenty-five; and the same, when so selected, to be used under such terms, conditions, and regulations, as the legislature of said state shall direct: *Provided,* That no salt spring, the right whereof now is, or hereafter shall be, confirmed or adjudged to any individual or individuals, shall, by this section, be granted to the said state: *And provided also,* That the legislature shall never sell or lease the same, at any one time, for a longer period than ten years, without the consent of Congress.

Third. That five per cent. of the net proceeds of the sale of lands lying within the said territory or state, and which shall be sold by Congress, from and after the first day of January next, after deducting all expenses incident to the same, shall be reserved for making public roads and canals, of which three fifths shall be applied to those objects within the state, under the direction of the legislature thereof; and the other two fifths in defraying, under the direction of Congress, the expenses to be incurred in making of a road or roads, canal or canals, leading to the said state.

Fourth. That four entire sections of land be, and the same are hereby, granted to the said state, for the purpose of fixing their seat of government thereon; which said sections shall, under the direction of the legislature of said state, be located, as near as may be, in one body, at any time, in such townships and ranges as the legislature aforesaid may select, on any of the public lands of the United States: *Provided,* That such locations shall be made prior to the public sale of the lands of the United States surrounding such location.

Fifth. That thirty-six sections, or one entire township, which shall be designated by the President of the United States, together with the other lands heretofore reserved for that purpose, shall be reserved for the use of a seminary of learning, and vested in the legislature of said state, to be appropriated solely to the use of such seminary by the said legislature: *Provided,* That the five foregoing propositions herein offered, are on the condition that the convention of the said state shall provide, by an ordinance, irrevocable without the consent of the United States, that every and each tract of land sold by the United States, from and after the first day of January next, shall remain exempt from any tax laid by order or under the authority of the state, whether for state, county, or township, or any other purpose whatever, for the term of five years from and after the day of sale; *And further,* That the bounty lands granted, or hereafter to be granted, for military services during the late war, shall, while they continue to be held by the patentees, or their heirs, remain exempt as aforesaid from taxation for the term of three years from and after the date of the patents respectively.

SEC. 7. *And be it further enacted,* That in case a constitution and state government shall be formed for the people of the said territory of Missouri, the said convention or representatives, as soon thereafter as may be, shall cause a true and attested copy of such constitution, or frame of state government, as shall be formed or provided, to be transmitted to Congress.

SEC. 8. *And be it further enacted,* That in all that territory ceded by France to the United States, under the name of Louisiana, which lies north of thirty-six degrees and thirty minutes north latitude, not included within the limits of the state, contemplated by this act, slavery and involuntary servitude, otherwise than in the punishment of crimes, whereof the parties shall have been duly convicted, shall be, and is hereby, forever prohibited: *Provided always,* That any person escaping into the same, from whom labour or service is lawfully claimed, in any state or territory of the United States, such fugitive may

be lawfully reclaimed and conveyed to the person claiming his or her labour or service as aforesaid.
Approved, March 6, 1820.

AN ACT FOR THE ESTABLISHMENT OF A TERRITORIAL GOVERNMENT IN FLORIDA

MARCH 30, 1822

Be it enacted by the Senate and House of Representatives of the United States of America, in Congress assembled, That all that territory ceded by Spain to the United States, known by the name of East and West Florida, shall constitute a territory of the United States, under the name of the territory of Florida, the government whereof shall be organized and administered as follows:

SEC. 2. *And be it further enacted,* That the executive power shall be vested in a governor, who shall reside in the said territory, and hold his office during the term of three years, unless sooner removed by the President of the United States. He shall be commander-in-chief of the militia of the said territory, and be ex officio superintendent of Indian affairs; and shall have power to grant pardons for offences against the said territory, and reprieves for those against the United States, until the decision of the President of the United States thereon shall be made known; and to appoint and commission all officers, civil and of the militia, whose appointments are not herein otherwise provided for, and which shall be established by law: he shall take care that the laws be faithfully executed.

SEC. 3. *And be it further enacted,* That the secretary of the territory shall also be appointed, who shall hold his office during the term of four years, unless sooner removed by the President of the United States; whose duty it shall be, under the direction of the governor, to record and preserve all the papers and proceedings of the executive, and all the acts of the governor and legislative council, and transmit authentic copies of the proceedings of the governor, in his executive department, every six months, to the President of the United States.

SEC. 4. *And be it further enacted,* That, in case of the death, removal, resignation, or necessary absence, of the governor of the said territory, the secretary thereof shall be, and he is hereby, authorized and required to execute all the powers, and perform all the duties, of the governor, during the vacancy occasioned by the removal, resignation, or necessary absence, of the said governor.

SEC. 5. *And be it further enacted,* That the legislative power shall be vested in the governor, and in thirteen of the most fit and discreet persons of the territory, to be called the legislative council, who shall be appointed annually, by the President of the United States, by and with the advice and consent of the Senate, from among the citizens of the United States residing there. The governor, by and with the advice and consent of the said legislative council, or a majority of them, shall have power to alter, modify, or repeal the laws which may be in force at the commencement of this act. Their legislative powers shall also extend to all the rightful subjects of legislation; but no law shall be valid which is inconsistent with the constitution and laws of the United States, or which shall lay any person under restraint, burthen, or disability, on account of his religious opinions, professions, or worship; in all which he shall be free to maintain his own, and not burthened with those of another. The governor shall publish, throughout the said territory, all the laws which shall be made, and shall, on or before the first day of December in each year, report the same to the President of the United States, to be laid before Congress, which, if disapproved by Congress, shall thenceforth be of no force. The governor and legislative council shall have no power over the primary disposal of the soil, nor to tax the lands of the United States, nor to interfere with the claims to lands within said territory: the legislative council shall hold a session once in each year, commencing its first session on the second Monday of June next, at Pensacola, and continue in session not longer than two months; and thereafter on the first Monday in May, in each and every year; but shall not continue longer in session than four weeks; to be held at such place in said territory as the governor and council shall direct. It shall be the duty of the governor to obtain all the information in his power in relation to the customs, habits, and dispositions, of the inhabitants of the said territory, and communicate the same, from time to time, to the President of the United States.

SEC. 6. *And be it further enacted,* That the judicial power shall be vested in two superior courts, and in such inferior courts and justices of the peace, as the legislative council of the territory may, from time to time, establish. There shall be a superior court for that part of the territory known as East Florida, to consist of one judge; he shall hold a court on the first Mondays in January, April, July, and October, in each year, at St. Augustine, and at such other times and places as the legislative council shall direct. There shall be a superior court for that part of the territory known as West Florida, to consist of one judge; he shall hold a court at Pensacola on the first Mondays in January, April, July, and October, in each year, and at such other times and places as the legislative council shall direct. Within its limits, herein described, each court shall have jurisdiction in all criminal cases, and exclusive jurisdiction in all capital cases, and original jurisdiction in all civil cases of the value of one hundred dollars, arising under, and cognisable by, the laws of the territory, now of force therein, or which may, at any time, be enacted by the legislative council thereof. Each judge shall appoint a clerk for his respective court, who shall reside, respectively, at St. Augustine and Pensacola, and they shall keep the records there. Each clerk shall receive for his services, in all cases arising under the territorial laws, such fees as may be established by the legislative council.

SEC. 7. *And be it further enacted,* That each of said superior courts shall, moreover, have and exercise the same jurisdiction within its limits, in all cases arising under the laws and constitution of the United States, which, by an act to establish the judicial *power* [courts] of the United States, approved the twenty-fourth day of September, one thousand seven hundred and eighty-nine, and "An act in addition to the act, entitled 'An act to establish the judicial courts of the United States,'" approved the second day of March, one thousand seven hundred and ninety-three, was vested in the court of the Kentucky district. And writs of error and appeal from the decisions in the said superior court, authorized by this section of this act, shall be made to the Supreme Court of the United States, in the same cases, and under the same regulations, as from the circuit courts of the United States. The clerks, respectively, shall keep the records at the places where the courts are held, and shall receive, in all cases arising under the laws and constitution of the United States, the same fees which the clerk of the Kentucky district received for similar services, whilst that court exercised the powers of the circuit and district courts. There shall be appointed, in the said territory, two persons learned in the law, to act as attorneys for the United States as well as for the territory; one for that part of the territory known as East Florida, the other for that part of the territory known as West Florida: to each of whom, in addition to his stated fees, shall be paid, annually, two hundred dollars, as a full compensation for all extra services. There shall also be appointed two marshals, one for each of the said superior courts, who shall each perform the same duties, be subject to the same regulations and penalties, and be entitled to the same fees, to which marshals in other districts are entitled for similar services; and shall, in addition, be paid the sum of two hundred dollars, annually, as a compensation for all extra services.

SEC. 8. *And be it further enacted,* That the governor, secretary, judges of the superior courts, district attorneys, marshals, and all general officers of the militia, shall be appointed by the President of the United States, by and with the advice and consent of the Senate. All judicial officers shall hold their offices for the term of four years, and no longer. The governor, secretary, judges, members of the legislative council, justices of the peace, and all other officers, civil and of the militia, before they enter upon the duties of their respective offices, shall take an oath or affirmation to support the constitution of the United States, and for the faithful discharge of the duties of their office; the governor, before the President of the United States, or before a judge of the Supreme or district court of the United States, or before such other person as the President of the United States shall authorize to administer the same; the secretary, judges, and members of the legislative council, before the governor, and all other officers, before such persons as the governor shall direct. The governor shall receive an annual salary of two thousand five hundred dollars; the secretary of one thousand five hundred dollars; and the judges of one thousand five hundred dollars, each; to be paid quarter yearly out of the treasury of the United States. The members of the legislative council shall receive three dollars each, per day, during their attendance in council, and three dollars for every twenty miles in going to, and returning from any meeting of the legislative council, once in each session, and no more. The members of the legislative council shall be privileged from arrest, except in cases of treason, felony, and breach of the peace, during their going to, attendance at, and returning from, each session of said council.

SEC. 9. *And be it further enacted,* That the following acts, that is to say:

"An act to provide for the punishment of certain crimes against the United States," approved April thirtieth, one thousand seven hundred and ninety, and all acts in addition or supplementary thereto, which are now in force:

"An act to provide for the punishment of [certain] crimes and offences committed within the Indian boundaries," approved March third, one thousand eight hundred and seventeen:

"An act in addition to the act for the punishment of certain crimes against the United States, and to repeal the acts therein mentioned," approved April twentieth, one thousand eight hundred and eighteen:

"An act for the punishment of [certain] crimes therein specified," approved January thirtieth, one thousand seven hundred and ninety-nine:

"An act respecting fugitives from justice and persons escaping from the service of their masters," approved twelfth February, one thousand seven hundred and ninety-three:

"An act to prohibit the carrying on the slave trade from the United States to any foreign place or country," approved March twenty-second, one thousand seven hundred and ninety-nine: [four]

"An act in addition to the act entitled 'An act to prohibit the carrying on the slave trade from the United States to any foreign place or country,'" approved May tenth, one thousand eight hundred:

"The act to prohibit the importation of slaves into any port or place within the jurisdiction of the United States, from and after the first day of January, in the year of our Lord one thousand eight hundred and eight," approved March second, one thousand eight hundred and seven:

"An act to prevent settlements being made on lands ceded to the United States until authorized by law," approved March third, one thousand eight hundred and seven:

"An act in addition to 'An act to prohibit the importation of slaves into any port or place within the jurisdiction of the United States, from and after the first day of January, in the year of our Lord one thousand eight hundred and eight, and to repeal certain parts of the same,'" approved April twentieth, one thousand eight hundred and eighteen:

"An act in addition to the acts prohibiting the slave trade," approved March third, one thousand eight hundred and nineteen:

"An act to establish the post-office of the United States:"

"An act further to alter and establish certain post-roads, and for the more secure carriage of the mail of the United States:"

"An act for the more general promulgation of the laws of the United States:"

"An act in addition to an act, entitled 'An act for the more general promulgation of the laws of the United States:'"

"An act to provide for the publication of the laws of the United States, and for other purposes:"

"An act to promote the progress of useful arts, and to repeal the act heretofore made for that purpose:"

"An act to extend the privilege of obtaining patents for useful discoveries and inventions to certain persons therein mentioned, and to enlarge and define the penalties for violating the rights of patentees:"

"An act for the encouragement of learning, by securing the copies of maps, charts, and books, to the authors and proprietors of such copies, during the time therein mentioned:"

"The act supplementary thereto, and for extending the benefits thereof to the arts of designing, engraving, and etching, historical and other prints:"

"An act to prescribe the mode in which the public acts, records, and judicial proceedings, in each state, shall be authenticated, so as to take effect in any other state:"

"An act supplementary to the act, entitled 'An act to prescribe the mode in which the public acts, records, and judicial proceedings, in each state, shall be acknowledged, so as to take effect in any other state:'"

"An act for establishing trading-houses with the Indian tribes," and the several acts continuing the same:

"An act making provision relative to rations for Indians, and their visits to the seat of government."

And the laws of the United States relating to the revenue and its collection, subject to the modification stipulated by the fifteenth article of the treaty of the twenty-second February, one thousand eight hundred and nine, in favour of Spanish vessels and their cargoes; and all other public laws of the United States, which are not repugnant to the provision of this act, shall extend to, and have full force and effect in, the territory aforesaid.

SEC. 10. *And be it further enacted,* That, to the end that the inhabitants may be protected in their liberty, property, and the exercise of their religion, no law shall ever be valid which shall impair, or in any way restrain, the freedom of religious opinions, professions, or worship. They shall be entitled to the benefit of the writ of habeas corpus. They shall be bailable in all cases, except for capital offences, where the proof is evident or the presumption great. All fines shall be moderate and proportioned to the offence; and excessive bail shall not be required, nor cruel nor unusual punishments inflicted. No ex post facto law, or law impairing the obligation of contracts, shall ever be passed; nor shall private property be taken for public uses without just compensation.

SEC. 11. *And be it further enacted,* That all free male white persons, who are housekeepers, and who shall have resided one year, at least, in the said territory, shall be qualified to act as grand and petit jurors in the courts of the said territory; and they shall, until the legislature thereof shall otherwise direct, be selected in such manner as the judges of the said courts shall respectively prescribe, so as to be most conducive to an impartial trial, and to be least burthensome to the inhabitants of the said territory.

SEC. 12. *And be it further enacted,* That it shall not be lawful for any person or persons to import or bring into the said territory, from any port or place without the limits of the United States, or cause or procure to be so imported or brought, or knowingly to aid or assist in so importing or bringing, any slave or slaves. And every person so offending, and being thereof convicted before any court within the said territory, having competent jurisdiction, shall forfeit and pay, for each and every slave so imported or brought, the sum of three hundred dollars, one moiety for the use of the United States, and the other moiety for the use of the person or persons who shall sue for the same; and every slave so imported or brought shall thereupon become entitled to, and receive, his or her freedom.

SEC. 13. *And be it further enacted,* That the laws in force in the said territory, at the commencement of this act, and not inconsistent with the provisions thereof, shall continue in force until altered, modified, or repealed, by the legislature.

SEC. 14. *And be it further enacted,* That the citizens of the said territory shall be entitled to one delegate to Congress, for the said territory, who shall possess the same powers heretofore granted to the delegates from the several territories of the United States. The said delegate shall be elected by such description of persons, at such times, and under such regulations, as the governor and legislative council may, from time to time, ordain and direct.

Approved, March 30, 1822.

AN ACT TO FIX THE WESTERN BOUNDARY LINE OF THE TERRITORY OF ARKANSAS, AND FOR OTHER PURPOSES

MAY 26, 1824

Be it enacted by the Senate and House of Representatives of the United States of America, in Congress assembled, That the western boundary line of the territory of Arkansas shall begin at a point forty miles west of the southwest corner of the state of Missouri, and run south to the right bank of the Red River, and thence, down the river, and with the Mexican boundary, to the line of the state of Louisiana, any law heretofore made, to the contrary notwithstanding.

SEC. 2. *And be it further enacted,* That the sum of two thousand dollars, to defray the expense of running and marking said boundary line, to be expended under the directions of the President of the United States, be, and the same hereby is, appropriated, to be paid out of any money in the treasury not otherwise appropriated.

SEC. 3. *And be it further enacted,* That so much of the appropriation of sixty-five thousand dollars, made by the act of the 3d of March, eighteen hundred and twenty-one, for carrying into effect the treaty of the eighteenth of October, eighteen hundred and twenty, with the Chactaw [Choctaw] Indians, as remains unexpended, shall, under the direction of the President of the United States, be employed for the purposes mentioned in the said act of 3d of March, eighteen hundred and twenty-one, any law to the contrary notwithstanding.

SEC. 4. *And be it further enacted*, That the sum of ten thousand dollars to be paid out of any money in the treasury not otherwise appropriated, be, and the same is hereby, appropriated, to defray the expenses of treating with the Chactaw [Choctaw] Indians, to obtain a modification of the treaty of October eighteenth, one thousand eight hundred and twenty.

Approved, May 26, 1824.

AN ACT TO AUTHORIZE THE PRESIDENT
OF THE UNITED STATES TO RUN AND MARK
A LINE DIVIDING THE TERRITORY OF FLORIDA
FROM THE STATE OF GEORGIA
MAY 4, 1826

Be it enacted by the Senate and House of Representatives of the United States of America, in Congress assembled, That the President of the United States of America be, and he is hereby, authorized, in conjunction with the constituted authorities of the state of Georgia, to cause to be run and distinctly marked the line dividing the territory of Florida, from the state of Georgia, from the junction of the rivers Chatahoochie and Flint, to the head of St. Mary's river: and for that purpose he is hereby authorized to appoint a commissioner, or surveyor, or both, as in his opinion may be necessary: *Provided*, That the line so to be run and marked, shall be run straight from the junction of said rivers Chatahoochie and Flint, to the point designated as the head of St. Mary's river, by the commissioners appointed under the third article of the treaty of friendship, limits, and navigation, between the United States of America and the King of Spain, made at San. Lorenzo el Real, on the seven and twentieth day of October, one thousand seven hundred and ninety-five: *And provided, also*, That the compensation to be allowed to the person or persons, so to be appointed by the President of the United States, shall not exceed in amount the compensation allowed by the government of Georgia to the person or persons appointed on its part, for the same object.

SEC. 2. *And be it further enacted*, That the person or persons, so to be appointed by the President of the United States, with such as have been or shall be appointed for the same purpose, on the part of the state of Georgia, after they, in conjunction, shall have run and distinctly marked said line, shall make two fair drafts, or maps thereof, both of which shall be certified by them, and one of which shall be deposited in the office of the Secretary of State for the United States, and the other delivered to the governor of Georgia.

SEC. 3. *And be it further enacted*, That, for the purpose of carrying this act into execution, the sum of five thousand dollars be, and hereby is, appropriated, to be paid out of any money in the treasury not otherwise appropriated.

Approved, May 4, 1826.

TREATY BETWEEN THE UNITED STATES
OF AMERICA AND THE WESTERN CHEROKEE
MAY 6, 1828
(EXCERPT)

ART. 1. The Western boundary of Arkansas shall be, and the same is, hereby defined, viz: A line shall be run, commencing on Red River, at the point where the Eastern Choctaw line strikes said River, and run due North with said line to the River Arkansas, thence in a direct line to the South West corner of Missouri.

. . . . . .

AN ACT TO AUTHORIZE THE PRESIDENT OF THE
UNITED STATES TO RUN AND MARK A LINE,
DIVIDING THE TERRITORY OF ARKANSAS
FROM THE STATE OF LOUISIANA
MAY 19, 1828

Be it enacted by the Senate and House of Representatives of the United States of America, in Congress assembled, That the President of the United States of America be, and he is hereby, authorized, in conjunction with the constituted authorities of the state of Louisiana, to cause to be run, and distinctly marked, the line dividing the territory of Arkansas from the state of Louisiana; commencing on the right bank of the Mississippi river, at latitude thirty-three degrees north, and running due west on that parallel of latitude, to where a line running due north from latitude thirty-two degrees north, on the Sabine river, will intersect the same. And, for that purpose, he is hereby authorized, to appoint a commissioner, or surveyor, or both, as in his opinion may be necessary: *Provided,* The compensation to be allowed to the person or persons so to be appointed by the President of the United States, shall not exceed in amount the compensation allowed by the government of Louisiana to the person or persons appointed, on its part, for the same object.

SEC. 2. *And be it further enacted,* That the person or persons, so to be appointed by the President of the United States, with such as have been or shall be appointed for the same purpose, on the part of the state of Louisiana, after they, in conjunction, shall have run, and distinctly marked said line, shall make two fair drafts, or maps thereof, both of which shall be certified by them, and one of which shall be deposited in the office of the Secretary of State for the United States, and the other delivered to the governor of Louisiana.

SEC. 3. *And be it further enacted,* That, for the purpose of carrying this act into execution, the sum of one thousand dollars be, and the same is hereby, appropriated, to be paid out of any money in the treasury, not otherwise appropriated.

Approved, May 19, 1828.

TREATY BETWEEN THE UNITED STATES OF AMERICA AND MEXICO
JANUARY 12, 1828
Treaty of Limits Between the United States of America and the United Mexican States

The limits of the United States of America with the bordering territories of Mexico having been fixed and designated by a solemn treaty concluded and signed at Washington on the twenty-second day of February, in the year of our Lord one thousand eight hundred and nineteen, between the respective Plenipotentiaries of the government of the United States of America on the one part and of that of Spain on the other: And whereas, the said treaty having been sanctioned at a period when Mexico constituted a part of the Spanish Monarchy, it is deemed necessary now to confirm the validity of the aforesaid treaty of limits, regarding it as still in force and binding between the United States of America and the United Mexican States.

With this intention, the President of the United States of America has appointed Joel Roberts Poinsett their Plenipotentiary; and the President of the United Mexican States their Excellencies Sebastian Camacho and José Ygnacio Esteva:

And the said Plenipotentiaries having exchanged their full powers, have agreed upon and concluded the following articles:

ARTICLE FIRST.

The dividing limits of the respective bordering territories of the United States of America and of the United Mexican States being the same as were agreed and fixed upon by the above-mentioned treaty of Washington concluded and signed on the twenty-second day of February in the year one thousand eight hundred and nineteen, the two high contracting parties will proceed forthwith to carry into full effect the third and fourth articles of said treaty, which are herein recited as follows:

ARTICLE SECOND.

The boundary line between the two countries, west of the Mississippi, shall begin on the Gulf of Mexico, at the mouth of the river Sabine, in the sea, continuing north, along the western bank of that river, to the 32d degree of latitude; thence, by a line due north, to the degree of latitude where it strikes the Rio Roxo of Natchitoches, or Red River; then, following the course of the Rio Roxo westward, to the degree of longitude 100 west from London and 23 from Washington; then, crossing the said Red River, and running thence, by a line due north, to the river Arkansas; thence, following the course of the southern bank of the Arkansas, to its source, in latitude 42 north; and thence, by that parallel of latitude, to the South Sea*. The whole being as laid down in Melish's map of the United States, published at Philadelphia, improved to the first of January, 1818. But if the source of the Arkansas river shall be found to fall north or south of latitude 42, then the line shall run from the said source due south or north, as the case may be, till it meets the said parallel of latitude 42, and thence, along the said parallel, to the South Sea: All the islands in the Sabine, and the said Red and Arkansas rivers, throughout the course thus described, to belong to the United States; but the use of the waters, and the navigation of the Sabine to the sea, and of the said rivers Roxo and Arkansas, throughout the extent of the said boundary, on their respective banks, shall be common to the respective inhabitants of both nations.

The two high contracting parties agree to cede and renounce all their rights, claims, and pretensions to the territories described by the said line; that is to say: the United States hereby cede to His Catholic Majesty, and renounce forever, all their rights, claims, and pretentions to the territories lying west and south of the above described line; and, in like manner, His Catholic Majesty cedes to the said United States, all his rights, claims, and pretentions to any territories east and north of the said line; and for himself, his heirs, and successors, renounces all claim to the said territories forever.

*Pacific Ocean

ARTICLE THIRD.

To fix this line with more precision, and to place the landmarks which shall designate exactly the limits of both nations, each of the contracting parties shall appoint a Commissioner and a Surveyor, who shall meet, before the termination of one year from the date of the ratification of this treaty, at Natchitoches, on the Red River, and proceed to run and mark the said line, from the mouth of the Sabine to the Red River, and from the Red River to the river Arkansas, and to ascertain the latitude of the source of the said river Arkansas, in conformity to what is agreed upon and stipulated, and the line of latitude 42, to the South Sea: they shall make out plans, and keep journals of their proceedings, and the result agreed upon by them shall be considered as part of this treaty, and shall have the same force as if it were inserted therein. The two governments will amicably agree respecting the necessary articles to be furnished to those persons, and also as to their respective escorts, should such be deemed necessary.

ARTICLE FOURTH.

The present Treaty shall be ratified, and the ratifications shall be exchanged at Washington, within the term of four months, or sooner, if possible.

In witness whereof, We, the respective Plenipotentiaries, have signed the same, and have hereunto affixed our respective seals.

Done at Mexico this twelfth day of January, in the Year of our Lord one thousand eight hundred and twenty eight, in the fifty-second year of the Independence of the United States of America, and in the eighth of that of the United Mexican States.

J.R. Poinsett	(Seal)
S. Camacho.	(Seal)
J.Y. Esteva	(Seal)

Additional Article to the Treaty of Limits concluded between the United States of America and the United Mexican States on the 12 day of January 1828.

The time having elapsed which was stipulated for the exchange of ratifications of the Treaty of Limits between the United Mexican States and the United States of America, signed in Mexico on the 12th of January 1828, and both Republics being desirous that it should be carried into full and complete effect with all due solemnity, the President of the United States of America has fully empowered on his part Anthony Butler a Citizen thereof and Chargé d'Affaires of the said States in Mexico. And the Vice-President of the United Mexican States, acting as President thereof, has in like manner fully empowered on his part their Excellencies Lucas Alaman, Secretary of State, and Foreign Relations, and Rafael Mangino Secretary of the Treasury, who after having exchanged their mutual powers found to be ample and in form have agreed and do hereby agree on the following article.

The ratifications of the Treaty of Limits concluded on the 12th of January of 1828, and shall be exchanged at the City of Washington within the term of one year counting from the date of this agreement and sooner should it be possible.

The present additional article shall have the same force and effect as if it had been inserted word for word in the aforesaid Treaty of the 12thof January of 1828, and shall be approved and ratified in the manner presribed by the Constitutions of the respective States.

In faith of which the said Plenipotentiaries have hereunto set their hands and affixed their respective seals. Done in Mexico the fifth of April of the year one thousand eight hundred thirty one, the fifty fifth of the Independence of the United States of America, and the eleventh of that of the United Mexican States.

(Seal)	A: Butler
(Seal)	Lucas Alaman
(Seal)	Rafael Mangino

AN ACT TO ASCERTAIN AND MARK THE LINE BETWEEN THE STATE OF ALABAMA AND THE TERRITORY OF FLORIDA, AND THE NORTHERN BOUNDARY OF THE STATE OF ILLINOIS, AND FOR OTHER PURPOSES
MARCH 2, 1831

Be it enacted by the Senate and House of Representatives of the United States of America, in Congress assembled, That the President of the United States be, and he is hereby, authorized to cause to be run and marked the boundary line between the state of Alabama and the territory of Florida, by the surveyors general of Alabama and Florida, on the thirty-first degree of north latitude; and it shall be the duty of the surveyor general of Florida to connect the public surveys on both sides with the line so run and marked.

SEC. 2. *And be it further enacted,* That patents shall be issued for such tracts of land as were sold and paid for at the land office at Tallahassee, in the territory of Florida, as are found to be situate within the limits of the district of lands subject to sale at Sparta, in Alabama, agreeably to the terms of the act organizing that district; and the said entries and sales shall be as valid, in every respect, as if they had been made in the land district of Alabama.

SEC. 3. *And be it further enacted,* That the President of the United States is hereby authorized to cause the surveyor general of the United States for the states of Illinois and Missouri, and the territory of Arkansas, to act as a commissioner on the part of the United States, whenever he shall be duly informed that the government of the state of Illinois shall have appointed a commissioner on its part, the two form a board, to ascertain, survey and mark the northern line of the state of Illinois, as defined in the act of Congress, entitled "An act to enable the people of the Illinois territory to form a constitution and state government, &c," passed the eighteenth of April, one thousand eight hundred and eighteen; and, in case of vacancy in said office of commissioner, or of his being unable to act from any cause, the President is authorized to fill such vacancy by the appointment of some other qualified person, whenever it may be necessary, until the object of the commission shall be attained.

SEC. 4. *And be it further enacted,* That the said board of commissioners shall have power to employ the necessary surveyors and labourers, and shall meet at such time and place as may be agreed upon by the President of the United States and the government of the state of Illinois, and proceed to ascertain, survey and mark the said northern line of the state of Illinois, and report their proceedings to the President of the United States, and the governor of the state of Illinois.

SEC. 5. *And be it further enacted,* That the President may allow to the said commissioner of the United States, such compensation for his services as shall seem to him reasonable: *Provided,* it does not exceed the allowance made by the state of Illinois to the commissioner on its part; and the said allowance, together with one-half of the necessary expenses of said board, and the surveyors and labourers, and the allowance to be made to the surveyors general of the state of Alabama and the territory of Florida, and the necessary expenses incurred by them in running and marking said line between said state and territory, shall be paid from the treasury of the United States, out of any money not otherwise appropriated; and, to enable the President to carry this act into effect, there is hereby appropriated the sum of two thousand dollars.

Approved, March 2, 1831.

AN ACT TO ATTACH THE TERRITORY OF THE UNITED STATES WEST OF THE MISSISSIPPI RIVER, AND NORTH OF THE STATE OF MISSOURI, TO THE TERRITORY OF MICHIGAN
JUNE 28, 1834

Be it enacted by the Senate and House of Representatives of the United States of America, in Congress assembled, That all that part of the territory of the United States bounded on the east by the Mississippi river, on the south by the state of Missouri, and a line drawn due west from the north-west corner of said state to the Missouri river; on the south-west and west by the Missouri river and the White Earth river, falling into the same; and on the north, by the northern boundary of the United States, shall be, and hereby is, for the purpose of temporary government, attached to, and made a part of, the territory of Michigan, and the inhabitants therein shall be entitled to the same privileges and immunities, and be subject to the same laws, rules, and regulations, in all respects, as the other citizens of Michigan territory.

Approved, June 28, 1834.

AN ACT ESTABLISHING THE TERRITORIAL GOVERNMENT OF WISCONSIN
APRIL 20, 1836

Be it enacted, by the Senate and House of Representatives of the United States of America in Congress assembled, That from and after the third day of July next, the country included within the following boundaries shall constitute a separate Territory, for the purposes of temporary government, by the name of Wisconsin; that is to say: Bounded on the east, by a line drawn from the northeast corner of the State of Illinois, through the middle of Lake Michigan, to a point in the middle of said lake, and opposite the main channel of Green Bay, and through said channel and Green Bay to the mouth of the Menomonie river; thence through the middle of the main channel of said river, to that head of said river nearest to the Lake of the Desert; thence in a direct line, to the middle of said lake; thence through the middle of the main channel of the Montreal river, to its mouth; thence with a direct line across Lake Superior, to where the territorial line of the United States last touches said lake northwest; thence on the north, with the said territorial line, to the White-earth river; on the west, by a line from the said boundary line following down the middle of the main channel of White-earth river, to the Missouri river, and down the middle of the main channel of the Missouri river to a point due west from the northwest corner of the State of Missouri; and on the south, from said point, due east to the northwest corner of the State of Missouri; and thence with the boundaries of the States of Missouri and Illinois, as already fixed by acts of Congress. And after the said third day of July next, all power and authority of the Government of Michigan in and over the Territory hereby constituted, shall cease: *Provided,* That nothing in this act contained shall be construed to impair the rights of person or property now appertaining to any Indians within the said Territory, so long as such rights shall remain unextinguished by treaty between the United States and such Indians, or to impair the obligations of any treaty now existing between the United States and such

Indians, or to impair or anywise to affect the authority of the Government of the United States to make any regulations respecting such Indians, their lands, property, or other rights, by treaty, or law, or otherwise, which it would have been competent to the Government to make if this act had never been passed: *Provided,* That nothing in this act contained shall be construed to inhibit the Government of the United States from dividing the Territory hereby established into one or more other Territories, in such manner, and at such times, as Congress shall, in its discretion, deem convenient and proper, or from attaching any portion of said Territory to any other State or Territory of the United States.

SEC. 2. *And be it further enacted,* That the Executive power and authority in and over the said Territory shall be vested in a Governor, who shall hold his office for three years, unless sooner removed by the President of the United States. The Governor shall reside within the said Territory, shall be commander-in-chief of the militia thereof, shall perform the duties and receive the emoluments of superintendent of Indian affairs, and shall approve of all laws passed by the Legislative Assembly before they shall take effect; he may grant pardons for offences against the laws of the said Territory, and reprieves for offences against the laws of the United States, until the decision of the President can be made known thereon; he shall commission all officers who shall be appointed to office under the laws of the said Territory, and shall take care that the laws be faithfully executed.

SEC. 3. *And be it further enacted,* That there shall be a Secretary of the said Territory, who shall reside therein, and hold his office for four years, unless sooner removed by the President of the United States; he shall record and preserve all the laws and proceedings of the Legislative Assembly hereinafter constituted, and all the acts and proceedings of the Governor in his executive department; he shall transmit one copy of the laws and one copy of the Executive proceedings on or before the first Monday in December in each year, to the President of the United States; and at the same time, two copies of the laws to the Speaker of the House of Representatives, for the use of Congress. And in case of the death, removal, resignation, or necessary absence, of the Governor from the Territory, the Secretary shall have, and he is hereby authorized and required to execute and perform, all the powers and duties of the Governor during such vacancy or necessary absence.

SEC. 4. *And be it further enacted,* That the Legislative power shall be vested in a Governor and a Legislative Assembly. The Legislative Assembly shall consist of a Council and House of Representatives. The Council shall consist of thirteen members, having the qualifications of voters as hereinafter prescribed, whose term of service shall continue four years. The House of Representatives shall consist of twenty-six members, possessing the same qualifications as prescribed for the members of the Council, and whose term of service shall continue two years. An apportionment shall be made, as nearly equal as practicable, among the several counties, for the election of the Council and Representatives, giving to each section of the Territory representation in the ratio of its population, Indians excepted, as nearly as may be. And the said members of the Council and House of Representatives shall reside in and be inhabitants of the district for which they may be elected. Previous to the first election, the Governor of the Territory shall cause the census or enumeration of the inhabitants of the several counties in the Territory to be taken and made by the sheriffs of the said counties, respectively, and returns thereof made by said sheriffs to the Governor. The first election shall be held at such time and place, and be conducted in such manner, as the Governor shall appoint and direct: and he shall, at the same time, declare the number of members of the Council and House of Representatives to which each of the counties is entitled under this act. The number of persons authorized to be elected having the greatest number of votes in each of the said counties for the Council, shall be declared, by the said Governor, to be duly elected to the said Council; and the person or persons having the greatest number of votes for the House of Representatives, equal to the number to which each county may be entitled, shall also be declared, by the Governor, to be duly elected: *Provided,* The Governor shall order a new election when there is a tie between two or more persons voted for, to supply the vacancy made by such tie. And the persons thus elected to the Legislative Assembly shall meet at such place on such day as he shall appoint; but, thereafter, the time, place, and manner of holding and conducting all elections by the people, and the apportioning the representation in the several counties to the Council and House of Representatives, according to population, shall be prescribed by law, as well as the day of the annual commencement of the session of the said Legislative Assembly; but no session, in any year, shall exceed the term of seventy-five days.

SEC. 5. *And be it further enacted,* That every free white male citizen of the United States, above the age of twenty-one years, who shall have been an inhabitant of said Territory at the time of its organization, shall be entitled to vote at the first election, and shall be eligible to any office within the said Territory; but the qualifications of voters at all subsequent elections shall be such as shall be determined by the Legislative Assembly: *Provided,* That the right of suffrage shall be exercised only by citizens of the United States.

SEC. 6. *And be it further enacted,* That the legislative power of the Territory shall extend to all rightful subjects of legislation; but no law shall be passed interfering with the primary disposal of the soil; no tax shall be imposed upon the property of the United States; nor shall the lands or other property of non-residents be taxed higher than the lands or other property of residents. All the laws of the Governor and Legislative Assembly shall be submitted to, and, if disapproved by the Congress of the United States, the same shall be null and of no effect.

SEC. 7. *And be it further enacted,* That all township officers and all county officers, except judicial officers, justices of the peace, sheriffs, and clerks of courts, shall be elected by the people, in such manner as may be provided by the Governor and Legislative Assembly. The Governor shall nominate, and, by and with the advice and consent of the Legislative Council, shall appoint, all judicial officers, justices of the peace, sheriffs, and all militia officers, except those of the staff, and all civil officers not herein provided for. Vacancies occurring in the recess of the Council shall be filled by appointments from the Governor, which shall expire at the end of the next session of the Legislative Assembly; but the said Governor may appoint, in the first instance, the aforesaid officers, who shall hold their offices until the end of the next session of the said Legislative Assembly.

SEC. 8. *And be it further enacted*, That no member of the Legislative Assembly shall hold or be appointed to any office created or the salary or emoluments of which shall have been increased whilst he was a member, during the term for which he shall have been elected, and for one year after the expiration of such term; and no person holding a commission under the United States, or any of its officers, except as a militia officer, shall be a member of the said Council, or shall hold any office under the Government of the said Territory.

SEC. 9. *And be it further enacted*, That the Judicial power of the said Territory shall be vested in a supreme court, district courts, probate courts, and in justices of the peace. The supreme court shall consist of a chief justice and two associate judges, any two of whom shall be a quorum, and who shall hold a term at the seat of Government of the said Territory, annually, and they shall hold their offices during good behaviour. The said Territory shall be divided into three judicial districts; and a district court or courts shall be held in each of the three districts, by one of the judges of the supreme court, at such times and places as may be prescribed by law. The jurisdiction of the several courts herein provided for, both appellate and original, and that of the probate courts, and of the justices of the peace, shall be as limited by law: *Provided, however*, That justices of the peace shall not have jurisdiction of any matter of controversy, when the title or boundaries of land may be in dispute, or where the debt or sum claimed exceeds fifty dollars. And the said supreme and district courts, respectively, shall possess chancery as well as common law jurisdiction. Each district court shall appoint its clerk, who shall keep his office at the place where the court may be held, and the said clerks shall also be the registers in chancery; and any vacancy in said office of clerk happening in the vacation of said court, may be filled by the judge of said district, which appointment shall continue until the next term of said court. And writs of error, bills of exception, and appeals in chancery causes, shall be allowed in all cases, from the final decisions of the said district courts to the supreme court, under such regulations as may be prescribed by law; but in no case removed to the supreme court, shall a trial by jury be allowed in said court. The supreme court may appoint its own clerk, and every clerk shall hold his office at the pleasure of the court by which he shall have been appointed. And writs of error and appeals from the final decisions of the said supreme court shall be allowed and taken to the Supreme Court of the United States, in the same manner, and under the same regulations, as from the circuit courts of the United States, where the value of the property, or the amount in controversy, to be ascertained by the oath or affirmation of either party, shall exceed one thousand dollars. And each of the said district courts shall have and exercise the same jurisdiction, in all cases arising under the constitution and laws of the United States as is vested in the circuit and district courts of the United States. And the first six days of every term of the said courts, or so much thereof as shall be necessary, shall be appropriated to the trial of causes arising under the said constitution and laws. And writs of error, and appeals from the final decisions of the said courts, in all such cases, shall be made to the supreme court of the

Territory, in the same manner as in other cases. The said clerks shall receive, in all such cases, the same fees which the clerk of the district court of the United States in the northern district of the State of New York receives for similar services.

SEC. 10. *And be it further enacted,* That there shall be an Attorney for the said Territory appointed, who shall continue in office four years, unless sooner removed by the President, and who shall receive the same fees and salary as the attorney of the United States for the Michigan Territory. There shall also be a Marshal for the Territory appointed, who shall hold his office for four years, unless sooner removed by the President, who shall execute all process issuing from the said courts when exercising their jurisdiction as circuit and district courts of the United States. He shall perform the same duties, be subject to the same regulations and penalties, and be entitled to the same fees, as the Marshal of the district court of the United States for the northern district of the State of New York; and shall, in addition, be paid the sum of two hundred dollars, annually, as a compensation for extra services.

SEC. 11. *And be it further enacted,* That the Governor, Secretary, Chief Justice and Associate Judges, Attorney, and Marshal, shall be nominated, and, by and with the advice and consent of the Senate, appointed by the President of the United States. The Governor and Secretary, to be appointed as aforesaid, shall, before they act, as such respectively take an oath or affirmation before some judge or justice of the peace in the existing Territory of Michigan, duly commissioned and qualified to administer an oath or affirmation, to support the constitution of the United States, and for the faithful discharge of the duties of their respective offices; which said oaths, when so taken, shall be certified by the person before whom the same shall have been taken, and such certificate shall be received and recorded by the said Secretary among the Executive proceedings. And, afterwards, the Chief Justice and associate Judges, and all other civil officers in said Territory, before they act as such, shall take a like oath or affirmation before the said Governor or Secretary, or some judge or justice of the Territory who may be duly commissioned and qualified, which said oath or affirmation shall be certified and transmitted by the person taking the same to the Secretary, to be by him recorded as aforesaid; and, afterwards, the like oath or affirmation shall be taken, certified, and recorded, in such manner and form as may be prescribed by law. The Governor shall receive an annual salary of two thousand five hundred dollars for his services as Governor and as superintendent of Indian affairs. The said Chief Justice and Associate Judges shall each receive an annual salary of eighteen hundred dollars. The Secretary shall receive an annual salary of twelve hundred dollars. The said salaries shall be paid quarter-yearly, at the Treasury of the United States. The members of the Legislative Assembly shall be entitled to receive three dollars each per day, during their attendance at the sessions thereof, and three dollars each for every twenty miles' travel in going to and returning from the said sessions, estimated according to the nearest usually-travelled route. There shall be appropriated, annually, the sum of three hundred and fifty dollars, to be expended by the Governor to defray the contingent expenses of the Territory, and there shall also be appropriated annually, a sufficient sum, to be expended by the Secretary of the Territory, and upon an estimate to be made by the

Secretary of the Treasury of the United States, to defray the expenses of the Legislative Assembly, the printing of the laws and other incidental expenses; and the Secretary of the Territory shall annually account to the Secretary of the Treasury of the United States for the manner in which the aforesaid sum shall have been expended.

SEC. 12. *And be it further enacted,* That the inhabitants of the said Territory shall be entitled to, and enjoy, all and singular the rights, privileges, and advantages, granted and secured to the people of the Territory of the United States northwest of the river Ohio, by the articles of the compact contained in the ordinance for the government of the said Territory, passed on the thirteenth day of July, one thousand seven hundred and eighty-seven; and shall be subject to all the conditions and restrictions and prohibitions in said articles of compact imposed upon the people of the said Territory. The said inhabitants shall also be entitled to all the rights, privileges, and immunities, heretofore granted and secured to the Territory of Michigan, and to its inhabitants, and the existing laws of the Territory of Michigan shall be extended over said Territory, so far as the same shall not be incompatible with the provisions of this act, subject, nevertheless, to be altered, modified, or repealed, by the Governor and Legislative Assembly of the said Territory of Wisconsin; and further, the laws of the United States are hereby extended over, and shall be in force in, said Territory, so far as the same, or any provisions thereof may be applicable.

SEC. 13. *And be it further enacted,* That the Legislative Assembly of the Territory of Wisconsin shall hold its first session at such time and place in said Territory as the Governor thereof shall appoint and direct; and at said session, or as soon thereafter as may by them be deemed expedient, the said Governor and Legislative Assembly shall proceed to locate and establish the seat of government for said Territory, at such place as they may deem eligible, which place, however, shall thereafter be subject to be changed by the said Governor and Legislative Assembly. And twenty thousand dollars, to be paid out of any money in the Treasury, not otherwise appropriated, is hereby given to the said Territory, which shall be applied by the Governor and Legislative Assembly to defray the expenses of erecting public buildings at the seat of government.

SEC. 14. *And be it further enacted,* That a Delegate to the House of Representatives of the United States, to serve for the term of two years, may be elected by the voters qualified to elect members of the Legislative Assembly, who shall be entitled to the same rights and privileges as have been granted to the Delegates from the several Territories of the United States to the said House of Representatives. The first election shall be held at such time and place or places, and be conducted in such manner, as the Governor shall appoint and direct. The person having the greatest number of votes shall be declared by the Governor to be duly elected, and a certificate thereof shall be given to the person so elected.

SEC. 15. *And be it further enacted,* That all suits, process, and proceedings, and all indictments and informations which shall be undetermined on the third day of July next, in the courts held by the additional judge for the Michigan Territory, in the counties of Brown and Iowa; and all suits, process and proceedings, and all indictments and informations which shall be undetermined on the said third day of July, in the county courts of the several counties of Crawford, Brown, Iowa, Dubuque, Milwalke [Milwaukie], and Des Moines, shall be transferred to be heard, tried, prosecuted, and determined, in the district courts hereby established, which may include the said counties.

SEC. 16. *And be it further enacted,* That all causes which shall have been or may be removed from the courts held by the additional judge for the Michigan Territory, in the counties of Brown and Iowa, by appeal or otherwise, into the supreme court for the Territory of Michigan, and which shall be undetermined therein on the third day of July next, shall be certified by the clerk of the said supreme court, and transferred to the supreme court of said Territory of Wisconsin, there to be proceeded in to final determination, in the same manner that they might have been in the said supreme court of the Territory of Michigan.

SEC. 17. *And be it further enacted,* That the sum of five thousand dollars be, and the same is hereby, appropriated, out of any money in the Treasury not otherwise appropriated, to be expended by and under the direction of the Legislative Assembly of said Territory, in the purchase of a library for the accommodation of said Assembly, and of the supreme court hereby established.

Approved, April 20, 1836.

AN AGREEMENT BETWEEN THE REPUBLIC OF TEXAS AND THE MEXICAN ARMY
MAY 14, 1836

Ejercito de Operationes

Articles of an agreement entered into between His Excellency David G. Burnet, President of the Republic of Texas, of the one part, and His Excellency General Antonio Lopez de Santa Anna, President General in Chief of the Mexican Army, of the other part.

ARTICLE 1ST

General Antonio Lopez de Santa Anna agrees that he will not take up arms, nor will he exercise his influence to cause them to be taken up, against the people of Texas, during the present war of Independence.

ARTICLE 2ND

All hostilities between the mexican and texian troops will cease immediately both on land and water.

ARTICLE 3RD

The mexican troops will evacuate the Territory of Texas, passing to the other side of the Rio Grande del Norte.

ARTICLE 4TH

The mexican army in its retreat shall not take the property of any person without his consent and just indemnification, using only such articles as may be necessary for its subsistence, in cases when the owner may not be present, and remitting to the Commander of the Army of Texas or to the commissioners to be appointed for the adjustment of such matters an account of the value of the property consumed — the place where taken and the name of the owner if it can be ascertained.

ARTICLE 5TH

That all private property including cattle, horses, negro slaves, or indentured persons of whatever denomination, that may have been captured by any portion of the mexican army, or may have taken refuge in the said army, since the commencement of the late invasion, shall be restored to the Commander of the Texian Army, or to such other persons as may be appointed by the Government of Texas to receive them.

ARTICLE 6TH

The troops of both armies will refrain from coming into contact with each other, and to this end, the Commander of the Army of Texas will be careful not to approach within a shorter distance of the mexican army than five leagues.

ARTICLE 7TH

The mexican army shall not make any other delay on its march than that which is necessary to take up their hospitals, baggage, etc., and to cross the river — any delay not necessary to these purposes to be considered an infraction of this agreement.

ARTICLE 8TH

By express to be immediately dispatched, this agreeement shall be sent to General Vicente Filisola and to General T.J. Rusk, commander of the Texian army, in order that they may be apprised of its stipulations, and to this end they will exchange engagements to comply with the same.

ARTICLE 9TH

That all Texian prisoners now in possession of the mexican army or its authorities be forthwith released, and furnished with free passports to return to their homes, in consideration of which a corresponding number of mexican prisoners, rank and file, now in possession of the Government of Texas, shall be immediately released — the remainder of the mexican prisoners that continue in possession of the Government of Texas, to be treated with due humanity — any extraordinary comforts that may be furnished them to be at the charge of the Government of Mexico.

ARTICLE 10TH

General Antonio Lopez de Santa Anna will be sent to Veracrus as soon as it shall be deemed proper.
The contracting parties sign this instrument for the above mentioned purposes, by duplicate at the Post of Velasco this 14th day of May 1836.

ANTONIO LOPEZ DE   JOHN COLLINSWORTH
SANTA ANA   Secretary of State.
  (Seal)
DAVID G. BURNET   BAILEY HARDEMAN
  (Seal)   Secy of Treasury.
                    P.W. GRAYSON
                    Atty General
                        (Seal)

AN ACT TO EXTEND THE WESTERN BOUNDARY
OF THE STATE OF MISSOURI TO THE MISSOURI RIVER
JUNE 7, 1836

Be it enacted by the Senate and House of Representatives of the United States of America in Congress assembled, That when the Indian title to all the lands lying between the State of Missouri and the Missouri river shall be extinguished, the jurisdiction over said lands shall be hereby ceded to the State of Missouri, and the western boundary of said State shall be then extended to the Missouri river, reserving to the United States the original right of soil in said lands, and of disposing of the same: *Provided,* That this act shall not take effect until the President shall by proclamation, declare that the Indian title to said

lands has been extinguished; nor shall it take effect until the State of Missouri shall have assented to the provisions of this act.
Approved, June 7, 1836.

AN ACT TO ESTABLISH THE NORTHERN BOUNDARY LINE OF THE STATE OF OHIO, AND TO PROVIDE FOR THE ADMISSION OF THE STATE OF MICHIGAN INTO THE UNION UPON THE CONDITIONS THEREIN EXPRESSED
JUNE 15, 1836

Be it enacted by the Senate and House of Representatives of the United States of America in Congress assembled, That the northern boundary line of the State of Ohio shall be established at, and shall be a direct line drawn from the southern extremity of Lake Michigan, to the most northerly cape of the Maumee (Miami) bay, after that line, so drawn, shall intersect the eastern boundary line of the State of Indiana; and from the said north cape of the said bay, northeast to the boundary line between the United States and the province of Upper Canada, in Lake Erie; and thence, with the said last mentioned line, to its intersection with the western line of the State of Pennsylvania.

SEC. 2. *And be it further enacted,* That the constitution and State Government which the people of Michigan have formed for themselves be, and the same is hereby, accepted, ratified, and confirmed; and that the said State of Michigan shall be, and is hereby, declared to be one of the United States of America, and is hereby admitted into the Union upon an equal footing with the original States, in all respects whatsoever: *Provided always,* and this admission is upon the express condition, that the said State shall consist of and have jurisdiction over all the territory included within the following boundaries, and over none other, to wit: Beginning at the point where the above described northern boundary of the State of Ohio intersects the eastern boundary of the State of Indiana, and running thence with the said boundary line of Ohio, as described in the first section of this act, until it intersects the boundary line between the United States and Canada, in Lake Erie; thence, with the said boundary line between the United States and Canada through the Detroit river, Lake Huron, and Lake Superior, to a point where the said line last touches Lake Superior; thence, in a direct line through Lake Superior, to the mouth of the Montreal river; thence through the middle of the main channel of the said river Montreal, to the middle of the Lake of the Desert; thence, in a direct line to the nearest head water of the Menomonie river; thence, through the middle of that fork of the said river first touched by the said line, to the main channel of the said Menomonie river; thence, down the centre of the main channel of the same, to the centre of the most usual ship channel of the Green bay of Lake Michigan; thence, through the centre of the most usual ship channel of the said bay to the middle of Lake Michigan; thence, through the middle of Lake Michigan, to the northern boundary of the State of Indiana, as that line was established by the act of Congress of the nineteenth of April eighteen hundred and sixteen; thence, due east, with the north boundary line of the said State of Indiana, to the northeast corner thereof; and thence, south, with the east boundary line of Indiana, to the place of beginning.

SEC. 3. *And be it further enacted,* That, as a compliance with the fundamental condition of admission contained in the last preceding section of this act, the boundaries of the said State of Michigan, as in that section described, declared, and established, shall receive the assent of a convention of delegates elected by the people of the said State, for the sole purpose of giving the assent herein required; and as soon as the assent herein required shall be given, the President of the United States shall announce the same by proclamation; and thereupon, and without any further proceeding on the part of Congress, the admission of the said State into the Union, as one of the United States of America, on an equal footing with the original States in all respects whatever, shall be considered as complete, and the Senators and Representatives who have been elected by the said State as its representative in the Congress of the United States, shall be entitled to take their seats in the Senate and House of Representatives respectively, without further delay.

SEC. 4. *And be it further enacted,* That nothing in this act contained, or in the admission of the said State into the Union as one of the United States of America upon an equal footing with the original States in all respects whatever, shall be so construed or understood as to confer upon the people, Legislature, or other authorities of the said State of Michigan, any authority or right to interfere with the sale by the United States, and under their authority, of the vacant and unsold lands within the limits of the said State, but that the subject of the public lands, and the interests which may be given to the said State therein, shall be regulated by future action between Congress, on the part of the United States, and the said State, or the authorities thereof. And the said State of Michigan shall in no case and under no pretence whatsoever, impose any tax, assessment or imposition of any description upon any of the lands of the United States within its limits.

Approved, June 15, 1836.

AN ACT FOR THE ADMISSION OF THE STATE OF ARKANSAS INTO THE UNION, AND TO PROVIDE FOR THE DUE EXECUTION OF THE LAWS OF THE UNITED STATES, WITHIN THE SAME, AND FOR OTHER PURPOSES
JUNE 15, 1836

Whereas, the people of the Territory of Arkansas, did, on the thirtieth day of January in the present year by a convention of delegates, called and assembled for that purpose, form for themselves a constitution and State Government, which constitution and State Government, so formed, is republican: and whereas, the number of inhabitants within the said Territory exceeds forty-seven thousand seven hundred persons, computed according to the rule prescribed by the constitution of the United States; and the said convention have, in their behalf, asked the Congress of the United States to admit the said Territory into the Union as a State, on an equal footing with the original States:

Be it enacted, by the Senate and House of Representatives of the United States of America in Congress assembled, That the State of Arkansas shall be one, and is hereby declared to be one of the United States of America, and admitted into the Union on an equal footing with the original States, in all respects whatever, and the said State shall consist of all the territory included within the following boundaries, to wit: beginning in the middle of the main channel of the Mississippi river, on the parallel of thirty-six degrees north latitude, running from thence west, with the said parallel of latitude, to the Saint Francis river; thence up the middle of the main channel of said river to the parallel of thirty-six degrees thirty minutes north; from thence west to the southwest corner of the State of Missouri; and from thence to be bounded on the west, to the north bank of Red river, by the lines described in the first article of the treaty between the United States and the Cherokee nation of Indians west of the Mississippi, made and concluded at the city of Washington, on the 26th* day of May, in the year of our Lord one thousand eight hundred and twenty-eight; and to be bounded on the south side of Red river by the Mexican boundary line, to the northwest corner of the State of Louisiana; thence east, with the Louisiana State line, to the middle of the main channel of the Mississippi river; thence up the middle of the main channel of the said river, to the thirty-sixth degree of north latitude, the point of beginning.

SEC. 2. *And be it further enacted,* That until the next general census shall be taken, the said State shall be entitled to one representative in the House of Representatives of the United States.

SEC. 3. *And be it further enacted,* That all the laws of the United States,

*Note: In this act of June 15, 1836 the treaty with the Western Cherokee is cited as May 26, 1828, but apparently should have been cited as May 6, 1828.

which are not locally inapplicable, shall have the same force and effect within the said State of Arkansas, as elsewhere within the United States.

SEC. 4. *And be it further enacted,* That the said State shall be one judicial district, and be called the Arkansas district; and a district court shall be held therein, to consist of one judge, who shall reside in the said district, and be called a district judge. He shall hold at the seat of Government of the said State, two sessions annually, on the first Mondays of April and November; and he shall, in all things, have and exercise the same jurisdiction and powers which were by law given to the judge of the Kentucky district under an act entitled "An act to establish the judicial courts of the United States." He shall appoint a clerk for the said district court, who shall reside and keep the records of the court at the place of holding the same; and shall receive, for the services performed by him, the same fees to which the clerk of the Kentucky district is entitled for similar services.

SEC. 5. *And be it further enacted,* That there shall be allowed to the judge of the said district court, the annual compensation of two thousand dollars, to commence from the date of his appointment, to be paid quarter-yearly at the Treasury of the United States.

SEC. 6. *And be it further enacted,* That there shall be appointed in the said district, a person learned in the law, to act as attorney for the United States, who shall, in addition to his stated fees, be paid by the United States two hundred dollars, as a full compensation for all extra services.

SEC. 7. *And be it further enacted,* That a marshall shall be appointed for the said district who shall perform the same duties, be subject to the same regulations and penalties, and be entitled to the same fees, as are prescribed to marshals in other districts; and he shall moreover be entitled to the sum of two hundred dollars annually, as a compensation for all extra services.

SEC. 8. *And be it further enacted,* That the State of Arkansas is admitted into the Union upon the express condition, that the people of the said State shall never interfere with the primary disposal of the public lands within the said State, nor shall they levy a tax on any of the lands of the United States within the said State; and nothing in this act shall be construed as an assent by Congress to all or to any of the propositions contained in the ordinance of the said convention of the people of Arkansas, nor to deprive the said State of Arkansas of the same grants, subject to the same restrictions, which were made to the State of Missouri by virtue of an act entitled "An act to authorize the people of the Missouri Territory to form a constitution and State government, and for the admission of such State into the Union, on an equal footing with the original States, and to prohibit slavery in certain Territories," approved the sixth day of March, one thousand eight hundred and twenty.

Approved, June 15, 1836.

AN ACT TO SETTLE AND ESTABLISH THE
NORTHERN BOUNDARY LINE OF THE STATE OF OHIO
JUNE 23, 1836

Be it enacted by the Senate and House of Representatives of the United States of America in Congress assembled, That the northern boundary of the State of Ohio shall be established by, and extend to, a direct line running from the southern extremity of Lake Michigan to the most northerly cape of the Miami bay; thence, northeast, to the northern boundary line of the United States; thence, with said line, to the Pennsylvania line.

SEC. 2. *And be it further enacted,* That the boundary line surveyed, marked, and designated, agreeably to "An act to authorize the President of the United States to ascertain and designate the northern boundary of the State of Indiana," approved March the second, eighteen hundred and twenty-seven, shall be deemed and taken as the east and west line mentioned in the constitution of the State of Indiana, drawn through a point ten miles north of the southern extreme of Lake Michigan, and shall be and for ever remain the northern boundary of said State.

SEC. 3. *And be it further enacted,* That the northern boundary line, ascertained, surveyed, and marked, agreeably to a law of Congress entitled "An act to ascertain and mark the line between the State of Alabama and the Territory of Florida, and the northern boundary of the State of Illinois, and for other purposes," approved March second, eighteen hundred and thirty-one, shall be deemed and taken as the line west from the middle of Lake Michigan, in north latitude forty-two degrees thirty minutes, to the middle of the Mississippi river, as defined in the act of Congress entitled "An act to enable the people of the Illinois Territory to form a constitution and State Government, and for the admission of such State into the Union on an equal footing with the original States," approved eighteenth of April, eighteen hundred and eighteen, and shall be and for ever remain the northern boundary line of said state.

Approved, June 23, 1836.

CONVENTION BETWEEN THE UNITED STATES OF
AMERICA AND THE REPUBLIC OF TEXAS
APRIL 25, 1838

Convention Between the United States of America and the Republic of Texas, for Marking the Boundary Between Them

Whereas the treaty of limits made and concluded on the twelfth day of January in the year of our Lord one thousand eight hundred and twenty eight between the United States of America on the one part and the United Mexican States on the other is binding upon the Republic of Texas, the same having been entered into at a time when Texas formed a part of the said United Mexican States:

And whereas it is deemed proper and expedient in order to prevent future disputes and collisions between the United States and Texas in regard to the boundary between the two countries as designated by the said treaty, that a portion of the same should be run and marked without unnecessary delay:

The President of the United States has appointed John Forsyth their plenipotentiary, and the President of the Republic of Texas has appointed Memucan Hunt its plenipotentiary:

And the said plenipotentiaries having exchanged their full powers, have agreed upon and concluded the following articles:

ART. 1. Each of the contracting parties shall appoint a commissioner and surveyor, who shall meet before the termination of twelve months from the exchange of the ratifications of this Convention at New Orleans and proceed to run and mark that portion of the said boundary which extends from the mouth of the Sabine, where that river enters the Gulph of Mexico to the Red River. They shall make out plans and keep journals of their proceedings and the result agreed upon by them shall be considered as part of this Convention and shall have the same force as if it were inserted therein. The two governments will amicably agree respecting the necessary articles to be furnished to those persons and also as to their respective escorts, should such be deemed necessary.

ART. 2. And it is agreed that until this line shall be marked out as is provided for in the foregoing article, each of the contracting parties shall continue to exercise jurisdiction in all territory over which its jurisdiction has hitherto been exercised, and that the remaining portion of the said boundary line shall be run and marked at such time hereafter as may suit the convenience of both the contracting parties, until which time each of the said parties shall exercise without the interference of the other within the territory of which the boundary shall not have been so marked and run, jurisdiction to the same extent to which it has been heretofore usually exercised.

ART. 3. The present Convention shall be ratified and the ratification shall be exchanged at Washington within the term of six months from the date hereof, or sooner if possible.

In witness whereof, we, the respective Plenipotentiaries, have signed the same, and have hereunto affixed our respective seals. Done at Washington, this twenty fifth day of April in the year of our Lord one thousand eight hundred and thirty eight, in the sixty second year of the Independence of the United States of America, and in the third of that of the Republic of Texas.

(Seal)   Memucan Hunt
(Seal)   John Forsyth

AN ACT TO DIVIDE THE
TERRITORY OF WISCONSIN AND TO ESTABLISH
THE TERRITORIAL GOVERNMENT OF IOWA
JUNE 12, 1838

Be it enacted by the Senate and House of Representatives of the United States of America in Congress assembled, That from and after the third day of July next, all that part of the present Territory of Wisconsin which lies west of the Mississippi river, and west of a line drawn due north from the head waters or sources of the Mississippi to the Territorial line, shall, for the purposes of temporary government, be and constitute a separate Territorial Government by the name of Iowa; and that from and after the said third day of July next, the present Territorial Government of Wisconsin shall extend only to that part of the present Territory of Wisconsin which lies east of the Mississippi river. And after the said third say of July next, all power and authority of the Government of Wisconsin in and over the Territory hereby constituted shall cease: *Provided,* That nothing in this act contained shall be construed to impair the rights of person or property now appertaining to any Indians within the said Territory, so long as such rights shall remain unextinguished by treaty between the United States and such Indians, or to impair the obligations of any treaty now existing between the United States and such Indians, or to impair or otherwise to affect the authority of the Government of the United States to make any regulations respecting such Indians, their lands, property, or other rights, by treaty or law, or otherwise, which it would have been competent to the Government to make if this act had never been passed: *Provided,* That nothing in this act contained shall be construed to inhibit the Government of the United States from dividing the Territory hereby established into one or more other Territories, in such manner and at such times as Congress shall, in its discretion, deem convenient and proper, or from attaching any portion of said Territory to any other state or Territory of the United States.

SEC. 2. *And be it further enacted,* That the executive power and authority in and over the said Territory of Iowa shall be vested in a Governor, who shall hold his office for three years, unless sooner removed by the President of the United States. The Governor shall reside within the said Territory, shall be commander-in-chief of the militia thereof, shall perform the duties and receive the emoluments of superintendent of Indian affairs, and shall approve of all laws passed by the Legislative Assembly before they shall take effect; he may grant pardons for offences against the laws of the said Territory, and reprieves for offences against the laws of the United States, until the decision of the President can be made known thereon; he shall commission all officers who shall be appointed to office under the laws of the said Territory, and shall take care that the laws be faithfully executed.

SEC. 3. *And be it further enacted,* That there shall be a Secretary of the said Territory, who shall reside therein, and hold his office for four years, unless sooner removed by the President of the United States; he shall record and preserve all the laws and proceedings of the Legislative Assembly hereinafter constituted, and all the acts and proceedings of the Governor in his executive department; he shall transmit one copy of the laws and one copy of the executive proceedings, on or before the first Monday in December in each year, to the President of the United States, and, at the same time, two copies of the laws to the Speaker of the House of Representatives, for the use of Congress. And in case of the death, removal, resignation, or necessary absence of the Governor from the Territory, the Secretary shall have, and he is hereby authorized and required to execute and perform all the powers and duties of the Governor during such vacancy or necessary absence, or until another Governor shall be duly appointed to fill such vacancy.

SEC. 4. *And be it further enacted*, That the legislative power shall be vested in the Governor and a Legislative Assembly. The Legislative Assembly shall consist of a Council and House of Representatives. The Council shall consist of thirteen members, having the qualifications of voters as hereinafter prescribed, whose term of service shall continue two years. The House of Representatives shall consist of twenty-six members possessing the same qualifications as prescribed for the members of the Council, and whose term of service shall continue one year. An apportionment shall be made as nearly equal as practicable, among the several counties, for the election of the Council and Representatives, giving to each section of the Territory representation in the ratio of its population, Indians excepted, as nearly as may be. And the said members of the council and House of Representatives shall reside in and be inhabitants of the district for which they may be elected. Previous to the first election, the Governor of the Territory shall cause the census or enumeration of the inhabitants of the several counties in the Territory to be taken, and made by the sheriffs of the said counties, respectively, unless the same shall have been taken within three months previous to the third day of July next, and returns thereof made by said sheriffs to the Governor. The first election shall be held at such time and place, and be conducted in such manner as the Governor shall appoint and direct; and he shall at the same time, declare the number of members of the Council and House of Representatives to which each of the counties or districts are entitled under this act. The number of persons authorized to be elected having the greatest number of votes in each of the said counties or districts for the Council, shall be declared by the said Governor to be duly elected to the said Council; and the person or persons having the greatest number of votes for the House of Representatives, equal to the number to which each county may be entitled, shall also be declared by the Governor to be duly elected: *Provided*, The Governor shall order a new election when there is a tie between two or more persons voted for, to supply the vacancy made by such tie. And the persons thus elected to the Legislative Assembly shall meet at such place, and on such day as he shall appoint; but thereafter the time, place, and manner of holding and conducting all elections by the people, and the apportioning the representation in the several counties to the Council and House of Representatives, according to population, shall be prescribed by laws, as well as the day of the annual commencement of the session of the said Legislative Assembly; but no session in any year shall exceed the term of seventy-five days.

SEC. 5. *And be it further enacted,* That every free white male citizen of the United States, above the age of twenty-one years, who shall have been an inhabitant of said Territory at the time of its organization, shall be entitled to vote at the first election, and shall be eligible to any office within the said Territory; but the qualifications of voters at all subsequent elections, shall be such as shall be determined by the Legislative Assembly: *Provided,* That the right of suffrage shall be exercised only by citizens of the United States.

SEC. 6. *And be it further enacted,* That the legislative power of the Territory shall extend to all rightful subjects of legislation; but no law shall be passed interfering with the primary disposal of the soil; no tax shall be imposed upon the property of the United States; nor shall the lands or other property of non-residents be taxed higher than the lands or other property of residents. All the laws of the Governor and Legislative Assembly shall be submitted to, and if disapproved by, the Congress of the United States, the same shall be null and of no effect.

SEC. 7. *And be it further enacted,* That all township officers, and all county officers, except judicial officers, justices of the peace, sheriffs, and clerks of courts, shall be elected by the people, in such manner as is now prescribed by the laws of the Territory of Wisconsin, or as may, after the first election, be provided by the Governor and Legislative Assembly of Iowa Territory. The Governor shall nominate and by and with the advice and consent of the Legislative Council, shall appoint all judicial officers, justices of the peace, sheriffs, and all militia officers, except those of the staff, and all civil officers not herein provided for. Vacancies occurring in the recess of the Council, shall be filled by appointments from the Governor, which shall expire at the end of the next session of the Legislative Assembly; but the said Governor may appoint, in the first instance, the aforesaid officers, who shall hold their offices until the end of the next session of the said Legislative Assembly.

SEC. 8. *And be it further enacted,* That no member of the Legislative Assembly shall hold, or be appointed to, any office created, or the salary and emoluments of which shall have been increased, whilst he was a member, during the term for which he shall have been elected, and for one year after the expiration of such term; and no person holding a commission or appointment under the United States, or any of its officers, except as a militia officer, shall be a member of the said Council or House of Representatives, or shall hold any office under the Government of the said Territory.

SEC. 9. *And be it further enacted,* That the judicial power of the said Territory shall be vested in a supreme court, district courts, probate courts, and in justices of the peace. The supreme court shall consist of a chief justice, and two associate judges, any two of whom shall be a quorum, and who shall hold a term at the seat of Government of the said Territory annually, and they shall hold their offices during the term of four years. The said Territory shall be divided into three judicial districts; and a district court or courts shall be held in each of the three districts, by one of the judges of the supreme court, at such times and places as may be prescribed by law; and the said judges shall, after their appointment, respectively, reside in the districts which shall be assigned to them. The jurisdiction of the several courts herein provided for, both appellate and original, and that of the probate courts, and of the justices of the peace, shall be as limited by law: *Provided, however,* That justices of the peace shall not have jurisdiction of any matter of controversy, when the title or boundaries of land may be in dispute, or where the debt or sum claimed exceeds fifty dollars. And the said supreme and district courts, respectively, shall possess a chancery as well as common law jurisdiction. Each district court shall appoint its clerk, who shall keep his office at the place where the court may be held, and the said clerks shall also be registers in chancery; and any vacancy in said office of clerk happening in the vacation of said court, may be filled by the judge of said district, which appointment shall continue until the next term of said court. And writs of error, bills of exception, and appeals in chancery causes, shall be allowed in all cases, from the final decisions of the said district courts to the supreme court under such regulations as may be prescribed by law; but in no case removed to the supreme court shall trial by jury be allowed in said court. The supreme court may appoint its own clerk, and every clerk shall hold his office at the pleasure of the court by which he shall have been appointed. And writs of error and appeals from the final decision of the said supreme court shall be allowed and taken to the Supreme Court of the United States, in the same manner and under the same regulations as from the circuit courts of the United States, where the value of the property, or the amount in controversy, to be ascertained by the oath or affirmation of either party, shall exceed one thousand dollars. And each of the said district courts shall have and exercise the same jurisdiction in all cases arising under the constitution and laws of the United States, as is vested in the circuit and district courts of the United States. And the first six days of every term of the said courts, or so much thereof as shall be necessary, shall be appropriated to the trial of causes arising under the said constitution and laws. And writs of error and appeals from the final decisions of the said courts, in all such cases, shall be made to the supreme court of the Territory, in the same manner as in other cases. The said clerks shall receive in all such cases, the same fees which the clerk of the district courts of Wisconsin Territory now receives for similar services.

SEC. 10. *And be it further enacted,* That there shall be an attorney for the said Territory appointed, who shall continue in office four years, unless sooner removed by the President, and who shall receive the same fees and salary as the attorney of the United States, for the present Territory of Wisconsin. There shall also be a marshal for the Territory appointed, who shall hold his office for four years, unless sooner removed by the President, who shall execute all process issuing from the said courts when exercising their jurisdiction as circuit and district courts of the United States. He shall perform the same duties, be subject to the same regulations and penalties, and be entitled to the same fees, as the marshal of the district court of the United States for the present Territory of Wisconsin; and shall, in addition, be paid the sum of two hundred dollars annually, as a compensation for extra services.

SEC. 11. *And be it further enacted,* That the governor, secretary, chief justice, and associate judges, attorney and marshal, shall be nominated, and by and with the advice and consent of the senate, appointed by the President of the United States. The Governor and secretary to be appointed as aforesaid, shall, before they act as such, respectively, take an oath or affirmation, before some judge or justice of the peace, in the existing Territory of Wisconsin, duly commissioned and qualified to administer an oath or affirmation, [or] before the chief justice, or some associate justice of the Supreme Court of the United States, to support the constitution of the United States, and for the faithful discharge of the duties of their respective offices, which said oaths when so taken, shall be certified by the person before whom the same shall have been taken, and such certificate shall be received and recorded by the said Secretary among the executive proceedings. And, afterwards, the chief justice and associate judges, and all other civil officers in said Territory, before they act as such, shall take a like oath or affirmation before the said Governor or secretary, or some judge or justice of the Territory who may be duly commissioned and qualified, which said oath or affirmation shall be certified and transmitted by the person taking the same to the Secretary, to be by him recorded as aforesaid; and, afterwards, the like oath or affirmation, shall be taken, certified, and recorded, in such manner and form as may be prescribed by law. The Governor shall receive an annual salary of fifteen hundred dollars as Governor, and one thousand dollars as superintendent of Indian affairs. The said chief justice and associate judges shall each receive an annual salary of fifteen hundred dollars. The secretary shall receive an annual salary of twelve hundred dollars. The said salaries shall be paid quarter-yearly at the Treasury of the United States. The members of the Legislative Assembly shall be entitled to receive three dollars each per day, during their attendance at the sessions thereof; and three dollars each for every twenty miles travel in going to and returning from, the said sessions, estimated according the the nearest usually travelled route. There shall be appropriated, annually, the sum of three hundred and fifty dollars, to be expended by the Governor to defray the contingent expenses of the Territory; and there shall also be appropriated, annually, a sufficient sum, to be expended by the Secretary of the Territory, and upon an estimate to be made by the Secretary of the Treasury of the United States, to defray the expenses of the Legislative Assembly, the printing of the laws, and other incidental expenses; and the Secretary of the Territory shall annually account to the Secretary of the Treasury of the United States, for the manner in which the aforesaid sum shall have been expended.

SEC. 12. *And be it further enacted,* That the inhabitants of the said Territory shall be entitled to all the rights, privileges and immunities heretofore granted and secured to the Territory of Wisconsin and to its inhabitants; and the existing laws of the Territory of Wisconsin shall be extended over said Territory, so far as the same be not incompatible with the provisions of this act, subject, nevertheless, to be altered, modified, or repealed, by the Governor and Legislative Assembly of the said Territory of Iowa; and further, the laws of the United States are hereby extended over, and shall be in force in said Territory, so far as the same, or any provisions thereof, may be applicable.

SEC. 13. *And be it further enacted,* That the Legislative Assembly of the Territory of Iowa shall hold its first session at such time and place in said Territory as the Governor thereof shall appoint and direct; and at said session, or as soon thereafter as may by them be deemed expedient, the said Governor and Legislative Assembly shall proceed to locate and establish the seat of Government for said Territory, at such place as they may deem eligible, which place, however, shall thereafter be subject to be changed by the said Governor and

Legislative Assembly. And the sum of twenty thousand dollars, out of any money in the Treasury not otherwise appropriated, is hereby granted to the said Territory of Iowa, which shall be applied by the Governor and Legislative Assembly thereof to defray the expenses of erecting public buildings at the seat of Government.

SEC. 14. *And be it further enacted,* That a delegate to the House of Representatives of the United States to serve for the term of two years, may be elected by the voters qualified to elect members of the Legislative Assembly, who shall be entitled to the same rights and privileges as have been granted to the delegates from the several Territories of the United States, to the said House of Representatives. The first election shall be held at such time and place or places, and be conducted in such manner as the Governor shall appoint and direct. The person having the greatest number of votes shall be declared by the Governor to be duly elected, and a certificate thereof shall be given to the person so elected.

SEC. 15. *And be it further enacted,* That all suits, process, and proceedings, and all indictments and informations, which shall be undetermined on the third day of July next, in the district courts of Wisconsin Territory, west of the Mississippi river, shall be transferred to be heard, tried, prosecuted and determined in the district courts hereby established, which may include the said counties.

SEC. 16. *And be it further enacted,* That all justices of the peace, constables, sheriffs, and all other executive and judicial officers, who shall be in office on the third day of July next, in that portion of the present Territory of Wisconsin which will then, by this act, become the Territory of Iowa, shall be, and are hereby authorized and required to continue to exercise and perform the duties of their respective offices, as officers of the Territory of Iowa, temporarily and until they, or others, shall be duly appointed to fill their places by the Territorial Government of Iowa, in the manner herein directed: *Provided,* That no officer shall hold or continue in office by virtue of this provision, over twelve months from the said third day of July next.

SEC. 17. *And be it further enacted,* That all causes which shall have been or may be removed from the courts held by the present Territory of Wisconsin, in the counties west of the Mississippi river, by appeal or otherwise, into the supreme court for the Territory of Wisconsin, and which shall be undetermined therein on the third day of July next, shall be certified by the clerk of the said supreme court, and transferred to the supreme court of said Territory of Iowa, there to be proceeded in to final determination, in the same manner that they might have been in the said supreme court of the Territory of Wisconsin.

SEC. 18. *And be it further enacted,* That the sum of five thousand dollars be, and the same is hereby appropriated, out of any money in the treasury not otherwise appropriated, to be expended by, and under the direction of, the Governor of said Territory of Iowa, in the purchase of a library, to be kept at the seat of Government, for the accommodation of the Governor, Legislative Assembly, judges, secretary, marshal, and attorney of said Territory, and such other persons as the Governor and Legislative Assembly shall direct.

SEC. 19. *And be it further enacted,* That from and after the day named in this act for the organization of the Territory of Iowa, the term of the members of the Council and House of Representatives of the Territory of Wisconsin shall be deemed to have expired, and an entirely new organization of the Council and House of Representatives of the Territory of Wisconsin as constitued by this act shall take place as follows: As soon as practicable after the passage of this act, the Governor of the Territory of Wisconsin shall apportion the thirteen members of the Council and twenty-six members of the House of Representatives among the several counties or districts comprised within said Territory, according to their population, as nearly as may be (Indians excepted). The first election shall be held at such time as the Governor shall appoint and direct; and shall be conducted, and returns thereof made, in all respects, according to the provisions of the laws of said Territory, and the Governor shall declare the persons having the greatest number of votes to be elected, and shall order a new election when there is a tie between two or more persons voted for, to supply the vacancy made by such tie. The persons thus elected shall meet at Madison, the seat of Government, on such day as he shall appoint, but thereafter the apportioning of the representation in the several counties to the Council and House of Representatives according to population, the day of their election, and the day for the commencement of the session of the Legislative Assembly, shall be prescribed by law.

SEC. 20. *And be it further enacted,* That temporarily, and until otherwise provided by law of the Legislative Assembly, the Governor of the Territory of Iowa may define the judicial districts of said Territory, and assign the judges who may be appointed for said Territory to the several districts, and also appoint the times for holding courts in the several counties in each district, by proclamation to be issued by him; but the Legislative Assembly, at their first, or any subsequent session, may organize, alter, or modify such judicial districts, and assign the judges and alter the times of holding the courts or any of them.

Approved, June 12, 1838.

AN ACT TO DEFINE AND ESTABLISH THE EASTERN BOUNDARY LINE OF THE TERRITORY OF IOWA

MARCH 3, 1839

Be it enacted by the Senate and House of Representatives of the United States of America in Congress assembled, That the middle or centre of the main channel of the river Mississippi shall be deemed, and is hereby declared, to be the eastern boundary line of the Territory of Iowa, so far or to such extent as the said Territory is bounded eastwardly by or upon said river: *Provided, however,* That the said Territory of Iowa shall have concurrent jurisdiction upon the said Mississippi river with any other conterminous State or Territory so far or to such extent as the said river shall form a common boundary between the aforesaid Territory of Iowa and any other such conterminous State or Territory.

Approved, March 3, 1839.

TREATY BETWEEN THE UNITED STATES OF AMERICA AND GREAT BRITAIN AUGUST 9, 1842

A Treaty to settle and define the Boundaries between the Territories of the United States and the possessions of Her Britannic Majesty, in North America: For the final Suppression of the African Slave Trade: and For the giving up of Criminals fugitive from justice, in certain cases.

Whereas certain portions of the line of boundary between the United States of America and the British Dominions in North America, described in the second article of the Treaty of Peace of 1783, have not yet been ascertained and determined, notwithstanding the repeated attempts which have been heretofore made for that purpose, and whereas it is now thought to be for the interest of both Parties, that, avoiding further discussion of their respective rights, arising in this respect under the said Treaty, they should agree on a conventional line in said portions of the said boundary, such as may be convenient to both Parties, with such equivalents and compensations, as are deemed just and reasonable: — And whereas by the Treaty concluded at Ghent, on the 24th day of December, 1814, between the United States and His Britannic Majesty, an article was agreed to and inserted of the following tenor, viz! "Art. 10. — whereas the Traffic in Slaves is irreconcilable with the principles of humanity and justice: And whereas both His Majesty and the United States are desirous of continuing their efforts to promote its entire abolition, it is hereby agreed that both the contracting Parties shall use their best endeavors to accomplish so desirable an object": and whereas, notwithstanding the laws which have at various times been passed by the two Governments, and the efforts made to suppress it, that criminal traffic is still prosecuted and carried on: And whereas the United States of America and Her Majesty the Queen of the United Kingdom of Great Britain and Ireland, are determined that, so far as may be in their power, it shall be effectually abolished: — And whereas it is found expedient for the better administration of justice and the prevention of crime within the Territories and jurisdiction of the two Parties, respectively, that persons committing the crimes hereinafter enumerated, and being fugitives from justice, should, under certain circumstances, be reciprocally delivered up: The

United States of America and Her Britannic Majesty, having resolved to treat on these several subjects, have for that purpose appointed their respective Plenipotentiaries to negotiate and conclude a Treaty, that is to say: the President of the United States has, on his part, furnished with full powers, Daniel Webster, Secretary of State of the United States; and Her Majesty the Queen of the United Kingdom of Great Britain and Ireland, has, on her part, appointed the Right honorable Alexander Lord Ashburton, a peer of the said United Kingdom, a member of Her Majesty's most honorable Privy Council, and Her Majesty's Minister Plenipotentiary on a Special Mission to the United States; who, after a reciprocal communication of their respective full powers, have agreed to and signed the following articles:

ARTICLE I.

It is hereby agreed and declared that the line of boundary shall be as follows: Beginning at the monument at the source of the river S⁣t Croix, as designated and agreed to by the Commissioners under the fifth article of the Treaty of 1794, between the Governments of the United States and Great Britain; thence, north, following the exploring line run and marked by the Surveyors of the two Governments in the years 1817 and 1818, under the fifth article of the Treaty of Ghent, to its intersection with the river S⁣t John, and to the middle of the channel thereof; thence, up the middle of the main channel of the said river S⁣t John, to the mouth of the river S⁣t Francis; thence up the middle of the channel of the said river S⁣t Francis, and of the lakes through which it flows, to the outlet of the Lake Pohenagamook; thence, southeasterly, in a straight line to a point on the northwest branch of the river S⁣t John, which point shall be ten miles distant from the mainbranch of the S⁣t John, in a straight line, and in the nearest direction; but if the said point shall be found to be less than seven miles from the nearest point of the summit or crest of the highlands that divide those rivers which empty themselves into the river Saint Lawrence from those which fall into the river Saint John, then the said point shall be made to recede down the said northwest branch of the river S⁣t John, to a point seven miles in a straight line from the said summit or crest; thence, in a straight line, in a course about south eight degrees west, to the point where the parallel of latitude of 46°25′ north, intersects the southwest branch of the S⁣t John's; thence, southerly, by the said branch, to the source thereof in the highlands at the Metjarmette Portage; thence, down along the said highlands which divide the waters which empty themselves into the river Saint Lawrence from those which fall into the Atlantic Ocean, to the head of Hall's Stream; thence, down the middle of said Stream, till the line thus run intersects the old line of boundary surveyed and marked by Valentine and Collins previously to the year 1774, as the 45ᵗʰ degree of north latitude, and which has been known and understood to be the line of actual division between the States of New York and Vermont on one side, and the British Province of Canada on the other; and, from said point of intersection, west along the said dividing line as heretofore known and understood, to the Iroquois or S⁣t Lawrence river.

ARTICLE II.

It is moreover agreed, that from the place where the joint Commissioners terminated their labors under the sixth article of the Treaty of Ghent, to wit: at a point in the Neebish Channel, near Muddy Lake, the line shall run into and along the ship channel between Saint Joseph and S! Tammany Islands, to the division of the channel at or near the head of S! Joseph's Island; thence, turning eastwardly and northwardly, around the lower end of S! George's or Sugar Island, and following the middle of the channel which divides S! George's from S! Joseph's Island; thence, up the east Neebish channel, nearest to S! George's Island, through the middle of Lake George; — thence, west of Jonas' Island, into S! Mary's river, to a point in the middle of that river, about one mile above S! George's or Sugar Island, so as to appropriate and assign the said Island to the United States; thence, adopting the line traced on the maps by the Commissioners, thro' the river S! Mary and Lake Superior, to a point north of Ile Royale in said Lake, one hundred yards to the north and east of Ile Chapeau, which last mentioned Island lies near the northeastern point of Ile Royale, where the line marked by the Commissioners terminates; and from the last mentioned point, southwesterly, through the middle of the Sound between Ile Royale and the northwestern mainland, to the mouth of Pigeon river, and up the said river to, and through, the north and south Fowl Lakes, to the Lakes of the height of land between Lake Superior and the Lake of the Woods; thence, along the water-communication to Lake Saisaginaga, and through that Lake; thence, to and through Cypress Lake, Lac du Bois Blanc, Lac la Croix, Little Vermilion Lake, and Lake Namecan, and through the several smaller lakes, straights, or streams, connecting the lakes here mentioned, to that point in Lac la Pluie, or Rainy Lake, at the Chaudière Falls, from which the Commissioners traced the line to the most northwestern point of the Lake of the Woods; — thence, along the said line to the said most northwestern point, being in latitude 49°23'55" north, and in longitude 95°14'38" west from the Observatory at Greenwich; thence, according to existing treaties, due south to its intersection with the 49th parallel of north latitude, and along that parallel to the Rocky Mountains. It being understood that all the water-communications, and all the usual portages along the line from Lake Superior to the Lake of the Woods; and also Grand Portage, from the shore of Lake Superior to the Pigeon river, as now actually used, shall be free and open to the use of the citizens and subjects of both countries.

ARTICLE III.

In order to promote the interest and encourage the industry of all the inhabitants of the countries watered by the river S! John and its tributaries, whether living within the State of Maine or the Province of New Brunswick, it is agreed that, where, by the provisions of the present treaty, the river S! John is declared to be the line of boundary, the navigation of the said river shall be free and open to both Parties, and shall in no way be obstructed by either: That all the produce of the forest, in logs, lumber, timber, boards, staves, or shingles, or of agriculture not being manufactured, grown on any of those parts of the State of Maine watered by the river S͏ͭ John, or by its tributaries, of which fact reasonable evidence shall, if required, be produced, shall have free access into and through the said river and its said tributaries, having their source within the State of Maine, to and from the seaport at the mouth of the said river S͏ͭ John's, and to and round the Falls of the said river, either by boats, rafts, or other conveyance: That when within the Province of New Brunswick, the said produce shall be dealt with as if it were the produce of the said province: That, in like manner, the inhabitants of the Territory of the Upper S͏ͭ John determined by this Treaty to belong to her Britannic Majesty, shall have free access to and through the river for their produce, in those parts where the said river runs wholly through the State of Maine: provided always, that this agreement shall give no right to either party to interfere with any regulations not inconsistent with the terms of this treaty which the Governments, respectively, of Maine or of New Brunswick, may make respecting the navigation of the said river, where both banks thereof shall belong to the same Party.

ARTICLE IV.

All grants of land heretofore made by either Party, within the limits of the territory which by this Treaty falls within the dominions of the other Party, shall be held valid, ratified, and confirmed to the persons in possession under such grants, to the same extent as if such territory had by this Treaty fallen within the dominions of the Party by whom such grants were made: And all equitable possessory claims, arising from a possession and improvement of any lot or parcel of land by the person actually in possession, or by those under whom such person claims, for more than six years before the date of this Treaty, shall, in like manner, be deemed valid, and be confirmed and quieted by a release to the person entitled thereto, of the title to such a lot or parcel of land, so described as best to include the improvements made thereon; and in all other respects the two contracting Parties agree to deal upon the most liberal principles of equity with the settlers actually dwelling upon the Territory falling to them, respectively, which has heretofore been in dispute between them.

ARTICLE V.

Whereas, in the course of the controversy respecting the disputed Territory on the northeastern boundary, some moneys have been received by the authorities of Her Britannic Majesty's Province of New Brunswick, with the intention of preventing depredations on the forests of the said Territory, which moneys were to be carried to a fund called the "Disputed Territory Fund", the proceeds whereof, it was agreed, should be hereafter paid over to the Parties interested, in the proportions to be determined by a final settlement of boundaries: It is hereby agreed, that a correct account of all receipts and payments on the said fund, shall be delivered to the Government of the United States, within six months after the ratification of this Treaty; and the proportion of the amount due thereon to the States of Maine and Massachusetts, and any bonds or securities appertaining thereto, shall be paid and delivered over to the Government of the United States; and the Government of the United States agrees to receive for the use of, and pay over to the States of Maine and Massachusetts, their respective portions of said Fund: And further to pay and satisfy said States, respectively, for all claims for expenses incurred by them in protecting the said heretofore disputed Territory, and making a survey thereof, in 1838; the Government of the United States agreeing with the States of Maine and Massachusetts to pay them the further sum of three hundred thousand dollars, in equal moieties, on account of their assent to the line of boundary described in this Treaty, and in consideration of the conditions and equivalents received therefor, from the Government of Her Britannic Majesty.

ARTICLE VI.

It is furthermore understood and agreed, that for the purpose of running and tracing those parts of the line between the source of the S! Croix and the S! Lawrence river, which will require to be run and ascertained, and for marking the residue of said line by proper monuments on the land, two Commissioners shall be appointed, one by the President of the United States, by and with the advice and consent of the Senate thereof, and one by Her Britannic Majesty: and the said commissioners shall meet at Bangor, in the State of Maine, on the first day of May next, or as soon thereafter as may be, and shall proceed to mark the line above described, from the source of the S! Croix to the river S! John; and shall trace on proper maps the dividing line along said river, and along the river S! Francis, to the outlet of the Lake Pohenagamook; and from the outlet of the said Lake, they shall ascertain, fix, and mark by proper and durable monuments on the land, the line described in the first article of this Treaty; and the said Commissioners shall make to each of their respective Governments a joint report or declaration, under their hands and seals, designating such line of boundary, and shall accompany such report or declaration with maps certified by them to be true maps of the new boundary.

ARTICLE VII.

It is further agreed, that the channels in the river S! Lawrence, on both sides of the Long Sault Islands and of Barnhart Island; the channels in the river Detroit, on both sides of the Island Bois Blanc, and between that Island and both the American and Canadian shores; and all the several channels and passages between the various Islands lying near the junction of the river S! Clair with the lake of that name, shall be equally free and open to the ships, vessels, and boats of both Parties.

ARTICLE VIII.

The Parties mutually stipulate that each shall prepare, equip, and maintain in service, on the coast of Africa, a sufficient and adequate squadron, or naval force of vessels, of suitable numbers and descriptions, to carry in all not less than eighty guns, to enforce, separately and respectively, the laws rights and obligations of each of the two countries, for the suppression of the Slave Trade, and said squadrons to be independent of each other, but the two Governments stipulating, nevertheless, to give such orders to the officers commanding their respective forces, as shall enable them most effectually to act in concert and coöperation, upon mutual consultation, as exigencies may arise, for the attainment of the true object of this article; copies of all such orders to be communicated by each Government to the other respectively.

ARTICLE IX.

Whereas, notwithstanding all efforts which may be made on the coast of Africa for Suppressing the Slave Trade, the facilities for carrying on that traffic and avoiding the vigilance of cruisers by the fraudulent use of flags, and other means, are so great, and the temptations for pursuing it, while a market can be found for Slaves, so strong, as that the desired result may be long delayed, unless all markets be shut against the purchase of African negroes, the Parties to this Treaty agree that they will unite in all becoming representations and remonstrances, with any and all Powers within whose dominions such markets are allowed to exist; and that they will urge upon all such Powers the propriety and duty of closing such markets effectually at once and forever.

ARTICLE X.

It is agreed that the United States and Her Britannic Majesty shall, upon mutual requisitions by them, or their Ministers, Officers, or authorities, respectively made, deliver up to justice, all persons who, being charged with the crime of murder, or assault with intent to commit murder, or Piracy, or arson, or robbery, or Forgery, or the utterance of forged paper, committed within the jurisdiction of either, shall seek an asylum, or shall be found, within the territories of the other: Provided, that this shall only be done upon such evidence of criminality as, according to the laws of the place where the fugitive or person so charged, shall be found, would justify his apprehension and commitment for trial, if the crime or offence had there been committed: And the respective Judges and other Magistrates of the two Governments, shall have power, jurisdiction, and authority, upon complaint made under oath, to issue a warrant for the apprehension of the fugitive or person so charged, that he may be brought before such Judges or other Magistrates, respectively, to the end that the evidence of criminality may be heard and considered; and if, on such hearing, the evidence be deemed sufficient to sustain the charge it shall be the duty of the examining Judge or Magistrate, to certify the same to the proper

Executive Authority, that a warrant may issue for the surrender of such fugitive. The expense of such apprehension and delivery shall be borne and defrayed by the Party who makes the requisition, and receives the fugitive.

ARTICLE XI.

The eighth article of this Treaty shall be in force for five years from the date of the exchange of the ratifications, and afterwards until one or the other Party shall signify a wish to terminate it. The tenth article shall continue in force until one or the other of the Parties shall signify its wish to terminate it, and no longer.

ARTICLE XII.

The present Treaty shall be duly ratified, and the mutual exchange of ratifications shall take place in London, within six months from the date hereof, or earlier if possible.

In Faith whereof, we, the respective Plenipotentiaries, have signed this Treaty, and have hereunto affixed our Seals.

Done in duplicate, at Washington, the ninth day of August, Anno Domini one thousand eight hundred and forty-two.

Dan Webster   Ashburton
(Seal)   (Seal)

AN ACT FOR THE ADMISSION OF THE STATES OF IOWA AND FLORIDA INTO THE UNION MARCH 3, 1845

Whereas, the people of the Territory of Iowa did, on the seventh day of October, eighteen hundred and forty-four, by a convention of delegates called and assembled for that purpose, form for themselves a constitution and State government; and whereas, the people of the Territory of Florida did, in like manner, by their delegates, on the eleventh day of January, eighteen hundred and thirty-nine, form for themselves a constitution and State government, both of which said constitutions are republican; and said conventions having asked the admission of their respective Territories into the Union as States, on equal footing with the original States:

Be it enacted by the Senate and House of Representatives of the United States of America in Congress assembled, That the States of Iowa and Florida be, and the same are hereby, declared to be States of the United States of America, and are hereby admitted into the Union on equal footing with the original States, in all respects whatsoever.

SEC. 2. *And be it further enacted*, That the following shall be the boundaries of the said State of Iowa, to wit: Beginning at the mouth of the Des Moines river, at the middle of the Mississippi, thence by the middle of the channel of that river to a parallel of latitude passing through the mouth of the Mankato, or Blue-Earth river, thence west along the said parallel of latitude to a point where it is intersected by a meridian line, seventeen degrees and thirty minutes west of the meridian of Washington city, thence due south to the northern boundary line of the State of Missouri, thence eastwardly following that boundary to the point at which the same intersects the Des Moines river, thence by the middle of the channel of that river to the place of beginning.

SEC. 3. *And be it further enacted*, That the said State of Iowa shall have concurrent jurisdiction on the river Mississippi, and every other river bordering on the said State of Iowa, so far as the said rivers shall form a common boundary to said State, and any other State or States now or hereafter to be formed or bounded by the same: Such rivers to be common to both: And that the said river Mississippi, and the navigable waters leading into the same, shall be common highways, and forever free as well to the inhabitants of said State, as to all other citizens of the United States, without any tax, duty, impost, or toll therefor, imposed by the said State of Iowa.

SEC. 4. *And be it further enacted*, That it is made and declared to be a fundamental condition of the admission of said State of Iowa into the Union, that so much of this act as relates to the said State of Iowa shall be assented to by a majority of the qualified electors at their township elections, in the manner and at the time prescribed in the sixth section of the thirteenth article of the constitution adopted at Iowa city the first day of November, anno Domini eighteen hundred and forty-four, or by the legislature of said State. And as soon as such assent shall be given, the President of the United States shall announce the same by proclamation; and therefrom and without further proceedings on the part of Congress the admission of the said State of Iowa into the Union, on an equal footing in all respects whatever with the original States, shall be considered as complete.

SEC. 5. *And be it further enacted*, That said State of Florida shall embrace the territories of East and West Florida, which by the treaty of amity, settlement and limits between the United States and Spain, on the twenty-second day of February, eighteen hundred and nineteen, were ceded to the United States.

SEC. 6. *And be it further enacted*, That until the next census and apportionment shall be made, each of said States of Iowa and Florida shall be entitled to one representative in the House of Representatives of the United States.

SEC. 7. *And be it further enacted*, That said States of Iowa and Florida are admitted into the Union on the express condition that they shall never interfere with the primary disposal of the public lands lying within them, nor levy any tax on the same whilst remaining the property of the United States: *Provided*, That the ordinance of the convention that formed the constitution of Iowa, and which is appended to the said constitution, shall not be deemed or taken to have any effect or validity, or to be recognised as in any manner obligatory upon the Government of the United States.

Approved, March 3, 1845.

TREATY BETWEEN THE UNITED STATES OF AMERICA AND GREAT BRITAIN
JUNE 15, 1846

The United States of America and Her Majesty the Queen of the United Kingdom of Great Britain and Ireland, deeming it to be desirable for the future welfare of both countries that the state of doubt and uncertainty which has hitherto prevailed respecting the sovereignty and government of the Territory on the northwest coast of America lying westward of the Rocky or Stony Mountains, should be finally terminated by an amicable compromise of the rights mutually asserted by the two Parties over the said Territory, have respectively named Plenipotentiaries to treat and agree concerning the terms of such settlement, that is to say: the President of the United States of America, has, on his part, furnished with Full Powers, James Buchanan, Secretary of State of the United States, and Her Majesty the Queen of the United Kingdom of Great Britain and Ireland, has, on her part, appointed the Right Honorable Richard Pakenham, a Member of Her Majesty's most honorable Privy Council, and Her Majesty's Envoy Extraordinary and Minister Plenipotentiary to the United States; who, after having communicated to each other their respective full Powers, found in good and due form, have agreed upon and concluded the following articles:

ARTICLE I.

From the point on the forty-ninth parallel of north latitude where the boundary laid down in existing treaties and conventions between the United States and Great Britain terminates, the line of boundary between the territories of the United States and those of Her Britannic Majesty shall be continued westward along the said forty-ninth parallel of north latitude to the middle of the channel which separates the continent from Vancouver's Island; and thence southerly through the middle of the said channel, and of Fuca's Straits to the Pacific Ocean; provided, however, that the navigation of the whole of the said channel and Straits south of the forty-ninth parallel of north latitude remain free and open to both Parties.

ARTICLE II.

From the point at which the forty-ninth parallel of north latitude shall be found to intersect the great northern branch of the Columbia River, the navigation of the said branch shall be free and open to the Hudson's Bay Company and to all British subjects trading with the same, to the point where the said branch meets the main stream of the Columbia, and thence down the said main stream to the Ocean, with free access into and through the said River or Rivers, it being understood that all the usual portages along the line thus described shall in like manner be free and open. In navigating the said River or Rivers, British subjects with their goods and produce, shall be treated on the same footing as citizens of the United States; it being however always understood that nothing in this article shall be construed as preventing, or intended to prevent, the Government of the United States from making any regulations respecting the navigation of the said River or Rivers, not inconsistent with the present treaty.

ARTICLE III.

In the future appropriation of the territory, south of the forty-ninth parallel of north latitude, as provided in the first article of this Treaty, the possessory rights of the Hudson's Bay Company and of all British subjects who may be already in the occupation of land or other property, lawfully acquired within the said Territory, shall be respected.

ARTICLE IV.

The farms, lands, and other property of every description belonging to the Puget's Sound Agricultural Company on the north side of the Columbia River, shall be confirmed to the said Company. In case however the situation of those farms and lands should be considered by the United States to be of public and political importance, and the United States' Government should signify a desire to obtain possession of the whole, or of any part thereof, the property so required shall be transferred to the said Government, at a proper valuation, to be agreed upon between the Parties.

ARTICLE V.

The present Treaty shall be ratified by the President of the United States, by and with the advice and consent of the Senate thereof, and by Her Britannic Majesty; and the ratifications shall be exchanged at London, at the expiration of six months from the date hereof, or sooner if possible.

In witness whereof, the respective Plenipotentiaries have signed the same, and have affixed thereto the seals of their arms.

Done at Washington the fifteenth day of June, in the year of our Lord one
thousand eight hundred and forty-six.

               (Seal)   James Buchanan
               (Seal)   Richard Pakenham.

AN ACT TO DEFINE THE BOUNDARIES OF THE STATE OF IOWA, AND TO REPEAL SO MUCH OF THE ACT OF THE THIRD OF MARCH, ONE THOUSAND EIGHT HUNDRED AND FORTY-FIVE AS RELATES TO THE BOUNDARIES OF IOWA

AUGUST 4, 1846

*Be it enacted by the Senate and House of Representatives of the United
States of America in Congress assembled,* That the following shall be, and they
are hereby, declared to be the boundaries of the State of Iowa, in lieu of those
prescribed by the second section of the act of the third of March, eighteen hundred and forty-five, entitled "An Act for the Admission of the States of Iowa
and Florida into the Union," viz. Beginning in the middle of the main channel
of the Mississippi River, at a point due east of the middle of the mouth of the
main channel of the Des Moines River; thence up the middle of the main channel of the said Des Moines River, to a point on said river where the northern
boundary line of the State of Missouri, as established by the constitution of
that State, adopted June twelfth, eighteen hundred and twenty, crosses the said
middle of the main channel of the said Des Moines River; thence, westwardly,
along the said northern boundary line of the State of Missouri, as established
at the time aforesaid, until an extension of said line intersect the middle of the
main channel of the Missouri River; thence, up the middle of the main channel
of the said Missouri River, to a point opposite the middle of the main channel
of the Big Sioux River, according to Nicollet's map; thence, up the main channel of the said Big Sioux River, according to said map, until it is intersected by
the parallel of forty-three degrees and thirty minutes north latitude; thence
east, along said parallel of forty-three degrees and thirty minutes, until said
parallel intersect the middle of the main channel of the Mississippi River;
thence, down the middle of the main channel of said Misssissippi River, to the
place of beginning.

    SEC. 2. *And be it further enacted,* That the question which has heretofore
been the subject-matter of controversy and dispute between the State of Missouri and the Territory of Iowa, respecting the precise location of the northern
boundary line of the State of Missouri, shall be, and the same is hereby,

referred to the Supreme Court of the United States for adjudication and settlement, in accordance with the act of the Legislature of Missouri, approved March twenty-five, eighteen hundred and forty-five, and the memorial of the Council and House of Representatives of the Territory of the Iowa, approved January seventeenth, eighteen hundred and forty-six, by which both parties have agreed to "the commencement and speedy determination of such suit as may be necessary to procure a final decision by the Supreme Court of the United States upon the true location of the northern boundary of that State;" and the said Supreme Court is hereby invested with all the power and authority necessary to the performance of the duty imposed by this section.

SEC. 3. *And be it further enacted,* That, until the next census and apportionment shall be made, the State of Iowa shall be entitled to two representatives in the House of Representatives of the United States.

SEC. 4. *And be it further enacted,* That so much of the act of the third of March, eighteen hundred and forty-five, entitled "An Act for the Admission of the States of Iowa and Florida into the Union," relating to the said State of Iowa, as is inconsistent with the provisions of this act, be and the same is hereby repealed.

Approved, August 4, 1846.

AN ACT TO ENABLE THE PEOPLE OF WISCONSIN TERRITORY TO FORM A CONSTITUTION AND STATE GOVERNMENT, AND FOR THE ADMISSION OF SUCH STATE INTO THE UNION
AUGUST 6, 1846

Be it enacted by the Senate and House of Representatives of the United States of America in Congress assembled, That the people of the Territory of Wisconsin be, and they are hereby, authorized to form a constitution and State government, for the purpose of being admitted into the Union on an equal footing with the original States in all respects whatsoever, by the name of the State of Wisconsin, with the following boundaries, to wit: Beginning at the northeast corner of the State of Illinois — that is to say, at a point in the centre of Lake Michigan where the line of forty-two degrees and thirty minutes of north latitude crosses the same; thence running with the boundary line of the State of Michigan, through Lake Michigan, Green Bay, to the mouth of the Menomonie River; thence up the channel of said river to the Brulé River; thence up said last mentioned river to Lake Brulé; thence along the southern shore of Lake Brulé in a direct line to the centre of the channel between Middle and South Islands, in the Lake of the Desert; thence in a direct line to the head-waters of the Montreal River, as marked upon the survey made by Captain Cramm; thence down the main channel of the Montreal River to the middle of Lake Superior; thence through the centre of Lake Superior to the mouth of the St. Louis River; thence up the main channel of said river to the first rapids in the same, above the Indian village, according to Nicollet's map; thence due south to the main branch of the River St. Croix; thence down the main channel of said river to the Mississippi; thence down the centre of the main channel of that river to the north-west corner of the State of Illinois; thence due east with the northern boundary of the State of Illinois to the place of beginning, as established by "An Act to enable the People of the Illinois Territory to form a Constitution and State Government, and for the Admission of such State into the Union on an equal Footing with the original States," approved April eighteen, eighteen hundred and eighteen.

SEC. 2. *And be it further enacted*, That, to prevent all disputes in reference to the jurisdiction of islands in the said Brulé and Menomonie Rivers, the line be so run as to include within the jurisdiction of Michigan all the islands in the Brulé and Menomonie Rivers, (to the extent in which said rivers are adopted as a boundary,) down to, and inclusive of, the Quinnesec Falls of the Menomonie; and from thence the line shall be so run as to include within the jurisdiction of Wisconsin all the islands in the Menomonie River, from the falls aforesaid down to the junction of said river with Green Bay: *Provided*, That the adjustment of boundary, as fixed in this act, between Wisconsin and Michigan shall not be binding on Congress, unless the same shall be ratified by the State of Michigan on or before the first day of June, one thousand eight hundred and forty-eight.

SEC. 3. *And be it further enacted*, That the said State of Wisconsin shall have concurrent jurisdiction on the Mississippi, and all other rivers and waters bordering on the said State of Wisconsin, so far as the same shall form a common boundary to said State and any other State or States now or hereafter to be formed or bounded by the same; and said river and waters, and the navigable waters leading into the same, shall be common highways, and forever free, as well to the inhabitants of said State as to all other citizens of the United States, without any tax, duty, impost, or toll, therefor.

SEC. 4. *And be it further enacted*, That from and after the admission of the State of Wisconsin into the Union, in pursuance of this act, the laws of the United States which are not locally inapplicable shall have the same force and effect within the State of Wisconsin as elsewhere within the United States; and said State shall constitute one district, and be called the District of Wisconsin; and a district court shall be held therein, to consist of one judge, who shall reside in the said district and be called a district judge. He shall hold, at the seat of government of said State, two sessions of said court annually, on the first Mondays in January and July; and he shall, in all things, have and exercise the same jurisdiction and powers which were by law given to the judge of the Kentucky District, under an act entitled "An Act to establish the Judicial Courts of the United States." He shall appoint a clerk for said district, who shall reside and keep the records of said court at the place of holding the same; and shall receive for the services performed by him the same fees to which the clerk of the

Kentucky District is by law entitled for similar services. There shall be allowed to the judge of said district court the annual compensation of fifteen hundred dollars, to commence from the date of his appointment, to be paid quarterly at the treasury of the United States.

SEC. 5. *And be it further enacted*, That there shall be appointed in said district a person learned in the law to act as attorney of the United States, who, in addition to the stated fees, shall be paid the sum of two hundred dollars annually by the United States, as a full compensation for all extra services; the said payment to be made quarterly at the treasury of the United States. And there shall also be appointed a marshal for said district, who shall perform the same duties, be subject to the same regulations and penalties, and be entitled to the same fees, as are prescribed and allowed to marshals in other districts; and shall, moreover, be allowed the sum of two hundred dollars annually, as a compensation for all extra services.

SEC. 6. *And be it further enacted*, That, until another census shall be taken and apportionment made, the State of Wisconsin shall be entitled to two representatives in the Congress of the United States.

SEC. 7. *And be it further enacted*, That the following propositions are hereby submitted to the convention which shall assemble for the purpose of forming a constitution for the State of Wisconsin, for acceptance or rejection; and if accepted by said convention, and ratified by an article in said constitution, they shall be obligatory on the United States:

First. That section numbered sixteen, in every township of the public lands in said State, and, where such section has been sold or otherwise disposed of, other lands equivalent thereto, and as contiguous as may be, shall be granted to said State for the use of schools.

Second. That the seventy-two sections or two entire townships of land set apart and reserved for the use and support of a university by an act of Congress, approved on the twelfth day of June, eighteen hundred and thirty-eight, entitled "An Act concerning a Seminary of Learning in the Territory of Wisconsin," are hereby granted and conveyed to the State, to be appropriated solely to the use and support of such university, in such manner as the Legislature may prescribe.

Third. That ten entire sections of land, to be selected and located under the direction of the Legislature, in legal divisions of not less than one quarter section, from any of the unappropriated lands belonging to the United States within the said State, are hereby granted to the said State, for the purpose of completing the public buildings of the said State, or for the erection of others at the seat of government, under the direction of the Legislature thereof.

Fourth. That all salt springs within said State, not exceeding twelve in number, with six sections of land adjoining, or as contiguous as may be to each, shall be granted to the State for its use; the same to be selected by the Legislature thereof, within one year after the admission of said State; and when so selected, to be used or disposed of on such terms, conditions, and regulations, as the Legislature shall direct: *Provided,* That no salt spring or land the right whereof is now vested in any individual or individuals, or which may hereafter be confirmed or adjudged to any individual or individuals, shall, by this section, be granted to said State.

Fifth. That five per cent. of the net proceeds of sales of all public lands lying within the said State, which have been or shall be sold by Congress, from and after the admission of said State into the Union, after deducting all the expenses incident to the same, shall be paid to the said State, for the purpose of making public roads and canals in the same, as the Legislature shall direct: *Provided,* That the foregoing propositions herein offered are on the condition that the said convention which shall form the constitution of said State shall provide, by a clause in said constitution, or an ordinance, irrevocable without the consent of the United States, that said State shall never interfere with the primary disposal of the soil within the same by the United States, nor with any regulations Congress may find necessary for securing the title in such soil to bona fide purchasers thereof; and that no tax shall be imposed on lands the property of the United States; and that in no case shall non-resident proprietors be taxed higher than residents.

Approved, August 6, 1846.

TREATY BETWEEN THE UNITED STATES
OF AMERICA AND THE MEXICAN REPUBLIC
FEBRUARY 2, 1848

In the name of Almighty God:

The United States of America, and the United Mexican States, animated by a sincere desire to put an end to the calamities of the war which unhappily exists between the two Republics, and to establish upon a solid basis relations of peace and friendship, which shall confer reciprocal benefits upon the citizens of both, and assure the concord, harmony and mutual confidence, wherein the two peoples should live, as good neighbours, have for that purpose appointed their respective Plenipotentiaries: that is to say, the President of the United States has appointed Nicholas P. Trist, a citizen of the United States, and the President of the Mexican Republic has appointed Don Luis Gonzaga Cuevas, Don Bernardo Couto, and Don Miguel Atristain, citizens of the said Republic; who, after a reciprocal communication of their respective full powers, have, under the protection of Almighty God, the author of Peace, arranged, agreed upon, and signed the following

Treaty of Peace, Friendship, Limits and Settlement between the United States of America and the Mexican Republic.

ARTICLE I.

There shall be firm and univeral peace between the United States of America and the Mexican Republic, and between their respective countries, territories, cities, towns and people, without exception of places or persons.

ARTICLE II.

Immediately upon the signature of this Treaty, a convention shall be entered into between a Commissioner or Commissioners appointed by the General in Chief of the forces of the United States, and such as may be appointed by the Mexican Government, to the end that a provisional suspension of hostilities shall take place, and that, in the places occupied by the said forces, constitutional order may be reestablished, as regards the political, administrative, and judicial branches, so far as this shall be permitted by the circumstances of military occupation.

ARTICLE III.

Immediately upon the ratification of the present treaty by the Government of the United States, orders shall be transmitted to the Commanders of their land and naval forces, requiring the latter, (provided this treaty shall then have been ratified by the Government of the Mexican Republic and the ratifications exchanged) immediately to desist from blockading any Mexican ports; and requiring the former (under the same condition) to commence, at the earliest moment practicable, withdrawing all troops of the United States then in the interior of the Mexican Republic, to points, that shall be selected by common agreement, at a distance from the sea-ports, not exceeding thirty leagues; and such evacuation of the interior of the Republic shall be completed with the least possible delay; the Mexican Government hereby binding itself to afford every facility in it's power for rendering the same convenient to the troops, on their march and in their new positions, and for promoting a good understanding between them and the inhabitants. In like manner, orders shall be despatched to the persons in charge of the Custom Houses at all ports occupied by the forces of the United States, requiring them (under the same condition) immediately to deliver possession of the same to the persons authorized by the Mexican Government to receive it, together with all bonds and evidences of debt for duties on importations and on exportations, not yet fallen due. Moreover, a faithful and exact account shall be made out, showing the entire amount of all duties on imports and on exports, collected at such Custom Houses, or elsewhere in Mexico, by authority of the United States, from and after the day of ratification of this treaty by the Government of the Mexican Republic; and also an account of the cost of collection; and such entire amount, deducting only the cost of collection, shall be delivered to the Mexican Government, at the City of Mexico, within three months after the exchange of ratifications.

The evacuation of the Capital of the Mexican Republic by the troops of the United States, in virtue of the above stipulation, shall be completed in one month after the orders there stipulated for shall have been received by the commander of said troops, or sooner if possible.

ARTICLE IV.

Immediately after the exchange of ratifications of the present treaty, all castles, forts, territories, places and possessions, which have been taken or occupied by the forces of the United States during the present war, within the limits of the Mexican Republic, as about to be established by the following Article, shall be definitively restored to the said Republic, together with all the artillery, arms, apparatus of war, munitions and other public property, which were in the said castles and forts when captured, and which shall remain there at the time when this treaty shall be duly ratified by the Government of the Mexican Republic. To this end, immediately upon the signature of this treaty, orders shall be despatched to the American officers commanding such castles and forts, securing against the removal or destruction of any such artillery, arms, apparatus of war, munitions or other public property. The City of Mexico, within the inner line of intrenchments surrounding the said City, is comprehended in the above stipulations, as regards the restoration of artillery, apparatus of war, &c.

The final evacuation of the territory of the Mexican Republic, by the forces of the United States, shall be completed in three months from the said exchange of ratifications, or sooner, if possible: the Mexican Government hereby engaging, as in the foregoing Article, to use all means in it's power for facilitating such evacuation, and rendering it convenient to the troops, and for promoting a good understanding between them and the inhabitants.

If, however, the ratification of this treaty by both parties should not take place in time to allow the embarcation of the troops of the United States to be completed before the commencement of the sickly season, at the Mexican Ports on the Gulf of Mexico; in such case a friendly arrangement shall be entered into between the General in Chief of the said troops and the Mexican Government, whereby healthy and otherwise suitable places at a distance from the ports not exceeding thirty leagues shall be designated for the residence of such troops as may not yet have embarked, until the return of the healthy season. And the space of time here referred to, as comprehending the sickly season, shall be understood to extend from the first day of May to the first day of November.

All prisoners of war taken on either side, on land or on sea, shall be restored as soon as practicable after the exchange of ratifications of this treaty. It is also agreed that if any Mexicans should now be held as captives by any savage tribe within the limits of the United States, as about to be established by the following Article, the Government of the said United States will exact the release of such captives, and cause them to be restored to their country.

ARTICLE V.

The Boundary line between the two Republics shall commence in the Gulf of Mexico, three leagues from land, opposite the mouth of the Rio Grande, otherwise called Rio Bravo del Norte, or opposite the mouth of it's deepest branch, if it should have more than one branch emptying directly into the sea; from thence, up the middle of that river, following the deepest channel, where it has more than one, to the point where it strikes the southern boundary of New Mexico; thence, westwardly, along the whole southern boundary of New Mexico (which runs north of the town called Paso) to it's western termination; thence, northward, along the western line of New Mexico, until it intersects the first branch of the river Gila; (or if it should not intersect any branch of that river, then, to the point on the said line nearest to such branch, and thence in a direct line to the same;) thence down the middle of the said branch and of the said river, until it empties into the Rio Colorado; thence, across the Rio Colorado, following the division line between Upper and Lower California, to the Pacific Ocean.

The southern and western limits of New Mexico, mentioned in this Article, are those laid down in the Map, entitled *"Map of the United Mexican States, as organized and defined by various acts of the Congress of said Republic, and constructed according to the best Authorities. Revised Edition. Published at New York in 1847 by J. Disturnell:"* of which Map a Copy is added to this treaty, bearing the signatures and seals of the Undersigned Plenipotentiaries. And, in order to preclude all difficulty in tracing upon the ground the limit separating Upper from Lower California, it is agreed that the said limit shall consist of a straight line, drawn from the middle of the Rio Gila, where it unites with the Colorado, to a point on the coast of the Pacific Ocean, distant one marine league due south of the southernmost point of the Port of San Diego, according to the plan of said port, made in the year 1782 by Don Juan Pantoja, second sailing master of the Spanish fleet, and published at Madrid in the year 1802, in the Atlas to the voyage of the schooners *Sutil* and *Mexicana:* of which plan a copy is hereunto added, signed and sealed by the respective plenipotentiaries.

In order to designate the Boundary line with due precision, upon authoritative maps, and to establish upon the ground landmarks which shall show the limits of both Republics, as described in the present Article, the two Governments shall each appoint a Commissioner and a Surveyor, who, before the expiration of one year from the date of the exchange of ratifications of this treaty, shall meet at the Port of San Diego, and proceed to run and mark the said boundary in it's whole course, to the Mouth of the Rio Bravo del Norte. They shall keep journals and make out plans of their operations; and the result, agreed upon by them, shall be deemed a part of this Treaty, and shall have the same force as if it were inserted therein. The two Governments will amicably agree regarding what may be necessary to these persons, and also as to their respective escorts, should such be necessary.

The Boundary line established by this Article shall be religiously respected by each of the two Republics, and no change shall ever be made therein, except by the express and free consent of both nations, lawfully given by the General Government of each, in conformity with it's own constitution.

ARTICLE VI.

The Vessels and citizens of the United States shall, in all time, have a free and uninterrupted passage by the Gulf of California, and by the River Colorado below it's confluence with the Gila, to and from their possessions situated north of the Boundary line defined in the preceding Article: it being understood, that this passage is to be by navigating the Gulf of California and the River Colorado, and not by land, without the express consent of the Mexican Government.

If, by the examinations which may be made, it should be ascertained to be practicable and advantageous to construct a road, canal or railway, which should, in whole or in part, run upon the river Gila, or upon it's right or it's left bank, within the space of one marine league from either margin of the river, the Governments of both Republics will form an agreement regarding it's construction, in order that it may serve equally for the use and advantage of both countries.

ARTICLE VII.

The river Gila, and the part of the Rio Bravo del Norte lying below the southern boundary of New Mexico, being, agreeably to the fifth Article, divided in the middle between the two Republics, the navigation of the Gila and of the Bravo below said boundary shall be free and common to the vessels and citizens of both countries; and neither shall, without the consent of the other, construct any work that may impede or interrupt, in whole or in part, the exercise of this right: not even for the purpose of favouring new methods of navigation. Nor shall any tax or contribution, under any denomination or title, be levied upon vessels or persons navigating the same, or upon merchandise or effects transported thereon, except in the case of landing upon one of their shores. If, for the purpose of making the said rivers navigable, or for maintaining them in such state, it should be necessary or advantageous to establish any tax or contribution, this shall not be done without the consent of both Governments.

The stipulations contained in the present Article shall not impair the territorial rights of either Republic, within it's established limits.

ARTICLE VIII.

Mexicans now established in territories previously belonging to Mexico, and which remain for the future within the limits of the United States, as defined by the present treaty, shall be free to continue where they now reside, or to remove at any time to the Mexican Republic, retaining the property which they possess in the said territories, or disposing thereof, and removing the proceeds wherever they please; without their being subjected, on this account, to any contribution, tax or charge whatever.

Those who shall prefer to remain in the said territories, may either retain the title and rights of Mexican citizens, or acquire those of citizens of the United States. But they shall be under the obligation to make their election within one year from the date of the exchange of ratifications of this treaty: and those who shall remain in the said territories, after the expiration of that year, without having declared their intention to retain the character of Mexicans, shall be considered to have elected to become citizens of the United States.

In the said territories, property of every kind, now belonging to Mexicans, not established there, shall be inviolably respected. The present owners, the heirs of these, and all Mexicans who may hereafter acquire said property by contract, shall enjoy with respect to it, guaranties equally ample as if the same belonged to citizens of the United States.

ARTICLE IX.

The Mexicans who, in the territories aforesaid, shall not preserve the character of citizens of the Mexican Republic, conformably with what is stipulated in the preceding article, shall be incorporated into the Union of the United States and be admitted, at the proper time (to be judged of by the Congress of the United States) to the enjoyment of all the rights of citizens of the United States according to the principles of the Constitution; and in the mean time shall be maintained and protected in the free enjoyment of their liberty and property, and secured in the free exercise of their religion without restriction.

ARTICLE X. *

ARTICLE XI.

Considering that a great part of the territories which, by the present Treaty, are to be comprehended for the future within the limits of the United States, is now occupied by savage tribes, who will hereafter be under the exclusive controul of the Government of the United States, and whose incursions within the territory of Mexico would be prejudicial in the extreme; it is solemnly agreed that all such incursions shall be forcibly restrained by the Government of the United States, whensoever this may be necessary; and that when they cannot be prevented, they shall be punished by the said Government, and satisfaction for the same shall be exacted: all in the same way, and with equal diligence and energy, as if the same incursions were meditated or committed within it's own territory against it's own citizens.

It shall not be lawful, under any pretext whatever, for any inhabitant of the United States, to purchase or acquire any Mexican or any foreigner residing in Mexico, who may have been captured by Indians inhabiting the territory of either of the two Republics, nor to purchase or acquire horses, mules, cattle or property of any kind, stolen within Mexican territory by such Indians.

*One of the amendments of the Senate struck out Article 10.

And, in the event of any person or persons, captured within Mexican Territory by Indians, being carried into the territory of the United States, the Government of the latter engages and binds itself in the most solemn manner, so soon as it shall know of such captives being within it's territory, and shall be able so to do, through the faithful exercise of it's influence and power, to rescue them and return them to their country, or deliver them to the agent or representative of the Mexican Government. The Mexican Authorities will, as far as practicable, give to the Government of the United States notice of such captures; and it's agent shall pay the expenses incurred in the maintenance and transmission of the rescued captives; who, in the mean time, shall be treated with the utmost hospitality by the American authorities at the place where they may be. But if the Government of the United States, before receiving such notice from Mexico, should obtain intelligence through any other channel, of the existence of Mexican captives within it's territory, it will proceed forthwith to effect their release and delivery to the Mexican agent, as above stipulated.

For the purpose of giving to these stipulations the fullest possible efficacy, thereby affording the security and redress demanded by their true spirit and intent, the Government of the United States will now and hereafter pass, without unnecessary delay, and always vigilantly enforce, such laws as the nature of the subject may require. And finally, the sacredness of this obligation shall never be lost sight of by the said Government, when providing for the removal of the Indians from any portion of the said territories, or for it's being settled by citizens of the United States; but on the contrary special care shall then be taken not to place it's Indian occupants under the necessity of seeking new homes, by committing those invasions which the United States have solemnly obliged themselves to restrain.

ARTICLE XII.

In consideration of the extension acquired by the boundaries of the United States, as defined in the fifth Article of the present Treaty, the Government of the United States engages to pay to that of the Mexican Republic the sum of fifteen Millions of Dollars.

Immediately after this treaty shall have been duly ratified by the Government of the Mexican Republic, the sum of three millions of dollars shall be paid to the said Government by that of the United States at the city of Mexico, in the gold or silver coin of Mexico. The remaining twelve millions of dollars shall be paid at the same place and in the same coin, in annual instalments of three millions of dollars each, together with interest on the same at the rate of six per centum per annum. This interest shall begin to run upon the whole sum of twelve millions, from the day of the ratification of the present treaty by the Mexican Government, and the first of the instalments shall be paid at the expiration of one year from the same day. Together with each annual instalment, as it falls due, the whole interest accruing on such instalment from the beginning shall also be paid.

ARTICLE XIII.

The United States engage moreover, to assume and pay to the claimants all the amounts now due them, and those hereafter to become due, by reason of the claims already liquidated and decided against the Mexican Republic, under the conventions between the two Republics severally concluded on the eleventh day of April eighteen hundred and thirty-nine, and on the thirtieth day of January eighteen hundred and forty three: so that the Mexican Republic shall be absolutely exempt for the future, from all expense whatever on account of the said claims.

ARTICLE XIV.

The United States do furthermore discharge the Mexican Republic from all claims of citizens of the United States, not heretofore decided against the Mexican Government, which may have arisen previously to the date of the signature of this treaty: which discharge shall be final and perpetual, whether the said claims be rejected or be allowed by the Board of Commissioners provided for in the following Article, and whatever shall be the total amount of those allowed.

ARTICLE XV.

The United States, exonerating Mexico from all demands on account of the claims of their citizens mentioned in the preceding Article, and considering them entirely and forever cancelled, whatever their amount may be, undertake to make satisfaction for the same, to an amount not exceeding three and one quarter millions of Dollars. To ascertain the validity and amount of those claims, a Board of Commissioners shall be established by the Government of the United States, whose awards shall be final and conclusive: provided that in deciding upon the validity of each claim, the board shall be guided and governed by the principles and rules of decision prescribed by the first and fifth Articles of the unratified convention, concluded at the City of Mexico on the twentieth day of November, one thousand eight hundred and forty-three; and in no case shall an award be made in favour of any claim not embraced by these principles and rules.

If, in the opinion of the said Board of Commissioners, or of the claimants, any books, records or documents in the possession or power of the Government of the Mexican Republic, shall be deemed necessary to the just decision of any claim, the Commissioners or the claimants, through them, shall, within such period as congress may designate, make an application in writing for the same, addressed to the Mexican Minister for Foreign Affairs, to be transmitted by the Secretary of State of the United States; and the Mexican Government engages, at the earliest possible moment after the receipt of such demand, to cause any of the books, records or documents, so specified, which shall be in their possession or power, (or authenticated Copies or extracts of the same) to be transmitted to the said Secretary of State, who shall immediately deliver them over to the said Board of Commissioners: provided that no such application shall be made, by, or at the instance of, any claimant, until the facts which it is expected to prove by such books, records or documents, shall have been stated under oath or affirmation.

ARTICLE XVI.

Each of the contracting parties reserves to itself the entire right to fortify whatever point within it's territory, it may judge proper so to fortify, for it's security.

ARTICLE XVII.

The Treaty of Amity, Commerce and Navigation, concluded at the city of Mexico on the fifth day of April A.D. 1831, between the United States of America and the United Mexican States, except the additional Article, and except so far as the stipulations of the said treaty may be incompatible with any stipulation contained in the present treaty, is hereby revived for the period of eight years from the day of the exchange of ratifications of this treaty, with the same force and virtue as if incorporated therein; it being understood that each of the contracting parties reserves to itself the right, at any time after the said period of eight years shall have expired, to terminate the same by giving one year's notice of such intention to the other party.

ARTICLE XVIII.

All supplies whatever for troops of the United States in Mexico, arriving at ports in the occupation of such troops, previous to the final evacuation thereof, although subsequently to the restoration of the Custom Houses at such ports, shall be entirely exempt from duties and charges of any kind: the Government of the United States hereby engaging and pledging it's faith to establish, and vigilantly to enforce, all possible guards for securing the revenue of Mexico, by preventing the importation under cover of this stipulation, of any articles, other than such, both in kind and in quantity, as shall really be wanted for the use and consumption of the forces of the United States during the time they may remain in Mexico. To this end, it shall be the duty of all officers and agents of the United States to denounce to the Mexican Authorities at the respective ports, any attempts at a fraudulent abuse of this stipulation, which they may know of or may have reason to suspect, and to give to such authorities all the aid in their power with regard thereto: and every such attempt, when duly proved and established by sentence of a competent tribunal, shall be punished by the confiscation of the property so attempted to be fraudulently introduced.

ARTICLE XIX.

With respect to all merchandise, effects and property whatsoever, imported into ports of Mexico whilst in the occupation of the forces of the United States, whether by citizens of either republic, or by citizens or subjects of any neutral nation, the following rules shall be observed:

I. All such merchandise, effects and property, if imported previously to the restoration of the Custom Houses to the Mexican Authorities, as stipulated for in the third Article of this treaty, shall be exempt from confiscation, although the importation of the same be prohibited by the Mexican tariff.

II. The same perfect exemption shall be enjoyed by all such merchandise, effects and property, imported subsequently to the restoration of the Custom Houses, and previously to the sixty days fixed in the following Article for the coming into force of the Mexican tariff at such ports respectively: the said merchandise, effects and property being, however, at the time of their importation, subject to the payment of duties, as provided for in the said following Article.

III. All merchandise, effects and property described in the two rules foregoing, shall, during their continuance at the place of importation, or upon their leaving such place for the interior, be exempt from all duty, tax or impost of every kind, under whatsoever title or denomination. Nor shall they be there subjected to any charge whatsoever upon the sale thereof.

IV. All merchandise, effects and property, described in the first and second rules, which shall have been removed to any place in the interior, whilst such place was in the occupation of the forces of the United States, shall, during their continuance therein, be exempt from all tax upon the sale or consumption thereof, and from every kind of impost or contribution, under whatsoever title or denomination.

V. But if any merchandise, effects or property, described in the first and second rules, shall be removed to any place not occupied at the time by the forces of the United States, they shall, upon their introduction into such place, or upon their sale or consumption there, be subject to the same duties, which, under the Mexican laws, they would be required to pay in such cases, if they had been imported in time of peace through the Maritime Custom Houses, and had there paid the duties conformably with the Mexican tariff.

VI. The owners of all merchandise, effects or property, described in the first and second rules, and existing in any port of Mexico, shall have the right to reship the same, exempt from all tax, impost or contribution whatever.

With respect to the metals, or other property exported from any Mexican port, whilst in the occupation of the forces of the United States, and previously to the restoration of the Custom House at such port, no person shall be required by the Mexican Authorities, whether General or State, to pay any tax, duty or contribution upon any such exportation, or in any manner to account for the same to the said Authorities.

ARTICLE XX.

Through consideration for the interests of commerce generally, it is agreed, that if less than sixty days should elapse between the date of the signature of this treaty and the restoration of the Custom Houses, comformably with the stipulation in the third Article, in such case, all merchandise, effects and property whatsoever, arriving at the Mexican ports after the restoration of the said Custom Houses, and previously to the expiration of sixty days after the day of the signature of this treaty, shall be admitted to entry; and no other duties shall be levied thereon than the duties established by the tariff found in force at such Custom Houses, at the time of the restoration of the same. And to all such merchandise, effects and property, the rules established by the preceding Article shall apply.

ARTICLE XXI.

If unhappily any disagreement should hereafter arise between the Governments of the two Republics, whether with respect to the interpretation of any stipulation in this treaty, or with respect to any other particular concerning the political or commercial relations of the two Nations, the said Governments, in the name of those Nations, do promise to each other, that they will endeavour in the most sincere and earnest manner, to settle the differences so arising, and to preserve the state of peace and friendship, in which the two countries are now placing themselves: using, for this end, mutual representations and pacific negotiations. And, if by these means, they should not be enabled to come to an agreement, a resort shall not, on this account, be had to reprisals, aggression or hostility of any kind, by the one Republic against the other, until the Government of that which deems itself aggrieved, shall have maturely considered, in the spirit of peace and good neighbourship, whether it would not be better that such difference should be settled by the arbitration of Commissioners appointed on each side, or by that of a friendly nation. And should such course be proposed by either party, it shall be acceded to by the other, unless deemed by it altogether incompatible with the nature of the difference, or the circumstances of the case.

ARTICLE XXII.

If (which is not to be expected, and which God forbid!) war should unhappily break out between the two Republics, they do now, with a view to such calamity, solemnly pledge themselves to each other and to the world, to observe the following rules: absolutely, where the nature of the subject permits, and as closely as possible in all cases where such absolute observance shall be impossible.

I. The merchants of either Republic, then residing in the other, shall be allowed to remain twelve months (for those dwelling in the interior) and six months (for those dwelling at the sea-ports) to collect their debts and settle their affairs; during which periods, they shall enjoy the same protection, and be on the same footing, in all respects, as the citizens or subjects of the most friendly nations; and, at the expiration thereof, or at any time before, they shall have full liberty to depart, carrying off all their effects, without molestation or hindrance: conforming therein to the same laws, which the citizens or subjects of the most friendly nations are required to conform to. Upon the entrance of the armies of either nation into the territories of the other, women and children, ecclesiastics, scholars of every faculty, cultivators of the earth, merchants, artizans, manufacturers and fishermen, unarmed and inhabiting unfortified towns, villages or places, and in general all persons whose occupations are for the common subsistence and benefit of mankind, shall be allowed to continue their respective employments, unmolested in their persons. Nor shall their houses or goods be burnt or otherwise destroyed: nor their cattle taken, nor, their fields wasted, by the armed force, into whose power, by the events of war, they may happen to fall; but if the necessity arise to take any thing from them for the use of such armed force, the same shall be paid for at an equitable price. All churches, hospitals, schools, colleges, libraries and other establishments for charitable and beneficent purposes, shall be respected, and all persons connected with the same protected in the discharge of their duties and the pursuit of their vocations.

II. In order that the fate of prisoners of war may be alleviated, all such practices as those of sending them into distant, inclement or unwholesome districts, or crowding them into close and noxious places, shall be studiously avoided. They shall not be confined in dungeons, prison-ships or prisons; nor be put in irons, or bound, or otherwise restrained in the use of their limbs. The officers shall enjoy liberty on their paroles, within convenient districts, and have comfortable quarters; and the common soldiers shall be disposed in cantonments, open and extensive enough for air and exercise, and lodged in barracks as roomy and good as are provided by the party in whose power they are for it's own troops. But if any officer shall break his parole by leaving the district so assigned him, or any other prisoner shall escape from the limits of his cantonment, after they shall have been designated to him, such individual, officer, or other prisoner shall forfeit so much of the benefit of this Article as provides for his liberty on parole or in cantonment. And if an officer so breaking his parole, or any common soldier so escaping from the limits assigned him, shall afterwards be found in arms, previously to his being regularly exchanged, the person so offending shall be dealt with according to the established laws of war. The officers shall be daily furnished by the party in whose power they are, with as many rations, and of the same articles as are allowed either in kind or by commutation, to officers of equal rank in it's own army; and all others shall be daily furnished with such ration as is allowed to a common soldier in it's own service: the value of all which supplies shall, at the close of the war, or at periods to be agreed upon between the respective commanders, be paid by the other party, on a mutal adjustment of accounts for the subsistence of prisoners; and such accounts shall not be mingled with or set off against any others, nor the balance due on them be withheld, as a compensation or reprisal for any cause whatever, real or pretended. Each party shall be allowed to keep a Commissary of prisoners, appointed by itself, with every cantonment of prisoners, in possession of the other; which Commissary shall see the prisoners as often as he pleases; shall be allowed to receive, exempt from all duties or taxes, and to distribute whatever comforts may be sent to them by their friends; and shall be free to transmit his reports in open letters to the party by whom he is employed.

And it is declared that neither the pretence that war dissolves all treaties, nor any other whatever, shall be considered as annulling or suspending the solemn convenant contained in this Article. On the contrary the state of war is precisely that for which it is provided; and during which it's stipulations are to be as sacredly observed as the most acknowledged obligations under the law of nature or nations.

ARTICLE XXIII.

This Treaty shall be ratified by the President of the United States of America, by and with the advice and consent of the Senate thereof; and by the President of the Mexican Republic, with the previous approbation of it's General Congress: and the ratifications shall be exchanged in the city of Washington or at the seat of government of Mexico, in four months from the date of the signature hereof, or sooner if practicable.

In faith whereof, we, the respective Plenipotentiaries, have signed this Treaty of Peace, Friendship, Limits and Settlement, and have hereunto affixed our seals respectively. Done in Quintuplicate at the city of Guadalupe Hidalgo on the second day of February in the Year of Our Lord one thousand eight hundred and forty-eight.

N.P. Trist.	(Seal)
Luis G. Cuevas	(Seal)
Bernardo Couto	(Seal)
Mig! Atristain	(Seal)

AN ACT GIVING THE CONSENT OF THE GOVERNMENT OF THE UNITED STATES TO THE STATE OF TEXAS TO EXTEND HER EASTERN BOUNDARY, SO AS TO INCLUDE WITHIN HER LIMITS ONE HALF OF SABINE PASS, SABINE LAKE, AND SABINE RIVER, AS FAR NORTH AS THE THIRTY-SECOND DEGREE OF NORTH LATITUDE

JULY 5, 1848

Be it enacted by the Senate and House of Representatives of the United States of America in Congress assembled, That this Congress consents that the legislature of the State of Texas may extend her eastern boundary so as to include within her limits one half of Sabine Pass, one half of Sabine Lake, also one half of Sabine River, from its mouth as far north as the thirty-second degree of north latitude.

Approved, July 5, 1848.

AN ACT TO ESTABLISH THE
TERRITORIAL GOVERNMENT OF OREGON
AUGUST 14, 1848

Be it enacted by the Senate and House of Representatives of the United States of America in Congress assembled, That from and after the passage of this act, all that part of the Territory of the United States which lies west of the summit of the Rocky Mountains, north of the forty-second degree of north latitude, known as the Territory of Oregon, shall be organized into and constitute a temporary government by the name of the Territory of Oregon: *Provided,* That nothing in this act contained shall be construed to impair the rights of person or property now pertaining to the Indians in said Territory, so long as such rights shall remain unextinguished by treaty between the United States and such Indians, or to affect the authority of the government of the United States to make any regulation respecting such Indians, their lands, property, or other rights, by treaty, law, or otherwise, which it would have been competent to the government to make if this act had never passed: *And provided, also,* That the title to the land, not exceeding six hundred and forty acres, now occupied as missionary stations among the Indian tribes in said Territory, together with the improvements thereon, be confirmed and established in the several religious societies to which said missionary stations respectively belong: *And provided further,* That nothing in this act contained shall be construed to inhibit the government of the United States from dividing said Territory into two or more Territories, in such manner and at such times as Congress shall deem convenient and proper, or from attaching any portion of said Territory to any other State or Territory of the United States.

SEC. 2. *And be it further enacted,* That the executive power and authority in and over said Territory of Oregon shall be vested in a governor, who shall hold his office for four years, and until his successor shall be appointed and qualified, unless sooner removed by the President of the United States. The governor shall reside within said Territory, shall be commander-in-chief of the militia thereof, shall perform the duties and receive the emoluments of superintendent of Indian affairs; he may grant pardons and respites for offences against the laws of said Territory, and reprieves for offences against the laws of the United States, until the decision of the President can be made known thereon; he shall commission all officers who shall be appointed to office under the laws of the said Territory, where, by law, such commissions shall be required, and shall take care that the laws be faithfully executed.

SEC. 3. *And be it further enacted,* That there shall be a secretary of said Territory, who shall reside therein, and hold his office for five years, unless sooner removed by the President of the United States; he shall record and preserve all the laws and proceedings of the legislative assembly hereinafter constituted, and all the acts and proceedings of the governor in his executive department; he shall transmit one copy of the laws and journals of the legislative assembly within thirty days after the end of each session, and one copy of the executive proceedings and official correspondence, semi-annually, on the first days of January and July in each year, to the President of the United States, and two copies of the laws to the President of the Senate and to the Speaker of the House of Representatives, for the use of Congress. And in case of the death, removal, resignation, or absence of the governor from the Territory, the secretary shall be, and he is hereby, authorized and required to execute and perform all the powers and duties of the governor during such vacancy or absence, or until another governor shall be duly appointed and qualified to fill such vacancy.

SEC. 4. *And be it further enacted,* That the legislative power and authority of said Territory shall be vested in a legislative assembly. The legislative assembly shall consist of a council and house of representatives. The council shall consist of nine members, having the qualifications of voters as hereinafter prescribed, whose term of service shall continue three years. Immediately after they shall be assembled, in consequence of the first election, they shall be divided as equally as may be into three classes. The seats of the members of council of the first class shall be vacated at the expiration of the first year; of the second class at the expiration of the second year; and of the third class at the expiration of the third year, so that one third may be chosen every year; and if vacancies happen by resignation or otherwise, the same shall be filled at the next ensuing election. The house of representatives shall, at its first session, consist of eighteen members, possessing the same qualifications as prescribed for members of the council, and whose term of service shall continue one year. The number of representatives may be increased by the legislative assembly from time to time, in proportion to the increase of qualified voters: *Provided,* That the whole number shall never exceed thirty. An apportionment shall be made, as nearly equal as practicable, among the several counties or districts, for the election of the council and representatives, giving to each section of the Territory representation in the ratio of its qualified voters, as nearly as may be. And the members of the council and of the house of representatives shall reside in and be inhabitants of the district, or county, or counties, for which they may be elected respectively. Previous to the first election, the governor shall cause a census or enumeration of the inhabitants and qualified voters of the several counties and districts of the Territory to be taken by such persons, and in such mode as the governor shall designate and appoint; and the persons so appointed shall receive a reasonable compensation therefor; and the first election shall be held at such time and places, and be conducted in such manner, both as to the persons who shall superintend such election, and the returns thereof, as the governor shall appoint and direct; and he shall, at the same time, declare the number of members of the council and house of representatives to which each of the counties or districts shall be entitled under this act; and the governor shall, by his proclamation, give at least sixty days' previous notice of such apportionment, and of the time, places, and manner of holding such election. The persons having the highest number of legal votes in each of said council districts for members of the council shall be declared by the governor to be duly elected to the council; and the persons having the highest number of legal votes for the house of representatives shall be declared by the governor to be duly elected members of said house: *Provided*, That, in case two or more persons voted for shall have an equal number of votes, and in case a vacancy shall otherwise occur in either branch of the legislative assembly, the governor shall order a new election; and the persons thus elected to the legislative assembly shall meet at such place, and on such day, within ninety days after such elections, as the governor shall appoint; but, thereafter, the time, place, and manner of holding and conducting all elections by the people, and the apportioning the representation in the several counties or districts to the council and house of representatives, according to the number of qualified voters, shall be prescribed by law, as well as the day of the commencement of the regular sessions of the legislative assembly: *Provided*, That no session in any one year shall exceed the term of sixty days, except the first session, which shall not be prolonged beyond one hundred days.

SEC. 5. *And be it further enacted*, That every white male inhabitant above the age of twenty-one years, who shall have been a resident of said Territory at the time of the passage of this act, and shall possess the qualifications hereinafter prescribed, shall be entitled to vote at the first election, and shall be eligible to any office within the said Territory; but the qualifications of voters and of holding office, at all subsequent elections, shall be such as shall be prescribed by the legislative assembly: *Provided*, That the right of suffrage and of holding office shall be exercised only by citizens of the United States above the age of twenty-one years, and those above that age who shall have declared, on oath, their intention to become such, and shall have taken an oath to support the constitution of the United States and the provisions of this act: *And provided further*, That no officer, soldier, seaman, or marine, or other person in the army or navy of the United States, or attached to troops in the service of the United States, shall be allowed to vote in said Territory, by reason of being on service therein, unless said Territory is and has been for the period of six months his permanent domicil: *Provided further*, That no person belonging to the army or navy of the United States shall ever be elected to or hold any civil office or appointment in said Territory.

SEC. 6. *And be it further enacted*, That the legislative power of the Territory shall extend to all rightful subjects of legislation not inconsistent with the constitution and laws of the United States; but no law shall be passed interfering with the primary disposal of the soil; no tax shall be imposed upon the property of the United States; nor shall the lands or other property of nonresidents be taxed higher than the lands or other property of residents. All the laws passed by the legislative assembly shall be submitted to the Congress of the United States, and if disapproved, shall be null and of no effect: *Provided,* That nothing in this act shall be construed to give power to incorporate a bank, or any institution with banking powers, or to borrow money in the name of the Territory, or to pledge the faith of the people of the same for any loan whatever, either directly or indirectly. No charter granting any privilege of making, issuing, or putting into circulation any notes or bills in the likeness of bank notes, or any bonds, scrip, drafts, bills of exchange or obligations, or granting any other banking powers or privileges, shall be passed by the legislative assembly; nor shall the establishment of any branch or agency of any such corporation, derived from other authority, be allowed in said Territory; nor shall said legislative assembly authorize the issue of any obligation, scrip, or evidence of debt by said Territory, in any mode or manner whatever, except certificates for services to said Territory: and all such laws, or any law or laws inconsistent with the provisions of this act, shall be utterly null and void; and all taxes shall be equal and uniform, and no distinction shall be made in the assessments between different kinds of property, but the assessments shall be according to the value thereof. To avoid improper influences which may result from intermixing in one and the same act such things as have no proper relation to each other, every law shall embrace but one object, and that shall be expressed in the title.

SEC. 7. *And be it further enacted,* That all township, district, and county officers, not herein otherwise provided for, shall be appointed or elected in such manner as shall be provided by the legislative assembly of the Territory of Oregon.

SEC. 8. *And be it further enacted,* That no member of the legislative assembly shall hold, or be appointed to, any office which shall have been created, or the salary or emoluments of which shall have been increased, while he was a member, during the term for which he was elected, and for one year after the expiration of such term; but this restriction shall not be applicable to members of the first legislative assembly; and no person holding a commission or appointment under the United States shall be a member of the legislative assembly, or shall hold any office under the government of said Territory.

SEC. 9. *And be it further enacted,* That the judicial power of said Territory shall be vested in a Supreme Court, District Courts, Probate Courts, and in justices of the peace. The Supreme Court shall consist of a chief justice and two associate justices, any two of whom shall constitute a quorum, and who shall hold a term at the seat of government of said Territory annually, and they shall hold their offices during the period of four years, and until their successors shall be appointed and qualified. The said Territory shall be divided into three judicial districts, and a District Court shall be held in each of said districts by one of the justices of the Supreme Court, at such times and places as may be prescribed by law; and the said judges shall, after their appointments, respectively, reside in the districts which shall be assigned them. The jurisdiction of the several courts herein provided for, both appellate and original, and that of the Probate Courts and of justices of the peace, shall be as limited by law: *Provided,* That justices of the peace shall not have jurisdiction of any case in which the title to land shall in any wise come in question, or where the debt or damages claimed shall exceed one hundred dollars; and the said Supreme and District Courts, respectively, shall possess chancery as well as common law jurisdiction. Each District Court, or the judge thereof, shall appoint its clerk, who shall also be the register in chancery, and shall keep his office at the place where the court may be held. Writs of error, bills of exception, and appeals, shall be allowed in all cases from the final decisions of said District Courts to the Supreme Court, under such regulations as may be prescribed by law; but in no case removed to the Supreme Court shall trial by jury be allowed in said court. The Supreme Court, or the justices thereof, shall appoint its own clerk, and every clerk shall hold his office at the pleasure of the Court for which he shall have been appointed. Writs of error and appeals from the final decisions of said Supreme Court shall be allowed, and may be taken to the Supreme Court of the United States, in the same manner and under the same regulations as from the Circuit Courts of the United States, where the value of the property or the amount in controversy, to be ascertained by the oath or affirmation of either party, or other competent witness, shall exceed two thousand dollars, and in all cases where the constitution of the United States, or acts of Congress, or a treaty of the United States, is brought in question; and each of the said District Courts shall have and exercise the same jurisdiction in all cases arising under the constitution of the United States, and the laws of said Territory, as is vested in the Circuit and District Courts of the United States; writs of error and appeal in all such cases shall be made to the Supreme Court of said Territory, the same as in other cases. Writs of error and appeals from the final decisions of said Supreme Court shall be allowed, and may be taken to the Supreme Court of the United States, in the same manner as from the Circuit Courts of the United States, where the value of the property, or the amount in controversy, shall exceed two thousand dollars; and each of said District Courts shall have and exercise the same jurisdiction in all cases arising under the constitution and laws of the United States, as is vested in the Circuit and District Courts of the United States, and also of all cases arising under the laws of the said Territory, and otherwise. The said clerk shall receive, in all such cases, the same fees which the clerks of the District Courts of the late Wisconsin Territory received for similar services.

SEC. 10. *And be it further enacted*, That there shall be appointed an attorney for said Territory, who shall continue in office for four years, and until his successor shall be appointed and qualified, unless sooner removed by the President, and who shall receive the same fees and salary as were provided by law for the attorney of the United States for the late Territory of Wisconsin. There shall also be a marshal for the Territory appointed, who shall hold his office for four years, and until his successor shall be appointed and qualified, unless sooner removed by the President, and who shall execute all processes issuing from the said courts, when exercising their jurisdiction as Circuit and District Courts of the United States; he shall perform the duties, be subject to the same regulations and penalties, and be entitled to the same fees, as were provided by law for the marshal of the District Court of the United States for the present [late] Territory of Wisconsin; and shall, in addition, be paid two hundred dollars annually as a compensation for extra services.

SEC. 11. *And be it further enacted*, That the governor, secretary, chief justice and associate justices, attorney, and marshal, shall be nominated, and, by and with the advice and consent of the Senate, appointed by the President of the United States. The governor and secretary, to be appointed as aforesaid, shall, before they act as such, respectively take an oath or affirmation, before the district judge, or some justice of the peace in the limits of said Territory, duly authorized to administer oaths and affirmations by the laws now in force therein, or before the chief justice or some associate justice of the Supreme Court of the United States, to support the constitution of the United States, and faithfully to discharge the duties of their respective offices; which said oaths, when so taken, shall be certified by the person by whom the same shall have been taken, and such certificates shall be received and recorded by the said secretary among the executive proceedings; and the chief justice and associate justice, and all other civil officers in said Territory, before they act as such, shall take a like oath or affirmation, before the said governor or secretary, or some judge or justice of the peace of the Territory, who may be duly commissioned and qualified; which said oath or affirmation shall be certified and transmitted by the person taking the same, to the secretary, to be by him recorded as aforesaid; and, afterwards, the like oath or affirmation shall be taken, certified, and recorded, in such manner and form as may be prescribed by law. The governor shall receive an annual salary of fifteen hundred dollars as governor, and fifteen hundred dollars as superintendent of Indian affairs. The chief justice and associate justices shall each receive an annual salary of two thousand dollars. The secretary shall receive an annual salary of fifteen hundred dollars. The said salaries shall be paid quarter-yearly, from the dates of the respective appointments, at the treasury of the United States; but no such payment shall be made until said officers shall have entered upon the duties of their respective appointments. The members of the legislative assembly shall be entitled to receive three dollars each per day during their attendance at the session thereof, and three dollars each for every twenty miles' travel in going to and returning from said sessions, estimated according to the nearest usually travelled route. And a chief clerk, one assistant clerk, a sergeant-at-arms, and door-keeper, may be chosen for each house; and the chief clerk shall receive five dollars per day, and the said other officers three dollars per day, during the session of the legislative assembly; but no other officers shall be paid by the United States: *Provided,* That there shall be but one session of the legislature annually, unless, on an extraordinary occasion, the governor shall think proper to call the legislature together. There shall be appropriated annually the sum of fifteen hundred dollars, to be expended by the governor to defray the contingent expenses of the Territory, including the salary of a clerk of the executive department; and there shall also be appropriated, annually, a sufficient sum to be expended by the Secretary of the Territory, and upon an estimate to be made by the Secretary of the Treasury of the United States, to defray the expenses of the legislative assembly, the printing of laws, and other incidental expenses; and the governor and secretary of the Territory shall, in the disbursement of all moneys intrusted to them, be governed soley by the instructions of the Secretary of the Treasury of the United States, and shall semiannually account to the said Secretary for the manner in which the aforesaid [sum] moneys shall have been expended; and no expenditure, to be paid out of money appropriated by Congress, shall be made by said legislative assembly for objects not specially authorized by the acts of Congress making the appropriations, nor beyond the sums thus appropriated for such objects.

SEC. 12. *And be it further enacted,* That the rivers and streams of water in said Territory of Oregon in which salmon are found, or to which they resort, shall not be obstructed by dams or otherwise, unless such dams or obstructions are so constructed as to allow salmon to pass freely up and down such rivers and streams.

SEC. 13. *And be it further enacted,* That the sum of ten thousand dollars be, and is hereby appropriated, to be expended under the direction of the President of the United States, in payment for the services and expenses of such persons as have been engaged by the provisional government of Oregon in conveying communications to and from the United States, and the purchase of presents for such of the Indian tribes as the peace and quietude of the country requires.

SEC. 14. *And be it further enacted,* That the inhabitants of said Territory shall be entitled to enjoy all and singular the rights, privileges, and advantages granted and secured to the people of the territory of the United States northwest of the River Ohio, by the articles of compact contained in the ordinance for the government of said territory, on the thirteenth day of July, seventeen hundred and eighty-seven; and shall be subject to all the conditions, and restrictions, and prohibitions in said articles of compact imposed upon the people of said territory; and the existing laws now in force in the Territory of Oregon, under the authority of the provisional government established by the people thereof, shall continue to be valid and operative therein, so far as the same be not incompatible with the constitution of the United States, and the principles and provisions of this act; subject, nevertheless, to be altered, modified, or repealed, by the legislative assembly of the said Territory of Oregon; but all laws heretofore passed in said Territory making grants of land, or otherwise affecting or incumbering the title to lands, shall be, and are hereby declared to be, null and void; and the laws of the United States are hereby extended over, and declared to be in force in, said Territory, so far as the same, or any provision thereof, may be applicable.

SEC. 15. *And be it further enacted,* That the legislative assembly of the Territory of Oregon shall hold its first session at such time and place in said Territory as the governor thereof shall appoint and direct; and at said first session, or as soon thereafter as they shall deem expedient, the legislative assembly shall proceed to locate and establish the seat of government for said Territory at such place as they may deem eligible; which place, however, shall thereafter be subject to be changed by said legislative assembly. And the sum of five thousand dollars, out of any money in the treasury not otherwise appropriated, is hereby appropriated and granted to said Territory of Oregon, to be there applied, by the governor, to the erection of suitable buildings at the seat of government.

SEC. 16. *And be it further enacted,* That a delegate to the House of Representatives of the United States, to serve for the term of two years, who shall be a citizen of the United States, may be elected by the voters qualified to elect members of the legislative assembly, who shall be entitled to the same rights and privileges as have been heretofore exercised and enjoyed by the delegates from the several other Territories of the United States to the said

House of Representatives; but the delegate first elected shall hold his seat only during the term of the Congress to which he shall be elected. The first election shall be held at such time and places, and be conducted in such manner, as the governor shall appoint and direct; of which, and the time, place, and manner of holding such elections, he shall give at least sixty days' notice by proclamation; and at all subsequent elections, the times, places, and manner of holding the elections shall be prescribed by law. The person having the greatest number of votes shall be declared by the governor to be duly elected, and a certificate thereof shall be given accordingly. The delegate from said Territory shall not be entitled to receive more than twenty-five hundred dollars at any one session of Congress, as a compensation for his mileage, in going to and returning from the seat of government of the United States, any act of Congress to the contrary notwithstanding.

SEC. 17. *And be it further enacted*, That all suits, process, and proceedings, civil and criminal, at law and in chancery, and all indictments and informations, which shall be pending and undetermined in the courts established by authority of the provisional government of Oregon, within the limits of said Territory, when this act shall take effect, shall be transferred to be heard, tried, prosecuted, and determined in the District Courts hereby established, which may include the counties or districts where any such proceeding may be pending. All bonds, recognizances, and obligations of every kind whatsoever, valid under the existing laws within the limits of said Territory, shall be valid under this act; and all crimes and misdemeansors against the laws in force within said limits may be prosecuted, tried, and punished in the courts established by this act; and all penalties, forfeitures, actions, and causes of action, may be recovered under this act, in like manner as they would have been under the laws in force within the limits composing said Territory at the time this act shall go into operation: *Provided*, That the laws, penalties, and forfeitures and punishments, by this section required to be enforced by the courts provided for by this act, shall not be inconsistent with the constitution of the United States: *And provided further*, That no right of action whatever shall accrue against any person for any act done in pursuance of any law heretofore passed by the temporary government, and which may be declared contrary to the constitution of the United States.

SEC. 18. *And be it further enacted*, That all justices of the peace, constables, sheriffs, and all other judicial and ministerial officers, who shall be in office within the limits of said Territory when this act shall take effect, shall be, and they are hereby, authorized and required to continue to exercise and perform the duties of their respective offices as officers of the Territory of Oregon until they or others shall be duly elected or appointed, and qualified to fill their places in the manner herein directed, or until their offices shall be abolished.

SEC. 19. *And be it further enacted*, That the sum of five thousand dollars be, and the same is hereby, appropriated out of any moneys in the treasury not otherwise appropriated, to be expended, by and under the direction of the said governor of the Territory of Oregon, in the purchase of a library, to be kept at the seat of government for the use of the governor, legislative assembly, judges of the Supreme Court, secretary, marshal, and attorney of said Territory, and such other persons, and under such regulations, as shall be prescribed by law.

SEC. 20. *And be it further enacted,* That when the lands in the said Territory shall be surveyed under the direction of the government of the United States, preparatory to bringing the same into market, sections numbered sixteen and thirty-six in each township in said Territory shall be, and the same is hereby, reserved for the purpose of being applied to schools in said Territory, and in the States and Territories hereafter to be erected out of the same.

SEC. 21. *And be it further enacted,* That, until otherwise provided for by law, the governor of said Territory may define the judicial districts of said Territory, and assign the judges who may be appointed for said Territory, to the several districts, and also appoint the times and places for holding courts in the several counties or subdivisions in each of said judicial districts by proclamation to be issued by him; but the legislative assembly, at their first or any subsequent session, may organize, alter, or modify such judicial districts, and assign the judges, and alter the time and places of holding the courts, as to them shall seem proper and convenient.

SEC. 22. *And be it further enacted,* That all officers to be appointed by the President, by and with the advice and consent of the Senate for the Territory of Oregon, who by virtue of the provisions of any law now existing, or which may be enacted during the present Congress, are required to give security for moneys that may be intrusted with them for disbursement, shall give such security at such time and place, and in such manner, as the Secretary of the Treasury may prescribe.

SEC. 23. *And be it further enacted,* That all the ports, harbors, shores, and waters of the main land of the Territory aforesaid shall constitute a collection district, to be called the District of Oregon; and a port of entry shall be established at Astoria, near the mouth of the Columbia River, and a collector of customs shall be appointed by the President, by and with the advice and consent of the Senate, to reside at such port of entry.

SEC. 24. *And be it further enacted,* That the President of the United States be, and he is hereby, authorized to establish such ports of delivery in the district created by this act, not exceeding two in number, (one of which shall be located of Puget's Sound,) as he may deem expedient, and may appoint, by and with the advice and consent of the Senate, surveyors to reside thereat.

SEC. 25. *And be it further enacted,* That the collector of said district shall be allowed a compensation of one thousand dollars per annum, and the fees allowed by law; and the compensation of any surveyor appointed in pursuance of this act shall not exceed five hundred dollars per annum, including in said sum the fees allowed by law; and the amount collected by any of said surveyors, for fees in any one year, exceeding the sum of five hundred dollars, shall be accounted for and paid into the treasury of the United States.

SEC. 26. *And be it further enacted,* That the revenue laws of the United States be, and are hereby, extended over the Territory of Oregon.

SEC. 27. *And be it further enacted,* That the sum of fifteen thousand dollars be, and the same is hereby, appropriated out of any moneys in the treasury not otherwise appropriated, to be expended under the direction of the Secretary of the Treasury, for the construction of lighthouses at Cape Disappointment and New Dungeness; and for the construction and anchoring of the requisite number of buoys, to indicate the channels at the mouth of the

Columbia River, and the approaches to the harbor of Astoria; the said buoys to be placed and anchored under the direction of such persons as the Secretary of the Treasury shall appoint.

Approved, August 14, 1848.

AN ACT TO ESTABLISH THE TERRITORIAL GOVERNMENT OF MINNESOTA

MARCH 3, 1849

Be it enacted by the Senate and House of Representatives of the United States of America in Congress assembled, That from and after the passage of this act, all that part of the territory of the United States which lies within the following limits, to wit: Beginning in the Mississippi River, at the point where the line of forty-three degrees and thirty minutes of north latitude crosses the same, thence running due west on said line, which is the northern boundary of the State of Iowa to the north-west corner of the said State of Iowa, thence southerly along the western boundary of said State to the point where said boundary strikes the Missouri River, thence up the middle of the main channel of the Missouri River to the mouth of the White-earth River, thence up the middle of the main channel of the White-earth River to the boundary line between the possessions of the United States and Great Britain; thence east and south along the boundary line between the possessions of the United States and Great Britain to Lake Superior; thence in a straight line to the northernmost point of the State of Wisconsin in Lake Superior; thence along the western boundary line of said State of Wisconsin to the Mississippi River; thence down the main channel of said river to the place of beginning, be, and the same is hereby, erected into a temporary government by the name of the Territory of Minnesota: *Provided,* That nothing in this act contained shall be construed to inhibit the government of the United States from dividing said Territory into two or more Territories, in such manner and at such times as Congress shall deem convenient and proper, or from attaching any portion of said Territory to any other State or Territory of the United States.

SEC. 2. *And be it further enacted,* That the executive power and authority in and over said Territory of Minnesota shall be vested in a governor, who shall hold his office for four years, and until his successor shall be appointed and qualified, unless sooner removed by the President of the United States. The governor shall reside within said Territory, shall be commander-in-chief of the militia thereof, shall perform the duties and receive the emoluments of superintendent of Indian affairs; he may grant pardons for offences against the laws of said Territory, and reprieves for offences against the laws of the United

States until the decision of the President can be made known thereon; he shall commission all officers who shall be appointed to office under the laws of the said Territory, and shall take care that the laws be faithfully executed.

SEC. 3. *And be it further enacted,* That there shall be a secretary of said Territory, who shall reside therein, and hold his office for four years, unless sooner removed by the President of the United States; he shall record and preserve all the laws and proceedings of the legislative assembly hereinafter constituted, and all the acts and proceedings of the governor in his executive department; he shall transmit one copy of the laws and one copy of the executive proceedings, on or before the first day of December in each year, to the President of the United States, and, at the same time, two copies of the laws to the Speaker of the House of Representatives, and the President of the Senate, for the use of Congress. And in case of the death, removal, resignation, or necessary absence of the governor from the Territory, the secretary shall be, and he is hereby, authorized and required to execute and perform all the powers and duties of the governor during such vacancy or necessary absence, or until another governor shall be duly appointed to fill such vacancy.

SEC. 4. *And be it further enacted,* That the legislative power and authority of said Territory shall be vested in the governor and a legislative assembly. The legislative assembly shall consist of a council and house of representatives. The council shall consist of nine members, having the qualifications of voters, as hereinafter prescribed, whose term of service shall continue two years. The house of representatives shall, at its first session, consist of eighteen members, possessing the same qualifications as prescribed for members of the council, and whose term of service shall continue one year. The number of councillors and representatives may be increased by the legislative assembly, from time to time, in proportion to the increase of population: *Provided,* That the whole number shall never exceed fifteen councillors and thirty-nine representatives. An apportionment shall be made, as nearly equal as practicable, among the several counties or districts, for the election of the council and representatives, giving to each section of the Territory representation in the ratio of its population, Indians excepted, as nearly as may be. And the members of the council and of the house of representatives shall reside in, and be inhabitants of, the district for which they may be elected respectively. Previous to the first election, the governor shall cause a census or enumeration of the inhabitants of the several counties and districts of the Territory to be taken, and the first election shall be held at such time and places, and be conducted in such manner, as the governor shall appoint and direct; and he shall, at the same time, declare the number of members of the council and house of representatives to which each of the counties or districts shall be entitled under this act. The number of persons authorized to be elected having the highest number of votes in each of said council districts for members of the council shall be declared by the governor to be duly elected to the council; and the person or persons authorized to be elected having the greatest number of votes for the house of representatives, equal to the number to which each county or district shall be entitled, shall be declared by the governor to be duly elected members of the house of representatives: *Provided,* That in case of a tie between two or more persons voted for, the governor shall order a new election to supply the vacancy made by such tie. And the persons thus elected to the legislative assembly shall meet at such place, and on such day, as the governor shall appoint; but thereafter, the time, place, and manner of holding and conducting all elections by the people, and the apportioning the representation in several counties or districts to the council and house of representatives according to the population, shall be prescribed by law, as well as the day of the commencement of the regular sessions of the legislative assembly: *Provided,* That no one session shall exceed the term of sixty days.

SEC. 5. *And be it further enacted,* That every free white male inhabitant above the age of twenty-one years, who shall have been a resident of said Territory at the time of the passage of this act, shall be entitled to vote at the first election, and shall be eligible to any office within the said Territory; but the qualifications of voters and of holding office, at all subsequent elections, shall be such as shall be prescribed by the legislative assembly: *Provided,* That the right of suffrage and of holding office shall be exercised only by citizens of the United States, and those who shall have declared, on oath, their intention to become such, and shall have taken an oath to support the Constitution of the United States and the provisions of this act.

SEC. 6. *And be it further enacted,* That the legislative power of the Territory shall extend to all rightful subjects of legislation, consistent with the Constitution of the United States and the provisions of this act; but no law shall be passed interfering with the primary disposal of the soil; no tax shall be imposed upon the property of the United States; nor shall the lands or other property of non-residents be taxed higher than the lands or other property of residents. All the laws passed by the legislative assembly and governor shall be submitted to the Congress of the United States, and, if disapproved, shall be null and of no effect.

SEC. 7. *And be it further enacted,* That all township, district, and county officers, not herein otherwise provided for, shall be appointed or elected, as the case may be, in such manner as shall be provided by the governor and legislative assembly of the Territory of Minnesota. The governor shall nominate, and, by and with the advice and consent of the legislative council, appoint, all officers not herein otherwise provided for; and in the first instance the governor alone may appoint all said officers, who shall hold their offices until the end of the next session of the legislative assembly.

SEC. 8. *And be it further enacted,* That no member of the legislative assembly shall hold or be appointed to any office which shall have been created, or the salary or emoluments of which shall have been increased, while he was a member, during the term for which he was elected, and for one year after the expiration of such term; and no person holding a commission or appointment under the United States, except postmasters, shall be a member of the legislative assembly, or shall hold any office under the government of said Territory.

SEC. 9. *And be it further enacted,* That the judicial power of said Territory shall be vested in a Supreme Court, District Courts, Probate Courts, and in justices of the peace. The Supreme Court shall consist of a chief justice and two associate justices, any two of whom shall constitute a quorum, and who shall hold a term at the seat of government of said Territory annually, and they shall hold their offices during the period of four years. The said Territory shall be divided into three judicial districts, and a District Court shall be held in each of said districts by one of the justices of the Supreme Court, at such times and places as may be prescribed by law; and the said judges shall, after their appointments, respectively, reside in the districts which shall be assigned them. The jurisdiction of the several courts herein provided for, both appellate and original, and that of the Probate Courts and of justices of the peace, shall be as limited by law: *Provided,* That the justices of the peace shall not have jurisdiction of any matter in controversy when the title or boundaries of land may be in dispute, or where the debt or sum claimed shall exceed one hundred dollars; and the said Supreme and District Courts, respectively, shall possess chancery as well as common law jurisdiction. Each District Court, or the judge thereof, shall appoint its clerk, who shall also be the register in chancery, and shall keep his office at the place where the court may be held. Writs of error, bills of exception and appeals, shall be allowed in all cases from the final decisions of said District Courts to the Supreme Court, under such regulations as may be prescribed by law, but in no case removed to the Supreme Court shall trial by jury be allowed in said court. The Supreme Court, or the justices thereof, shall appoint its own clerk, and every clerk shall hold his office at the pleasure of the court for which he shall have been appointed. Writs of error and appeals from the final decisions of said Supreme Court shall be allowed, and may be taken to the Supreme Court of the United States, in the same manner and under the same regulations as from the Circuit Courts of the United States, where the value of the property, or the amount in controversy, to be ascertained by the oath or affirmation of either party, or other competent witness, shall exceed one thousand dollars; and each of the said District Courts shall have and exercise the same jurisdiction, in all cases arising under the Constitution and laws of the United States, as is vested in the Circuit and District Courts of the United States; and the first six days of every term of said courts, or so much thereof as shall be necessary, shall be appropriated to the trial of causes arising under the said Constitution and laws; and writs of error and appeal in all such cases shall be made to the Supreme Court of said Territory, the same as in other cases. The said clerk shall receive, in all such cases, the same fees which the clerks of the District Courts of the late Wisconsin Territory received for similar services.

SEC. 10. *And be it further enacted,* That there shall be appointed an attorney for said Territory, who shall continue in office for four years, unless sooner removed by the President, and who shall receive the same fees and salary as the attorney of the United States for the late Territory of Wisconsin received. There shall also be a marshal for the Territory appointed, who shall hold his office for four years, unless sooner removed by the President, and who shall execute all processes issuing from the said courts, when exercising their jurisdiction as Circuit and District Courts of the United States; he shall perform the duties, be subject to the same regulations and penalties, and be entitled to the same fees, as the marshal of the District Court of the United States for the late Territory of Wisconsin; and shall in addition, be paid two hundred dollars annually as a compensation for extra services.

SEC. 11. *And be it further enacted,* That the governor, secretary, chief justice, and associate justices, attorney, and marshal, shall be nominated, and, by and with the advice and consent of the Senate, appointed by the President of the United States. The governor and secretary, to be appointed as aforesaid, shall, before they act as such, respectively take an oath or affirmation, before the district judge, or some justice of the peace in the limits of said Territory, duly authorized to administer oaths and affirmations by the laws now in force therein, or before the chief justice or some associate justice of the Supreme Court of the United States, to support the Constitution of the United States, and faithfully to discharge the duties of their respective offices; which said oaths, when so taken, shall be certified by the person by whom the same shall have been taken, and such certificates shall be received and recorded by the said secretary among the executive proceedings; and the chief justice and associate justices, and all other civil officers in said Territory, before they act as such, shall take a like oath or affirmation, before the said governor or secretary, or some judge or justice of the peace of the Territory, who may be duly commissioned and qualified, which said oath or affirmation shall be certified and transmitted, by the person taking the same, to the secretary, to be by him recorded as aforesaid; and afterwards, the like oath or affirmation shall be taken, certified, and recorded in such manner and form as may be prescribed by law. The governor shall receive an annual salary of fifteen hundred dollars as governor, and one thousand dollars as superintendent of Indian affairs. The chief justice and associate justices shall each receive an annual salary of eighteen hundred dollars. The secretary shall receive an annual salary of eighteen hundred dollars. The said salaries shall be paid quarter-yearly, at the treasury of the United States. The members of the legislative assembly shall be entitled to receive three dollars each per day during their attendance at the sessions thereof, and three dollars each for every twenty miles travel in going to and returning from the said sessions, estimated according to the nearest usually travelled route. There shall be appropriated, annually, the sum of one thousand dollars, to be expended by the governor to defray the contingent expenses of the Territory; and there shall also be appropriated, annually, a sufficient sum, to be expended by the Secretary of the Territory, and upon an estimate to be made by the Secretary of the Treasury of the United States, to defray the expenses of the legislative assembly, the printing of the laws, the other incidental expenses; and the Secretary of the Territory shall annually account to the Secretary of the Treasury of the United States for the manner in which the aforesaid sum shall have been expended.

SEC. 12. *And be it further enacted,* That the inhabitants of the said Territory shall be entitled to all the rights, privileges, and immunities heretofore granted and secured to the Territory of Wisconsin and to its inhabitants; and the laws in force in the Territory of Wisconsin at the date of admission of the State of Wisconsin shall continue to be valid and operative therein, so far as the same be not incompatible with the provisions of this act, subject, nevertheless, to be altered, modified, or repealed, by the governor and legislative assembly of the said Territory of Minnesota; and the laws of the United States are hereby extended over and declared to be in force in said Territory, so far as the same, or any provision thereof, may be applicable.

SEC. 13. *And be it further enacted,* That the legislative assembly of the Territory of Minnesota shall hold its first session at Saint Paul; and at said first session the governor and legislative assembly shall locate and establish a temporary seat of government for said Territory at such place as they may deem eligible; and shall, at such time as they shall see proper, prescribe by law the manner of locating the permanent seat of government of said Territory by a vote of the people. And the sum of twenty thousand dollars, out of any money in the treasury not otherwise appropriated, is hereby appropriated and granted to said Territory of Minnesota, to be applied, by the governor and legislative assembly, to the erection of suitable public buildings at the seat of government.

SEC. 14. *And be it further enacted*, That a delegate to the House of Representatives of the United States, to serve for the term of two years, may be elected by the voters qualified to elect members of the legislative assembly, who shall be entitled to the same rights and privileges as are exercised and enjoyed by the delegates from'the several other Territories of the United States to the said House of Representatives. The first election shall be held at such times and places, and be conducted in such manner, as the governor shall appoint and direct; and at all subsequent elections, the times, places, and manner of holding the elections shall be prescribed by law. The person having the greatest number of votes shall be declared by the governor to be duly elected, and a certificate thereof shall be given accordingly.

SEC. 15. *And be it further enacted*, That all suits, process, and proceedings, civil and criminal, at law and in chancery, and all indictments and informations, which shall be pending and undetermined in the courts of the Territory of Wisconsin, within the limits of said Territory of Minnesota, when this act shall take effect, shall be transferred to be heard, tried, prosecuted, and determined in the District Courts hereby established, which may include the counties or districts where any such proceedings may be pending. All bonds, recognizances, and obligations, of every kind whatsoever, valid under the existing laws within the limits of said Territory, shall be valid under this act; and all crimes and misdemeanors against the laws in force within said limits may be prosecuted, tried, and punished in the courts established by this act; and all penalties, forfeitures, actions, and causes of action, may be recovered under this act, the same as they would have been under the laws in force within the limits composing said Territory at the time this act shall go into operation.

SEC. 16. *And be it further enacted*, That all justices of the peace, constables, sheriffs, and all other judicial and ministerial officers, who shall be in office within the limits of said Territory, when this act shall take effect, shall be, and they are hereby, authorized and required to continue to exercise and perform the duties of their respective offices as officers of the Territory of Minnesota, temporarily, and until they, or others, shall be duly appointed and qualified to fill their places in the manner herein directed, or until their offices shall be abolished.

SEC. 17. *And be it further enacted*, That the sum of five thousand dollars be, and the same is hereby, appropriated, out of any moneys in the treasury not otherwise appropriated, to be expended by and under the direction of the said governor of the Territory of Minnesota, in the purchase of a library, to be kept at the seat of government, for the use of the governor, legislative assembly, judges of the Supreme Court, secretary, marshal, and attorney of said Territory, and such other persons and under such regulations as shall be prescribed by law.

SEC. 18. *And be it further enacted,* That when the lands in the said Territory shall be surveyed under the direction of the government of the United States, preparatory to bringing the same into market, sections numbered sixteen and thirty-six in each township in said Territory shall be, and the same are hereby, reserved for the purpose of being applied to schools in said Territory, and in the States and Territories hereafter to be erected out of the same.

SEC. 19. *And be it further enacted,* That temporarily, and until otherwise provided by law, the governor of said Territory may define the judicial districts of said Territory, and assign the judges who may be appointed for said Territory to the several districts, and also appoint the times and places for holding courts in the several counties or subdivisions in each of said judicial districts, by proclamation to be issued by him; but the legislative assembly, at their first or any subsequent session, may organize, alter, or modify such judicial districts, and assign the judges, and alter the times and places of holding the courts, as to them shall seem proper and convenient.

SEC. 20. *And be it further enacted,* That every bill which shall or may pass the council and house or representatives shall, before it becomes a law, be presented to the governor of the Territory; if he approve, he shall sign it, but if not, he shall return it, with his objections, to the house in which it originated; which shall cause the objections to be entered at large upon their journal, and proceed to reconsider it. If, after such reconsideration, two thirds of that house shall agree to pass the bill, it shall be sent, together with the objections, to the other house, by which it shall also be reconsidered, and if approved by two thirds of that house, it shall become a law; but in all such cases the votes of both houses shall be determined by yeas and nays, and the names of the persons voting for and against the bill shall be entered on the journal of each house, respectively. If any bill shall not be returned by the governor within three days (Sundays excepted) after it shall have been presented to him, the same shall be a law, in like manner as if he had signed it, unless the legislative assembly, by adjournment, prevent it; in which case it shall not become a law.

Approved, March 3, 1849.

AN ACT PROPOSING TO THE STATE OF TEXAS THE ESTABLISHMENT OF HER NORTHERN AND WESTERN BOUNDARIES, THE RELINQUISHMENT BY THE SAID STATE OF ALL TERRITORY CLAIMED BY HER EXTERIOR TO SAID BOUNDARIES, AND OF ALL HER

CLAIMS UPON THE UNITED STATES, AND TO

ESTABLISH A TERRITORIAL GOVERNMENT

FOR NEW MEXICO

SEPTEMBER 9, 1850

Be it enacted by the Senate and House of Representatives of the United States of America in Congress assembled, That the following propositions shall be, and the same hereby are, offered to the State of Texas, which, when agreed to by the said State, in an act passed by the general assembly, shall be binding and obligatory upon the United States, and upon the said State of Texas: *Provided,* The said agreement by the said general assembly shall be given on or before the first day of December, eighteen hundred and fifty:

FIRST. The State of Texas will agree that her boundary on the north shall commence at the point at which the meridian of one hundred degrees west from Greenwich is intersected by the parallel of thirty-six degrees thirty minutes north latitude, and shall run from said point due west to the meridian of one hundred and three degrees west from Greenwich; thence her boundary shall run due south to the thirty-second degree of north latitude; thence on the said parallel of thirty-two degrees of north latitude to the Rio Bravo del Norte, and thence with the channel of said river to the Gulf of Mexico.

SECOND. The State of Texas cedes to the United States all her claim to territory exterior to the limits and boundaries which she agrees to establish by the first article of this agreement.

THIRD. The State of Texas relinquishes all claim upon the United States for liability of the debts of Texas, and for compensation or indemnity for the surrender to the United States of her ships, forts, arsenals, custom-houses, custom-house revenue, arms and munitions of war, and public buildings with their sites, which became the property of the United States at the time of the annexation.

FOURTH. The United States, in consideration of said establishment of boundaries, cession of claim to territory, and relinquishment of claims, will pay to the State of Texas the sum of ten millions of dollars in a stock bearing five per cent. interest, and redeemable at the end of fourteen years, the interest payable half-yearly at the treasury of the United States.

FIFTH. Immediately after the President of the United States shall have been furnished with an authentic copy of the act of the general assembly of Texas accepting these propositions, he shall cause the stock to be issued in favor of the State of Texas, as provided for in the fourth article of this agreement: *Provided, also,* That no more than five millions of said stock shall be issued until the creditors of the State holding bonds and other certificates of stock of Texas for which duties on imports were specially pledged, shall first file at the treasury of the United States releases of all claim against the United States for or on account of said bonds or certificates in such form as shall be prescribed by the Secretary of the Treasury and approved by the President of the United States: *Provided,* That nothing herein contained shall be construed to impair or qualify any thing contained in the third article of the second section of the "joint resolution for annexing Texas to the United States," approved March first, eighteen hundred and forty-five, either as regards the number of States that may hereafter be formed out of the State of Texas, or otherwise.

SEC. 2. *And be it further enacted,* That all that portion of the Territory of the United States bounded as follows: Beginning at a point in the Colorado River where the boundary line with the republic of Mexico crosses the same; thence eastwardly with the said boundary line to the Rio Grande; thence following the main channel of said river to the parallel of the thirty-second degree of north latitude; thence east with said degree to its intersection with the one hundred and third degree of longitude west of Greenwich; thence north with said degree of longitude to the parallel of thirty-eighth degree of north latitude; thence west with said parallel to the summit of the Sierra Madre; thence south with the crest of said mountains to the thirty-seventh parallel of north latitude; thence west with said parallel to its intersection with the boundary line of the State of California; thence with said boundary line to the place of beginning — be, and the same is hereby, erected into a temporary government, by the name of the Territory of New Mexico: *Provided,* That nothing in this act contained shall be construed to inhibit the government of the United States from dividing said Territory into two or more Territories, in such manner and at such times as Congress shall deem convenient and proper, or from attaching any portion thereof to any other Territory or State: *And provided, further,* That, when admitted as a State, the said Territory, or any portion of the same, shall be received into the Union, with or without slavery, as their constitution may prescribe at the time of their admission.

SEC. 3. *And be it further enacted,* That the executive power and authority in and over said Territory of New Mexico shall be vested in a governor, who shall hold his office for four years, and until his successor shall be appointed and qualified, unless sooner removed by the President of the United States. The governor shall reside within said Territory, shall be commander-in-chief of the militia thereof, shall perform the duties and receive the emoluments of superintendent of Indian affairs, and shall approve all laws passed by the legislative assembly before they shall take effect; he may grant pardons for offences against the laws of said Territory, and reprieves for offences against the laws of the United States, until the decision of the President can be made known thereon; he shall commission all officers who shall be appointed to office under the laws of the said Territory, and shall take care that the laws be faithfully executed.

SEC. 4. *And be it further enacted,* That there shall be a secretary of said Territory, who shall reside therein, and hold his office for four years, unless sooner removed by the President of the United States; he shall record and preserve all the laws and proceedings of the legislative assembly hereinafter constituted, and all the acts and proceedings of the governor in his executive department; he shall transmit one copy of the laws and one copy of the executive proceedings, on or before the first day of December in each year, to the President of the United States, and, at the same time, two copies of the laws to the Speaker of the House of Representatives and the President of the Senate, for the use of Congress. And, in case of the death, removal, resignation, or other necessary absence of the governor from the Territory, the secretary shall have, and he is hereby authorized and required to execute and perform all the powers and duties of the governor during such vacancy or necessary absence, or until another governor shall be duly appointed to fill such vacancy.

SEC. 5. *And be it further enacted,* That the legislative power and authority of said Territory shall be vested in the governor and a legislative assembly. The legislative assembly shall consist of a Council and House of Representatives. The Council shall consist of thirteen members, having the qualifications of voters as hereinafter prescribed, whose term of service shall continue two years. The House of Representatives shall consist of twenty-six members, possessing the same qualifications as prescribed for members of the Council, and whose term of service shall continue one year. An apportionment shall be made, as nearly equal as practicable, among the several counties or districts, for the election of the Council and House of Representatives, giving to each section of the Territory representation in the ratio of its population, (Indians excepted,) as nearly as may be. And the members of the Council and of the House of Representatives shall reside in, and be inhabitants of, the district for which they may be elected respectively. Previous to the first election, the governor shall cause a census or enumeration of the inhabitants of the several counties and districts of the Territory to be taken, and the first election shall be held at such time and places, and be conducted in such manner, as the governor shall appoint and direct; and he shall, at the same time, declare the number of the members of the Council and House of Representatives to which each of the counties or districts shall be entitled under this act. The number of persons authorized to be elected having the highest number of votes in each of said Council districts, for members of the Council, shall be declared by the governor to be duly elected to the Council; and the person or persons authorized to be elected having the greatest number of votes for the House of Representatives, equal to the number to which each county or district shall be entitled, shall be declared by the governor to be duly elected members of the House of Representatives: Provided, That in case of a tie between two or more persons voted for, the governor shall order a new election to supply the vacancy made by such tie. And the persons thus elected to the legislative assembly shall meet at such place and on such day as the governor shall appoint; but thereafter, the time, place, and manner of holding and conducting all elections by the people, and the apportioning the representation in the several counties or districts to the Council and House of Representatives according to the population, shall be prescribed by law, as well as the day of the commencement of the regular sessions of the legislative assembly: *Provided,* That no one session shall exceed the term of forty days.

SEC. 6. *And be it further enacted,* That every free white male inhabitant, above the age of twenty-one years, who shall have been a resident of said Territory at the time of the passage of this act, shall be entitled to vote at the first election, and shall be eligible to any office within the said Territory; but the qualifications of voters and of holding office, at all subsequent elections, shall be such as shall be prescribed by the legislative assembly: *Provided,* That the right of suffrage, and of holding office, shall be exercised only by citizens of the United States, including those recognized as citizens by the treaty with the republic of Mexico, concluded February second, eighteen hundred and forty-eight.

SEC. 7. *And be it further enacted,* That the legislative power of the Territory shall extend to all rightful subjects of legislation, consistent with the Constitution of the United States and the provisions of this act; but no law shall be passed interfering with the primary disposal of the soil; no tax shall be imposed upon the property of the United States; nor shall the lands or other property of non-residents be taxed higher than the lands or other property of residents. All the laws passed by the legislative assembly and governor shall be submitted to the Congress of the United States, and, if disapproved, shall be null and of no effect.

SEC. 8. *And be it further enacted,* That all township, district, and county officers, not herein otherwise provided for, shall be appointed or elected, as the case may be, in such manner as shall be provided by the governor and legislative assembly of the Territory of New Mexico. The governor shall nominate, and, by and with the advice and consent of the legislative Council, appoint, all officers not herein otherwise provided for; and in the first instance the governor alone may appoint all said officers, who shall hold their offices until the end of the first session of the legislative assembly, and shall lay off the necessary districts for members of the Council and House of Representatives, and all other officers.

SEC. 9. *And be it further enacted,* That no member of the legislative assembly shall hold, or be appointed to, any office which shall have been created, or the salary or emoluments of which shall have been increased while he was a member, during the term for which he was elected, and for one year after the expiration of such term; and no person holding a commission or appointment under the United States, except postmasters, shall be a member of the legislative assembly, or shall hold any office under the government of said Territory.

SEC. 10. *And be it further enacted,* That the judicial power of said Territory shall be vested in a Supreme Court, District Courts, Probate Courts, and in justices of the peace. The Supreme Court shall consist of a chief justice and two associate justices, any two or whom shall constitute a quorum, and who shall hold a term at the seat of government of said Territory annually, and they shall hold their offices during the period of four years. The said Territory shall be divided into three judicial districts, and a District Court shall be held in each of said districts by one of the justices of the Supreme Court, at such time and place as may be prescribed by law; and the said judges shall, after their appointments, respectively, reside in the districts which shall be assigned them. The jurisdiction of the several courts herein provided for, both appellate and original, and that of the Probate Courts and of justices of the peace, shall be as limited by law: *Provided,* That justices of the peace shall not have jurisdiction of any matter in controversy when the title or boundaries of land may be in dispute, or where the debt or sum claimed shall exceed one hundred dollars; and the said Supreme and District Courts, respectively, shall possess chancery as well as common law jurisdiction. Each District Court, or the judge thereof, shall appoint its clerk, who shall also be the register in chancery, and shall keep his office at the place where the court may be held. Writs of error, bills of exception, and appeals, shall be allowed in all cases from the final decisions of said District Courts to the Supreme Court, under such regulations as may be prescribed by law, but in no case removed to the Supreme Court shall trial by jury be allowed in said court. The Supreme Court, or the justices thereof, shall appoint its own clerk, and every clerk shall hold his office at the pleasure of the court for which he shall have been appointed. Writs or error and appeals from the final decisions of said Supreme Court shall be allowed, and may be taken to the Supreme Court of the United States, in the same manner and under the same regulations as from the Circuit Courts of the United States, where the value of the property or the amount in controversy, to be ascertained by the oath or affirmation of either party, or other competent witness, shall exceed one thousand dollars; except only that in all cases involving title to slaves, the said writs of error or appeals shall be allowed and decided by the said Supreme Court without regard to the value of the matter, property, or title in controversy; and except also that a writ of error or appeal shall also be allowed to the Supreme Court of the United States from the decision of the said Supreme Court created by this act, or of any judge thereof, or of the District Courts created by this act, or of any judge thereof, upon any writ of habeas corpus involving the question of personal freedom; and each of the said District Courts shall have and exercise the same jurisdiction in all cases arising under the Constitution and laws of the United States as is vested in the Circuit and District Courts of the United States; and the said Supreme and District Courts of the said Territory, and the respective judges thereof, shall and may grant writs of habeas corpus in all cases in which the same are grantable by the judges of the United States in the District of Columbia; and the first six days of every term of said courts, or so much thereof as shall be necessary, shall be appropriated to the trial of causes arising under the said Constitution and laws; and writs of error and appeals in all such cases shall be made to the Supreme Court of said Territory, the same as in other cases. The said clerk shall receive in all such cases the same fees which the clerks of the District Courts of Oregon Territory now receive for similar services.

SEC. 11. *And be it further enacted,* That there shall be appointed an attorney for said Territory, who shall continue in office for four years, unless sooner removed by the President, and who shall receive the same fees and salary as the attorney of the United States for the present Territory of Oregon. There shall also be a marshal for the Territory appointed, who shall hold his office for four years, unless sooner removed by the President, and who shall execute all processes issuing from the said courts when exercising their jurisdiction as Circuit and District Courts of the United States: he shall perform the duties, be subject to the same regulations and penalties, and be entitled to the same fees as the marshal of the District Court of the United States for the present Territory of Oregon, and shall, in addition, be paid two hundred [dollars] annually as a compensation for extra services.

SEC. 12. *And be it further enacted,* That the governor, secretary, chief justice and associate justices, attorney and marshal, shall be nominated, and, by and with the advice and consent of the Senate, appointed by the President of the United States. The governor and secretary, to be appointed as aforesaid, shall, before they act as such, respectively take an oath or affirmation, before the district judge, or some justice of the peace in the limits of said Territory, duly authorized to administer oaths and affirmations by the laws in force therein, or before the chief justice or some associate justice of the Supreme Court of the United States, to support the Constitution of the United States, and faithfully to discharge the duties of their respective offices; which said oaths, when so taken, shall be certified by the person by whom the same have been taken, and such certificates shall be received and recorded by the said secretary among the executive proceedings; and the chief justice and associate justices, and all other civil officers in said Territory, before they act as such, shall take a like oath or affirmation, before the said governor or secretary, or some judge or justice of the peace of the Territory, who may be duly commissioned and qualified, which said oath or affirmation shall be certified and transmitted, by the person taking the same, to the secretary, to be by him recorded as aforesaid; and afterwards, the like oath or affirmation shall be taken, certified, and recorded, in such manner and form as may be prescribed by law. The governor shall receive an annual salary of fifteen hundred dollars as governor, and one thousand dollars as superintendent of Indian affairs. The chief justice and associate justices shall each receive an annual salary of eighteen hundred dollars. The secretary shall receive an annual salary of eighteen hundred dollars. The said salaries shall be paid quarter-yearly, at the treasury of the United States. The members of the legislative assembly shall be entitled to receive three dollars each per day during their attendance at the sessions thereof, and three dollars each for every twenty miles' travel in going to and returning from the said sessions, estimated according to the nearest usually travelled route. There shall be appropriated annually the sum of one thousand dollars, to be expended by the governor, to defray the contingent expenses of the Territory; there shall also be appropriated annually a sufficient sum to be expended by the secretary of the Territory, and upon an estimate to be made by the Secretary of the Treasury of the United States, to defray the expenses of the legislative assembly, the printing of the laws, and other incidental expenses; and the secretary of the Territory shall annually account to the Secretary of the Treasury of the United States for the manner in which the aforesaid sum shall have been expended.

SEC. 13. *And be it further enacted,* That the legislative assembly of the Territory of New Mexico shall hold its first session at such time and place in said Territory as the Governor thereof shall appoint and direct; and at said first session, or as soon thereafter as they shall deem expedient, the governor and legislative assembly shall proceed to locate and establish the seat of government for said Territory at such place as they may deem eligible; which place, however, shall thereafter be subject to be changed by the said governor and legislative assembly.

SEC. 14. *And be it further enacted,* That a delegate to the House of Representatives of the United States, to serve during each Congress of the United States, may be elected by the voters qualified to elect members of the legislative assembly, who shall be entitled to the same rights and privileges as are exercised and enjoyed by the delegates from the several other Territories of the United States to the said House of Representatives. The first election shall be held at such time and places, and be conducted in such manner, as the governor shall appoint and direct; and at all subsequent elections, the times, places, and manner of holding the elections shall be prescribed by law. The person having the greatest number of votes shall be declared by the governor to be duly elected, and a certificate thereof shall be given accordingly: *Provided,* That such delegate shall receive no higher sum for mileage than is allowed by law to the delegate from Oregon.

SEC. 15. *And be it further enacted,* That when the lands in said Territory shall be surveyed under the direction of the government of the United States, preparatory to bringing the same into market, sections numbered sixteen and thirty-six in each township in said Territory shall be, and the same are hereby, reserved for the purpose of being applied to schools in said Territory, and in the States and Territories hereafter to be erected out of the same.

SEC. 16. *And be it further enacted,* That temporarily and until otherwise provided by law, the governor of said Territory may define the judicial districts of said Territory, and assign the judges who may be appointed for said Territory to the several districts, and also appoint the times and places for holding courts in the several counties or subdivision in each of said judicial districts, by proclamation to be issued by him; but the legislative assembly, at their first or any subsequent session, may organize, alter, or modify such judicial districts, and assign the judges, and alter the times and places of holding the courts, as to them shall seem proper and convenient.

SEC. 17. *And be it further enacted,* That the Constitution, and all laws of the United States which are not locally inapplicable, shall have the same force and effect within the said Territory of New Mexico as elsewhere within the United States.

SEC. 18. *And be it further enacted,* That the provisions of this act be, and they are hereby, suspended until the boundary between the United States and the State of Texas shall be adjusted; and when such adjustment shall have been effected, the President of the United States shall issue his proclamation, declaring this act to be in full force and operation, and shall proceed to appoint the officers herein provided to be appointed in and for said Territory.

SEC. 19. *And be it further enacted,* That no citizen of the United States shall be deprived of his life, liberty, or property, in said Territory, except by the judgement of his peers and the laws of the land.

Approved, September 9, 1850.

AN ACT TO ESTABLISH A
TERRITORIAL GOVERNMENT FOR UTAH
SEPTEMBER 9, 1850

Be it enacted by the Senate and House of Representatives of the United States of America in Congress assembled, That all that part of the territory of the United States included within the following limits, to wit: bounded on the west by the State of California, on the north by the Territory of Oregon, and on the east by the summit of the Rocky Mountains, and on the south by the thirty-seventh parallel of north latitude, be, and the same is hereby, created into a temporary government, by the name of the Territory of Utah; and, when admitted as a State, the said Territory, or any portion of the same, shall be received into the Union, with or without slavery, as their constitution may prescribe at the time of their admission: *Provided,* That nothing in this act contained shall be construed to inhibit the government of the United States from dividing said Territory into two or more Territories, in such manner and at such times as Congress shall deem convenient and proper, or from attaching any portion of said Territory to any other State or Territory of the United States.

SEC. 2. *And be it further enacted,* That the executive power and authority in and over said Territory of Utah shall be vested in a governor, who shall hold his office for four years, and until his successor shall be appointed and qualified, unless sooner removed by the President of the United States. The governor shall reside within said Territory, shall be commander-in-chief of the militia thereof, shall perform the duties and receive the emoluments of superintendent of Indian affairs, and shall approve all laws passed by the legislative assembly before they shall take effect: he may grant pardons for offences against the laws of said Territory, and reprieves for offences against the laws of the United States,until the decision of the President can be made known thereon; he shall commission all officers who shall be appointed to office under the laws of the said Territory, and shall take care that the laws be faithfully executed.

SEC. 3. *And be it further enacted,* That there shall be a secretary of said Territory, who shall reside therein, and hold his office for four years, unless sooner removed by the President of the United States: he shall record and preserve all the laws and proceedings of the legislative assembly hereinafter constituted, and all the acts and proceedings of the governor in his executive department; he shall transmit one copy of the laws and one copy of the executive proceedings, on or before the first day of December in each year, to the President of the United States, and, at the same time, two copies of the laws to the Speaker of the House of Representatives, and the President of the Senate, for the use of Congress. And in the case of the death, removal, resignation, or other necessary absence of the governor from the Territory, the secretary shall have, and he is hereby authorized and required to execute and perform, all the powers and duties of the governor during such vacancy or necessary absence, or until another governor shall be duly appointed to fill such vacancy.

SEC. 4. *And be it further enacted,* That the legislative power and authority of said Territory shall be vested in the governor and a legislative assembly. The legislative assembly shall consist of a Council and House of Representatives. The Council shall consist of thirteen members, having the qualifications of voters as hereinafter prescribed, whose term of service shall continue two years. The House of Representatives shall consist of twenty-six members, possessing the same qualifications as prescribed for members of the Council, and whose term of service shall continue one year. An apportionment shall be made, as nearly equal as practicable, among the several counties or districts, for the election of the Council and House of Representatives, giving to each section of the Territory representation in the ratio of its population, Indians excepted, as nearly as may be. And the members of the Council and of the House of Representatives shall reside in, and be inhabitants of, the district for which they may be elected respectively. Previous to the first election, the governor shall cause a census or enumeration of the inhabitants of the several counties and districts of the Territory to be taken, and the first election shall be held at such time and places, and be conducted in such manner, as the governor shall appoint and direct; and he shall, at the same time, declare the number of members of the Council and House of Representatives to which each of the counties or districts shall be entitled under this act. The number of persons authorized to be elected having the highest number of votes in each of said Council districts for members of the Council, shall be declared by the governor to be duly elected to the Council; and the person or persons authorized to be elected having the highest number of votes for the House of Representatives, equal to the number to which each county or district shall be entitled, shall be declared by the governor to be duly elected members of the House of Representatives: *Provided,* That in case of a tie between two or more persons voted for, the governor shall order a new election to supply the vacancy made by such a tie. And the persons thus elected to the legislative assembly shall meet at such place, and on such day, as the governor shall appoint; but thereafter, the time, place, and manner of holding and conducting all elections by the people, and the apportioning the representation in the several counties or districts to the Council and House of Representatives, according to population, shall be prescribed by law, as well as the day of the commencement of the regular sessions of the legislative assembly: *Provided,* That no one session shall exceed the term of forty days.

SEC. 5. *And be it further enacted,* That every free white male inhabitant above the age of twenty-one years, who shall have been a resident of said Territory at the time of the passage of this act, shall be entitled to vote at the first election, and shall be eligible to any office within the said Territory; but the qualifications of voters and of holding office, at all subsequent elections, shall be such as shall be prescribed by the legislative assembly: *Provided,* That the right of suffrage and of holding office shall be exercised only by citizens of the United States, including those recognized as citizens by the treaty with the republic of Mexico, concluded February second, eighteen hundred and forty-eight.

SEC. 6. *And be it further enacted,* That the legislative power of said Territory shall extend to all rightful subjects of legislation, consistent with the

Constitution of the United States and the provisions of this act; but no law shall be passed interfering with the primary disposal of the soil; no tax shall be imposed upon the property of the United States; nor shall the lands or other property of non-residents be taxed higher than the lands or other property of residents. All the laws passed by the legislative assembly and governor shall be submitted to the Congress of the United States, and, if disapproved, shall be null and of no effect.

SEC. 7. *And be it further enacted,* That all township, district, and county officers, not herein otherwise provided for, shall be appointed or elected, as the case may be, in such manner as shall be provided by the governor and legislative assembly of the territory of Utah. The governor shall nominate, and, by and with the advice and consent of the legislative Council, appoint all officers not herein otherwise provided for; and in the first instance the governor alone may appoint all said officers, who shall hold their offices until the end of the first session of the legislative assembly, and shall lay off the necessary districts for members of the Council and House of Representatives, and all other offices.

SEC. 8. *And be it further enacted,* That no member of the legislative assembly shall hold or be appointed to any office which shall have been created, or the salary or emoluments of which shall have been increased while he was a member, during the term for which he was elected, and for one year after the expiration of such term; and no person holding a commission or appointment under the United States, except postmasters, shall be a member of the legislative assembly, or shall hold any office under the government of said Territory.

SEC. 9. *And be it further enacted,* That the judicial power of said Territory shall be vested in a Supreme Court, District Courts, Probate Courts, and in justices of the peace. The Supreme Court shall consist of a chief justice and two associate justices, any two of whom shall constitute a quorum, and who shall hold a term at the seat of government of said Territory annually, and they shall hold their offices during the period of four years. The said Territory shall be divided into three judicial districts, and a District Court shall be held in each of said districts by one of the justices of the Supreme Court, at such time and place as may be prescribed by law; and the said judges shall, after their appointments, respectively, reside in the districts which shall be assigned them. The jurisdiction of the several courts herein provided for, both appellate and original, and that of the Probate Courts and of justices of the peace, shall be as limited by law: *Provided,* That justices of the peace shall not have jurisdiction of any matter in controversy when the title or boundaries of land may be in dispute, or where the debt or sum claimed shall exceed one hundred dollars; and the said Supreme and District Courts, respectively, shall possess chancery as well as common law jurisdiction. Each District Court, or the judge thereof, shall appoint its clerk, who shall also be the register in chancery, and shall keep his office at the place where the court may be held. Writs of error, bills of exception, and appeals shall be allowed in all cases from the final decisions of said District Courts to the Supreme Court, under such regulations as may be prescribed by law; but in no case removed to the Supreme Court shall trial by jury be allowed in said court. The Supreme Court, or the justices thereof, shall appoint its own clerk, and every clerk shall hold his office at the pleasure of the court for which he shall have been appointed. Writs of error, and appeals from the final decisions of said Supreme Court, shall be allowed, and may be taken to the Supreme Court of the United States, in the same manner and under the same regulations as from the Circuit Courts of the United States, where the value of the property or the amount in controversy, to be ascertained by the oath or affirmation of either party, or other competent witness, shall exceed one thousand dollars, except only that, in all cases involving title to slaves, the said writs of error or appeals shall be allowed and decided by the said Supreme Court, without regard to the value of the matter, property, or title in controversy; and except, also, that a writ of error or appeal shall also be allowed to the Supreme Court of the United States, from the decisions of the said Supreme Court created by this act, or of any judge thereof, or of the District Courts created by this act, or of any judge thereof, upon any writ of habeas corpus involving the question of personal freedom; and each of the said District Courts shall have and exercise the same jurisdiction in all cases arising under the Constitution and laws of the United States as is vested in the Circuit and District Courts of the United States; and the said Supreme and District Courts of the said Territory, and the respective judges thereof, shall and may grant writs of habeas corpus in all cases in which the same are granted by the judges of the United States in the District of Columbia; and the first six days of every term of said courts, or so much thereof as shall be necessary, shall be appropriated to the trial of causes arising under the said Constitution and laws; and writs of error and appeal, in all such cases, shall be made to the Supreme Court of said Territory, the same as in other cases. The said clerk shall receive in all such cases the same fees which the clerks of the District Courts of Oregon Territory now receive for similar services.

SEC. 10. *And be it further enacted,* That there shall be appointed an attorney for said Territory, who shall continue in office for four years, unless sooner removed by the President, and who shall receive the same fees and salary as the attorney of the United States for the present Territory of Oregon. There shall also be a marshal for the Territory appointed, who shall hold his office for four years, unless sooner removed by the President, and who shall execute all processes issuing from the said courts, when exercising their jurisdiction as Circuit and District Courts of the United States: he shall perform the duties, be subject to the same regulation and penalties, and be entitled to the same fees as the marshal of the District Court of the United States for the present Territory of Oregon; and shall, in addition, be paid two hundred dollars annually as a compensation for extra services.

SEC. 11. *And be it further enacted,* That the governor, secretary, chief justice and associate justices, attorney and marshal, shall be nominated, and, by and with the advice and consent of the Senate, appointed by the President of the United States. The governor and secretary to be appointed as aforesaid shall, before they act as such, respectively, take an oath or affirmation, before the district judge, or some justice of the peace in the limits of said Territory, duly authorized to administer oaths and affirmations by the laws now in force therein, or before the chief justice or some associate justice of the Supreme Court of the United States, to support the Constitution of the United States, and faithfully to discharge the duties of their respective offices; which said oaths, when so taken, shall be certified by the person by whom the same shall have been taken, and such certificates shall be received and recorded by the said secretary among the executive proceedings; and the chief justice and associate justices, and all other civil officers in said Territory, before they act as such, shall take a like oath or affirmation, before the said governor or secretary, or some judge or justice of the peace of the Territory who may be duly commissioned and qualified, which said oath or affirmation shall be certified and transmitted, by the person taking the same, to the secretary, to be by him recorded as aforesaid; and afterwards, the like oath or affirmation shall be taken, certified, and recorded, in such manner and form as may be prescribed by law. The governor shall receive an annual salary of fifteen hundred dollars as governor, and one thousand dollars as superintendent of Indian affairs. The chief justice and associate justices shall each receive an annual salary of eighteen hundred dollars. The secretary shall receive an annual salary of eighteen hundred dollars. The said salaries shall be paid quarter-yearly, at the treasury of the United States. The members of the legislative assembly shall be entitled to receive three dollars each per day during their attendance at the sessions thereof, and three dollars each for twenty miles' travel, in going to and returning from the said sessions, estimated according to the nearest usually travelled route. There shall be appropriated annually the sum of one thousand dollars, to be expended by the governor, to defray the contingent expenses of the Territory. There shall also be appropriated, annually, a sufficient sum, to be expended by the secretary of the Territory, and upon an estimate to be made by the Secretary of the Treasury of the United States, to defray the expenses of the legislative assembly, the printing of the laws, and other incidental expenses; and the secretary of the Territory shall annually account to the Secretary of the Treasury of the United States for the manner in which the aforesaid sum shall have been expended.

SEC. 12. *And be it further enacted,* That the legislative assembly of the Territory of Utah shall hold its first session at such time and place in said Territory as the governor thereof shall appoint and direct; and at said first session, or as soon thereafter as they shall deem expedient, the governor and legislative assembly shall proceed to locate and establish the seat of government for said Territory at such place as they may deem eligible; which place, however, shall thereafter be subject to be changed by the said governor and legislative assembly. And the sum of twenty thousand dollars, out of any money in the treasury not otherwise appropriated, is hereby appropriated and granted to said Territory of Utah to be applied by the governor and legislative assembly to the erection of suitable public buildings at the seat of government.

SEC. 13. *And be it further enacted,* That a delegate to the House of Representatives of the United States, to serve during each Congress of the United States, may be elected by the voters qualified to elect members of the legislative assembly, who shall be entitled to the same rights and privileges as are exercised and enjoyed by the delegates from the several other Territories of the United States to the said House of Representatives. The first election shall be held at such time and places, and be conducted in such manner, as the governor shall appoint and direct; and at all subsequent elections, the times, places, and manner of holding the elections shall be prescribed by law. The person having the greatest number of votes shall be declared by the governor to be duly elected, and a certificate thereof shall be given accordingly: *Provided,* That said delegate shall receive no higher sum for mileage than is allowed by law to the delegate from Oregon.

SEC. 14. *And be it further enacted,* That the sum of five thousand dollars be, and the same is hereby, appropriated out of any moneys in the treasury not otherwise appropriated, to be expended by and under the direction of the said governor of the territory of Utah, in the purchase of a library, to be kept at the seat of government for the use of the governor, legislative assembly, judges of the Supreme Court, secretary, marshal, and attorney of said Territory, and such other persons, and under such regulations, as shall be prescribed by law.

SEC. 15. *And be it further enacted,* That when the lands in the said Territory shall be surveyed under the direction of the government of the United States, preparatory to bringing the same into market, sections numbered sixteen and thirty-six in each township in said Territory shall be, and the same are hereby, reserved for the purpose of being applied to schools in said Territory, and in the States and Territories hereafter to be erected out of the same.

SEC. 16. *And be it further enacted,* That temporarily, and until otherwise provided by law, the governor of said Territory may define the judicial districts of said Territory, and assign the judges who may be appointed for said Territory to the several districts, and also appoint the times and places for holding courts in the several counties or subdivisions in each of said judicial districts, by proclamation to be issued by him; but the legislative assembly, at their first or any subsequent session, may organize, alter, or modify such judicial districts, and assign the judges, and alter the times and places of holding the courts, as to them shall seem proper and convenient.

SEC. 17. *And be it further enacted,* That the Constitution and laws of the United States are hereby extended over and declared to be in force in said Territory of Utah, so far as the same, or any provision thereof, may be applicable.

Approved, September 9, 1850.

AN ACT TO ESTABLISH THE
TERRITORIAL GOVERNMENT OF WASHINGTON
MARCH 2, 1853

Be it enacted by the Senate and House of Representatives of the United States of America in Congress assembled, That from and after the passage of this act, all that portion of Oregon Territory lying and being south of the forty-ninth degree of north latitude, and north of the middle of the main channel of the Columbia River, from its mouth to where the forty-sixth degree of north latitude crosses said river, near Fort Wallawalla, thence with said forty-sixth degree of latitude to the summit of the Rocky Mountains, be organized into and constitute a temporary government by the name of the Territory of Washington: *Provided,* That nothing in this act contained shall be construed to affect the authority of the government of the United States to make any regulation respecting the Indians of said Territory, their lands, property, or other rights, by treaty, law or otherwise, which it would have been competent to the government to make if this act had never been passed: *Provided further,* That the title to the land, not exceeding six hundred and forty acres, now occupied as missionary stations among the Indian tribes in said Territory, or that may have been so occupied as missionary stations prior to the passage of the act establishing the Territorial government of Oregon, together with the improvements thereon, be, and is hereby, confirmed and established to the several religious societies to which said missionary stations respectively belong.

SEC. 2. *And be it further enacted,* That the executive power and authority in and over said Territory of Washington shall be vested in a governor, who shall hold his office for four years, and until his successor shall be appointed and qualified, unless sooner removed by the President of the United States. The governor shall reside in said Territory, shall be the commander-in-chief of the militia thereof, shall perform the duties and receive the emoluments of Superintendent of Indian affairs; he may grant pardons and remit fines and forfeitures for offences against the laws of said Territory, and respites for offences against the laws of the United States until the decision of the President can be made known thereon; he shall commission all officers who shall be appointed to office under the laws of the said Territory, where, by law, such commissions shall be required, and shall take care that the laws be faithfully executed.

SEC. 3. *And be it further enacted,* That there shall be a Secretary of said Territory, who shall reside therein, and hold his office for four years, unless sooner removed by the President of the United States; he shall record and preserve all the laws and proceedings of the Legislative Assembly hereinafter constituted, and all the acts and proceedings of the Governor in his Executive department; he shall transmit one copy of the laws and journals of the Legislative Assembly within thirty days after the end of each session, and one copy of the executive proceedings and official correspondence semi-annually, on the first days of January and July in each year, to the President of the United States, and two copies of the laws to the President of the Senate and to the Speaker of the House of Representatives, for the use of Congress. And in case of the death, removal, resignation, or absence of the Governor from the Territory, the Secretary shall be, and he is hereby, authorized and required to execute and perform all the powers and duties of the Governor during such vacancy or absence, or until another Governor shall be duly appointed and qualified to fill such vacancy.

SEC. 4. *And be it further enacted,* That the Legislative power and authority of said Territory shall be vested in a Legislative Assembly, which shall consist of a Council and House of Representatives. The Council shall consist of nine members, having the qualifications of voters, as hereinafter prescribed, whose term of service shall continue three years. Immediately after they shall be assembled, in consequence of their first election, they shall be divided as equally as may be into three classes. The seats of the members of Council of the first class, shall be vacated at the expiration of the first year, of the second class at the expiration of the second year, and of the third class at the expiration of the third year, so that one third may be chosen every year; and if vacancies happen, by resignation or otherwise, the same shall be filled at the next ensuing election. The House of Representatives shall, at its first session, consist of eighteen members, possessing the same qualifications as prescribed for members of the Council, and whose term of service shall continue one year. The number of representatives may be increased by the Legislative Assembly, from time to time, in proportion to the increase of qualified voters. *Provided*, That the whole number shall never exceed thirty. An apportionment shall be made, as nearly as practicable, among the several counties or districts, for the election of the Council and Representatives, giving to each section of the Territory representation in the ratio of its qualified voters, as nearly as may be. And the members of the Council and of the House of Representatives shall reside in, and be inhabitants of, the district or county or counties, for which they may be elected, respectively. Previous to the first election, the Governor shall cause a census or enumeration of the inhabitants and qualified voters of the several counties and districts of the Territory to be taken, by such persons, and in such mode, as the Governor shall designate and appoint; and the persons so appointed shall receive a reasonable compensation therefor. And the first election shall be held at such time and places, and be conducted in such manner, both as to the persons who shall superintend such election and the returns thereof, as the Governor shall appoint and direct; and he shall at the same time declare the number of members of the Council and House of Representatives to which each of the counties or districts shall be entitled under this act; and the Governor shall, by his proclamation, give at least sixty days' previous notice of such apportionment, and of the time, places, and manner of holding such election. The persons having the highest number of legal votes in each of said council districts for members of the Council shall be declared by the Governor to be duly elected to the Council, and the persons having the highest number of legal votes for the House of Representatives shall be declared by the Governor to be duly elected members of said House: *Provided*, That in case two or more persons voted for shall have an equal number of votes, and in case a vacancy shall otherwise occur in either branch of the Legislative Assembly, the Governor shall order a new election; and the persons thus elected to the Legislative Assembly shall meet at such place, and on such day, within ninety days after such elections, as the Governor shall appoint. But thereafter the time, place, and manner of holding and conducting all elections by the people, and the apportioning the representation in the several counties or districts to the Council and House of Representatives, according to the number of qualified voters, shall be prescribed by law, as well as the day of the commencement of the regular session of the Legislative Assembly: *Provided*, That no session in any one year shall exceed the term of sixty days, except the first session, which shall not exceed one hundred days.

SEC. 5. *And be it further enacted,* That every white male inhabitant above the age of twenty-one years, who shall have been a resident of said Territory at the time of the passage of this act, and shall possess the qualifications hereinafter prescribed, shall be entitled to vote at the first election, and shall be eligible to any office within the said Territory; but the qualifications of voters and of holding office at all subsequent elections shall be such as shall be prescribed by the Legislative Assembly: *Provided,* That the right of suffrage and of holding office shall be exercised only by citizens of the United States above the age of twenty-one years, and those above that age who shall have declared on oath their intention to become such, and shall have taken an oath to support the Constitution of the United States and the provisions of this act: *And provided further,* That no officer, soldier, seaman, mariner, or other person in the army or navy of the United States, or attached to troops in the service of the United States, shall be allowed to vote in said Territory, by reason of being on service therein, unless said Territory is, and has been for the period of six months, his permanent domicil: *Provided further,* That no person belonging to the army or navy of the United States shall ever be elected to or hold any civil office or appointment in said Territory.

SEC. 6. *And be it further enacted,* That the Legislative power of the Territory shall extend to all rightful subjects of legislation not inconsistent with the Constitution and laws of the United States. But no law shall be passed interfering with the primary disposal of the soil; no tax shall be imposed upon the property of the United States; nor shall the lands or other property of nonresidents be taxed higher than the lands or other property of residents. All the laws passed by the Legislative Assembly shall be submitted to the Congress of the United States, and, if disapproved, shall be null and of no effect: *Provided,* That nothing in this act shall be construed to give power to incorporate a bank or any institution with banking powers, or to borrow money in the name of the Territory, or to pledge the faith of the people of the same for any loan whatever, directly or indirectly. No charter granting any privileges of making, issuing, or putting into circulation any notes or bills in the likeness of banknotes, or any bonds, scrip, drafts, bills of exchange, or obligations, or granting any other banking powers or privileges, shall be passed by the Legislative Assembly; nor shall the establishment of any branch or agency of any such corporation, derived from other authority, be allowed in said Territory; nor shall said Legislative Assembly authorize the issue of any obligation, scrip, or evidence of debt, by said Territory, in any mode or manner whatever, except certificates for service to said Territory. And all such laws, or any law or laws inconsistent with the provisions of this act, shall be utterly null and void. And all taxes shall be equal and uniform; and no distinctions shall be made in the assessments between different kinds of property, but the assessments shall be according to the value thereof. To avoid improper influences, which may result from intermixing in one and the same act such things as have no proper relation to each other, every law shall embrace but one object, and that shall be expressed in the title.

SEC. 7. *And be it further enacted,* That all township, district, and county officers not herein otherwise provided for, shall be appointed or elected in such manner as shall be provided by the Legislative Assembly of the Territory of Washington.

SEC. 8. *And be it further enacted,* That no member of the Legislative Assembly shall hold or be appointed to any office which shall have been created, or the salary or emoluments of which shall have been increased while he was a member, during the term for which he was elected and for one year after the expiration of such term; but this restriction shall not be applicable to members of the first Legislative Assembly; and no person holding a commission or appointment under the United States shall be a member of the Legislative Assembly, or shall hold any office under the government of said Territory.

SEC. 9. *And be it further enacted*, That the judicial power of said Territory shall be vested in a supreme court, district courts, probate courts, and in justices of the peace. The supreme court shall consist of a chief justice and two associate justices, any two of whom shall constitute a quorum, and who shall hold a term at the seat of government of said Territory annually, and they shall hold their offices during the period of four years, and until their successor shall be appointed and qualified. The said Territory shall be divided into three judicial districts, and a district court shall be held in each of said districts by one of the justices of the supreme court, at such times and places as may be prescribed by law; and the said judges shall, after their appointments, respectively reside in the districts which shall be assigned them. The jurisdiction of the several courts herein provided for, both appellate and original, and that of the probate courts and of justices of the peace, shall be as limited by law: *Provided*, That justices of the peace shall not have jurisdiction of any case in which the title to land shall in any wise come in question, or where the debt or damages claimed shall exceed one hundred dollars; and the said supreme and district courts, respectively shall possess chancery as well as common-law jurisdiction. Each district court, or the judge thereof, shall appoint its clerk, who shall also be the register in chancery, and shall keep his office at the place where the court may be held. Writs of error, bills of exception, and appeals, shall be allowed in all cases from the final decisions of said district court to the supreme court under such regulations as may be prescribed by law; but in no case removed to the supreme court shall trial by jury be allowed in said court. The supreme court, or the justices thereof, shall appoint its own clerk, and every clerk shall hold his office at the pleasure of the court for which he shall have been appointed. Writs of error, and appeals from the final decisions of said supreme court, shall be allowed, and may be taken to the Supreme Court of the United States, in the same manner and under the same regulations as from the circuit court of the United States, where the value of the property, or the amount in controversy, to be ascertained by the oath or affirmation of either party, or other competent witness, shall exceed two thousand dollars, and in all cases where the constitution of the United States, or acts of Congress, or a treaty of the United States, is brought in question; and each of the said district courts shall have and exercise the same jurisdiction in all cases arising under the constitution of the United States and the laws of said Territory, as is vested in the circuit and district courts of the United States; writs of error and appeal in all such cases shall be made to the supreme court of said Territory the same as in other cases. Writs of error, and appeals from the final decisions of said supreme court, shall be allowed and may be taken to the supreme court of the United States in the same manner as from the circuit courts of the United States, where the value of the property, or the amount in controversy, shall exceed two thousand dollars, and each of said district courts shall have and exercise the same jurisdiction, in all cases arising under the constitution and laws of the United States, as is vested in the circuit and district courts of the United States; and also of all cases arising under the laws of said Territory, and otherwise. The said clerk shall receive in all such cases the same fees which the clerks of the district courts of the Territory of Oregon receive for similar services.

SEC. 10. *And be it further enacted,* That there shall be appointed an attorney for said Territory, who shall continue in office for four years and until his successor shall be appointed and qualified, unless sooner removed by the President, and who shall receive the same fees and salary as is provided by law for the attorney of the United States for the Territory of Oregon. There shall also be a marshal for the Territory appointed, who shall hold his office for four years and until his successor shall be appointed and qualified, unless sooner removed by the President, and who shall execute all processes issuing from the said courts when exercising their jurisdiction as circuit and district courts of the United States; he shall perform the duties, be subject to the same regulation and penalties, and be entitled to the same fees, as are provided by law for the marshal of the Territory of Oregon, and shall, in addition, be paid the sum of two hundred dollars annually as a compensation for extra services.

SEC. 11. *And be it further enacted,* That the governor, secretary, chief justice, and associate justices, attorney, and marshal, shall be nominated, and, by and with the advice and consent of the Senate, appointed by the President of the United States. The governor and secretary to be appointed as aforesaid shall, before they act as such, respectively take an oath or affirmation before the district judge, or some justice of the peace in the limits of said Territory duly authorized to administer oaths and affirmations by the laws in force therein, or before the chief justice or some associate justice of the supreme court of the United States, to support the constitution of the United States, and faithfully to discharge the duties of their respective offices, which said oaths, when so taken, shall be certified by the person before whom the same shall have been taken; and such certificates shall be received and recorded by the said Secretary among the executive proceedings; and the Chief Justice and Associate Justices, and all other civil officers in said Territory, before they act as such, shall take a like oath or affirmation before the said Governor or Secretary, or some judge or justice of the peace of the Territory who may be duly commissioned and qualified, which said oath or affirmation shall be certified and transmitted, by the person taking the same, to the Secretary, to be by him recorded as aforesaid; and afterwards, the like oath or affirmation shall be taken, certified and recorded in such manner and form as may be prescribed by law. The Governor shall receive an annual salary of fifteen hundred dollars as Governor, and fifteen hundred dollars as Superintendent of Indian affairs. The Chief Justice, and Associate Justices, shall each receive an annual salary of two thousand dollars. The Secretary shall receive an annual salary of fifteen hundred dollars. The said salaries shall be paid quarterly, from the dates of the respective appointments, at the Treasury of the United States; but no such payment shall be made until said officers shall have entered upon the duties of their respective appointments. The members of the legislative assembly shall be entitled to receive three dollars each per day during their attendance at the session thereof, and three dollars each for every twenty miles' travel in going to and returning from said sessions, estimated according to the nearest usually travelled route. And a chief clerk, one assistant clerk, a sergeant-at-arms, and door-keeper, may be chosen for each house; and the chief clerk shall receive five dollars per day, and the said other officers three dollars per day, during the session of the legislative assembly; but no other officers shall be paid by the United States: *Provided*, That there shall be but one session of the legislative assembly annually, unless, on an extraordinary occasion, the Governor shall deem it expedient and proper to call the legislature together. There shall be appropriated, annually, the sum of fifteen hundred dollars, to be expended by the Governor, to defray the contingent expenses of the Territory, including the salary of a clerk of the executive department; and there shall also be appropriated, annually, a sufficient sum to be expended by the Secretary of the Territory, and upon an estimate to be made by the Secretary of the Treasury of the United States, to defray the expenses of the legislative assembly, the printing of the laws, and other incidental expenses; and the Governor and Secretary of the Territory shall, in the disbursement of all moneys intrusted to them, be governed solely by the instructions of the Secretary of the Treasury of the United States, and shall, semi-annually, account to the said Secretary for the manner in which the aforesaid sums of money shall have been expended; and no expenditure, to be paid out of money appropriated by Congress, shall be made by said legislative assembly for objects not specially authorized by the acts of Congress making the appropriations, nor beyond the sums thus appropriated for such objects.

SEC. 12. *And be it further enacted*, That the laws now in force in said Territory of Washington, by virtue of the legislation of Congress in reference to the Territory of Oregon, which have been enacted and passed subsequent to the first day of September, eighteen hundred and forty-eight, applicable to the said Territory of Washington, together with the legislative enactments of the Territory of Oregon, enacted and passed prior to the passage of, and not inconsistent with, the provisions of this act, and applicable to the said Territory of Washington, be, and they are hereby, continued in force in said Territory of Washington until they shall be repealed or amended by future legislation.

SEC. 13. *And be it further enacted*, That the legislative assembly of the Territory of Washington shall hold its first session at such time and place in said Territory as the Governor thereof shall appoint and direct; and at said first session, or as soon thereafter as they shall deem expedient, the legislative assembly shall proceed to locate and establish the seat of government for said Territory, at such place as they may deem eligible; 'which place, however, shall thereafter be subject to be changed by said legislative assembly. And the sum of five thousand dollars, out of any money in the Treasury not otherwise appropriated, is hereby appropriated and granted to said Territory of Washington, to be there applied by the Governor to the erection of suitable buildings at the seat of government.

SEC. 14. *And be it further enacted*, That a delegate to the House of Representatives of the United States, to serve for the term of two years, who shall be a citizen of the United States, may be elected by the voters qualified to elect members of the legislative assembly, who shall be entitled to the same rights and privileges as have been heretofore exercised and enjoyed by the delegates

from the several other Territories of the United States to the House of Representatives, but the delegate first elected shall hold his seat only during the term
of the Congress to which he shall be elected. The first election shall be held at
such time, and places, and be conducted in such manner, as the Governor shall
appoint and direct; of which, and the time, place, and manner of holding such
elections, he shall give at least sixty days' notice by proclamation; and at all
subsequent elections the time, places, and manner of holding the elections shall
be prescribed by law. The person having the greatest number of votes shall be
declared by the Governor to be duly elected, and a certificate thereof shall be
given accordingly. The delegate from said Territory shall be entitled to receive .
the same per diem compensation and mileage at present allowed the delegate
from the Territory of Oregon.

SEC. 15. *And be it further enacted,* That all suits, plaints, process, and
proceedings, civil and criminal, at law and in chancery, and all indictments and
informations, which shall be pending and undetermined in the courts established within and for said Territory of Oregon, by act of Congress, entitled "An
act to establish the territorial government of Oregon," approved August fourteen, one thousand eight hundred and forty-eight, wherein the venue in said
cases, suits at law, or in chancery, or criminal proceedings, shall be included
within the limits hereinbefore declared and established for the said Territory
of Washington; then, and in that case, said actions so pending in the Supreme
or Circuit Courts of the Territory of Oregon shall be, by the clerks of said
courts, duly certified to the proper courts of said Territory of Washington; and
thereupon said causes shall, in all things concerning the same, be proceeded on,
and judgements, verdicts, decrees, and sentences rendered thereon, in the same
manner as if the said Territory had not been divided. All bonds, recognizances,
and obligations of every kind whatsoever, valid, under the existing laws,
within the limits of said Territory of Oregon, shall be held valid under this act,
and all crimes and misdemeanors against the laws now in force within the said
limits of the Territory of Washington may be prosecuted, tried, and punished
in the courts established by this act, and all penalties, forfeitures, actions, and
causes of action, may be recovered and enforced, under this act, before the
Supreme and Circuit Courts established by this act as aforesaid: *Provided,*
That no right of action whatever shall accrue against any person for any act
done in pursuance of any law heretofore passed by the legislative assembly of
the Territory of Oregon, and which may be declared contrary to the Constitution or laws of the United States.

SEC. 16. *And be it further enacted,* That all justices of the peace, constables, sheriffs, and other judicial and ministerial officers, who shall be in
office within the limits of said Territory of Washington when this act shall take
effect, shall be and they are hereby authorized and required to continue to exercise and perform the duties of their respective offices, as officers of said Territory, until they or others shall be duly elected or appointed, and qualified,
to fill their places in the manner herein directed, or until their offices shall be
abolished.

SEC. 17. *And be it further enacted,* That the sum of five thousand dollars
be, and the same is hereby, appropriated out of any moneys in the Treasury
not otherwise appropriated, to be expended, by and under the direction of the

Governor of Washington, in the purchase of a library, to be kept at the seat of government for the use of the Governor, legislative assembly, Judges of the Supreme Court, secretary, marshal, and Attorney of said Territory, and such other persons, and under such regulations, as shall be prescribed by law.

SEC. 18. *And be it further enacted,* That until otherwise provided for by law, the Governor of said Territory may define the judicial districts of said Territory, and assign the judges who may be appointed for said Territory to the several districts, and also appoint the times and places for holding courts in the several counties or subdivisions in each of said judicial districts by proclamation, to be issued by him; but the legislative assembly, at their first or any subsequent session, may organize, alter, or modify such judicial districts, and assign the judges, and alter the times and places of holding the courts, as to them shall seem expedient and proper.

SEC. 19. *And be it further enacted,* That all officers to be appointed by the President, by and with the advice and consent of the Senate, for the Territory of Washington, who, by virtue of the provisions of any law of Congress now existing, or which may be enacted during the present session of Congress, are required to give security for moneys that may be intrusted with them for disbursement, shall give such security at such time and place, and in such manner, as the Secretary of the Treasury may prescribe.

SEC. 20. *And be it further enacted,* That when the lands in said Territory shall be surveyed under the direction of the Government of the United States, preparatory to bringing the same into market or otherwise disposing thereof, sections numbered sixteen and thirty-six in each township in said Territory shall be, and the same are hereby, reserved for the purpose of being applied to common schools in said Territory. And in all cases where said sections sixteen and thirty-six, or either or any of them, shall be occupied by actual settlers prior to survey thereof, the County Commissioners of the counties in which said sections so occupied as aforesaid are situated, be, and they are hereby, authorized to locate other lands to an equal amount in sections, or fractional sections, as the case may be, within their respective counties, in lieu of said sections so occupied as aforesaid.

SEC. 21. *And be it further enacted,* That the Territory of Oregon and the Territory of Washington shall have concurrent jurisdiction over all offences committed on the Columbia River, where said river forms a common boundary between said Territories.

Approved, March 2, 1853.

TREATY BETWEEN THE UNITED STATES
OF AMERICA AND MEXICO
DECEMBER 30, 1853

In the Name of Almighty God.

The Republic of Mexico and the United States of America desiring to remove every cause of disagreement, which might interfere in any manner with the better friendship and intercourse between the two Countries; and especially, in respect to the true limits which should be established, when notwithstanding what was covenanted in the Treaty of Guadalupe Hidalgo in the Year 1848, opposite interpretations have been urged, which might give occasion to questions of serious moment: to avoid these, and to strengthen and more firmly maintain the peace, which happily prevails between the two Republics, the President of the United States has for this purpose, appointed James Gadsden Envoy Extraordinary and Minister Plenipotentiary of the same near the Mexican Government, and the President of Mexico has appointed as Plenipotentiary "ad hoc" His Excellency Don Manuel Diez de Bonilla Cavalier Grand Cross of the National and Distinguished Order of Guadalupe, and Secretary of State and of the Office of Foreign Relations, and Don Jose Salazar Ylarregui and General Mariano Monterde as Scientific Commissioner invested with Full powers for this Negotiation who having communicated their respective Full Powers, and finding them in due and proper form, have agreed upon the Articles following:

ARTICLE I.

The Mexican Republic agrees to designate the following as her true limits with the United States for the future, Retaining the same dividing line between the two California's, as already defined and established according to the 5th Article of the Treaty of Guadalupe Hidalgo, the limits between the two Republics shall be as follows: Beginning in the Gulf of Mexico, three leagues from land, opposite the mouth of the Rio Grande as provided in the fifth article of the Treaty of Guadalupe Hidalgo, thence as defined in the said article, up the middle of that river to the point where the parallel of 31°47' north latitude crosses the same, thence due west one hundred miles, thence south to the parallel of 31°20' north latitude, thence along the said parallel of 31°20' to the 111th meridian of longitude west of Greenwich, thence in a straight line to a point on the Colorado river twenty english miles below the junction of the Gila and Colorado rivers, thence up the middle of the said river Colorado until it intersects the present line between the United States and Mexico.

For the performance of this portion of the Treaty each of the two Governments shall nominate one Commissioner to the end that, by common consent, the two thus nominated having met in the City of Paso del Norte, three months after the exchange of the ratifications of this Treaty may proceed to survey and mark out upon the land the dividing line stipulated by this article, where it shall not have already been surveyed and established by the Mixed Commission according to the Treaty of Guadalupe keeping a Journal and making proper plans of their operations. For this purpose if they should Judge it necessary. The contracting Parties shall be at liberty each to unite to its respective Commissioner, scientific or other assistants, such as Astronomers and Surveyors whose concurrence shall not be considered necessary for the settlement and ratification of a true line of division between the two Republics; that line shall be alone established upon which the Commissioners may fix, their consent in this particular being considered decisive and an integral part of this Treaty, without necessity of ulterior ratification or approval, and without room for interpretation of any kind by either of the Parties contracting.

The dividing line thus established shall in all time be faithfully respected by the two Governments without any variation therein, unless of the express and free consent of the two, given in conformity to the principles of the Law of Nations, and in accordance with the Constitution of each country respectively.

In consequence, the stipulation in the 5th Article of the Treaty of Guadalupe upon the Boundary line therein described is no longer of any force, wherein it may conflict with that here established, the said line being considered annulled and abolished wherever it may not coincide with the present, and in the same manner remaining in full force where in accordance with the same.

ARTICLE II.

The government of Mexico hereby releases the United States from all liability on account of the obligations contained in the eleventh article of the Treaty of Guadalupe Hidalgo, and the said article and the thirty-third article of the treaty of amity, commerce and navigation between the United States of America and the United Mexican States concluded at Mexico, on the fifth day of April, 1831, are hereby abrogated.

ARTICLE III.

In consideration of the foregoing stipulations, the government of the United States agrees to pay to the government of Mexico, in the city of New York, the sum of ten millions of dollars, of which seven millions shall be paid immediately upon the exchange of the ratifications of this treaty, and the remaining three millions as soon as the boundary line shall be surveyed, marked, and established.

ARTICLE IV.

The Provisions of the 6th and 7th articles of the Treaty of Guadalupe Hidalgo having been rendered nugatory for the most part by the Cession of Territory granted in the First Article of this Treaty, the said Articles are hereby abrogated and annulled and the provisions as herein expressed substituted therefor. The Vessels and Citizens of the United States shall in all Time have free and uninterrupted passage through the Gulf of California to and from their possessions situated North of the Boundary line of the Two Countries. It being understood that this passage is to be by navigating the Gulf of California and the river Colorado, and not by land, without the express consent of the

Mexican Government, and precisely the same provisions, stipulations and restrictions in all respects are hereby agreed upon and adopted and shall be scrupulously observed and enforced by the Two Contracting Governments in reference to the Rio Colorado, so far and for such distance as the middle of that River is made their common Boundary Line, by the First Article of this Treaty.

The several provisions, stipulations and restrictions contained in the 7th Article of the Treaty of Guadalupe Hidalgo, shall remain in force only so far as regards the Rio Bravo del Norte below the initial of the said Boundary provided in the First Article of this Treaty; that is to say, below the intersection of the 31° 47'.30'.' parallel of Latitude with the Boundary Line established by the late Treaty dividing said river from its mouth upwards according to the fifth Article of the Treaty of Guadalupe.

ARTICLE V.

All the provisions of the eighth and ninth, sixteenth and seventeenth articles of the Treaty of Guadalupe Hidalgo shall apply to the Territory ceded by the Mexican Republic in the first Article of the present Treaty and to all the rights of persons and property both civil and ecclesiastical within the same, as fully and as effectually as if the said Articles were herein again recited and set forth.

ARTICLE VI.

No Grants of Land within the Territory ceded by the first Article of this Treaty bearing date subsequent to the day twenty-fifth of September — when the Minister and Subscriber to this Treaty on the part of the United States proposed to the Government of Mexico to terminate the question of Boundary, will be considered valid or be recognized by the United States, or will any Grants made previously be respected or be considered as obligatory which have not been located and duly recorded in the Archives of Mexico.

ARTICLE VII.

Should there at any future period (which God forbid) occur any disagreement between the two Nations which might lead to a rupture of their relations and reciprocal peace, they bind themselves in like manner to procure by every possible method the adjustment of every difference, and should they still in this manner not succeed, never will they proceed to a declaration of War, without having previously paid attention to what has been set forth in Article 21 of the Treaty of Guadalupe for similar cases; which Article as well as the 22d is here re-affirmed.

ARTICLE VIII.

The Mexican government having the 5th of February 1853 authorized the early construction of a plank and railroad across the Isthmus of Tehuantepec, and to secure the stable benefits of said transit way to the persons and merchandise of the citizens of Mexico and the United States, it is stipulated that neither government will interpose any obstacle to the transit of persons and merchandise of both nations; and at no time shall higher charges be made on the transit of persons and property of citizens of the United States than may be made on the persons and property of other foreign nations, nor shall any interest in said transit way, nor in the proceeds thereof, be transferred to any foreign government.

The United States by its Agents shall have the right to transport across the Isthmus, in closed bags, the mails of the United States not intended for distribution along the line of communication; also the effects of the United States government and its citizens, which may be intended for transit, and not for distribution on the Isthmus, free of custom-house or other charges by the Mexican government. Neither passports nor letters of security will be required of persons crossing the Isthmus and not remaining in the country.

When the construction of the railroad shall be completed, the Mexican government agrees to open a port of entry in addition to the port of Vera Cruz, at or near the terminus of said road on the Gulf of Mexico.

The two governments will enter into arrangements for the prompt transit of troops and munitions of the United States, which that government may have occasion to send from one part of its territory to another, lying on opposite sides of the continent.

The Mexican government having agreed to protect with its whole power the prosecution, preservation and security of the work, the United States may extend its protection as it shall judge wise to it when it may feel sanctioned and warranted by the public or international law.

ARTICLE IX.

This Treaty shall be ratified, and the respective ratifications shall be exchanged at the City of Washington, within the exact period of six months from the date of its signature or sooner if possible.

In testimony whereof, We the Plenipotentiaries of the contracting parties have hereunto affixed our hand and seals at Mexico the Thirtieth (30th) day of December in the Year of Our Lord one thousand eight hundred and fifty three, in the thirty-third year of the Independence of the Mexican Republic, and the seventy eighth of that of the United States.

JAMES GADSDEN	(Seal)
MANUEL DIEZ de	
BONILLA	(Seal)
JOSÉ SALAZAR YLARREGUI	(Seal)
J. MARIANO MONTERDE	(Seal)

AN ACT TO ORGANIZE THE TERRITORIES
OF NEBRASKA AND KANSAS
MAY 30, 1854

Be it enacted by the Senate and House of Representatives of the United States of America in Congress assembled, That all that part of the territory of the United States included within the following limits, except such portions thereof as are hereinafter expressly exempted from the operations of this act, to wit: beginning at a point in the Missouri River where the fortieth parallel of north latitude crosses the same; thence west on said parallel to the east boundary of the Territory of Utah, on the summit of the Rocky Mountains; thence on said summit northward to the forty-ninth parallel of north latitude; thence east on said parallel to the western boundary of the territory of Minnesota; thence southward on said boundary to the Missouri River; thence down the main channel of said river to the place of beginning, be, and the same is hereby, created into a temporary government by the name of the Territory of Nebraska; and when admitted as a State or States, the said Territory, or any portion of the same, shall be received into the Union with or without slavery, as their constitution may prescribe at the time of their admission: *Provided,* That nothing in this act contained shall be construed to inhibit the government of the United States from dividing said Territory into two or more Territories, in such manner and at such times as Congress shall deem convenient and proper, or from attaching any portion of said Territory to any other State or Territory of the United States: *Provided further,* That nothing in this act contained shall be construed to impair the rights of person or property now pertaining to the Indians in said Territory, so long as such rights shall remain unextinguished by treaty between the United States and such Indians, or to include any territory which, by treaty with any Indian tribe, is not, without the consent of said tribe, to be included within the territorial limits or jurisdiction of any State or Territory; but all such territory shall be excepted out of the boundaries, and constitute no part of the Territory of Nebraska, until said tribe shall signify their assent to the President of the United States to be included within the said Territory of Nebraska, or to affect the authority of the government of the United States to make any regulations respecting such Indians, their lands, property, or other rights, by treaty, law, or otherwise, which it would have been competent to the government to make if this act had never passed.

SEC. 2. *And be it further enacted,* That the executive power and authority in and over said Territory of Nebraska shall be vested in a Governor, who shall hold his office for four years, and until his successor shall be appointed and qualified, unless sooner removed by the President of the United States. The Governor shall reside within said Territory, and shall be commander-in-chief of the militia thereof. He may grant pardons and respites for offences against the laws of said Territory, and reprieves for offences against the laws of the United States, until the decision of the President can be made known thereon; he shall commission all officers who shall be appointed to office under the laws of the said Territory, and shall take care that the laws be faithfully executed.

SEC. 3. *And be it further enacted,* That there shall be a Secretary of said Territory, who shall reside therein, and hold his office for five years, unless sooner removed by the President of the United States; he shall record and preserve all the laws and proceedings of the Legislative Assembly hereinafter constituted, and all the acts and proceedings of the Governor in his executive department; he shall transmit one copy of the laws and journals of the Legislative Assembly within thirty days after the end of each session, and one copy of the executive proceedings and official correspondence semi-annually, on the first days of January and July in each year to the President of the United States, and two copies of the laws to the President of the Senate and to the Speaker of the House of Representatives, to be deposited in the libraries of Congress; and in case of the death, removal, resignation, or absence of the Governor from the Territory, the Secretary shall be, and he is hereby, authorized and required to execute and perform all the powers and duties of the Governor during such vacancy or absence, or until another Governor shall be duly appointed and qualified to fill such vacancy.

SEC. 4. *And be it further enacted,* That the legislative power and authority of said Territory shall be vested in the Governor and a Legislative Assembly. The Legislative Assembly shall consist of a Council and House of Representatives. The Council shall consist of thirteen members, having the qualifications of voters, as hereinafter prescribed, whose term of service shall continue two years. The House of Representatives shall, at its first session, consist of twenty-six members, possessing the same qualifications as prescribed for members of the Council, and whose term of service shall continue one year. The number of representatives may be increased by the Legislative Assembly, from time to time, in proportion to the increase of qualified voters: *Provided,* That the whole number shall never exceed thirty-nine. An apportionment shall be made, as nearly equal as practicable, among the several counties or districts, for the election of the council and representatives, giving to each section of the Territory representation in the ratio of its qualified voters as nearly as may be. And the members of the Council and of the House of Representatives shall reside in, and be inhabitants of, the district or county, or counties for which they may be elected, respectively. Previous to the first election, the Governor shall cause a census, or enumeration of the inhabitants and qualified voters of the several counties and districts of the Territory, to be taken by such persons and in such mode as the Governor shall designate and appoint; and the persons so appointed shall receive a reasonable compensation therefor. And the first election shall be held at such time and places, and be conducted in such manner, both as to the persons who shall superintend such election and the returns thereof, as the Governor shall appoint and direct; and he shall at the same time declare the number of members of the Council and House of Representatives to which each of the counties or districts shall be entitled under this act. The persons having the highest number of legal votes in each of said council districts for members of the Council, shall be declared by the Governor to be duly elected to the Council; and the persons having the highest number of legal votes for the House of Representatives, shall be declared by the Governor to be duly elected members of said house: *Provided,* That in case two or more persons voted for shall have an equal number of votes, and in case a vacancy shall otherwise occur in either branch of the Legislative Assembly, the Governor shall order a new election; and the persons thus elected to the Legislative Assembly shall meet at such place and on such day as the Governor shall appoint; but thereafter, the time, place, and manner of holding and conducting all elections by the people, and the apportioning and representation in the several counties or districts to the Council and House of Representatives, according to the number of qualified voters, shall be prescribed by law, as well as the day of the commencement of the regular sessions of the Legislative Assembly: *Provided,* That no session in any one year shall exceed the term of forty days, except the first session, which may continue sixty days.

SEC. 5. *And be it further enacted,* That every free white male inhabitant above the age of twenty-one years who shall be an actual resident of said Territory, and shall possess the qualifications hereinafter prescribed, shall be entitled to vote at the first election, and shall be eligible to any office within the said Territory; but the qualifications of voters, and of holding office, at all subsequent elections, shall be such as shall be prescribed by the Legislative Assembly: *Provided,* That the right of suffrage and of holding office shall be exercised only by the citizens of the United States and those who shall have declared on oath their intention to become such, and shall have taken an oath to support the Constitution of the United States and the provisions of this act: *And provided further,* That no officer, soldier, seaman, or marine, or other person in the army or navy of the United States, or attached to troops in the service of the United States, shall be allowed to vote or hold office in said Territory, by reason of being on service therein.

SEC. 6. *And be it further enacted,* That the legislative power of the Territory shall extend to all rightful subjects of legislation consistent with the Constitution of the United States and the provisions of this act; but no law shall be passed interfering with the primary disposal of the soil; no tax shall be imposed upon the property of the United States; nor shall the lands or other property of non-residents be taxed higher than the lands or other property of residents. Every bill which shall have passed the Council and House of Representatives of the said Territory shall, before it become a law, be presented to the Governor of the Territory; if he approve, he shall sign it; but if not, he shall return it with his objections to the house in which it originated, who shall enter the objections at large on their journal, and proceed to reconsider it. If, after such reconsideration, two thirds of that house shall agree to pass the bill, it shall be sent, together with the objections, to the other house, by which it shall likewise be reconsidered, and if approved by two thirds of that house, it shall become a law. But in all such cases the votes of both houses shall be determined by yeas and nays, to be entered on the journal of each house respectively. If any bill shall not be returned by the Governor within three days (Sundays excepted) after it shall have been presented to him, the same shall be a law in like manner as if he had signed it, unless the Assembly, by adjournment, prevents its return, in which case it shall not be a law.

SEC. 7. *And be it further enacted,* That all township, district, and county officers, not herein otherwise provided for, shall be appointed or elected, as the case may be, in such manner as shall be provided by the Governor and Legislative Assembly of the Territory of Nebraska. The Governor shall nominate, and, by and with the advice and consent of the Legislative Council, appoint all officers not herein otherwise provided for; and in the first instance the Governor alone may appoint all said officers, who shall hold their offices until the end of the first session of the Legislative Assembly; and shall lay off the necessary districts for members of the Council and House of Representatives, and all other officers.

SEC. 8. *And be it further enacted,* That no member of the Legislative Assembly shall hold, or be appointed to, any office which shall have been created, or the salary or emoluments of which shall have been increased, while he was a member, during the term for which he was elected, and for one year after the expiration of such term; but this restriction shall not be applicable to members of the first Legislative Assembly; and no person holding a commission or appointment under the United States, except Postmasters, shall be a member of the Legislative Assembly, or hold any office under the government of said Territory.

SEC. 9. *And be it further enacted,* That the judicial power of said Territory shall be vested in a Supreme Court, District Courts, Probate Courts, and in Justices of the Peace. The Supreme Court shall consist of a chief justice and two associate justices, any two of whom shall constitute a quorum, and who shall hold a term at the seat of government of said Territory annually, and they shall hold their offices during the period of four years, and until their successor shall be appointed and qualified. The said Territory shall be divided into three judicial districts, and a district court shall be held in each of said districts by one of the justices of the Supreme Court, at such times and places as may be prescribed by law; and the said judges shall, after their appointments, respectively, reside in the districts which shall be assigned them. The jurisdiction of the several courts herein provided for, both appellate and original, and that of the probate courts and of justices of the peace, shall be as limited by law: *Provided,* That justices of the peace shall not have jurisdiction of any matter in controversy when the title or boundaries of land may be in dispute, or where the debt or sum claimed shall exceed one hundred dollars; and the said supreme and district courts, respectively, shall possess chancery as well as common law jurisdiction. Each District Court, or the judge thereof, shall appoint its clerk, who shall also be the register in chancery, and shall keep his office at the place where the court may be held. Writs of error, bills of exception, and appeals, shall be allowed in all cases from the final decisions of said district courts to the Supreme Court, under such regulations as may be prescribed by law; but in no case removed to the Supreme Court shall trial by jury be allowed in said court. The Supreme Court, or the justices thereof, shall appoint its own clerk, and every clerk shall hold his office at the pleasure of the court for which he shall have been appointed. Writs of error, and appeals from the final decisions of said Supreme Court, shall be allowed, and may be taken to the Supreme Court of the United States, in the same manner and under the same regulations as from the circuit courts of the United States, where the value of the property, or the amount in controversy, to be ascertained by the oath or affirmation of either party, or other competent witness, shall exceed one thousand dollars; except only that in all cases involving title to slaves, the said writs of error, or appeals shall be allowed and decided by the said Supreme Court, without regard to the value of the matter, property, or title in controversy; and except also that a writ or error or appeal shall also be allowed to the Supreme Court of the United States, from the decision of the said Supreme Court created by this act, or of any judge thereof, or of the district courts created by this act, or of any judge thereof, upon any writ of *habeas corpus*, involving the question of personal freedom: *Provided*, that nothing herein contained shall be construed to apply to or affect the provisions to the "act respecting fugitives from justice, and persons escaping from the service of their masters," approved February twelfth, seventeen hundred and ninety-three, and the "act to amend and supplementary to the aforesaid act," approved September eighteen, eighteen hundred and fifty; and each of the said district courts shall have and exercise the same jurisdiction in all cases arising under the Constitution and Laws of the United States as is vested in the Circuit and District Courts of the United States; and the said Supreme and District Courts of the said Territory, and the respective judges thereof, shall and may grant writs of *habeas corpus* in all cases in which the same are granted by the judges of the United States in the District of Columbia; and the first six days of every term of said courts, or so much thereof as shall be necessary, shall be appropriated to the trial of causes arising under the said constitution and laws, and writs of error and appeal in all such cases shall be made to the Supreme Court of said Territory, the same as in other cases. The said clerk shall receive in all such cases the same fees which the clerks of the district courts of Utah Territory now receive for similar services.

SEC. 10. *And be it further enacted,* That the provisions of an act entitled "An act respecting fugitives from justice, and persons escaping from the service of their masters," approved February twelve, seventeen hundred and ninety-three, and the provisions of the act entitled "An act to amend, and supplementary to, the aforesaid act," approved September eighteen, eighteen hundred and fifty, be, and the same are hereby, declared to extend to and be in full force within the limits of said Territory of Nebraska.

SEC. 11. *And be it further enacted,* That there shall be appointed an Attorney for said Territory, who shall continue in office for four years, and until his successor shall be appointed and qualified, unless sooner removed by the President, and who shall receive the same fees and salary as the Attorney of the United States for the present Territory of Utah. There shall also be a Marshal for the Territory appointed, who shall hold his office for four years, and until his successor shall be appointed and qualified, unless sooner removed by the President, and who shall execute all processes issuing from the said courts when exercising their jurisdiction as Circuit and District Courts of the United States; he shall perform the duties, be subject to the same regulation and penalties, and be entitled to the same fees, as the Marshal of the District Court of the United States for the present Territory of Utah, and shall, in addition, be paid two hundred dollars annually as a compensation for extra services.

SEC. 12. *And be it further enacted,* That the Governor, Secretary, Chief Justice, and Associate Justices, Attorney and Marshal, shall be nominated, and, by and with the advice and consent of the Senate, appointed by the President of the United States. The Governor and Secretary to be appointed as aforesaid, shall, before they act as such, respectively take an oath or affirmation before the District Judge or some Justice of the Peace in the limits of said Territory, duly authorized to administer oaths and affirmations by the laws now in force therein, or before the Chief Justice, or some Associate Justice of the Supreme Court of the United States, to support the Constitution of the United States, and faithfully to discharge the duties of their respective offices, which said oaths, when so taken, shall be certified by the person by whom the same shall have been taken; and such certificates shall be received and recorded by the said Secretary among the Executive proceedings; and the Chief Justice and Associate Justices, and all other civil officers in said Territory, before they act as such, shall take a like oath or affirmation before the said Governor or Secretary, or some Judge or Justice of the Peace of the Territory, who may be duly commissioned and qualified, which said oath or affirmation shall be certified and transmitted by the person taking the same to the Secretary, to be by him recorded as aforesaid; and, afterwards, the like oath or affirmation shall be taken, certified, and recorded, in such manner and form as may be prescribed by law. The Governor shall receive an annual salary of two thousand five hundred dollars. The Chief Justice and Associate Justices shall each receive an annual salary of two thousand dollars. The Secretary shall receive an annual salary of two thousand dollars. The said salaries shall be paid quarter-yearly, from the dates of the respective appointments, at the Treasury of the United States; but no such payment shall be made until said officers shall have entered upon the duties of their respective appointments. The members of the Legislative Assembly shall be entitled to receive three dollars each per day during their attendance at the sessions thereof, and three dollars each for every twenty miles' travel in going to and returning from the said sessions, estimated according to the nearest usually travelled route; and an additional allowance of three dollars shall be paid to the presiding officer of each house for each day he shall so preside. And a chief clerk, one assistant clerk, a sergeant-at-arms, and doorkeeper, may be chosen for each house; and the chief clerk shall receive four dollars per day, and the said other officers three dollars per day, during the session of the Legislative Assembly; but no other officers shall be paid by the United States: *Provided,* That there shall be but one session of the Legislature annually, unless, on an extraordinary occasion, the Governor shall think proper to call the legislature together. There shall be appropriated, annually, the usual sum, to be expended by the Governor, to defray the contingent expenses of the Territory, including the salary of a clerk of the Executive Department; and there shall also be appropriated, annually, a sufficient sum, to be expended by the Secretary of the Territory, and upon an estimate to be made by the Secretary of the Treasury of the United States, to defray the expenses of the Legislative Assembly, the printing of the laws, and other incidental expenses; and the Governor and Secretary of the Territory shall, in the disbursement of all moneys intrusted to them, be governed solely by the instructions of the Secretary of the Treasury of the United States, and shall, semi-annually, account to the said Secretary for the manner in which the aforesaid moneys shall have been expended; and no expenditure shall be made by said Legislative Assembly for objects not specially authorized by the acts of Congress, making the appropriations, nor beyond the sums thus appropriated for such objects.

SEC. 13. *And be it further enacted,* That the Legislative Assembly of the

Territory of Nebraska shall hold its first session at such time and place in said Territory as the Governor thereof shall appoint and direct; and at said first session, or as soon thereafter as they shall deem expedient, the Governor and Legislative Assembly shall proceed to locate and establish the seat of government for said Territory at such place as they may deem eligible; which place, however, shall thereafter be subject to be changed by the said Governor and Legislative Assembly.

SEC. 14. *And be it further enacted,* That a delegate to the House of Representatives of the United States, to serve for the term of two years, who shall be a citizen of the United States, may be elected by the voters qualified to elect members of the Legislative Assembly, who shall be entitled to the same rights and privileges as are exercised and enjoyed by the delegates from the several other Territories of the United States to the said House of Representatives, but the delegate first elected shall hold his seat only during the term of the Congress to which he shall be elected. The first election shall be held at such time and places, and be conducted in such manner, as the Governor shall appoint and direct; and at all subsequent elections the times, places, and manner of holding the elections, shall be prescribed by law. The person having the greatest number of votes shall be declared by the Governor to be duly elected; and a certificate thereof shall be given accordingly. That the Constitution, and all Laws of the United States which are not locally inapplicable, shall have the same force and effect within the said Territory of Nebraska as elsewhere within the United States, except the eighth section of the act preparatory to the admission of Missouri into the Union, approved March sixth, eighteen hundred and twenty, which, being inconsistent with the principle of non-intervention by Congress with slavery in the States and Territories, as recognized by the legislation of eighteen hundred and fifty, commonly called the Compromise Measures, is hereby declared inoperative and void; it being the true intent and meaning of this act not to legislate slavery into any Territory or State, nor to exclude it therefrom, but to leave the people thereof perfectly free to form and regulate their domestic institutions in their own way, subject only to the Constitution of the United States: *Provided,* That nothing herein contained shall be construed to revive or put in force any law or regulation which may have existed prior to the act of sixth March, eighteen hundred and twenty, either protecting, establishing, prohibiting, or abolishing slavery.

SEC. 15. *And be it further enacted,* That there shall hereafter be appropriated, as has been customary for the Territorial governments, a sufficient amount, to be expended under the direction of the said Governor of the Territory of Nebraska, not exceeding the sums heretofore appropriated for similar objects, for the erection of suitable public buildings at the seat of government, and for the purchase of a library, to be kept at the seat of government for the use of the Governor, Legislative Assembly, Judges of the Supreme Court, Secretary, Marshal, and Attorney of said Territory, and such other persons, and under such regulations, as shall be prescribed by law.

SEC. 16. *And be it further enacted,* That when the lands in the said Territory shall be surveyed under the direction of the government of the United States, preparatory to bringing the same into market, sections numbered sixteen and thirty-six in each township in said Territory shall be, and the same are hereby, reserved for the purpose of being applied to schools in said Territory, and in the States and Territories hereafter to be erected out of the same.

SEC. 17. *And be it further enacted,* That, until otherwise provided by law, the Governor of said Territory may define the Judicial Districts of said Territory, and assign the judges who may be appointed for said Territory to the several districts; and also appoint the times and places for holding courts in the several counties or subdivisions in each of said Judicial Districts by proclamation, to be issued by him; but the Legislative Assembly, at their first or any subsequent session, may organize, alter, or modify such Judicial Districts, and assign the judges, and alter the times and places of holding the courts, as to them shall seem proper and convenient.

SEC. 18. *And be it further enacted,* That all officers to be appointed by the President, by and with the advice and consent of the Senate, for the Territory of Nebraska, who, by virtue of the provisions of any law now existing, or which may be enacted during the present Congress, are required to give security for moneys that may be intrusted with them for disbursement, shall give such security, at such time and place, and in such manner, as the Secretary of the Treasury may prescribe.

SEC. 19. *And be it further enacted,* That all that part of the Territory of the United States included within the following limits, except such portions thereof as are hereinafter expressly exempted from the operations of this act, to wit, beginning at a point on the western boundary of the State of Missouri, where the thirty-seventh parallel of north latitude crosses the same; thence west on said parallel to the eastern boundary of New Mexico; thence north on said boundary to latitude thirty-eight; thence following said boundary westward to the east boundary of the Territory of Utah, on the summit of the Rocky Mountains; thence northward on said summit to the fortieth parallel of latitude; thence east on said parallel to the western boundary of the State of Missouri; thence south with the western boundary of said State to the place of beginning, be, and the same is hereby, created into a temporary government by the name of the Territory of Kansas; and when admitted as a State or States, the said Territory, or any portion of the same, shall be received into the Union with or without slavery, as their Constitution may prescribe at the time of their admission: *Provided,* That nothing in this act contained shall be construed to inhibit the government of the United States from dividing said Territory into two or more Territories, in such manner and at such times as Congress shall deem convenient and proper, or from attaching any portion of said Territory to any other State or Territory of the United States: *Provided further,* That nothing in this act contained shall be construed to impair the rights of person or property now pertaining to the Indians in said Territory, so long as such rights shall remain unextinguished by treaty between the United States and such Indians, or to include any territory which, by treaty with any Indian tribe, is not, without the consent of said tribe, to be included within the territorial limits or jurisdiction of any State or Territory; but all such territory shall be excepted out of the boundaries, and constitute no part of the Territory of Kansas, until said tribe shall signify their assent to the President of the United States to be included within the said Territory of Kansas, or to affect the authority of the government of the United States to make any regulation respecting such

Indians, their lands, property, or other rights, by treaty, law, or otherwise, which it would have been competent to the government to make if this act had never passed.

SEC. 20. *And be it further enacted,* That the executive power and authority in and over said Territory of Kansas shall be vested in a Governor, who shall hold his office for four years, and until his successor shall be appointed and qualified, unless sooner removed by the president of the United States. The Governor shall reside within said Territory, and shall be commander-in-chief of the militia thereof. He may grant pardons and respites for offences against the laws of said Territory, and reprieves for offences against the laws of the United States, until the decision of the President can be made known thereon; he shall commission all officers who shall be appointed to office under the laws of the said Territory, and shall take care that the laws be faithfully executed.

SEC. 21. *And be it further enacted,* That there shall be a Secretary of said Territory, who shall reside therein, and hold his office for five years, unless sooner removed by the President of the United States; he shall record and preserve all the laws and proceedings of the Legislative Assembly hereinafter constituted, and all the acts and proceedings of the Governor in his Executive Department; he shall transmit one copy of the laws and journals of the Legislative Assembly within thirty days after the end of each session, and one copy of the executive proceedings and official correspondence semi-annually, on the first days of January and July in each year, to the President of the United States, and two copies of the laws to the President of the Senate and to the Speaker of the House of Representatives, to be deposited in the libraries of Congress; and, in case of the death, removal, resignation, or absence of the Governor from the Territory, the Secretary shall be, and he is hereby, authorized and required to execute and perform all the powers and duties of the Governor during such vacancy or absence, or until another Governor shall be duly appointed and qualified to fill such vacancy.

SEC. 22. *And be it further enacted,* That the legislative power and authority of said Territory shall be vested in the Governor and a Legislative Assembly. The Legislative Assembly shall consist of a Council and House of Representatives. The Council shall consist of thirteen members, having the qualifications of voters, as hereinafter prescribed, whose term of service shall continue two years. The House of Representatives shall, at its first session, consist of twenty-six members, possessing the same qualifications as prescribed for members of the Council, and whose term of service shall continue one year. The number of representatives may be increased by the Legislative Assembly, from time to time, in proportion to the increase of qualified voters: *Provided,* That the whole number shall never exceed thirty-nine. An apportionment shall be made, as nearly equal as practicable, among the several counties or districts, for the election of the Council and Representatives, giving to each section of the Territory representation in the ratio of its qualified voters as nearly as may be. And the members of the Council and of the House of Representatives shall reside in, and be inhabitants of, the district or county, or counties, for which they may be elected, respectively. Previous to the first election, the Governor shall cause a census, or enumeration of the inhabitants and qualified voters of the several counties and districts of the Territory, to be taken by such persons and in such mode as the Governor shall designate and appoint; and the persons so appointed shall receive a reasonable compensation therefor. And the first election shall be held at such time and place, and be conducted in such manner, both as to the persons who shall superintend such election and the returns thereof, as the Governor shall appoint and direct; and he shall at the same time declare the number of members of the Council and House of Representatives to which each of the counties or districts shall be entitled under this act. The persons having the highest number of legal votes in each of said Council Districts for members of the Council, shall be declared by the Governor to be duly elected to the Council; and the persons having the highest number of legal votes for the House of Representatives, shall be declared by the Governor to be duly elected members of said house: *Provided*, That in case two or more persons voted for shall have an equal number of votes, and in case a vacancy shall otherwise occur in either branch of the Legislative Assembly, the Governor shall order a new election; and the persons thus elected to the Legislative Assembly shall meet at such place and on such day as the Governor shall appoint; but thereafter, the time, place, and manner of holding and conducting all elections by the people, and the apportioning the representation in the several counties or districts to the Council and House of Representatives, according to the number of qualified voters, shall be prescribed by law, as well as the day of the commencement of the regular sessions of the Legislative Assembly: *Provided*, That no session in any one year shall exceed the term of forty days, except the first session, which may continue sixty days.

SEC. 23. *And be it further enacted*, That every free white male inhabitant above the age of twenty-one years, who shall be an actual resident of said Territory, and shall possess the qualifications hereinafter prescribed, shall be entitled to vote at the first election, and shall be eligible to any office within the said Territory; but the qualifications of voters, and of holding office, at all subsequent elections, shall be such as shall be prescribed by the Legislative Assembly: Provided, That the right of suffrage and of holding office shall be exercised only by citizens of the United States, and those who shall have declared, on oath, their intention to become such, and shall have taken an oath to support the Constitution of the United States and the provisions of this act: *And, provided further*, That no officer, soldier, seaman, or marine, or other person in the army or navy of the United States, or attached to troops in the service of the United States, shall be allowed to vote or hold office in said Territory by reason of being on service therein.

SEC. 24. *And be it further enacted*, That the legislative power of the Territory shall extend to all rightful subjects of the legislation consistent with the Constitution of the United States and the provisions of this act; but no law shall be passed interfering with the primary disposal of the soil; no tax shall be imposed upon the property of the United States; nor shall the lands or other property of non-residents be taxed higher than the lands or other property of residents. Every bill which shall have passed the Council and House of Representatives of the said Territory shall, before it become a law, be presented to the Governor of the Territory; if he approve, he shall sign it; but if not, he shall return it with his objections to the house in which it originated, who shall enter the objections at large on their journal, and proceed to reconsider it. If, after such reconsideration, two thirds of that house shall agree to pass the bill, it shall be sent, together with the objections, to the other house, by which it shall likewise be reconsidered, and, if approved by two thirds of that house, it shall become a law. But in all such cases the votes of both houses shall be determined by yeas and nays, to be entered on the journal of each house, respectively. If any bill shall not be returned by the Governor within three days (Sundays excepted) after it shall have been presented to him, the same shall be a law in like manner as if he had signed it, unless the Assembly, by adjournment, prevent its return, in which case it shall not be a law.

SEC. 25. *And be it further enacted,* That all township, district, and county officers, not herein otherwise provided for, shall be appointed or elected as the case may be, in such manner as shall be provided by the Governor and Legislative Assembly of the Territory of Kansas. The Governor shall nominate, and, by and with the advice and consent of the Legislative Council, appoint all officers not herein otherwise provided for; and, in the first instance, the Governor alone may appoint all said officers, who shall hold their offices until the end of the first session of the Legislative Assembly; and shall lay off the necessary districts for members of the Council and House of Representatives, and all other officers.

SEC. 26. *And be it further enacted,* That no member of the Legislative Assembly shall hold, or be appointed to, any office which shall have been created, or the salary or emoluments of which shall have been increased, while he was member, during the term for which he was elected, and for one year after the expiration of such term; but this restriction shall not be applicable to members of the first Legislative Assembly; and no person holding a commission or appointment under the United States, except postmasters, shall be a member of the Legislative Assembly, or shall hold any office under the government of said Territory.

SEC. 27. *And be it further enacted,* That the judicial power of said Territory shall be vested in a supreme court, district courts, probate courts, and in justices of the peace. The Supreme Court shall consist of [a] chief justice and two associate justices, any two of whom shall constitute a quorum, and who shall hold a term at the seat of government of said Territory annually; and they shall hold their offices during the period of four years, and until their successors shall be appointed and qualified. The said Territory shall be divided into three judicial districts, and a district court shall be held in each of said districts by one of the justices of the Supreme Court, at such times and places as may be prescribed by law; and the said judges shall, after their appointments, respectively, reside in the districts which shall be assigned them. The jurisdiction of the several courts herein provided for, both appellate and original, and that of the probate courts and of justices of the peace, shall be as limited by law: *Provided,* That justices of the peace shall not have jurisdiction of any matter in controversy when the title or boundaries of land may be in dispute, or where the debt or sum claimed shall exceed one hundred dollars; and the said supreme and district courts, respectively, shall possess chancery as well as common law jurisdiction. Each District Court, or the judge thereof, shall appoint its clerk, who shall also be the register in chancery, and shall keep his office at the place where the court may be held. Writs of error, bills of exception, and appeals, shall be allowed in all cases from the final decisions of said district courts to the Supreme Court, under such regulations as may be prescribed by law; but in no case removed to the Supreme Court shall trial by jury be allowed in said court. The Supreme Court, or the justices thereof, shall appoint its own clerk, and every clerk shall hold his office at the pleasure of the court for which he shall have been appointed. Writs of error, and appeals from the final decisions of said supreme court, shall be allowed, and may be taken to the Supreme Court of the United States, in the same manner and under the same regulations as from the Circuit Courts of the United States, where the value of the property, or the amount in controversy, to be ascertained by the oath or affirmation of either party, or other competent witness, shall exceed one thousand dollars; except only that in all cases involving title to slaves, the said writs of error or appeals shall be allowed and decided by said supreme court, without regard to the value of the matter, property, or title in controversy; and except also that a writ of error or appeal shall also be allowed to the Supreme Court of the United States, from the decision of the said supreme court created by this act, or of any judge thereof, or of the district courts created by this act, or of any judge thereof, upon any writ of habeas corpus, involving the question of personal freedom: *Provided*, That nothing herein contained shall be construed to apply to or affect the provisions of the "act respecting fugitives from justice, and persons escaping from the service of their masters," approved February twelfth, seventeen hundred and ninety-three, and the "act to amend and supplementary to the aforesaid act," approved September eighteenth, eighteen hundred and fifty; and each of the said district courts shall have and exercise the same jurisdiction in all cases arising under the Constitution and laws of the United States as is vested in the Circuit and District Courts of the United States; and the said supreme and district courts of the said Territory, and the respective judges thereof, shall and may grant writs of habeas corpus in all cases in which the same are granted by the judges of the United States in the District of Columbia; and the first six days of every term of said courts, or so much thereof as may be necessary, shall be appropriated to the trial of causes arising under the said Constitution and laws, and writs of error and appeal in all such cases shall be made to the Supreme Court of said Territory, the same as in other cases. The said clerk shall receive the same fees in all such cases, which the clerks of the district courts of Utah Territory now receive for similar services.

SEC. 28. *And be it further enacted*, That the provisions of the act entitled "An act respecting fugitives from justice, and persons escaping from the service of their masters," approved February twelfth, seventeen hundred and ninety-three, and the provisions of the act entitled "An act to amend, and supplementary to, the aforesaid act," approved September eighteenth, eighteen hundred and fifty, be, and the same are hereby, declared to extend to and be in full force within the limits of the said Territory of Kansas.

SEC. 29. *And be it further enacted*, That there shall be appointed an attorney for said Territory, who shall continue in office for four years, and until his successor shall be appointed and qualified, unless sooner removed by the President, and who shall receive the same fees and salary as the Attorney of the United States for the present Territory of Utah. There shall also be a marshal for the Territory appointed, who shall hold his office for four years, and until his successor shall be appointed and qualified, unless sooner removed by the President, and who shall execute all processes issuing from the said courts when exercising their jurisdiction as Circuit and District Courts of the United States; he shall perform the duties, be subject to the same regulations and penalties, and be entitled to the same fees, as the Marshal of the District Court of the United States for the present Territory of Utah, and shall, in addition, be paid two hundred dollars annually as a compensation for extra services.

SEC. 30. *And be it further enacted,* That the Governor, Secretary, Chief Justice, and Associate Justices, Attorney, and Marshal, shall be nominated, and, by and with the advice and consent of the Senate, appointed by the President of the United States. The Governor and Secretary to be appointed as aforesaid shall, before they act as such, respectively take an oath or affirmation before the district judge or some justice of the peace in the limits of said Territory, duly authorized to administer oaths and affirmations by the laws now in force therein, or before the Chief Justice or some Associate Justice of the Supreme Court of the United States, to support the Constitution of the United States, and faithfully to discharge the duties of their respective offices, which said oaths, when so taken, shall be certified by the person by whom the same shall have been taken; and such certificates shall be received and recorded by the said secretary among the executive proceedings; and the Chief Justice and Associate Justices, and all other civil officers in said Territory, before they act as such, shall take a like oath or affirmation before the said Governor or Secretary, or some Judge or Justice of the Peace of the Territory who may be duly commissioned and qualified, which said oath or affirmation shall be certified and transmitted by the person taking the same to the Secretary, to be by him recorded as aforesaid; and, afterwards, the like oath or affirmation shall be taken, certified, and recorded, in such manner and form as may be prescribed by law. The Governor shall receive an annual salary of two thousand five hundred dollars. The Chief Justice and Associate Justices shall receive an annual salary of two thousand dollars. The Secretary shall receive an annual salary of two thousand dollars. The said salaries shall be paid quarter-yearly, from the dates of the respective appointments, at the Treasury of the United States; but no such payment shall be made until said officers shall have entered upon the duties of their respective appointments. The members of the Legislative Assembly shall be entitled to receive three dollars each per day during their attendance at the sessions thereof, and three dollars each for every twenty miles' travel in going to and returning from the said sessions, estimated according to the nearest usually travelled route; and an additional allowance of three dollars shall be paid to the presiding officer of each house for each day he shall so preside. And a chief clerk, one assistant clerk, a sergeant-at-arms, and doorkeeper, may be chosen for each house; and the chief clerk shall receive four dollars per day, and the said other officers three dollars per day, during the session of the Legislative Assembly; but no other officers shall be paid by the United States: *Provided,* That there shall be but one session of the Legislature annually, unless, on an extraordinary occasion, the Governor shall think proper to call the Legislature together. There shall be appropriated annually, the usual sum, to be expended by the Governor, to defray the contingent expenses of the Territory, including the salary of a clerk of the Executive

Department and there shall also be appropriated, annually, a sufficient sum, to be expended by the Secretary of the Territory, and upon an estimate to be made by the Secretary of the Treasury of the United States, to defray the expenses of the Legislative Assembly, the printing of the laws, and other incidental expenses; and the Governor and Secretary of the Territory shall, in the disbursement of all moneys intrusted to them, be governed solely by the instructions of the secretary of the Treasury of the United States, and shall, semi-annually, account to the said secretary for the manner in which the aforesaid moneys shall have been expended; and no expenditure shall be made by said Legislative Assembly for objects not specially authorized by the acts of Congress making the appropriations, nor beyond the sums thus appropriated for such objects.

SEC. 31. *And be it further enacted*, That the seat of government of said Territory is hereby located temporarily at Fort Leavenworth; and that such portions of the public buildings as may not be actually used and needed for military purposes, may be occupied and used, under the direction of the Governor and Legislative Assembly, for such public purposes as may be required under the provisions of this act.

SEC. 32. *And be it further enacted*, That a delegate to the House of Representatives of the United States, to serve for the term of two years, who shall be a citizen of the United States, may be elected by the voters qualified to elect members of the Legislative Assembly, who shall be entitled to the same rights and privileges as are exercised and enjoyed by the delegates from the several other Territories of the United States to the said House of Representatives, but the delegate first elected shall hold his seat only during the term of the Congress to which he shall be elected. The first election shall be held at such time and places, and be conducted in such manner, as the Governor shall appoint and direct; and at all subsequent elections, the times, places, and manner of holding the elections shall be prescribed by law. The person having the greatest number of votes shall be declared by the Governor to be duly elected, and certificate thereof shall be given accordingly. That the Constitution, and all laws of the United States which are not locally inapplicable, shall have the same force and effect within the said Territory of Kansas as elsewhere within the United States, except the eighth section of the act preparatory to the admission of Missouri into the Union, approved March sixth, eighteen hundred and twenty, which, being inconsistent with the principle of non-intervention by Congress with slavery in the States and Territories, as recognized by the legislation of eighteen hundred and fifty, commonly called the Compromise Measures, is hereby declared inoperative and void; it being the true intent and meaning of this act not to legislate slavery into any Territory or State, nor to exclude it therefrom, but to leave the people thereof perfectly free to form and regulate their domestic institutions in their own way, subject only to the Constitution of the United States: *Provided*, That nothing herein contained shall be construed to revive or put in force any law or regulation which may have existed prior to the act of sixth of March, eighteen hundred and twenty, either protecting, establishing, prohibiting, or abolishing slavery.

SEC. 33. *And be it further enacted*, That there shall hereafter be appropriated, as has been customary for the territorial governments, a sufficient amount, to be expended under the direction of the said Governor of the Territory of Kansas, not exceeding the sums heretofore appropriated for similar objects, for the erection of suitable public buildings at the seat of government, and for the purchase of a library, to be kept at the seat of government for the use of the Governor, Legislative Assembly, Judges of the Supreme Court, Secretary, Marshal, and Attorney of said Territory, and such other persons, and under such regulations, as shall be prescribed by law.

SEC. 34. *And be it further enacted,* That when the lands in the said Territory shall be surveyed under the direction of the government of the United States, preparatory to bringing the same into market, sections numbered sixteen and thirty-six in each township in said Territory shall be, and the same are hereby, reserved for the purpose of being applied to schools in said Territory, and in the States and Territories hereafter to be erected out of the same.

SEC. 35. *And be it further enacted,* That, until otherwise provided by law, the Governor of said Territory may define the Judicial Districts of said Territory, and assign the judges who may be appointed for said Territory to the several districts; and also appoint the times and places for holding courts in the several counties or subdivisions in each of said judicial districts by proclamation, to be issued by him; but the Legislative Assembly, at their first or any subsequent session, may organize, alter, or modify such judicial districts, and assign the judges, and alter the times and places of holding the courts as to them shall seem proper and convenient.

SEC. 36. *And be it further enacted,* That all officers to be appointed by the President, by and with the advice and consent of the Senate, for the Territory of Kansas, who, by virtue of the provisions of any law now existing, or which may be enacted during the present Congress, are required to give security for moneys that may be intrusted with them for disbursement, shall give such security, at such time and place, and in such manner as the Secretary of the Treasury may prescribe.

SEC. 37. *And be it further enacted,* That all treaties, laws, and other engagements made by the government of the United States with the Indian tribes inhabiting the territories embraced within this act, shall be faithfully and rigidly observed, notwithstanding any thing contained in this act; and that the existing agencies and superintendencies of said Indians be continued with the same powers and duties which are now prescribed by law, except that the President of the United States may, at his discretion, change the location of the office of superintendent.

Approved, May 30, 1854.

AN ACT DECLARING THE
SOUTHERN BOUNDARY OF NEW MEXICO
AUGUST 4, 1854

Be it enacted by the Senate and House of Representatives of the United States of America in Congress assembled, That, until otherwise provided by law, the territory acquired under the late treaty with Mexico, commonly known as the Gadsden treaty, be, and the same is hereby incorporated with the territory of "New Mexico," subject to all the laws of said last named territory.

Approved, August 4, 1854.

AN ACT TO AUTHORIZE THE PEOPLE OF THE
TERRITORY OF MINNESOTA TO FORM A
CONSTITUTION AND STATE GOVERNMENT,
PREPARATORY TO THEIR ADMISSION
IN THE UNION ON AN EQUAL FOOTING
WITH THE ORIGINAL STATES
FEBRUARY 26, 1857

Be it enacted by the Senate and House of Representatives of the United States of America in Congress assembled, That the inhabitants of that portion of the Territory of Minnesota which is embraced within the following limits, to wit: Beginning at the point in the centre of the main channel of the Red River of the North, where the boundary line between the United States and the British possessions crosses the same; thence up the main channel of said river to that of the Boix des Sioux River; thence [up] the main channel of said river to Lake Travers; thence up the centre of said lake to the southern extremity thereof; thence in a direct line to the head of Big Stone Lake; thence through its centre to its outlet; thence by a due south line to the north line of the State of Iowa; thence east along the northern boundary of said State to the main channel of the Mississippi River; thence up the main channel of said river, and following the boundary line of the State of Wisconsin, until the same intersects the Saint Louis River; thence down said river to and through Lake Superior, on the boundary line of Wisconsin and Michigan, until it intersects the dividing line between the United States and the British possessions; thence up Pigeon

River, and following said dividing line to the place of beginning—be and they are hereby authorized to form for themselves a Constitution and State Government, by the name of the State of Minnesota, and to come into the Union on an equal footing with the original States, according to the federal constitution.

SEC. 2. *And be it further enacted*, That the said State of Minnesota shall have concurrent jurisdiction on the Mississippi and all other rivers and waters bordering on the said State of Minnesota, so far as the same shall form a common boundary to said State and any other State or States now or hereafter to be formed or bounded by the same; and said river and waters, and the navigable waters leading into the same, shall be common highways, and forever free, as well to the inhabitants of said State as to all other citizens of the United States, without any tax, duty, impost, or toll, therefor.

SEC. 3. *And be it further enacted*, That on the first Monday in June next, the legal voters in each representative district, then existing within the limits of the proposed State, are hereby authorized to elect two delegates for each representative to which said district may be entitled according to the apportionment for representatives to the territorial legislature, which election for delegates shall be held and conducted, and the returns made, in all respects in conformity with the laws of said Territory regulating the election of representatives; and the delegates so elected shall assemble at the capitol of said Territory on the second Monday in July next, and first determine, by a vote, whether it is the wish of the people of the proposed State to be admitted into the Union at that time; and if so, shall proceed to form a constitution, and take all necessary steps for the establishment of a State government, in conformity with the federal constitution, subject to the approval and ratification of the people of the proposed State.

SEC. 4. *And be it further enacted*, That in the event said convention shall decide in favor of the immediate admission of the proposed State into the Union, it shall be the duty of the United States' marshal for said Territory to proceed to take a census or enumeration of the inhabitants within the limits of the proposed State, under such rules and regulations as shall be prescribed by the Secretary of the Interior, with the view of ascertaining the number of representatives to which said State may be entitled in the Congress of the United States; and said State shall be entitled to one representative and such additional representatives as the population of the State shall, according to the census, show it would be entitled to according to the present ratio of representation.

SEC. 5. *And be it further enacted*, That the following propositions be, and the same are hereby offered to the said convention of the people of Minnesota for their free acceptance or rejection, which, if accepted by the convention, shall be obligatory on the United States and upon the said State of Minnesota, to wit:

First. That sections numbered sixteen and thirty-six in every township of public lands in said State, and where either of said sections, or any part thereof, has been sold or otherwise been disposed of, other lands, equivalent thereto and as contiguous as may be, shall be granted to said State for the use of schools.

Second. That seventy-two sections of land shall be set apart and reserved for the use and support of a State university, to be selected by the Governor of said State, subject to the approval of the Commissioner of the General Land-Office, and to be appropriated and applied in such manner as the legislature of said State may prescribe for the purpose aforesaid, but for no other purpose.

Third. That ten entire sections of land, to be selected by the Governor of said State, in legal subdivisions, shall be granted to said State for the purpose of completing the public buildings, or for the erection of others at the seat of government, under the direction of the legislature thereof.

Fourth. That all salt springs within said State, not exceeding twelve in number, with six sections of land adjoining, or as contiguous as may be to each, shall be granted to said State for its use; the same to be selected by the Governor thereof within one year after the admission of said State, and when so selected, to be used or disposed of on such terms, conditions, and regulations as the legislature shall direct: *Provided,* That no salt spring or land, the right whereof is now vested in any individual or individuals, or which may be hereafter confirmed or adjudged to any individual or individuals, shall, by this article, be granted to said State.

Fifth. That five per centum of the net proceeds of sales of all public lands lying within said State, which shall be sold by Congress after the admission of the said State into the Union, after deducting all the expenses incident to the same, shall be paid to said State, for the purpose of making public roads and internal improvements, as the legislature shall direct: *Provided,* The foregoing propositions herein offered are on the condition that the said convention which shall form the constitution of said State shall provide, by a clause in said constitution, or an ordinance, irrevocable without the consent of the United States, that said State shall never interfere with the primary disposal of the soil within the same, by the United States, or with any regulations Congress may find necessary for securing the title in said soil to *bona fide* purchasers thereof; and that no tax shall be imposed on lands belonging to the United States, and that in no case shall non-resident proprietors be taxed higher than residents.

Approved, February 26, 1857.

AN ACT TO AUTHORIZE THE PRESIDENT OF THE UNITED STATES, IN CONJUNCTION WITH THE STATE OF TEXAS, TO RUN AND MARK THE BOUNDARY LINES BETWEEN THE TERRITORIES OF THE UNITED STATES AND THE STATE OF TEXAS JUNE 5, 1858

Be it enacted by the Senate and House of Representatives of the United States of America in Congress assembled, That the President of the United

States be, and he hereby is, authorized and empowered to appoint a suitable person or persons, who, in conjunction with such person or persons as may be appointed by and on behalf of the State of Texas for the same purpose, shall run and mark the boundary lines between the Territories of the United States and the State of Texas: Beginning at the point where the one hundredth degree of longitude west from Greenwich crosses Red River, and running thence north to the point where said one hundredth degree of longitude intersects the parallel of thirty-six degrees thirty minutes north latitude; and thence west with the said parallel of thirty-six degrees and thirty minutes north latitude to the point where it intersects the one hundred and third degree of longitude west from Greenwich; and thence south with the said one hundred and third degree of longitude to the thirty-second parallel of north latitude; and thence west with the said thirty-second degree of north latitude to the Rio Grande.

SEC. 2. *And be it further enacted,* That such landmarks shall be established at the said point of beginning on Red River, and at the other corners, and on the said several lines of said boundary, as may be agreed on by the President of the United States, or those acting under his authority, and the said State of Texas, or those acting under its authority.

SEC. 3. *Be it further enacted,* That the sum of eighty thousand dollars, or so much thereof as may be necessary, be, and the same hereby is, appropriated, out of any money in the treasury not otherwise appropriated, to carry out the provisions of this act: *Provided,* That the person or persons appointed and employed on the part and behalf of Texas are to be paid by the said State: *Provided further,* That no persons, except a superintendent or commissioner, shall be appointed or employed in this service by the United States but such as are required to make the necessary observations and surveys to ascertain such line and erect suitable monuments thereon and make return of the same.

Approved, June 5, 1858.

AN ACT FOR THE ADMISSION
OF OREGON INTO THE UNION
FEBRUARY 14, 1859

Whereas the people of Oregon have framed, ratified, and adopted a constitution of State government which is republican in form, and in conformity with the Constitution of the United States, and have applied for admission into the Union on an equal footing with the other States: Therefore—

Be it enacted by the Senate and House of Representatives of the United States of America in Congress assembled, That Oregon be, and she is hereby, received into the Union on an equal footing with the other States in all respects whatever, with the following boundaries: In order that the boundaries of the State may be known and established, it is hereby ordained and declared that the State of Oregon shall be bounded as follows, to wit: Beginning one marine league at sea due west from the point where the forty-second parallel of north latitude intersects the same; thence northerly, at the same distance from the line of the coast, lying west and opposite the State, including all islands within the jurisdiction of the United States, to a point due west and opposite the middle of the north ship channel of the Columbia River; thence easterly, to and up the middle channel of said river, and, where it is divided by islands, up the middle of the widest channel thereof, to a point near Fort Walla-Walla, where the forty-sixth parallel of north latitude crosses said river; thence east, on said parallel, to the middle of the main channel of the Shoshones or Snake River; thence up the middle of the main channel of said river, to the mouth of the Owyhee River; thence due south, to the parallel of latitude forty-two degrees north; thence west, along said parallel, to the place of beginning, including jurisdiction in civil and criminal cases upon the Columbia River and Snake River, concurrently with States and Territories of which those rivers form a boundary in common with this State.

SEC. 2. *And be it further enacted,* That the said State of Oregon shall have concurrent jurisdiction on the Columbia and all other rivers and waters bordering on the said State of Oregon so far as the same shall form a common boundary to said State, and any other State or States now or hereafter to be formed or bounded by the same; and said rivers and waters, and all the navigable waters of said State, shall be common highways and forever free, as well as to the inhabitants of said State as to all other citizens of the United States, without any tax, duty, impost, or toll therefor.

SEC. 3. *And be it further enacted,* That, until the next census and apportionment of representatives, the State of Oregon shall be entitled to one representative in the Congress of the United States.

SEC. 4. *And be it further enacted,* That the following propositions be, and the same are hereby, offered to the said people of Oregon for their free acceptance or rejection, which, if accepted, shall be obligatory on the United States and upon the said State of Oregon, to wit: First. That sections numbered sixteen and thirty-six in every township of public lands in said State, and where either of said sections, or any part thereof, has been sold or otherwise been disposed of, other lands equivalent thereto, and as contiguous as may be, shall be granted to said State for the use of schools. Second. That seventy-two sections of land shall be set apart and reserved for the use and support of a State university, to be selected by the governor of said State, subject to the approval of the Commissioner of the General Land-Office, and to be appropriated and applied in such manner as the legislature of said State may prescribe for the purpose aforesaid, but for no other purpose. Third. That ten entire sections of land, to be selected by the governor of said State, in legal subdivisions, shall be granted to said State for the purpose of completing the public buildings, or for the erection of others at the seat of government, under the direction of the legislature thereof. Fourth. That all salt springs within said State, not exceeding twelve in number, with six sections of land adjoining, or as contiguous as may be to each, shall be granted to said State for its use, the same to be selected by the governor thereof within one year after the admission of said State, and when so selected, to be used or disposed of on such terms, conditions, and regulations as the legislature shall direct: *Provided,* That no salt spring or land, the right whereof is now vested in any individual or individuals, or which may be hereafter confirmed or adjudged to any individual or individuals, shall by this article be granted to said State. Fifth. That five per centum of the net proceeds of sales of all public lands lying within said State which shall be sold by Congress after the admission of said State into the Union, after deducting all the expenses incident to the same, shall be paid to said State, for the purpose of making public roads and internal improvements, as the legislature shall direct: *Provided,* That the foregoing propositions, hereinbefore offered, are on the condition that the people of Oregon shall provide by an ordinance, irrevocable without the consent of the United States, that said State shall never interfere with the primary disposal of the soil within the same by the United States, or with any regulations Congress may find necessary for securing the title in said soil to bona fide purchasers thereof; and that in no case shall nonresident proprietors be taxed higher than residents. Sixth. And that the said State shall never tax the lands or the property of the United States in said State: *Provided, however,* That in case any of the lands herein granted to the State of Oregon have heretofore been confirmed to the Territory of Oregon for the purposes specified in this act, the amount so confirmed shall be deducted from the quantity specified in this act.

SEC. 5. *And be it further enacted,* That, until Congress shall otherwise direct, the residue of the Territory of Oregon shall be, and is hereby, incorporated into, and made a part of the Territory of Washington.

Approved, February 14, 1859.

AN ACT TO AUTHORIZE THE PRESIDENT OF THE UNITED STATES IN CONJUNCTION WITH THE STATE OF CALIFORNIA, TO RUN AND MARK THE BOUNDARY LINES BETWEEN THE TERRITORIES OF THE UNITED STATES AND THE STATE OF CALIFORNIA
MAY 26, 1860

Be it enacted by the Senate and House of Representatives of the United States of America in Congress assembled, That the President of the United

States be, and he hereby is, authorized and empowered to appoint a suitable person or persons, who, in conjunction with such person or persons as may be appointed on behalf of the State of California for the same purpose, shall run and mark the boundary lines between the Territories of the United States and the State of California; commencing at the point of intersection of the forty-second degree of north latitude with the one hundred and twentieth degree of longitude west from Greenwich, and running south on the line of said one hundred and twentieth degree of west longitude until it intersects the thirty-ninth degree of north latitude; thence running in a straight line in a southeasterly direction to the river Colorado at a point where it intersects the thirty-fifth degree of north latitude.

SEC. 2. *And be it further enacted,* That such landmarks shall be established at the said point of beginning, and at the other corners and on the several lines of said boundary as may be agreed on by the President of the United States, or those acting under his authority, and the said State of California or those acting under its authority: *Provided,* That the person or persons appointed and employed on the part and behalf of the State of California are to be paid by the said State: *Provided, further,* that no persons except a superintendent or commissioner shall be appointed or employed in this service by the United States, but such as are required to make the necessary observations and surveys, to ascertain such line and erect suitable monuments thereon, and make return of the same.

Approved, May 26, 1860.

AN ACT FOR THE ADMISSION
OF KANSAS INTO THE UNION
JANUARY 29, 1861

Whereas the people of the Territory of Kansas, by their representatives in Convention assembled, at Wyandott, in said Territory, on the twenty-ninth day of July, one thousand eight hundred and fifty-nine, did form for themselves a constitution and State government, republican in form, which was ratified and adopted by the people at an election held for that purpose on Tuesday, the fourth day of October, one thousand eight hundred and fifty-nine, and the said Convention has, in their name and behalf, asked the Congress of the United States to admit the said Territory into the Union as a State, on an equal footing with the other States: Therefore

Be it enacted by the Senate and House of Representatives of the United States of America in Congress assembled, That the State of Kansas shall be, and is hereby declared to be, one of the United States of America, and admitted into the Union on an equal footing with the original States in all respects whatever. And the said State shall consist of all the territory included within the following boundaries, to wit: Beginning at a point on the western boundary of the State of Missouri, where the thirty-seventh parallel of north latitude crosses the same; thence west on said parallel to the twenty-fifth meridian of longitude west from Washington; thence north on said meridian to the fortieth parallel of latitude; thence east on said parallel to the western boundary of the State of Missouri; thence south with the western boundary of said State to the place of beginning: *Provided*, That nothing contained in the said constitution respecting the boundary of said State shall be construed to impair the rights of person or property now pertaining to the Indians in said Territory, so long as such rights shall remain unextinguished by treaty between the United States and such Indians, or to include any territory which, by treaty with such Indian tribe, is not, without the consent of said tribe, to be included within the territorial limits or jurisdiction of any State or Territory; but all such territory shall be excepted out of the boundaries, and constitute no part of the State of Kansas, until said tribe shall signify their assent to the President of the United States to be included within said State, or to affect the authority of the Government of the United States to make any regulation respecting such Indians, their lands, property, or other rights, by treaty, law, or otherwise, which it would have been competent to make if this act had never passed.

SEC. 2. *And be it further enacted*, That until the next general apportionment of Representatives the State of Kansas shall be entitled to one Representative in the House of Representatives of the United States.

SEC. 3. *And be it further enacted*, That nothing in this act shall be construed as an assent by Congress to all or to any of the propositions or claims contained in the ordinance of said constitution of the people of Kansas, or in the resolutions thereto attached; but the following propositions are hereby offered to the said people of Kansas for their free acceptance or rejection, which, if accepted, shall be obligatory on the United States and upon the said State of Kansas, to wit: First, That sections numbered sixteen and thirty-six in every township of public lands in said State, and where either of said sections or any part thereof has been sold or otherwise been disposed of, other lands, equivalent thereto and as contiguous as may be, shall be granted to said State for the use of schools. Second, That seventy-two sections of land shall be set apart and reserved for the use and support of a State University, to be selected by the Governor of said State, subject to the approval of the Commissioner of the General Land Office, and to be appropriated and applied in such manner as the Legislature of said State may prescribe for the purpose aforesaid, but for no other purpose. Third, That ten entire sections of land, to be selected by the Governor of said State, in legal subdivisions, shall be granted to said State for the purpose of completing the public buildings, or for the erection of others at the seat of government, under the direction of the Legislature thereof. Fourth, That all salt springs within said State, not exceeding twelve in number, with six sections of land adjoining or as contiguous as may be to each, shall be granted to said State for its use, the same to be selected by the Governor thereof within one year after the admission of said State, and when so selected to be used or disposed of on such terms, conditions, and regulations as the Legislature shall direct: *Provided*, That no salt spring or land, the right whereof is now vested in any individual or individuals, or which may be hereafter confirmed or adjudged to any individual or individuals, shall by this article be granted to said State. Fifth, That five per centum of the net proceeds of sales of all public lands lying within said State, which shall be sold by Congress after the admission of said State into the Union, after deducting all the expenses incident to the same, shall be paid to said State for the purpose of making public roads and internal improvements, or for other purposes, as the Legislature shall direct: *Provided*, That the foregoing propositions hereinbefore offered are on the condition that the people of Kansas shall provide by an ordinance, irrevocable without the consent of the United States, that said State shall never interfere with the primary disposal of the soil within the same by the United States, or with any regulations Congress may find necessary for securing the title in said soil to bona fide purchasers thereof. Sixth, And that the said State shall never tax the lands or the property of the United States in said State: *Provided, however*, That in case any of the lands herein granted to the State of Kansas have heretofore been confirmed to the Territory of Kansas for the purposes specified in this act, the amount so confirmed shall be deducted from the quantity specified in this act.

SEC. 4. *And be it further enacted*, That from and after the admission of the State of Kansas, as hereinbefore provided, all the laws of the United States, which are not locally inapplicable, shall have the same force and effect within that State as in other States of the Union; and the said State is hereby constituted a judicial district of the United States, within which a district court, with the like powers and jurisdiction as the district court of the United States for the district of Minnesota, shall be established; the judge, attorney, and marshal of the United States for the said district of Kansas shall reside within the same, and shall be entitled to the same compensation as the judge, attorney, and marshal of the district of Minnesota; and in all cases of appeal or writ of error heretofore prosecuted, and now pending in the Supreme Court of the United States, upon any record from the supreme court of Kansas Territory, the mandate of execution or order of further proceedings shall be directed by the Supreme Court of the United States to the district court of the United States for the district of Kansas, or to the supreme court of the State of Kansas, as the nature of such appeal or writ of error may require; and each of those courts shall be the successor of the supreme court of Kansas Territory, as to all such cases, with full power to hear and determine the same, and to award mesne or final process therein.

SEC. 5. *And be it further enacted*, That the judge of the district court for the district of Kansas shall hold two regular terms of the said court annually, at the seat of government of the said State, to commence on the second Mondays of April and October in each year.

Approved, January 29, 1861.

AN ACT TO PROVIDE A TEMPORARY GOVERNMENT FOR THE TERRITORY OF COLORADO
FEBRUARY 28, 1861

Be it enacted by the Senate and House of Representatives of the United States of America in Congress assembled, That all that part of the territory of the United States included within the following limits, viz: commencing on the thirty-seventh parallel of north latitude, where the twenty-fifth meridian of longitude west from Washington crosses the same; thence north on said meridian to the forty-first parallel of north latitude; thence along said parallel west to the thirty-second meridian of longitude west from Washington; thence south on said meridian to the northern line of New Mexico; thence along the thirty-seventh parallel of north latitude to the place of beginning, be and the same is hereby erected into a temporary government by the name of the Territory of Colorado: *Provided,* That nothing in this act contained shall be construed to impair the rights of person or property now pertaining to the Indians in said Territory, so long as such rights shall remain unextinguished by treaty between the United States and such Indians, or to include any territory which, by treaty with any Indian tribe, is not, without the consent of said tribe, to be included within the territorial limits or jurisdiction of any State or Territory; but all such territory shall be excepted out of the boundaries and constitute no part of the Territory of Colorado until said tribe shall signify their assent to the President of the United States to be included within the said Territory, or to affect the authority of the Government of the United States to make any regulations respecting such Indians, their lands, property, or other rights, by treaty, law, or otherwise, which it would have been competent for the Government to make if this act had never passed: *Provided further,* That nothing in this act contained shall be construed to inhibit the Government of the United States from dividing said Territory into two or more Territories, in such manner and at such times as Congress shall deem convenient and proper, or from attaching any portion thereof to any other Territory or State.

SEC. 2. *And be it further enacted,* That the executive power and authority in and over said Territory of Colorado shall be vested in a governor, who shall hold his office for four years, and until his successor shall be appointed and qualified, unless sooner removed by the President of the United States. The governor shall reside within said Territory, shall be commander-in-chief of the militia thereof, shall perform the duties and receive the emoluments of superintendent of Indian affairs, and shall approve all laws passed by the legislative assembly before they shall take effect; he may grant pardons for offences against the laws of said Territory, and reprieves for offences against the laws of the United States, until the decision of the President can be made known thereon; he shall commission all officers who shall be appointed to office under the laws of said Territory, and shall take care that the laws be faithfully executed.

SEC. 3. *And be it further enacted,* That there shall be a secretary of said Territory, who shall reside therein, and hold his office for four years, unless sooner removed by the President of the United States; he shall record and preserve all the laws and proceedings of the legislative assembly hereinafter constituted, and all the acts and proceedings of the governor, in his executive department; he shall transmit one copy of the laws and one copy of the executive proceedings, on or before the first day of December in each year, to the President of the United States, and, at the same time, two copies of the laws to the Speaker of the House of Representatives and the President of the Senate for the use of Congress. And in case of the death, removal, or resignation, or other necessary absence of the governor from the Territory, the secretary shall have, and he is hereby authorized and required to execute and perform all the powers and duties of the governor during such vacancy or necessary absence, or until another governor shall be duly appointed to fill such vacancy.

SEC. 4. *And be it further enacted,* That the legislative power and authority of said Territory shall be vested in the governor and a legislative assembly. The legislative assembly shall consist of a council and house of representatives. The council shall consist of nine members, which may be increased to thirteen, having the qualifications of voters as hereinafter prescribed, whose term of service shall continue two years. The house or representatives shall consist of thirteen members, which may be increased to twenty-six, possessing the same qualifications as prescribed for members of the council, and whose term of service shall continue one year. An apportionment shall be made, as nearly equal as practicable, among the several counties or districts for the election of the council and house of representatives, giving to each section of the Territory representation in the ratio of its population (Indians excepted) as nearly as may be; and the members of the council and of the house of representatives shall reside in, and be inhabitants of, the district for which they may be elected, respectively. Previous to the first election the governor shall cause a census or enumeration of the inhabitants of the several counties and districts of the Territory to be taken; and the first election shall be held at such time and places and be conducted in such manner as the governor shall appoint and direct; and he shall, at the same time, declare the number of the members of the council and house of representatives to which each of the counties or districts shall be entitled under this act. The number of persons authorized to be elected, having the highest number of votes in each of said council districts for members of the council, shall be declared by the governor to be duly elected to the council; and the person or persons authorized to be elected having the greatest number of votes for the house of representatives, equal to the number to which each county or district shall be entitled, shall be declared by the governor to be elected members of the house of representatives: *Provided,* That in case of a tie between two or more persons voted for, the governor shall order a new election, to supply the vacancy made by such tie. And the persons thus elected to the legislative assembly shall meet at such place and on such day as the governor shall appoint; but thereafter the time, place, and manner of holding and conducting all elections by the people, and the apportioning the representation in the several counties or districts to the council and house of representatives, according to the population, shall be prescribed by law, as well as the day of the commencement of the regular sessions of the legislative assembly:

Provided, That no one session shall exceed the term of forty days, except the first, which may be extended to sixty days, but no longer.

SEC. 5. *And be it further enacted,* That every free white male citizen of the United States above the age of twenty-one years, who shall have been a resident of said Territory at the time of the passage of this act, including those recognized as citizens by the treaty with the Republic of Mexico, concluded February two, eighteen hundred and forty-eight, and the treaty negotiated with the same country on the thirtieth day of December, eighteen hundred and fifty-three, shall be entitled to vote at the first election, and shall be eligible to any office within the said Territory; but the qualifications of voters and of holding office at all subsequent elections shall be such as shall be prescribed by the legislative assembly.

SEC. 6. *And be it further enacted,* That the legislative power of the Territory shall extend to all rightful subjects of legislation consistent with the Constitution of the United States and the provisions of the act; but no law shall be passed interfering with the primary disposal of the soil; no tax shall be imposed upon the property of the United States; nor shall the lands or other property of non-residents be taxed higher than the lands or other property of residents; nor shall any law be passed impairing the rights of private property; nor shall any discrimination be made in taxing different kinds of property; but all property subject to taxation shall be in proportion to the value of the property taxed.

SEC. 7. *And be it further enacted,* That all township, district, and county officers, not herein otherwise provided for, shall be appointed or elected, as the case may be, in such manner as shall be provided by the governor and legislative assembly of the Territory. The governor shall nominate and, by and with the advice and consent of the legislative council, appoint all officers not herein otherwise provided for; and in the first instance the governor alone may appoint all said officers, who shall hold their offices until the end of the first session of the legislative assembly, and shall lay off the necessary districts for members of the council and house of representatives, and all other officers.

SEC. 8. *And be it further enacted,* That no member of the legislative assembly shall hold or be appointed to any office which shall have been created, or the salary or emoluments of which shall have been increased, while he was a member, during the term for which he was elected, and for one year after the expiration of such term; and no person holding a commission or appointment under the United States, except postmasters, shall be a member of the legislative assembly, or shall hold any office under the government of said Territory.

SEC. 9. *And be it further enacted,* That the judicial power of said Territory shall be vested in a supreme court, district courts, probate courts, and in justices of the peace. The supreme court shall consist of a chief justice and two associate justices, any two of whom shall constitute a quorum, and who shall hold a term at the seat of government of said Territory annually; and they shall hold their offices during the period of four years. The said Territory shall be divided into three judicial districts, and a district court shall be held in each of said districts by one of the justices of the supreme court at such time and place as may be prescribed by law; and the said judges shall, after their appointments, respectively, reside in the districts which shall be assigned them. The jurisdiction of the several courts herein provided for, both appellate and original, and that of the probate courts and of the justices of the peace, shall be as limited by law: *Provided,* That justices of the peace and probate courts shall not have jurisdiction of any matter in controversy when the title or boundaries of land may be in dispute, or where the debt or sum claimed shall exceed one hundred dollars; and the said supreme and district courts, respectively, shall possess chancery as well as common law jurisdiction; and authority for redress of all wrongs committed against the Constitution or laws of the United States, or of the Territory, affecting persons or property. Each district court or the judge thereof shall appoint its clerk, who shall also be the register in chancery, and shall keep his office at the place where the court may be held. Writs of error, bills of exception, and appeals, shall be allowed in all cases from the final decisions of said district courts to the supreme court, under such regulations as may be prescribed by law; but in no case removed to the supreme court shall trial by jury be allowed in said court. The supreme court, or the justices thereof, shall appoint its own clerk, and every clerk shall hold his office at the pleasure of the court for which he shall have been appointed. Writs of error and appeals from the final decisions of said supreme court shall be allowed, and may be taken to the Supreme Court of the United States, in the same manner and under the same regulations as from the circuit courts of the United States, where the value of the property or the amount in controversy, to be ascertained by the oath or affirmation of either party, or other competent witness, shall exceed one thousand dollars; and each of the said district courts shall have and exercise the same jurisdiction, in all cases arising under the Constitution and laws of the United States, as is vested in the circuit and district courts of the United States; and the said supreme and district courts of the said Territory, and the respective judges thereof, shall and may grant writs of habeas corpus in all cases in which the same are grantable by the judges of the United States in the District of Columbia; and the first six days of every term of said courts, or so much therof as shall be necessary, shall be appropriated to the trial of causes arising under the said Constitution and laws, and writs of error and appeals in all such cases shall be made to the supreme court of said Territory the same as in other cases. The said clerk shall receive in all such cases the same fees which the clerks of the district courts of Oregon Territory receive for similar services.

SEC. 10. *And be it further enacted,* That there shall be appointed an attorney for said Territory, who shall continue in office for four years, unless sooner removed by the President, and who shall receive the same fees and salary as the attorney of the United States for the late Territory of Oregon. There shall also be a marshal for the Territory appointed, who shall hold his office for four years, unless sooner removed by the President, and who shall execute all processes issuing from the said courts when exercising their jurisdiction as circuit and district courts of the United States; he shall perform the duties, be subject to the same regulations and penalties, and be entitled to the same fees as the marshal of the district court of the United States for the late Territory of Oregon, and shall, in addition, be paid two hundred dollars annually as a compensation for extra services.

SEC. 11. *And be it further enacted*, That the governor, secretary, chief justice, and associate justices, attorney, and marshal, shall be nominated and, by and with the advice and consent of the Senate, appointed by the President of the United States. The governor and secretary to be appointed as aforesaid shall, before they act as such, respectively take an oath or affirmation before the district judge or some justice of the peace in the limits of said Territory duly authorized to administer oaths and affirmations by the laws now in force therein, or before the chief justice or some associate justice of the Supreme Court of the United States, to support the Constitution of the United States, faithfully to discharge the duties of their respective offices, which said oaths, when so taken, shall be certified by the person by whom the same shall have been taken; and such certificates shall be received and recorded by the secretary among the executive proceedings; and the chief justice and associate justices, and all other civil officers in said Territory, before they act as such, shall take a like oath or affirmation before the said governor or secretary, or some judge or justice of the peace of the Territory who may be duly commissioned and qualified, which said oath or affirmation shall be certified and transmitted by the person taking the same to the secretary, to be by him recorded as aforesaid; and afterwards the like oath or affirmation shall be taken, certified, and recorded in such manner and form as may be prescribed by law. The governor shall receive an annual salary of fifteen hundred dollars as governor, and one thousand dollars as superintendent of Indian affairs; the chief justice and associate justices shall each receive an annual salary of eighteen hundred dollars; the secretary shall receive an annual salary of eighteen hundred dollars. The said salaries shall be paid quarter-yearly at the Treasury of the United States. The members of the legislative assembly shall be entitled to receive three dollars each per day during their attendance at the session thereof, and three dollars for every twenty miles' travel in going to and returning from the said sessions, estimated according to the nearest usually travelled route. There shall be appropriated annually the sum of one thousand dollars, to be expended by the governor, to defray the contingent expenses of the Territory. There shall also be appropriated annually a sufficient sum, to be expended by the secretary of the Territory, and upon an estimate to be made by the Secretary of the Treasury of the United States, to defray the expenses of the legislative assembly, the printing of the laws, and other incidental expenses; and the secretary of the Territory shall annually account to the Secretary of the Treasury of the United States for the manner in which the aforesaid sum shall have been expended.

SEC. 12. *And be it further enacted*, That the legislative assembly of the Territory of Colorado shall hold its first session at such time and place in said Territory as the governor thereof shall appoint and direct; and at said first session, or as soon thereafter as they shall deem expedient, the governor and legislative assembly shall proceed to locate and establish the seat of government for said Territory at such place as they may deem eligible; which place, however, shall thereafter be subject to be changed by the said governor and legislative assembly.

SEC. 13. *And be it further enacted*, That a delegate to the House of Representatives of the United States, to serve during each Congress of the

United States, may be elected by the voters qualified to elect members of the legislative assembly, who shall be entitled to the same rights and privileges as are exercised and enjoyed by the delegates from the several other Territories of the United States to the said House of Representatives. The first election shall be held at such time and places and be conducted in such manner as the governor shall appoint and direct; and at all subsequent elections the times, places, and manner of holding elections shall be prescribed by law. The person having the greatest number of votes shall be declared by the governor to be duly elected, and a certificate thereof shall be given accordingly.

SEC. 14. *And be it further enacted*, That when the land in the said Territory shall be surveyed, under the direction of [the] Government of the United States, preparatory to bringing the same into market, sections numbered sixteen and thirty-six in each township in said Territory shall be and the same are hereby reserved for the purpose of being applied to schools in the States hereafter to be erected out of the same.

SEC. 15. *And be it further enacted*, That temporarily, and until otherwise provided by law, the governor of said Territory may define the judicial districts of said Territory, and assign the judges who may be appointed for said Territory to the several districts, and also appoint the times and places for holding courts in the several counties or subdivisions in each of said judicial districts by proclamation to be issued by him; but the legislative assembly at their first or any subsequent session may organize, alter, or modify such judicial districts, and assign the judges, and alter the times and places of holding the courts, as to them shall seem proper and convenient.

SEC. 16. *And be it further enacted*, That the Constitution and all laws of the United States which are not locally inapplicable shall have the same force and effect within the said Territory of Colorado as elsewhere within the United States.

SEC. 17. *And be it further enacted*, That the President of the United States, by and with the advice and consent of the Senate, shall be and he is hereby authorized to appoint a surveyor general for Colorado, who shall locate his office at such place as the Secretary of the Interior shall from time to time direct, and whose duties, powers, obligations, responsibilities, compensation, and allowances for clerk hire, office rent, fuel, and incidental expenses, shall be the same as those of the surveyor general of New Mexico, under the direction of the Secretary of the Interior, and such instructions as he may from time to time deem it advisable to give him.

Approved, February 28, 1861.

AN ACT TO ORGANIZE
THE TERRITORY OF NEVADA
MARCH 2, 1861

Be it enacted by the Senate and House of Representatives of the United States of America in Congress assembled, That all that part of the territory of the United States, included within the following limits, to wit: — beginning at the point of intersection of the forty-second degree of north latitude with the thirty-ninth degree of longitude west from Washington; thence, running south on the line of said thirty-ninth degree of west longitude, until it intersects the northern boundary line of the Territory of New Mexico; thence due west to the dividing ridge separating the waters of Carson Valley from those that flow into the Pacific; thence on said dividing ridge northwardly to the forty-first degree of north latitude; thence due north to the southern boundary line of the State of Oregon; thence due east to the place of beginning, be, and the same is hereby, erected into a temporary government by the name of the Territory of Nevada: *Provided,* That so much of the Territory within the present limits of the State of California shall not be included within this Territory until the State of California shall assent to the same by an act irrevocable without the consent of the United States: *Provided, further,* That nothing in this act contained shall be construed to impair the rights of person or property now pertaining to the Indians in said Territory, so long as such rights shall remain unextinguished by treaty between the United States and such Indians, or to include any territory which, by treaty with any Indian tribe, is not, without the consent of said tribe, to be included within the territorial limits or jurisdiction of any State or Territory; but all territory shall be excepted out of the boundaries and constitute no part of the Territory of Nevada, until said tribe shall signify their assent to the President of the United States to be included within the said Territory, or to affect the authority of the Government of the United States to make any regulations respecting such Indians, their lands, property, or other rights, by treaty, law, or otherwise, which it would have been competent for the Government to make if this act had never passed: *Provided, further,* That nothing in this act contained shall be constructed to inhibit the Government of the United States from dividing said Territory into two or more Territories, in such manner and at such times as Congress shall deem convenient and proper, or from attaching any portion thereof to any other Territory or State.

SEC. 2. *And be it further enacted,* That the executive power and authority in and over said Territory of Nevada shall be vested in a governor, who shall hold his office for four years, and until his successor shall be appointed and qualified, unless sooner removed by the President of the United States. The governor shall reside within said Territory, shall be commander-in-chief of the militia thereof, shall perform the duties and receive the emoluments of superintendent of Indian Affairs, and shall approve all laws passed by the legislative assembly before they shall take effect; he may grant pardons for offences against the laws of said Territory, and reprieves for offences against the laws of the United States until the decision of the President can be made known thereon; he shall commission all officers who shall be appointed to office under the laws of said Territory, and shall take care that the laws be faithfully executed.

SEC. 3. *And be it further enacted,* That there shall be a secretary of said Territory, who shall reside therein, and hold his office for four years, unless sooner removed by the President of the United States; he shall record and preserve all the laws and proceedings of the legislative assembly hereinafter constituted, and all the acts and proceedings of the governor, in his executive department; he shall transmit one copy of the laws and one copy of the executive proceedings, on or before the first day of December in each year, to the President of the United States, and at the same time two copies of the laws to the Speaker of the House of Representatives and the President of the Senate, for the use of Congress; and in case of the death, removal, or resignation, or other necessary absence of the governor from the Territory, the secretary shall have, and he is hereby authorized and required, to execute and perform all the powers and duties of the governor during such vacancy or necessary absence, or until another governor shall be duly appointed to fill such vacancy.

SEC. 4. *And be it further enacted,* That the legislative power and authority of said Territory shall be vested in the governor and a legislative assembly. The legislative assembly shall consist of a Council and House of Representatives. The Council shall consist of nine members, which may be increased to thirteen, having the qualifications of voters as hereinafter prescribed, whose term of service shall continue two years. The House of Representatives shall consist of thirteen members, which may be increased to twenty-six, possessing the same qualifications as prescribed for members of the Council, and whose term of service shall continue one year. An apportionment shall be made, as nearly equal as practicable, among the several counties or districts for the election of the Council and House or Representatives, giving to each section of the Territory representation in the ratio of its population (Indians excepted), as nearly as may be; and the members of the Council and of the House of Representatives shall reside in, and be inhabitants of, the district for which they may be elected, respectively. Previous to the first election, the Governor shall cause a census or enumeration of the inhabitants of the several counties and districts of the Territory to be taken; and the first election shall be held at such time and places, and be conducted in such manner, as the Governor shall appoint and direct; and he shall, at the same time, declare the number of the members of the Council and House of Representatives to which each of the counties or districts shall be entitled under this act. The number of persons authorized to be elected having the highest number of votes in each of said council districts for members of the Council shall be declared by the Governor to be duly elected to the Council; and the person or persons authorized to be elected having the greatest number of votes for the House of Representatives, equal to the number to which each county or district shall be entitled, shall be declared by the Governor to be elected members of the House of Representatives: *Provided,* That in case of a tie between two or more persons voted for, the Governor shall order a new election to supply the vacancy made by such tie. And the persons thus elected to the legislative assembly shall meet at such place and on such day as the Governor shall appoint; but thereafter, the time, place, and manner of holding and conducting all elections by the people, and the apportioning the representatives, in the several counties or districts to the Council and House of Representatives, according to the population, shall be prescribed by law, as well as the day of the commencement of the regular sessions of the legislative assembly: *Provided*, That no one session shall exceed the term of forty days, except the first, which may be extended to sixty days, but no longer.

SEC. 5. *And be it further enacted*, That every free white male inhabitant of the United States above the age of twenty-one years, who shall have been a resident of said Territory at the time of the passage of this act, shall be entitled to vote at the first election, and shall be eligible to any office within the said Territory; but the qualifications of voters and of holding office at all subsequent elections shall be such as shall be prescribed by the Legislative Assembly: *Provided*, That the right of suffrage and of holding office shall be exercised only by citizens of the United States and those who shall have declared on oath their intention to become such, and shall have taken an oath to support the Constitution of the United States.

SEC. 6. *And be it further enacted*, That the legislative power of the Territory shall extend to all rightful subjects of legislation consistent with the Constitution of the United States and the provisions of this act; but no law shall be passed interfering with the primary disposal of the soil; no tax shall be imposed upon the property of the United States; nor shall the lands or other property of non-residents be taxed higher than the lands or other property of residents; nor shall any law be passed impairing the rights of private property; nor shall any discrimination be made in taxing different kinds of property; but all property subject to taxation shall be in proportion to the value of the property taxed.

SEC. 7. *And be it further enacted*, That all township, district, and county officers, not herein otherwise provided for, shall be appointed or elected, as the case may be, in such manner as shall be provided by the governor and legislative assembly of the Territory. The governor shall nominate and, by and with the advice and consent of the legislative council, appoint all officers not herein otherwise provided for; and, in the first instance, the governor alone may appoint all said officers, who shall hold their offices until the end of the first session of the legislative assembly, and shall lay off the necessary districts for members of the council and house of representatives, and all other officers.

SEC. 8. *And be it further enacted*, That no member of the legislative assembly shall hold or be appointed to any office which shall have been created, or the salary or emoluments of which shall have been increased while he was a member, during the term for which he was elected, and for one year after the expiration of such term; and no person holding a commission or appointment under the United States, except postmasters, shall be a member of the legislative assembly, or shall hold any office under the government of said Territory.

SEC. 9. *And be it further enacted*, That the judicial power of said Territory shall be vested in a supreme court, district courts, probate courts, and in justices of the peace. The supreme court shall consist of a chief justice and two associate justices, any two of whom shall constitute a quorum, and who shall hold a term at the seat of government of said Territory annually, and they shall hold their offices during the period of four years. The said Territory shall be divided into three judicial districts, and a district court shall be held in each of said districts by one of the justices of the supreme court, at such time and place as may be prescribed by law; and the said judges shall, after their appointments, respectively, reside in the districts which shall be assigned them. The jurisdiction of the several courts herein provided for, both appellate and original, and that of the probate courts and of the justices of the peace, shall be as limited by law: *Provided*, That justices of the peace shall not have jurisdiction of any matter in controversy when the title of boundaries of land may be in dispute, or where the debt or sum claimed shall exceed one hundred dollars; and the said supreme and district courts, respectively, shall possess chancery as well as common-law jurisdiction; and authority for redress of all wrongs committed against the Constitution or laws of the United States, or of the Territory, affecting persons or property. Each district court, or the judge thereof, shall appoint its clerk, who shall also be the register in chancery, and shall keep his office at the place where the court may be held. Writs of error, bills of exception, and appeals, shall be allowed in all cases from the final decisions of said district courts to the supreme court, under such regulations as may be prescribed by law; but in no case removed to the supreme court shall trial by jury be allowed in said court. The supreme court, or the justices thereof, shall appoint its own clerk, and every clerk shall hold his office at the pleasure of the court for which he shall have been appointed. Writs of error and appeals from the final decisions of said supreme court, shall be allowed, and may be taken to the Supreme Court of the United States, in the same manner and under the same regulations as from the circuit courts of the United States, where the value of the property, or the amount in controversy, to be ascertained by the oath or affirmation of either party, or other competent witness, shall exceed one thousand dollars; and each of the said district courts shall have and exercise the same jurisdiction in all cases arising under the Constitution and laws of the United States as is vested in the circuit and district courts of the United States; and the said supreme and district courts of the said Territory, and the respective judges thereof, shall and may grant writs of habeas corpus in all cases in which the same are grantable by the judges of the United States in the District of Columbia; and the first six days of every term of said courts, or so much thereof as shall be necessary, shall be appropriated to the trial of causes arising under the said Constitution and laws; and writs of error and appeals in all such cases shall be made to the supreme court of said Territory the same as in other cases. The said clerk shall receive in all such cases, the same fees which the clerks of the district courts of Utah Territory now receive for similar services.

SEC. 10. *And be it further enacted*, That there shall be appointed an attorney for said Territory, who shall continue in office for four years, unless sooner removed by the President, and who shall receive the same fees and salary as the attorney of the United States for the present Territory of Utah. There shall also be a marshal for the Territory appointed, who shall hold his office for four years, unless sooner removed by the President, and who shall execute all processes issuing from the said courts when exercising their jurisdiction as circuit and district courts of the United States; he shall perform the duties, be subject to the same regulations and penalties, and be entitled to the same fees as the marshal of the district court of the United States for the present Territory of Utah, and shall, in addition, be paid two hundred dollars annually as a compensation for extra services.

SEC. 11. *And be it further enacted,* That the governor, secretary, chief justice and associate justices, attorney, and marshals, shall be nominated and, by and with the advice and consent of the Senate, appointed by the President of the United States. The governor and secretary to be appointed as aforesaid shall, before they act as such, respectively take an oath or affirmation before the district judge, or some justice of the peace in the limits of said Territory duly authorized to administer oaths and affirmations by the laws now in force therein, or before the Chief Justice or some associate justice of the Supreme Court of the United States, to support the Constitution of the United States and faithfully to discharge the duties of their respective offices; which said oaths, when so taken, shall be certified by the person by whom the same shall have been taken, and such certificates shall be received and recorded by the secretary among the executive proceedings; and the chief justice and associate justices, and all other civil officers in said Territory, before they act as such, shall take a like oath or affirmation before the said governor or secretary, or some judge or justice of the peace of the Territory who may be duly commissioned and qualified, which said oath or affirmation shall be certified and transmitted by the person taking the same to the secretary, to be by him recorded as aforesaid; and afterwards the like oath or affirmation shall be taken, certified, and recorded in such manner and form as may be prescribed by law. The governor shall receive an annual salary of fifteen hundred dollars as governor, and one thousand dollars as superintendent of Indian Affairs; the chief justice and associate justices shall each receive an annual salary of eighteen hundred dollars; the secretary shall receive an annual salary of eighteen hundred dollars. The said salaries shall be paid quarter-yearly at the Treasury of the United States. The members of the legislative assembly shall be entitled to receive three dollars each per day during their attendance at the session thereof, and three dollars for every twenty miles' travel in going to and returning from the said sessions, estimated according to the nearest usually travelled route. There shall be appropriated annually the sum of one thousand dollars, to be expended by the governor to defray the contingent expenses of the Territory. There shall also be appropriated annually a sufficient sum, to be expended by the Secretary of the Territory, and upon an estimate to be made by the Secretary of the Treasury of the United States, to defray the expenses of the legislative assembly, the printing of the laws, and other incidental expenses; and the secretary of the Territory shall annually account to the Secretary of the Treasury of the United States for the manner in which the aforesaid sum shall have been expended.

SEC. 12. *And be it further enacted,* That the legislative assembly of the Territory of Nevada shall hold its first session at such time and place in said Territory as the governor thereof shall appoint and direct; and at said first session, or as soon thereafter as they shall deem expedient, the governor and legislative assembly shall proceed to locate and establish the seat of government for said Territory at such place as they may deem eligible; which place, however, shall thereafter be subject to be changed by the said governor and legislative assembly.

SEC. 13. *And be it further enacted,* That a delegate to the House of Representatives of the United States, to serve during each Congress of the United States, may be elected by the voters qualified to elect members of the legislative assembly, who shall be entitled to the same rights and privileges as are exercised and enjoyed by the delegates from the several other Territories of the United States to the said House of Representatives. The first election shall be held at such time and places, and be conducted in such manner, as the governor shall appoint and direct; and at all subsequent elections, the times, places, and manner of holding elections shall be prescribed by law. The person having the greatest number of votes shall be declared by the governor to be duly elected, and a certificate thereof shall be given accordingly.

SEC. 14. *And be it further enacted,* That when the land in said Territory shall be surveyed, under the direction of the Government of the United States, preparatory to bringing the same into market, sections numbered sixteen and thirty-six in each township in said Territory shall be, and the same is hereby, reserved for the purpose of being applied to schools in the States hereafter to be erected out of the same.

SEC. 15. *And be it further enacted,* That temporarily, and until otherwise provided by law, the governor of said Territory may define the judicial districts of said Territory and assign the judges who may be appointed for said Territory to the several districts, and also appoint the times and places for holding courts in the several counties or subdivisions in each of said judicial districts, by proclamation to be issued by him; but the legislative assembly, at their first or any subsequent session, may organize, alter, or modify such judicial districts, and assign the judges, and alter the times and places of holding the courts, as to them shall seem proper and convenient.

SEC. 16. *And be it further enacted,* That the Constitution and all laws of the United States which are not locally inapplicable shall have the same force and effect within the said Territory of Nevada as elsewhere within the United States.

SEC. 17. *And be it further enacted,* That the President of the United States, by and with the advice and consent of the Senate, shall be, and he is hereby, authorized to appoint a surveyor general for Nevada, who shall locate his office at such place as the Secretary of the Interior shall from time to time direct, and whose duties, powers, obligations, responsibilities, compensation, and allowances for clerk hire, office rent, fuel, and incidental expenses, shall be the same as those of the surveyor general of New Mexico, under the direction of the Secretary of the Interior, and such instructions as he may from time to time deem it advisable to give him.

Approved, March 2, 1861.

AN ACT TO PROVIDE A TEMPORARY GOVERNMENT FOR THE TERRITORY OF DAKOTA, AND TO CREATE THE OFFICE OF SURVEYOR GENERAL THEREIN MARCH 2, 1861

Be it enacted by the Senate and House of Representatives of the United States of America in Congress assembled, That all that part of the territory of the United States included within the following limits, namely: commencing at a point in the main channel of the Red River of the North, where the forty-ninth degree of north latitude crosses the same; thence up the main channel of the same, and along the boundary of the State of Minnesota, to Big Stone lake; thence along the boundary line of the said State of Minnesota to the Iowa line; thence along the boundary line of the State of Iowa to the point of intersection between the Big Sioux and Missouri rivers; thence up the Missouri river, and along the boundary line of the Territory of Nebraska, to the mouth of the Niobrara or Running Water river; thence following up the same, in the middle of the main channel thereof, to the mouth of the Keha Paha or Turtle Hill river; thence up said river to the forty-third parallel of north latitude; thence due west to the present boundary of the Territory of Washington; thence along the boundary line of Washington Territory, to the forty-ninth degree of north latitude; thence east, along said forty-ninth degree of north latitude, to the place of beginning, be, and the same is hereby, organized into a temporary government, by the name of the Territory of Dakota: *Provided,* That nothing in this act contained shall be construed to impair the rights of person or property now pertaining to the Indians in said Territory, so long as such rights shall remain unextinguished by treaty between the United States and such Indians, or to include any territory which, by treaty with any Indian tribe, is not, without the consent of said tribe, to be included within the territorial limits or jurisdiction of any State or Territory; but all such territory shall be excepted out of the boundaries and constitute no part of the Territory of Dakota, until said tribe shall signify their assent to the President of the United States to be included within the said Territory, or to affect the authority of the government of the United States to make any regulations respecting such Indians, their lands, property, or other rights, by treaty, law, or otherwise, which it would have been competent for the government to make if this act had never passed: *Provided, further,* That nothing in this act contained shall be construed to inhibit the government of the United States from dividing said Territory into two or more Territories, in such manner and at such times as Congress shall deem convenient and proper, or from attaching any portion thereof to any other Territory or State.

SEC. 2. *And be it further enacted,* That the executive power and authority in and over said Territory of Dakota, shall be vested in a governor, who shall hold his office for four years, and until his successor shall be appointed and qualified, unless sooner removed by the President of the United States. The governor shall reside within said Territory, shall be commander-in-chief of the militia thereof, shall perform the duties and receive the emoluments of superintendent of Indian affairs, and shall approve all laws passed by the legislative assembly before they shall take effect; he may grant pardons for offences against the laws of said Territory, and reprieves for offences against the laws of the United States until the decision of the President can be made known thereon; he shall commission all officers who shall be appointed to office under the laws of said Territory, and shall take care that the laws be faithfully executed.

SEC. 3. *And be it further enacted*, That there shall be a secretary of said Territory, who shall reside therein, and hold his office for four years, unless sooner removed by the President of the United States; he shall record and preserve all the laws and proceedings of the legislative assembly hereinafter constituted, and all the acts and proceedings of the governor, in his executive department; he shall transmit one copy of the laws, and one copy of the executive proceedings, on or before the first day of December in each year, to the President of the United States, and, at the same time, two copies of the laws to the Speaker of the House of Representatives and the President of the Senate, for the use of Congress; and in case of the death, removal, or resignation, or other necessary absence of the governor from the Territory, the secretary shall have, and he is hereby authorized and required, to execute and perform all the powers and duties of the governor during such vacancy or necessary absence, or until another governor shall be duly appointed to fill such vacancy.

SEC. 4. *And be it further enacted*, That the legislative power and authority of said Territory shall be vested in the governor and a legislative assembly. The legislative assembly shall consist of a council and house of representatives. The council shall consist of nine members, which may be increased to thirteen having the qualifications of voters as hereinafter prescribed, whose term of service shall continue two years. The house of representatives shall consist of thirteen members, which may be increased to twenty-six, possessing the same qualifications as prescribed for members of the council, and whose term of service shall continue one year. An apportionment shall be made, as nearly equal as practicable, among the several counties or districts for the election of the council and house of representatives, giving to each section of the Territory representation in the ratio of its population, (Indians excepted) as nearly as may be; and the members of the council and of the house or representatives shall reside in, and be inhabitants of, the district for which they may be elected, respectively. Previous to the first election, the governor shall cause a census or enumeration of the inhabitants of the several counties and districts of the Territory to be taken; and the first election shall be held at such time and places, and be conducted in such manner, as the governor shall appoint and direct; and he shall, at the same time, declare the number of the members of the council and house of representatives to which each of the counties or districts shall be entitled under this act. The number of persons authorized to be elected, having the highest number of votes in each of said council districts, for members of the council, shall be declared by the governor to be duly elected to the council; and the person or persons authorized to be elected having the greatest number of votes for the house of representatives, equal to the number to which each county or district shall be entitled, shall be declared by the governor to be elected members of the house of representatives: *Provided*, That in case of a tie between two or more persons voted for, the governor shall order a new election, to supply the vacancy made by such tie. And the persons thus elected to the legislative assembly shall meet at such place and on such day as the governor shall appoint; but thereafter, the time, place, and manner of holding and conducting all elections by the people, and the apportioning the representation in the several counties or districts to the council and house of representatives, according to the population, shall be prescribed by law, as well as the day of the commencement of the regular sessions of the legislative assembly: *Provided*, That no one session shall exceed the term of forty days, except the first, which may be extended to sixty days, but no longer.

SEC. 5. *And be it further enacted*, That every free white male inhabitant of the United States above the age of twenty-one years, who shall have been a resident of said Territory at the time of the passage of this act, shall be entitled to vote at the first election, and shall be eligible to any office within the said Territory; but the qualifications of voters and of holding office at all subsequent elections shall be such as shall be prescribed by the legislative assembly: *Provided*, That the right of suffrage and of holding office shall be exercised only by citizens of the United States and those who shall have declared on oath their intention to become such, and shall have taken an oath to support the Constitution of the United States.

SEC. 6. *And be it further enacted*, That the legislative power of the Territory shall extend to all rightful subjects of legislation consistent with the Constitution of the United States and the provisions of this act; but no law shall be passed interfering with the primary disposal of the soil; no tax shall be imposed upon the property of the United States; nor shall the lands or other property of non-residents be taxed higher than the lands or other property of residents; nor shall any law be passed impairing the rights of private property; nor shall any discrimination be made in taxing different kinds of property; but all property subject to taxation shall be in proportion to the value of the property taxed.

SEC. 7. *And be it further enacted*, That all township, district, and county officers, not herein otherwise provided for, shall be appointed or elected, as the case may be, in such manner as shall be provided by the governor and legislative assembly of the Territory. The governor shall nominate and, by and with the advice and consent of the legislative council, appoint all officers not herein otherwise provided for; and, in the first instance, the governor alone may appoint all said officers, who shall hold their offices until the end of the first session of the legislative assembly, and shall lay off the necessary districts for members of the council and house of representatives, and all other officers.

SEC. 8. *And be it further enacted*, That no member of the legislative assembly shall hold or be appointed to any office which shall have been created, or the salary or emoluments of which shall have been increased while he was a member, during the term for which he was elected, and for one year after the expiration of such term; and no person holding a commission or appointment under the United States, except postmasters, shall be a member of the legislative assembly, or shall hold any office under the government of said Territory.

SEC. 9. *And be it further enacted*, That the judicial power of said Territory shall be vested in a supreme court, district courts, probate courts, and in justices of the peace. The supreme court shall consist of a chief justice and two associate justices, any two of whom shall constitute a quorum, and who shall hold a term at the seat of government of said Territory annually, and they shall hold their offices during the period of four years. The said Territory shall be divided into three judicial districts, and a district court shall be held in each of said districts by one of the justices of the supreme court, at such time and place as may be prescribed by law; and the said judges shall, after their appointments, respectively, reside in the districts which shall be assigned them. The jurisdiction of the several courts herein provided for, both appellate and original, and that of the probate courts and of the justices of the peace, shall be as limited by law: *Provided*, That justices of the peace shall not have jurisdiction of any matter in controversy when the title or boundaries of land may be in dispute, or where the debt or sum claimed shall exceed one hundred dollars; and the said supreme and district courts, respectively, shall possess chancery as well as common-law jurisdiction, and authority for redress of all wrongs committed against the Constitution or laws of the United States, or of the Territory, affecting persons or property. Each district court, or the judge thereof, shall appoint its clerk, who shall also be the register in chancery, and shall keep his office at the place where the court may be held. Writs of error, bills of exception, and appeals, shall be allowed in all cases from the final decisions of said district courts to the supreme court, under such regulations as may be prescribed by law; but in no case removed to the supreme court shall trial by jury be allowed in said court. The supreme court, or the justices thereof, shall appoint its own clerk, and every clerk shall hold his office at the pleasure of the court for which he shall have been appointed. Writs of error and appeals from the final decisions of said supreme court shall be allowed, and may be taken to the Supreme Court of the United States, in the same manner and under the same regulations as from the circuit courts of the United States, where the value of the property, or the amount in controversy, to be ascertained by the oath or affirmation of either party, or other competent witness, shall exceed one thousand dollars; and each of the said district courts shall have and exercise the same jurisdiction, in all cases arising under the Constitution and laws of the United States as is vested in circuit and district courts of the United States; and the said supreme and district courts of the said Territory, and the respective judges thereof, shall and may grant writs of habeas corpus in all cases in which the same are grantable by the judges of the United States in the District of Columbia; and the first six days of every term of said courts, or so much thereof as shall be necessary shall be appropriated to the trial of causes arising under the said Constitution and laws; and writs of error and appeals in all such cases shall be made to the supreme court of said Territory the same as in other cases. The said clerk shall receive, in all such cases, the same fees which the clerks of the district courts of Nebraska Territory now receive for similar services.

SEC. 10. *And be it further enacted*, That there shall be appointed an attorney for said Territory, who shall continue in office for four years, unless sooner removed by the President, and who shall receive the same fees and salary as the attorney of the United States for the present Territory of Nebraska. There shall also be a marshal for the Territory appointed, who shall hold his office for four years, unless sooner removed by the President, and who shall execute all processes issuing from the said courts when exercising their jurisdiction as circuit and district courts of the United States; he shall perform the duties, be subject to the same regulations and penalties, and be entitled to the same fees as the marshal of the district court of the United States for the present Territory of Nebraska, and shall, in addition, be paid two hundred dollars annually as a compensation for extra services.

SEC. 11. *And be it further enacted,* That the governor, secretary, chief justice and associate justices, attorney, and marshal, shall be nominated and, by and with the advice and consent of the Senate, appointed by the President of the United States. The governor and secretary to be appointed as aforesaid shall, before they act as such, respectively take an oath or affirmation before the district judge, or some justice of the peace in the limits of said Territory duly authorized to administer oaths and affirmations by the laws now in force therein, or before the chief justice or some associate justice of the Supreme Court of the United States, to support the Constitution of the United States and faithfully to discharge the duties of their respective offices; which said oaths, when so taken, shall be certified by the person by whom the same shall have been taken; and such certificates shall be received and recorded by the secretary among the executive proceedings; and the chief justice and associate justices, and all other civil officers in said Territory, before they act as such, shall take a like oath or affirmation before the said governor or secretary, or some judge or justice of the peace of the Territory who may be duly commissioned and qualified, which said oath or affirmation shall be certified and transmitted by the person taking the same to the secretary, to be by him recorded as aforesaid; and afterwards the like oath or affirmation shall be taken, certified, and recorded in such manner and form as may be prescribed by law. The governor shall receive an annual salary of fifteen hundred dollars as governor, and one thousand dollars as superintendent of Indian affairs; the chief justice and associate justices shall each receive an annual salary of eighteen hundred dollars; the secretary shall receive an annual salary of eighteen hundred dollars. The said salaries shall be paid quarter-yearly at the Treasury of the United States. The members of the legislative assembly shall be entitled to receive three dollars each per day during their attendance at the session thereof, and three dollars for every twenty miles' travel in going to and returning from the said sessions, estimated according to the nearest usually travelled route. There shall be appropriated annually the sum of one thousand dollars, to be expended by the governor, to defray the contingent expenses of the Territory. There shall also be appropriated annually a sufficient sum, to be expended by the secretary of the Territory, and upon an estimate to be made by the Secretary of the Treasury of the United States, to defray the expenses of the legislative assembly, the printing of the laws, and other incidental expenses; and the secretary of the Territory shall annually account to the Secretary of the Treasury of the United States for the manner in which the aforesaid sum shall have been expended.

SEC. 12. *And be it further enacted,* That the legislative assembly of the

Territory of Dakota shall hold its first session at such time and place in said Territory as the governor thereof shall appoint and direct; and at said first session, or as soon thereafter as they shall deem expedient, the governor and legislative assembly shall proceed to locate and establish the seat of government for said Territory at such place as they may deem eligible; which place, however, shall thereafter be subject to be changed by the said governor and legislative assembly.

SEC. 13. *And be it further enacted,* That a delegate to the House of Representatives of the United States, to serve during each Congress of the United States, may be elected by the voters qualified to elect members of the legislative assembly, who shall be entitled to the same rights and privileges as are exercised and enjoyed by the delegates from the several other Territories of the United States to the said House of Representatives. The first election shall be held at such time and places, and be conducted in such manner, as the governor shall appoint and direct; and at all subsequent elections, the times, places, and manner of holding elections shall be prescribed by law. The person having the greatest number of votes shall be declared by the governor to be duly elected, and a certificate thereof shall be given accordingly.

SEC. 14. *And be it further enacted,* That when the land in said Territory shall be surveyed, under the direction of the government of the United States, preparatory to bringing the same into market, sections numbered sixteen and thirty-six in each township in said Territory shall be, and the same are hereby, reserved for the purpose of being applied to schools in the States hereafter to be erected out of the same.

SEC. 15. *And be it further enacted,* That temporarily, and until otherwise provided by law, the governor of said Territory may define the judicial districts of said Territory and assign the judges who may be appointed for said Territory to the several districts, and also appoint the times and places for holding courts in the several counties or subdivisions in each of said judicial districts by proclamation to be issued by him; but the legislative assembly, at their first or any subsequent session, may organize, alter, or modify such judicial districts, and assign the judges, and alter the times and places of holding the courts, as to them shall seem proper and convenient.

SEC. 16. *And be it further enacted,* That the Constitution and all laws of the United States which are not locally inapplicable shall have the same force and effect within the said Territory of Dakota as elsewhere within the United States.

SEC. 17. *And be it further enacted,* That the President of the United States, by and with the advice and consent of the Senate, shall be, and he is hereby, authorized to appoint a surveyor-general for Dakota, who shall locate his office at such place as the Secretary of the Interior shall from time to time direct, and whose duties, powers, obligations, responsibilities, compensation, and allowances for clerk hire, office rent, fuel, and incidental expenses, shall be the same as those of the surveyor-general of Nebraska and Kansas, under the direction of the Secretary of the Interior, and such instructions as he may from time to time deem it advisable to give him.

SEC. 18. *And be it further enacted,* That so much of the public lands of the United States in the Territory of Dakota, west of its eastern boundary and east and north of the Niobrara, or Running Water river, be formed into a land district, to be called the Yancton district, at such time as the President may direct, the land office for which shall be located at such point as the President may direct, and shall be removed from time to time to other points within said district whenever, in his opinion, it may be expedient.

SEC. 19. *And be it further enacted*, That the President be, and he is hereby, authorized to appoint, by and with the advice and consent of the Senate, a register and receiver for said district, who shall respectively be required to reside at the site of said office, and who shall have the same powers, perform the same duties, and be entitled to the same compensation, as are or may be prescribed by law in relation to other land-offices of the United States.

SEC. 20. *And be it further enacted*, That the river in said Territory heretofore known as the "River aux Jacques," or "James river," shall hereafter be called the Dakota river.

SEC. 21. *And be it further enacted*, That, until Congress shall otherwise direct, that portion of the Territories of Utah and Washington between the forty-first and forty-third degrees of north latitude, and east of the thirty-third meridian of longitude west from Washington, shall be, and is hereby, incorporated into and made a part of the Territory of Nebraska.

Approved, March 2, 1861.

AN ACT TO SECURE HOMESTEADS TO ACTUAL SETTLERS ON THE PUBLIC DOMAIN

MAY 20, 1862

Be it enacted by the Senate and House of Representatives of the United States of America in Congress assembled, That any person who is the head of a family, or who has arrived at the age of twenty-one years, and is a citizen of the United States, or who shall have filed his declaration of intention to become such, as required by the naturalization laws of the United States, and who has never borne arms against the United States Government or given aid and comfort to its enemies, shall, from and after the first January, eighteen hundred and sixty-three, be entitled to enter one quarter section or less quantity of unappropriated public lands, upon which said person may have filed a preëmption claim, or which may, at the time the application is made, be subject to preëmption at one dollar and twenty-five cents, or less, per acre; or eighty acres or less of such unappropriated lands, at two dollars and fifty cents per acre, to be located in a body, in conformity to the legal subdivisions of the public lands, and after the same shall have been surveyed: *Provided*, That any person owning and residing on land may, under the provisions of this act, enter other land lying contiguous to his or her said land, which shall not, with the land so already owned and occupied, exceed in the aggregate one hundred and sixty acres.

SEC. 2. *And be it further enacted,* That the person applying for the benefit of this act shall, upon application to the register of the land office in which he or she is about to make such entry, make affidavit before the said register or receiver that he or she is the head of a family, or is twenty-one years or more of age, or shall have performed service in the army or navy of the United States, and that he has never borne arms against the Government of the United States or given aid and comfort to its enemies, and that such application is made for his or her exclusive use and benefit, and that said entry is made for the purpose of actual settlement and cultivation, and not either directly or indirectly for the use or benefit of any other person or persons whomsoever; and upon filing the said affidavit with the register or receiver, and on payment of ten dollars, he or she shall thereupon be permitted to enter the quantity of land specified: *Provided, however,* That no certificate shall be given or patent issued therefor until the expiration of five years from the date of such entry; and if, at the expiration of such time, or at any time within two years thereafter, the person making such entry; or, if he be dead, his widow; or in case of her death, his heirs or devisee; or in case of a widow making such entry, her heirs or devisee, in case of her death; shall prove by two credible witnesses that he, she, or they have resided upon or cultivated the same for the term of five years immediately succeeding the time of filing the affidavit aforesaid, and shall make affidavit that no part of said land has been alienated, and that he has borne true allegiance to the Government of the United States; then, in such case, he, she, or they, if at that time a citizen of the United States, shall be entitled to a patent, as in other cases provided for by law: *And provided, further,* That in case of the death of both father and mother, leaving an infant child, or children, under twenty-one years of age, the right and fee shall enure to the benefit of said infant child or children; and executor, administrator, or guardian may, at any time within two years after the death of the surviving parent, and in accordance with the laws of the State in which such children for the time being have their domicil, sell said land for the benefit of said infants, but for no other purpose; and the purchaser shall acquire the absolute title by the purchase, and be entitled to a patent from the United States, on payment of the office fees and sum of money herein specified.

SEC. 3. *And be it further enacted,* That the register of the land office shall note all such applications on the tract books and plats of his office, and keep a register of all such entries, and make return thereof to the General Land Office, together with the proof upon which they have been founded.

SEC. 4. *And be it further enacted,* That no lands acquired under the provisions of this act shall in any event become liable to the satisfaction of any debt or debts contracted prior to the issuing of the patent therefor.

SEC. 5. *And be it further enacted,* That if, at any time after the filing of the affidavit, as required in the second section of this act, and before the expiration of the five years aforesaid, it shall be proven, after due notice to the settler, to the satisfaction of the register of the land office, that the person having filed such affidavit shall have actually changed his or her residence, or abandoned the said land for more than six months at any time, then and in that event the land so entered shall revert to the government.

SEC. 6. *And be it further enacted,* That no individual shall be permitted to acquire title to more than one quarter section under the provisions of this act; and that the Commissioner of the General Land Office is hereby required to prepare and issue such rules and regulations, consistent with this act, as shall be necessary and proper to carry its provisions into effect; and that the registers and receivers of the several land offices shall be entitled to receive the same compensation for any lands entered under the provisions of this act that they are now entitled to receive when the same quantity of land is entered with money, one half to be paid by the person making the application at the time of so doing, and the other half on the issue of the certificate by the person to whom it may be issued; but this shall not be construed to enlarge the maximum of compensation now prescribed by law for any register or receiver: *Provided,* That nothing contained in this act shall be so construed as to impair or interfere in any manner whatever with existing preëmption rights: *And provided, further,* That all persons who may have filed their applications for a preëmption right prior to the passage of this act, shall be entitled to all privileges of this act: *Provided, further,* That no person who has served, or may hereafter serve, for a period of not less than fourteen days in the army or navy of the United States, either regular or volunteer, under the laws thereof, during the existence of an actual war, domestic or foreign, shall be deprived of the benefits of this act on account of not having attained the age of twenty-one years.

SEC. 7. *And be it further enacted,* That the fifth section of the act entitled "An act in addition to an act more effectually to provide for the punishment of certain crimes against the United States, and for other purposes," approved the third of March, in the year eighteen hundred and fifty-seven, shall extend to all oaths, affirmations, and affidavits, required or authorized by this act.

SEC. 8. *And be it further enacted,* That nothing in this act shall be so construed as to prevent any person who has availed him or herself of the benefits of the first section of this act, from paying the minimum price, or the price to which the same may have graduated, for the quantity of land so entered at any time before the expiration of the five years, and obtaining a patent therefor from the government, as in other cases provided by law, on making proof of settlement and cultivation as provided by existing laws granting preëmption rights.

Approved, May 20, 1862.

AN ACT TO EXTEND THE TERRITORIAL LIMITS
OF THE TERRITORY OF NEVADA
JULY 14, 1862

Be it enacted by the Senate and House of Representatives of the United States of America in Congress assembled, That all that part of the territory of the United States included within the following limits, namely: beginning at the point of intersection of the forty-second degree of north latitude with the thirty-eighth degree of longitude west from Washington; thence running south on the said thirty-eighth degree of west longitude until it intersects the northern boundary line of New Mexico; thence due west to the thirty-ninth degree of longitude west from Washington; thence with said thirty-ninth degree north to the intersection of said forty-second degree of north latitude; thence east with said forty-second degree of north latitude to the place of beginning, be, and the same is hereby, attached to and made a part of the Territory of Nevada, subject to the limitations, restrictions, and provisions of the act organizing the Territory of Nevada.

Approved, July 14, 1862.

AN ACT FOR THE ADMISSION OF THE STATE
OF "WEST VIRGINIA" INTO THE UNION,
AND FOR OTHER PURPOSES
DECEMBER 31, 1862

Whereas the people inhabiting that portion of Virginia known as West Virginia did, by a Convention assembled in the city of Wheeling on the twenty-sixth of November, eighteen hundred and sixty-one, frame for themselves a Constitution with a view of becoming a separate and independent State; and whereas at a general election held in the counties composing the territory aforesaid on the third day of May last, the said Constitution was approved and adopted by the qualified voters of the proposed State; and whereas the Legislature of Virginia, by an act passed on the thirteenth day of May, eighteen hundred and sixty-two, did give its consent to the formation of a new State within the jurisdiction of the said State of Virginia, to be known by the name of West Virginia, and to embrace the following named counties, to wit: Hancock, Brooke, Ohio, Marshall, Wetzel, Marion, Monongalia, Preston, Taylor, Tyler, Pleasants, Ritchie, Doddridge, Harrison, Wood, Jackson, Wirt, Roane, Calhoun, Gilmer, Barbour, Tucker, Lewis, Braxton, Upshur, Randolph,

Mason, Putnam, Kanawha, Clay, Nicholas, Cabell, Wayne, Boone, Logan, Wyoming, Mercer, McDowell, Webster, Pocahontas, Fayette, Raleigh, Greenbrier, Monroe, Pendleton, Hardy, Hampshire, and Morgan; and whereas both the Convention and the Legislature aforesaid have requested that the new State should be admitted into the Union, and the Constitution aforesaid being republican in form, Congress doth hereby consent that the said forty-eight counties may be formed into a separate and independent State. Therefore —

Be it enacted by the Senate and House of Representatives of the United States of America in Congress assembled, That the State of West Virginia be, and is hereby, declared to be one of the United States of America, and admitted into the Union on an equal footing with the original States in all respects whatever, and until the next general census shall be entitled to three members in the House of Representatives of the United States: *Provided, always,* That this act shall not take effect until after the proclamation of the President of the United States hereinafter provided for.

It being represented to Congress that since the Convention of the twenty-sixth of November, eighteen hundred and sixty-one, that framed and proposed the Constitution for the said State of West Virginia, the people thereof have expressed a wish to change the seventh section of the eleventh article of said Constitution by striking out the same and inserting the following in its place, viz: "The children of slaves born within the limits of this State after the fourth day of July, eighteen hundred and sixty-three, shall be free; and that all slaves within the said State who shall, at the time aforesaid, be under the age of ten years, shall be free when they arrive at the age of twenty-one years; and all slaves over ten and under twenty-one years shall be free when they arrive at the age of twenty-five years; and no slave shall be permitted to come into the State for permanent residence therein:" Therefore —

SEC. 2. *Be it further enacted,* That whenever the people of West Virginia shall, through their said Convention, and by a vote to be taken at an election to be held within the limits of the said State, at such time as the Convention may provide, make, and ratify the change aforesaid, and properly certify the same under the hand of the president of the Convention, it shall be lawful for the President of the United States to issue his proclamation stating the fact, and thereupon this act shall take effect and be in force from and after sixty days from the date of said proclamation.

Approved, December 31, 1862.

AN ACT TO PROVIDE A TEMPORARY GOVERNMENT
FOR THE TERRITORY OF ARIZONA,
AND FOR OTHER PURPOSES
FEBRUARY 24, 1863

Be it enacted by the Senate and House of Representatives of the United States of America in Congress assembled, That all that part of the present Territory of New Mexico situate west of a line running due south from the point where the southwest corner of the Territory of Colorado joins the northern boundary of the Territory of New Mexico to the southern boundary line of said Territory of New Mexico be, and the same is hereby, erected into a temporary government by the name of the Territory of Arizona: *Provided,* That nothing contained in the provisions of this act shall be construed to prohibit the Congress of the United States from dividing said Territory or changing its boundaries in such manner and at such time as it may deem proper: *Provided, further,* That said government shall be maintained and continued until such time as the people residing in said Territory shall, with the consent of Congress, form a State government, republican in form, as prescribed in the Constitution of the United States, and apply for and obtain admission into the Union as a State, on an equal footing with the original States.

SEC. 2. *And be it further enacted,* That the government hereby authorized shall consist of an executive, legislative, and judicial power. The executive power shall be vested in a governor. The legislative power shall consist of a council of nine members, and a house of representatives of eighteen. The judicial power shall be vested in a supreme court, to consist of three judges, and such inferior courts as the legislative council may by law prescribe; there shall also be a secretary, a marshal, a district attorney, and a surveyor-general for said Territory, who, together with the governor and judges of the supreme court, shall be appointed by the President, by and with the advice and consent of the Senate, and the term of office for each, the manner of their appointment, and the powers, duties, and the compensation of the governor, legislative assembly, judges of the supreme court, secretary, marshal, district attorney, and surveyor-general aforesaid, with their clerks, draughtsman, deputies, and sergeant-at-arms, shall be such as are conferred upon the same officers by the act organizing the Territorial government of New Mexico, which subordinate officers shall be appointed in the same manner, and not exceed in number those created by said act; and acts amendatory thereto, together with all legislative enactments of the Territory of New Mexico not inconsistent with the provisions of this act, are hereby extended to and continued in force in the said Territory of Arizona, until repealed or amended by future legislation: *Provided,* That no salary shall be due or paid the officers created by this act until they have entered upon the duties of their respective offices within the said Territory.

SEC. 3. *And be it further enacted,* That there shall neither be slavery nor involuntary servitude in the said Territory, otherwise than in the punishment of crimes, whereof the parties shall have been duly convicted; and all acts and parts of acts, either of Congress or of the Territory of New Mexico, establishing, regulating, or in any way recognizing the relation of master and slave in said Territory, are hereby repealed.

Approved, February 24, 1863.

AN ACT TO PROVIDE A TEMPORARY GOVERNMENT FOR THE TERRITORY OF IDAHO
MARCH 3, 1863

Be it enacted by the Senate and House of Representatives of the United States of America in Congress assembled, That all that part of the territory of the United States included within the following limits, to wit: Beginning at a point in the middle channel of the Snake River where the northern boundary of Oregon intersects the same; then follow down said channel of Snake River to a point opposite the mouth of the Kooskooskia, or Clear Water River; thence due north to the forty-ninth parallel of latitude; thence east along said parallel to the twenty-seventh degree of longitude west of Washington; thence south along said degree of longitude to the northern boundary of Colorado Territory; thence west along said boundary to the thirty-third degree of longitude west of Washington; thence north along said degree to the forty-second parallel of latitude; thence west along said parallel to the eastern boundary of the State of Oregon; thence north along said boundary to place of beginning. And the same is hereby created into a temporary government, by the name of the Territory of Idaho: *Provided,* That nothing in this act contained shall be construed to inhibit the Government of the United States from dividing said Territory or changing its boundaries in such manner and at such time as Congress shall deem convenient and proper, or from attaching any portion of said Territory to any other state or territory of the United States: *Provided, further,* That nothing in this act contained shall be construed to impair the rights of person or property now pertaining to the Indians in said Territory, so long as such rights shall remain unextinguished by treaty between the United States and such Indians, or to include any territory which, by treaty with any Indian tribes, is not, without the consent of said tribe, to be included within the territorial limits or jurisdiction of any state or territory; but all such territory shall be excepted out of the boundaries, and constitute no part of the Territory of Idaho, until said tribe shall signify their assent to the President of the United States to be included within said Territory, or to affect the authority of the Government of the United States to make any regulations respecting such Indians, their lands, property, or other rights, by treaty, law, or otherwise, which it would have been competent for the Government to make if this act had never passed.

SEC. 2. *And be it further enacted*, That the executive power and authority in and over said Territory of Idaho shall be vested in a governor, who shall hold his office for four years, and until his successor shall be appointed and qualified, unless sooner removed by the President of the United States. The governor shall reside within said Territory, and shall be commander-in-chief of the militia, and superintendent of Indian affairs thereof. He may grant pardons and respites for offences against the laws of said Territory, and reprieve for offences against the laws of the United States until the decision of the President of the United States can be made known thereon; he shall commission all officers who shall be appointed to office under the laws of the said Territory, and shall take care that the laws be faithfully executed.

SEC. 3. *And be it further enacted*, That there shall be a secretary of said Territory, who shall reside therein, and shall hold his office for four years, unless sooner removed by the President of the United States; he shall record and preserve all laws and proceedings of the legislative assembly hereinafter constituted, and all the acts and proceedings of the governor in his executive department; he shall transmit one copy of the laws and journals of the legislaive assembly within thirty days after the end of each session, and one copy of the executive proceedings and official correspondence semiannually, on the first days of January and July in each year, to the President of the United States, and two copies of the laws to the President of the Senate and to the Speaker of the House of Representatives for the use of Congress; and in case of the death, removal, resignation, or absence of the governor from the Territory, the secretary shall be, and he is hereby, authorized and required to execute and perform all the powers and duties of the governor during such vacancy or absence, or until another governor shall be duly appointed and qualified to fill such vacancy.

SEC. 4. *And be it further enacted*, That the legislative power and authority of said Territory shall be vested in the governor and a legislative assembly. The legislative assembly shall consist of a council and house of representatives. The council shall consist of seven members having the qualifications of voters as hereinafter prescribed, whose term of service shall continue two years. The house of representatives shall, at its first session, consist of thirteen members possessing the same qualifications as prescribed for the members of the council, and whose term of service shall continue one year. The number of representatives may be increased by the legislative assembly, from time to time, to twenty six, in proportion to the increase of qualified voters; and the council, in like manner, to thirteen. An apportionment shall be made as nearly equal as practicable among the several counties or districts for the election of the council and representatives, giving to each section of the Territory representation in the ratio of its qualified voters as nearly as may be. And the members of the council and of the house of representatives shall reside in, and be inhabitants of, the district or county, or counties, for which they may be elected respectively. Previous to the first election, the governor shall cause a census or enumeration of the inhabitants and qualified voters of the several counties and districts of the Territory to be taken by such persons and in such mode as the governor shall designate and appoint, and the persons so appointed shall receive a reasonable compensation therefor. And the first election shall be held at such time and places, and be conducted in such manner both as to the persons who shall superintend such election and the returns thereof, as the governor shall appoint and direct; and he shall, at the same time, declare the number of members of the council and house of representatives to which each of the counties or districts shall be entitled under this act. The persons having the highest number of legal votes in each of said council districts for members of the council shall be declared by the governor to be duly elected to the council; and the persons having the highest number of legal votes for the house of representatives shall be declared by the governor to be duly elected members of said house: *Provided*, That in case two or more persons voted for shall have an equal number of votes, and in case a vacancy shall otherwise occur in either branch of the legislative assembly, the governor shall order a new election; and the persons thus elected to the legislative assembly shall meet at such place and on such day as the governor shall appoint; but thereafter the time, place, and manner of holding and conducting all elections by the people, and the apportioning the representation in the several counties or districts to the council and house of representatives, according to the number of qualified voters, shall be prescribed by law, as well as the day of the commencement of the regular sessions of the legislative assembly: *Provided*, That no session in any one year shall exceed the term of forty days, except the first session, which may continue sixty days.

SEC. 5. *And be it further enacted*, That every free white male inhabitant above the age of twenty-one years, who shall have been an actual resident of said Territory at the time of the passage of this act, shall be entitled to vote at the first election, and shall be eligible to any office within the said Territory; but the qualifications of voters, and holding office, at all subsequent elections, shall be such as shall be prescribed by the legislative assembly.

SEC. 6. *And be it further enacted*, That the legislative power of the Territory shall extend to all rightful subjects of legislation consistent with the Constitution of the United States and the provisions of this act; but no law shall be passed interfering with the primary disposal of the soil; no tax shall be imposed upon the property of the United States, nor shall the lands or other property of non-residents be taxed higher than the lands or other property of residents. Every bill which shall have passed the council and house of representatives of the said Territory shall, before it becomes a law, be presented to the governor of the Territory; if he approve, he shall sign it; but if not, he shall return it, with his objections, to the house in which it originated, who shall enter the objections at large upon their journal and proceed to reconsider it. If, after such reconsideration, two thirds of that house shall agree to pass the bill, it shall be sent, together with the objections, to the other house, by which it shall likewise be reconsidered; and if approved by two thirds of that house, it shall become a law. But in all such cases the votes of both houses shall be determined by yeas and nays, to be entered on the journal of each house respectively. If any bill shall not be returned by the governor within three days (Sunday excepted) after it shall have been presented to him, the same shall be a law in like manner as if he had signed it, unless the assembly, by adjournment, prevent its return; in which case it shall not be a law: *Provided*, That whereas slavery is prohibited in said territory by act of Congress of June nineteenth, eighteen hundred and sixty-two, nothing herein contained shall be construed to authorize or permit its existence therein.

SEC. 7. *And be it further enacted,* That all township, district, and county officers, not herein otherwise provided for, shall be appointed or elected, as the case may be, in such manner as shall be provided by the governor and legislative assembly of the Territory of Idaho. The governor shall nominate and, by and with the advice and consent of the legislative council, appoint all officers not herein otherwise provided for; and in the first instance the governor alone may appoint all said officers, who shall hold their offices until the end of the first session of the legislative assembly, and shall lay off the necessary districts for members of the council and house of representatives, and all other officers.

SEC. 8. *And be it further enacted,* That no member of the legislative assembly shall hold or be appointed to any office which shall have been created, or the salary or emoluments of which shall have been increased, while he was a member, during the term for which he was elected, and for one year after the expiration of such term; but this restriction shall not be applicable to members of the first legislative assembly; and no person holding a commission or appointment under the United States, except postmasters, shall be a member of the legislative assembly, or shall hold any office under the government of said Territory.

SEC. 9. *And be it further enacted,* That the judicial power of said territory shall be vested in a supreme court, district courts, probate courts, and in justices of the peace. The supreme court shall consist of a chief justice and two associate justices, any two of whom shall constitute a quorum, and who shall hold a term at the seat of government of said Territory annually; and they shall hold their offices during the period of four years, and until their successors shall be appointed and qualified. The said Territory shall be divided into three judicial districts, and a district court shall be held in each of said districts by one of the justices of the supreme court at such times and places as may be prescribed by law; and the said judges shall, after their appointments, respectively, reside in the districts which shall be assigned them. The jurisdiction of the several courts herein provided for, both appellate and original, and that of the probate courts and of justices of the peace, shall be limited by law: *Provided,* That justices of the peace shall not have jurisdiction of any matter in controversy when the title or boundaries of land may be in dispute, or where the debt or sum claimed shall exceed one hundred dollars; and the said supreme and district courts, respectively, shall possess chancery as well as common-law jurisdiction. Each district court, or the judge thereof, shall appoint its clerk, who shall also be the register in chancery, and shall keep his office at the place where the court may be held. Writs of error, bills of exception, and appeals, shall be allowed in all cases from the final decisions of said district courts to the supreme court, under such regulations as may be prescribed by law. The supreme court, or the justices thereof, shall appoint its own clerk, and every clerk shall hold his office at the pleasure of the court for which he shall have been appointed. Writs of error and appeals from the final decisions of said supreme court shall be allowed, and may be taken to the supreme court of the United States, in the same manner and under the same regulations as from the circuit courts of the United States, where the value of the property or the amount in controversy, to be ascertained by the oath or affirmation of either party, or other competent witnesses, shall exceed one thousand dollars, except that a writ of error or appeal shall be allowed to the supreme court of the United States from the decision of the said supreme court created by this act, or of any judge thereof, or of the district courts created by this act, or of any judge thereof, upon any writs of habeas corpus involving the question of personal freedom. And each of the said district courts shall have and exercise the same jurisdiction, in all cases arising under the Constitution and laws of the United States, as is vested in the circuit and district courts of the United States; and the first six days of every term of said courts, or so much thereof as shall be necessary, shall be appropriated to the trial of causes arising under the said Constitution and laws; and writs of error and appeal in all such cases shall be made to the supreme court of said Territory, the same as in other cases. The said clerks shall receive, in all such cases, the same fees which clerks of the district courts of Washington Territory now receive for similar services.

SEC. 10. *And be it further enacted,* That there shall be appointed an attorney for said territory, who shall continue in office four years, and until his successor shall be appointed and qualified, unless sooner removed by the President of the United States, and who shall receive the same fees and salary as the attorney of the United States for the present Territory of Washington. There shall also be a marshal for the Territory appointed, who shall hold his office for four years, and until his successor shall be appointed and qualified, unless sooner removed by the President of the United States, and who shall execute all processes issuing from the said courts when exercising their jurisdiction as circuit and district courts of the United States; he shall perform the duties, be subject to the same regulations and penalties, and be entitled to the same fees as the marshal of the district court of the United States for the present Territory of Washington, and shall, in addition, be paid two hundred dollars annually as a compensation for extra services.

SEC. 11. *And be it further enacted,* That the governor, secretary, chief justice, and associate justices, attorney, and marshal, shall be appointed by the President of the United States, by and with the advice and consent of the Senate. The governor and secretary to be appointed as aforesaid, shall, before they act as such, respectively, take an oath or affirmation before the district judge or some justice of the peace in the limits of said Territory duly authorized to administer oaths and affirmations by the laws now in force therein, or before the chief justice or some associate justice of the supreme court of the United States, to support the Constitution of the United States, and faithfully to discharge the duties of their respective offices, which said oaths, when so taken, shall be certified by the person by whom the same shall have been taken; and such certificates shall be received and recorded by the said secretary among the executive proceedings; and the chief justice and associate justices, and all civil officers in said Territory, before they act as such, shall take a like oath or affirmation before the said governor or secretary, or some judge or justice of the peace of the Territory, who may be duly commissioned and qualified, which said oath or affirmation shall be certified and transmitted by the person taking the same to the secretary, to be by him recorded as aforesaid; and afterwards the like oath or affirmation shall be taken, certified, and recorded in such manner and form as may be prescribed by law. The governor shall receive an annual salary of two thousand five hundred dollars, the chief justice and associate justices shall receive an annual salary of two thousand five hundred dollars, the secretary shall receive an annual salary of two thousand dollars; the said salaries shall be paid quarter-yearly, from the dates of the respective appointments, at the treasury of the United States; but no payment shall be made until said officers shall have entered upon the duties of their respective appointments. The members of the legislative assembly shall be entitled to receive four dollars each per day, during their attendance at the sessions thereof, and four dollars each for every twenty miles' travel in going to and returning from said sessions, estimated according to the nearest usually travelled route, and an additional allowance of four dollars per day shall be paid to the presiding officer of each house for each day he shall so preside. And a chief clerk, one assistant clerk, one engrossing and one enrolling clerk, a sergeant-at-arms and doorkeeper may be chosen for each house; and the chief clerk shall receive four dollars per day, and the said other officers three dollars per day, during the session of the legislative assembly; but no other officers shall be paid by the United States: *Provided*, That there shall be but one session of the legislative assembly annually, unless, on an extraordinary occasion, the governor shall think proper to call the legislative assembly together. There shall be appropriated annually the usual sum to be expended by the governor to defray the contingent expenses of the Territory, including the salary of the clerk of the executive department; and there shall also be appropriated annually a sufficient sum, to be expended by the secretary of the Territory, and upon an estimate to be made by the Secretary of the Treasury of the United States, to defray the expenses of the legislative assembly, the printing of the laws, and other incidental expenses; and the governor and secretary of the Territory shall, in the disbursement of all moneys intrusted to them, be governed solely by the instructions of the Secretary of the Treasury of the United States, and shall, semiannually, account to the said Secretary for the manner in which the aforesaid moneys shall have been expended; and no expenditure shall be made by said legislative assembly for objects not specially authorized by the acts of Congress making the appropriations, nor beyond the sums thus appropriated for such objects.

SEC. 12. *And be it further enacted*, That the legislative assembly of the Territory of Idaho shall hold its first session at such time and place in said Territory as the governor thereof shall appoint and direct; and at said first session, or as soon thereafter as they shall deem expedient, the governor and legislative assembly shall proceed to locate and establish the seat of government for said Territory at such place as they may deem eligible: *Provided*, That the seat of government fixed by the governor and legislative assembly shall not be at any time changed, except by an act of the said assembly duly passed, and which shall be approved, after due notice, at the first general election thereafter, by a majority of the legal votes cast on that question.

SEC. 13. *And be it further enacted*, That a delegate to the House of Representatives of the United States, to serve for the term of two years, who shall be a citizen of the United States, may be elected by the voters qualified to elect members of the legislative assembly, who shall be entitled to the same rights and privileges as are exercised and enjoyed by the delegates from the several other territories of the United States to the said House of Representatives; but the delegate first elected shall hold his seat only during the term of the Congress to which he shall be elected. The first election shall be held at such time and places, and be conducted in such manner as the governor shall appoint and direct; and at all subsequent elections the times, places, and manner of holding the elections shall be prescribed by law. The person having the greatest number of legal votes shall be declared by the governor to be duly elected, and a certificate thereof shall be given accordingly. That the Constitution and all laws of the United States which are not locally inapplicable shall have the same force and effect within the said Territory of Idaho as elsewhere within the United States.

SEC. 14. *And be it further enacted,* That when the lands in the said Territory shall be surveyed, under the direction of the government of the United States, preparatory to bringing the same into market, sections numbered sixteen and thirty-six in each township in said territory shall be, and the same are hereby, reserved for the purpose of being applied to schools in said Territory, and in the states and territories hereafter to be erected out of the same.

SEC. 15. *And be it further enacted,* That, until otherwise provided by law, the governor of said Territory may define the judicial districts of said Territory, and assign the judges who may be appointed for said Territory to the several districts, and also appoint the times and places for holding courts in the several counties or subdivisions in each of said judicial districts, by proclamation to be issued by him; but the legislative assembly, at their first or any subsequent session, may organize, alter, or modify such judicial districts, and assign the judges, and alter the times and places of holding the courts, as to them shall seem proper and convenient.

SEC. 16. *And be it further enacted,* That all officers to be appointed by the President of the United States, by and with the advice and consent of the Senate, for the Territory of Idaho, who, by virtue of the provisions of any law now existing, or which may be enacted by Congress, are required to give security for moneys that may be intrusted with them for disbursement, shall give such security at such time and in such manner as the Secretary of the Treasury may prescribe.

SEC. 17. *And be it further enacted,* That all treaties, laws, and other engagements made by the Government of the United States with the Indian tribes inhabiting the Territory embraced within the provisions of this act, shall be faithfully and rigidly observed, anything contained in this act to the contrary notwithstanding; and that the existing agencies and superintendencies of said Indians be continued with the same powers and duties which are now prescribed by law, except that the President of the United States may, at his discretion, change the location of the office of said agencies or superintendents.

Approved, March 3, 1863.

AN ACT TO ENABLE THE PEOPLE OF NEVADA
TO FORM A CONSTITUTION AND STATE
GOVERNMENT, AND FOR THE ADMISSION OF SUCH
STATE INTO THE UNION ON AN EQUAL FOOTING
WITH THE ORIGINAL STATES
MARCH 21, 1864

Be it enacted by the Senate and House of Representatives of the United States of America in Congress assembled, That the inhabitants of that portion of the territory of Nevada included in the boundaries hereinafter designated be, and they are hereby, authorized to form for themselves, out of said territory, a state government, with the name aforesaid, which said state, when formed, shall be admitted into the Union upon an equal footing with the original states, in all respects whatsoever.

SEC. 2. *And be it further enacted,* That the said state of Nevada shall consist of all the territory included within the following boundaries, to wit: Commencing at a point formed by the intersection of the thirty-eighth degree of longitude west from Washington with the thirty-seventh degree of north latitude; thence due west along said thirty-seventh degree of north latitude to the eastern boundary line of the state of California; thence in a northwesterly direction along the said eastern boundary line of the state of California to the forty-third degree of longitude west from Washington; thence north along said forty-third degree of west longitude and said eastern boundary line of the state of California to the forty-second degree of north latitude; thence due east along the said forty-second degree of north latitude to a point formed by its intersection with the aforesaid thirty-eighth degree of longitude west from Washington; thence due south down said thirty-eighth degree of west longitude to the place of beginning.

SEC. 3. *And be it further enacted,* That all persons qualified by law to vote for representatives to the general assembly of said territory, at the date of the passage of this act shall be qualified to be elected, and they are authorized to vote for and choose representatives to form a convention, under such rules and regulations as the governor of said territory may prescribe; and also to vote upon the acceptance or rejection of such constitution as may be formed by said convention, under such rules and regulations as the said convention may prescribe; and if any of said citizens are enlisted in the army of the United States, and are still within said territory, they shall be permitted to vote at their place of rendezvous; and [if] any are absent from said territory, by reason of their enlistment in the army of the United States, they shall be permitted to vote at their place of service, under the rules and regulations in each case to be prescribed as aforesaid; and the aforesaid representatives to form the aforesaid convention shall be apportioned among the several counties in said territory in proportion to the population as near as may be; and said apportionment shall be made for said territory by the governor, United States district-attorney, and chief justice thereof, or any two of them; and the governor of said territory shall, by proclamation on or before the first Monday of May next, order an election of the representatives as aforesaid to be held on the first Monday in June thereafter throughout the territory, and such election shall be conducted in the same manner as is prescribed by the laws of said territory regulating elections therein for members of the house of representatives, and the number of members to said convention shall be the same as now constitute both branches of the legislature of the aforesaid territory.

SEC. 4. *And be it further enacted,* That the members of the convention, thus elected, shall meet at the capital of said territory on the first Monday in July next, and, after organization, shall declare, on behalf of the people of said territory, that they adopt the constitution of the United States. Whereupon the said convention shall be, and it is hereby, authorized to form a constitution and state government for said territory: *Provided,* That the constitution, when formed, shall be republican, and not repugnant to the constitution of the United States, and the principles of the Declaration of Independence: *And provided further,* That said convention shall provide, by an ordinance irrevocable, without the consent of the United States and people of said state: —

First. That there shall be neither slavery nor involuntary servitude in the said state, otherwise than in the punishment of crimes, whereof the party shall have been duly convicted.

Second. That perfect toleration of religious sentiment shall be secured, and no inhabitant of said state shall ever be molested in person or property on account of his or her mode of religious worship.

Third. That the people inhabiting said territory do agree and declare that they forever disclaim all right and title to the unappropriated public lands lying within said territory, and that the same shall be and remain at the sole and entire disposition of the United States; and that the lands belonging to citizens of the United States residing without the said state shall never be taxed higher than the land belonging to the residents thereof; and that no taxes shall be imposed by said state on lands or property therein belonging to, or which may hereafter be purchased by, the United States.

SEC. 5. *And be it further enacted,* That in case a constitution and state government shall be formed for the people of said territory of Nevada, in compliance with the provisions of this act, *that* said convention forming the same shall provide by ordinance for submitting said constitution to the people of said state for their ratification or rejection at an election to be held on the second Tuesday of October, one thousand eight hundred and sixty-four, at such places and under such regulations as may be prescribed therein, at which election the lawful voters of said new state shall vote directly for or against the proposed constitution, and the returns of said election shall be made to the acting governor of the territory, who, with the United States district-attorney and chief justice of said territory, or any two of them, shall canvass the same, and if a majority of legal votes shall be cast for said constitution in said proposed state, the said acting governor shall certify the same to the President of the United States, together with a copy of said constitution and ordinances; whereupon it shall be the duty of the President of the United States to issue his proclamation declaring the state admitted into the Union on an equal footing with the original states, without any further action whatever on the part of congress.

SEC. 6. *And be it further enacted*, That until the next general census shall be taken said state of Nevada shall be entitled to one representative in the house of representatives of the United States, which representative, together with the governor and state and other officers provided for in said constitution, may be elected on the same day a vote is taken for or against the proposed constitution and state government.

SEC. 7. *And be it further enacted*, That sections numbers sixteen and thirty-six, in every township, and where such sections have been sold or otherwise disposed of by any act of congress, other lands equivalent thereto in legal subdivisions of not less than one quarter-section, and as contiguous as may be, shall be, and are hereby, granted to said state for the support of common schools.

SEC. 8. *And be it further enacted*, That provided the state of Nevada shall be admitted into the Union, in accordance with the foregoing provisions of this act, *that* twenty entire sections of the unappropriated public lands within said state, to be selected and located by direction of the legislature thereof, on or before the first day of January, anno Domini eighteen hundred and sixty-eight, shall be, and they are hereby, granted, in legal subdivisions of not less than one hundred and sixty acres, to said state, for the purpose of erecting public buildings at the capital of said state, for legislative and judicial purposes, in such manner as the legislature shall prescribe.

SEC. 9. *And be it further enacted*, That twenty other entire sections of land, as aforesaid, to be selected and located as aforesaid, in legal subdivisions, as aforesaid, shall be, and they are hereby, granted to said state for the purpose of erecting a suitable building for a penitentiary or state prison in the manner aforesaid.

SEC. 10. *And be it further enacted*, That five percentum of the proceeds of the sales of all public lands lying within said state, which shall be sold by the United States subsequent to the admission of said state into the Union, after deducting all the expenses incident to the same, shall be paid to the said state for the purpose of making and improving public roads, constructing ditches or canals, to effect a general system of irrigation of the agricultural land in the state, as the legislature shall direct.

SEC. 11. *And be it further enacted*, That from and after the admission of the said state of Nevada into the Union, in pursuance of this act, the laws of the United States, not locally inapplicable, shall have the same force and effect within the said state as elsewhere within the United States, and said state shall constitute one judicial district, and be called the district of Nevada.

Approved, March 21, 1864.

AN ACT TO ENABLE THE PEOPLE OF NEBRASKA TO FORM A CONSTITUTION AND STATE GOVERNMENT, AND FOR THE ADMISSION OF SUCH STATE INTO THE UNION ON AN EQUAL FOOTING WITH THE ORIGINAL STATES

APRIL 19, 1864

Be it enacted by the Senate and House of Representatives of the United States of America in Congress assembled, That the inhabitants of that portion of the territory of Nebraska included in the boundaries hereinafter designated be, and they are hereby, authorized to form for themselves a constitution and state government, with the name aforesaid, which state, when so formed, shall be admitted into the Union as hereinafter provided.

SEC. 2. *And be it further enacted,* That the said state of Nebraska shall consist of all the territory included within the following boundaries, to wit: Commencing at a point formed by the intersection of the western boundary of the state of Missouri with the fortieth degree of north latitude; extending thence due west along said fortieth degree of north latitude to a point formed by its intersection with the twenty-fifth degree of longitude west from Washington; thence north along said twenty-fifth degree of longitude to a point formed by its intersection with the forty-first degree of north latitude; thence west along said forty-first degree of north latitude to a point formed by its intersection with the twenty-seventh degree of longitude west from Washington; thence north along said twenty-seventh degree of west longitude to a point formed by its intersection with the forty-third degree of north latitude; thence east along said forty-third degree of north latitude to the Reya Paha river; thence down the middle of the channel of said river, with its meanderings, to its junction with the Niobrara river; thence down the middle of the channel of said Niobrara river, and following the meanderings thereof, to its junction with the Missouri river; thence down the middle of the channel of said Missouri river, and following the meanderings thereof, to the place of beginning.

SEC. 3. *And be it further enacted,* That all persons qualified by law to vote for representatives to the general assembly of said territory shall be qualified to be elected; and they are hereby authorized to vote for and choose representatives to form a convention, under such rules and regulations as the governor of said territory may prescribe, and also to vote upon the acceptance or rejection of such constitution as may be formed by said convention, under such rules and regulations as said convention may prescribe; and if any of said citizens are enlisted in the army of the United States, and are still within said territory, they shall be permitted to vote at their place of rendevous; and if any are absent from said territory, by reason of their enlistment in the army of the United States, they shall be permitted to vote at their place of service, under the rules and regulations in each case to be prescribed as aforesaid; and the aforesaid representatives to form the aforesaid convention shall be apportioned among the several counties in said territory in proportion to the population as near as may be, and said apportionment shall be made for said territory by the governor, United States district attorney, and chief justice thereof, or any two of them. And the governor of said territory shall, by proclamation, on or before the first Monday of May next, order an election of the representatives aforesaid to be held on the first Monday in June thereafter throughout the territory; and such election shall be conducted in the same manner as is prescribed by the laws of said territory regulating elections therein for members of the house of representatives; and the number of members to said convention shall be the same as now constitute both branches of the legislature of the aforesaid territory.

SEC. 4. *And be it further enacted,* That the members of the convention thus elected shall meet at the capital of said territory on the first Monday in July next, and after organization shall declare, on behalf of the people of said territory, that they adopt the constitution of the United States; whereupon the said convention shall be, and it is hereby, authorized to form a constitution and state government: *Provided,* That the constitution when formed shall be republican, and not repugnant to the constitution of the United States and the principles of the Declaration of Independence: *And provided, further,* That said constitution shall provide, by an article forever irrevocable, without the consent of the Congress of the United States:

First. That slavery or involuntary servitude shall be forever prohibited in said state.

Second. That perfect toleration of religious sentiment shall be secured, and no inhabitant of said state shall ever be molested in person or property on account of his or her mode of religious worship.

Third. That the people inhabiting said territory do agree and declare that they forever disclaim all right and title to the unappropriated public lands lying within said territory, and that the same shall be and remain at the sole and entire disposition of the United States, and that the lands belonging to citizens of the United States residing without the said state shall never be taxed higher than the land belonging to residents thereof; and that no taxes shall be imposed by said state on lands or property therein belonging to or which may hereafter be purchased by the United States.

SEC. 5. *And be it further enacted,* That in case a constitution and state government shall be formed for the people of said territory of Nebraska, in compliance with the provisions of this act, that said convention forming the same shall provide by ordinance for submitting said constitution to the people of said state for their ratification or rejection at an election to be held on the second Tuesday of October, one thousand eight hundred and sixty-four, at such places and under such regulations as may be prescribed therein, at which election the qualified voters, as hereinbefore provided, shall vote directly for or against the proposed constitution, and the returns of said election shall be made to the acting governor of the territory, who, together with the United States district attorney and chief justice of the said territory, or any two of them, shall canvass the same, and if a majority of legal votes shall be cast for said constitution in said proposed state, the said acting governor shall certify the same to the President of the United States, together with a copy of said constitution and ordinances; whereupon it shall be the duty of the President of the United States to issue his proclamation declaring the state admitted into the Union on an equal footing with the original states, without any further action whatever on the part of congress.

SEC. 6. *And be it further enacted,* That until the next general census shall be taken said state of Nebraska shall be entitled to one representative in the house of representatives of the United States, which representative, together with the governor and state and other officers provided for in said constitution, may be elected on the same day a vote is taken for or against the proposed constitution and state government.

SEC. 7. *And be it further enacted,* That sections numbered sixteen and thirty-six in every township, and when such sections have been sold or otherwise disposed of by any act of congress, other lands equivalent thereto, in legal subdivisions of not less than one quarter section, and as contiguous as may be, shall be, and are hereby, granted to said state for the support of common schools.

SEC. 8. *And be it further enacted,* That provided the state of Nebraska shall be admitted into the union in accordance with the foregoing provisions of this act, that twenty entire sections of the unappropriated public lands within said state, to be selected and located by direction of the legislature thereof, on or before the first day of January, anno Domini eighteen hundred and sixty-eight, shall be and they are hereby granted, in legal subdivisions of not less than one hundred and sixty acres, to said state for the purpose of erecting public buildings at the capital of said state for legislative and judicial purposes, in such manner as the legislature shall prescribe.

SEC. 9. *And be it further enacted,* That fifty other entire sections of land, as aforesaid, to be selected and located as aforesaid, in legal subdivisions as aforesaid, shall be, and they are hereby, granted to said state for the purpose of erecting a suitable building for a penitentiary or state prison in the manner aforesaid.

SEC. 10. *And be it further enacted,* That seventy-two other sections of land shall be set apart and reserved for the use and support of a state university, to be selected in manner as aforesaid, and to be appropriated and applied as the legislature of said state may prescribe for the purpose named, and for no other purpose.

SEC. 11. *And be it further enacted,* That all salt springs within said state, not exceeding twelve in number, with six sections of land adjoining, or as contiguous as may be to each, shall be granted to said state for its use, the said land to be selected by the governor thereof, within one year after the admission of the state, and when so selected to be used or disposed of on such terms, conditions, and regulations as the legislature shall direct: *Provided,* That no salt spring or lands, the right whereof is now vested in any individual or individuals, or which hereafter shall be confirmed or adjudged to any individual or individuals, shall, by this act, be granted to said state.

SEC. 12. *And be it further enacted,* That five per centum of the proceeds of the sales of all public lands lying within said state, which have been or shall be sold by the United States prior or subsequent to the admission of said state into the Union, after deducting all expenses incident to the same, shall be paid to the said state for the support of common schools.

SEC. 13. *And be it further enacted*, That from and after the admission of the said state of Nebraska into the Union in pursuance of this act, the laws of the United States, not locally inapplicable, shall have the same force and effect within the said state as elsewhere within the United States; and said state shall constitute one judicial district, and be called the district of Nebraska.

SEC. 14. *And be it further enacted*, That any unexpended balance of the appropriations for said territorial legislative expenses of Nebraska remaining for the fiscal years eighteen hundred and sixty-three and eighteen hundred and sixty-four, or so much thereof as may be necessary, shall be applied to and used for defraying the expenses of said convention and for the payment of the members thereof, under the same rules, regulations, and rates as are now provided by law for the payment of the territorial legislature.

Approved, April 19, 1864.

AN ACT TO PROVIDE A TEMPORARY GOVERNMENT FOR THE TERRITORY OF MONTANA
MAY 26, 1864

Be it enacted by the Senate and House of Representatives of the United States of America in Congress assembled, That all that part of the territory of the United States included within the limits, to wit: Commencing at a point formed by the intersection of the twenty-seventh degree of longitude west from Washington with the forty-fifth degree of north latitude; thence due west on said forty-fifth degree of latitude to a point formed by its intersection with the thirty-fourth degree of longitude west from Washington; thence due south along said thirty-fourth degree of longitude to its intersection with the forty-fourth degree and thirty minutes of north latitude; thence due west along said forty-fourth degree and thirty minutes of north latitude to a point formed by its intersection with the crest of the Rocky Mountains; thence following the crest of the Rocky Mountains northward till its intersection with the Bitter Root Mountains; thence northward along the crest of said Bitter Root Mountains to its intersection with the thirty-ninth degree of longitude west from Washington; thence along said thirty-ninth degree of longitude northward to the boundary line of the British possessions; thence eastward along said boundary line to the twenty-seventh degree of longitude west from Washington; thence southward along said twenty-seventh degree of longitude to the place of beginning, be, and the same is hereby, created into a temporary government by the name of the Territory of Montana: *Provided*, That nothing in this act contained shall be construed to inhibit the government of the United States from dividing said territory or changing its boundaries in such manner and at such time as congress shall deem convenient and proper, or from attaching any portion of said territory to any other state or territory of the

United States: *Provided, further,* That nothing in this act contained shall be construed to impair the rights of person or property now pertaining to the Indians in said territory so long as such rights shall remain unextinguished by treaty between the United States and such Indians, or to include any territory which, by treaty with any Indian tribes, is not, without the consent of said tribe, to be included within the territorial limits or jurisdiction of any state or territory; but all such territory shall be excepted out of the boundaries, and constitute no part of the Territory of Montana, until said tribe shall signify their assent to the President of the United States to be included within said territory, or to affect the authority of the government of the United States to make any regulations respecting such Indians, their lands, property, or other rights, by treaty, law, or otherwise, which it would have been competent for the government to make if this act had never passed.

SEC. 2. *And be it further enacted,* That the executive power and authority in and over said Territory of Montana shall be vested in a governor, who shall hold his office for four years, and until his successor shall be appointed and qualified, unless sooner removed by the President of the United States. The governor shall reside within said territory, and shall be commander-in-chief of the militia and superintendent of Indian affairs thereof. He may grant pardons and respites for offences against the laws of said territory, and reprieve for offences against the laws of the United States until the decision of the President of the United States can be made known thereon; he shall commission all officers who shall be appointed to office under the laws of the said territory, and shall take care that the laws be faithfully executed.

SEC. 3. *And be it further enacted,* That there shall be a secretary of said territory, who shall reside therein and hold his office for four years, unless sooner removed by the President of the United States; he shall record and preserve all laws and proceedings of the legislative assembly hereinafter constituted, and all the acts and proceedings of the governor in his executive department; he shall transmit one copy of the laws and journals of the legislative assembly within thirty days after the end of each session, and one copy of the executive proceedings and official correspondence semi-annually, on the first days of January and July in each year, to the President of the United States, and two copies of the laws to the president of the senate and to the speaker of the house of representatives, for the use of congress. And in case of the death, removal, resignation, or absence of the governor from the territory, the secretary shall be, and he is hereby, authorized and required to execute and perform all the powers and duties of the governor during such vacancy or absence, or until another governor shall be duly appointed and qualified to fill such vacancy.

SEC. 4. *And be it further enacted,* That the legislative power and authority of said territory shall be vested in the governor and a legislative assembly. The legislative assembly shall consist of a council and house of representatives. The council shall consist of seven members, having the qualifications of voters, as hereinafter prescribed, whose term of service shall continue two years. The house of representatives shall, at its first session, consist of thirteen members, possessing the same qualifications as prescribed for the members of the council, and whose term of service shall continue one year. The number of representatives may be increased by the legislative assembly, from time to time, to twenty-six, in proportion to the increase of qualified voters; and the council, in like manner, to thirteen. An apportionment shall be made, as nearly equal as practicable, among the several counties or districts for the election of the council and representatives, giving to each section of the territory representation in the ratio of its qualified voters as nearly as may be. And the members of the council and of the house of representatives shall reside in, and be inhabitants of, the district or county or counties for which they may be elected respectively. Previous to the first election the governor shall cause a census or enumeration of the inhabitants and qualified voters of the several counties and districts of the territory to be taken by such persons and in such mode as the governor shall designate and appoint, and the person so appointed shall receive a reasonable compensation therefor. And the first election shall be held at such time and places, and be conducted in such manner, both as to the persons who shall superintend such election and the returns thereof, as the governor shall appoint and direct; and he shall at the same time declare the number of members of the council and house of representatives to which each of the counties or districts shall be entitled under this act. The persons having the highest number of legal votes in each of said council districts, respectively, for members of the council, shall be declared by the governor to be duly elected to the council; and the persons having the highest number of legal votes for the house of representatives in each of said representative districts, respectively, shall be declared by the governor to be duly elected members of said house: *Provided,* That in case two or more persons voted for shall have an equal number of votes, and in case a vacancy shall otherwise occur in either branch of the legislative assembly, the governor shall order a new election. And the persons thus elected to the legislative assembly shall meet at such place and on such day as the governor shall appoint; but thereafter the time, place, and manner of holding and conducting all elections by the people, and the apportioning the representation in the several counties or districts to the council and house of representatives, according to the number of qualified voters, shall be prescribed by law, as well as the day of the commencement of the regular sessions of the legislative assembly: *Provided,* That no session in any one year shall exceed the term of forty days, except the first session, which may continue sixty days.

SEC. 5. *And be it further enacted,* That all citizens of the United States, and those who have declared their intentions to become such, and who are otherwise described and qualified under the fifth section of the act of congress providing for a temporary government for the territory of Idaho, approved March third, eighteen hundred and sixty-three, shall be entitled to vote at said first election, and shall be eligible to any office within the said territory; but the qualifications of voters, and of holding office, at all subsequent elections, shall be such as shall be prescribed by the legislative assembly.

SEC. 6. *And be it further enacted,* That the legislative power of the territory shall extend to all rightful subjects of legislation consistent with the constitution of the United States and the provisions of this act; but no law shall be passed interfering with the primary disposal of the soil; no tax shall be imposed upon the property of the United States, nor shall the lands or other property of non-residents be taxed higher than the lands or other property of residents. Every bill which shall have passed the council and house of representatives of the said territory shall, before it becomes a law, be presented to the governor of the territory. If he approve, he shall sign it; but if not, he shall return it, with his objections, to the house in which it originated, who shall enter the objections at large upon their journal, and proceed to reconsider it. If, after such reconsideration, two thirds of that house shall agree to pass the bill, it shall be sent, together with the objections, to the other house, by which it shall likewise be reconsidered, and, if approved by two thirds of that house, it shall become a law. But in all such cases the votes of both houses shall be determined by yeas and nays, to be entered on the journal of each house, respectively. If any bill shall not be returned by the governor within three days (Sunday excepted) after it shall have been presented to him, the same shall be a law, in like manner as if he had signed it, unless the assembly, by adjournment, prevent its return; in which case it shall not be a law: *Provided*, That whereas slavery is prohibited in said territory by act of congress of June nineteenth, eighteen hundred and sixty-two, nothing herein contained shall be construed to authorize or permit its existence therein.

SEC. 7. *And be it further enacted*, That all township, district, and county officers, not herein otherwise provided for, shall be appointed or elected, as the case may be, in such manner as shall be provided by the governor and legislative assembly of the Territory of Montana. The governor shall nominate, and, by and with the advice and consent of the legislative council, appoint all officers not herein otherwise provided for; and in the first instance the governor alone may appoint all said officers, who shall hold their offices until the end of the first session of the legislative assembly, and shall lay off the necessary districts for members of the council and house of representatives, and all other officers.

SEC. 8. *And be it further enacted*, That no member of the legislative assembly shall hold or be appointed to any office which shall have been created, or the salary or emoluments of which shall have been increased while he was a member, during the term for which he was elected, and for one year after the expiration of such term; but this restriction shall not be applicable to members of the first legislative assembly. And no person holding a commission or appointment under the United States, except postmasters, shall be a member of the legislative assembly, or shall hold any office under the government of said territory.

SEC. 9. *And be it further enacted*, That the judicial power of said territory shall be vested in a supreme court, district courts, probate courts, and in justices of the peace. The supreme court shall consist of a chief-justice and two associate justices, any two of whom shall constitute a quorum, and who shall hold a term at the seat of government of said territory annually; and they shall hold their offices during the period of four years, and until their successors shall be appointed and qualified. The said territory shall be divided into three judicial districts, and a district court shall be held in each of said districts by one of the justices of the supreme court at such times and places as may be prescribed by law; and the said judges shall, after their appointments, respectively, reside in the districts which shall be assigned them. The jurisdiction of the several courts herein provided for, both appellate and original, and that of the probate courts and of justices of the peace, shall be limited by law: *Provided,* That justices of the peace shall not have jurisdiction of any matter in controversy when the title of land may be in dispute, or where the debt or sum claimed shall exceed one hundred dollars; and the said supreme and district courts, respectively, shall possess chancery as well as comon-law jurisdiction. Each district court, or the judge thereof, shall appoint its clerk, who shall also be the register in chancery, and shall keep his office at the place where the court may be held. Writs of error, bills of exceptions, and appeals, shall be allowed in all cases from the final decisions of said district courts to the supreme court, under such regulations as may be prescribed by law. The supreme court, or the justices thereof, shall appoint its own clerk; and every clerk shall hold his office at the pleasure of the court for which he shall have been appointed. Writs of error and appeals from the final decisions of said supreme court shall be allowed, and may be taken to the supreme court of the United States, in the same manner and under the same regulations as from the circuit courts of the United States, where the value of the property, or the amount in controversy, to be ascertained by the oath or affirmation of either party, or other competent witnesses, shall exceed one thousand dollars, except that a writ of error or appeal shall be allowed to the supreme court of the United States from the decision of the said supreme court created by this act, or of any judge thereof, or of the district courts created by this act, or of any judge thereof, upon any writs of habeas corpus involving the question of personal freedom. And each of the said district courts shall have and exercise the same jurisdiction, in all cases arising under the constitution and laws of the United States, as is vested in the circuit and district courts of the United States; and the first six days of every term of said courts, or so much thereof as shall be necessary, shall be appropriated to the trial of causes arising under the said constitution and laws; and writs of error and appeal in all such cases shall be made to the supreme court of said territory the same as in other cases. The said clerks shall receive, in all such cases, the same fees which the clerks of the district courts of Washington Territory now receive for similar services.

SEC. 10. *And be it further enacted,* That there shall be appointed an attorney for said territory, who shall continue in office four years, and until his successor shall be appointed and qualified, unless sooner removed by the President of the United States, and who shall receive the same fees and salary as the attorney of the United States for the present Territory of Washington. There shall also be a marshal for the territory appointed, who shall hold his office for four years, and until his successor shall be appointed and qualified, unless sooner removed by the President of the United States, and who shall execute all processes issuing from the said courts when exercising their jurisdiction as circuit and district courts of the United States. He shall perform the duties, be subject to the same regulations and penalties, and be entitled to the same fees as the marshal of the district court of the United States for the present Territory of Washington, and shall, in addition, be paid two hundred dollars annually as a compensation for extra services. There shall also be appointed by the President of the United States, by and with the advice and consent of the Senate, a surveyor-general for said territory, who shall locate his office at such place as the Secretary of the Interior shall from time to time direct, and whose duties, powers, obligations, responsibilities, compensation, and allowances for clerk-hire, office-rent, fuel, and incidental expenses, shall be the same as those of the surveyor-general of New Mexico, under the direction of the Secretary of the Interior, and such instructions as he may from time to time deem advisable to give.

SEC. 11. *And be it further enacted,* That the governor, secretary, chief justice, and associate justices, attorney, and marshal shall be appointed by the President of the United States, by and with the advice and consent of the Senate. The governor and secretary to be appointed as aforesaid shall, before they act as such, respectively, take an oath or affirmation before the district judge, or some justice of the peace in the limits of said territory, duly authorized to administer oaths and affirmations by the laws now in force therein, or before the chief justice or some associate justice of the supreme court of the United States, to support the constitution of the United States, and faithfully to discharge the duties of their respective offices; which said oaths, when so taken, shall be certified by the person by whom the same shall have been taken; and such certificates shall be received and recorded by the said secretary among the executive proceedings; and the chief justice and associate justices, and all civil officers in said territory, before they act as such, shall take a like oath or affirmation before the said governor and secretary, or some judge or justice of the peace of the territory who may be duly commissioned and qualified, or before the chief justice or some associate justice of the supreme court of the United States, which said oath or affirmation shall be certified and transmitted by the person taking the same to the secretary, to be by him recorded as aforesaid; and afterwards the like oath or affirmation shall be taken, certified, and recorded in such manner and form as may be prescribed by law. And any person who has heretofore been appointed chief justice or associate justice of the Territory of Idaho, who has not yet taken the oath of office, as prescribed by the act organizing said territory, may take said oath or affirmation before the chief justice or some associate justice of the supreme court of the United States. The governor shall receive an annual salary of two thousand five hundred dollars; the chief justice and associate justices shall receive an annual salary of two thousand five hundred dollars; the secretary shall receive an annual salary of two thousand dollars. The said salaries shall be paid quarter-yearly from the dates of the respective appointments at the treasury of the United States; but no payment shall be made until said officers shall have entered upon the duties of their respective appointments. The members of the legislative assembly shall be entitled to receive four dollars each per day during their attendance at the sessions thereof, and four dollars each for every twenty miles' travel in going to and returning from said sessions, estimated according to the nearest usually travelled route; and an additional allowance of four dollars per day shall be paid to the presiding officer of each house for each day he shall so preside. And a chief clerk, one assistant clerk, one engrossing and one enrolling clerk, a sergeant-at-arms, and doorkeeper may be chosen for each house; and the chief clerk shall receive four dollars per day, and the said other officers three dollars per day during the session of the legislative assembly; but no other officers shall be paid by the United States: *Provided,* That there shall be but one session of the legislative assembly annually, unless, on an extraordinary occasion, the governor shall think proper to call the legislative assembly together. There shall be appropriated annually the usual sum, to be expended by the governor, to defray the contingent expenses of the territory, including the salary of the clerk of the executive department. And there shall also be appropriated annually a sufficient sum, to be expended by the secretary of the territory, and upon an estimate to be made by the Secretary of the Treasury of the United States, to defray the expenses of the legislative assembly, the printing of the laws, and other incidental expenses. And the governor and secretary of the territory shall, in the disbursement of all moneys intrusted to them, be governed solely by the instructions of the Secretary of the Treasury of the United States, and shall semi-annually account to the said secretary for the manner in which the aforesaid moneys shall have been expended; and no expenditure shall be made by said legislative assembly for objects not specially authorized by the acts of congress making the appropriations, nor beyond the sums thus appropriated for such objects.

SEC. 12. *And be it further enacted,* That the legislative assembly of the Territory of Montana shall hold its first session at such time and place in said territory as the governor thereof shall appoint and direct; and at said first session, or as soon thereafter as they shall deem expedient, the governor and legislative assembly shall proceed to locate and establish the seat of government for said territory at such place as they may deem eligible: *Provided,* That the seat of government fixed by the governor and legislative assembly shall not be at any time changed except by an act of the said assembly duly passed, and which shall be approved, after due notice, at the first general election thereafter, by a majority of the legal votes cast on that question.

SEC. 13. *And be it further enacted,* That a delegate to the house of representatives of the United States, to serve for the term of two years, who shall be a citizen of the United States, may be elected by the voters qualified to elect members of the legislative assembly, who shall be entitled to the same rights and privileges as are exercised and enjoyed by the delegates from the several other territories of the United States to the said house of representatives; but the delegate first elected shall hold his seat only during the term of the congress to which he shall be elected. The first election shall be held at such time and places, and be conducted in such manner, as the governor shall appoint and direct; and at all subsequent elections the time and places, and manner of holding the elections, shall be prescribed by law. The person having the greatest number of legal votes shall be declared by the governor to be duly elected, and a certificate thereof shall be given accordingly. That the constitution and all laws of the United States, which are not locally inapplicable, shall have the same force and effect within the said Territory of Montana as elsewhere within the United States.

SEC. 14. *And be it further enacted,* That when the lands in the said territory shall be surveyed under the direction of the government of the United States, preparatory to bringing the same into market, sections numbered sixteen and thirty-six in each township in said territory shall be, and the same are hereby, reserved for the purpose of being applied to schools in said territory and in the states and territories hereafter to be erected out of the same.

SEC. 15. *And be it further enacted,* That, until otherwise provided by law, the governor of said territory may define the judicial districts of said territory, and assign the judges who may be appointed for said territory to the several districts, and also appoint the times and places for holding courts in the several counties or subdivisions in each of said judicial districts, by proclamation to be issued by him; but the legislative assembly, at their first or any subsequent session, may organize, alter, or modify such judicial districts, and assign the judges, and alter the times and places of holding the courts, as to them shall seem proper and convenient.

SEC. 16. *And be it further enacted,* That all officers to be appointed by the President of the United States, by and with the advice and consent of the Senate, for the Territory of Montana, who, by virtue of the provisions of any law now existing, or which may be enacted by congress, are required to give security for moneys that may be intrusted with them for disbursement, shall give such security at such time and in such manner as the Secretary of the Treasury may prescribe.

SEC. 17. *And be it further enacted,* That all treaties, laws, and other engagements made by the government of the United States with the Indian tribes inhabiting the territory embraced within the provisions of this act, shall be faithfully and rigidly observed, anything contained in this act to the contrary notwithstanding; and that the existing agencies and superintendencies of said Indians be continued, with the same powers and duties which are now prescribed by law, except that the President of the United States may, at his discretion, change the location of the office of said agencies or superintendents.

SEC. 18. *And be it further enacted,* That, until congress shall otherwise direct, all that part of the Territory of Idaho included within the following boundaries, to wit: Commencing at a point formed by the intersection of the thirty-third degree of longitude west from Washington with the forty-first degree of north latitude; thence along said thirty-third degree of longitude to the crest of the Rocky Mountains; thence northward along the said crest of the Rocky Mountains to its intersection with the forty-fourth degree and thirty minutes of north latitude; thence eastward along said forty-fourth degree thirty minutes north latitude to the thirty-fourth degree of longitude west from Washington; thence northward along said thirty-fourth degree of longitude to its intersection with the forty-fifth degree north latitude; thence eastward along said forty-fifth degree of north latitude to its intersection with the twenty-seventh degree of longitude west from Washington; thence south along said twenty-seventh degree of longitude west from Washington to the forty-first degree north latitude; thence west along said forty-first degree of latitude to the place of beginning, shall be, and is hereby, incorporated temporarily into and made part of the Territory of Dakota.

Approved, May 26, 1864.

AN ACT CONCERNING THE BOUNDARIES
OF THE STATE OF NEVADA
MAY 5, 1866

Be it enacted by the Senate and House of Representatives of the United States of America in Congress assembled, That, as provided for and consented to in the constitution of the State of Nevada, all that territory and tract of land adjoining the present eastern boundary of the State of Nevada, and lying between the thirty-seventh and the forty-second degrees of north latitude and west of the thirty-seventh degree of longitude west of Washington, is hereby added to and made a part of the State of Nevada.

SEC. 2. *And be it further enacted,* That there is hereby added to and made a part of the State of Nevada all that extent of territory lying within the following boundaries to wit: Commencing on the thirty-seventh degree of north latitude at the thirty-seventh degree of longitude west from Washington; and running thence south on said degree of longitude to the middle of the river Colorado of the West; thence down the middle of said river to the eastern boundary of the State of California; thence northwesterly along said boundary of California to the thirty-seventh degree of north latitude; and thence east along said degree of latitude to the point of beginning: *Provided,* That the territory mentioned in this section shall not become a part of the State of Nevada until said State shall, through its legislature consent thereto: *And provided further,* That all possessory rights acquired by citizens of the United States to mining claims, discovered, located, and originally recorded in compliance with the rules and regulations adopted by miners in the Pah-Ranagat and other mining districts in the Territory incorporated by the provisions of this act into the State of Nevada shall remain as valid subsisting mining claims; but nothing herein contained shall be so construed as granting a title in fee to any mineral lands held by possessory titles in the mining States and Territories.

Approved, May 5, 1866.

AN ACT TO PROVIDE A TEMPORARY GOVERNMENT
FOR THE TERRITORY OF WYOMING
JULY 25, 1868

Be it enacted by the Senate and House of Representatives of the United States of America in Congress assembled, That all that part of the United States described as follows: Commencing at the intersection of the twenty-seventh meridian of longitude west from Washington with the forty-fifth degree of north latitude, and running thence west to the thirty-fourth meridian of west longitude, thence south to the forty-first degree of north latitude, thence east to the twenty-seventh meridian of west longitude, and thence north to the place of beginning, be, and the same is hereby, organized into a temporary government by the name of the Territory of Wyoming: *Provided*, That nothing in this act shall be construed to impair the rights of person or property now pertaining to the Indians in said Territory, so long as such rights shall remain unextinguished by treaty between the United States and such Indians: *Provided, further*, That nothing in this act contained shall be construed to inhibit the government of the United States from dividing said Territory into two or more Territories, in such manner and at such time as Congress shall deem convenient and proper, or from attaching any portion thereof to any other Territory or State.

SEC. 2. *And be it further enacted*, That the executive power and authority in and over said Territory of Wyoming shall be vested in a governor, who shall hold his office for four years, and until his successor shall be appointed and qualified, unless sooner removed by the President of the United States with the advice and consent of the Senate. The governor shall reside within said Territory, shall be commander-in-chief of the militia thereof, shall perform the duties and receive the emoluments of superintendent of Indian affairs, and shall approve all laws passed by the legislative assembly before they shall take effect, unless the same shall pass by a two-thirds vote as provided in section six of this act; he may grant pardons for offences against the laws of said Territory, and reprieves for offences against the laws of the United States, until the decision of the President can be made known thereon; he shall commission all officers who shall be appointed to office under the laws of said Territory, and shall take care that the laws be faithfully executed.

SEC. 3. *And be it further enacted*, That there shall be a secretary of said Territory, who shall reside therein and hold his office for four years, unless sooner removed by the President of the United States, with the consent of the Senate; he shall record and preserve all the laws and the proceedings of the legislative assembly hereinafter constituted, and all acts and proceedings of the governor in his executive department; he shall transmit one copy of the laws and one copy of the executive proceedings on or before the first day of December in each year to the President of the United States, and, at the same time, two copies of the laws to the Speaker of the House of Representatives and the President of the Senate for the use of Congress; and in case of the death, removal, resignation, or other necessary absence of the governor from the Territory, the secretary shall have, and he is hereby authorized and required to execute and perform, all the powers and duties of the governor during such vacancy or absence, or until another governor shall be appointed to fill such vacancy.

SEC. 4. *And be it further enacted*, That the legislative power and authority of said Territory shall be vested in the governor and legislative assembly. The legislative assembly shall consist of a council and house of representatives. The council shall consist of nine members, which may be increased to thirteen, having the qualifications of voters as hereinafter prescribed, whose term of service shall continue two years. The house of representatives shall consist of thirteen

members, which may be increased to twenty-seven, possessing the same qualifications as prescribed for members of the council, and whose term of service
shall continue one year. An apportionment shall be made by the governor as
nearly equal as practicable among the several counties or districts for the election of the council and house of representatives, giving to each section of the
Territory representation in the ratio of their population, (excepting Indians not
taxed,) as nearly as may be, and the members of the council and house of representatives shall reside in and be inhabitants of the districts for which they may
be elected, respectively. Previous to the first election the governor shall cause
a census or enumeration of the inhabitants of the several counties or districts
of the Territory to be taken, and the first election shall be held at such times
and places, and be conducted in such manner as the governor shall appoint and
direct, and he shall at the same time declare the number of the members of the
council and house of representatives to which each of the counties or districts
shall be entitled under this act. The number of persons authorized to be elected,
having the highest number of votes in each of said council districts for members
of the council, shall be declared by the governor duly elected to the council;
and the person or persons authorized to be elected having the greatest number
of votes for the house of representatives equal to the number to which each
county or district shall be entitled, shall be declared by the governor to be
elected members of the house of representatives: *Provided*, That in case of a
tie between two or more persons voted for, the governor shall order a new election, to supply the vacancy made by such tie vote. And the persons thus elected
to the legislative assembly shall meet at such place and on such day as the
governor shall appoint; but thereafter the time, place, and manner of holding
and conducting elections by the people, and the apportioning the representation in the several counties or districts to the council and house of representatives, according to the population, shall be prescribed by law, as well as the
day of the commencement of the regular sessions of the legislative assembly:
Provided, That no one session shall exceed the term of forty days, except the
first, which may be extended to sixty days, but no longer.

SEC. 5. *And be it further enacted*, That every male citizen of the United
States above the age of twenty-one years, *and* [including] persons who shall
have declared their intention to become citizens of the United States, who shall
have been a resident of the said Territory at the time of the passage of this act,
shall be entitled to vote at the first and all subsequent elections in the Territory,
and shall be eligible to hold any office in said Territory. And the legislative
assembly shall not at any time abridge the right of suffrage, or to hold office,
on account of the race, color, or previous condition of servitude of any resident
of the Territory: Provided, That the right of suffrage and of holding office shall
be exercised only by citizens of the United States, and those who shall have
declared on oath before a competent court of record their intention to become
such, and shall have taken an oath to support the Constitution and government
of the United States.

SEC. 6. *And be it further enacted*, [That] the legislative power of the Territory shall extend to all rightful subjects of legislation consistent with the Constitution of the United States and the provisions of this act; but no law shall
be passed interfering with the primary disposal of the soil; no tax shall be

imposed upon the property of the United States, nor shall the lands or other property on non-residents be taxed higher than the lands or other property of residents, nor shall any law be passed impairing the rights of private property, nor shall any unequal discrimination be made in taxing different kinds of property, but all property subject to taxation shall be taxed in proportion to its value. Every bill which shall have passed the council and the house of representatives of said Territory shall, before it becomes a law, be presented to the governor of the Territory. If he approve, he shall sign it; but if not, he shall return it with his objections to the house in which it originated, who shall enter the objections at large upon their journal and proceed to reconsider it. If, after such reconsideration, two-thirds of that house shall agree to pass the bill, it shall be sent, together with the objections, to the other house, by which it shall likewise be reconsidered; and if approved by two-thirds of that house it shall become a law. But in all such cases the votes of both houses shall be determined by yeas and nays, to be entered on the journal of each house respectively. If any bill shall not be returned by the governor within five days (Sunday excepted) after it shall have been presented to him, the same shall be a law in like manner as if he had signed it, unless the assembly, by adjournment, prevent its return, in which case it shall not be a law.

SEC. 7. *And be it further enacted,* That all township, district, and county officers, not herein otherwise provided for, shall be appointed or elected, as the case may be, in such manner as shall be provided by the governor and legislative assembly of the Territory. The governor shall nominate and by and with the consent of the council appoint all officers not herein otherwise provided for, and in the first instance the governor alone may appoint all such officers, who shall hold their offices until the end of the first session of the legislative assembly; and he shall lay off the necessary districts for members of the council and house of representatives, and all other officers.

SEC. 8. *And be it further enacted,* That no member of the legislative assembly shall hold or be appointed to any office which shall have been created, or the salary or emoluments of which shall have been increased while he was a member, during the term for which he was elected, and for one year after the expiration of such term; and no person holding a commission or appointment under the United States, except postmasters, shall be a member of the legislative assembly, or shall hold any office under the government of said Territory.

SEC. 9. *And be it further enacted,* That the judicial power of said Territory shall be vested in a supreme court, district courts, probate courts, and justices of the peace. The supreme court shall consist of a chief justice and two associate justices, any two of whom shall constitute a quorum, and who shall hold a term at the seat of government of said Territory annually, and they shall hold their offices for four years, unless sooner removed by the President with the consent of the Senate of the United States. The said Territory shall be divided into three judicial districts, and a district court shall be held in each of said districts by one of the justices of the supreme court, at such time and place as may be prescribed by law; and said judges shall after their appointments, respectively, reside in the districts which shall be assigned them. The jurisdiction of the several courts herein provided for, both appellate and original, and that of the probate courts, and of the justices of the peace, shall be as limited by law: *Provided,* That justices of the peace shall not have jurisdiction of any matter in controversy when the title or boundaries of land may be in dispute, or where the debt or sum claimed shall exceed one hundred dollars; and the said supreme and district courts, respectively, shall possess chancery as well as common law jurisdiction and authority for redress of all wrongs committed against the Constitution or laws of the United States or of the Territory affecting persons or property. Each district court, or the judge thereof, shall appoint its clerk, who shall also be the register in chancery, and shall keep his office where the court may be held. Writs of error, bills of exception, and appeals shall be allowed in all cases from the final decisions of said district courts to the supreme court under such regulations as may be prescribed by law, but in no case removed to the supreme court shall trial by jury be allowed in said court. The supreme court, or the justices thereof, shall appoint its own clerks, and every clerk shall hold his office at the pleasure of the court for which he shall have been appointed. Writs of error and appeal from the final decision of said supreme court shall be allowed and may be taken to the Supreme Court of the United States, in the same manner and under the same regulations as from the circuit courts of the United States, where the value of the property or the amount in controversy, to be ascertained by the oath or affirmation of either party, or other competent witness, shall exceed one thousand dollars; and each of the said district courts shall have and exercise the same jurisdiction in all cases arising under the Constitution and laws of the United States, as is vested in the circuit and district courts of the United States; and the said supreme and district courts of said Territory, and the respective judges thereof, shall and may grant writs of habeas corpus in all cases in which the same are grantable by the judges of the United States in the District of Columbia; and the first six days of every term of said courts, or so much thereof as shall be necessary, shall be appropriated to the trial of causes arising under the said Constitution and laws; and writs of error and appeals in all such cases shall be made to the supreme court of said Territory, the same as in other cases. The said clerk shall receive in all such cases the same fees which the clerks of the district courts of Dakota Territory now receive for similar services.

SEC. 10. *And be it further enacted,* That there shall be appointed an attorney for said Territory, who shall continue in office for four years, unless sooner removed by the President with the consent of the Senate, and who shall receive the same fees and salary as is now received by the attorney of the United States for the Territory of *Dacotah* [Dakota]. There shall also be a marshal for the Territory appointed, who shall hold his office for four years, unless sooner removed by the President with the consent of the Senate, and who shall execute all processes issuing from the said courts when exercising their jurisdiction as circuit and district courts of the United States; he shall perform the duties, be subject to the same regulations and penalties, and be entitled to the same fees as the marshal of the district court of the United States for the present Territory of Dakota, and shall, in addition, be paid two hundred dollars annually as a compensation for extra services.

SEC. 11. *And be it further enacted,* That the governor, secretary, chief justice and associate justices, attorney, and marshal, shall be nominated, and, by and with the advice and consent of the Senate, appointed by the President of the United States. The governor and secretary to be appointed as aforesaid shall, before they act as such, respectively, take an oath or affirmation before the district judge, or some justice of the peace in the limits of said Territory duly authorized to administer oaths and affirmations by the laws now in force therein, or before the Chief Justice, or some associate justice of the Supreme Court of the United States, to support the Constitution of the United States, and faithfully to discharge the duties of their respective offices, which said oaths when so taken shall be certified by the person by whom the same shall have been taken; and such certificates shall be received and recorded by the secretary among the executive proceedings, and the chief justice, and associate justices, and all other civil officers in said Territory, before they act as such, shall take a like oath or affirmation before the said governor or secretary, or some judge or justice of the peace of the Territory, who may be duly commissioned and qualified, which said oath or affirmation shall be certified and transmitted by the person taking the same to the secretary to be recorded by him as aforesaid, and afterwards the like oath or affirmation shall be taken, certified, and recorded in such manner and form as may be prescribed by law. The governor shall receive an annual salary of two thousand dollars as governor, and one thousand dollars as superintendent of Indian affairs; the chief justice and the associate justices shall each receive an annual salary of twenty-five hundred dollars, and the secretary shall receive an annual salary of eighteen hundred dollars. The said salaries shall be payable quarter-yearly at the treasury of the United States. The members of the legislative assembly shall be entitled to receive four dollars each per day during their attendance at the session thereof, and three dollars for every twenty miles' travel in going to and returning from the said sessions, estimating the distance by the nearest travelled route. There shall be appropriated annually the sum of one thousand dollars, to be expended by the governor, to defray the contingent expenses of the Territory. There shall also be appropriated annually a sufficient sum, to be expended by the secretary, and upon an estimate to be made by the Secretary of the Treasury of the United States, to defray the expenses of the legislative assembly, the printing of the laws, and other incidental expenses; and the secretary of the Territory shall annually account to the Secretary of the Treasury of the United States for the manner in which the aforesaid sum shall have been expended.

SEC. 12. *And be it further enacted,* That the legislative assembly of the Territory of Wyoming shall hold its first session at such time and place in said Territory as the governor thereof shall appoint and direct; and at said first session, or as soon thereafter as they shall deem expedient, the governor and legislative assembly shall proceed to locate and establish the seat of government for said Territory at such place as they may deem eligible; which place, however, shall thereafter be subject to be changed by the said governor and legislative assembly.

SEC. 13. *And be it further enacted,* That a delegate to the House of Representatives of the United States, to serve during each Congress of the United States, may be elected by the voters qualified to elect members of the legislative assembly, who shall be entitled to the same rights and privileges as are exercised and enjoyed by the delegates from the several other Territories of the United States in the said House of Representatives. The first election shall be held at such time and places, and be conducted in such manner, as the governor shall appoint and direct; and at all subsequent elections the time, place, and manner of holding elections shall be prescribed by law. The person having the greatest number of votes of the qualified electors as hereinbefore provided, shall be declared by the governor elected, and a certificate thereof shall be accordingly given.

SEC. 14. *And be it further enacted,* That sections numbered sixteen and thirty-six in each township in said Territory shall be, and the same are hereby, reserved for the purpose of being applied to public schools in the State or States hereafter to be erected out of the same.

SEC. 15. *And be it further enacted,* That temporarily and until otherwise provided by law the governor of said Territory may define the judicial districts of said Territory, and assign the judges who may be appointed for the said Territory to the several districts, and also appoint the times and places for holding courts in the several counties or subdivisions in each of said judicial districts by proclamation to be issued by him; but the legislative assembly, at their first or any subsequent session, may organize, alter, or modify such judicial districts and assign the judges and alter the times and places of holding the courts as to them shall seem proper and convenient.

SEC. 16. *And be it further enacted,* That the Constitution and all laws of the United States which are not locally inapplicable, shall have the same force and effect within the said Territory of Wyoming as elsewhere within the United States.

SEC. 17. *And be it further enacted,* That this act shall take effect from and after the time when the executive and judicial officers herein provided for shall have been duly appointed and qualified: *Provided,* That all general territorial laws of the Territory of Dakota in force in any portion of said Territory of Wyoming at the time this act shall take effect shall be and continue in force throughout the said Territory until repealed by the legislative authority of said Territory, except such laws as relate to the possession or occupation of mines or mining claims.

Approved, July 25, 1868.

AN ACT TO RE-DEFINE A PORTION OF THE BOUNDARY LINE BETWEEN THE STATE OF NEBRASKA AND THE TERRITORY OF DAKOTA

APRIL 28, 1870

Be it enacted by the Senate and House of Representatives of the United States of America in Congress assembled, That so soon as the State of

Nebraska, through her legislature, has given her consent thereto, the centre of the main channel of the Missouri river shall be the boundary line between the State of Nebraska and the Territory of Dakota, between the following points, to wit: Commencing at a point in the centre of said main channel, north of the west line of section twenty-four in township twenty-nine north, of range eight east of the sixth principal meridian, and running along the same to a point west of the most northerly portion of fractional section seventeen, of township twenty-nine north, of range nine east of said meridian, in the State of Nebraska, as meandered and shown by the plats and surveys of said sections originally made and now on file in the general land office.

SEC. 2. *And be it further enacted,* That the respective jurisdictions of the said State and Territory (and of the United States) shall extend to and over all of the territory, within their limits, according to the line herein designated, to all intents and purposes as fully and completely as if no change had taken place in the channel of said Missouri river. And the Secretary of the Interior is hereby authorized and required to cause to be made all necessary surveys and meanderings, and to order the transfer of all plats, papers, and documents which may be necessary in the premises.

Approved, April 28, 1870.

AN ACT TO READJUST THE WESTERN BOUNDARY
OF DAKOTA TERRITORY
FEBRUARY 17, 1873

Be it enacted by the Senate and House of Representatives of the United States of America in Congress assembled, That all that portion of Dakota Territory lying west of the one hundred and eleventh meridian of longitude which, by an erroneous definition of the boundaries of said Territory by a former act of Congress, remains detached and distant from Dakota proper some two hundred miles, be, and the same is hereby, attached to the adjoining territory of Montana.

Approved, February 17, 1873.

AN ACT TO ENABLE THE PEOPLE OF COLORADO TO FORM A CONSTITUTION AND STATE GOVERNMENT, AND FOR THE ADMISSION OF THE SAID STATE INTO THE UNION ON AN EQUAL FOOTING WITH THE ORIGINAL STATES MARCH 3, 1875

Be it enacted by the Senate and House of Representatives of the United States of America in Congress assembled, That the inhabitants of the Territory of Colorado included in the boundaries hereinafter designated be, and they are hereby, authorized to form for themselves, out of said Territory, a State government, with the name of the State of Colorado; which State, when formed, shall be admitted into the Union upon an equal footing with the original States in all respects whatsoever, as hereinafter provided.

SEC. 2. That the said State of Colorado shall consist of all the territory included within the following boundaries, to wit: Commencing on the thirty-seventh parallel of north latitude where the twenty-fifth meridian of longitude west from Washington crosses the same; thence north, on said meridian, to the forty-first parallel of north latitude; thence along said parallel west to the thirty-second meridian of longitude west from Washington; thence south on said meridian, to the thirty-seventh parallel of north latitude; thence along said thirty-seventh parallel of north latitude, to the place of beginning.

SEC. 3. That all persons qualified by law to vote for representatives to the general assembly of said Territory, at the date of the passage of this act, shall be qualified to be elected, and they are hereby authorized to vote for and choose representatives to form a convention under such rules and regulations as the governor of said Territory, the chief justice, and the United States attorney thereof may prescribe; and also to vote upon the acceptance or rejection of such constitution as may be formed by said convention, under such rules and regulations as said convention may prescribe; and the aforesaid representatives to form the aforesaid convention shall be apportioned among the several counties in said Territory in proportion to the vote polled in each of said counties at the last general election as near as may be; and said apportionment shall be made for said Territory by the governor, United States district attorney, and chief justice thereof, or any two of them; and the governor of said Territory shall, by proclamation, order an election of the representatives aforesaid to be held throughout the Territory at such time as shall be fixed by the governor, chief justice, and United States attorney, or any two of them, which proclamation shall be issued within ninety days next after the first day of September, eighteen hundred and seventy-five, and at least thirty days prior to the time of said election; and such election shall be conducted in the same manner as is prescribed by the laws of said Territory regulating elections therein for members of the house of representatives; and the number of members to said convention shall be the same as now constitutes both branches of the legislature of the aforesaid Territory.

SEC. 4. That the members of the convention thus elected shall meet at the capital of said Territory, on a day to be fixed by said governor, chief justice, and United States attorney, not more than sixty days subsequent to the day of election, which time of meeting shall be contained in the aforesaid proclamation mentioned in the third section of this act, and, after organization, shall declare, on behalf of the people of said Territory, that they adopt the Constitution of the United States; whereupon the said convention shall be, and is hereby, authorized to form a constitution and State government for said Territory: *Provided,* That the constitution shall be republican in form, and make no distinction in civil or political rights on account of race or color, except Indians not taxed, and not be repugnant to the Constitution of the United States and the principles of the Declaration of Independence: *And provided further,* That said convention shall provide, by an ordinance irrevocable without the consent of the United States and the people of said State, first, that perfect toleration of religious sentiment shall be secured, and no inhabitant of said State shall ever be molested, in person or property, on account of his or her mode of religious worship; secondly, that the people inhabiting said Territory do agree and declare that they forever disclaim all right and title to the unappropriated public lands lying within said Territory, and that the same shall be and remain at the sole and entire disposition of the United States, and that the lands belonging to citizens of the United States residing without the said State shall never be taxed higher than the lands belonging to residents thereof, and that no taxes shall be imposed by the State on lands or property therein belonging to, or which may hereafter be purchased by the United States.

SEC. 5. That in case the constitution and State government shall be formed for the people of said Territory of Colorado, in compliance with the provisions of this act, said convention forming the same shall provide, by ordinance, for submitting said constitution to the people of said State for their ratification or rejection, at an election, to be held at such time, in the month of July, eighteen hundred and seventy-six, and at such places and under such regulations as may be prescribed by said convention, at which election the lawful voters of said new State shall vote directly for or against the proposed constitution; and the returns of said election shall be made to the acting governor of the Territory, who, with the chief justice and United States attorney of said Territory, or any two of them, shall canvass the same; and if a majority of legal votes shall be cast for said constitution in said proposed State, the said acting governor shall certify the same to the President of the United States, together with a copy of said constitution and ordinances; whereupon it shall be the duty of the President of the United States to issue his proclamation declaring the State admitted into the Union on an equal footing with the original States, without any further action whatever on the part of Congress.

SEC. 6. That until the next general census said State shall be entitled to one Representative in the House of Representatives of the United States, which Representative, together with the governor and State and other officers provided for in said constitution, shall be elected on a day subsequent to the adoption of the constitution, and to be fixed by said constitutional convention; and until said State officers are elected and qualified under the provisions of the constitution, the territorial officers shall continue to discharge the duties of their respective offices.

SEC. 7. That sections numbered sixteen and thirty-six in every township, and where such sections have been sold or otherwise disposed of by any act of Congress, other lands, equivalent thereto, in legal subdivisions of not more than one quarter section, and as contiguous as may be, are hereby granted to said State for the support of common schools.

SEC. 8. That, provided the State of Colorado shall be admitted into the Union in accordance with the foregoing provisions of this act, fifty entire sections of the unappropriated public lands within said State, to be selected and located by direction of the legislature thereof, and with the approval of the President, on or before the first day of January, eighteen hundred and seventy-eight, shall be, and are hereby, granted, in legal subdivisions of not less than one quarter section, to said State for the purpose of erecting public buildings at the capital of said State for legislative and judicial purposes, in such manner as the legislature shall prescribe.

SEC. 9. That fifty other entire sections of land as aforesaid, to be selected and located and with the approval as aforesaid, in legal subdivisions as aforesaid, shall be, and they are hereby, granted to said State for the purpose of erecting a suitable building for a penitentiary or State prison in the manner aforesaid.

SEC. 10. That seventy-two other sections of land shall be set apart and reserved for the use and support of a State university, to be selected and approved in manner as aforesaid, and to be appropriated and applied as the legislature of said State may prescribe for the purpose named and for no other purpose.

SEC. 11. That all salt-springs within said State, not exceeding twelve in number, with six sections of land adjoining, and as contiguous as may be to each, shall be granted to said State for its use, the said land to be selected by the governor of said State within two years after the admission of the State, and when so selected to be used and disposed of on such terms, conditions, and regulations as the legislature shall direct: *Provided*, That no salt-spring or lands the right whereof is now vested in any individual or individuals, or which hereafter shall be confirmed or adjudged to any individual or individuals, shall by this act be granted to said State.

SEC. 12. That five per centum of the proceeds of the sales of agricultural public lands lying within said State which shall be sold by the United States subsequent to the admission of said State into the Union, after deducting all the expenses incident to the same, shall be paid to the said State for the purpose of making such internal improvements within said State as the legislature thereof may direct: *Provided*, That this section shall not apply to any lands disposed of under the homestead-laws of the United States, or to any lands now or hereafter reserved for public or other uses.

SEC. 13. That any balance of the appropriations for the legislative expenses of said Territory of Colorado remaining unexpended shall be applied to and used for defraying the expenses of said convention, and for the payment of the members thereof, under the same rules and regulations and rates as are now provided by law for the payment of the territorial legislature.

SEC. 14. That the two sections of land in each township herein granted for the support of common schools shall be disposed of only at public sale and at a price not less than two dollars and fifty cents per acre, the proceeds to constitute a permanent school-fund, the interest of which to be expended in the support of common schools.

SEC. 15. That all mineral-lands shall be excepted from the operation and grants of this act.

Approved, March 3, 1875.

AN ACT GIVING THE CONSENT OF CONGRESS TO AN AGREEMENT OR COMPACT ENTERED INTO BETWEEN THE STATES OF NEW YORK AND VERMONT RESPECTING THE BOUNDARY BETWEEN SAID STATES APRIL 7, 1880

Whereas, the general assembly of the State of Vermont at its October session, anno Domini eighteen hundred and seventy-six, passed an act which was approved on the twenty-seventh day of November of the same year, declaring that "all that portion of the town of Fair Haven, in the county of Rutland, and State of Vermont, lying westerly from the middle of the deepest channel of Poultney River as it now runs, and between the middle of the deepest channel of said river and the west line of the State of Vermont as at present established, is hereby ceded and relinquished to the State of New York in full and absolute right and jurisdiction." And also declaring that "this act shall not take effect until the State of New York shall have assented to the same, nor until the same shall have been approved by an act of the Congress of the United States"; and

Whereas "the people of the State of New York represented in senate and assembly" did by act approved March twentieth, anno Domini eighteen hundred and seventy-nine, enact that "sovereignty and jurisdiction over all that portion of the town of Fair Haven, in the county of Rutland and State of Vermont, lying westerly from the middle of the deepest channel of Poultney River, as it now runs, and between the middle of the deepest channel of said river and the west line of the State of Vermont, as at present established", "and the same is described in an act of the legislature of the State of Vermont entitled 'An act annexing that portion of the town of Fair Haven, lying west of the Poultney River, to the State of New York' and approved by the governor of the said State of Vermont November twenty-seventh, anno Domini eighteen hundred and seventy-six, and the cession of the same to the State of New York is hereby accepted by the State of New York"; and also enacting that "this act shall take effect when the Congress of the United States shall consent to such cession and annexation": Therefore,

Be it enacted by the Senate and House of Representatives of the United States of America in Congress assembled, That the consent of the Congress of the United States is hereby given to the said agreement, compact, and cession, and every part and article thereof.

Approved, April 7, 1880.

AN ACT TO EXTEND THE NORTHERN BOUNDARY
OF THE STATE OF NEBRASKA
MARCH 28, 1882

Be it enacted by the Senate and House of Representatives of the United States of America in Congress assembled, That the northern boundary of the State of Nebraska shall be, and hereby is, subject to the provisions hereinafter contained, extended so as to include all that portion of the Territory of Dakota lying south of the forty-third parallel of north latitude and east of the Keyapaha River and west of the main channel of the Missouri River; and when the Indian title to the lands thus described shall be extinguished, the jurisdiction over said lands shall be, and hereby is, ceded to the State of Nebraska, and subject to all the conditions and limitations provided in the act of Congress admitting Nebraska into the Union, and the northern boundary of the State shall be extended to said forty-third parallel as fully and effectually as if said lands had been included in the boundaries of said State at the time of its admission to the Union; reserving to the United States the original right of soil in said lands and of disposing of the same: *Provided,* That this act, so far as jurisdiction is concerned, shall not take effect until the President shall, by proclamation, declare that the Indian title to said lands has been extinguished, nor shall it take effect until the State of Nebraska shall have assented to the provisions of this act; and if the State of Nebraska shall not by an act of its legislature consent to the provisions of this act within two years after the passage hereof, this act shall cease and be of no effect.

Approved, March 28, 1882.

AN ACT TO PROVIDE FOR THE DIVISION OF DAKOTA INTO TWO STATES AND TO ENABLE THE PEOPLE OF NORTH DAKOTA, SOUTH DAKOTA, MONTANA, AND WASHINGTON TO FORM CONSTITUTIONS AND STATE GOVERNMENTS AND TO BE ADMITTED INTO THE UNION ON AN EQUAL FOOTING WITH THE ORIGINAL STATES, AND TO MAKE DONATIONS OF PUBLIC LANDS TO SUCH STATES FEBRUARY 22, 1889

Be it enacted by the Senate and House of Representatives of the United States of America in Congress assembled, That the inhabitants of all that part of the area of the United States now constituting the Territories of Dakota, Montana, and Washington, as at present described, may become the States of North Dakota, South Dakota, Montana, and Washington, respectively, as hereinafter provided.

SEC. 2. The area comprising the Territory of Dakota shall, for the purposes of this act, be divided on the line of the seventh standard parallel produced due west to the western boundary of said Territory; and the delegates elected as hereinafter provided to the constitutional convention in districts north of said parallel shall assemble in convention, at the time prescribed in this act, at the city of Bismark; and the delegates elected in districts south of said parallel shall, at the same time, assemble in convention at the city of Sioux Falls.

SEC. 3. That all persons who are qualified by the laws of said Territories to vote for representatives to the legislative assemblies thereof, are hereby authorized to vote for and choose delegates to form conventions in said proposed States; and the qualifications for delegates to such conventions shall be such as by the laws of said Territories respectively persons are required to possess to be eligible to the legislative assemblies thereof; and the aforesaid delegates to form said conventions shall be apportioned within the limits of the proposed States, in such districts as may be established as herein provided, in proportion to the population in each of said counties and districts, as near as may be, to be ascertained at the time of making said apportionments by the persons hereinafter authorized to make the same, from the best information obtainable, in each of which districts three delegates shall be elected, but no elector shall vote for more than two persons for delegates to such conventions; that said apportionments shall be made by the governor, the chief-justice, and the secretary of said Territories; and the governors of said Territories shall, by proclamation, order an election of the delegates aforesaid in each of said proposed States, to be held on the Tuesday after the second Monday in May, eighteen hundred and eighty-nine, which proclamation shall be issued on the fifteenth day of April, eighteen hundred and eighty-nine; and such election shall be conducted, the returns made, the result ascertained, and the certificates to persons elected to such convention issued in the same manner as is prescribed by the laws of the said Territories regulating elections therein for Delegates to Congress; and the number of votes cast for delegates in each precinct shall also be returned. The number of delegates to said conventions respectively shall be seventy-five; and all persons resident in said proposed States, who are qualified voters of said Territories as herein provided, shall be entitled to vote upon the election of delegates, and under such rules and regulations as said conventions may prescribe, not in conflict with this act, upon the ratification or rejection of the constitutions.

SEC. 4. That the delegates to the conventions elected as provided for in this act shall meet at the seat of government of each of said Territories, except the delegates elected in South Dakota, who shall meet at the city of Sioux Falls, on the fourth day of July, eighteen hundred and eighty-nine, and, after organization, shall declare, on behalf of the people of said proposed States, that they adopt the Constitution of the United States; whereupon the said conventions shall be, and are hereby, authorized to form constitutions and States governments for said proposed States, respectively. The constitutions shall be republican in form, and make no distinction in civil or political rights on account of race or color, except as to Indians not taxed, and not be repugnant to the Constitution of the United States and the principles of the Declaration of Independence. And said conventions shall provide, by ordinance irrevocable without the consent of the United States and the people of said States:

First. That perfect toleration of religious sentiment shall be secured and that no inhabitant of said States shall ever be molested in person or property on account of his or her mode of religious worship.

Second. That the people inhabiting said proposed States do agree and declare that they forever disclaim all right and title to the unappropriated public lands lying within the boundaries thereof, and to all lands lying within said limits owned or held by any Indian or Indian tribes; and that until the title thereto shall have been extinguished by the United States, the same shall be and remain subject to the disposition of the United States, and said Indian lands shall remain under the absolute jurisdiction and control of the Congress of the United States; that the lands belonging to citizens of the United States residing without the said States shall never be taxed at a higher rate than the lands belonging to residents thereof; that no taxes shall be imposed by the States on lands or property therein belonging to or which may hereafter be purchased by the United States or reserved for its use. But nothing herein, or in the ordinances herein provided for, shall preclude the said States from taxing as other lands are taxed any lands owned or held by any Indian who has severed his tribal relations, and has obtained from the United States or from any person a title thereto by patent or other grant, save and except such lands as have been or may be granted to any Indian or Indians under any act of Congress containing a provision exempting the lands thus granted from taxation; but said ordinances shall provide that all such lands shall be exempt from taxation by said States so long and to such extent as such act of Congress may prescribe.

Third. That the debts and liabilities of said Territories shall be assumed and paid by said States, respectively.

Fourth. That provision shall be made for the establishment and maintenance of systems of public schools, which shall be open to all the children of said States, and free from sectarian control.

SEC. 5. That the convention which shall assemble at Bismark shall form a constitution and State government for a State to be known as North Dakota, and the convention which shall assemble at Sioux Falls shall form a constitution and State government for a State to be known as South Dakota: *Provided,* That at the election for delegates to the constitutional convention in South Dakota, as hereinbefore provided, each elector may have written or printed on his ballot the words "For the Sioux Falls constitution," or the words "against the Sioux Falls constitution," and the votes on this question shall be returned and canvassed in the same manner as for the election provided for in section three of this act; and if a majority of all votes cast on this question shall be "for the Sioux Falls constitution" it shall be the duty of the convention which may assemble at Sioux Falls, as herein provided, to resubmit to the people of South Dakota, for ratification or rejection at the election hereinafter provided for in this act, the constitution framed at Sioux Falls and adopted November third, eighteen hundred and eighty-five, and also the articles and propositions separately submitted at that election, including the question of locating the temporary seat of government, with such changes only as relate to the name and boundary of the proposed State, to the re-apportionment of the judicial and legislative districts, and such amendments as may be necessary in order to comply with the provisions of this act; and if a majority of the votes cast on the ratification or rejection of the constitution shall be for the constitution irrespective of the articles separately submitted, the State of South Dakota shall be admitted as a State in the Union under said constitution as hereinafter provided; but the archives, records, and books of the Territory of Dakota shall remain at Bismarck, the capital of North Dakota, until an agreement in reference thereto is reached by said States. But if at the election for delegates to the constitutional convention in South Dakota a majority of all the votes cast at that election shall be "against the Sioux Falls constitution", then and in that event it shall be the duty of the convention which will assemble at the city of Sioux Falls on the fourth day of July, eighteen hundred and eighty-nine, to proceed to form a constitution and State government as provided in this act the same as if that question had not been submitted to a vote of the people of South Dakota.

SEC. 6. It shall be the duty of the constitutional conventions of North Dakota and South Dakota to appoint a joint commission, to be composed of not less than three members of each convention, whose duty it shall be to assemble at Bismarck, the present seat of government of said Territory, and agree upon an equitable division of all property belonging to the Territory of Dakota, the disposition of all public records, and also adjust and agree upon the amount of the debts and liabilities of the Territory, which shall be assumed and paid by each of the proposed States of North Dakota and South Dakota; and the agreement reached respecting the Territorial debts and liabilities shall be incorporated in the respective constitutions, and each of said States shall obligate itself to pay its proportion of such debts and liabilities the same as if they had been created by such States respectively.

SEC. 7. If the constitutions formed for both North Dakota and South Dakota shall be rejected by the people at the elections for the ratification or rejection of their respective constitutions as provided for in this act, the Territorial government of Dakota shall continue in existence the same as if this act had not been passed. But if the constitution formed for either North Dakota or South Dakota shall be rejected by the people, that part of the Territory so rejecting its proposed constitution shall continue under the Territorial government of the present Territory of Dakota, but shall, after the State adopting its constitution is admitted into the Union, be called by the name of the Territory of North Dakota or South Dakota, as the case may be: *Provided*, That if either of the proposed States provided for in this act shall reject the constitution which may be submitted for ratification or rejection at the election provided therefor, the governor of the Territory in which such proposed constitution was rejected shall issue his proclamation reconvening the delegates elected to the convention which formed such rejected constitution, fixing the time and place at which said delegates shall assemble; and when so assembled they shall proceed to form another constitution or to amend the rejected constitution, and shall submit such new constitution or amended constitution to the people of the proposed State for ratification or rejection, at such time as said convention may determine; and all the provisions of this act, so far as applicable, shall apply to such convention so reassembled and to the constitution which may be formed, its ratification or rejection, and to the admission of the proposed State.

SEC. 8. That the constitutional convention which may assemble in South Dakota shall provide by ordinance for resubmitting the Sioux Falls constitution of eighteen hundred and eighty-five, after having amended the same as provided in section five of this act, to the people of South Dakota for ratification or rejection at an election to be held therein on the first Tuesday in October, eighteen hundred and eighty-nine; but if said constitutional convention is authorized and required to form a new constitution for South Dakota it shall provide for submitting the same in like manner to the people of South Dakota for ratification or rejection at an election to be held in said proposed State on the said first Tuesday in October. And the constitutional conventions which may assemble in North Dakota, Montana, and Washington shall provide in like manner for submitting the constitutions formed by them to the people of said proposed States, respectively, for ratification or rejection at elections to be held in said proposed States on the said first Tuesday in October. At the elections provided for in this section the qualified voters of said proposed States shall vote directly for or against the proposed constitutions, and for or against any articles or propositions separately submitted. The returns of said elections shall be made to the secretary of each of said Territories, who, with the governor and chief-justice thereof, or any two of them, shall canvass the same; and if a majority of the legal votes cast shall be for the constitution the governor shall certify the result to the President of the United States, together with a statement of the votes cast thereon and upon separate articles or propositions, and a copy of said constitution, articles, propositions, and ordinances. And if the constitutions and governments of said proposed States are republican in form, and if all the provisions of this act have been complied with in the formation thereof, it shall be the duty of the President of the United States to issue his proclamation announcing the result of the election in each, and thereupon the proposed States which have adopted constitutions and formed State governments as herein provided shall be deemed admitted by Congress into the Union under and by virtue of this act on an equal footing with the original States from and after the date of said proclamation.

SEC. 9. That until the next general census, or until otherwise provided by law, said States shall be entitled to one Representative in the House of Representatives of the United States, except South Dakota, which shall be entitled to two; and the Representatives to the Fifty-first Congress, together with the governors and other officers provided for in said constitutions, may be elected on the same day of the election for the ratification or rejection of the constitutions; and until said State officers are elected and qualified under the provisions of each constitution and the States, respectively, are admitted into the Union, the Territorial officers shall continue to discharge the duties of their respective offices in each of said Territories.

SEC. 10. That upon the admission of each of said States into the Union sections numbered sixteen and thirty-six in every township of said proposed States, and where such sections, or any parts thereof, have been sold or otherwise disposed of by or under the authority of any act of Congress, other lands equivalent thereto, in legal subdivisions of not less than one-quarter section, and as contiguous as may be to the section in lieu of which the same is taken, are hereby granted to said States for the support of common schools, such indemnity lands to be selected within said States in such manner as the legislature may provide, with the approval of the Secretary of the Interior: *Provided,* That the sixteenth and thirty-sixth sections embraced in permanent reservations for national purposes shall not, at any time, be subject to the grants nor to the indemnity provisions of this act, nor shall any lands embraced in Indian, military, or other reservations of any character be subject to the grants or to the indemnity provisions of this act until the reservation shall have been extinguished and such lands be restored to, and become a part of, the public domain.

SEC. 11. That all lands herein granted for educational purposes shall be disposed of only at public sale, and at a price not less than ten dollars per acre, the proceeds to constitute a permanent school-fund, the interest of which only shall be expended in the support of said schools. But said lands may, under such regulations as the legislatures shall prescribe, be leased for periods of not more than five years, in quantities not exceeding one section to any one person or company; and such land shall not be subject to pre-emption, homestead entry, or any other entry under the land laws of the United States, whether surveyed or unsurveyed, but shall be reserved for school purposes only.

SEC. 12. That upon the admission of each of said States into the Union, in accordance with the provisions of this act, fifty sections of the unappropriated public lands within said States, to be selected and located in legal subdivisions as provided in section ten of this act, shall be, and are hereby, granted to said States for the purpose of erecting public buildings at the capital of said States for legislative, executive, and judicial purposes.

SEC. 13. That five per centum of the proceeds of the sales of public lands lying within said States which shall be sold by the United States subsequent to the admission of said States into the Union, after deducting all the expenses incident to the same, shall be paid to the said States, to be used as a permanent fund, the interest of which only shall be expended for the support of common schools within said States, respectively.

SEC. 14. That the lands granted to the Territories of Dakota and Montana by the act of February eighteenth, eighteen hundred and eighty-one, entitled "An act to grant lands to Dakota, Montana, Arizona, Idaho, and Wyoming for university purposes," are hereby vested in the States of South Dakota, North Dakota, and Montana, respectively, if such States are admiited into the Union, as provided in this act, to the extent of the full quantity of seventy-two sections to each of said States, and any portion of said lands that may not have been selected by either of said Territories of Dakota or Montana may be selected by the respective States aforesaid; but said act of February eighteenth, eighteen hundred and eighty-one, shall be so amended as to provide that none of said lands shall be sold for less than ten dollars per acre, and the proceeds shall constitute a permanent fund to be safely invested and held by said States severally, and the income thereof be used exclusively for university purposes. And such quantity of the lands authorized by the fourth section of the act of July seventeenth, eighteen hundred and fifty-four, to be reserved for university purposes in the Territory of Washington, as, together with the lands confirmed to the vendees of the Territory by the act of March fourteenth, eighteen hundred and sixty-four, will make the full quantity of seventy-two entire sections, are hereby granted in like manner to the State of Washington for the purposes of a university in said State. None of the lands granted in this section shall be sold at less than ten dollars per acre; but said lands may be leased in the same manner as provided in section eleven of this act. The schools, colleges, and universities provided for in this act shall forever remain under the exclusive control of the said States, respectively, and no part of the proceeds arising from the sale or disposal of any lands herein granted for educational purposes shall be used for the support of any sectarian or denominational school, college, or university. The section of land granted by the act of June sixteenth, eighteen hundred and eighty, to the Territory of Dakota, for an asylum for the insane shall, upon the admission of said State of South Dakota into the Union, become the property of said State.

SEC. 15. That so much of the lands belonging to the United States as have been acquired and set apart for the purpose mentioned in "An act appropriating money for the erection of a penitentiary in the Territory of Dakota," approved March second, eighteen hundred and eighty-one, together with the buildings thereon, be, and the same is hereby, granted, together with any unexpended balances of the moneys appropriated therefor by said act, to said State of South Dakota, for the purposes therein designated; and the States of North Dakota and Washington shall, respectively, have like grants for the same purpose, and subject to like terms and conditions as provided in said act of March second, eighteen hundred and eighty-one, for the Territory of Dakota. The penitentiary at Deer Lodge City, Montana, and all lands connected therewith and set apart and reserved therefor, are hereby granted to the State of Montana.

SEC. 16. That ninety thousand acres of land, to be selected and located as provided in section ten of this act, are hereby, granted to each of said States, except to the State of South Dakota, to which one hundred and twenty thousand acres are granted, for the use and support of agricultural colleges in said States, as provided in the acts of Congress making donations of lands for such purpose.

SEC. 17. That in lieu of the grant of land for purposes of internal improvement made to new States by the eighth section of the act of September fourth, eighteen hundred and forty-one, which act is hereby repealed as to the States provided for by this act, and in lieu of any claim or demand by the said States, or either of them, under the act of September twenty-eighth, eighteen hundred and fifty, and section twenty four hundred and seventy-nine of the Revised Statutes, making a grant of swamp and overflowed lands to certain States, which grant it is hereby declared is not extended to the States provided for in this act, and in lieu of any grant of saline lands to said States, the following grants of land are hereby made, to wit:

To the State of South Dakota: For the school of mines, forty thousand acres; for the reform school, forty thousand acres; for the deaf and dumb asylum, forty thousand acres; for the agricultural college, forty thousand acres; for the university, forty thousand acres; for State normal schools, eighty thousand acres; for public buildings at the capital of said State, fifty thousand acres, and for such other educational and charitable purposes as the legislature of said State may determine, one hundred and seventy thousand acres; in all five hundred thousand acres.

To the State of North Dakota a like quantity of land as is in this section granted to the State of South Dakota, and to be for like purposes, and in like proportion as far as practicable.

To the State of Montana: For the establishment and maintenance of a school of mines, one hundred thousand acres; for State normal schools, one hundred thousand acres; for agricultural colleges, in addition to the grant hereinbefore made for that purpose, fifty thousand acres; for the establishment of a state reform school, fifty thousand acres; for the establishment of a deaf and dumb asylum, fifty thousand acres; for public buildings at the capital of the State, in addition to the grant hereinbefore made for that purpose, one hundred and fifty thousand acres.

To the State of Washington: For the establishment and maintenance of a scientific school, one hundred thousand acres; for State normal schools, one hundred thousand acres; for public buildings at the State capital, in addition to the grant hereinbefore made for that purpose, one hundred thousand acres; for State charitable, educational, penal, and reformatory institutions, two hundred thousand acres.

That the States provided for in this act shall not be entitled to any further or other grants of land for any purpose than as expressly provided in this act. And the lands granted by this section shall be held, appropriated, and disposed of exclusively for the purposes herein mentioned, in such manner as the legislatures of the respective States may severally provide.

SEC. 18. That all mineral lands shall be exempted from the grants made by this act. But if sections sixteen and thirty-six, or any subdivision or portion of any smallest subdivision thereof in any township shall be found by the

Department of the Interior to be mineral lands, said States are hereby authorized and empowered to select, in legal subdivisions, an equal quantity of other unappropriated lands in said States, in lieu thereof, for the use and the benefit of the common schools of said States.

SEC. 19. That all lands granted in quantity or as indemnity by this act shall be selected, under the direction of the Secretary of the Interior, from the surveyed, unreserved, and unappropriated public lands of the United States within the limits of the respective States entitled thereto. And there shall be deducted from the number of acres of land donated by this act for specific objects to said States the number of acres in each heretofore donated by Congress to said Territories for similar objects.

SEC. 20. That the sum of twenty thousand dollars, or so much thereof as may be necessary, is hereby appropriated, out of any money in the Treasury not otherwise appropriated, to each of said Territories for defraying the expenses of the said conventions, except to Dakota, for which the sum of forty thousand dollars is so appropriated, twenty thousand dollars each for South Dakota and North Dakota, and for the payment of the members thereof, under the same rules and regulations and at the same rates as are now provided by law for the payment of the Territorial legislatures. Any money hereby appropriated not necessary for such purpose shall be covered into the Treasury of the United States.

SEC. 21. That each of said States, when admitted as aforesaid, shall constitute one judicial district, the names thereof to be the same as the names of the States, respectively: and the circuit and district courts therefor shall be held at the capital of such State for the time being, and each of said districts shall, for judicial purposes, until otherwise provided, be attached to the eighth judicial circuit, except Washington and Montana, which shall be attached to the ninth judicial circuit. There shall be appointed for each of said districts one district judge, one United States attorney, and one United States marshal. The judge of each of said districts shall receive a yearly salary of three thousand five hundred dollars, payable in four equal installments, on the first days of January, April, July, and October of each year, and shall reside in the district. There shall be appointed clerks of said courts in each district, who shall keep their offices at the capital of said State. The regular terms of said courts shall be held in each district, at the place aforesaid, on the first Monday in April and the first Monday in November of each year, and only one grand jury and one petit jury shall be summoned in both said circuit and district courts. The circuit and district courts for each of said districts, and the judges thereof, respectively, shall possess the same powers and jurisdiction, and perform the same duties required to be performed by the other circuit and district courts and judges of the United States, and shall be governed by the same laws and regulations. The Marshal, district attorney, and clerks of the circuit and district courts of each of said districts, and all other officers and persons performing duties in the administration of justice therein, shall severally possess the powers and perform the duties lawfully possessed and required to be performed by similar officers in other districts of the United States; and shall, for the services they may perform, receive the fees and compensation allowed by law to other similar officers and persons performing similar duties in the State of Nebraska.

SEC. 22. That all cases of appeal or writ of error heretofore prosecuted and now pending in the Supreme Court of the United States upon any record from the supreme court of either of the Territories mentioned in this act, or that may hereafter lawfully be prosecuted upon any record from either of said courts may be heard and determined by said Supreme Court of the United States. And the mandate of execution or of further proceedings shall be directed by the Supreme Court of the United States to the circuit or district court hereby established within the State succeeding the Territory from which such record is or may be pending, or to the supreme court of such State, as the nature of the case may require: *Provided,* That the mandate of execution or of further proceedings shall, in cases arising in the Territory of Dakota, be directed by the Supreme Court of the United States to the circuit or district court of the district of South Dakota, or to the supreme court of the State of South Dakota, or to the circuit or district court of the district of North Dakota, or to the supreme court of the State of North Dakota, or to the supreme court of the Territory of North Dakota, as the nature of the case may require. And each of the circuit, district, and State courts, herein named, shall, respectively, be the successor of the supreme court of the Territory, as to all such cases arising within the limits embraced within the jurisdiction of such courts respectively with full power to proceed with the same, and award mesne or final process therein; and that from all judgments and decrees of the supreme court of either of the Territories mentioned in this act, in any case arising within the limits of any of the proposed States prior to admission, the parties to such judgment shall have the same right to prosecute appeals and writs of error to the Supreme Court of the United States as they shall have had by law prior to the admission of said State into the Union.

SEC. 23. That in respect to all cases, proceedings, and matters now pending in the supreme or district courts of either of the Territories mentioned in this act at the time of the admission into the Union of either of the States mentioned in this act, and arising within the limits of any such State, whereof the circuit or district courts by this act established might have had jurisdiction under the laws of the United States had such courts existed at the time of the Commencement of such cases, the said circuit and district courts, respectively, shall be the successors of said supreme and district courts of said Territory; and in respect to all other cases, proceedings and matters pending in the supreme or district courts of any of the Territories mentioned in this act at the time of the admission of such Territory into the Union, arising within the limits of said proposed State, the courts established by such state shall, respectively, be the successors of said supreme and district Territorial courts; and all the files, records, indictments, and proceedings relating to any such cases, shall be transferred to such circuit, district, and State courts, respectively, and the same shall be proceeded with therein in due course of law; but no writ, action, indictment, cause or proceeding now pending, or that prior to the admission of any of the States mentioned in this act, shall be pending in any Territorial court in any of the Territories mentioned in this act, shall abate by the admission of any such State into the Union, but the same shall be transferred and proceeded with in the proper United States circuit, district or State court, as the case may be: *Provided, however,* That in all civil actions, causes, and proceedings, in which the United States is not a party, transfers shall not be made to the circuit and district courts of the United States, except upon written request of one of the parties to such action or proceeding filed in the proper court; and in the absence of such request such cases shall be proceeded with in the proper State courts.

SEC. 24. That the constitutional conventions may, by ordinance, provide for the election of officers for full State governments, including members of the legislatures and Representatives in the Fifty-first Congress; but said State governments shall remain in abeyance until the States shall be admitted into the Union, respectively, as provided in this act. In case the constitution of any of said proposed States shall be ratified by the people, but not otherwise, the legislature thereof may assemble, organize, and elect two Senators of the United States; and the governor and secretary of state of such proposed State shall certify the election of the Senators and Representatives in the manner required by law; and when such State is admitted into the Union, the Senators and Representatives shall be entitled to be admitted to seats in Congress, and to all the rights and privileges of Senators and Representatives of other States in the Congress of the United States; and the officers of the State governments formed in pursuance of said constitutions, as provided by the constitutional conventions, shall proceed to exercise all the functions of such State officers; and all laws in force made by said Territories, at the time of their admission into the Union, shall be in force in said States, except as modified or changed by this act or by the constitutions of the States, respectively.

SEC. 25. That all acts or parts of acts in conflict with the provisions of this act, whether passed by the legislatures of said Territories or by Congress, are hereby repealed.

Approved, February 22, 1889.

AN ACT TO PROVIDE A TEMPORARY GOVERNMENT FOR THE TERRITORY OF OKLAHOMA, TO ENLARGE THE JURISDICTION OF THE UNITED STATES COURT IN THE INDIAN TERRITORY, AND FOR OTHER PURPOSES

MAY 2, 1890

Be it enacted by the Senate and House of Representatives of the United States of America in Congress assembled, SEC. 1. That all that portion of the United States now known as the Indian Territory, except so much of the same as is actually occupied by the five civilized tribes, and the Indian tribes within the Quapaw Indian Agency, and except the unoccupied part of the Cherokee outlet, together with that portion of the United States known as the Public Land Strip, is hereby erected into a temporary government by the name of the Territory of Oklahoma. The portion of the Indian Territory included in said Territory of Oklahoma is bounded by a line drawn as follows: Commencing at a point where the ninety-eighth meridian crosses the Red River, thence by said meridian to the point where it crosses the Canadian River, thence along said river to the west line of the Seminole country, thence along said line to the north fork of the Canadian River, thence down said river to the west line of the Creek country, thence along said line to the northwest corner of the Creek country, thence along the north line of the Creek country, to the ninety-sixth meridian, thence northward by said meridian to the southern boundary line of Kansas, thence west along said line to the Arkansas River, thence down said river to the north line of the land occupied by the Ponca tribe of Indians from which point the line runs so as to include all the lands occupied by the Ponca, Tonkawa, Otoe and Missouria, and the Pawnee tribes of Indians until it strikes the south line of the Cherokee outlet which it follows westward to the east line of the State of Texas, thence by the boundary line of the State of Texas to the point of beginning; the Public Land Strip which is included in said Territory of Oklahoma is bounded east by the one-hundredth meridian, south by Texas, west by New Mexico, north by Colorado and Kansas. Whenever the interest of the Cherokee Indians in the land known as the Cherokee outlet shall have been extinguished and the President shall make proclamation thereof, said outlet shall thereupon and without further legislation, become a part of the Territory of Oklahoma. Any other lands within the Indian Territory not embraced within these boundaries shall hereafter become a part of the Territory of Oklahoma whenever the Indian nation or tribe owning such lands shall signify to the President of the United States in legal manner its assent that such lands shall so become a part of said Territory of Oklahoma, and the President shall thereupon make proclamation to that effect.

Congress may at any time hereafter change the boundaries of said Territory, or attach any portion of the same to any other State or Territory of the United States without the consent of the inhabitants of the Territory hereby created: *Provided,* That nothing in this act shall be construed to impair any right now pertaining to any Indians or Indian tribe in said Territory under the laws, agreements, and treaties of the United States, or to impair the rights of person or property pertaining to said Indians, or to affect the authority of the Government of the United States to make any regulation or to make any law respecting said Indians, their lands, property, or other rights which it would have been competent to make or enact if this act had not been passed.

SEC. 2. That the executive power of the Territory of Oklahoma shall be vested in a governor, who shall hold his office for four years, and until his successor shall be appointed and qualified, unless sooner removed by the President of the United States. The governor shall reside within said Territory; shall be commander-in-chief of the militia thereof; he may grant pardons for offenses against the laws of said Territory, and reprieves for offenses against the laws of the United States, until the decision of the President can be made known thereon; he shall commission all officers who shall be appointed to office under the laws of said Territory, and shall take care that the laws be faithfully executed.

SEC. 3. That there shall be a secretary of said Territory, who shall reside therein and hold his office for four years unless sooner removed by the President of the United States; he shall record and preserve all the laws and the proceedings of the legislative assembly hereinafter constituted, and all acts and proceedings of the governor in his executive department; he shall transmit one copy of the laws and journals of the legislative assembly, within thirty days after the end of each session thereof, to the President of the United States and to the Secretary of the Interior and, at the same time, two copies of the laws and journals of the legislative assembly to the Speaker of the House of Representatives and the President of the Senate for the use of Congress; and in case of the death, removal, resignation, or other necessary absence of the governor from the Territory, the secretary shall execute all the powers and perform all the duties of governor during such vacancy or absence, or until another governor is appointed and qualified.

SEC. 4. That the legislative power and authority of said Territory shall be vested in the governor and legislative assembly. The legislative assembly shall consist of a council and a house of representatives. The council shall consist of thirteen members, having the qualifications of voters as hereinafter prescribed, whose term of service shall continue two years. The house of representatives shall consist of twenty-six members, possessing the same qualifications as prescribed for members of the council, and whose term of service shall continue two years, and the sessions of the legislative assembly shall be biennial and shall be limited to sixty days' duration: *Provided, however,* That the duration of the first session of said legislative assembly may continue one hundred and twenty days.

That for the purpose of facilitating the organization of a temporary government in the Territory of Oklahoma, seven counties are hereby established therein, to be known, until after the first election in the Territory, as the First County, the Second County, the Third County, the Fourth County, the Fifth County, and the Sixth County, the boundaries of which shall be fixed by the governor of the Territory until otherwise provided by the legislative assembly thereof. The county seat of the First County shall be at Guthrie. The county seat of the Second County shall be at Oklahoma City. The county seat of the Third County shall be at Norman. The county seat of the Fourth County shall be at El Reno. The county seat of the Fifth County shall be at Kingfisher City. The county seat of the Sixth County shall be at Stillwater. The Seventh County shall embrace all that portion of the Territory lying west of the one hundredth meridian, known as the Public Land Strip, the county seat of which shall be at Beaver: *Provided,* That the county seats located by this act may be changed in such manner as the Territorial legislature may provide.

At the first election for members of the legislative assembly the people of each county may vote for a name for such county, and the name which receives the greatest number of votes shall be the name of such county. If two or more counties should select the same name, the county which casts the greatest number of votes for such name shall be entitled to the same, and the names receiving the next highest number of votes in the other counties shall be the names of such counties. An apportionment shall be made by the governor as nearly equal as practicable among the several counties or districts for the election of the council and house of representatives, giving to each section of the Territory representation in the ratio of its population (excepting Indians not taxed) as nearly as may be, and the members of the council and house of representatives shall reside in and be inhabitants of the district for which they may be elected, respectively. Previous to the first election the governor shall cause a census or enumeration of the inhabitants of the several counties or districts of the Territory to be taken, unless the same shall have been taken and published by the United States, in which case such census and enumeration shall be adopted, and the first election shall be held at such times and places and be conducted in such manner, both as to the persons who superintend such election and the returns thereof, as the governor shall appoint and direct, and he shall at the same time declare the number of the members of the council and house of representatives to which each of the counties or districts shall be entitled, as shown by the census herein provided for. The number of persons authorized to be elected, having the highest number of legal votes in each of said council districts for members of the council, shall be declared by the governor to be duly elected to the council, and the person or persons authorized to be elected, having the greatest number of votes for the house of representatives equal to the number to which each county or district shall be entitled, shall be declared by the governor to be elected members of the house of representatives: *Provided,* That in case two or more persons voted for have an equal number of votes, and in case a vacancy otherwise occurs in either branch of the legislative assembly, the governor shall order a new election, and the persons thus elected to the legislative assembly shall meet at such place on such day as the governor shall appoint, but after such first election, however, the time, place, and manner of holding elections by the people, and the apportionment of representation, and the day of the commencement of the regular sessions of the legislative assembly shall be prescribed by law: *Provided, however,* That the governor shall have power to call the legislative assembly together by proclamation, on an extraordinary occasion at any time.

SEC. 5. That all male citizens of the United States above the age of twenty-one years, and all male persons of foreign birth over said age who shall have twelve months prior thereto declared their intention to become citizens of the United States, as now required by law, who are actual residents at the time of the passage of this act of that portion of said Territory which was declared by the proclamation of the President to be open for settlement on the twenty-second day of April, anno Domini eighteen hundred and eighty-nine, and of that portion of said Territory heretofore known as the Public Land Strip, shall be entitled to vote at the first election in the Territory. At every subsequent election the qualifications of voters and of holding office shall be such as may be prescribed by the legislative assembly, subject, however, to the following restrictions on the power of the legislative assembly, namely: First. The right of suffrage and of holding office shall be exercised only by citizens of the United States above the age of twenty-one years and by persons of foreign birth above that age who have declared, on oath, before a competent court of record, as required by the naturalization laws of the United States their intention to become citizens, and have taken an oath to support the Constitution of the United States, and who shall have been residents of the United States for the term of twelve months before the election at which they offer to vote. Second, There shall be no denial of the elective franchise or of holding office to a citizen on account of race, color, or previous condition of servitude. Third. No officer, soldier, seaman, marine, or other person in the Army or Navy, or attached to troops in the service of the United States, shall be allowed to vote in said Territory by reason of being on service therein. Fourth. No person belonging to the Army or Navy shall be elected to, or hold, any civil office or appointment in said Territory.

SEC. 6. That the legislative power of the Territory shall extend to all rightful subjects of legislation not inconsistent with the Constitution and laws of the United States, but no law shall be passed interfering with the primary disposal of the soil: no tax shall be imposed upon the property of the United States, nor shall the lands or other property of non-residents be taxed higher than the lands or other property of residents, nor shall any law be passed impairing the right to private property, nor shall any unequal discrimination be made in taxing different kinds of property, but all property subject to the taxation shall be taxed in proportion to its value: *Provided,* That nothing herein shall be held to prohibit the levying and collecting license or special taxes in the Territory from persons engaged in any business therein, if the legislative power shall consider such taxes necessary. Every bill which shall have passed the council and the house of representatives of said Territory shall, before it becomes a law, be presented to the governor of the Territory. If he approve he shall sign it, but if not, he shall return it with his objections to the house in which it originated, who shall enter the objections at large upon their journal and proceed to reconsider it. If, after such reconsideration, two-thirds of that house shall agree to pass the bill, it shall be sent, together with the objections, to the other house, by which it shall likewise be reconsidered, and if approved by two-thirds of that house it shall become a law. But in all such cases the vote of both houses shall be determined by yeas and nays to be entered on the journal of each house, respectively. If any bill shall not be returned by the governor within five days (Sunday excepted) after it shall have been presented to him, the same shall be a law in like manner as if he had signed it, unless the assembly, by adjournment, prevent its return, in which case it shall not be a law.

SEC. 7. That all township, district, and county officers, not herein otherwise provided for, shall be appointed or elected, as the case may be, in such manner as shall be provided by the governor and legislative assembly of the Territory. The governor shall nominate and, by and with the advice and consent of the council, appoint all officers not herein otherwise provided for, and in the first instance the governor alone may appoint all such officers, who shall hold their offices until the end of the first session of the legislative assembly; and he shall lay off the necessary districts for members of the council and house of representatives, and all other officers, and whenever a vacancy happens from resignation or death, during the recess of the legislative council in any office which is filled by appointment of the governor, by and with the advice and consent of the council, the governor shall fill such vacancy by granting a commission, which shall expire at the end of the next session of the legislative council. It is further provided that the legislative assembly shall not authorize the issuing any bond, script, or evidence of debt by the Territory, or any county, city, town, or township therein for the construction of any railroad.

SEC. 8. That no member of the legislative assembly shall hold or be appointed to any office which has been created or the salary or emoluments of which have been increased while he was a member, during the term for which he was elected and for one year after the expiration of such term, but this restriction shall not be applicable to members of the first legislative assembly provided for by this act; and no person holding a commission or appointment under the United States, except postmasters, shall be a member of the legislative assembly, or shall hold any office under the government of said Territory.

SEC. 9. That the judicial power of said Territory shall be vested in a supreme court, district courts, probate courts, and justices of the peace. The supreme court shall consist of a chief-justice and two associate justices, any two of whom shall constitute a quorum. They shall hold their offices for four years, and until their successors are appointed and qualified, and they shall hold a term annually at the seat of government of said Territory. The jurisdiction of the several courts herein provided for, both appellate and original, and that of the probate courts and of the justices of the peace, shall be as limited by law: *Provided,* That justices of the peace, who shall be elected in such manner as the legislative assembly may provide by law, shall not have jurisdiction of any matter in controversy when the title or boundaries of land may be in dispute, or where the debt or sum claimed shall exceed one hundred dollars; and the said supreme and district courts, respectively, shall possess chancery as well as common law jurisdiction and authority for redress of all wrongs committed against the Constitution or laws of the United States or of the Territory affecting persons or property. Said Territory shall be divided into three judicial districts, and a district court shall be held in each county in said district thereof by one of the justices of the supreme court, at such time and place as may be prescribed by law, and each judge after assignment shall reside in the district to which he is assigned. The supreme court shall define said judicial districts, and shall fix the times and places at each county seat in each district where the district court shall be held and designate the judge who shall preside therein. And the territory not embraced in organized counties shall be attached for judicial purposes to such organized county or counties as the supreme court may determine. The supreme court of said Territory shall appoint its own clerk, who shall hold his office at the pleasure of the court for which he is appointed. Each district court shall appoint its clerk, who shall also be the register in chancery, and shall keep his office where the court may be held. Writs of error, bills of exception, and appeals shall be allowed in all cases from the final decisions of said district courts to the supreme court under such regulations as may be prescribed by law, but in no case removed to the supreme court shall trial by jury be allowed in said court. Writs of error and appeals from the final decisions of said supreme court shall be allowed and may be taken to the Supreme Court of the United States in the same manner and under the same regulations as from the circuit courts of the United States, where the value of the property or the amount in controversy, to be ascertained by oath or affirmation of either party or other competent witness, shall exceed five thousand dollars; and each of the said district courts shall have and exercise, exclusive of any court heretofore established, the same jurisdiction in all cases arising under the Constitution and laws of the United States as is vested in the circuit and district courts of the United States. In addition to the jurisdiction otherwise conferred by this act, said district courts shall have and exercise exclusive original jurisdiction over all offenses against the laws of the United States committed within that portion of the Cherokee Outlet not embraced within the boundaries of said Territory of Oklahoma as herein defined, and in all civil cases between citizens of the United States residing in such portion of the Cherokee Outlet, or between citizens of the United States, or of any State or Territory, and any citizen of or person or persons residing or found therein, when the value of the thing in controversy or damages or money claimed shall exceed one hundred dollars; writs of error, bills of exceptions, and appeals shall in all such cases, civil and criminal, be allowed from the district courts to the supreme court in like manner, and be proceeded with in like manner as in cases arising within the limits of said Territory. For all judicial purposes as herein defined such portion of the Cherokee Outlet not embraced within the boundaries of the Territory of Oklahoma shall be attached to, and be a part of, one of the judicial districts of said Territory as may be designated by the Supreme court. All acts and parts of acts heretofore enacted, conferring jurisdiction upon United States courts held beyond and outside the limits of the Territory of Oklahoma as herein defined, as to all causes of action or offenses in said Territory, and in that portion of the Cherokee Outlet herein before referred to, are hereby repealed, and such jurisdiction is hereby given to the supreme and district courts in said Territory; but all actions commenced in such courts, and crimes committed in said Territory and in the Cherokee Outlet, prior to the passage of this act, shall be tried and prosecuted, and proceeded with until finally disposed of, in the courts now having jurisdiction thereof, as if this act had not been passed. The said supreme and district courts of said Territory, and the respective judges thereof, shall and may grant writs of mandamus and habeas corpus in all cases authorized by law; and the first six days of every term of said courts, or so much thereof as shall be necessary, shall be appropriated to the trial of causes arising under the said Constitution and laws; and writs of error and appeals in all such cases shall be made to the supreme court of said Territory, as in other cases.

SEC. 10. Persons charged with any offense or crime in the Territory of Oklahoma, and for whose arrest a warrant has been issued, may be arrested by the United States marshal or any of his deputies, wherever found in said Territory, but in all cases the accused shall be taken, for preliminary examination, before a United States commissioner, or a justice of the peace of the county, whose office is nearest to the place where the offense or crime was committed.

All offenses committed in said Territory, if committed within any organized county, shall be prosecuted and tried within said county, and if committed within territory not embraced in any organized county, shall be prosecuted and tried in the county to which such territory shall be attached for judicial purposes. And all civil actions shall be instituted in the county in which the defendant, or either of them, resides or may be found; and when such actions arise within any portion of said Territory, not organized as a county, such actions shall be instituted in the county to which such territory is attached for judicial purposes; but any case, civil or criminal, may be removed, by change of venue, to another county.

SEC. 11. That the following chapters and provisions of the Compiled Laws of the State of Nebraska, in force November first, eighteen hundred and eighty-nine, in so far as they are locally applicable, and not in conflict with the laws of the United States or with this act, are hereby extended to and put in force in the Territory of Oklahoma until after the adjournment of the first session of the legislative assembly of said Territory, namely: the provisions of articles two, three, and four of chapter two, entitled "Agriculture;" of chapter four, entitled "Animals;" of chapter six, entitled "Assignments;" of chapter seven, entitled "Attorneys;" of chapter ten, entitled "Bonds and oaths-official;" of chapter twelve, entitled "Chattel mortgages;" of chapter fourteen, entitled "Cities of the second class and villages;" of chapter fifteen, entitled "Common law;" of chapter sixteen, entitled "Corporations;" of chapter eighteen, entitled "Countys and county officers;" of sections fifteen and sixteen of article six of the constitution of said State, and of chapter twenty of said laws, entitled "Courts-probate;" of chapter twenty-three, entitled "Decedents;" of chapter twenty-four, entitled "Deputies;" of chapter twenty-five, entitled "Divorce and alimony;" of chapter twenty-six, entitled "Elections;" of chapter twenty-eight, entitled "Fees;" of chapter thirty-two, entitled "Frauds;" of chapter thirty-four, entitled "Guardians and wards;" of chapter thirty-six, entitled "Homesteads;" of chapter forty-one, entitled "Instruments negotiable;" of chapter forty-four, entitled "Interest;" of chapter forty-six, entitled "Jails;" of chapter fifty, entitled "Liquors;" but no licenses shall be issued under this chapter; of chapter fifty-two, entitled "Marriage;" of chapter fifty-three, entitled "Married women;" of chapter fifty-four, entitled "Mechanics' and laborers' liens;" of chapter sixty-one, entitled "Notaries public;" of chapter sixty-two, entitled "Oaths and affirmations;" of chapter sixty-three, entitled "Occupying claimants;" of article one of chapter seventy-two, entitled "Railroads;" of chapter seventy-three, entitled "Real estate;" and the provisions of part two of said laws, entitled "Code of civil procedure," and of part three thereof, entitled "Criminal code."

The governor of said Territory is authorized to divide each county into election precincts and into such political sub-divisions other than school districts as may be required by the laws of the State of Nebraska; and he is hereby authorized to appoint all officers of such counties and subdivisions thereof as he shall deem necessary, and all election officers until their election or appointment shall be provided for by the legislative assembly, but not more than two of the judges or inspectors of election in any election precinct shall be members of the same political party, and the candidates of each political party who may be voted for at such election may designate one person who shall be present at the counting and canvassing of the votes cast in each precinct.

The supreme and district courts of said Territory shall have the same power to enforce the laws of the State of Nebraska hereby extended to and put in force in said Territory as courts of like jurisdiction have in said State; but county courts and justices of the peace shall have and exercise the jurisdiction which is authorized by said laws of Nebraska: *Provided,* That the jurisdiction of justices of the peace in said Territory shall not exceed the sum of one hundred dollars, and county courts shall have jurisdiction in all cases where the sum or matter in demand exceeds the sum of one hundred dollars.

SEC. 12. That jurisdiction is hereby conferred upon the district courts in the Territory of Oklahoma over all controversies arising between members or citizens of one tribe or nation of Indians and the members or citizens of other tribes or nations in the Territory of Oklahoma, and any citizen or member of one tribe or nation who may commit any offense or crime in said Territory against the person or property of a citizen or member of another tribe or nation shall be subject to the same punishment in the Territory of Oklahoma as he would be if both parties were citizens of the United States; and any person residing in the Territory of Oklahoma, in whom there is Indian blood, shall have the right to invoke the aid of courts therein for the protection of his person or property, as though he were a citizen of the United States: *Provided,* That nothing in this act contained shall be so construed as to give jurisdiction to the courts established in said Territory in controversies arising between Indians of the same tribe, while sustaining their tribal relation.

SEC. 13. That there shall be appointed for said Territory a person learned in the law, who shall act as attorney for the United States, and shall continue in office for four years, and until his successor is appointed and qualified, unless sooner removed by the President. Said attorney shall receive a salary at the rate of two hundred and fifty dollars annually. There shall be appointed a marshal for said Territory, who shall hold his office for four years, and until his successor is appointed and qualified, unless sooner removed by the President, and who shall execute all process issuing from the said courts when exercising their jurisdiction as circuit and district courts of the United States; he shall have the power and perform the duties and be subject to the same regulations and penalties imposed by law on the marshal of the United States, and be entitled to a salary at the rate of two hundred dollars a year. There shall be allowed to the attorney, marshal, clerks of the supreme and district courts the same fees as are prescribed for similar services by such persons in chapter sixteen, title Judiciary, of the Revised Statutes of the United States.

SEC. 14. That the governor, secretary, chief-justice, and associate justices, attorney, and marshal shall be nominated and, by and with the advice and consent of the Senate, appointed by the President of the United States. The governor and Secretary to be appointed as aforesaid shall, before they act as such, respectively take an oath or affirmation before the district judge, or some justice of the peace, or other officer in the limits of said Territory duly authorized to administer oaths and affirmations by the laws now in force therein, or before the Chief-Justice or some associate justice of the Supreme Court of the United States, to support the Constitution of the United States and faithfully to discharge the duties of their respective offices, which said oaths, when so taken, shall be certified by the person by whom the same shall have been taken; and such certificates shall be received and recorded by the secretary among the executive proceedings, and the chief-justice and associate justices, and all other civil officers in said Territory, before they act as such, shall take a like oath or affirmation before the said governor or secretary, or some judge or justice of the peace of the Territory, who may be duly commissioned and qualified, which said oath or affirmation shall be certified and transmitted by the person taking the same to the secretary, to be recorded by him as aforesaid, and afterwards the like oath or affirmation shall be taken, certified, and recorded in such manner and form as may be prescribed by law. The governor shall receive an annual salary of two thousand six hundred dollars as governor; the chief-justice and associate justices shall receive an annual salary of three thousand dollars, and the Secretary shall receive an annual salary of one thousand eight hundred dollars. The said salaries shall be payable quarter-yearly at the Treasury of the United States. The members of the legislative assembly shall be entitled to receive four dollars each per day during their attendance at the sessions, and four dollars for each and every twenty miles traveled in going to and returning from said sessions, estimating the distance by the nearest travelled route. There shall be appropriated annually the sum of one thousand dollars, to be expended by the governor to defray the contingent expenses of the Territory. There shall also be appropriated annually a sufficient sum, to be expended by the secretary, and upon an estimate to be made by the Secretary of the Treasury of the United States, to defray the expenses of the legislative assembly, of the courts, the printing of the laws, and other incidental expenses; and the secretary of the Territory shall annually account to the Secretary of the Treasury of the United States for the manner in which the aforesaid sum shall have been expended.

SEC. 15. That the legislative assembly of the Territory of Oklahoma shall hold its first session at Guthrie, in said Territory, at such time as the governor thereof shall appoint and direct; and at said first session, or as soon thereafter as they shall deem expedient, the governor and legislative assembly shall proceed to locate and establish the seat of government for said Territory at such place as they may deem eligible, which place, however, shall thereafter be subject to be changed by the said governor and legislative assembly.

SEC. 16. That a Delegate to the House of Representatives of the United States, to serve during each Congress of the United States, may be elected by the voters qualified to elect members of the legislative assembly, who shall be entitled to the same rights and privileges as are exercised and enjoyed by the Delegates from the several other Territories of the United States in the said House of Representatives. The first election shall be held at such time and place, and be conducted in such manner as the governor shall appoint and direct, after at least sixty days' notice, to be given by proclamation, and at all subsequent elections the time, place, and manner of holding elections shall be prescribed by law. The person having the greatest number of votes of the qualified electors, as hereinbefore provided, shall be declared by the governor elected, and a certificate thereof shall be accordingly given.

SEC. 17. That the provisions of title sixty-two of the Revised Statutes of the United States relating to national banks, and all amendments thereto, shall have the same force and effect in the Territory of Oklahoma as elsewhere in the United States: *Provided,* That persons otherwise qualified to act as directors shall not be required to have resided in said Territory for more than three months immediately preceding their election as such.

SEC. 18. That sections numbered sixteen and thirty-six in each township in said Territory shall be, and the same are hereby, reserved for the purpose of being applied to public schools in the State or States hereafter to be erected out of the same. In all cases where the sections sixteen and thirty-six, or either of them, are occupied by actual settlers prior to survey thereof, the county commissioners of the counties in which such sections are so occupied are authorized to locate other lands, to an equal amount, in sections or fractional sections, as the case may be, within their respective counties, in lieu of the sections so occupied.

All the lands embraced in that portion of the Territory of Oklahoma heretofore known as the Public Land Strip, shall be open to settlement under the provisions of the homestead laws of the United States, except section twenty-three hundred and one of the Revised Statutes, which shall not apply; but all actual and bona fide settlers upon and occupants of the lands in said Public Land Strip at the time of the passage of this act shall be entitled to have preference to and hold the lands upon which they have settled under the homestead laws of the United States, by virtue of their settlement and occupancy of said lands, and they shall be credited with the time they have actually occupied their homesteads, respectively, not exceeding two years, on the time required under said laws to perfect title as homestead settlers.

The lands within said Territory of Oklahoma, acquired by cession of the Muscogee (or Creek) Nation of Indians, confirmed by act of Congress approved March first, eighteen hundred and eighty-nine, and also the lands acquired in pursuance of an agreement with the Seminole Nation of Indians by re-lease and conveyance, dated March sixteenth, eighteen hundred and eighty-nine, which may hereafter be open to settlement, shall be disposed of under the provisions of sections twelve, thirteen, and fourteen of the "Act making appropriations for the current and contingent expenses of the Indian Department, and for fulfilling treaty stipulations with various Indian tribes, for the year ending June thirtieth, eighteen hundred and ninety, and for other purposes," approved March second, eighteen hundred and eighty-nine, and under section two of an "Act to ratify and confirm an agreement with the Muscogee (or Creek) Nation of Indians in the Indian Territory, and for other purposes," approved March first, eighteen hundred and eighty-nine: *Provided, however,* That each settler under and in accordance with the provisions of said acts shall, before receiving a patent for his homestead on the land hereafter opened to settlement as aforesaid, pay to the United States for the land so taken by him, in addition to the fees provided by law, the sum of one dollar and twenty-five cents per acre.

Whenever any of the other lands within the Territory of Oklahoma, now occupied by any Indian tribe, shall by operation of law or proclamation of the President of the United States, be open to settlement, they shall be disposed of to actual settlers only, under the provisions of the homestead law, except section twenty-three hundred and one of the Revised Statutes of the United States, which shall not apply: *Provided, however,* That each settler, under and in accordance with the provisions of said homestead laws, shall before receiving a patent for his homestead pay to the United States for the land so taken by him, in addition to the fees provided by law, a sum per acre equal to the amount which has been or may be paid by the United States to obtain a relinquishment of the Indian title or interest therein, but in no case shall such payment be less than one dollar and twenty-five cents per acre. The rights of honorably discharged soldiers and sailors in the late civil war, as defined and described in sections twenty-three hundred and four and twenty-three hundred and five of the Revised Statutes of the United States, shall not be abridged except as to such payment. All tracts of land in Oklahoma Territory which have been set apart for school purposes, to educational societies, or missionary boards at work among the Indians, shall not be open for settlement, but are hereby granted to the respective educational societies or missionary boards for whose use the same has been set apart. No part of the land embraced within the Territory hereby created shall inure to the use or benefit of any railroad corporation, except the rights of way and land for stations heretofore granted to certain railroad corporations. Nor shall any provision of this act or any act of any officer of the United States, done or performed under the provisions of this act or otherwise, invest any corporation owning or operating any railroad in the Indian Territory, or Territory created by this act, with any land or right to any land in either of said Territories, and this act shall not apply to or affect any land which, upon any condition on becoming a part of the public domain, would inure to the benefit of, or become the property of, any railroad corporation.

SEC. 19. That portion of the Territory of Oklahoma heretofore known as the Public Land Strip is hereby declared a public land district, and the President of the United States is hereby empowered to locate a land office in said district, at such place as he shall select, and to appoint in conformity with existing law a register and receiver of said land office. He may also, whenever he shall deem it necessary, establish another additional land district within said Territory, locate a land office therein, and in like manner appoint a register and receiver thereof. And the Commissioner of the General Land Office shall, when directed by the President, cause the lands within the Territory to be properly surveyed and subdivided where the same has not already been done.

SEC. 20. That the procedure in applications, entries, contests, and adjudications in the Territory of Oklahoma shall be in form and manner prescribed under the homestead laws of the United States, and the general principles and provisions of the homestead laws, except as modified by the provisions of this act and the acts of Congress approved March first and second, eighteen hundred and eighty-nine, heretofore mentioned, shall be applicable to all entries made in said Territory, but no patent shall be issued to any person who is not a citizen of the United States at the time of making final proof.

All persons who shall settle on land in said Territory, under the provisions of the homestead laws of the United States, and of this act, shall be required to select the same in square form as nearly as may be; and no person who shall at the time be seized in fee simple of a hundred and sixty acres of land in any State or Territory, shall hereafter be entitled to enter land in said Territory of Oklahoma. The provisions of sections twenty-three hundred and four and twenty-three hundred and five of the Revised Statutes of the United States shall, except so far as modified by this act, apply to all homestead settlements in said Territory.

SEC. 21. That any person, entitled by law to take a homestead in said

Territory of Oklahoma, who has already located and filed upon, or shall hereafter locate and file upon, a homestead within the limits described in the President's proclamation of April first, eighteen hundred and eighty-nine, and under and in pursuance of the laws applicable to the settlement of the lands opened for settlement by such proclamation, and who has complied with all the laws relating to such homestead settlement, may receive a patent therefor at the expiration of twelve months from date of locating upon said homestead upon payment to the United States of one dollar and twenty-five cents per acre for land embraced in such homestead.

SEC. 22. That the provisions of title thirty-two, chapter eight of the Revised Statutes of the United States relating to "reservation and sale of town sites on the public lands" shall apply to the lands open, or to be opened to settlement in the Territory of Oklahoma, except those opened to settlement by the proclamation of the President on the twenty-second day of April, eighteen hundred and eighty-nine: *Provided,* That hereafter all surveys for town sites in said Territory shall contain reservations for parks (of substantially equal area if more than one park) and for schools and other public purposes, embracing in the aggregate not less than ten nor more than twenty acres; and patents for such reservations, to be maintained for such purposes, shall be issued to the towns respectively when organized as municipalities: *Provided further,* That in case any lands in said Territory of Oklahoma, which may be occupied and filed upon as a homestead, under the provisions of law applicable to said Territory, by a person who is entitled to perfect his title thereto under such laws, are required for town-site purposes, it shall be lawful for such person to apply to the Secretary of the Interior to purchase the lands embraced in said homestead or any part thereof for town-site purposes. He shall file with the application a plat of such proposed town-site, and if such plat shall be approved by the Secretary of the Interior, he shall issue a patent to such person for land embraced in said town-site, upon the payment of the sum of ten dollars per acre for all the lands embraced in such town-site, except the lands to be donated and maintained for public purposes as provided in this section. And the sums so received by the Secretary of the Interior shall be paid over to the proper authorities of the municipalities when organized, to be used by them for school purposes only.

SEC. 23. That there shall be reserved public highways four rods wide between each section of land in said Territory, the section lines being the center of said highways; but no deduction shall be made, where cash payments are provided for, in the amount to be paid for each quarter section of land by reason of such reservation. But if the said highway shall be vacated by any competent authority, the title to the respective strips shall inure to the then owner of the tract of which it formed a part by the original survey.

SEC. 24. That it shall be unlawful for any person, for himself or any company, association, or corporation, to directly or indirectly procure any person to settle upon any lands open to settlement in the Territory of Oklahoma, with intent thereafter of acquiring title thereto; and any title thus acquired shall be void; and the parties to such fraudulent settlement shall severally be guilty of a misdemeanor, and shall be punished upon indictment, by imprisonment not exceeding twelve months, or by a fine not exceeding one thousand dollars, or by both such fine and imprisonment, in the discretion of the court.

SEC. 25. That inasmuch as there is a controversy between the United States and the State of Texas as to the ownership of what is known as Greer County, it is hereby expressly provided that this act shall not be construed to apply to said Greer County until the title to the same has been adjudicated and determined to be in the United States; and in order to provide for a speedy and final judicial determination of the controversy aforesaid the Attorney-General of the United States is hereby authorized and directed to commence in the name and on behalf of the United States, and prosecute to a final determination, a proper suit in equity in the Supreme Court of the United States against the State of Texas, setting forth the title and claim of the United States to the tract of land lying between the North and South Forks of the Red River where the Indian Territory and the State of Texas adjoin, east of the one hundredth degree of longitude, and claimed by the State of Texas as within its boundary and a part of its land, and designated on its map as Greer County, in order that the rightful title to said land may be finally determined, and the court, on the trial of the case may, in its discretion, so far as the ends of justice will warrant, consider any evidence heretofore taken and received by the Joint Boundary Commission under the act of Congress approved January thirty-first, eighteen hundred and eighty-five; and said case shall be advanced on the docket of said court, and proceeded with to its conclusion as rapidly as the nature and circumstances of the case permit.

SEC. 26. That the following sums, or so much thereof as may be necessary, are hereby appropriated, out of any money in the Treasury not otherwise appropriated, to be disbursed under the direction of the Secretary of the Interior, in the same manner that similar appropriations are disbursed in the other Territories of the United States, namely:

To pay the expenses of the first legislative assembly of said Territory, including the printing of the session laws thereof, the sum of forty thousand dollars.

To pay the salaries of the governor, the judges of the supreme court, the secretary of the Territory, the marshal, the attorney, and other officers whose appointment is provided for in this act, for the remainder of the fiscal year ending June thirtieth, eighteen hundred and ninety, the sum of twenty thousand dollars.

To pay for the rent of buildings for the legislative and executive offices, and for the supreme and district courts; to provide jails, and support prisoners; to pay mileage and per diem of jurors and witnesses; to provide books, records, and stationary for the executive and judicial offices for the remainder of the fiscal year ending June thirtieth, eighteen hundred and ninety, the sum of fifteen thousand dollars.

To enable the governor to take a census of the inhabitants of said Territory, as required by law, the sum of five thousand dollars.

To be expended by the governor in temporary support and aid of common school education in said Territory, as soon as a system of public schools shall have been established by the legislative assembly, the sum of fifty thousand dollars.

SEC. 27. That the provisions of this act shall not be so construed as to invalidate or impair any legal claims or rights of persons occupying any portion of said Territory, under the laws of the United States, but such claims shall be adjudicated by the Land Department, or the courts, in accordance with their respective jurisdictions.

SEC. 28. That the Constitution and all the laws of the United States not locally inapplicable shall, except so far as modified by this act, have the same force and effect as elsewhere within the United States; and all acts and parts of acts in conflict with the provisions of this act are as to their effect in said Territory of Oklahoma hereby repealed: *Provided*, That section eighteen hundred and fifty of the Revised Statutes of the United States shall not apply to the Territory of Oklahoma.

SEC. 29. That all that part of the United States which is bounded on the north by the State of Kansas, on the east by the States of Arkansas and Missouri, on the south by the State of Texas, and on the west and north by the Territory of Oklahoma as defined in the first section of this act, shall, for the purposes of this act, be known as the Indian Territory; and the jurisdiction of the United States court established under and by virtue of an act entitled "An act to establish a United States court in the Indian Territory, and for other purposes," approved March first, eighteen hundred and eighty-nine, is hereby limited to and shall extend only over the Indian Territory as defined in this section; that the court established by said act shall, in addition to the jurisdiction conferred thereon by said act, have and exercise within the limits of the Indian Territory jurisdiction in all civil cases in the Indian Territory, except cases over which the tribal courts have exclusive jurisdiction; and in all cases on contracts entered into by citizens of any tribe or nations with citizens of the United States in good faith and for valuable consideration, and in accordance with the laws of such tribe or nation, and such contracts shall be deemed valid and enforced by such courts; and in all cases over which jurisdiction is conferred by this act or may hereafter be conferred by act of Congress; and the provisions of this act hereinafter set forth shall apply to said Indian Territory only.

SEC. 30. That for the purpose of holding terms of said court, said Indian Territory is hereby divided into three divisions, to be known as the first, second, and third division. The first division shall consist of the country occupied by the Indian tribes in the Quapaw Indian Agency and all that part of the Cherokee country east of the ninety-sixth meridian and all of the Creek country; and the place for holding said court therein shall be at Muskogee. The second division shall consist of the Choctaw country, and the place for holding said court therein shall be at South McAlister. The third division shall consist of the Chickasaw and Seminole countries, and the place for holding said court therein shall be at Ardmore. That the Attorney-General of the United States may, if in his judgement it shall be necessary, appoint an assistant attorney for said court. And the clerk of said court shall appoint a deputy clerk in each of said divisions in which said clerk does not himself reside at the place in such division where the terms of said court are to be held. Such deputy clerk shall keep his office and reside at the place appointed for holding said court in the division of such residence, and shall keep the records of said court for such division, and in the absence of the clerk may exercise all the official powers of the clerk within the division for which he is appointed: *Provided*, That the appointment of such deputies shall be approved by said United States court in the

Indian Territory, and may be annulled by said court at its pleasure, and the clerk shall be responsible for the official acts and negligence of his respective deputies. The judge of said court shall hold at least two terms of said court each year in each of the divisions aforesaid, at such regular times as said judge shall fix and determine, and shall be paid his actual traveling expenses and subsistence while attending and holding court at places other than Muscogee. And jurors for each term of said court, in each division, shall be selected and summoned in the manner provided in said act, three jury commissioners to be selected by said court for each division, who shall possess all the qualifications and perform in said division all the duties required of the jury commissioners provided for in said act. All prosecutions for crimes or offenses hereafter committed in said Indian Territory shall be cognizable within the division in which such crime or offense shall have been committed. And all civil suits shall be brought in the division in which the defendant or defendants reside or may be found; but if there be two or more defendants residing in different divisions, the action may be brought in any division in which either of the defendants resides or may be found. And all cases shall be tried in the division in which the process is returnable as herein provided, unless said judge shall direct such case to be removed to one of the other divisions: *Provided, however,* That the judicial tribunals of the Indian nations shall retain exclusive jurisdiction in all civil and criminal cases arising in the country in which members of the nation by nativity or by adoption shall be the only parties; and as to all such cases the laws of the State of Arkansas extended over and put in force in said Indian Territory by this act shall not apply.

SEC. 31. That certain general laws of the State of Arkansas in force at the close of the session of the general assembly of that State of eighteen hundred and eighty-three, as published in eighteen hundred and eighty-four in the volume known as Mansfield's Digest of the Statutes of Arkansas, which are not locally inapplicable or in conflict with this act or with any law of Congress, relating to the subjects specially mentioned in this section, are hereby extended over and put in force in the Indian Territory until Congress shall otherwise provide, that is to say, the provisions of the said general statutes of Arkansas relating to administration, chapter one, and the United States court in the Indian Territory herein referred to shall have and exercise the powers of courts of probate under said laws; to public administrators, chapter two, and the United States marshal of the Indian Territory shall perform the duties imposed by said chapter on the sheriffs in said State; to arrest and bail, civil, chapter seven; to assignment for benefit of creditors, chapter eight; to attachments, chapter nine; to attorneys at law, chapter eleven; to bills of exchange and promissory notes, chapter fourteen; to civil rights, chapter eighteen; to common and statute law of England, chapter twenty; to contempts, chapter twenty-six; to municipal corporations, chapter twenty-nine, division one; to costs, chapter thirty; to descents and distributions, chapter forty-nine; to divorce, chapter fifty-two, and said court in the Indian Territory shall exercise the powers of the circuit courts of Arkansas under this chapter; to dower, chapter fifty-two; to evidence, chapter fifty-nine; to execution, chapter sixty; to fees, chapter sixty-three; to forcible entry and detainer, chapter sixty-seven; to frauds, statute of, chapter sixty-eight; to fugitives from justice, chapter sixty-nine; to gaming contracts, chapter seventy; to guardians, curators, and wards, chapter seventy-three, and said court in the Indian Territory shall appoint guardians and curators; to habeas corpus, chapter seventy-four; to injunction, chapter eighty-one; to insane persons and drunkards, chapter eighty-two, and said court in the Indian Territory shall exercise the powers of the probate courts of Arkansas under this chapter; to joint and several obligations and contracts, chapter eighty-seven; to judgements and decrees, chapter eighty-eight; to judgements summary, chapter eighty-nine; to jury, chapter ninety; to landlord and tenant, chapter ninety-two; to legal notices and advertisements, chapter ninety-four; to liens, chapter ninety-six; to limitations, chapter ninety-seven; to mandamus and prohibition, chapter one hundred; to marriage contracts, chapter one hundred and two; to marriages, chapter one hundred and three; to married women, chapter one hundred and four; to money and interest, chapter one hundred and nine; to mortgages, chapter one hundred and ten; to notaries public, chapter one hundred and eleven, and said court in the Indian Territory shall appoint notaries public under this chapter; to partition and sale of lands, chapter one hundred and fifteen; to pleadings and practice, chapter one hundred and nineteen; to recorders, chapter one hundred and twenty-six; to replevin, chapter one hundred and twenty-eight; to venue, change of, chapter one hundred and fifty-three; and to wills and testaments, chapter one hundred and fifty-five; and wherever in said laws of Arkansas the courts of record of said State are mentioned the said court in the Indian Territory shall be substituted therefor; and wherever the clerks of said courts are mentioned in said laws the clerk of said court in the Indian Territory and his deputies, respectively, shall be substituted therefor; and wherever the sheriff of the county is mentioned in said laws the United States marshal of the Indian Territory shall be substituted therefor, for the purpose, in each of the cases mentioned, of making said laws of Arkansas applicable to the Indian Territory.

That no attachment shall issue against improvements on real estate while the title to the land is vested in any Indian nation, except where such improvements have been made by persons, companies, or corporations operating coal or other mines, railroads, or other industries under lease or permission of law of an Indian national council, or charter, or law of the United States.

That executions upon judgements obtained in any other than Indian courts shall not be valid for the sale or conveyance of title to improvements made upon lands owned by an Indian nation, except in the cases wherein attachments are provided for. Upon a return of nulla bona, upon an execution upon any judgement against an adopted citizen of any Indian tribe, or against any person residing in the Indian country and not a citizen thereof, if the judgement debtor shall be the owner of any improvements upon real estate within the Indian Territory in excess of one hundred and sixty acres occupied as a homestead, such improvements may be subjected to the payment of such judgement by a decree of the court in which such judgement was rendered. Proceedings to subject such property to the payment of judgements may be by petition, of which the judgement debtor shall have notice as in the original suit. If on the hearing the court shall be satisfied from the evidence that the judgement debtor is the owner of improvements on real estate, subject to the payment of said judgement, the court may order the same sold, and the proceeds, or so much thereof as may be necessary to satisfy said judgement and costs, applied to the payment of said judgement; or if the improvement is of sufficient rental value to discharge the judgement within a reasonable time the court may appoint a receiver, who shall take charge of such property and apply the rental receipts thereof to the payment of such judgement, under such regulations as the court may prescribe. If under such proceeding any improvement is sold only citizens of the tribe in which said property is situate may become the purchaser thereof.

The Constitution of the United States and all general laws of the United States which prohibit crimes and misdemeanors in any place within the sole and exclusive jurisdiction of the United States, except in the District of Columbia, and all laws relating to national banking associations shall have the same force and effect in the Indian Territory as elsewhere in the United States; but nothing in this act shall be so construed as to deprive any of the courts of the civilized nations of exclusive jurisdiction over all cases arising wherein members of said nations, whether by treaty, blood, or adoption, are the sole parties, nor so as to interfere with the right and power of said civilized nations to punish said members for violation of the statutes and laws enacted by their national councils where such laws are not contrary to the treaties and laws of the United States.

SEC. 32. That the word "county," as used in any of the laws of Arkansas which are put in force in the Indian Territory by the provisions of this act, shall be construed to embrace the territory within the limits of a judicial division in said Indian Territory; and whenever in said laws of Arkansas the word "county" is used, the words "judicial division" may be substituted therefor, in said Indian Territory, for the purposes of this act. And whenever in said laws of Arkansas the word "State" or the words "State of Arkansas" are used, the word "Territory," or the words "Indian Territory," may be substituted therefor, for the purposes of this act, and for the purpose of making said laws of Arkansas applicable to the said Indian Territory; but all prosecutions therein shall run in the name of the "United States."

SEC. 33. That the provisions of chapter forty-five of the said general laws of Arkansas, entitled "Criminal law," except as to the crimes and misdemeanor mentioned in the provisos to this section, and the provisions of chapter forty-six of said general laws of Arkansas, entitled "Criminal Procedure," as far as they are applicable, are hereby extended over and put in force in the Indian Territory, and jurisdiction to enforce said provisions is hereby conferred upon the United States court therein: *Provided,* That in all cases where the laws of the United States and the said criminal laws of Arkansas have provided for the punishment of the same offenses the laws of the United States shall govern as to such offenses: *And provided further,* That the United States circuit and district courts, respectively, for the western district of Arkansas and the eastern district of Texas, respectively, shall continue to exercise exclusive jurisdiction as now provided by law in the Indian Territory as defined in this act, in their respective districts as heretofore established, over all crimes and misdemeanors against the laws of the United States applicable to the said Territory, which are punishable by said laws of the United States by death or by imprisonment at hard labor, except as otherwise provided in the following sections of this act.

SEC. 34. That original jurisdiction is hereby conferred upon the United States court in the Indian Territory to enforce the provisions of title twenty-eight, chapters three and four, of the Revised Statutes of the United States in said Territory, except the offenses defined and embraced in sections twenty-one hundred and forty-two and twenty-one hundred and forty-three: *Provided*, That as to the violations of the provisions of section twenty-one hundred and thirty-nine of said Revised Statutes, and jurisdiction of said court in the Indian Territory shall be concurrent with the jurisdiction exercised in the enforcement of such provisions by the United States courts for the western district of Arkansas and the eastern district of Texas: *Provided*, That all violations of said chapters three and four, prior to the passage of this act, shall be prosecuted in the said United States courts, respectively, the same as if this act had not been passed.

SEC. 35. That exclusive original jurisdiction is hereby conferred upon the United States court in the Indian Territory to enforce the provisions of chapter four, title seventy, of the Revised Statutes of the United States entitled "Crimes against justice," in all cases where the crimes mentioned therein are committed in any judicial proceeding in the Indian Territory and where such crimes affect or impede the enforcement of the laws in the courts established in said Territory: *Provided*, That all violations of the provisions of said chapter prior to the passage of this act shall be prosecuted in the United States courts for the Western district of Arkansas and the eastern district of Texas, respectively, the same as if this act had not been passed.

SEC. 36. That jurisdiction is hereby conferred upon the United States court in the Indian Territory over all controversies arising between members or citizens of one tribe or nation of Indians and the members or citizens of other tribes or nations in the Indian Territory, and any citizen or member of one tribe or nation who may commit any offense or crime against the person or property of a citizen or member of another tribe or nation shall be subject to the same punishment in the Indian Territory as he would be if both parties were citizens of the United States. And any member or citizen of any Indian tribe or nation in the Indian Territory shall have the right to invoke the aid of said court therein for the protection of his person or property as against any person not a member of the same tribe or nation, as though he were a citizen of the United States.

SEC. 37. That if any person shall, in the Indian Territory, open, carry on, promote, make or draw, publicly or privately, any lottery, or scheme of chance of any kind or description, by whatever name, style or title the same may be denominated or known, or shall, in said Territory, vend, sell, barter or dispose of any lottery ticket or tickets, order or orders, device or devices, of any kind, for, or representing any number of shares or any interest in any lottery or scheme of chance, or shall open or establish as owner or otherwise any lottery or scheme of chance in said Territory, or shall be in any wise concerned in any lottery or scheme of chance, by acting as owner or agent in said Territory, for or on behalf of any lottery or scheme of chance, to be drawn, paid or carried on, either out of or within said Territory, every such person shall be deemed guilty of a misdemeanor, and, on conviction thereof, shall be fined for the first offense, not exceeding five hundred dollars, and for the second offense shall, on conviction, be fined not less than five hundred dollars and not exceeding five thousand, and he may be imprisoned, in the discretion of the court, not exceeding one year. And jurisdiction to enforce the provisions of this section is hereby conferred upon the United States court in said Indian Territory, and all persons therein, including Indians and members and citizens of Indian tribes and nations, shall be subject to its provisions and penalties.

SEC. 38. The clerk and deputy clerks of said United States court shall have the power within their respective divisions to issue marriage licenses or certificates and to solemnize marriages. They shall keep copies of all marriage licenses or certificates issued by them, and a record book in which shall be recorded all licenses or certificates after the marriage has been solemnized, and all persons authorized by law to solemnize marriages shall return the license or certificate, after executing the same, to the clerk or deputy clerk who issued it, together with his return thereon. They shall also be ex-officio recorders within their respective divisions, and as such they shall perform such duties as are required of recorders of deeds under the said laws of Arkansas, and receive the fees and compensation therefor which are provided in said laws of Arkansas for like service: *Provided,* That all marriages heretofore contracted under the laws or tribal customs of any Indian nation now located in the Indian Territory are hereby declared valid, and the issue of such marriages shall be deemed legitimate and entitled to all inheritances of property or other rights, the same as in the case of the issue of other forms of lawful marriage: *Provided further,* That said chapter one hundred and three of said laws of Arkansas shall not be construed so as to interfere with the operation of the laws governing marriage enacted by any of the civilized tribes, nor to confer any authority upon any officer of said court to unite a citizen of the United States in marriage with a member of any of the civilized nations until the preliminaries to such marriage shall have first been arranged according to the laws of the nation of which said Indian person is a member: *And provided further,* That where such marriage is required by law of an Indian nation to be of record, the certificate of such marriage shall be sent for record to the proper officer, as provided in such law enacted by the Indian nation.

SEC. 39. That the United States court in the Indian Territory shall have all the powers of the United States circuit courts or circuit court judges to appoint commissioners within said Indian Territory, who shall be learned in the law, and shall be known as United States commissioners; but not exceeding three commissioners shall be appointed for any one division, and such commissioners when appointed shall have, within the district to be designated in the order appointing them, all the powers of commissioners of circuit courts of the United States. They shall be ex officio notaries public, and shall have power to solemnize marriages. The provisions of chapter ninety-one of the said laws of Arkansas, regulating the jurisdiction and procedure before justices of the peace, are hereby extended over the Indian Territory; and said commissioners shall exercise all the powers conferred by the laws of Arkansas upon justices of the peace within their districts; but they shall have no jurisdiction to try any cause where the value of the thing or the amount in controversy exceeds one hundred dollars.

Appeals may be taken from the final judgement of said commissioners to the United States court in said Indian Territory in all cases and in the same manner that appeals may be taken from the final judgements of justices of the peace under the provisions of said chapter ninety-one. The said court may appoint a constable for each of the commissioner's districts designated by the court, and the constable so appointed shall perform all the duties required of constables under the provision of chapter twenty-four and other laws of the State of Arkansas. Each commissioner and constable shall execute to the United States, for the security of the public, a good and sufficient bond, in the sum of five thousand dollars, to be approved by the judge appointing him, conditioned that he will faithfully discharge the duties of his office and account for all moneys coming into his hands, and he shall take an oath to support the Constitution of the United States and to faithfully perform the duties required of him.

The appointments of United States commissioners by said court held at Muscogee, in the Indian Territory, heretofore made, and all acts in pursuance of law and in good faith performed by them, are hereby ratified and validated.

SEC. 40. That persons charged with any offense or crime in the Indian Territory, and for whose arrest a warrant has been issued, may be arrested by the United States marshal or any of his deputies, wherever found in said Territory, but in all cases the accused shall be taken, for preliminary examination, before the commissioner in the judicial division whose office or place of business is nearest by the route usually travelled to the place where the offense or crime was committed; but this section shall apply only to crimes or offenses over which the courts located in the Indian Territory have jurisdiction: *Provided,* That in all cases where persons have been brought before a United States commissioner in the Indian Territory for preliminary examination, charged with the commission of any crime therein, and where it appears from the evidence that a crime has been committed, and that there is probable cause to believe the accused guilty thereof, but that the crime is one over which the courts in the Indian Territory have no jurisdiction, the accused shall not, on that account, be discharged, but the case shall be proceeded with as provided in section ten hundred and fourteen of the Revised Statutes of the United States.

SEC. 41. That the judge of the United States court in the Indian Territory shall have the same power to extradite persons who have taken refuge in the Indian Territory, charged with crimes in the States or other Territories of the United States, that may now be exercised by the governor of Arkansas in that State, and he may issue requisitions upon governors of States and other Territories for persons who have committed offenses in the Indian Territory, and who have taken refuge in such States or Territories.

SEC. 42. That appeals and writs of error may be taken and prosecuted from the decisions of the United States court in the Indian Territory to the Supreme Court of the United States in the same manner and under the same regulations as from the circuit courts of the United States, except as otherwise provided in this act.

SEC. 43. That any member of any Indian tribe or nation residing in the Indian Territory may apply to the United States court therein to become a citizen of the United States, and such court shall have jurisdiction thereof and shall hear and determine such application as provided in the statutes of the

United States; and the Confederated Peoria Indians residing in the Quapaw Indian Agency, who have heretofore or who may hereafter accept their land in severalty under any of the allotment laws of the United States, shall be deemed to be, and are hereby, declared to be citizens of the United States from and after the selection of their allotments, and entitled to all the rights, privileges, and benefits as such, and parents are hereby declared from time to time to have been and to be the legal guardians of their minor children without process of court: *Provided*, That the Indians who become citizens of the United States under the provisions of this act do not forfeit or lose any rights or privileges they enjoy or are entitled to as members of the tribe or nation to which they belong.

SEC. 44. That the following sum, or so much thereof as may be necessary, is hereby appropriated, out of any money in the Treasury not otherwise appropriated, to be disbursed under the direction of the Attorney-General of the United States, in the same manner that similar appropriations are disbursed in the other Territories of the United States, namely:

To pay the actual traveling and other expenses of the judge of the United States court holding court in said Indian Territory other than at Muscogee; to pay for the rent of buildings for the court; to provide jails and support prisoners; to pay mileage and per diem of jurors and witnesses; to provide books, records, and stationary for the judicial offices for the remainder of the fiscal year ending June thirtieth, eighteen hundred and ninety, the sum of ten thousand dollars.

Approved, May 2, 1890.

AN ACT TO PROVIDE FOR THE ADMISSION OF THE STATE OF IDAHO INTO THE UNION

JULY 3, 1890

Whereas, The people of the Territory of Idaho did, on the fourth day of July, eighteen hundred and eighty-nine, by a convention of delegates called and assembled for that purpose, form for themselves a constitution, which constitution was ratified and adopted by the people of said Territory at an election held therefor on the first Tuesday in November, eighteen hundred and eighty-nine, which constitution is republican in form and is in conformity with the Constitution of the United States; and

Whereas, Said convention and the people of said Territory have asked the admission of said Territory into the Union of States on an equal footing with the original States in all respects whatever: Therefore,

Be it enacted by the Senate and House of Representatives of the United States of America in Congress assembled, That the State of Idaho is hereby declared to be a State of the United States of America, and is hereby declared admitted into the Union on an equal footing with the original States in all respects whatever; and that the constitution which the people of Idaho have formed for themselves be, and the same is hereby, accepted, ratified, and confirmed.

SEC. 2. That the said State shall consist of all the Territory described as follows: Beginning at the intersection of the thirty-ninth meridian with the boundary-line between the United States and the British Possessions, then following said meridian south until it reaches the summit of the Bitter Root Mountains; thence southeastward along the crest of the Bitter Root range and the continental divide until it intersects the meridian of thirty-four degrees of longitude; thence southward on this meridian to the forty-second parallel of latitude; thence west on this parallel of latitude to its intersection with a meridian drawn through the mouth of the Owyhee River; north on this meridian to the mouth of the Owyhee River; thence down the mid-channel of the Snake River to the mouth of the Clearwater River; and thence north on the meridian which passes through the mouth of the Clearwater to the boundary-line between the United States and the British Possessions, and east on said boundary-line to the place of beginning.

SEC. 3. That until the next general census, or until otherwise provided by law, said State shall be entitled to one Representative in the House of Representatives of the United States and the election of the Representative to the Fifty-first Congress and the Representative to the Fifty-second Congress shall take place at the time and be conducted and certified in the same manner as is provided in the constitution of the State for the election of State, district, and other officers in the first instance. The law of the Territory of Idaho for the registration of voters shall apply to the first election of State, District, and other officers held after the admission of the State of Idaho. County and precinct officers elected at the first election held after the admission of the State Idaho, shall assume the duties of their respective offices on the Monday of January eighteen hundred and ninety-one.

SEC. 4. That sections numbered sixteen and thirty-six in every township of said State, and where such sections, or any parts thereof, have been sold or otherwise disposed of by or under the authority of any act of Congress, other lands equivalent thereto, in legal subdivisions of not less than one quarter section, and as contiguous as may be to the section in lieu of which the same is taken, are hereby granted to said State for the support of common schools, such indemnity lands to be selected within said State in such manner as the legislature may provide, with the approval of the Secretary of the Interior.

SEC. 5. That all lands herein granted for educational purposes shall be disposed of only at public sale, the proceeds to constitute a permanent school fund, the interest of which only shall be expended in the support of said schools. But said lands may, under such regulations as the legislature shall prescribe, be leased for periods of not more than five years, and such lands shall not be subject to pre-emption, homestead entry, or any other entry under the land laws of the United States, whether surveyed or unsurveyed, but shall be reserved for school purposes only.

SEC. 6. That fifty sections of the unappropriated public lands within said

State, to be selected and located in legal subdivisions as provided in section four of this act, shall be, and are hereby, granted to said State for the purpose of erecting public buildings at the capital of said State for legislative, executive, and judicial purposes.

SEC. 7. That five per centum of the proceeds of the sales of public lands lying within said State which shall be sold by the United States subsequent to the admission of said State into the Union, after deducting all the expenses incident to the same, shall be paid to the said State, to be used as a permanent fund, the interest of which only shall be expended for the support of the common schools within said State.

SEC. 8. That the lands granted to the Territory of Idaho by the act of February eighteenth, eighteen hundred and eighty-one, entitled "An act to grant lands to Dakota, Montana, Arizona, Idaho, and Wyoming for university purposes," are hereby vested in the State of Idaho to the extent of the full quantity of seventy-two sections to said State, and any portion of said lands that may not have been selected by said Territory of Idaho may be selected by the said State; but said act of February eighteenth, eighteen hundred and eighty-one, shall be so amended as to provide that none of said lands shall be sold for less than ten dollars per acre, and the proceeds shall constitute a permanent fund to be safely invested and held by said State, and the income thereof be used exclusively for university purposes. The schools, colleges, and universities provided for in this act shall forever remain under the exclusive control of the said State, and no part of the proceeds arising from the sale or disposal of any lands herein granted for educational purposes shall be used for the support of any sectarian or denominational school, college, or university.

SEC. 9. That the penitentiary at Boise City, Idaho, and all lands connected therewith and set apart and reserved therefor, and unexpended appropriations of money therefor, and the personal property of the United States now being in the Territory of Idaho, which has been in use in the said Territory in the administration of the Territorial government, including books and records and the property used at the constitutional convention which convened at Boise City, in the month of July, eighteen hundred and eighty-nine, are hereby granted and donated to the State of Idaho.

SEC. 10. That ninety thousand acres of land, to be selected and located as provided in section four of this act, are hereby granted to said State for the use and support of an agricultural college in said State, as provided in the acts of Congress making donations of lands for such purposes.

SEC. 11. That in lieu of the grant of land for purposes of internal improvement made to the new States by the eighth section of the act of September fourth, eighteen hundred and forty-one, which section is hereby repealed as to the State of Idaho, and in lieu of any claim or demand by the said State under the act of September twenty-eighth eighteen hundred and fifty, and section twenty four hundred and seventy-nine of the Revised Statutes, making a grant of swamp and overflowed lands to certain States, which grant it is hereby declared is not extended to the State of Idaho, and in lieu of any grant of saline lands to said state the following grants of lands are hereby made, to wit: To the State of Idaho: For the establishment and maintenance of a scientific school, one hundred thousand acres; for State normal schools, one hundred thousand acres; for the support and maintenance of the insane-asylum located at Black-foot, fifty thousand acres; for the support and maintenance of the State University located at Moscow, fifty thousand acres; for the support and maintenance of the penitentiary located at Boise City, fifty thousand acres; for other State, charitable, educational, penal, and reformatory institutions, one hundred and fifty thousand acres. None of the lands granted by this act shall be sold for less than ten dollars an acre.

SEC. 12. That the State of Idaho shall not be entitled to any further or other grants of land for any purpose than as expressly provided in this act. And the lands granted by this section shall be held, appropriated, and disposed of exclusively for the purpose herein mentioned, in such manner as the legislature of the State may provide.

SEC. 13. That all mineral lands shall be exempted from the grants by this act. But if sections sixteen and thirty-six, or any subdivision, or portion of any smallest subdivision thereof in any township shall be found by the Department of the Interior to be mineral lands, the said State is hereby authorized and empowered to select, in legal subdivisions, an equal quantity of other unappropriated lands in said State, in lieu thereof, for the use and the benefit of the common schools of said State.

SEC. 14. That all lands granted in quantity or as indemnity by this act shall be selected, under the direction of the Secretary of the Interior, from the surveyed unreserved, and unappropriated public lands of the United States within the limits of the State entitled thereto. And there shall be deducted from the number of acres of land donated by this act for specific objects to said State the number of acres heretofore donated by Congress to said Territory for similar objects.

SEC. 15. That the sum of twenty eight thousand dollars, or so much thereof as may be necessary, is hereby appropriated, out of any money in the Treasury not otherwise appropriated, for defraying the expenses of said convention and for the payment of the members thereof, under the same rules and regulations and at the same rates as are now provided by law for the payment of the Territorial legislatures, and for elections held therefor and thereunder. Any money hereby appropriated not necessary for such purpose shall be covered into the Treasury of the United States.

SEC. 16. That the said State shall constitute a judicial district, the name thereof to be the same as the name of the State; and the circuit and district courts therefor shall be held at the capital of the State for the time being, and the said district shall, for judicial purposes, until otherwise provided, be attached to the ninth judicial circuit. There shall be appointed for said district one district judge, one United States attorney, and one United States marshal. The judge of the said district shall receive a yearly salary of three thousand five hundred dollars, payable in four equal installments, on the first days of January, April, July, and October of each year, and shall reside in the district. There shall be appointed clerks of said courts, in the said district, who shall keep their offices at the capital of said State. The regular terms of said courts shall be held in said district, at the place aforesaid, on the first Monday in April and the first Monday in November of each year, and only one grand jury and one petit jury shall be summoned in both said circuit and district courts. The circuit and district courts for said district, and the judges thereof, respectively, shall possess the same powers and jurisdiction, and perform the same duties required to be performed by the other circuit and district courts and judges of the United States, and shall be governed by the same laws and regulations. The marshal, district attorney, and clerks of the circuit and district courts of said district, and all other officers and persons performing duties in the administration of justice therein, shall severally possess the powers and perform the duties lawfully possessed and required to be performed by similar officers in other districts of the United States; and shall, for the services they may perform, receive the fees and compensation allowed by law to other similar officers and persons performing similar duties in the State of Oregon.

SEC. 17. That all cases of appeal or writ of error heretofore prosecuted and now pending in the Supreme Court of the United States upon any record from the supreme court of said Territory, or that may hereafter lawfully be prosecuted upon any record from said court, may be heard and determined by said Supreme Court of the United States; and the mandate of execution or of further proceedings shall be directed by the Supreme Court of the United States to the circuit or district court hereby established within the said State from or to the supreme court of such State, as the nature of the case may require. And the circuit, district, and State courts herein named shall, respectively, be the successors of the supreme court of the Territory, as to all such cases arising within the limits embraced within the jurisdiction of such courts, respectively, with full power to proceed with the same, and award mesne or final process therein; and that from all judgements and decrees of the supreme court of the Territory mentioned in this act, in any case arising within the limits of the proposed State prior to admission, the parties to such judgement shall have the same right to prosecute appeals and writs of error to the Supreme Court of the United States as they shall have had by law prior to the admission of said State into the Union.

SEC. 18. That in respect to all cases, proceedings, and matters now pending in the supreme or district courts of the said Territory at the time of the admission into the Union of the State of Idaho and arising within the limits of such State, whereof the circuit or district courts by this act established might have had jurisdiction under the laws of the United States had such courts existed at the time of the commencement of such cases, the said circuit and district courts, respectively, shall be the successors of said supreme and district courts of said Territory; and in respect to all other cases, proceedings, and matters pending in the supreme or district courts of said Territory at the time of the admission of such Territory into the Union, arising within the limits of said State, the courts established by such State shall, respectively, be the successors of said supreme and district Territorial courts; and all the files, records, indictments, and proceedings relating to any such cases shall be transferred to such circuit, district, and State courts, respectively, and the same shall be proceeded with therein in due course of law; but no writ, action, indictment, cause, or proceeding now pending, or that prior to the admission of the State shall be pending, in any Territorial court in said Territory, shall abate by the admission of such State into the Union, but the same shall be transferred and proceeded within the proper United States circuit, district, or State court as the case may be: *Provided, however,* That in all civil actions, causes, and proceedings in which the United States is not a party transfers shall not be made to the circuit and district courts of the United States, except upon written request of one of the parties to such action or proceeding filed in the proper court; and in the absence of such request such cases shall be proceeded with in the proper State courts.

SEC. 19. That from and after the admission of said State into the Union, in pursuance of this act, the laws of the United States not locally inapplicable shall have the same force and effect within the said State as elsewhere within the United States.

SEC. 20. That the legislature of the said State may elect two Senators of the United States as is provided by the constitution of said State, and the Senators and Representatives of said State shall be entitled to seats in Congress and to all the rights and privileges of Senators and Representatives of other States in the Congress of the United States.

SEC. 21. That until the State officers are elected and qualified under the provisions of the constitution of said State, the officers of the Territory of Idaho shall discharge the duties of their respective offices under the constitution of the State, in the manner and form as therein provided; and all laws in force made by said Territory, at the time of its admission into the Union, shall be in force in said State, except as modified or changed by this act or by the constitution of the State.

SEC. 22. That all acts or parts of acts in conflict with the provisions of this act, whether passed by legislature of said Territory or by Congress, are hereby repealed.

Approved, July 3, 1890.

AN ACT TO PROVIDE FOR THE ADMISSION OF THE STATE OF WYOMING INTO THE UNION, AND FOR OTHER PURPOSES

JULY 10, 1890

Whereas, the people of the Territory of Wyoming did, on the thirtieth day of September, eighteen hundred and eighty-nine, by a convention of delegates called and assembled for that purpose, form for themselves a constitution, which constitution was ratified and adopted by the people of said Territory at the election held therefor on the first Tuesday in November, eighteen hundred and eighty-nine, which constitution is republican in form and is in conformity with the Constitution of the United States; and

Whereas, said convention and the people of the said Territory have asked the admission of said Territory into the Union of States on an equal footing with the original States in all respects whatever; Therefore,

Be it enacted by the Senate and House of Representatives of the United States of America in Congress assembled, That the State of Wyoming is hereby declared to be a State of the United States of America, and is hereby declared admitted into the Union on an equal footing with the original States in all respects whatever; and that the constitution which the people of Wyoming have formed for themselves be, and the same is hereby, accepted, ratified, and confirmed.

SEC. 2. That the said State shall consist of all the territory included within the following boundaries, to wit: Commencing at the intersection of the twenty-seventh meridian of longitude west from Washington with the forty-fifth degree of north latitude and running thence west to the thirty-fourth meridian of west longitude; thence south to the forty-first degree of north latitude; thence east to the twenty-seventh meridian of west longitude, and thence north to the place of beginning: *Provided,* That nothing in this act contained shall repeal or affect any act of Congress relating to the Yellowstone National Park, or the reservation of the park as now defined, or as may be hereafter defined or extended, or the power of the United States over it; and nothing contained in this act shall interfere with the right and ownership of the United States in said park and reservation as it now is or may hereafter be defined or extended by law; but exclusive legislation, in all cases whatsoever, shall be exercised by the United States, which shall have exclusive control and jurisdiction over the same; but nothing in this proviso contained shall be construed to prevent the service within said park of civil and criminal process lawfully issued by the authority of said State; and the said State shall not be entitled to select indemnity school lands for the sixteenth and thirty-sixth sections that may be in said park reservation as the same is now defined or may be hereafter defined.

SEC. 3. That until the next general census, or until otherwise provided by law, said State shall be entitled to one Representative in the House of Representatives of the United States, and the election of the Representative to the Fifty-first Congress and the Representative to the Fifty-second Congress shall take place at the time and be conducted and certified in the same manner as is provided in the constitution of the State for the election of State, district, and other officers.

SEC. 4. That sections numbered sixteen and thirty-six in every township of said proposed State, and where such sections, or any parts thereof, have been sold or otherwise disposed of by or under the authority of any act of Congress, other lands equivalent thereto, in legal subdivisions of not less than one quarter section, and as contiguous as may be to the section in lieu of which the same is taken, are hereby granted to said State for the support of common schools, such indemnity lands to be selected within said State in such manner as the legislature may provide, with the approval of the Secretary of the Interior: *Provided,* That section six of the act of Congress of August ninth, eighteen hundred and eighty-eight, entitled "An act to authorize the leasing of the school and university lands in the Territory of Wyoming, and for other purposes," shall apply to the school and university indemnity lands of the said State of Wyoming so far as applicable.

SEC. 5. That all lands herein granted for educational purposes shall be disposed of only at public sale, the proceeds to constitute a permanent school fund, the interest of which only shall be expended in the support of said schools. But said lands may, under such regulations as the legislature shall prescribe, be leased for periods of not more than five years, in quantities not exceeding one section to any one person or company; and such land shall not be subject to preemption, homestead entry, or any other entry under the land laws of the United States, whether surveyed or unsurveyed, but shall be reserved for school purposes only.

SEC. 6. That fifty sections of the unappropriated public lands within said State, to be selected and located in legal subdivisions as provided in section four of this act, shall be, and are hereby, granted to said State for the purpose of erecting public buildings at the capital of said State.

SEC. 7. That five per centum of the proceeds of the sales of public lands lying within said State which shall be sold by the United States subsequent to the admission of said State into the Union, after deducting all the expenses incident to the same, shall be paid to the said State, to be used as a permanent fund, the interest of which only shall be expended for the support of the common schools within said State.

SEC. 8. That the lands granted to the Territory of Wyoming by the act of February eighteenth, eighteen hundred and eighty-one, entitled "An act to grant lands to Dakota, Montana, Arizona, Idaho, and Wyoming for university purposes," are hereby vested in the State of Wyoming, to the extent of the full quantity of seventy-two sections to said State, and any portion of said lands that may not have been selected by said Territory of Wyoming may be selected by the said State; but said act of February eighteenth, eighteen hundred and eighty-one, shall be so amended as to provide that none of said lands shall be sold for less than ten dollars per acre, and the proceeds shall constitute a permanent fund to be safely invested and held by said State and the income thereof be used exclusively for university purposes. The schools, colleges, and universities provided for in this act shall forever remain under the exclusive control of the said State, and no part of the proceeds arising from the sale or disposal of any lands herein granted for educational purposes shall be used for the support of any sectarian or denominational school, college, or university. The section of land granted by the act of May twenty-eighth, eighteen hundred and eighty-eight, to the Territory of Wyoming for a fish hatchery and other public purposes shall, upon the admission of said State of Wyoming into the Union, become the property of said State.

SEC. 9. That the penitentiary at Laramie City, Wyoming, and all lands connected therewith and set apart and reserved therefor, and the personal property of the United States now being in the Territory of Wyoming and which has been in use in the said Territory in the administration of the Territorial government, including books and records, and the property used at the Constitutional Convention which convened at Cheyenne, in the month of September, eighteen hundred and eighty-nine, are hereby granted and donated, and unexpended appropriations of money therefor, are hereby granted and donated to the State of Wyoming.

SEC. 10. That ninety thousand acres of land, to be selected and located as provided in section four of this act, are hereby granted to said State for the use and support of an agriculture college in said State as provided in the acts of Congress making donations of lands for such purpose.

SEC. 11. That in lieu of the grant of land for purposes of internal improvement made to new States by the eighth section of the act of September fourth, eighteen hundred and forty-one, which section is hereby repealed as to the State of Wyoming, and in lieu of any claim or demand by the said State under the act of September twenty-eighth, eighteen hundred and fifty, and section twenty-four hundred and seventy-nine of the Revised Statutes, making a grant of swamp and overflowed lands to certain States, which grant it is hereby declared is not extended to the State of Wyoming, and in lieu of any grant of saline lands to said State, the following grants of land are hereby made, to wit:

To the State of Wyoming: For the establishment and maintenance and support in the said State of the insane asylum in Uinta County, thirty thousand acres; for the penal, reform, or educational institution in course of construction in Carbon County, thirty thousand acres; for the penitentiary in Albany County, thirty thousand acres; for the fish-hatchery in Albany County, five thousand acres; for the deaf, dumb, and blind asylum in Laramie County, thirty thousand acres; for the poor farm in Fremont County, ten thousand acres; for a hospital for miners who shall become disabled or incapacitated to labor while working in the mines of the State, thirty thousand acres; for public buildings at the capital of the State, in addition to those hereinbefore granted for that purpose, seventy-five thousand acres; for State charitable, educational, penal, and reformatory institutions, two hundred and sixty thousand acres, making a total of five hundred thousand acres: *Provided,* That none of the lands granted by this act shall be sold for less than ten dollars per acre.

SEC. 12. That the State of Wyoming shall not be entitled to any further or other grants of land for any purpose than as expressly provided in this act; and the lands granted by this section shall be held, appropriated, and disposed of exclusively for the purposes herein mentioned, in such manner as the legislature of the State may provide.

SEC. 13. That all mineral lands shall be exempted from the grants made by this act. But if sections sixteen and thirty-six, or any subdivision or portion of any smallest subdivision thereof in any township, shall be found by the Department of the Interior to be mineral lands, said State is hereby authorized and empowered to select, in legal subdivisions, an equal quantity of other unappropriated lands in said State in lieu thereof, for the use and the benefit of the common schools of said State.

SEC. 14. That all lands granted in quantity or as indemnity by this act shall be selected, under the direction of the Secretary of the Interior, from the surveyed, unreserved and unappropriated public lands of the United States within the limits of the State entitled thereto. And there shall be deducted from the number of acres of land donated by this act for specific objects to said State the number of acres heretofore donated by Congress to said Territory for similar objects.

SEC. 15. That the sum of thirty thousand dollars, or so much thereof as may be necessary, is hereby appropriated, out of any money in the Treasury not otherwise appropriated, to said Territory for defraying the expenses of the said convention and for the payment of the members thereof, under the same rules and regulations and at the same rates as are now provided by law for the payment of the Territorial legislatures, and for the elections held therefor and thereunder. Any money hereby appropriated not necessary for such purpose shall be covered into the Treasury of the United States.

SEC. 16. That the said State, when admitted as aforesaid, shall constitute a judicial district, the name thereof to be the same as the name of the State; and the circuit and district courts therefor shall be held at the capital of the State for the time being, and the said district shall, for judicial purposes, until otherwise provided, be attached to the eighth judicial circuit. There shall be appointed for said district one district judge, one United States attorney, and one United States marshal. The judge of said district shall receive a yearly salary of three thousand five hundred dollars, payable in four equal installments, on the first days of January, April, July, and October of each year and shall reside in the district.

There shall be appointed clerks of said courts in the said district, who shall keep their offices at the capital of said State. The regular terms of said courts shall be held in said district at the place aforesaid on the first Monday in April and the first Monday in November of each year, and only one grand jury and one petit jury shall be summoned in both said circuit and district courts. The circuit and district courts for said district, and the judges thereof, respectively shall possess the same powers and jurisdiction, and perform the same duties required to be performed by the other circuit and district courts and judges of the United States, and shall be governed by the same laws and regulations. The marshal, district attorney, and clerks of the circuit and district courts of said district, and all other officers and persons performing duties in the administration of justice therein, shall severally possess the powers and perform the duties lawfully possessed and required to be performed by similar officers in other districts of the United States; and shall, for the services they may perform, receive the fees and compensation allowed by law to other similar officers and persons performing similar duties in the State of Oregon.

SEC. 17. That all cases of appeal or writ of error heretofore prosecuted and now pending in the Supreme Court of the United States upon any record from the supreme court of said Territory, or that may hereafter lawfully be prosecuted upon any record from said courts, may be heard and determined by said Supreme Court of the United States. And the mandate of execution of further proceedings shall be directed by the Supreme Court of the United States to the circuit or district court hereby established within the said State from or to the supreme court of such State, as the nature of the case may require. And the circuit, district, and State courts herein named shall, respectively, be the successor of the supreme court of the Territory, as to all such cases arising within the limits embraced within the jurisdiction of such courts, respectively, with full power to proceed with the same, and award mesne or final process therein; and that from all judgments and decrees of the supreme court of the Territory mentioned in this act, in any case arising within the limits of the proposed State prior to admission, the parties to such judgment shall have the same right to prosecute appeals and writs of error to the Supreme Court of the United States as they shall have had by law prior to the admission of said State into the Union.

SEC. 18. That in respect to all cases, proceedings, and matters now pending in the supreme or district courts of the said Territory at the time of the admission into the Union of the State of Wyoming and arising within the limits of such State, whereof the circuit or district court by this act established might have had jurisdiction under the laws of the United States had such courts existed at the time of commencement of such cases, the said circuit and district court, respectively, shall be the successors of said supreme and district courts of said Territory; and in respect to all other cases, proceedings, and matters pending in the supreme or district courts of the said Territory at the time of the admission of such Territory into the Union, arising within the limits of said State, the courts established by such State shall, respectively, be the successors of said supreme and district Territorial courts; and all the files, records, indictments, and proceedings relating to any such cases shall be transferred to such circuit, district, and State courts, respectively, and the same shall be proceeded with therein in due course of law; but no writ, action, indictment, cause, or proceeding now pending, or that prior to the admission of the State shall be pending, in any Territorial court in said Territory shall abate by the admission of such State into the Union, but the same shall be transferred and proceeded with in the proper United States circuit, district, or State court, as the case may be: *Provided, however,* That in all civil actions, causes, and proceedings in which the United States is not a party, transfers shall not be made to the circuit and district court of the United States except upon written request of one of the parties to such action or proceeding filed in the proper court; and in the absence of such request such cases shall be proceeded with in the proper State courts.

SEC. 19. That the legislature of the said State may elect two Senators of the United States as is provided by the constitution of said State, and the Senators and Representatives of said State shall be entitled to be admitted to seats in Congress and to all the rights and privileges of Senators and Representatives of other States in the Congress of the United States.

SEC. 20. That until the State officers are elected and qualified under the provisions of the constitution of said State, the officers of the Territory of Wyoming shall discharge the duties of their respective offices under the constitution of the State, in the manner and form as therein provided.

SEC. 21. That from and after the admission of said State into the Union, in pursuance of this act, the laws of the United States, not locally inapplicable, shall have the same force and effect within the said State as elsewhere within the United States; and all laws in force made by said Territory, at the time of its admission into the Union, until amended or repealed, shall be in force in said State, except as modified or changed by this act or by the constitution of the State, and all acts or parts of acts in conflict with the provisions of this act, whether passed by a legislature of said Territory or by Congress, are hereby repealed.

Approved, July 10, 1890.

AN ACT TO ENABLE THE PEOPLE OF UTAH TO FORM A CONSTITUTION AND STATE GOVERNMENT, AND TO BE ADMITTED INTO THE UNION ON AN EQUAL FOOTING WITH THE ORIGINAL STATES JULY 16, 1894

Be it enacted by the Senate and House of Representatives of the United States of America in Congress assembled, That the inhabitants of all that part of the area of the United States now constituting the Territory of Utah, as at present described, may become the State of Utah, as hereinafter provided.

SEC. 2. That all male citizens of the United States over the age of twenty-one years, who have resided in said Territory for one year next prior to such election, are hereby authorized to vote for and choose delegates to form a convention in said Territory. Such delegates shall possess the qualifications of such electors; and the aforesaid convention shall consist of one hundred and seven delegates, apportioned among the several counties within the limits of the proposed State as follows: Beaver County, two delegates; Box Elder County, four delegates; Cache County, eight delegates; Davis County, three delegates; Emery County, three delegates; Garfield County, one delegate; Grand County, one delegate; Iron County, one delegate; Juab County, three delegates; Kane County, one delegate; Millard County, two delegates; Morgan County, one delegate; Piute County, one delegate; Rich County, one delegate; Salt Lake County, twenty-nine delegates, thus apportioned, to wit: Salt Lake City, first precinct, four delegates; second precinct, six delegates; third precinct, five delegates; fourth precinct, three delegates; fifth precinct, three delegates; all other precincts in said county, outside of Salt Lake City, eight delegates; San Juan County, one delegate; San Pete County, seven delegates; Sevier County, three delegates; Summit County, four delegates; Tooele County, two delegates; Uintah County, one delegate; Utah County, twelve delegates; Wasatch County, two delegates; Washington County, two delegates; Wayne County, one delegate, and Weber County, eleven delegates; and the governor of said Territory shall, on the first day of August, eighteen hundred and ninety-four, issue a proclamation ordering an election of the delegates aforesaid in said Territory to be held on the Tuesday next after the first Monday in November following. The board of commissioners known as the Utah commission is hereby authorized and required to cause a new and complete registration of voters of said Territory to be made under the provisions of the laws of the United States and said Territory, except that the oath required for registration under said laws shall be so modified as to test the qualifications of the electors as prescribed in this Act; such new registration to be made as nearly conformable with the provisions of such laws as may be; and such election for delegates shall be conducted, the returns made, the result ascertained, and the certificate of persons elected to such convention issued in the same manner as is prescribed by the laws of said Territory regulating elections therein of members of the legislature. Persons possessing the qualifications entitling them to vote for delegates under this Act shall be entitled to vote on the ratification or rejection of the constitution, under such rules or regulations as said convention may prescribe, not in conflict with this Act.

SEC. 3. That the delegates to the convention thus elected shall meet at the seat of government of said Territory on the first Monday in March, eighteen hundred and ninety-five, and, after organization, shall declare on behalf of the people of said proposed State that they adopt the Constitution of the United States, whereupon the said convention shall be, and is hereby, authorized to form a constitution and State government for said proposed State.

The constitution shall be republican in form, and make no distinction in civil or political rights on account of race or color, except as to Indians not taxed, and not to be repugnant to the Constitution of the United States and the principles of the Declaration of Independence. And said convention shall provide, by ordinance irrevocable without the consent of the United States and the people of said State—

First. That perfect toleration of religious sentiment shall be secured, and that no inhabitant of said State shall ever be molested in person or property on account of his or her mode of religious worship: *Provided,* That polygamous or plural marriages are forever prohibited.

Second. That the people inhabiting said proposed State do agree and declare that they forever disclaim all right and title to the unappropriated public lands lying within the boundaries thereof; and to all lands lying within said limits owned or held by any Indian or Indian tribes; and that until the title thereto shall have been extinguished by the United States, the same shall be and remain subject to the disposition of the United States, and said Indian lands shall remain under the absolute jurisdiction and control of the Congress of the United States; that the lands belonging to citizens of the United States residing without the said State shall never be taxed at a higher rate than the lands belonging to residents thereof; that no taxes shall be imposed by the State on lands or property therein belonging to or which may hereafter be purchased by the United States or reserved for its use; but nothing herein, or in the ordinance herein provided for, shall preclude the said State from taxing, as other lands are taxed, any lands owned or held by any Indian who has severed his tribal relations and has obtained from the United States or from any person a title thereto by patent or other grant, save and except such lands as have been or may be granted to any Indian or Indians under any Act of Congress containing a provision exempting the lands thus granted from taxation; but said ordinance shall provide that all such lands shall be exempt from taxation by said State so long and to such extent as such Act of Congress may prescribe.

Third. That the debts and liabilities of said Territory, under authority of the legislative assembly thereof, shall be assumed and paid by said State.

Fourth. That provision shall be made for the establishment and maintenance of a system of public schools, which shall be open to all the children of said State and free from sectarian control.

SEC. 4. That in case a constitution and State government shall be formed in compliance with the provisions of this Act, the convention forming the same shall provide by ordinance for submitting said constitution to the people of said State for its ratification or rejection, at an election to be held on the

Tuesday next after the first Monday in November, eighteen hundred and ninety-five, at which election the qualified voters of said proposed State shall vote directly for or against the proposed constitution, and for or against any provisions separately submitted. The return of said election shall be made to the said Utah commission, who shall cause the same to be canvassed, and if a majority of the votes cast on that question shall be for the constitution, shall certify the result to the President of the United States, together with a statement of the votes cast thereon, and upon separate articles or propositions, and a copy of said constitution, articles, propositions, and ordinances. And if the constitution and government of said proposed State are republican in form, and if all the provisions of this Act have been complied with in the formation thereof, it shall be the duty of the President of the United States to issue his proclamation announcing the result of said election, and thereupon the proposed State of Utah shall be deemed admitted by Congress into the Union, under and by virtue of this Act, on an equal footing with the original States, from and after the date of said proclamation.

SEC. 5. That until the next general census, or until otherwise provided by law, said State shall be entitled to one Representative in the House of Representatives of the United States, which Representative in the Fifty-fourth Congress, together with the governor and other officers provided for in said constitution, may be elected on the same day of the election for the adoption of the constitution; and until said State officers are elected and qualified under the provisions of the constitution, and the State is admitted into the Union, the Territorial officers shall continue to discharge the duties of the respective offices in said Territory.

SEC. 6. That upon the admission of said State into the Union, sections numbered two, sixteen, thirty-two, and thirty-six in every township of said proposed State, and where such sections or any part thereof have been sold or otherwise disposed of by or under the authority of any Act of Congress other lands equivalent thereto, in legal subdivisions of not less than one quarter section and as contiguous as may be to the section in lieu of which the same is taken, are hereby granted to said State for the support of common schools, such indemnity lands to be selected within said State in such manner as the legislature may provide, with the approval of the Secretary of the Interior: *Provided*, That the second, sixteenth, thirty-second, and thirty-sixth sections embraced in permanent reservations for national purposes shall not, at any time, be subject to the grants nor to the indemnity provisions of this Act, nor shall any lands embraced in Indian, military, or other reservations of any character be subject to the grants or to the indemnity provisions of this Act until the reservation shall have been extinguished and such lands be restored to and become a part of the public domain.

SEC. 7. That upon the admission of said State into the Union, in accordance with the provisions of this Act, one hundred sections of the unappropriated lands within said State to be selected and located in legal subdivisions as provided in section six of this Act, shall be, and are hereby, granted to said State for the purpose of erecting public buildings at the capital of said State, when permanently located, for legislative, executive, and judicial purposes.

SEC. 8. That lands to the extent of two townships in quantity, authorized by the third section of the Act of February twenty-one, eighteen hundred and fifty-five, to be reserved for the establishment of the University of Utah, are hereby granted to the State of Utah for university purposes, to be held and used in accordance with the provisions of this section; and any portion of said lands that may not have been selected by said Territory may be selected by said State. That in addition to the above, one hundred and ten thousand acres of land, to be selected and located as provided in the foregoing section of this Act, and including all saline lands in said State, are hereby granted to said State, for the use of the said university, and two hundred thousand acres for the use of an agricultural college therein. That the proceeds of the sale of said lands, or any portion thereof, shall constitute permanent funds, to be safely invested and held by said State; and the income thereof to be used exclusively for the purpose of such university and agricultural college respectively.

SEC. 9. That five per centum of the proceeds of the sales of public lands lying within said State, which shall be sold by the United States subsequent to the admission of said State into the Union, after deducting all the expenses incident to the same, shall be paid to the said State, to be used as a permanent fund, the interest of which only shall be expended for the support of the common schools within said State.

SEC. 10. That the proceeds of lands herein granted for educational purposes, except as hereinafter otherwise provided, shall constitute a permanent school fund, the interest of which only shall be expended for the support of said schools, and such land shall not be subject to preëmption, homestead entry, or any other entry under the land laws of the United States, whether surveyed or unsurveyed, but shall be surveyed for school purposes only.

SEC. 11. The schools, colleges, and university provided for in this Act shall forever remain under the exclusive control of said State, and no part of the proceeds arising from the sale or disposal of any lands herein granted for educational purposes, or of the income thereof, shall be used for the support of any sectarian or denominational school, college, or university.

SEC. 12. That in lieu of the grant of land for purposes of internal improvement made to new States by the eighth section of the Act of September fourth, eighteen hundred and forty-one, which section is hereby repealed as to said State, and in lieu of any claim or demand by the State of Utah under the Act of September twenty-eighth, eighteen hundred and fifty, and section twenty-four hundred and seventy-nine of the Revised Statutes, making a grant of swamp and overflowed lands to certain States, which grant it is hereby declared is not extended to said State of Utah, the following grants of land are hereby made to said State for the purposes indicated, namely:

For the establishment of permanent water reservoirs for irrigating purposes, five hundred thousand acres; for the establishment and maintenance of an insane asylum, one hundred thousand acres; for the establishment and maintenance of a school of mines in connection with the university, one hundred thousand acres; for the establishment and maintenance of a deaf and dumb asylum, one hundred thousand acres; for the establishment and maintenance of a reform school, one hundred thousand acres; for establishment and maintenance of State normal schools, one hundred thousand acres; for the establishment and maintenance of an institution for the blind, one hundred thousand acres; for a miners' hospital for disabled miners, fifty thousand acres. The United States penitentiary near Salt Lake City and all lands and appurtenances connected therewith and set apart and reserved therefor are hereby granted to the State of Utah.

The said State of Utah shall not be entitled to any further or other grants of land for any purpose than as expressly provided in this Act; and the lands granted by this section shall be held, appropriated, and disposed of exclusively for the purposes herein mentioned, in such manner as the legislature of the State may provide.

SEC. 13. That all land granted in quantity or as indemnity by this Act shall be selected under the direction of the Secretary of the Interior, from the unappropriated public lands of the United States within the limits of said State of Utah.

SEC. 14. That the State of Utah shall constitute one judicial district, which shall be called the district of Utah, and the circuit and district courts thereof shall be held at the capital of this State for the time being. The judge of said district shall receive a yearly salary of five thousand dollars, payable monthly, and shall reside in his district. There shall be appointed clerks of said courts, who shall keep their offices at the capital of said State. There shall be appointed for said district one district judge, one United States attorney, and one United States marshal. The regular terms of said courts shall be held at the place aforesaid on the first Monday in April and the first Monday in November of each year. For judicial purposes, the district of Utah shall be attached to the eighth judicial circuit, and only one grand jury and one petit jury shall be summoned in both of said courts.

SEC. 15. That the circuit and district courts for the district of Utah and the judges thereof, respectively, shall possess the same powers and jurisdiction and perform the same duties possessed and required to be performed by the other circuit and district courts and judges of the United States, and shall be governed by the same laws and regulations.

SEC. 16. That the marshal, district attorney, and clerks of the circuit and district courts of the said district of Utah, and all other officers and other persons performing duty in the administration of justice therein, shall severally possess the powers and perform the duties lawfully possessed and required to be performed by similar officers in other districts of the United States, and shall, for the services they may perform, receive the same fees and compensation allowed by law to other similar officers and persons performing similar duties.

SEC. 17. That the convention herein provided for shall have the power to provide, by ordinance, for the transfer of actions, cases, proceedings, and matters pending in the supreme or district courts of the Territory of Utah at the time of the admission of the said State into the Union, to such courts as shall be established under the constitution to be thus formed, or to the circuit or district court of the United States for the district of Utah; and no indictment, action, or proceeding shall abate by reason of any change in the courts, but shall be proceeded with in the State or United States courts according to the laws thereof, respectively. That all cases of appeal or writ of error heretofore prosecuted and now pending in the Supreme Court of the United States upon any record from the supreme court of said Territory, or that may hereafter lawfully be prosecuted upon any record from said court, may be heard and determined by said Supreme Court of the United States; and the mandate of execution or of further proceedings shall be directed by the Supreme Court of the United States to the circuit or district court hereby established within the said State from or to the supreme court of such State, as the nature of the case may require. And the circuit, district, and State courts herein named shall, respectively, be the successors of the supreme court of the Territory as to all such cases arising within the limits embraced within the jurisdiction of such courts, respectively, with full power to proceed with the same, and award mesne or final process therein; and that from all judgments and decrees of the supreme court of the Territory, mentioned in this Act, in any case arising within the limits of the proposed State prior to admission, the parties to such judgment shall have the same right to prosecute appeals and writs of error to the Supreme Court of the United States as they shall have had by law prior to the admission of said State into the Union.

SEC. 18. That the sum of thirty thousand dollars, or so much thereof as may be necessary, is hereby appropriated out of any money in the Treasury not otherwise appropriated to said Territory for defraying the expenses of said convention and for the payment of the members thereof, under the same rules and regulations and at the same rates as are now provided by law for the payment of the Territorial legislature.

SEC. 19. That the constitutional convention may by ordinance provide for the election of officers for a full State government, including members of the legislature and Representative in the Fifty-fourth Congress, at the time for the election for the ratification or rejection of the constitution; but the said State government shall remain in abeyance until the State shall be admitted into the Union as proposed by this Act. In case the constitution of said State shall be ratified by the people, but not otherwise, the legislature thereof may assemble, organize, and elect two Senators of the United States in the manner now prescribed by the laws of the United States; and the governor and secretary of state of the proposed State shall certify the election of the Senators and Representative in the manner required by law, and when such State is admitted into the Union as provided in this Act, the Senators and Representative shall be entitled to be admitted to seats in Congress, and to all rights and privileges of Senators and Representatives of other States in the Congress of the United States; and the State government formed in pursuance of said constitution, as provided by the constitutional convention, shall proceed to exercise all the functions of State officers; and all laws in force made by said Territory at the time of its admission into the Union shall be in force in said State, except as modified or changed by this Act or by the constitution of the State; and the laws of the United States shall have the same force and effect within the said State as elsewhere within the United States.

SEC. 20. That all Acts or parts of Acts in conflict with the provisions of this Act, whether passed by the legislature of said Territory or by Congress, are hereby repealed.

Approved, July 16, 1894.

AN ACT TO GIVE THE CONSENT OF CONGRESS TO A COMPACT ENTERED INTO BETWEEN THE STATES OF SOUTH DAKOTA AND NEBRASKA RESPECTING THE BOUNDARY BETWEEN SAID STATES

JULY 24, 1897

Whereas commissioners duly appointed on the part of the State of South Dakota and commissioners duly appointed on the part of the State of Nebraska, for the purpose of settling the boundary line between said States, have ascertained said boundary line and reported the same, as by law required; and

Whereas the legislature of the State of South Dakota and the legislature of the State of Nebraska have, by acts duly passed, approved and adopted, subject to the consent of Congress, the boundary line ascertained and reported by said commission; and

Whereas the governor of the State of South Dakota and the governor of the State of Nebraska, duly authorized by acts of the legislatures of said States, have entered into and signed, in behalf of their respective States, the following compact:

"Wherefore, This compact, made and entered into by and between Honorable Andrew E. Lee, governor of the State of South Dakota, in behalf of said State of South Dakota, and Honorable Silas A. Holcomb, governor of Nebraska, in behalf of said State of Nebraska,

"Witnesseth, That, subject to the consent of Congress, the center of the main channel of the Missouri River is hereby established as, and declared to be, the boundary line between the State of Nebraska and the State of South Dakota between the following points, that is to say, between a point in the center of the channel of the Missouri River directly north of the west line of Dixon County, Nebraska, and a point in the center of said channel directly south of the east line of Clay County, South Dakota.

"In witness whereof we have hereunto set our hands and have caused the great seals of our respective States to be affixed hereto.

"Done at the city of Lincoln, the capital of the State of Nebraska, this 3d day of June, 1897.

"SILAS A. HOLCOMB,
"Governor of the State of Nebraska.

"Attest:
> "W.F. PORTER,
>> "Secretary of State.

"Done at the city of Pierre, the capital of the State of South Dakota, this 7th day of June, 1897.

> "ANDREW E. LEE.
> "Governor of the State of South Dakota.

"Attest:
> "WILLIAM H. RODDLE,
>> "Secretary of State,
> "By PHILIP LAWRENCE,
>> "Assistant Secretary of State."

Therefore,

Be it enacted by the Senate and House of Representatives of the United States of America in Congress assembled, That the consent of the Congress of the United States is hereby given to the said compact, and all its declarations are hereby confirmed.

Approved, July 24, 1897.

JOINT RESOLUTION RATIFYING AGREEMENT BETWEEN TENNESSEE AND VIRGINIA WITH REFERENCE TO THE BOUNDARY LINE OF SAID STATES

MARCH 3, 1901

Resolved by the Senate and House of Representatives of the United States of America in Congress assembled, That a recent compact or agreement having been made by and between the States of Tennessee and Virginia, whereby the State of Tennessee, by an act of its legislature approved January twenty-eighth, nineteen hundred and one, ceded to the State of Virginia certain territory specifically described in said act and being the northern half of the main street between the cities of Bristol, Virginia, and Bristol, Tennessee, and the State of Virginia, by act of its general assembly, approved February ninth, nineteen hundred and one, having accepted said cession of the State of Tennessee, the consent of Congress is hereby given to said contract or agreement between said States fixing the boundary line between said States as shown by said acts referred to, and the same is hereby ratified.

Approved, March 3, 1901.

AN ACT TO EXTEND THE WESTERN BOUNDARY LINE
OF THE STATE OF ARKANSAS
FEBRUARY 10, 1905

Be it enacted by the Senate and House of Representatives of the United States of America in Congress assembled, That the consent of the United States is hereby given for the State of Arkansas to extend her western boundary line so as to include all that strip of land in the Indian Territory lying and being situate between the Arkansas State line adjacent to the city of Fort Smith, Arkansas, and the Arkansas and Poteau rivers, described as follows, namely: Beginning at a point on the south bank of the Arkansas River one hundred paces east of the old Fort Smith, where the western boundary line of the State of Arkansas crosses the said river, and running southwesterly along the south bank of the Arkansas River to the mouth of the Poteau; thence at right angles with the Poteau River to the center of the current of said river; thence southerly up the middle of the current of the Poteau River (except where the Arkansas State line intersects the Poteau River) to a point in the middle of the current of the Poteau River opposite the mouth of Mill Creek, and where it is intersected by the middle of the current of Mill Creek; thence up the middle of Mill Creek to the Arkansas State line; thence northerly along the Arkansas State line to the point of beginning: *Provided,* That nothing in this Act shall be construed to impair any right now pertaining to any Indian tribe or tribes in said part of said Indian Territory under the laws, agreements, or treaties of the United States, or to affect the authority of the Government of the United States to make any regulations or to make any law respecting said Indians or their lands which it would have been competent to make or enact if this Act had not been passed.

Approved, February 10, 1905.

AN ACT ESTABLISHING THAT PORTION
OF THE BOUNDARY LINE BETWEEN THE STATE
OF SOUTH DAKOTA AND THE STATE OF NEBRASKA
SOUTH OF UNION COUNTY, SOUTH DAKOTA
MARCH 1, 1905

Be it enacted by the Senate and House of Representatives of the United States of America in Congress assembled, That the portion of the boundary line between the State of South Dakota and the State of Nebraska lying and being south of Union County, South Dakota, shall be in the middle of the main channel of the Missouri River as now existing, and the compact between said States establishing said boundary line is hereby approved.

Approved, March 1, 1905.

AN ACT TO ENABLE THE PEOPLE OF OKLAHOMA AND OF THE INDIAN TERRITORY TO FORM A CONSTITUTION AND STATE GOVERNMENT AND BE ADMITTED INTO THE UNION ON AN EQUAL FOOTING WITH THE ORIGINAL STATES; AND TO ENABLE THE PEOPLE OF NEW MEXICO AND OF ARIZONA TO FORM A CONSTITUTION AND STATE GOVERNMENT AND BE ADMITTED INTO THE UNION ON AN EQUAL FOOTING WITH THE ORIGINAL STATES JUNE 16, 1906

Be it enacted by the Senate and House of Representatives of the United States of America in Congress assembled, That the inhabitants of all that part of the area of the United States now constituting the Territory of Oklahoma and the Indian Territory, as at present described, may adopt a constitution and become the State of Oklahoma, as hereinafter provided: *Provided,* That nothing contained in the said constitution shall be construed to limit or impair the rights of person or property pertaining to the Indians of said Territories (so long as such rights shall remain unextinguished) or to limit or affect the authority of the Government of the United States to make any law or regulation respecting such Indians, their lands, property, or other rights by treaties, agreement, law, or otherwise, which it would have been competent to make if this Act had never been passed.

SEC. 2. That all male persons over the age of twenty-one years, who are citizens of the United States, or who are members of any Indian nation or tribe in said Indian Territory and Oklahoma, and who have resided within the limits of said proposed State for at least six months next preceding the election, are hereby authorized to vote for and choose delegates to form a constitutional convention for said proposed State; and all persons qualified to vote for said delegates shall be eligible to serve as delegates; and the delegates to form such convention shall be one hundred and twelve in number, fifty-five of whom shall be elected by the people of the Territory of Oklahoma, and fifty-five by the people of Indian Territory, and two shall be elected by the electors residing in the Osage Indian Reservation in the Territory of Oklahoma; and the governor, the chief justice, and the secretary of the Territory of Oklahoma shall apportion the Territory of Oklahoma into fifty-six districts, as nearly equal in population as may be, except that such apportionment shall include as one district the Osage Indian Reservation, and the governor, the chief justice, and the secretary of the Territory of Oklahoma shall appoint an election commissioner who shall establish voting precincts in said Osage Indian Reservation, and shall appoint the judges for election in said Osage Indian Reservation; and two delegates shall be elected from said Osage district; and the Commissioner to the Five Civilized Tribes, and two judges of the United States courts for the Indian Territory, to be designated by the President, shall constitute a board, which shall apportion the said Indian Territory into fifty-five districts, as nearly equal in population as may be, and one delegate shall be elected from each of said districts; and the governor of said Oklahoma Territory, together with the judge senior in service of the United States courts in Indian Territory, shall, by proclamation in which such apportionment shall be fully specified and announced, order an election of the delegates aforesaid in said proposed State at a time designated by them within six months after the approval of this Act, which proclamation shall be issued at least sixty days prior to the time of holding said election of delegates. The election for delegates in the Territory of Oklahoma and in said Indian Territory shall be conducted, the returns made, the result ascertained, and the certificates of all persons elected to such convention issued in the same manner as is prescribed by the laws of the Territory of Oklahoma regulating elections for Delegates to Congress. That the election laws of the Territory of Oklahoma now in force, as far as applicable and not in conflict with this Act, including the penal laws of said Territory of Oklahoma relating to elections and illegal voting, are hereby extended to and put in force in said Indian Territory until the legislature of said proposed State shall otherwise provide, and until all persons offending against said laws in the election aforesaid shall have been dealt with in the manner therein provided. And the United States courts of said Indian Territory shall have the same power to enforce the laws of the Territory of Oklahoma, hereby extended to and put in force in said Territory, as have the courts of the Territory of Oklahoma: *Provided, however,* That said board to apportion districts in Indian Territory shall, for the purpose of said election, appoint an election commissioner for each district who shall distribute all ballots and election supplies to the several precincts in his district, receive the election returns from the judges in precincts, and deliver the same to the canvassing board herein named, establish and define the necessary election precincts, and appoint three judges of election for each precinct, not more than two of whom shall be of the same political party, which judges may appoint the necessary clerk or clerks; that said judges of election, so appointed, shall supervise the election in their respective precincts, and canvass and make due return of the vote cast, to the election commissioner for said district who shall deliver said returns, poll books, and ballots to said board, which shall constitute the ultimate and final canvassing board of said election, and they shall issue certificates of election to all persons elected to such convention from the various districts of the Indian Territory, and their certificates of election shall be prima facie evidence as to the election of delegates: *Provided further*, That in said Indian Territory and Osage Indian Reservation, nominations for delegate to said constitutional convention may be made by convention, by the Republican, Democratic, and People's Party, or by petition in the manner provided by the laws of the Territory of Oklahoma; and certificates and petitions of nomination in said Indian Territory shall be filed with the districting and canvassing board who shall perform the duties of election commissioner under said law, and shall prepare, print, and distribute all ballots, poll books, and election supplies necessary for the holding of said election under said laws. The capital of said State shall temporarily be at the city of Guthrie, in the present Territory of Oklahoma and shall not be changed therefrom previous to anno Domini nineteen hundred and thirteen, but said capital shall, after said year, be located by the electors of said State at an election to be provided for by the legislature: *Provided, however*, That the legislature of said State, except as shall be necessary for the convenient transaction of the public business of said State at said capital, shall not appropriate any public moneys of the State for the erection of buildings for capitol purposes during such period.

SEC. 3. That the delegates to the convention thus elected shall meet at the seat of government of said Oklahoma Territory on the second Tuesday after their election, excluding the day of election in case such day shall be Tuesday, but they shall not receive compensation for more than sixty days of service, and, after organization, shall declare, on behalf of the people of said proposed State, that they adopt the Constitution of the United States; whereupon the said convention shall, and is hereby authorized to, form a constitution and State government for said proposed State. The constitution shall be republican in form, and make no distinction in civil or political rights on account of race or color, and shall not be repugnant to the Constitution of the United States and the principles of the Declaration of Independence. And said convention shall provide in said constitution—

First. That perfect toleration of religious sentiment shall be secured, and that no inhabitant of said State shall ever be molested in person or property on account of his or her mode of religious worship, and that polygamous or plural marriages are forever prohibited.

Second. That the manufacture, sale, barter, giving away, or otherwise furnishing, except as hereinafter provided, of intoxicating liquors within those parts of said State now known as the Indian Territory and the Osage Indian Reservation and within any other parts of said State which existed as Indian reservations on the first day of January, nineteen hundred and six, is prohibited for a period of twenty-one years from the date of the admission of said State into the Union, and thereafter until the people of said State shall otherwise provide by amendment of said constitution and proper State legislation. Any person, individual or corporate, who shall manufacture, sell, barter, give away, or otherwise furnish any intoxicating liquor of any kind, including beer, ale, and wine, contrary to the provisions of this section, or who shall, within the above-described portions of said State, advertise for sale or solicit the purchase of any such liquors, or who shall ship or in any way convey such liquors from other parts of said State into the portions hereinbefore described, shall be punished, on conviction thereof, by fine not less than fifty dollars and by imprisonment not less than thirty days for each offense: *Provided,* That the legislature may provide by law for one agency under the supervision of said State in each incorporated town of not less than two thousand population in the portions of said State hereinbefore described; and if there be no incorporated town of two thousand population in any county in said portions of said State, such county shall be entitled to have one such agency, for the sale of such liquors for medicinal purposes; and for the sale, for industrial purposes, of alcohol which shall have been denaturized by some process approved by the United States Commissioner of Internal Revenue; and for the sale of alcohol for scientific purposes to such scientific institutions, universities, and colleges as are authorized to procure the same free of tax under the laws of the United States; and for the sale of such liquors to any apothecary who shall have executed an approved bond, in a sum not less than one thousand dollars, conditioned that none of such liquors shall be used or disposed of for any purpose other than in the compounding of prescriptions or other medicines, the sale of which would not subject him to the payment of the special tax required of liquor dealers by the United States, and the payment of such special tax by any person within the parts of said State hereinabove defined shall constitute prima facie evidence of his intention to violate the provisions of this section. No sale shall be made except upon the sworn statement of the applicant in writing setting forth the purpose for which the liquor is to be used, and no sale shall be made for medicinal purposes except sales to apothecaries as hereinabove provided unless such statement shall be accompanied by a bona fide prescription signed by a regular practicing physician, which prescription shall not be filled more than once. Each sale shall be duly registered, and the register thereof, together with the affidavits and prescriptions pertaining thereto, shall be open to inspection by any officer or citizen of said State at all times during business hours. Any person who shall knowingly make a false affidavit for the purpose aforesaid shall be deemed guilty of perjury. Any physician who shall prescribe any such liquor, except for treatment of disease which after his own personal diagnosis he shall deem to require such treatment, shall, upon conviction thereof, be punished for each offense by fine of not less than two hundred dollars or by imprisonment for not less than thirty days, or by both such fine and imprisonment; and any person connected with any such agency who shall be convicted of making any sale or other disposition of liquor contrary to these provisions shall be punished by imprisonment for not less than one year and one day. Upon the admission of said State into the Union these provisions shall be immediately enforceable in the courts of said State.

    Third. That the people inhabiting said proposed State do agree and declare that they forever disclaim all right and title in or to any unappropriated public lands lying within the boundaries thereof, and to all lands lying within said limits owned or held by any Indian, tribe, or nation; and that until the title to any such public land shall have been extinguished by the United States, the same shall be and remain subject to the jurisdiction, disposal, and control of the United States. That land belonging to citizens of the United States residing without the limits of said State shall never be taxed at a higher rate than the land belonging to residents thereof; that no taxes shall be imposed by the State on lands or property belonging to or which may hereafter be purchased by the United States or reserved for its use.

Fourth. That the debts and liabilities of said Territory of Oklahoma shall be assumed and paid by said State.

Fifth. That provisions shall be made for the establishment and maintenance of a system of public schools, which shall be open to all the children of said State and free from sectarian control; and said schools shall always be conducted in English: *Provided,* That nothing herein shall preclude the teaching of other languages in said public schools: *And provided further,* That this shall not be construed to prevent the establishment and maintenance of separate schools for white and colored children.

Sixth. That said State shall never enact any law restricting or abridging the right of suffrage on account of race, color, or previous condition of servitude.

SEC. 4. That in case a constitution and State government shall be formed in compliance with the provisions of this Act the convention forming the same shall provide by ordinance for submitting said constitution to the people of said proposed State for its ratification or rejection at an election to be held at a time fixed in said ordinance, at which election the qualified voters for said proposed State shall vote directly for or against the proposed constitution, and for or against any provisions separately submitted. The returns of said election shall be made to the secretary of the Territory of Oklahoma, who, with the chief justice thereof and the senior judge of the United States court of appeals for the Indian Territory, shall canvass the same; and if a majority of the legal votes cast on that question shall be for the constitution the governor of Oklahoma Territory and the judge senior in service of the United States court of appeals for the Indian Territory shall certify the result to the President of the United States, together with the statement of the votes cast thereon, and upon separate articles or propositions and a copy of said constitution, articles, propositions, and ordinances. And if the constitution and government of said proposed State are republican in form, and if the provisions in this Act have been complied with in the formation thereof, it shall be the duty of the President of the United States, within twenty days from the receipt of the certificate of the result of said election and the statement of votes cast thereon and a copy of said constitution, articles, propositions, and ordinances, to issue his proclamation announcing the result of said election; and thereupon the proposed State of Oklahoma shall be deemed admitted by Congress into the Union, under and by virtue of this Act, on an equal footing with the original States. The original of said constitution, articles, propositions, and ordinances, and the election returns, and a copy of the statement of the votes cast at said election, shall be forwarded and turned over by the secretary of the Territory of Oklahoma to the State authorities of said State.

SEC. 5. That the sum of one hundred thousand dollars, or so much thereof as may be necessary, is hereby appropriated, out of any money in the Treasury not otherwise appropriated, for the defraying of the expenses of the elections provided for in this Act, and said convention, and for the payment of the members thereof, under the same rules and regulations and at the same rates as are now provided by law for the payment of the Territorial legislature of the Territory of Oklahoma, and the disbursements of the money appropriated by this section shall be made by the secretary of the Territory of Oklahoma.

SEC. 6. That until the next general census, or until otherwise provided by law, the said State of Oklahoma shall be entitled to five Representatives in the House of Representatives of the United States, to be elected from the following-described districts, the boundaries of which shall remain the same until the next general census:

That district numbered one shall comprise the counties of Grant, Kay, Garfield, Noble, Pawnee, Kingfisher, Logan, Payne, Lincoln, and the territory comprising the Osage and Kansas Indian reservations.

That district numbered two shall comprise the counties of Oklahoma, Canadian, Blaine, Caddo, Custer, Dewey, Day, Woods, Woodward, and Beaver.

That district numbered three shall (with the exception of that part of the recording district numbered twelve, which is in the Cherokee and Creek nations) comprise all the territory now constituting the Cherokee, Creek, and Seminole nations, and the Indian reservations lying northeast of the Cherokee Nation, within said State.

That district numbered four shall comprise all that territory now constituting the Choctaw Nation, that part of recording district numbered twelve which is in the Cherokee and Creek nations, that part of recording district numbered twenty-five which is in the Chickasaw Nation, and the territory comprising recording districts numbered sixteen, twenty-one, twenty-two, and twenty-six, in the Indian Territory.

That district numbered five shall comprise the counties of Greer, Roger Mills, Kiowa, Washita, Comanche, Cleveland, and Pottawatomie, and the territory comprising recording districts numbered seventeen, eighteen, nineteen, and twenty, in the Chickasaw Nation, Indian Territory.

And the said Representatives, together with the governor and other officers provided for in said constitution, shall be elected on the same day of the election for the ratification or rejection of the constitution; and until said officers are elected and qualified under the provisions of such constitution and the said State is admitted into the Union, the Territorial officers of Oklahoma Territory shall continue to discharge the duties of their respective offices in said Territory.

SEC. 7. That upon the admission of the State into the Union sections numbered sixteen and thirty-six, in every township in Oklahoma Territory, and all indemnity lands heretofore selected in lieu thereof, are hereby granted to the State for the use and benefit of the common schools: *Provided*, That sections sixteen and thirty-six embraced in permanent reservations for national purposes shall not at any time be subject to the grant nor the indemnity provisions of this Act, nor shall any lands embraced in Indian, military, or other reservations of any character, nor shall land owned by Indian tribes or individual members of any tribe be subjected to the grants or to the indemnity provisions of this Act until the reservation shall have been extinguished and such lands be restored to and become a part of the public domain: *Provided*, That there is sufficient untaken public land within said State to cover this grant: *And provided*, That in case any of the lands herein granted to the State of

Oklahoma have heretofore been confirmed to the Territory of Oklahoma for the purposes specified in this Act, the amount so confirmed shall be deducted from the quantity specified in this Act.

There is hereby appropriated, out of any money in the Treasury not otherwise appropriated, the sum of five million dollars for the use and benefit of the common schools of said State in lieu of sections sixteen and thirty-six, and other lands of the Indian Territory. Said appropriation shall be paid by the Treasurer of the United States at such time and to such person or persons as may be authorized by said State to receive the same under laws to be enacted by said State, and until said State shall enact such laws said appropriation shall not be paid, but said State shall be allowed interest thereon at the rate of three per centum per annum, which shall be paid to said State for the use and benefit of its public schools. Said appropriation of five million dollars shall be held and invested by the said State, in trust, for the use and benefit of said schools, and the interest thereon shall be used exclusively in the support and maintenance of said schools: *Provided,* That nothing in this Act contained shall repeal or affect any Act of Congress relating to the Sulphur Springs Reservation as now defined or as may be hereafter defined or extended, or the power of the United States over it or any other lands embraced in the State hereafter set aside by Congress as a national park, game preserve, or for the preservation of objects of archaeological or ethnological interest; and nothing contained in this Act shall interfere with the rights and ownership of the United States in any land hereafter set aside by Congress as national park, game preserve, or other reservation, or in the said Sulphur Springs Reservation, as it now is or may be hereafter defined or extended by law; but exclusive legislation, in all cases whatsoever, shall be exercised by the United States, which shall have exclusive control and jurisdiction over the same; but nothing in this proviso contained shall be construed to prevent the service within said Sulphur Springs Reservation or national parks, game preserves, and other reservations hereafter established by law, of civil and criminal processes lawfully issued by the authority of said State, and said State shall not be entitled to select indemnity school lands for the thirteenth, sixteenth, thirty-third, and thirty-sixth sections that may be embraced within the metes and bounds of the national park, game preserve, and other reservation or the said Sulphur Springs Reservation, as now defined or may be hereafter defined.

SEC. 8. That section thirteen in the Cherokee Outlet, the Tonkawa Indian Reservation, and the Pawnee Indian Reservation, reserved by the President of the United States by proclamation issued August nineteenth, eighteen hundred and ninety-three, opening to settlement the said lands, and by any Act or Acts of Congress since said date, and section thirteen in all other lands which have been or may be opened to settlement in the Territory of Oklahoma, and all lands heretofore selected in lieu thereof, is hereby reserved and granted to said State for the use and benefit of the University of Oklahoma and the University Preparatory School, one-third; of the normal schools now established or hereafter to be established, one-third; and of the Agricultural and Mechanical College and the Colored Agricultural Normal University, one-third. The said lands or the proceeds thereof as above apportioned shall be divided between the institutions as the legislature of said State may prescribe: *Provided,* That the said lands so reserved or the proceeds of the sale thereof shall be safely kept or invested and held by said State, and the income thereof, interest, rentals, or otherwise, only shall be used exclusively for the benefit of said educational institutions. Such educational institutions shall remain under the exclusive control of said State, and no part of the proceeds arising from the sale or disposal of any lands herein granted for educational purposes, or the income or rentals thereof, shall be used for the support of any religious or sectarian school, college, or university.

That section thirty-three, and all lands heretofore selected in lieu thereof, heretofore reserved under said proclamation, and Acts for charitable and penal institutions and public buildings, shall be apportioned and disposed of as the legislature of said State may prescribe.

Where any part of the lands granted by this Act to the State of Oklahoma are valuable for minerals, which terms shall also include gas and oil, such lands shall not be sold by the said State prior to January first, nineteen hundred and fifteen; but the same may be leased for periods not exceeding five years by the State officers duly authorized for that purpose, such leasing to be made by public competition after not less than thirty days' advertisement in the manner to be prescribed by law, and all such leasing shall be done under sealed bids and awarded to the highest responsible bidder. The leasing shall require and the advertisement shall specify in each case a fixed royalty to be paid by the successful bidder, in addition to any bonus offered for the lease, and all proceeds from leases shall be covered into the fund to which they shall properly belong, and no transfer or assignment of any lease shall be valid or confer any right in the assignee without the consent of the proper State authorities in writing: *Provided, however,* That agricultural lessees in possession of such lands shall be reimbursed by the mining lessees for all damage done to said agricultural lessees' interest therein by reason of such mining operations. The legislature of the State may prescribe additional legislation governing such leases not in conflict herewith.

SEC. 9. That said sections sixteen and thirty-six, and lands taken in lieu thereof, herein granted for the support of the common schools, if sold, may be appraised and sold at public sale in one hundred and sixty acre tracts or less, under such rules and regulations as the legislature of the said State may prescribe, preference right to purchase at the highest bid being given to the lessee at the time of such sale, the proceeds to constitute a permanent school fund, the interest of which only shall be expended in the support of such schools. But said lands may, under such regulations as the legislature may prescribe, be leased for periods not to exceed ten years; and such lands shall not be subject to homestead entry or any other entry under the land laws of the United States, whether surveyed or unsurveyed, but shall be reserved for school purposes only.

SEC. 10. That said sections thirteen and thirty-three, aforesaid, if sold, may be appraised and sold at public sale, in one hundred and sixty acre tracts or less, under such rules and regulations as the legislature of said State may prescribe, preference right to purchase at the highest bid being given to the lessee at the time of such sale, but such lands may be leased for periods of not more than five years, under such rules and regulations as the legislature shall prescribe, and until such time as the legislature shall prescribe such rules these and all other lands granted to the State shall be leased under existing rules and regulations, and shall not be subject to homestead entry or any other entry under the land laws of the United States, whether surveyed or unsurveyed, but shall be reserved for designated purposes only, and until such time as the legislature shall prescribe as aforesaid such lands shall be leased under existing rules: *Provided*, That before any of the said lands shall be sold, as provided in sections nine and ten of this Act, the said lands and the improvements thereon shall be appraised by three disinterested appraisers, who shall be non-residents of the county wherein the land is situated, to be designated as the legislature of said State shall prescribe, and the said appraisers shall make a true appraisement of said lands at the actual cash value thereof, exclusive of improvements, and shall separately appraise all permanent improvements thereon at their fair and reasonable value, and in case the leaseholder does not become the purchaser, the purchaser at said sale shall, under such rules and regulations as the legislature may prescribe, pay to or for the leaseholder the appraised value of said improvements, and to the State the amount bid for the said lands, exclusive of the appraised value of improvements; and at said sale no bid for any tract at less than the appraisement thereof shall be accepted.

SEC. 11. That an amount equal to five per centum of the proceeds of the sales of public lands lying within said State shall be paid to the said State, to be used as a permanent fund, the interest only of which shall be expended for the support of the common schools within said State.

SEC. 12. That in lieu of the grant of land for purposes of internal improvement made to new States by the eighth section of the Act of September fourth, eighteen hundred and forty-one, which section is hereby repealed as to said State, and in lieu of any claim or demand of the State of Oklahoma under the Act of September twenty-eighth, eighteen hundred and fifty, and section twenty-four hundred and seventy-nine of the Revised Statutes, making a grant of swamp and overflowed lands, which grant it is hereby declared is not extended to said State of Oklahoma, the following grant of land is hereby made to said State from public lands of the United States within said State, for the purposes indicated, namely: For the benefit of the Oklahoma University, two hundred and fifty thousand acres; for the benefit of the University Preparatory School, one hundred and fifty thousand acres; for the benefit of the Agricultural and Mechanical College, two hundred and fifty thousand acres; for the benefit of the Colored Agricultural and Normal University, one hundred thousand acres; for the benefit of normal schools, now established or hereafter to be established, three hundred thousand acres. The lands granted by this section shall be selected by the board for leasing school lands of the Territory of Oklahoma immediately upon the approval of this Act. Said selections as soon as made shall be certified to the Secretary of the Interior, and the lands so selected shall be thereupon withdrawn from homestead entry.

SEC. 13. That said State when admitted as aforesaid shall constitute two judicial districts, to be known as the eastern district of Oklahoma and the western district of Oklahoma; the said Indian Territory shall constitute said eastern district, and the said Oklahoma Territory shall constitute said western district. The circuit and district courts for the eastern district shall be held one term at Muscogee, one term at Vinita, one term at Tulsa, one term at South McAlester, one term at Chickasha, and one term at Ardmore, each year, and the circuit and district courts of the western district shall be held one term at Guthrie, one term at Oklahoma City, and one term at Enid, and one term at Lawton, each year, for the time being. And the said districts shall, for judicial purposes, until otherwise provided, be attached to the eighth judicial circuit. There shall be appointed for each of said districts one district judge, one United States attorney, and one United States marshal. There shall be appointed a clerk for each of said districts, who shall keep his office at Muscogee and Guthrie, respectively, for the time being. The regular term of said courts shall be held at the places designated in this Act, at Muscogee on the first Monday in January and at Vinita on the first Monday in March and at Tulsa on the first first Monday in April; at South McAlester on the first Monday in June; at Ardmore on the first Monday in October; at Chickasha on the first Monday of November; at Guthrie on the first Monday in January; at Oklahoma City on the first Monday in March; at Enid on the first Monday in June, and at Lawton on the first Monday in October, in each year, and one grand jury shall be summoned in each year in each of said circuit and district courts. The circuit and district courts for each of said districts, and the judges thereof, respectively, shall possess the same powers and jurisdiction and perform the same duties required to be performed by the other circuit and district courts and judges of the United States, and shall be governed by the same laws and regulations. The marshal, district attorney, and clerk of each of the circuit and district courts of said districts, and all other officers and persons performing duties in the administration of justice therein, shall severally possess the powers and perform the duties lawfully required to be performed by similar officers in other districts of the United States, and shall, for the services they may perform, receive the fees and compensation now allowed by law to officers performing similar services for the United States in other districts of the United States; and that the laws in force in the Territory of Oklahoma, as far as applicable, shall extend over and apply to said State until change by the legislature thereof.

SEC. 14. That all prosecutions for crimes or offenses hereafter committed in either of said judicial districts as hereby constituted shall be cognizable within the district in which committed, and all prosecutions for crimes or offenses committed before the passage of this Act in which indictments have not yet been found or proceedings instituted shall be cognizable within the judicial district as hereby constituted in which such crimes or offenses were committed.

SEC. 15. That all appeals or writs of error taken from the supreme court of Oklahoma Territory, or the United States court of appeals in the Indian Territory to the Supreme Court of the United States or the United States circuit court of appeals for the eighth circuit, previous to the final admission of such State shall be prosecuted to final determination as though this Act had not been passed. And all cases in which final judgement has been rendered in such Territorial appellate courts which appeals or writs of error might be had except for the admission of such State may still be sued out, taken, and prosecuted to the Supreme Court of the United States or the United States circuit court of appeals under the provisions of existing laws, and there held and determined in like manner, and in either case the Supreme Court of the United States, or the

United States circuit court of appeals, in the event of reversal shall remand the said causes to either the State supreme court or other final appellate court of said State, or the United States circuit and district courts of said State, as the case may require: *Provided,* That the time allowed by existing law for appeals and writs of error from appellate courts of said Territories shall not be enlarged hereby, and all appeals and writs of error not sued out from the final judgements of said courts at the time of the admission of such State shall be taken within six months from such time.

SEC. 16. That all causes pending in the supreme and district courts of Oklahoma Territory and in the United States courts and in the United States court of appeals in the Indian Territory arising under the Constitution, laws, or treaties of the United States, or affecting ambassadors, ministers, or consuls of the United States, or of any country or State, or of admiralty or of maritime jurisdiction, or in which the United States may be a party, or between citizens of the same State claiming lands under grants from different States; and in all cases where there is a controversy between citizens of said Territories prior to admission and citizens of different States, or between citizens of different States, or between a citizen of any State and citizens or subjects of any foreign State or country, and in which cases of diversity of citizenship there shall be more than two thousand dollars in controversy, exclusive of interest and costs, shall be transferred to the proper United States circuit or district court for final disposition: *Provided,* That said transfer shall not be made in any case where the United States is not a party except on application of one of the parties in the court in which the cause is pending, at or before the second term of such court, after the admission of said State, supported by oath, showing that the case is one which may be so transferred, the proceedings to effect such transfer, except as to time and parties, to be the same as are now provided by law for the removal of causes from a State court to a circuit court of the United States; and in causes transferred from the appellate courts of said Territories the circuit court of the United States in such State shall first determine such appellate matters as the successor of and with all the power of said Territorial appellate courts, and shall thereafter proceed under its original jurisdiction of such causes. All final judgments and decrees rendered in such circuit and district courts in such transferred cases may be reviewed by the Supreme Court of the United States or by the United States circuit court of appeals in the same manner as is now provided by law with reference to existing United States circuit and district courts.

SEC. 17. That all causes pending in the supreme court of said Territory of Oklahoma and in the United States court of appeals in the Indian Territory not transferred to the United States circuit and district courts in said State of Oklahoma shall be proceeded with, held, and determined by the supreme or other final appellate court of such State as the successor of said Territorial supreme court and appellate court, subject to the same right to review upon appeal or error to the Supreme Court of the United States now allowed from the supreme or appellate courts of a State under existing laws. Jurisdiction of all cases pending in the courts of original jurisdiction in said Territories not transferred to the United States circuit and district courts shall devolve upon and be exercised by the courts of original jurisdiction created by said State.

SEC. 18. That the supreme court or other court of last resort of said State shall be deemed to be the successor of said Territorial appellate courts and shall take and possess any and all jurisdiction as such, not herein otherwise specifically provided for, and shall receive and retain the custody of all books, dockets, records, and files not transferred to other courts, as herein provided, subject to the duty to furnish transcripts of all book entries in any specific case transferred to complete the record thereof.

SEC. 19. That the courts of original jurisdiction of such State shall be deemed to be the successor of all courts of original jurisdiction of said Territories and as such shall take and retain custody of all records, dockets, journals, and files of such courts except in cases transferred therefrom, as herein provided; the files and papers in such transferred cases shall be transferred to the proper United States circuit or district court, together with a transcript of all book entries to complete the record in such particular case so transferred.

SEC. 20. That all cases pending in the district courts of Oklahoma Territory and in the United States courts for the Indian Territory at the time said Territories become a State not transferred to the United States circuit or district courts in the State of Oklahoma shall be proceeded with, held, and determined by the courts of said State, the successors of said district courts of the Territory of Oklahoma and United States courts for the Indian Territory, with the right to prosecute appeals or writs of error to the supreme court of said State, and also with the same right to prosecute appeals or writs of error from the final determination in said cases made by the supreme court of said State of Oklahoma to the Supreme Court of the United States, as now provided by law for appeals and writs of error from the supreme court of a State to the Supreme Court of the United States.

SEC. 21. That the constitutional convention may by ordinance provide for the election of officers for a full State government, including members of the legislature and five Representatives to Congress, and shall constitute the Osage Indian Reservation a separate county, and provide that it shall remain a separate county until the lands in the Osage Indian Reservation are allotted in severalty and until changed by the legislature of Oklahoma, and designate the county seat thereof, and shall provide rules and regulations and define the manner of conducting the first election for officers in said county. Such State government shall remain in abeyance until the State shall be admitted into the Union and the election for State officers held, as provided for in this Act. The State legislature when organized shall elect two Senators of the United States, in the manner now prescribed by the laws of the United States, and the governor and secretary of said State shall certify the election of the Senators and Representatives in the manner required by law; and said Senators and Representatives shall be entitled to be admitted to seats in Congress and to all the rights and privileges of Senators and Representatives of other States in the Congress of the United States. And the officers of the State government formed in pursuance of said constitution, as provided by said constitutional convention, shall proceed to exercise all the functions of such State officers; and all laws in force in the Territory of Oklahoma at the time of the admission of said State into the Union shall be in force throughout said State, except as modified or changed by this Act or by the constitution of the State, and the laws of the

United States not locally inapplicable shall have the same force and effect within said State as elsewhere within the United States.

SEC. 22. That the constitutional convention provided for herein shall, by ordinance irrevocable, accept the terms and conditions of this Act.

SEC. 23. That the inhabitants of all that part of the area of the United States now constituting the Territories of Arizona and New Mexico, as at present described, may become the State of Arizona, as hereinafter provided.

SEC. 24. That at the general election to be held on the sixth day of November, nineteen hundred and six, all the electors of said Territories, respectively, qualified to vote at such election, are hereby authorized to vote for and choose delegates to form a convention for said Territories. The aforesaid convention shall consist of one hundred and ten delegates, sixty-six of which delegates shall be elected to said convention by the people of the Territory of New Mexico and forty-four by the people of the Territory of Arizona; and the governors, chief justices, and secretaries of each of said Territories, respectively, shall apportion the delegates to be thus elected from their respective Territories, as nearly as may be, equitably among the several counties thereof in accordance with the voting population as shown by the vote cast for Delegate in Congress in the respective Territories in nineteen hundred and four.

That at the said general election and on the same ballots on which the names of candidates to the convention aforesaid are printed, there shall be submitted to said qualified electors of each of said Territories a question which shall be stated on the ballot in substance and form as follows:

"Shall Arizona and New Mexico be united to form one State?"

☐ Yes. ☐ No.

Electors desiring to vote in the affirmative shall place a cross mark in the square to the left of the word "Yes," and those desiring to vote in the negative shall place a cross mark in the square to the left of the word "No" in the form above prescribed. The governors and secretaries of the respective Territories shall certify and transmit, as soon as may be practicable, the results of said election each to the other and likewise to the Secretary of the Interior, and if it appears from the returns thus certified that a majority of the qualified electors in each of said Territories who voted on the question aforesaid at such election voted in favor of the union of New Mexico and Arizona as one State, then, and not otherwise, the inhabitants of that part of the area of the United States now constituting the Territories of Arizona and New Mexico as at present described may become the State of Arizona as hereinafter provided; but if in either of said Territories a majority of the qualified electors voting on the question aforesaid at such election shall appear by such certified returns to have voted against the union of said Territories then, and in that event, section twenty-three and all succeeding sections of this Act shall thereafter be null and void and of no effect, excepting that the appropriation made in section forty-one hereof shall be and remain available for defraying all and every kind and character of expense incurred on account of the election of delegates to the convention and the submission of the question aforesaid.

The governors of said Territories, respectively, shall, within thirty days after the approval of this Act, by proclamation in which the aforesaid apportionment of delegates to the convention shall be fully specified and announced and the aforesaid question to be voted on by the electors shall be clearly stated, order that the delegates aforesaid in their respective Territories shall be voted for and the question aforesaid shall be submitted to the qualified electors in each of said Territories as herein required at the aforesaid general election. Such election for delegates shall be conducted, the returns made and the certificates of persons elected to such convention issued, as near as may be in the same manner as is prescribed by the laws of said Territories, respectively, regulating elections therein of members of the legislature: *Provided,* That if it appears from the returns that a majority of the qualified electors in the Territory of Arizona who voted on the question at the election voted in favor of the union of New Mexico and Arizona as one State, then, and not otherwise, the secretary or other proper officer of the said Territory of Arizona into whose hands the result of said election finally comes, shall immediately transmit and certify the result as to the election of delegates to the convention to the secretary of the Territory of New Mexico at Santa Fe, and if it appears from the returns from the election held in New Mexico that a majority of the qualified voters aforesaid voted in favor of joint statehood, then in that event the secretary of said Territory of New Mexico shall make up a temporary roll of the convention from the certified returns from both of said Territories, and he shall call the convention to order at the time herein required, and said convention when so called to order and organized shall be the sole judge of the election and qualifications of its own members. Persons possessing the qualifications entitling them to vote at the aforesaid general election shall be entitled to vote on the ratification or rejection of the constitution if submitted to the people of said Territories hereunder, and on the election of all officials whose election is taking place at the same time, under such rules and regulations as said convention may prescribe, not in conflict with this Act.

SEC. 25. That if a majority in each of said Territories at the election aforesaid shall vote for joint statehood, and not otherwise, the delegates to the convention thus elected shall meet in the hall of the house of representatives of the Territory of New Mexico, in the city of Santa Fe therein, at twelve o'clock noon on Monday, December third, nineteen hundred and six, but they shall not receive compensation for more than sixty days of service, and after organization shall declare on behalf of the people of said proposed State that they adopt the Constitution of the United States, whereupon the said convention shall be, and is hereby, authorized to form a constitution and State government for said proposed State. The constitution shall be republican in form, and make no distinction in civil or political rights on account of race or color, except as to Indians not taxed, and shall not be repugnant to the Constitution of the United States and the principles of the Declaration of Independence. And said convention shall provide, by ordinance irrevocable without the consent of the United States and the people of said State—

First. That perfect toleration of religious sentiment shall be secured, and that no inhabitants of said State shall ever be molested in person or property on account of his or her mode of religious worship; and that polygamous or plural marriages and the sale, barter, or giving of intoxicating liquors to Indians are forever prohibited.

Second. That the people inhabiting said proposed State do agree and declare that they forever disclaim all right and title to the unappropriated and ungranted public lands lying within the boundaries thereof and to all lands lying within said limits owned or held by any Indian or Indian tribes, except as hereinafter provided, and that until the title thereto shall have been extinguished by the United States the same shall be and remain subject to the disposition of the United States, and such Indian lands shall remain under the absolute jurisdiction and control of the Congress of the United States; that the lands and other property belonging to citizens of the United States residing without the said State shall never be taxed at a higher rate than the lands and other property belonging to residents thereof; that no taxes shall be imposed by the State on lands or property therein belonging to or which may hereafter be purchased by the United States or reserved for its use; but nothing herein, or in the ordinance herein provided for, shall preclude the said State from taxing, as other lands and other property are taxed, any lands and other property owned or held by any Indian who has severed his tribal relations and has obtained from the United States or from any person a title thereto by patent or other grant, save and except such lands as have been or may be granted to any Indian or Indians under any Act of Congress containing a provision exempting the lands thus granted from taxation, but said ordinance shall provide that all such lands shall be exempt from taxation by said State so long and to such extent as such Act of Congress may prescribe.

Third. That the debts and liabilities of said Territory of Arizona and of said Territory of New Mexico shall be assumed and paid by said State, and that said State shall be subrogated to all the rights of indemnity and reimbursement which either of said Territories now has.

Fourth. That provision shall be made for the establishment and maintenance of a system of public schools, which shall be open to all the children of said State and free from sectarian control; and that said schools shall always be conducted in English: *Provided*, That nothing in this Act shall preclude the teaching of other languages in said public schools.

Fifth. That said State shall never enact any law restricting or abridging the right of suffrage on account of race, color, or previous condition or servitude, and that ability to read, write, and speak the English language sufficiently well to conduct the duties of the office without the aid of an interpreter shall be a necessary qualification for all State officers.

Sixth. That the capital of said State shall temporarily be at the city of Santa Fe, in the present Territory of New Mexico, and shall not be changed therefrom previous to anno Domini nineteen hundred and fifteen, but the permanent location of said capital may, after said year, be fixed by the electors of said State, voting at an election to be provided for by the legislature.

SEC. 26. That in case a constitution and State government shall be formed in compliance with the provisions of this Act, the convention forming the same shall provide by ordinance for submitting said constitution to the people of said proposed State for its ratification or rejection, at an election to be held at a time fixed in said ordinance, which shall be not less than sixty days nor more than ninety days from the adjournment of the convention, at which election the qualified voters of said proposed State shall vote directly for or against the proposed constitution and for or against any provisions thereof separately submitted. The returns of said election shall be made by the election officers direct to the secretary of the Territory of New Mexico at Santa Fe; who, with the governors and chief justices of said Territories, or any four of them, shall meet at said city of Santa Fe on the third Monday after said election and shall canvass the same; and if a majority of the legal votes on that question shall be for the constitution the said canvassing board shall certify the result to the President of the United States, together with the statement of the votes cast thereon, and upon separate articles or propositions, and a copy of said constitution, articles, propositions, and ordinances. And if the constitution and government of said proposed State are republican in form, and if the provisions in this Act have been complied with in the formation thereof, it shall be the duty of the President of the United States, within twenty days from the receipt of the certificate of the result of said election and the statement of the votes cast thereon and a copy of said constitution, articles, propositions, and ordinances from said board, to issue his proclamation announcing the result of said election, and thereupon the proposed State shall be deemed admitted by Congress into the Union, under and by virtue of this Act, under the name of Arizona, on an equal footing with the original States, from and after the date of said proclamation.

The original of said constitution, articles, propositions, and ordinances, and the election returns, and a copy of the statement of the votes cast at said election shall be forwarded and turned over by the secretary of the Territory of New Mexico to the State authorities.

SEC. 27. That until the next general census, or until otherwise provided by law, said State shall be entitled to two Representatives in the House of Representatives of the United States, which Representatives, together with the governor and other officers provided for in said constitution, and also all other State and county officers, shall be elected on the same day of the election for the adoption of the constitution; and until said State officers are elected and qualified under the provisions of the constitution, and the State is admitted into the Union, the Territorial officers of said Territories, respectively, including delegates to Congress, shall continue to discharge the duties of their respective offices in said Territories until their successors are duly elected and qualified.

SEC. 28. That upon the admission of said State into the Union there is hereby granted unto it, including the sections thereof heretofore granted, four sections of public land in each township in the proposed State for the support of free public nonsectarian common schools, to wit: Sections numbered thirteen, sixteen, thirty-three, and thirty-six, and where such sections or any parts thereof have been sold or otherwise disposed of by or under the authority of any Act of Congress other lands equivalent thereto, in legal subdivisions of not less than one quarter section and as contiguous as may be to the section in lieu of which the same is taken; such indemnity lands to be selected within said respective portions of said State in the manner provided in this Act: *Provided*, That the thirteenth, sixteenth, thirty-third, and thirty-sixth sections embraced in permanent reservations for national purposes shall not at any time be subject to the grants nor to the indemnity provisions of this Act, but other lands equivalent thereto may be selected for such school purposes in lieu thereof; nor shall any lands embraced in Indian, military, or other reservations of any character be subject to the grants of this Act, but such reservation lands shall be subject to the indemnity provisions of this Act: *Provided*, That nothing in this Act contained shall repeal or affect any Act of Congress relating to the Casa Grande Ruin as now defined or as may be hereafter defined or extended, or the power of the United States over it, or any other lands embraced in the State hereafter set aside by Congress as a national park, game preserve, or for the preservation of objects of archaeological or ethnological interest; and nothing contained in this Act shall interfere with the rights and ownership of the United States in any land hereafter set aside by Congress as national park, game preserve, or other reservation, or in the said Casa Grande Ruin as it now is or may be hereafter defined or extended by law, but exclusive legislation, in all cases whatsoever, shall be exercised by the United States, which shall have exclusive control and jurisdiction over the same; but nothing in this proviso contained shall be construed to prevent the service within said Casa Grande Ruin, or national parks, game preserves, and other reservations hereafter established by law, of civil and criminal processes lawfully issued by the authority of said State; and said lands shall not be subject at any time to the school grants of this Act that may be embraced within the metes and bounds of the national park, game preserve, and other reservation, or the said Casa Grande Ruin, as now defined or may be hereafter defined; but other lands equivalent thereto may be selected for such school purposes hereinbefore provided in lieu thereof.

SEC. 29. That three hundred sections of the unappropriated nonmineral public lands within said State, to be selected and located in legal subdivisions, as provided in this Act, are hereby granted to said State for the purpose of erecting legislative, executive, and judicial public buildings in the same, and for the payment of the bonds heretofore or hereafter issued therefor.

SEC. 30. That the lands granted to the Territory of Arizona by the Act of February eighteenth, eighteen hundred and eighty-one, entitled "An Act to grant lands to Dakota, Montana, Arizona, Idaho, and Wyoming for university purposes," are hereby vested in the proposed State to the extent of the full quantity of seventy-five sections, and any portion of said lands that may not have been selected by said Territory of Arizona may be selected by the said State. In addition to the foregoing, and in addition to all lands heretofore granted for such purpose, there shall be, and hereby is, granted to said State, to take effect when the same is admitted to the Union, three hundred sections of land, to be selected from the public domain within said State in the same manner as provided in this Act, and the proceeds of all such lands shall constitute a permanent fund, to be safely invested and held by said State, and the income thereof be used exclusively for university purposes. The schools, colleges, and universities provided for in this Act shall forever remain under the exclusive control of the said State, and no part of the proceeds arising from the sale or disposal of any lands herein granted for educational purposes shall be used for the support of any sectarian or denominational school, college or university.

SEC. 31. That nothing in this Act shall be so construed, except where the same is so specifically stated, as to repeal any grant of land heretofore made by any Act of Congress to either of said Territories, but such grants are hereby ratified and confirmed in and to said State, and all of the land that may not, at the time of the admission of said State into the Union, have been selected and segregated from the public domain, may be so selected and segregated in the manner provided in this Act.

SEC. 32. That five per centum of the proceeds of the sales of public lands lying within said State which shall be sold by the United States subsequent to the admission of said State into the Union, after deducting all the expenses incident to the same, shall be paid to the said State to be used as a permanent fund, the interest of which only shall be expended for the support of the common schools within said State. And there is hereby appropriated, out of any moneys in the Treasury not otherwise appropriated, the sum of five million dollars for the use and benefit of the common schools of said State. Said appropriation shall be paid by the Treasurer of the United States at such time and to such person or persons as may be authorized by said State to receive the same under laws to be enacted by said State, and until said State shall enact such laws said appropriation shall not be paid. Said appropriation of five million dollars shall be held inviolable and invested by said State, in trust, for the use and benefit of said schools.

SEC. 33. That all lands herein granted for educational purposes may be appraised and disposed of only at public sale, the proceeds to constitute a permanent school fund, the income from which only shall be expended in the support of said schools. But said lands may, under such regulations as the legislature shall prescribe, be leased for periods of not more than ten years, and such common school land shall not be subject to preemption, homestead entry, or any other entry under the land laws of the United States, whether surveyed or unsurveyed, but shall be reserved for school purposes only.

SEC. 34. That in lieu of the grant of land for purposes of internal improvement made to new States by the eighth section of the Act of September fourth, eighteen hundred and forty-one, which section is hereby repealed as to the proposed State, and in lieu of any claim or demand by the said State under the Act of September twenty-eighth, eighteen hundred and fifty, and section twenty-four hundred and seventy-nine of the Revised Statutes, making a grant of swamp and overflowed lands to certain States, which grant it is hereby declared is not extended to the said State, and in lieu of any grant of saline lands to said State, save as heretofore made, the following grants of land from public lands of the United States within said State are hereby made, to wit:

For the establishment and maintenance and support of insane asylums in the said State, two hundred thousand acres; for penitentiaries, two hundred thousand acres; for schools for the deaf, dumb, and the blind, two hundred thousand acres; for miners' hospitals for disabled miners, one hundred thousand acres; for normal schools, two hundred thousand acres; for State charitable, penal, and reformatory institutions, two hundred thousand acres; for agricultural and mechanical colleges, three hundred thousand acres: *Provided,* That the two national appropriations heretofore annually paid to the two agricultural and mechanical colleges of said Territories, respectively, shall, until the further order of Congress, continue to be paid to said State for the use of said respective institutions; for schools of mines, two hundred thousand acres; for military institutes, two hundred thousand acres.

SEC. 35. That all lands granted in quantity or as indemnity by this Act shall be selected, under the direction of the Secretary of the Interior, from the unappropriated public lands of the United States within the limits of the said State, by a commission composed of the governor, surveyor-general, and attorney-general of said State; and no fees shall be charged for passing the title to the same or for the preliminary proceedings thereof.

SEC. 36. That all mineral lands shall be exempted from the grants made by this Act; but if any portion thereof shall be found by the Department of the Interior to be mineral lands, said State, by the commission provided for in section thirty-five hereof, under the direction of the Secretary of the Interior, is hereby authorized and empowered to select, in legal subdivisions, an equal quantity of other unappropriated lands in said State in lieu thereof.

SEC. 37. That the said State, when admitted as aforesaid, shall constitute two judicial districts, to be named, respectively, the eastern and western districts of Arizona, the boundaries of said districts to be the same as the boundaries of said Territories, respectively, and the circuit and district court of said districts shall be held, respectively, at Albuquerque and Phoenix for the time being, and the said districts shall, for judicial purposes, until otherwise provided, be attached to the ninth judicial circuit. There shall be appointed for each of said districts one district judge, one United States attorney, and one United States marshal. The judge of each of said districts shall receive a yearly salary the same as other similar judges of the United States, payable as provided for by law, and shall reside in the district to which he is appointed. There shall be appointed clerks of said courts, who shall keep their offices at said Albuquerque and Phoenix in said State. The regular terms of said courts shall be held in said districts, at the places aforesaid, on the first Monday in April and the first Monday in November of each year, and one grand jury shall be summoned in each year in each of said circuit and district courts. The circuit and district courts for said districts, and the judges thereof, respectively, shall possess the same powers and jurisdiction and perform the same duties required to be performed by the other circuit and district courts and judges of the United States, and shall be governed by the same laws and regulations. The marshal, district attorney, and clerks of the circuit and district courts of said districts, and all other officers and persons performing duties in the administration of justice therein, shall severally possess the powers and perform the duties lawfully possessed and required to be performed by similar officers in other districts of the United States, and shall, for the services they may perform, receive the fees and compensation now allowed by law to officers performing similar services for the United States in the Territories of Arizona and New Mexico, respectively.

SEC. 38. That all cases of appeal or writ of error heretofore prosecuted and now pending in the Supreme Court of the United States upon any record from the supreme court of either of said Territories, or that may hereafter lawfully be prosecuted upon any record from said courts, may be heard and determined by said Supreme Court of the United States. And the mandate of execution or of further proceedings shall be directed by the Supreme Court of the United States to the circuit or district courts, respectively, hereby established within the said State or to the supreme court of such State, as the nature of the case may require. And the circuit, district, and State courts herein named shall, respectively, be the successors of the supreme courts of the said Territories as to all such cases arising within the limits of embraced within the jurisdiction of such courts, respectively, with full power to proceed with the same and award mesne or final process therein; and that from all judgments and decrees of the supreme courts of the said Territories mentioned in this Act, in any case arising within the limits of the proposed State prior to admission, the parties to such judgment shall have the same right to prosecute appeals and writs of error to the Supreme Court of the United States or to the circuit court of appeals as they shall have had by law prior to the admission of said State into the Union.

SEC. 39. That in respect to all cases, proceedings, and matters now pending in the supreme or district courts of the said Territories at the time of the admission into the Union of the said State, and arising within the limits of such State, whereof the circuit or district courts by this Act established might have had jurisdiction under the laws of the United States had such courts existed at the time of the commencement of such cases, the said circuit and district courts, respectively, shall be the successors of said supreme and district courts of said Territories, respectively; and in respect to all other cases, proceedings, and matters pending in the supreme or district courts of the said Territories at the time of the admission of such Territories into the Union, arising within the limits of said State, the courts established by such State shall, respectively, be the successors of said supreme and district Territorial courts; and all the files, records, indictments, and proceedings relating to any such cases shall be transferred to such circuit, district, and State courts, respectively, and the same shall be proceeded with therein in due course of law; but no writ, action, indictment, cause, or proceeding now pending, or that prior to the admission of the State shall be pending, in any Territorial court in said Territories shall abate by the admission of such State into the Union, but the same shall be transferred and proceeded with in the proper United States circuit, district, or State court, as the case may be: *Provided, however,* That in all civil actions, causes, and proceedings in which the United States is not a party transfers shall not be made to the circuit and district courts of the United States except upon cause shown by written request of one of the parties to such action or proceeding filed in the proper court; and in the absence of such request such cases shall be proceeded with in the proper State courts.

SEC. 40. That the constitutional convention shall by ordinance provide for the election of officers for a full State government, including members of the legislature and two Representatives in Congress, at the time for the election for the ratification or rejection of the constitution; one of which Representatives shall be chosen from a Congressional district comprised of the present territory of Arizona, to be known as the First Congressional district, and the other from a Congressional district comprised of the remainder of said State, to be known as the Second Congressional district; but the said State government shall remain in abeyance until the State shall be admitted into the Union as proposed by this Act. In case the constitution of said State shall be ratified by a majority of the qualified voters of said Territories voting at the election held therefor as hereinbefore provided, but not otherwise, the legislature thereof may assemble at Santa Fe, organize, and elect two Senators of the United States in the manner now prescribed by the laws of the United States; and the governor and secretary of state of the proposed State shall certify the election of the Senators and Representatives in the manner required by law, and when such State is admitted into the Union, as provided in this Act, the Senators and Representatives shall be entitled to be admitted to seats in Congress and to all rights and privileges of Senators and Representatives of other States in the Congress of the United States; and the officers of the State government formed in pursuance of said constitution, as provided by the constitutional convention, shall proceed to exercise all the functions of State officers; and all laws of said Territories in force at the time of their admission into the Union shall be in force in the respective portions of said State until changed by the legislature of said State, except as modified or changed by this Act or by the constitution of the State; and the laws of the United States shall have the same force and effect within the said States as elsewhere within the United States.

SEC. 41. That the sum of one hundred and fifty thousand dollars, or so much thereof as may be necessary, is hereby appropriated, out of any money in the Treasury not otherwise appropriated, for defraying all and every kind and character of expense incident to the elections and conventions provided for in this Act; that is, the payment of the expenses of holding the election for members of the constitutional convention and the submission of the question of joint statehood and the election for the ratification of the constitution, at the same rates that are paid for similar services under the Territorial laws, respectively, and for the payment of the mileage for and salaries of members of the constitutional convention at the same rates that are paid the said Territorial legislatures under national law, and for the payment of all proper and necessary expenses, officers, clerks, and messengers thereof, and printing and other expenses incident thereto: *Provided,* That any expense incurred in excess of said sum of one hundred and fifty thousand dollars shall be paid by said State. The said money shall be expended under the direction of the Secretary of the Interior, and shall be forwarded, to be locally expended in the present Territory of Arizona and the present Territory of New Mexico, through the respective secretaries of said Territories, as may be necessary and proper, in the discretion of the Secretary of the Interior, in order to carry out the full intent and meaning of this Act.

Approved, June 16, 1906.

AN ACT TO ENABLE THE PEOPLE OF NEW MEXICO TO FORM A CONSTITUTION AND STATE GOVERNMENT AND BE ADMITTED INTO THE UNION ON AN EQUAL FOOTING WITH THE ORIGINAL STATES; AND TO ENABLE

THE PEOPLE OF ARIZONA TO FORM A CONSTITUTION AND STATE GOVERMENT AND BE ADMITTED INTO THE UNION ON AN EQUAL FOOTING WITH THE ORIGINAL STATES JUNE 20, 1910

Be it enacted by the Senate and House of Representatives of the United States of America in Congress assembled, That the qualified electors of the Territory of New Mexico are hereby authorized to vote for and choose delegates to form a constitutional convention for said Territory for the purpose of framing a constitution for the proposed State of New Mexico. Said convention shall consist of one hundred delegates; and the governor, chief justice, and secretary of said Territory shall apportion the delegates to be thus selected, as nearly as may be, equitably among the several counties thereof in accordance with the voting population, as shown by the vote cast at the election for Delegate in Congress in said Territory in nineteen hundred and eight: *Provided,* That in the event that any new counties shall have been added after said election, the apportionment for delegates shall be made proportionate to the vote cast within the various precincts contained in the area of such new counties so created, and the proportionate number of delegates so apportioned shall be deducted from the original counties out of which such counties shall have been created.

The governor of said Territory shall, within thirty days after the approval of this Act, by proclamation, in which the aforesaid apportionment of delegates to the convention shall be fully specified and announced, order an election of the delegates aforesaid on a day designated by him in said proclamation, not earlier than sixty nor later than ninety days after the approval of this Act. Such election for delegates shall be held and conducted, the returns made, and the certificates of persons elected to such convention issued, as nearly as may be, in the same manner as is prescribed by the laws of said Territory regulating elections therein of members of the legislature existing at the time of the last election of said members of the legislature; and the provisions of said laws in all respects, including the qualifications of electors and registration, are hereby made applicable to the election herein provided for; and said convention, when so called to order and organized, shall be the sole judge of the election and qualifications of its own members. Qualifications to entitle persons to vote on the ratification or rejection of the constitution formed by said convention when said constitution shall be submitted to the people of said Territory hereunder shall be the same as the qualifications to entitle persons to vote for delegates to said convention.

SEC. 2. That the delegates to the convention thus elected shall meet in the hall of the house of representatives in the capital of the Territory of New Mexico at twelve o'clock noon on the fourth Monday after their election, and they shall receive compensation for the period they actually are in session, but not for more than sixty days in all. After organization they shall declare on behalf of the people of said proposed State that they adopt the Constitution of the United States, whereupon the said convention shall be, and is hereby, authorized to form a constitution and provide for a state government for said proposed State, all in the manner and under the conditions contained in this Act. The constitution shall be republican in form and make no distinction in civil or political rights on account of race or color, and shall not be repugnant to the Constitution of the United States and the principles of the Declaration of Independence.

And said convention shall provide, by an ordinance irrevocable without the consent of the United States and the people of said State —

First. That perfect toleration of religious sentiment shall be secured, and that no inhabitant of said State shall ever be molested in person or property on account of his or her mode of religious worship; and that polygamous or plural marriages, or polygamous cohabitation, and the sale, barter, or giving of intoxicating liquors to Indians and the introduction of liquors into Indian country, which term shall also include all lands now owned or occupied by the Pueblo Indians of New Mexico, are forever prohibited.

Second. That the people inhabiting said proposed State do agree and declare that they forever disclaim all right and title to the unappropriated and ungranted public lands lying within the boundaries thereof and to all lands lying within said boundaries owned or held by any Indian or Indian tribes the right or title to which shall have been acquired through or from the United States or any prior sovereignty, and that until the title of such Indian or Indian tribes shall have been extinguished the same shall be and remain subject to the disposition and under the absolute jurisdiction and control of the Congress of the United States; that the lands and other property belonging to citizens of the United States residing without the said State shall never be taxed at a higher rate than the lands and other property belonging to residents thereof; that no taxes shall be imposed by the State upon lands or property therein belonging to or which may hereafter be acquired by the United States or reserved for its use; but nothing herein, or in the ordinance herein provided for, shall preclude the said State from taxing, as other lands and other property are taxed, any lands and other property outside of an Indian reservation owned or held by any Indian, save and except such lands as have been granted or acquired as aforesaid or as may be granted or confirmed to any Indian or Indians under any Act of Congress, but said ordinance shall provide that all such lands shall be exempt from taxation by said State so long and to such extent as Congress has prescribed or may hereafter prescribe.

Third. That the debts and liabilities of said Territory of New Mexico and the debts of the counties thereof which shall be valid and subsisting at the time of the passage of this Act shall be assumed and paid by said proposed State, and that said State shall, as to all such debts and liabilities, be subrogated to all the rights, including rights of indemnity and reimbursement, existing in favor of the said Territory or of any of the several counties thereof at the time of the passage of this Act: *Provided,* That nothing in this Act shall be construed as validating or in any manner legalizing any territorial, county, municipal, or other bonds, obligations, or evidences of indebtedness of said Territory or the counties or municipalities thereof which now are or may be invalid or illegal at the time said proposed State is admitted, nor shall the legislature of said proposed State pass any law in any manner validating or legalizing the same.

Fourth. That provision shall be made for the establishment and maintenance of a system of public schools, which shall be open to all the children of said State and free from sectarian control, and that said schools shall always be conducted in English.

Fifth. That said State shall never enact any law restricting or abridging the right of suffrage on account of race, color, or previous condition of servitude, and that ability to read, write, speak, and understand the English language sufficiently well to conduct the duties of the office without the aid of an interpreter shall be a necessary qualification for all State officers and members of the state legislature.

Sixth. That the capital of said State shall, until changed by the electors voting at an election provided for by the legislature of said State for that purpose, be at the city of Santa Fe, but no election shall be called or provided for prior to the thirty-first day of December, nineteen hundred and twenty-five.

Seventh. That there be and are reserved to the United States, with full acquiescence of the State, all rights and powers for the carrying out of the provisions by the United States of the Act of Congress entitled "An Act appropriating the receipts from the sale and disposal of public lands in certain States and Territories to the construction of irrigation works for the reclamation of arid lands," approved June seventeenth, nineteen hundred and two, and Acts amendatory thereof or supplementary thereto, to the same extent as if said State had remained a Territory.

Eighth. That whenever hereafter any of the lands contained within Indian reservations or allotments in said proposed State shall be alloted, sold, reserved, or otherwise disposed of, they shall be subject for a period of twenty-five years after such allotment, sale, reservation, or other disposal to all the laws of the United States prohibiting the introduction of liquor into the Indian country; and the terms "Indian" and "Indian country" shall include the Pueblo Indians of New Mexico and the lands now owned or occupied by them.

Ninth. That the State and its people consent to all and singular the provisions of this Act concerning the lands hereby granted or confirmed to the State, the terms and conditions upon which said grants and confirmations are made, and the means and manner of enforcing such terms and conditions, all in every respect and particular as in this Act provided.

All of which ordinance described in this section shall, by proper reference, be made a part of any constitution that shall be formed hereunder, in such terms as shall positively preclude the making by any future constitutional amendment of any change or abrogation of the said ordinance in whole or in part without the consent of Congress.

SEC. 3. That when said constitution shall be formed as aforesaid the convention forming the same shall provide for the submission of said constitution to the people of New Mexico for ratification at an election which shall be held on a day named by said convention not earlier than sixty nor later than ninety days after said convention adjourns, at which election the qualified voters of New Mexico shall vote directly for or against said constitution and for or against any provisions thereof separately submitted. The returns of said election shall be made by the election officers direct to the secretary of the Territory of New Mexico at Santa Fe, who, with the governor and the chief justice of said Territory, shall constitute a canvassing board, and they, or any two of them, shall meet at said city of Santa Fe on the third Monday after said election and shall canvass the same. If a majority of the legal votes cast at said election shall reject the constitution, the said canvassing board shall forthwith certify said result to the governor of said Territory, together with the statement of votes cast upon the question of the ratification or rejection of said constitution and also a statement of the votes cast for or against such provisions thereof as were separately submitted to the voters at said election; whereupon the governor of said Territory shall, by proclamation, order the constitutional convention to reassemble at a date not later than twenty days after the receipt by said governor of the documents showing the rejection of the constitution by the people, and thereafter a new constitution shall be framed and the same proceedings shall be taken in regard thereto in like manner as if said constitution were being originally prepared for submission and submitted to the people.

SEC. 4. That when said constitution and such provisions thereof as have been separately submitted shall have been duly ratified by the people of New Mexico as aforesaid a certified copy of the same shall be submitted to the President of the United States and to Congress for approval, together with the statement of the votes cast thereon and upon any provisions thereof which were separately submitted to and voted upon by the people. And if Congress and the President approve said constitution and the said separate provisions thereof, or, if the President approves the same and Congress fails to disapprove the same during the next regular session thereof, then and in that event the President shall certify said facts to the governor of New Mexico, who shall, within thirty days after the receipt of said notification from the President of the United States, issue his proclamation for the election of the state and county officers, the members of the state legislature and Representatives in Congress, and all other officers provided for in said constitution, all as hereinafter provided; said election to take place not earlier than sixty days nor later than ninety days after said proclamation by the governor of New Mexico ordering the same.

SEC. 5. That said constitutional convention shall, by ordinance, provide that in case of the ratification of said constitution by the people, and in case the President of the United States and Congress approve the same, or in case the President approves the same and Congress fails to act in its next regular session, all as hereinbefore provided, an election shall be held at the time named in the proclamation of the governor of New Mexico, provided for in the preceding section, at which election officers for a full state government, including a governor, members of the legislature, two Representatives in Congress, to be elected at large from said State, and such other officers as such constitutional convention shall prescribe, shall be chosen by the people. Such election shall be held, the returns thereof made, canvassed, and certified to by the secretary of said Territory in the same manner as in this Act prescribed for the making of the returns, the canvassing and certification of the same of the election for the ratification or rejection of said constitution, as hereinbefore provided, and the qualifications of voters at said election for all state officers, members of the legislature, county officers, and Representatives in Congress, and other officers prescribed by said constitution shall be made the same as the qualifications of voters at the election for the ratification or rejection of said constitution as hereinbefore provided. When said election of said state and county officers, members of the legislature, and Representatives in Congress, and other officers above provided for shall be held and the returns thereof made, canvassed, and certified as hereinbefore provided, the governor of the Territory of New Mexico shall certify the result of said election, as canvassed and certified as herein provided, to the President of the United States, who thereupon shall immediately issue his proclamation announcing the result of said election so ascertained, and upon the issuance of said proclamation by the President of the United States the proposed State of New Mexico shall be deemed admitted by Congress into the Union, by virtue of this Act, on an equal footing with the other States. Until the issuance of said proclamation by the President of the United States, and until the said State is so admitted into the Union and said officers are elected and qualified under the provisions of the Constitution, the county and territorial officers of said Territory, including the Delegate in Congress thereof elected at the general election in nineteen hundred and eight, shall continue to discharge the duties of their respective offices in and for said Territory: *Provided,* That no session of the territorial legislative assembly shall be held in nineteen hundred and eleven.

SEC. 6. That in addition to sections sixteen and thirty-six, heretofore granted to the Territory of New Mexico, sections two and thirty-two in every township in said proposed State not other-wise appropriated at the date of the passage of this Act are hereby granted to the said State for the support of common schools; and where sections two, sixteen, thirty-two, and thirty-six, or any parts thereof, are mineral, or have been sold, reserved, or other-wise appropriated or reserved by or under the authority of any Act of Congress, or are wanting or fractional in quantity or where settlement thereon with a view to preemption or homestead, or improvement thereof with a view to desert-land entry has been made heretofore or hereafter, and before the survey thereof in the field, the provisions of sections twenty-two hundred and seventy-five and twenty-two hundred and seventy-six of the Revised Statutes are hereby made applicable thereto and to the selection of lands in lieu thereof to the same extent as if sections two and thirty-two, as well as sections sixteen and thirty-six, were mentioned therein: *Provided, however,* That the area of such indemnity selections on account of any fractional township shall not in any event exceed an area which, when added to the area of the above-named sections returned by the survey as in place, will equal four sections for fractional townships containing seventeen thousand two hundred and eighty acres or more, three sections for such townships containing eleven thousand five hundred and twenty acres or more, two sections for such townships containing five thousand seven hundred and sixty acres or more, nor one section for such township containing six hundred and forty acres or more: *And provided further,* That the grants of sections two, sixteen, thirty-two, and thirty-six to said State, within national forests now existing or proclaimed, shall not vest the title to said sections in said State until the part of said national forests embracing any of said sections is restored to the public domain; but said granted sections shall be administered as a part of said forests, and at the close of each fiscal year there shall be paid by the Secretary of the Treasury to the State, as income for its common-school fund, such proportion of the gross proceeds of all the national forests within said State as the area of lands hereby granted to said State for school purposes which are situate within said forest reserves, whether surveyed or unsurveyed, and for which no indemnity has been selected, may bear to the total area of all the national forests with said State, the area of said sections when unsurveyed to be determined by the Secretary of the Interior, by protraction or otherwise, the amount necessary for such payments being appropriated and made available annually from any money in the Treasury not otherwise appropriated.

SEC. 7. That in lieu of the grant of land for purposes of internal improvements made to new States by the eighth section of the Act of September fourth, eighteen hundred and forty-one, and in lieu of the swamp-land grant made by the Act of September twenty-eighth, eighteen hundred and fifty, and section twenty-four hundred and seventy-nine of the Revised Statutes, and in lieu of the grant of thirty thousand acres for each Senator and Representative in Congress, made by the Act of July second, eighteen hundred and sixty-two, Twelfth Statutes at Large, page five hundred and three, which grants are hereby declared not to extend to the said State, and in lieu of the grant of saline lands heretofore made to the Territory of New Mexico for university purposes by section three of the Act of June twenty-first, eighteen hundred and ninety-eight, which is hereby repealed, except to the extent of such approved selections of such saline lands as may have been made by said Territory prior to the passage of this Act, the following grants of lands are hereby made, to wit:

For university purposes, two hundred thousand acres; for legislative, executive, and judicial public buildings heretofore erected in said Territory or to be hereafter erected in the proposed State, and for the payment of the bonds heretofore or hereafter issued therefor, one hundred thousand acres; for insane asylums, one hundred thousand acres; for penitentiaries, one hundred thousand acres; for schools and asylums for the deaf, dumb, and the blind, one hundred thousand acres; for miners' hospitals for disabled miners, fifty thousand acres; for normal schools, two hundred thousand acres; for state charitable, penal, and reformatory institutions, one hundred thousand acres; for agricultural and mechanical colleges, one hundred and fifty thousand acres; and the national appropriation heretofore annually paid for the agricultural and mechanical college to said Territory shall, until further order of Congress, continue to be paid to said State for the use of said institution; for school of mines, one hundred and fifty thousand acres; for military institutes, one hundred thousand acres; and for the payment of the bonds and accrued interest thereon issued by Grant and Santa Fe Counties, New Mexico, which said bonds were validated, approved, and confirmed by Act of Congress of January sixteenth, eighteen hundred and ninety-seven (Twenty-ninth statutes, page four hundred and eighty-seven), one million acres: *Provided,* That if there shall remain any of the one million acres of land so granted, or of the proceeds of the sale or lease thereof, or rents, issues, or profits therefrom, after the payment of said debts, such remainder of lands and the proceeds of sales thereof shall be added to and become a part of the permanent school fund of said State, the income therefrom only to be used for the maintenance of the common schools of said State.

SEC. 8. That the schools, colleges, and universities provided for in this Act shall forever remain under the exclusive control of the said State, and no part of the proceeds arising from the sale or disposal of any lands granted herein for educational purposes shall be used for the support of any sectarian or denominational school, college, or university.

SEC. 9. That five per centum of the proceeds of sales of public lands lying within said State, which shall be sold by the United States subsequent to the admission of said State into the Union, after deducting all the expenses incident to such sales, shall be paid to the said State to be used as a permanent inviolable fund, the interest of which only shall be expended for the support of the common schools within said State.

SEC. 10. That it is hereby declared that all lands hereby granted, including those which, having been heretofore granted to the said Territory, are hereby expressly transferred and confirmed to the said State, shall be by the said State held in trust, to be disposed of in whole or in part only in manner as herein provided and for the several objects specified in the respective granting and confirmatory provisions, and that the natural products and money proceeds of any of said lands shall be subject to the same trusts as the lands producing the same.

Disposition of any of said lands, or of any money or thing of value directly or indirectly derived therefrom, for any object other than that for which such particular lands, or the lands from which such money or thing of value shall have been derived, were granted or confirmed, or in any manner contrary to the provisions of this Act, shall be deemed a breach of trust.

No mortgage or other incumbrance of the said lands, or any thereof, shall be valid in favor of any person or for any purpose or under any circumstances whatsoever. Said lands shall not be sold or leased, in whole or in part, except to the highest and best bidder at a public auction to be held at the county seat of a county wherein the lands to be affected, or the major portion thereof, shall lie, notice of which public auction shall first have been duly given by advertisement, which shall set forth the nature, time, and place of the transaction to be had, with a full description of the lands to be offered, and be published once each week for not less than ten successive weeks in a newspaper of general circulation published regularly at the state capital, and in that newspaper of like circulation which shall then be regularly published nearest to the location of such lands so offered; nor shall any sale or contract for the sale of any timber or other natural product of such lands be made, save at the place, in the manner, and after the notice by publication thus provided for sales and leases of the lands themselves: *Provided*, That nothing herein contained shall prevent said proposed State from leasing any of said lands referred to in this section for a term of five years or less without said advertisements herein required.

All lands, leaseholds, timber, and other products of land before being offered shall be appraised at their true value, and no sale or other disposal thereof shall be made for a consideration less than the value so ascertained, nor in any case less than the minimum price hereinafter fixed, nor upon credit unless accompanied by ample security, and the legal title shall not be deemed to have passed until the consideration shall have been paid.

Lands east of the line between ranges eighteen and nineteen east of the New Mexico principal meridian shall not be sold for less than five dollars per acre, and land west of said line shall not be sold for less than three dollars per acre, and no lands which are or shall be susceptible of irrigation under any projects now or hereafter completed or adopted by the United States under legislation for the reclamation of lands, or under any other project for the reclamation of lands, shall be sold at less than twenty-five dollars per acre: *Provided,* That said State, at the request of the Secretary of the Interior, shall from time to time relinquish such of its lands to the United States as at any time are needed for irrigation works in connection with any such government project. And other lands in lieu thereof are hereby granted to said State, to be selected from lands of the character named and in the manner prescribed in section eleven of this Act.

There is hereby reserved to the United States and exempted from the operation of any and all grants made or confirmed by this Act to said proposed State all land actually or prospectively valuable for the development of water powers or power for hydroelectric use or transmission and which shall be ascertained and designated by the Secretary of the Interior within five years after the proclamation of the President declaring the admission of the State; and no lands so reserved and excepted shall be subject to any disposition whatsoever by said State, and any conveyance or transfer of such land by said State or any officer thereof shall be absolutely null and void within the period above named; and in lieu of the land so reserved to the United States and excepted from the operation of any of said grants, there be, and is hereby, granted to the proposed State an equal quantity of land to be selected from land of the character named and in the manner prescribed in section eleven of this Act.

A separate fund shall be established for each of the several objects for which the said grants are hereby made or confirmed, and whenever any moneys shall be in any manner derived from any of said land the same shall be deposited by the state treasurer in the fund corresponding to the grant under which the particular land producing such moneys were by this Act conveyed or confirmed. No moneys shall ever be taken from one fund for deposit in any other, or for any object other than that for which the land producing the same was granted or confirmed. The state treasurer shall keep all such moneys invested in safe interest-bearing securities, which securities shall be approved by the governor and secretary of state of said proposed State, and shall at all times be under a good and sufficient bond or bonds conditioned for the faithful performance of his duties in regard thereto as defined by this Act and the laws of the State not in conflict herewith.

Every sale, lease, conveyance, or contract of or concerning any of the lands hereby granted or confirmed, or the use thereof or the natural products thereof, not made in substantial conformity with the provisions of this Act shall be null and void, any provision of the constitution or laws of the said State to the contrary notwithstanding.

It shall be the duty of the Attorney-General of the United States to prosecute in the name of the United States and its courts such proceedings at law or in equity as may from time to time be necessary and appropriate to enforce the provisions hereof relative to the application and disposition of the said lands and the products thereof and the funds derived therefrom.

Nothing herein contained shall be taken as in limitation of the power of the State or of any citizen thereof to enforce the provisions of this Act.

SEC. 11. That all lands granted in quantity or as indemnity by this Act shall be selected, under the direction and subject to the approval of the Secretary of the Interior, from the surveyed, unreserved, unappropriated, and non-mineral public lands of the United States within the limits of said State, by a commission composed of the governor, surveyor-general, or other officer exercising the functions of a surveyor-general, and the attorney-general of the said State; and after its admission into the Union said State may procure public lands of the United States within its boundaries to be surveyed with a view to satisfying any public-land grants made to said State in the same manner prescribed for the procurement of such surveys by Washington, Idaho, and other States by the Act of Congress approved August eighteenth, eighteen hundred and ninety-four (Twenty-eighth Statutes at Large, page three hundred and ninety-four), and the provisions of said Act, in so far as they relate to such surveys and the preference right of selection, are hereby extended to the said State of New Mexico. The fees to be paid to the register and receiver for each final location or selection of one hundred and sixty acres made hereunder shall be one dollar.

SEC. 12. That all grants of lands heretofore made by any Act of Congress to said Territory, except to the extent modified or repealed by this Act, are hereby ratified and confirmed to said State, subject to the provisions of this Act: *Provided, however,* That nothing in this Act contained shall, directly or indirectly, affect any litigation now pending and to which the United States is a party, or any right or claim therein asserted.

SEC. 13. That the State, when admitted as aforesaid, shall constitute one judicial district, and the circuit and district courts of said district shall be held at the capital of said State, and the said district shall, for judicial purposes, be attached to the eighth judicial circuit. There shall be appointed for said district one district judge, one United States attorney, and one United States marshal. The judge of said district shall receive a yearly salary the same as other similar judges of the United States, payable as provided for by law, and shall reside in the district to which he is appointed. There shall be appointed clerks of said courts, who shall keep their offices at the capital of said State. The regular terms of said courts shall be held on the first Monday in April and the first Monday in October of each year. The circuit and district courts for said district, and the judges thereof, respectively, shall possess the same powers and jurisdiction and perform the same duties required to be performed by the other circuit and district courts and judges of the United States, and shall be governed by the same laws and regulations. The marshal, district attorney, and the clerks of the circuit and district courts of said district, and all other officers and persons performing duties in the administration of justice therein, shall severally possess the powers and perform the duties lawfully possessed and required to be performed by similar officers in other districts of the United States, and shall, for the services they may perform, receive the fees and compensation now allowed by law to officers performing similar services for the United States in the Territory of New Mexico.

SEC. 14. That all cases of appeal or writ of error and all other proceedings heretofore lawfully prosecuted and now pending in the Supreme Court of the United States or in the proper circuit court of appeals upon any record from the supreme court of said Territory, and all cases of appeal or writ of error and all other proceedings heretofore lawfully prosecuted and now pending in the Supreme Court of the United States upon any record from a district court of said Territory or in any matter of habeas corpus upon any return or order of a district judge thereof, and all and singular the cases aforesaid which, hereafter shall be so lawfully prosecuted and remain pending in the Supreme Court of the United States or in the proper circuit court of appeals, may be heard and determined by the Supreme Court of the United States or the proper circuit court of appeals, as the case may be. And the mandate of execution or of further proceedings shall be directed by the Supreme Court of the United States or the circuit court of appeals to the circuit or district court, hereby established within the said State, or to the supreme court of such State, as the nature of the case may require. And the circuit, district, and state courts herein named shall respectively be the successors of the supreme court and of the district courts of the said Territory as to all such cases arising within the limits embraced within the jurisdiction of said courts, respectively, with full power to proceed with the same and award mesne or final process therein; and that from all judgements and decrees or other determinations of any court of the said Territory, in any case begun prior to admission, the parties to such cause shall have the same right to prosecute appeals and writs of error to the Supreme Court of the United States or to the circuit court of appeals as they would have had by law prior to the admission of said State into the Union.

SEC. 15. That the said circuit or the said district court, as the case may be, shall have jurisdiction to hear and determine all trials, proceedings, and questions arising, or which may be raised, in any case or controversy pending in any of the courts other than the supreme court of the said Territory at the date of its admission as a State, the case being such that, under the laws of the United States touching the jurisdictions of federal courts, it might properly have been begun in or (as a separable controversy or otherwise) removed to said circuit or said district court, had they been established when the litigation of such case or controversy was commenced. Should such case or controversy be such that, if begun within a State, it would have fallen within the exclusive original cognizance of a circuit or district court of the United States sitting therein, it shall be transferred to the one or the other of said courts sitting within said State of New Mexico, with due regard for the general provisions of law defining their respective jurisdictions; but should such case or controversy be by nature one of those which under such general jurisdictional provisions fall within the concurrent but not the exclusive jurisdiction of such courts, then such transfer may be had upon application of any party to such case or controversy, to be made as nearly as may be in the manner now provided for removal of cases from state to federal courts, and not later than sixty days after the lodgement of the record of such case or controversy in the proper court of the State, as herein provided. All cases and controversies pending at the admission of the State, and not transferable to the said çircuit or district court under the foregoing provisions, shall be heard and determined by the proper court of the State. All files, records, and proceedings relating to any such pending cases or controversies shall be transferred to such circuit, district, and state courts, respectively, in such wise and so authenticated or proven as such courts shall, respectively, by rule direct, and upon transfer of any case or controversy, as herein provided, the same shall be proceeded with in due course of law; and no writ, action, indictment, information, cause, or proceeding pending in any court of the said Territory at the time of its admission as a State shall abate or be deemed ineffective by reason of such admission, but the same shall be transferred and proceeded with in the proper circuit or district court of the United States, or state court, as the case may be: *Provided, however,* That all cases pending and undisposed of in the supreme court of the said Territory at the time of the admission thereof as a State be transferred, together with the records thereof, to the highest appellate court of the State, and shall be heard and determined thereby, and appeal to and writ of error from the Supreme Court of the United States shall lie to review all such cases in accordance with the rules and principles applicable to the review by that tribunal of cases determined by state courts: *Provided further,* That all cases so pending in said territorial supreme court in which the United States is a party or which, if instituted within a State, would have fallen within the exclusive original cognizance of a circuit or district court of the United States, shall, with the records appertaining thereto, be transferred to the circuit court of appeals for the eighth circuit, and be there heard and decided; and any such case which, if finally decided by the supreme court of the Territory, would have been in any manner reviewable by the Supreme Court of the United States, may in like manner and with like effect be so reviewed after final decision thereof by said circuit court of appeals. Transfers of all files and records from the said territorial supreme court to the highest appellate court of the State and to the said circuit court of appeals, shall be accomplished in such manner and under such proofs and authentications as the two last-mentioned courts shall respectively by rule prescribe.

All civil causes of action and all criminal offenses which shall have arisen or been committed prior to the admission of said Territory as a State, but as to which no suit, action, or prosecution shall be pending at the date of such admission, shall be subject to prosecution in the courts of said State and the said circuit or district courts of the United States sitting therein, and to review in the appellate courts of such respective sovereignties in like manner and to the same extent as if said State had been created and such circuit, district, and state courts had been established prior to the accrual of such causes of action and the commission of such offenses; and in effectuation of this provision such of the said criminal offenses as shall have been committed against the laws of the said Territory shall be tried and punished by the appropriate courts of the said State, and such as shall have been committed against the laws of the United States shall be tried and punished in the circuit or district courts of the United States.

All suits and actions brought by the United States in which said Territory is named as a party defendant, which shall be pending in any court of said

Territory at the date of its admission hereunder, shall be transferred as herein provided; and the said State shall be substituted therein and become a party defendant thereto in lieu of said Territory.

SEC. 16. That the members of the legislature elected at the election hereinbefore provided for may assemble at Santa Fe, organize, and elect two Senators of the United States in the manner now prescribed by the Constitution and laws of the United States; and the governor and secretary of state of the proposed State shall certify the election of the Senators and Representatives in the manner required by law; and the Senators and Representatives so elected shall be entitled to be admitted to seats in Congress and to all rights and privileges of Senators and Representatives of other States in the Congress of the United States; and the officers of the state government formed in pursuance of said constitution, as provided by the constitutional convention, shall proceed to exercise all the functions of state officers; and all laws of said Territory in force at the time of its admission into the Union shall be in force in said State until changed by the legislature of said State, except as modified or changed by this Act or by the constitution of the State; and the laws of the United States shall have the same force and effect within the said State as elsewhere within the United States.

SEC. 17. That the sum of one hundred thousand dollars, or so much thereof as may be necessary, is hereby appropriated, out of any money in the Treasury not otherwise appropriated, for defraying all and every kind and character of expense incident to the elections and convention provided for in this Act; that is, the payment of the expenses of holding the election for members of the constitutional convention and the election for the ratification of the constitution, at the same rates that are paid for similar services under the territorial laws, and for the payment of the mileage for and salaries of members of the constitutional convention at the same rates that are paid to members of the said territorial legislature under national law, and for the payment of all proper and necessary expenses, officers, clerks, and messengers thereof, and printing and other expenses incident thereto: *Provided,* That any expense incurred in excess of said sum of one hundred thousand dollars shall be paid by said State. The said money shall be expended under the direction of the Secretary of the Interior, and shall be forwarded, to be locally expended in the present Territory of New Mexico, through the secretary of said Territory as may be necessary and proper, in the discretion of the Secretary of the Interior, in order to carry out the full intent and meaning of this Act.

SEC. 18. That all saline lands in the proposed State of New Mexico are hereby reserved from entry, location, selection, or settlement until such time as Congress shall hereafter provide for their disposition.

SEC. 19. That the qualified electors of the Territory of Arizona are hereby authorized to vote for and choose delegates to form a constitutional convention for said Territory for the purpose of framing a constitution for the proposed State of Arizona. Said convention shall consist of fifty-two delegates; and the governor, chief justice, and secretary of said Territory shall apportion the delegates to be thus selected, as nearly as may be, equitably among the several counties thereof in accordance with the voting population as shown by the vote cast at the election for Delegate in Congress in said Territory in nineteen hundred and eight.

A qualified elector within the meaning of this section shall be any male citizen of the United States of the age of twenty-one years who shall have resided in the Territory at least twelve months next preceding the date fixed for the election of delegates to the constitutional convention, as herein provided for, and who shall possess in other respects the qualifications of an elector as provided by title twenty, Revised Statutes of Arizona, August second, nineteen hundred and one. Within ten days after the issuance of the governor's proclamation ordering the election of delegates to the constitutional convention, as herein provided, the board of supervisors of each county of the Territory shall meet and authorize and require a reregistration of the qualified electors of said county: *Provided, however,* That there need not be a reregistration of the qualified electors whose names appear on the great register of said county for the year nineteen hundred and eight, but all such names, together with such as may be registered under the provisions of this section, shall constitute the great register of said county and be used at each of the elections herein provided for; and so far as the same is consistent with the provisions of this Act, such registration, as also the making up, printing, distribution, and use of such great register, shall in all respects conform to and be governed by the provisions of chapter three of said title twenty, Revised Statutes of Arizona, nineteen hundred and one. And the provisions of this section shall apply to all voters at all elections for the election of delegates to the constitutional convention and for the ratification of the constitution, for state officers, members of the state legislature, Representatives in Congress, and all other officers named in said constitution or in any manner herein provided for or mentioned.

The governor of said Territory shall, within thirty days after the approval of this Act, by proclamation, in which the aforesaid apportionment of delegates to the convention shall be fully specified and announced, order an election of the delegates aforesaid on a day, designated by him in said proclamation, not earlier than sixty nor later than ninety days after the approval of this Act. Such election for delegates shall be held and conducted, the returns made, and the certificates of persons elected to such convention issued, as nearly as may be, in the same manner as is prescribed by the laws of said Territory regulating elections therein of members of the legislature existing at the time of the last election of said members of the legislature; and the provisions of said laws in all respects, including the qualifications of electors and registration, are hereby made applicable to the election herein provided for; and said convention when so called to order and organized shall be the sole judge of the election and qualifications of its own members. Qualifications to entitle persons to vote on the ratification or rejection of the constitution formed by said convention when said constitution shall be submitted to the people of said Territory hereunder shall be the same as the qualifications to entitle persons to vote for delegates to said convention.

SEC. 20. That the delegates to the convention thus elected shall meet in the hall of the house of representatives in the capital of the Territory of Arizona at twelve o'clock noon on the fourth Monday after their election and they shall receive compensation for the period they actually are in session, but not for more than sixty days in all; after organization they shall declare on behalf of the people of said proposed State that they adopt the Constitution of the United

States, whereupon the said convention shall be, and is hereby, authorized to form a constitution and provide for a state government for said proposed State, all in the manner and under the conditions contained in this Act. The constitution shall be republican in form and make no distinction in civil or political rights on account of race or color, and shall not be repugnant to the Constitution of the United States and the principles of the Declaration of Independence.

And said convention shall provide by an ordinance irrevocable without the consent of the United States and the people of said State —

First. That perfect toleration of religious sentiment shall be secured, and that no inhabitant of said State shall ever be molested in person or property on account of his or her mode of religious worship; and that polygamous or plural marriages, or polygamous cohabitation, and the sale, barter, or giving of intoxicating liquors to Indians, and the introduction of liquors into Indian country are forever prohibited.

Second. That the people inhabiting said proposed State do agree and declare that they forever disclaim all right and title to the unappropriated and ungranted public lands lying within the boundaries thereof and to all lands lying within said boundaries owned or held by any Indian or Indian tribes, the right or title to which shall have been acquired through or from the United States or any prior sovereignty, and that until the title of such Indian or Indian tribes shall have been extinguished the same shall be and remain subject to the disposition and under the absolute jurisdiction and control of the Congress of the United States; that the lands and other property belonging to citizens of the United States residing without the said State shall never be taxed at a higher rate than the lands and other property belonging to residents thereof; that no taxes shall be imposed by the State upon lands or property therein belonging to or which may hereafter be acquired by the United States or reserved for its use; but nothing herein, or in the ordinance herein provided for, shall preclude the said State from taxing as other lands and other property are taxed any lands and other property outside of an Indian reservation owned or held by any Indian, save and except such lands as have been granted or acquired as aforesaid or as may be granted or confirmed to any Indian or Indians under any Act of Congress, but said ordinance shall provide that all such lands shall be exempt from taxation by said State so long and to such extent as Congress has prescribed or may hereafter prescribe.

Third. That the debts and liabilities of said Territory of Arizona, and the debts of the counties thereof, which shall be valid and subsisting at the time of the passage of this Act, shall be assumed and paid by said proposed State, and that said State shall, as to all such debts and liabilities, be subrogated to all the rights, including rights of indemnity and reimbursement, existing in favor of said Territory or of any of the several counties thereof at the time of the passage of this Act: *Provided,* That nothing in this Act shall be construed as validating or in any manner legalizing any territorial, county, municipal, or other bonds, obligations, or evidences of indebtedness of said Territory or the counties or muncipalities thereof which now are or may be invalid or illegal at the time said proposed State is admitted, nor shall the legislature of said proposed State pass any law in any manner validating or legalizing the same.

Fourth. That provisions shall be made for the establishment and maintenance of a system of public schools which shall be open to all the children of said State and free from sectarian control; and that said schools shall always be conducted in English.

Fifth. That said State shall never enact any law restricting or abridging the right of suffrage on account of race, color, or previous condition of servitude, and that ability to read, write, speak, and understand the English language sufficiently well to conduct the duties of the office without the aid of an interpreter shall be a necessary qualification for all state officers and members of the state legislature.

Sixth. That the capital of said State shall, until changed by the electors voting at an election provided for by the legislature of said State for that purpose, be at the city of Phoenix, but no election shall be called or provided for prior to the thirty-first day of December, nineteen hundred and twenty-five.

Seventh. That there be and are reserved to the United States, with full acquiescence of the State, all rights and powers for the carrying out of the provisions by the United States of the Act of Congress entitled "An Act appropriating the receipts from the sale and disposal of public lands in certain States and Territories to the construction of irrigation works for the reclamation of arid lands," approved June seventeenth, nineteen hundred and two, and Acts amendatory thereof or supplementary thereto, to the same extent as if said State had remained a Territory.

Eighth. That whenever hereafter any of the lands contained within Indian reservations or allotments in said proposed State shall be allotted, sold, reserved, or otherwise disposed of, they shall be subject, for a period of twenty-five years after such allotment, sale, reservation, or other disposal, to all the laws of the United States prohibiting the introduction of liquor into the Indian country.

Ninth. That the State and its people consent to all and singular the provisions of this Act concerning the lands hereby granted or confirmed to the State, the terms and conditions upon which said grants and confirmations are made, and the means and manner of enforcing such terms and conditions, all in every respect and particular as in this Act provided.

All of which ordinance described in this section shall, by proper reference, be made a part of any constitution that shall be formed hereunder, in such terms as shall positively preclude the making by any future constitutional amendment of any change or abrogation of the said ordinance in whole or in part without the consent of Congress.

SEC. 21. That when said constitution shall be formed, as aforesaid, the convention forming the same shall provide for the submission of said constitution to the people of Arizona for ratification at an election which shall be held on a day named by said convention not earlier than sixty nor later than ninety days after said convention adjourns, at which election the qualified voters of Arizona shall vote directly for or against said constitution and for or against any provisions thereof separately submitted. The returns of said election shall be made by the election officers direct to the secretary of the Territory of Arizona at Phoenix, who, with the governor and chief justice of said Territory, shall constitute a canvassing board, and they, or any two of them, shall meet at said city of Phoenix on the third Monday after said election and shall canvass the same. If a majority of the legal votes cast at said election shall reject the constitution, the said canvassing board shall forthwith certify said result to the governor of said Territory, together with the statement of votes cast upon the question of the ratification or rejection of said constitution and also a statement of the votes cast for or against such provisions thereof as were separately submitted to the voters at said election; whereupon the governor of said Territory shall, by proclamation, order the constitutional convention to reassemble at a date not later than twenty days after the receipt by said governor of the documents showing the rejection of the constitution by the people, and thereafter a new constitution shall be framed and the same proceedings shall be taken in regard thereto in like manner as if said constitution were being originally prepared for submission and submitted to the people.

SEC. 22. That when said constitution and such provisions thereof as have been separately submitted shall have been duly ratified by the people of Arizona, as aforesaid, a certified copy of the same shall be submitted to the President of the United States and to Congress for approval, together with the statement of the votes cast thereon and upon any provisions thereof which were separately submitted to and voted upon by the people. And if Congress and the President approve said constitution and the said separate provisions thereof, if any, or if the President approves the same and Congress fails to disapprove the same during the next regular session thereof, then and in that event the President shall certify said facts to the governor of Arizona, who shall, within thirty days after the receipt of said notification from the President of the United States, issue his proclamation for the election of the state and county officers, the members of the state legislature, and Representative in Congress, and all other officers provided for in said constitution, all as hereinafter provided; said election to take place not earlier than sixty days nor later than ninety days after said proclamation by the governor of Arizona ordering the same.

SEC. 23. That said constitutional convention shall, by ordinance, provide that in case of the ratification of said constitution by the people, and in case the President of the United States and Congress approve the same, or in case the President approves the same and Congress fails to act in its next regular session, all as hereinbefore provided, an election shall be held at the time named in the proclamation of the governor of Arizona, provided for in the preceding section, at which election of officers for a full state government, including a governor, members of the legislature, one Representative in Congress, and such other officers as such constitutional convention shall prescribe, shall be chosen by the people. Such election shall be held, the returns thereof made, canvassed, and certified to by the secretary of said Territory, in the same manner as in this Act prescribed for the making of the returns, the canvassing and certification of the same of the election for the ratification or rejection of said constitution, as hereinbefore provided, and the qualifications of voters at said election for all state officers, members of the legislature, county officers, and Representative in Congress, and other officers prescribed by said constitution shall be made the same as the qualifications of voters at the election for the ratification or rejection of said constitution, as hereinbefore provided. When said election of state and county officers, members of the legislature, and Representative in Congress, and other officers above provided for shall be held and the returns thereof made, canvassed, and certified, as hereinbefore provided, the governor of the Territory of Arizona shall certify the result of said election as canvassed and certified, as herein provided, to the President of the United States, who thereupon shall immediately issue his proclamation announcing the result of said election so ascertained, and upon the issuance of said proclamation by the President of the United States the proposed State of Arizona shall be deemed admitted by Congress into the Union by virtue of this Act on an equal footing with the other States. Until the issuance of said proclamation by the President of the United States, and until the said State is so admitted into the Union and said officers are elected and qualified under the provisions of the constitution, the county and territorial officers of said Territory, including the Delegate in Congress thereof elected in the general election in nineteen hundred and eight, shall continue to discharge the duties of their respective offices in and for said Territory: *Provided,* That no session of the territorial legislative assembly shall be held in nineteen hundred and eleven.

SEC. 24. That in addition to sections sixteen and thirty-six, heretofore reserved for the Territory of Arizona, sections two and thirty-two in every township in said proposed State not otherwise appropriated at the date of the passage of this Act are hereby granted to the said State for the support of common schools; and where sections two, sixteen, thirty-two, and thirty-six, or any parts thereof, are mineral, or have been sold, reserved, or otherwise appropriated or reserved by or under the authority of any Act of Congress, or are wanting or fractional in quantity, or where settlement thereon with a view to preemption or homestead, or improvement thereof with a view to desert-land entry has been made heretofore or hereafter, and before the survey thereof in the field, the provisions of section twenty-two hundred and seventy-five and twenty-two hundred and seventy-six of the Revised Statutes, and Acts amendatory thereof or supplementary thereto, are hereby made applicable thereto and to the selection of lands in lieu thereof to the same extent as if sections two and thirty-two, as well as sections sixteen and thirty-six, were mentioned therein: *Provided, however,* That the area of such indemnity selections on account of any fractional township shall not in any event exceed an area which, when added to the area of the above-named sections returned by the survey as in place, will equal four sections for fractional townships containing seventeen thousand two hundred and eighty acres or more, three sections for such townships containing eleven thousand five hundred and twenty acres or more, two sections for such townships containing five thousand seven hundred and sixty acres or more, nor one section for such townships containing six hundred and forty acres or more: *And provided further,* That the grants of sections two, sixteen, thirty-two, and thirty-six to said State, within national forests now existing or proclaimed, shall not vest the title to said sections in said State until the part of said national forests embracing any of said sections is restored to the public domain; but said granted sections shall be administered as a part of said forests, and at the close of each fiscal year there shall be paid by the Secretary of the Treasury to the State, as income for its common-school fund, such proportion of the gross proceeds of all the national forests within said

State as the area of lands hereby granted to said State for school purposes which are situated within said forest reserves, whether surveyed or unsurveyed, and for which no indemnity has been selected, may bear to the total area of said sections when unsurveyed to be determined by the Secretary of the Interior, by protraction or otherwise, the amount necessary for such payments being appropriated and made available annually from any money in the Treasury not otherwise appropriated.

SEC. 25. That in lieu of the grant of land for purposes of internal improvements made to new States by the eighth section of the Act of September fourth, eighteen hundred and forty-one, and in lieu of the swamp-land grant made by the Act of September twenty-eighth, eighteen hundred and fifty, and section twenty-four hundred and seventy-nine of the Revised Statutes, and in lieu of the grant of thirty thousand acres for each Senator and Representative in Congress, made by the Act of July second, eighteen hundred and three, which grants are hereby declared not to extend to the said State, the following grants are hereby made, to wit:

For university purposes, two hundred thousand acres; for legislative, executive, and judicial public buildings heretofore erected in said Territory or to be hereafter erected in the proposed State, and for the payment of the bonds heretofore or hereafter issued therefor, one hundred thousand acres; for penitentiaries, one hundred thousand acres; for insane asylums, one hundred thousand acres; for school and asylums for the deaf, dumb, and the blind, one hundred thousand acres; for miners' hospitals for disabled miners, fifty thousand acres; for normal schools, two hundred thousand acres; for state charitable, penal, and reformatory institutions, one hundred thousand acres; for agricultural and mechanical colleges, one hundred and fifty thousand acres; and the national appropriation heretofore annually paid for the agricultural and mechanical college to said Territory shall, until further order of Congress, continue to be paid to said State for the use of said institution; for school of mines, one hundred and fifty thousand acres; for military institutes, one hundred thousand acres; and for the payment of the bonds and accrued interest thereon issued by Maricopia, Pima, Yavapai, and Coconino counties, Arizona, which said bonds were validated, approved, and confirmed by the Act of Congress of June sixth, eighteen hundred and ninety-six (Twenty-ninth Statutes, page two hundred and sixty-two), one million acres: *Provided,* That if there shall remain any of the one million acres of land so granted, or of the proceeds of the sale or lease thereof, or rents, issues, or other profits therefrom, after the payment of said debts, such remainder of lands and the proceeds of sales thereof shall be added to and become a part of the permanent school fund of said State, the income therefrom only to be used for the maintenance of the common schools of said State.

SEC. 26. That the schools, colleges, and universities provided for in this Act shall forever remain under the exclusive control of the said State, and no part of the proceeds arising from the sale or disposal of any lands granted herein for educational purposes shall be used for the support of any sectarian or denominational school, college, or university.

SEC. 27. That five per centum of the proceeds of sales of public lands lying within said State which shall be sold by the United States subsequent to the admission of said State into the Union, after deducting all the expenses incident to the such sales, shall be paid to the said State to be used as a permanent inviolable fund, the interest of which only shall be expended for the support of the common schools within said State.

SEC. 28. That it is hereby declared that all lands hereby granted, including those which, having been heretofore granted to the said Territory, are hereby expressly transferred and confirmed to the said State, shall be by the said State held in trust, to be disposed of in whole or in part only in manner as herein provided and for the several objects specified in the respective granting and confirmatory provisions, and that the natural products and money proceeds of any of said lands shall be subject to the same trusts as the lands producing the same.

Disposition of any of said lands, or of any money or thing of value directly or indirectly derived therefrom, for any object other than for which such particular lands, or the lands from which such money or thing of value shall have been derived, were granted or confirmed, or in any manner contrary to the provisions of this Act, shall be deemed a breach of trust.

No mortgage or other incumbrance of the said lands, or any thereof, shall be valid in favor of any person or for any purpose or under any circumstances whatsoever. Said lands shall not be sold or leased, in whole or in part, except to the highest and best bidder at a public auction to be held at the county seat of the county wherein the lands to be affected, or the major portion thereof, shall lie, notice of which public auction shall first have been duly given by advertisement, which shall set forth the nature, time, and place of the transaction to be had, with a full description of the lands to be offered, and be published once each week for not less than ten successive weeks in a newspaper of general circulation published regularly at the state capital, and in that newspaper of like circulation which shall then be regularly published nearest to the location of such lands so offered; nor shall any sale or contract for the sale of any timber or other natural product of such lands be made, save at the place, in the manner, and after the notice by publication thus provided for sales and leases of the lands themselves: *Provided*, That nothing herein contained shall prevent said proposed State from leasing any of said lands referred to in this section for a term of five years or less without said advertisement herein required.

All lands, leaseholds, timber, and other products of land, before being offered, shall be appraised at their true value, and no sale or other disposal thereof shall be made for a consideration less than the value so ascertained, nor in any case less than the minimum price hereinafter fixed, nor upon credit unless accompanied by ample security, and the legal title shall not be deemed to have passed until the consideration shall have been paid.

No lands shall be sold for less than three dollars per acre, and no lands which are or shall be susceptible of irrigation under any projects now or hereafter completed or adopted by the United States under legislation for the reclamation of lands, or under any other project for the reclamation of lands, shall be sold at less than twenty-five dollars per acre: *Provided*, That said State, at the request of the Secretary of the Interior, shall from time to time relinquish such of its lands to the United States as at any time are needed for irrigation works in connecting with any such government project. And other lands in lieu thereof are hereby granted to said State, to be selected from lands of the character named and in the manner prescribed in section twenty-four of this Act.

There is hereby reserved to the United States and excepted from the operation of any and all grants made or confirmed by this Act to said proposed State all land actually or prospectively valuable for the development of water powers or power for hydro-electric use or transmission and which shall be ascertained and designated by the Secretary of the Interior within five years after the proclamation of the President declaring the admission of the State; and no lands so reserved and excepted shall be subject to any disposition whatsoever by said State, and any conveyance or transfer of such land by said State or any officer thereof shall be absolutely null and void within the period above named; and in lieu of the land so reserved to the United States and excepted from the operation of any of said grants there be, and is hereby, granted to the proposed State an equal quantity of land to be selected from land of the character named and in the manner prescribed in section twenty-four of this Act.

A separate fund shall be established for each of the several objects for which the said grants are hereby made or confirmed, and whenever any moneys shall be in any manner derived from any of said land the same shall be deposited by the state treasurer in the fund corresponding to the grant under which the particular land producing such moneys was by this Act conveyed or confirmed. No moneys shall ever be taken from one fund for deposit in any other, or for any object other than that for which the land producing the same was granted or confirmed. The state treasurer shall keep all such moneys invested in safe, interest-bearing securities, which securities shall be approved by the governor and secretary of state of said proposed State, and shall at all times be under a good and sufficient bond or bonds conditioned for the faithful performance of his duties in regard thereto, as defined by this Act and the laws of the State not in conflict herewith.

Every sale, lease, conveyance, or contract of or concerning any of the lands hereby granted or confirmed, or the use thereof or the natural products thereof, not made in substantial conformity with the provisions of this Act shall be null and void, any provision of the constitution or laws of the said State to the contrary notwithstanding.

It shall be the duty of the Attorney-General of the United States to prosecute, in the name of the United States and in its courts, such proceedings at law or in equity as may from time to time be necessary and appropriate to enforce the provisions hereof relative to the application and disposition of the said lands and the products thereof and the funds derived therefrom.

Nothing herein contained shall be taken as in limitation of the power of the State or of any citizen thereof to enforce the provisions of this Act.

SEC. 29. That all lands granted in quantity, or as indemnity, by this Act, shall be selected, under the direction and subject to the approval of the Secretary of the Interior, from the surveyed, unreserved, unappropriated, and nonmineral public lands of the United States within the limits of said State, by a commission composed of the governor, surveyor-general or other officer exercising the functions of a surveyor-general, and the attorney-general of the said State; and after its admission into the Union said State may procure public lands of the United States within its boundaries to be surveyed with a view to satisfying any public land grants made to said State in the same manner prescribed for the procurement of such surveys by Washington, Idaho, and other States by the Act of Congress approved August eighteenth, eighteen hundred and ninety-four (Twenty-eighth Statutes at Large, page three hundred and ninety-four), and the provisions of said Act, in so far as they relate to such surveys and the preference right of selection, are hereby extended to the said State of Arizona. The fees to be paid to the register and receiver for each final location or selection of one hundred and sixty acres made hereunder shall be one dollar.

SEC. 30. That all grants of lands heretofore made by any Act of Congress to said Territory, except to the extent modified or repealed by this Act, are hereby ratified and confirmed to said State, subject to the provisions of this Act: *Provided, however,* That nothing in this Act contained shall, directly or indirectly, affect any litigation now pending and to which the United States is a party, or any right or claim therein asserted.

SEC. 31. That the said State, when admitted as aforesaid, shall constitute one judicial district, and the circuit and district courts of said district shall be held at the capital of said State, and the said district shall, for judicial purposes, be attached to the ninth judicial circuit. There shall be appointed for said district one district judge, one United States attorney, and one United States marshal. The judge of said district shall receive a yearly salary the same as other similar judges of the United States, payable as provided for by law, and shall reside in the district to which he is appointed. There shall be appointed clerks of said courts, who shall keep their offices at the capital of said State. The regular terms of said courts shall be held on the first Monday in April and the first Monday in October of each year. The circuit and district courts for said district, and the judges thereof, respectively, shall possess the same powers and jurisdiction and perform the same duties required to be performed by the other circuit and district courts and judges of the United States, and shall be governed by the same laws and regulations. The marshal, district attorney, and the clerks of the circuit and district courts of said district, and all other officers and persons performing duties in the administration of justice therein, shall severally possess the powers and perform the duties lawfully possessed and required to be performed by similar officers in other districts of the United States, and shall, for the services they perform, receive the fees and compensation now allowed by law to officers performing similar services for the United States in the Territory of Arizona.

SEC. 32. That all cases of appeal or writ of error and all other proceedings heretofore lawfully prosecuted and now pending in the Supreme Court of the United States or in the proper circuit court of appeals upon any record from the supreme court of said Territory, and all cases of appeal or writ of error and all other proceedings heretofore lawfully prosecuted and now pending in the Supreme Court of the United States upon any record from a district court of said Territory or, in any matter of habeas corpus, upon any return or order of a district judge thereof, and all and singular the cases aforesaid which, hereafter shall be so lawfully prosecuted and remain pending in the Supreme Court of the United States or in the proper circuit court of appeals, may be heard and determined by the Supreme Court of the United States or the proper circuit court of appeals, as the case may be. And the mandate of execution or of further proceedings shall be directed by the Supreme Court of the United States or the circuit court of appeals to the circuit or district court hereby established within the said State, or to the supreme court of such State, as the nature of the case may require. And the circuit, district, and state courts herein named shall, respectively, be the successors of the supreme court and of the district courts of said Territory as to all such cases arising within the limits embraced within the jurisdiction of said courts, respectively, with full power to proceed with the same and award mesne or final process therein; and that from all judgements and decrees or other determinations of any court of the said Territory, in any case begun prior to admission, the parties to such cause shall have the same right to prosecute appeals, writs of error, and petitions for review to the Supreme Court of the United States or to the circuit court of appeals as they would have had by law prior to the admission of said State into the Union.

SEC. 33. That the said circuit or the said district courts, as the case may be, shall have jurisdiction to hear and determine all trials, proceedings, and questions arising, or which may be raised, in any case or controversy pending in any of the courts other than the supreme court of the said Territory at the date of its admission as a State, the case being such that, under the laws of the United States touching the jurisdictions of federal courts, it might properly have been begun in or (as a separable controversy or otherwise) removed to said circuit or said district court had they been established when the litigation of such case or controversy was commenced. Should such case or controversy be such that, if begun within a State, it would have fallen within the exclusive original cognizance of a circuit or district court of the United States sitting therein, it shall be transferred to the one or the other of said courts sitting within the said State of Arizona, with due regard for the general provisions of law defining their respective jurisdictions; but should such case or controversy be by nature one of those which under such general jurisdictional provisions fall within the concurrent, but not the exclusive, jurisdiction of such courts, then such transfer may be had upon application of any party to such case or controversy, to be made as nearly as may be in the manner now provided for removal of cases from state to federal courts, and not later than sixty days after the lodgment of the record of such case or controversy in the proper court of the State as herein provided. All cases and controversies pending at the admission of the State, and not transferable to the said circuit or district court under the foregoing provision, shall be heard and determined by the proper court of the State. All files, records, and proceedings relating to any such pending cases or controversies shall be transferred to such circuit, district, and state courts, respectively, in such wise and so authenticated or proven as such courts shall respectively by rule direct, and upon transfer of any case or controversy as herein provided the same shall be proceeded with in due course of law; and no writ, action, indictment, information, cause, or proceeding pending in any court of the said Territory at the time of its admission as a State shall abate or be deemed ineffective by reason of such admission, but the same shall be transferred and proceeded with in the proper circuit or district court of the United States or state court, as the case may be: *Provided, however,* That all cases pending and undisposed of in the supreme court of the said Territory at the time of the admission thereof as a State shall be transferred, together with the records thereof, to the highest appellate court of the State, and shall be heard and determined thereby, and appeal to and writ of error from the Supreme Court of the United States shall lie to review all such cases in accordance with the rules and principles applicable to the review by that tribunal of cases determined by state courts: *Provided further,* That all cases pending in said territorial supreme court in which the United States is a party or which, if instituted within a State, would have fallen within the exclusive original cognizance of a circuit or district court of the United States shall, with the records appertaining thereto, be transferred to the circuit court of appeals for the ninth circuit, and be there heard and decided; and any such case which, if finally decided by the supreme court of the Territory, would have been in any manner reviewable by the Supreme Court of the United States may, in like manner and with like effect, be so reviewed after final decision thereof by said circuit court of appeals. Transfers of all files and records from the said territorial supreme court to the highest appellate court of the State and to the said circuit court of appeals shall be accomplished in such manner and under such proofs and authentications as the two last-mentioned courts shall respectively by rule prescribe.

All civil causes of action and all criminal offenses which shall have arisen or been committed prior to the admission of said Territory as a State, but as to which no suit, action, or prosecution shall be pending at the date of such admission, shall be subject to prosecution in the courts of said State and the said circuit or district courts of the United States sitting therein, and to review in the appellate courts of such respective sovereignties in like manner and to the same extent as if said State had been created and such circuit, district, and state courts had been established prior to the accrual of such causes of action and the commission of such offenses; and in effectuation of this provision such of the said criminal offenses as shall have been committed against the laws of the said Territory shall be tried and punished by the appropriate courts of the said State, and such as shall have been committed against the laws of the United States shall be tried and punished in the circuit or district courts of the United States.

All suits and actions brought by the United States in which said Territory is named as a party defendant which shall be pending in any court of said Territory at the date of its admission hereunder shall be transferred as herein provided, and the said State shall be substituted therein and become a party defendant thereto in lieu of said Territory.

SEC. 34. That the members of the legislature elected at the election hereinbefore provided for may assemble at Phoenix, organize, and elect two Senators of the United States in the manner now prescribed by the Constitution and laws of the United States; and the governor and secretary of state of the proposed State shall certify the election of the Senators and Representative in the manner required by law, and the Senators and Representative so elected shall be entitled to be admitted to seats in Congress and to all rights and privileges of

Senators and Representatives of other States in the Congress of the United States; and the officers of the state government formed in pursuance of said constitution, as provided by the constitutional convention, shall proceed to exercise all the functions of state officers; and all laws of said Territory in force at the time of its admission into the Union shall be in force in said State until changed by the legislature of said State, except as modified or changed by this Act or by the constitution of the State; and the laws of the United States shall have the same force and effect within the said State as elsewhere within the United States.

SEC. 35. That the sum of one hundred thousand dollars, or so much thereof as may be necessary, is hereby appropriated, out of any money in the Treasury not otherwise appropriated, for defraying all and every kind and character of expense incident to the elections and convention provided for in this Act; that is, the payment of the expenses of holding the election for members of the constitutional convention and the election for the ratification of the constitution, at the same rates that are paid for similar services under the territorial laws, and for the payment of the mileage for and salaries of members of the constitutional convention, at the same rates that are paid to members of the said territorial legislature under national law, and for the payment of all proper and necessary expenses, officers, clerks, and messengers thereof, and printing and other expenses incident thereto: *Provided*, That any expense incurred in excess of said sum of one hundred thousand dollars shall be paid by said State. The said money shall be expended under the direction of the Secretary of the Interior, and shall be forwarded to be locally expended in the present Territory of Arizona, through the secretary of said Territory, as may be necessary and proper in the discretion of the Secretary of the Interior, in order to carry out the full intent and meaning of this Act.

Approved, June 20, 1910.

JOINT RESOLUTION REAFFIRMING
THE BOUNDARY LINE BETWEEN TEXAS
AND THE TERRITORY OF NEW MEXICO
FEBRUARY 16, 1911

Whereas the constitutional convention recently held in the Territory of New Mexico submitted for acceptance or rejection the draft of a proposed constitution for the State of New Mexico, to be voted upon by the voters of said proposed new State on the twenty-first day of January, nineteen hundred and eleven, which proposed constitution contains a clause attempting to annul and set aside the boundary lines heretofore legally run, marked, established, and ratified by the United States and the State of

Texas, said lines between the Territory of New Mexico and the State of Texas, having been run by John H. Clark, the boundary commissioner acting for the United States in eighteen hundred and fifty-nine and eighteen hundred and sixty, the said lines being now known and recognized as the Clark lines; and

Whereas the United States and the State of Texas have patented land based upon the Clark lines as the boundary between Texas and the Territory of New Mexico: Therefore be it

Resolved by the Senate and House of Representatives of the United States of America in Congress assembled, That any provision of said proposed constitution that in any way tends to annul or change the boundary lines between the State of Texas and the Territory or State of New Mexico shall be of no force or effect, but shall be construed so as not in any way to change, affect, or alter the said boundary lines known as the Clark lines and heretofore run and marked by him as a commissioner on the part of the United States and concurred in by the State of Texas, and the former ratification of said Clark lines, by the United States by the Act approved March third, eighteen hundred and ninety-one, and the State of Texas by the joint resolution passed March twenty-fifth, eighteen hundred and ninety-one, shall be held and deemed a conclusive location and settlement of said boundary lines.

SEC. 2. That the President of the United States is hereby authorized, in conjunction with the State of Texas, to reestablish and re-mark the boundary lines heretofore established and marked by John H. Clark between New Mexico and the State of Texas, and for such purpose he is hereby authorized and empowered to appoint a commissioner, who, in conjunction with such commissioner as may be appointed by and on behalf of the State of Texas for the same purpose, shall re-mark the boundary between the Territory of New Mexico and the State of Texas as follows: Beginning at the point where the one hundred and third degree of longitude west from Greenwich intersects the parallel of thirty-six degrees and thirty minutes north latitude, as determined and fixed by John H. Clark, the commissioner on the part of the United States in the years eighteen hundred and fifty-nine and eighteen hundred and sixty; thence south with the line run by said Clark for the said one hundred and third degree of longitude to the thirty-second parallel of north latitude to the point marked by said Clark as the southeast corner of New Mexico; and thence west with the thirty-second degree of north latitude as determined by said Clark to the Rio Grande.

SEC. 3. That the part of the line run and marked by monuments along the thirty-second parallel of north latitude and that part of the line marked by monuments along the one hundred and third degree of longitude west from Greenwich, the same being the east and west and north and south lines between Texas and New Mexico, and run by authority of the Act of Congress approved June fifth, eighteen hundred and fifty-eight, and known as the Clark lines, which said lines run by said Clark have been confirmed, as aforesaid, by the Act of Congress approved March third, eighteen hundred and ninety-one, and the joint resolution of the Legislature of Texas passed March twenty-fifth, eighteen hundred and ninety-one, shall remain the true boundary lines of Texas and New Mexico: *Provided,* That it shall be the duty of the commissioners appointed under this Act to re-mark said old Clark monuments and line where they can be found and identified by the original monuments now on the ground, or where monuments are now missing or the lines can not be found but their original position can be shown by competent parol evidence or by the topographic maps or field notes made by said Clark, the monuments so found or their position so identified shall determine the true position and course of the boundary lines as marked by said Clark to the full extent of the survey made by him, and where no survey was actually originally made on said lines it shall be the duty of the said commissioners to run a straight line between the nearest points determined by the Clark map, field notes, and survey, and when said straight lines have been so run, marked, and agreed upon by the commissioners they shall thereafter form the true boundary lines.

SEC. 4. That the sum of twenty thousand dollars, or so much thereof as may be necessary, be, and the same is hereby, appropriated, out of any money in the Treasury not otherwise appropriated, to carry out the purposes of this Act: *Provided,* That the person or persons appointed and employed on the part of the State of Texas shall be paid by the said State.

Approved, February 16, 1911.

AN ACT TO STOP INJURY TO THE PUBLIC GRAZING LANDS BY PREVENTING OVERGRAZING AND SOIL DETERIORATION, TO PROVIDE FOR THEIR ORDERLY USE, IMPROVEMENT, AND DEVELOPMENT, TO STABILIZE THE LIVESTOCK INDUSTRY DEPENDENT UPON THE PUBLIC RANGE, AND FOR OTHER PURPOSES

JUNE 28, 1934

Be it enacted by the Senate and House of Representatives of the United States of America in Congress assembled, That in order to promote the highest use of the public lands pending its final disposal, the Secretary of the Interior is authorized, in his discretion, by order to establish grazing districts or additions thereto and/or to modify the boundaries thereof, not exceeding in the aggregate an area of eighty million acres of vacant, unappropriated, and unreserved lands from any part of the public domain of the United States (exclusive of Alaska), which are not in national forests, national parks and monuments, Indian reservations, revested Oregon and California Railroad grant lands, or revested Coos Bay Wagon Road grant lands, and which in his opinion are chiefly valuable for grazing and raising forage crops: *Provided,* That no lands withdrawn or reserved for any other purpose shall be included in any such district except with the approval of the head of the department having jurisdiction thereof. Nothing in this Act shall be construed in any way to diminish, restrict, or impair any right which has been heretofore or may be hereafter initiated under existing law validly affecting the public lands, and which is maintained pursuant to such law except as otherwise expressly provided in this Act, nor to affect any land heretofore or hereafter surveyed which, except for the provisions of this Act, would be a part of any grant to any State, nor as limiting or restricting the power or authority of any State as to matters within its jurisdiction. Whenever any grazing district is established pursuant to this Act, the Secretary shall grant to owners of land adjacent to such district, upon application of any such owner, such rights-of-way over the lands included in such district for stock-driving purposes as may be necessary for the convenient access by any such owner to marketing facilities or to lands not within such district owned by such person or upon which such person has stock-grazing rights. Neither this Act nor the Act of December 29, 1916 (39 Stat. 862; U.S.C., title 43, secs. 291 and following), commonly known as the "Stock Raising Homestead Act", shall be construed as limiting the authority or policy of Congress or the President to include in national forests public lands of the character described in section 24 of the Act of March 3, 1891 (26 Stat. 1103; U.S.C., title 16, sec. 471), as amended, for the purposes set forth in the Act of June 4, 1897 (30 Stat. 35; U.S.C., title 16, sec. 475), or such other purposes as Congress may specify. Before grazing districts are created in any State as herein provided, a hearing shall be held in the State, after public notice thereof shall have been given, at such location convenient for the attendance of State officials, and the settlers, residents, and livestock owners of the vicinity, as may be determined by the Secretary of the Interior. No such district shall be established until the expiration of ninety days after such notice shall have been given, nor until twenty days after such hearing shall be held: *Provided, however,* That the publication of such notice shall have the effect of withdrawing all public lands within the exterior boundary of such proposed grazing districts from all forms of entry of settlement. Nothing in this Act shall be construed as in any way altering or restricting the right to hunt or fish within a grazing district in accordance with the laws of the United States or of any State, or as vesting in any permittee any right whatsoever to interfere with hunting or fishing within a grazing district.

SEC. 2. The Secretary of the Interior shall make provision for the protection, administration, regulation, and improvement of such grazing districts as may be created under the authority of the foregoing section, and he shall make such rules and regulations and establish such service, enter into such cooperative agreements, and do any and all things necessary to accomplish the purposes of this Act and to insure the objects of such grazing districts, namely, to regulate their occupancy and use, to preserve the land and its resources from destruction or unnecessary injury, to provide for the orderly use, improvement, and development of the range; and the Secretary of the Interior is authorized to continue the study of erosion and flood control and to perform such work as may be necessary amply to protect and rehabilitate the areas subject to the provisions of this Act, through such funds as may be made available for that purpose, and any willful violation of the provisions of this Act or of such rules and regulations thereunder after actual notice thereof shall be punishable by a fine of not more than $500.

SEC. 3. That the Secretary of the Interior is hereby authorized to issue or cause to be issued permits to graze livestock on such grazing districts to such bona fide settlers, residents, and other stock owners as under his rules and regulations are entitled to participate in the use of the range, upon the payment annually of reasonable fees in each case to be fixed or determined from time to time: *Provided,* That grazing permits shall be issued only to citizens of the United States or to those who have filed the necessary declarations of intention to become such, as required by the naturalization laws and to groups, associations, or corporations authorized to conduct business under the laws of the State in which the grazing district is located. Preference shall be given in the issuance of grazing permits to those within or near a district who are landowners engaged in the livestock business, bona fide occupants or settlers, or owners of water or water rights, as may be necessary to permit the proper use of lands, water or water rights owned, occupied, or leased by them, except that until July 1, 1935, no preference shall be given in the issuance of such permits to any such owner, occupant, or settler, whose rights were acquired between January 1, 1934, and December 31, 1934, both dates inclusive, except that no permittee complying with the rules and regulations laid down by the Secretary of the Interior shall be denied the renewal of such permit, if such denial will impair the value of the grazing unit of the permittee, when such unit is pledged as security for any bona fide loan. Such permits shall be for a period of not more than ten years, subject to the preference right of the permittees to renewal in the discretion of the Secretary of the Interior, who shall specify from time to time numbers of stock and seasons of use. During periods of range depletion due to severe drought or other natural causes, or in case of a general epidemic of disease, during the life of the permit, the Secretary of the Interior is hereby authorized, in his discretion to remit, reduce, refund in whole or in part, or authorize postponement of payment of grazing fees for such depletion period so long as the emergency exists: *Provided further,* That nothing in this Act shall be construed or administered in any way to diminish or impair any right to the possession and use of water for mining, agriculture, manufacturing, or other purposes which has heretofore vested or accrued under existing law validly affecting the public lands or which may be hereafter initiated or acquired and maintained in accordance with such law. So far as consistent with the purposes and provisions of this Act, grazing privileges recognized and acknowledged shall be adequately safeguarded, but the creation of a grazing district or the issuance of a permit pursuant to the provisions of this Act shall not create any right, title, interest, or estate in or to the lands.

SEC. 4. Fences, wells, reservoirs, and other improvements necessary to the care and management of the permitted livestock may be constructed on the public lands within such grazing districts under permit issued by the authority of the Secretary, or under such cooperative arrangement as the Secretary may approve. Permittees shall be required by the Secretary of the Interior to comply with the provisions of law of the State within which the grazing district is located with respect to the cost and maintenance of partition fences. No permit shall be issued which shall entitle the permittee to the use of such improvements constructed and owned by a prior occupant until the applicant has paid to such prior occupant the reasonable value of such improvements to be determined under rules and regulations of the Secretary of the Interior. The decision of the Secretary in such cases is to be final and conclusive.

SEC. 5. That the Secretary of the Interior shall permit, under regulations to be prescribed by him, the free grazing within such districts of livestock kept for domestic purposes; and provided that so far as authorized by existing law or laws hereinafter enacted, nothing herein contained shall prevent the use of timber, stone, gravel, clay, coal, and other deposits by miners, prospectors for mineral, bona fide settlers and residents, for firewood, fencing, buildings, mining, prospecting, and domestic purposes within areas subject to the provisions of this Act.

SEC. 6. Nothing herein contained shall restrict the acquisition, granting or use of permits or rights-of-way within grazing districts under existing law; or ingress or egress over the public lands in such districts for all proper and lawful purposes; and nothing herein contained shall restrict prospecting, locating, developing, mining, entering, leasing, or patenting the mineral resources of such districts under law applicable thereto.

SEC. 7. That the Secretary is hereby authorized, in his discretion, to examine and classify any lands within such grazing districts which are more valuable and suitable for the production of agricultural crops than native grasses and forage plants, and to open such lands to homestead entry in tracts not exceeding three hundred and twenty acres in area. Such lands shall not be subject to settlement or occupation as homesteads until after same have been classified and opened to entry after notice to the permittee by the Secretary of the Interior, and the lands shall remain a part of the grazing district until patents are issued therefor, the homesteader to be, after his entry is allowed, entitled to the possession and use thereof: *Provided,* That upon the application of any person qualified to make homestead entry under the public-land laws, filed in the land office of the proper district, the Secretary of the Interior shall cause any tract not exceeding three hundred and twenty acres in any grazing district to be classified, and such application shall entitle the applicant to a preference right to enter such lands when opened to entry as herein provided.

SEC. 8. That where such action will promote the purposes of the district or facilitate its administration, the Secretary is authorized and directed to accept on behalf of the United States any lands within the exterior boundaries of a district as a gift, or, when public interest will be benefited thereby, he is authorized and directed to accept on behalf of the United States title to any privately owned lands within the exterior boundaries of said grazing district, and in exchange therefor to issue patent for not to exceed and equal value of surveyed grazing district land or of unreserved surveyed public land in the same State or within a distance of not more than fifty miles within the adjoining State nearest the base lands: *Provided,* That before any such exchange shall be effected, notice of the contemplated exchange, describing the lands involved, shall be published by the Secretary of the Interior once each week for four successive weeks in some newspaper of general circulation in the county or counties in which may be situated the lands to be accepted, and in the same manner in some like newspaper published in any county in which may be situated any lands to be given in such exchange; lands conveyed to the United States under this Act shall, upon acceptance of title, become public lands and parts of the grazing district within whose exterior boundaries they are located: *Provided further,* That either party to an exchange may make reservations of minerals, easements, or rights of use, the values of which shall be duly considered in determining the values of the exchanged lands. Where reservations are made in lands conveyed to the United States, the right to enjoy them shall be subject to such reasonable conditions respecting ingress and egress and the use of the surface of the land as may be deemed necessary by the Secretary of the Interior. Where mineral reservations are made in lands conveyed by the United States, it shall be so stipulated in the patent, and any person who acquires the right to mine and remove the reserved mineral deposits may enter and occupy so much of the surface as may be required for all purposes incident to the mining and removal of the minerals therefrom, and may mine and remove such minerals, upon payment to the owner of the surface for damages caused to the land and improvements thereon. Upon application of any State to exchange lands within or without the boundary of a grazing district the Secretary of the Interior is authorized and directed, in the manner provided for the exchange of privately owned lands in this section, to proceed with such exchange at the earliest practicable date and to cooperate fully with the State to that end, but no State shall be permitted to select lieu lands in another State.

SEC. 9. The Secretary of the Interior shall provide, by suitable rules and regulations, for cooperation with local associations of stockmen, State land officials, and official State agencies engaged in conservation or propagation of wild life interested in the use of the grazing districts. The Secretary of the Interior shall provide by appropriate rules and regulations for local hearings on appeals from the decisions of the administrative officer in charge in a manner similar to the procedure in the land department. The Secretary of the Interior shall also be empowered to accept contributions toward the administration, protection, and improvement of the district, moneys so received to be covered into the Treasury as a special fund, which is hereby appropriated and made available until expended, as the Secretary of the Interior may direct, for payment of expenses incident to said administration, protection, and improvement, and for refunds to depositors of amounts contributed by them in excess of their share of the cost.

SEC. 10. That, except as provided in sections 9 and 11 hereof, all moneys received under the authority of this Act shall be deposited in the Treasury of the United States as miscellaneous receipts, but 25 per centum of all moneys received from each grazing district during any fiscal year is hereby made available, when appropriated by the Congress, for expenditure by the Secretary of the Interior for the construction, purchase, or maintenance of range improvements, and 50 per centum of the money received from each grazing district during any fiscal year shall be paid at the end thereof by the Secretary of the Treasury to the State in which said grazing district is situated, to be expended as the State legislature may prescribe for the benefit of the county or counties in which the grazing district is situated: *Provided*, That if any grazing district is in more than one State or county, the distributive share to each from the proceeds of said district shall be proportional to its area therein.

SEC. 11. That when appropriated by Congress, 25 per centum of all moneys received from each grazing district on Indian lands ceded to the United States for disposition under the public-land laws during any fiscal year is hereby made available for expenditure by the Secretary of the Interior for the construction, purchase, or maintenance of range improvements; and an additional 25 per centum of the money received from grazing during each fiscal year shall be paid at the end thereof by the Secretary of the Treasury to the State in which said lands are situated, to be expended as the State legislature may prescribe for the benefit of public schools and public roads of the county or counties in which such grazing lands are situated. And the remaining 50 per centum of all money received from such grazing lands shall be deposited to the credit of the Indians pending final disposition under applicable laws, treaties, or agreements. The applicable public land laws as to said Indian ceded lands within a district created under this Act shall continue in operation, except that each and every application for nonmineral title to said lands in a district created under this Act shall be allowed only if in the opinion of the Secretary of the Interior the land is of the character suited to disposal through the Act under which application is made and such entry and disposal will not affect adversely the best public interest, but no settlement or occupation of such lands shall be permitted until ninety days after allowance of an application.

SEC. 12. That the Secretary of the Interior is hereby authorized to cooperate with any department of the Government in carrying out the purposes of this Act, and in the coordination of range administration, particularly where the same stock grazes part time in a grazing district and part time in a national forest or other reservation.

SEC. 13. That the President of the United States is authorized to reserve by proclamation and place under national-forest administration in any State where national forests may be created or enlarged by Executive order any unappropriated public lands lying within watersheds forming a part of the national forests which, in his opinion, can best be administered in connection with existing national-forest administration units, and to place under the Interior Department administration any lands within national forest, principally valuable for grazing, which, in his opinion, can best be administered under the provisions of this Act: *Provided*, That such reservations or transfers shall not interfere with legal rights acquired under any public-land laws so long as such rights are legally maintained. Lands placed under the national-forest administration under the authority of this Act shall be subject to all the laws and regulations relating to national forests, and lands placed under the Interior Department administration shall be subject to all public-land laws and regulations applicable to grazing districts created under authority of this Act. Nothing in this section shall be construed so as to limit the powers of the President (relating to reorganizations in the executive departments) granted by title 4 of the Act entitled "An Act making appropriations for the Treasury and Post Office Departments for the fiscal year ending June 30, 1934, and for other purposes", approved March 3, 1933.

SEC. 14. That section 2455 of the Revised Statutes, as amended, is amended to read as follows:

"SEC. 2455. Nothwithstanding the provisions of section 2357 of the Revised Statutes (U.S.C., title 43, sec. 678) and of the Act of August 30, 1890 (26 Stat. 391), it shall be lawful for the Secretary of the Interior to order into market and sell at public auction, at the land office of the district in which the land is situated, for not less than the appraised value, any isolated or disconnected tract or parcel of the public domain not exceeding seven hundred and sixty acres which, in his judgement, it would be proper to expose for sale after at least thirty days' notice by the land office of the district in which such land may be situated: *Provided,* That for a period of not less than thirty days after the highest bid has been received, any owner or owners of contiguous land shall have a preference right to buy the offered lands at such highest bid price, and where two or more persons apply to exercise such preference right the Secretary of the Interior is authorized to make an equitable division of the land among such applicants, but in no case shall the adjacent land owner or owners be required to pay more than three times the appraised price: *Provided further,* That any legal subdivisions of the public land, not exceeding one hundred and sixty acres, the greater part of which is mountainous or too rough for cultivation, may, in the discretion of the said Secretary, be ordered into the market and sold pursuant to this section upon the application of any person who owns land or holds a valid entry of lands adjoining such tract, regardless of the fact that such tract may not be isolated or disconnected within the meaning of this section: *Provided further,* That this section shall not defeat any valid right which has already attached under any pending entry or location. The word 'person' in this section shall be deemed to include corporations, partnerships, and associations."

SEC. 15. The Secretary of the Interior is further authorized in his discretion, where vacant, unappropriated, and unreserved lands of the public domain are situated in such isolated or disconnected tracts of six hundred and forty acres or more as not to justify their inclusion in any grazing district to be established pursuant to this Act, to lease any such lands to owners of lands contiguous thereto for grazing purposes, upon application therefor by any such owner, and upon such terms and conditions as the Secretary may prescribe.

SEC. 16. Nothing in this Act shall be construed as restricting the respective States from enforcing any and all statutes enacted for police regulation, nor shall the police power of the respective States be, by this Act, impaired or restricted, and all laws heretofore enacted by the respective States or any thereof, or that may hereafter be enacted as regards public health or public welfare, shall at all times be in full force and effect: *Provided, however,* That nothing in this section shall be construed as limiting or restricting the power and authority of the United States.

Approved, June 28, 1934.

Bibliography

De Voto, Bernard. *The Course of Empire*. Boston: Houghton Mifflin Company, 1952.

Harrison, Gordon F. and Coder, John P., prepared under the direction of the Senate Committee on Rules and Administration, Eighty Seventh Congress. *Senate Manual Containing the Standing Rules, Orders, Laws, and Resolutions Affecting the Business of the United States Senate*. Washington, DC: United States Government Printing Office, 1961.

Merk, Frederick. *History of the Westward Movement*. New York: Alfred A. Knopf, 1978.

Miller, Hunter, ed. *Treaties and Other International Acts of the United States of America*, Vols. 1–7. Washington, DC: United States Government Printing Office, 1937.

Nevins, Allen and Commager, Henry Steele. *A Short History of the United States*. New York: Random House, 1945.

Philbrick, Francis S. *The Rise of the West 1754–1830*. New York: Harper & Row, 1965.

Shipton, Clifford K. and Mooney, James E. *The American Bibliography of Charles Evans — National Index of American Imprints Through 1800, The Short-Title Evans (Vol. Two)*. American Antiquarian Society and Barre Publishers, 1969.

Silverberg, Robert. *To the Western Shore: Growth of the United States 1776–1853*. New York: Doubleday, 1971.

United States Department of the Interior, Geological Survey in conjunction with the Bureau of Land Management. *A Map of the United States of American Showing the Extent of Public Land Surveys*. Washington, DC: United States Geological Survey, 1965.

Van Zandt, Franklin K. United States Department of the Interior, Geological Survey. *Boundaries of the United States and the Several States, Bulletin 1212*. Washington, DC: United States Government Printing Office, 1966.

Index

417

N